ᵀᴴᴱ ILIAD & ᵀᴴᴱ ODYSSEY

THE ILIAD &
THE ODYSSEY

HOMER

Translated by Samuel Butler
Introduction by Michael Dirda

BARNES & NOBLE
NEW YORK

Cover design by Jo Obarowski

Barnes & Noble, Inc.
122 Fifth Avenue
New York, NY 10011

ISBN-13: 978-1-4351-1043-4

Printed and bound in China

1 3 5 7 9 10 8 6 4 2

Contents

INTRODUCTION

Homer's two epic poems, the *Iliad* and the *Odyssey*, stand with the supreme masterworks of world literature, yet the stories they tell are among the first that many of us ever hear. When I was a small boy, my steel-worker father would perch me on his lap and make my eyes grow wide with tales of a ten-years-long war fought over the most beautiful woman in the world and won by a sneaky trick, then go on to describe a one-eyed Cyclops, the Sirens and their irresistible singing, a huge whirlpool and a six-headed monster, the witch Circe who turned sailors into swine, magical winds and a despised beggar who cast off his rags to take bloody revenge with a bow no one but he could string. At that time these episodes from the Trojan War and Odysseus's long voyage home struck me as the best stories in the world. Many years and many stories later, I haven't changed my mind.

Few other works, apart from the Bible, Shakespeare's plays, and perhaps Ovid's *Metamorphoses* (that sourcebook of ancient myth) have so deeply entered our cultural bloodstream. In Dante's *Inferno* Ulysses—the Latin form of Odysseus—reappears as a restless quester after knowledge who sails to the edge of the world and beyond. Christopher Marlowe captured Helen's beauty in two famous lines: "Was this the face that launched a thousand ships/And burned the topless towers of Ilium?" Myriad paintings, sculptures, ballets, and operas have drawn on Homer's stories. Even Rider Haggard (author of that classic boys' adventure *King Solomon's Mines*) and Andrew Lang (of fairy tale fame) teamed up to write *The World's Desire*, wherein Ulysses—searching for Helen in Egypt—falls prey to an incarnation of Haggard's celebrated *femme fatale* Ayesha, better known as She-Who-Must-Be-Obeyed. James Joyce's *Ulysses* slyly modernizes the *Odyssey*, and Derek Walcott's book-length poem *Omeros* gives Homer a Caribbean accent.

WHEN PEOPLE THINK OF TROY, THEY USUALLY THINK FIRST OF THE TROJAN Horse. Yet that incident plays no part in the *Iliad*, which focuses on "the anger of Achilles" and its consequences. Only in the *Odyssey* does the blind bard Demodocus, while reciting poems about Troy, mention Odysseus's clever stratagem. Virgil adds further details in the *Aeneid* (first century B.C.E.), his Latin epic about the adventures of Aeneas and the founding of Rome. Yet the episode of the gigantic hollow horse packed with armed warriors was known in full throughout ancient times because Homer's poems made up only two parts of an epic cycle about Troy. These other poems are lost, aside from their titles and a few fragments, but we do know the general outline of what they contained:

Cypria relates the story of the Judgment of Paris, in which the Trojan prince of that name must award a golden apple to the fairest of three goddesses. He chooses Aphrodite because she promises that in return he will possess the most beautiful woman in the world. Before long, Paris has run off with Helen, the wife of Menelaus, and returned to Troy.

The *Iliad* is the poem we know. To reclaim his errant wife and take revenge, Menelaus enlists his brother Agamemnon as the general of a Greek army that sails to Troy in a thousand ships. The *Iliad* proper actually begins nine years into the siege, when everyone is growing restive and tempers are strained. The poem opens with an out-of control quarrel—over a concubine—between the somewhat supercilious Agamemnon and his deadliest fighter, Achilles. Feeling that his honor has been sullied, Achilles retreats to his tent and threatens to simply go home. Much of the epic then describes the ebb and flow of battle, and that admirable family-man Hector emerging as the great champion of Troy. (Hector means "the wall of his people.") But when this Trojan prince kills Achilles's best friend, Patroclus, the sulky Greek warrior vows a bloodfest in revenge. Many men die, including Hector, whose corpse is abused and mutilated. Bereft, the aged Trojan King Priam begs for the body of his son and Achilles—in a touching moment of humane understanding and personal transcendence—allows the old man to take it back into Troy for burial. The poem then ends with the funeral of Hector, "tamer of horses." Alas, the war itself will continue.

Aithiopis describes more of the war and ends with the death and funeral of Achilles, who had chosen a brief but glorious life over a long and obscure one. This poem also includes an account of Achilles' battle with Penthisilea, the queen of the Amazons, who had come to aid the Trojans and with whom he fell in love—when it was too late.

Ilias Parva, or *Little Iliad*, focuses on the subterfuge of the Trojan Horse as a means to enter Troy and includes the contest between the sturdy Ajax and wily Odysseus over Achilles's armor. (Odysseus wins the armor; Ajax then goes temporarily mad and eventually kills himself out of shame.)

Iliu Persis, or *The Sack of Troy*, relates the actual taking of the city and the general massacre that followed, including the killing of Hector's father, Priam, and infant son, Astyanax, as well as the rape of Cassandra, the prophetess whom no one ever believes. Hector's wife Andromache becomes the concubine of Neoptolemus, the son of Achilles.

The *Nostoi* survey the "homecomings" of the various heroes, including that of Agamemnon who is immediately murdered by his faithless wife Clytemnestra and her lover Aegisthus. (This story, followed by the revenge of Electra and Orestes for the slaying of their father, provides the plot for Aeschylus's three-play sequence, *The Oresteia*. Zeus refers to Agamemnon's murder at the beginning of the *Odyssey*.)

The Odyssey is the *"nostos,"* or homeward voyage, of the resourceful and crafty Odysseus, the man of many turns. He suffers and endures much—including the loss of at least 600 men and twelve ships—before he finally lands on his home island of Ithaca, alone. There he discovers that 108 suitors have been laying siege to his wife Penelope, hoping she will choose one as her new husband, but in the meantime eating and drinking up everything in his household. Disguised as a beggar, and with the help of his now grown son, Telemachus, Odysseus eventually slaughters these interlopers, cleanses his house of their pollution, and looks forward to a life of quiet and rest.

Telegonia caps the cycle with a bizarre minuet-like neatness. Telegonus, Odysseus's son by the enchantress Circe, accidentally kills his father and then marries Penelope, while Telemachus, Odysseus's son by Penelope, in due course marries Circe. They all live happily together on the enchantress's magical isle.

All these poems were apparently known in ancient times, though the *Iliad* and the *Odyssey* towered above the others in artistry and repute. Indeed, together this pair assumed a place in Greek culture somewhat comparable to the Bible, Torah, or Koran as a kind of sacred scripture. Their author might be referred to as simply "The Poet." Homer provided a code of conduct, a compendium of inspirational example, a history of the "founding fathers" of Greece, a guide to storytelling and oratory, a source for Athenian drama and poetry, and, not least, the common fount of wisdom for statesmen and ordinary citizens. Rhapsodes—*aoidoi*—memorized the poems in their entirety and they were regularly recited at festivals. Plato's *Republic* actually ends with a vision of the Homeric heroes in the afterlife (where most choose to be reincarnated as eagles or lions, but Odysseus wishes to come back as a perfectly ordinary man). In his *Poetics* Aristotle refers to Homer's poems as complementary models of narrative construction: "the *Iliad* is at once simple and 'pathetic' and the *Odyssey* complex (for 'recognition' scenes run through it) and at the same time 'ethical.'" Alexander the Great, it is said, carried the *Iliad* with him while on campaign.

By the second century B.C.E., Lucian's satirical *True History* was poking fun at Homer: Lucian visits the Isles of the Blessed and runs into Odysseus, who surreptitiously asks him to take a love letter to Calypso, expressing regret for turning down the offer of immortality and saying he'll be seeing her soon. Around the same time the famous Library of Alexandria was editing and providing annotations ("scholia") for the two poems. Even now we possess more early manuscripts of *The Iliad* and *The Odyssey* than of any other works from antiquity.

Yet, sadly, knowledge of the Homeric poems, except in the Byzantine Empire, was soon lost for a thousand years. By the end of the fourth century A.D. knowledge of Greek began to die out in western Europe. During the Middle Ages writers and thinkers only knew Homer from summaries, or gained a skewed sense of the *Iliad* from two Latin works of late antiquity (fourth to sixth century A.D.): Dictys the Cretan's supposed *Diary of the Trojan War*, told from the Greek side, and Dares the Phrygian's *History of the Destruction of Troy*, related from the Trojan point of view. These inspired several medieval romances on the so-called "matter of Troy."

Homer finally started his comeback in 1354 when the Italian poet Petrarch procured a Byzantine manuscript of the *Iliad* and the *Odyssey*. It was translated into Latin, since Petrarch couldn't read Greek (his friend Boccaccio did learn the language). In 1488 the first printed editions in Greek appeared and more and more scholars began to study the recovered language in earnest. In 1598, George Chapman brought out an English version of the first 10 books of the *Iliad* and eventually went on to translate the remainder, as well as the *Odyssey*.

Since the rebirth of Greek studies during the Renaissance, the English-speaking world has been steadily fascinated by Hellenism and by Homer in particular. The great seventeenth-century epic, *Paradise Lost*, opens by deliberately echoing the *Iliad*'s invocation of the Muse and, despite its orotund Latinate diction, possesses a strength and grandeur almost equal to its pagan model. The blind Milton naturally identified with the reputedly blind Homer.

During the eighteenth century Alexander Pope produced the equivalent of a bestseller with his rendering of the *Iliad* into heroic couplets. Several distinguished modern classicists—Jasper Griffin and Bernard Knox, for instance—rate Pope's *Iliad* the finest translation of Homer in the language. (Pope's *Odyssey* is uneven, since much of it was written by two helpers.) Pope's contemporary, the classical scholar Richard Bentley, reportedly observed, "A pretty poem, Mr. Pope, but you must not call it Homer." Yet Pope's verse possessed real strength: "Now on the field Ulysses stands alone/The Greeks all fled, the Trojans pouring on;/But stands collected in himself and whole. . . ."

During the later eighteenth century scholarship started to revolutionize our historical understanding of Homer. F.A. Wolf, in his *Prologemenon ad Homerum* (1795), argued that the poems had been composed orally during a time when the Greeks were unacquainted with writing, then passed down for four centuries through recitation until they could be set down on papyrus. The artistic unity of the works is largely due to the work of editors.

By the time Queen Victoria ascended her throne, Homer had become a central text in British education, a sourcebook for the heroic ideals of empire, and the preferred recreation of noble minds. William Gladstone himself, the most eminent prime minister of nineteenth-century England, actually published seven books about Homer and was a leading figure in Homeric scholarship, despite sometimes crackpot attempts to see ancient customs as fundamentally Christian. By contrast, his contemporary, the poet and essayist Matthew Arnold, brought out what is still regarded as one of literary criticism's most brilliant works, "On Translating Homer." In this essay Arnold, after critiquing a recent rendering of the poems (by Francis Newman, the brother of John Henry, Cardinal Newman), rattled off what he regarded as Homer's four primary qualities as a writer: The general effect of Homer, he tells us, is "that of a most rapidly moving poet, that of a poet most plain and direct in his style, and that of a poet most plain and direct in his ideas, that of a poet eminently noble."

The iconoclast Samuel Butler agreed with those principles, except perhaps for the last. This wit ("Man is a jelly which quivers so much as to run about"), novelist (*The Way of All Flesh*), visionary (the Utopian *Erewhon*), and amateur Greek scholar grew obsessed with Homer. The *Odyssey*, he became convinced, was written by a woman—in fact, it was written by a "young, headstrong and unmarried" girl of aristocratic birth resident in what is now Trapania, Sicily. According to Butler's *The Authoress of the Odyssey*, she even portrays herself in the poem as the lovely princess Nausicaa. On the surface, all this sounds deranged. But as Alexander Pope notes in the very leisurely introduction to his translation of the *Iliad*, there is a legend that Homer, while in Egypt, actually stole his poems from a woman named, improbably, Phantasia. Butler took this notion seriously—but only for the *Odyssey*—and developed it, and at the least inspired Robert Graves to create one of his most unusual historical novels, *Homer's Daughter*.

Whatever its truth, Butler's theory underscores the significant differences in tone, construction, and character of the *Iliad* and the *Odyssey*. The former is grand, somber, and heartbreaking, while the latter is almost a fairy tale, the adventures of a Greek trickster. In fact, many scholars now believe that the *Odyssey* may have been influenced by Near Eastern epics like *Gilgamesh* and the kind of folktales gathered together in the *Arabian Nights*; it almost certainly borrowed some of Odysseus's close calls from an earlier epic about Jason and the Argonauts. At heart, the *Iliad* is tragic, while the *Odyssey* seems a kind of romance, almost a picaresque novel.

In effect, Butler's own translations, relying on a straightforward, quick-paced prose, transformed the epics into works of Victorian fiction. Even now such an approach makes his version—reprinted in this volume—an ideal introduction to Homer: clear, direct, and invitingly readable.

THERE HAS LONG BEEN CONSIDERABLE SPECULATION AND BITTER CONTROVERSY about the dating, historicity, authorship, and method of composition of *The Iliad* and *The Odyssey*. It is now generally believed that Homer's poems, though written down in the seventh or eighth century B.C.E., were composed using "oral formulas," and describe a world similar to that of the "bronze-age" Mycenean culture of 1200 B.C.E., centered at Knossos and Pylos. Excavations at Hissarlik in Turkey—first begun by Heinrich von Schliemann in the 1860s—continue to unearth the remains of a great city that may have been Troy. Scholars have attempted, more or less seriously, to trace Odysseus's voyage and identify the islands he visited.

Even though the *Iliad* takes place in a single small geographical area and covers only 55 days of the war, Homer manages to suggest vast tracts of time and history. He does this through the back-stories of his combatants, the retelling of myths and legends, the input of the gods, and through his brilliant similes. Repeatedly, he illuminates a martial scene by comparing it to something homely and familiar:

> As countless swarms of flies buzz around a herdsman's home-stead in the time of spring when the pails are drenched with milk, even so did the Achaeans swarm on to the plain to charge the Trojans and destroy them.

> As a horse, stabled and full fed, breaks loose and gallops gloriously over the plain to the place where he is wont to bathe in the fair-flowing river—he holds his head high, and his mane

streams upon his shoulders as he exults in his strength and flies like the wind to the haunts and feeding ground of the mares— even so went forth Paris from high Pergamus, gleaming like sunlight in his armor, and he laughed aloud as he sped swiftly on his way.

Open to any page of Homer, and there is never anything vague or less than concrete. Each detail is presented in sharp focus in an orderly fashion.

Just so are all the major characters distinct personalities, from the petulant goddess Aphrodite to the equally petulant Achilles, a James Dean or Jim Morrison of the battlefield. As the critic Mark Van Doren observed: "Achilles will die young, yet he looks and moves like one who will live forever." While sulking, the killing machine diverts himself by playing on a stolen lyre and "singing the feats of heroes." (Even for the heroes of Troy, the real heroic age is already in the past.) He only returns to the battle out of a desire to revenge the death of his friend Patroclus. To many readers, the most admirable character in the poem is the stoically resigned Hector, happiest with his wife and child—little Astyanax is frightened by the plume on his father's helmet—but duty-bound to fight for his city. Each man will have his *aristeia*—his moment of glory, when he sweeps through battlefield like a thresher through wheat. Both fight knowing that fate is against them: Hector recognizes that Troy will eventually fall, Achilles' knows that he is doomed to an early death. But there is no self-pity in either of them. As Achilles tells Priam's son Lycaon, who has been bartering for his life:

Talk not to me of ransom. Until Patroclus fell I preferred to give the Trojans quarter, and sold beyond the sea many of those whom I had taken alive; but now not a man shall live of those whom heaven delivers into my hands before the city of Ilium— and of all Trojans it will fare hardest with the sons of Priam. Therefore, my friend, you too shall die. Why should you whine in this way? Patroclus fell, and he was a better man than you are. I too—see you not how I am great and goodly? I am son to a noble father and have a goddess for my mother, but the hands of doom and death overshadow me all as surely. The day will come, either at dawn or dark, or at the noontide, when one shall take my life also in battle, either with his spear, or with an arrow sped from his bow.

At which point Lycaon gives up pleading and is killed. As Oliver Taplin has written, "The *Iliad* is not so much concerned with what people do, as with the way they do it, above all the way they face suffering and death."

By contrast, the *Odyssey* is pitched at a much less intense level. Its first word, "*andra,*" means man, and the poem really does focus on the fortunes and vicissitudes of its hero, as he tries to reach home. (His *nostos* is, so to speak, fueled by nostalgia.) Resourceful, cautious, and omnicompetent, Odysseus seems far more modern than Achilles or Agamemnon. He wants his glory to be recognized—why else would he finally reveal his real name to the blinded Polyphemus?—but his real talent is for survival. To do that requires all his talent for wariness and cunning. Over the course of the poem Odysseus smoothly gives out one phony account after another of who he is; sometimes he's Phoenician, other times a brother of Idomineus, and, with Polyphemus the Cyclops, he's at first Nobody at all. Above all, he's the man of many parts—even flirting with Athene and braving the land of the dead to consult the prophet Tiresias. For while arguably greater men, like Achilles, Agamemnon, Ajax, and Hector die, Odysseus lives. There is his triumph, even if it lacks tragic grandeur.

While the *Iliad* focuses on "men at war," living in makeshift camps as they fight before the walls of Troy or along the banks of the Scamander river, the *Odyssey* for all its geographical restlessness is surprisingly domestic. It shows us a world largely at peace, and its great theme is hospitality, nearly the opposite of Achilles's anger. In ancient times, households extended hospitality—*xeinia*—to weary strangers and travelers. Or were supposed to. Penelope's suitors abuse this privilege; the Cyclops inverts it (he doesn't feed his guests—he eats them), Circe and Calypso bend it to their sensual purposes. How often does Odysseus land on an island and wonder what kind of welcome he will receive? And is there any other classical hero who talks so much about hunger, his belly, and the need for food?

The Phaeacians, who dwell in a kind of Greek Shangri-la, entertain the half-drowned stranger with honor—and it is to them that Odysseus eventually tells his true story. Those celebrated Sinbad-like adventures occupy only books nine through twelve of this twenty-four-book epic. Most of the second half of the poem takes place on Ithaca, and offers even greater, if quieter thrills: the moment when Odysseus's old dog, Argus, who has waited twenty years, recognizes his master; the moment when the nurse Euyclea touches the tell-tale scar and knows the identity of the stranger before her; the dramatic moment when the reviled beggar carefully examines the great bow for dry rot, then suddenly strings it and plucks it like a lyre, before notching an arrow: "Dogs, did you think that I should not come from Troy? You have wasted my substance, have forced my womenservants to lie with you, and have wooed my wife while I was still living. You have feared neither God nor man, and now you shall die."

And they do. Every last one.

WHAT, IN THE END, DOES ONE TAKE AWAY FROM THE *ILIAD* AND THE *ODYSSEY*? The immensely influential eighteenth-century classical scholar Johann Joachim Winckelmann spoke of *"eine edle Einfalt und eine stille Grosse"*—a noble simplicity and a calm greatness. The critic Guy Davenport aptly points to Homer's "wonderfully generous mind," impartially accepting the world in all its diversity. Others might stress his wisdom about the contagious nature of war, or his depiction of Odysseus as the first modern man. But I think Ezra Pound got it right when he stressed Homer's perennial freshness. After more than 2,500 years, the *Iliad* and the *Odyssey* still speak to us, unforgettably, about nearly everything in life that matters.

Michael Dirda, who received the 1993 Pulitzer Prize for criticism, is the author of the memoir *An Open Book* and of four collections of essays: *Readings*, *Bound to Please*, *Book by Book*, and *Classics for Pleasure*.

THE
ILIAD

Contents

PREFACE

The headmaster of one of our foremost public schools told me not long since that he had been asked what canons he thought it most essential to observe in translating from English into Latin. His answer was that in the first place the Latin must be idiomatic, in the second it must flow, and in the third it must keep as near as it could to the English from which it was being translated.

I said, "Then you hold that if either the Latin or the English must perforce give place, it is the English that should yield rather than the Latin?"

This, he replied, was his opinion; and surely the very sound canons above given apply to all translation. The genius of the language into which a translation is being made is the first thing to be considered; if the original was readable, the translation must be so also, or however good it may be as a construe, it is not a translation.

It follows that a translation should depart hardly at all from the modes of speech current in the translator's own times, inasmuch as nothing is readable, for long, which affects any other diction than that of the age in which it is written. We know the charm of the Elizabethan translations, but he who would attempt one that shall vie with these must eschew all Elizabethanisms that are not good Victorianisms also.

For the charm of the Elizabethans does not lie in their Elizabethanisms; these are but as the mosses and lichens which Time will grow upon our Victorian literature as surely as he has grown them upon the Elizabethan—upon such of it, at least, as has not been jerry-built. Shakespeare tells us that it is Time's glory to stamp the seal of time on aged things. No doubt; but he will have no hands stamp it save his own; he will rot an artificial ruin, but he will not glorify it; if he is to hallow any work it must be frankly secular when he deigns to take it in hand—by this I mean honestly after the manner of its own age and country. The Elizabethans probably knew this too well to know that they knew it, but whether they knew it or no they did not lard a crib with Chaucerisms and think that they were translating. They aimed fearlessly and without taint of affectation at making a dead author living to a generation other than his own. To do this they transfused their blood into his cold veins, and quickened him with their own livingness.

Then the life is theirs not his? In part no doubt it is so; but if they have loved him well enough, his life will have entered into them and possessed them. They will have given him of their life, and he will have paid them in their own coin. If, however, the mouth of the ox who treads out the corn may not be muzzled, and if there is to be a certain give and take between a dead author and his translator, it follows that a translator should be allowed greater liberty when the work he is translating belongs to an age and country widely remote from his own. For a poem's prosperity is like a jest's—it is in the ear of him that hears it. It takes two people to say a thing—a sayee as well as a sayer—and by parity of reasoning a poem's original audience and environment are integral parts of the poem itself. Poem and audience are as ego and nonego; they blend into one another. Change either, and some corresponding change, spiritual rather than literal, will be necessary in the other, if the original harmony between them is to be preserved.

Happily in the cases both of the *Iliad* and the *Odyssey* we can see clearly enough that the audiences did not differ so widely from ourselves as we might expect after an interval of some three thousand years. But they differ, especially in the case of the *Iliad*, and the difference necessitates a greater amount of freedom on the part of a translator than would be tolerable if it did not exist.

Freedom of another kind is further involved in the initial liberty of rendering in prose a work that was composed in verse. Prose differs from verse much as singing from speaking or dancing from walking, and what is right in the one is often wrong in the other. Prose, for example, does not permit that iteration of epithet and title, sometimes due merely to the requirements of meter, and sometimes otiose, which abounds in the *Iliad* without in any way disfiguring it. We look, indeed, for the iteration and enjoy it. We are never weary of being told that Juno is white-armed, Minerva gray-eyed, and Agamemnon king of men; but had Homer written in prose he would not have told us these things so often. Therefore, though frequently allowing common form epithets and titles to recur, I have not less frequently suppressed them.

Lest, however, the reader should imagine that I have departed from the letter of the *Iliad* more than I have, I will give the first fifty lines or so of the best prose translation that has yet been made—I mean that of Messrs. Leaf, Lang, and Myers, to which throughout my work I have been greatly indebted. Often have they saved me from error, and rarely have I found occasion to differ from them as to the meaning of a passage. I do not believe that I have translated a single paragraph without reference to them, but this said, a comparison of their opening paragraphs with my own will show the kind of way in which I differ from them as to the manner in which Homer should be translated.

Their translation (here, by Dr. Leaf) opens thus:

> Sing, goddess, the wrath of Achilles Peleus' son, the ruinous wrath that brought on the Achaians woes innumerable, and hurled down into Hades many strong souls of heroes, and gave their bodies to be a prey to dogs and all winged fowls; and so the counsel of Zeus wrought out its accomplishment from the day when strife first parted Atreides king of men and noble Achilles.
>
> Who then among the gods set the twain at strife and variance? Even the son of Leto and of Zeus; for he in anger at the king sent a sore plague upon the host, that the folk began to perish, because Atreides had done dishonour to Chryses the priest. For he had come to the Achaians' fleet ships to win his daughter's freedom, and brought

a ransom beyond telling; and bare in his hands the fillet of Apollo the Far-darter upon a golden staff; and made his prayer unto all the Achaians, and most of all to the two sons of Atreus, orderers of the host: "Ye sons of Atreus and all ye well-greaved Achaians, now may the gods that dwell in the mansions of Olympus grant you to lay waste the city of Priam, and to fare happily homeward; only set ye my dear child free, and accept the ransom in reverence to the son of Zeus, far-darting Apollo."

Then all the other Achaians cried assent, to reverence the priest and accept his goodly ransom; yet the thing pleased not the heart of Agamemnon son of Atreus, but he roughly sent him away, and laid stern charge upon him, saying, "Let me not find thee, old man, amid the hollow ships, whether tarrying now or returning again hereafter, lest the staff and fillet of the god avail thee naught. And her will I not set free; nay, ere that shall old age come on her in our house, in Argos, far from her native land, where she shall ply the loom and serve my couch. But depart, provoke me not, that thou mayest the rather go in peace."

So said he, and the old man was afraid and obeyed his word, and fared silently along the shore of the loud-sounding sea. Then went that aged man apart and prayed aloud to King Apollo, whom Leto of the fair locks bare, "Hear me, god of the silver bow, that standest over Chryse and holy Killa, and rulest Tenedos with might, O Smintheus! If ever I built a temple gracious in thine eyes, or if ever I burnt to thee fat flesh of thighs of bulls or goats, fulfil thou this my desire; let the Danaans pay by thine arrows for my tears."

So spake he in prayer, and Phoebus Apollo heard him, and came down from the peaks of Olympus wroth at heart, bearing on his shoulders his bow and covered quiver. And the arrows clanged upon his shoulders in his wrath, as the god moved; and he descended like to night. Then he sate him aloof from the ships, and let an arrow fly; and there was heard a dread clanging of the silver bow. First did he assail the mules and fleet dogs, but afterward, aiming at the men his piercing dart, he smote; and the pyres of the dead burnt continually in multitude.

I have given the foregoing extract with less compunction, by reason of the reflection, ever present with me, that not a few readers—nor these the least cultured—will prefer Dr. Leaf's translation to my own. Throughout my work I have taken the same kind of liberties as those that the reader will readily detect if he compares Dr. Leaf's rendering with mine. But I do not believe that I have anywhere taken greater ones. The difference between us in the prayer of Chryses, where Dr. Leaf translates "If ever I built a temple," etc., while I render "If ever I decked your temple with garlands," etc., is not a case in point, for it is due to my preferring Liddell and Scott's translation. I very readily admit that Dr. Leaf has in the main kept more closely to the words of Homer, but I believe him to have lost more of the spirit of the original through his abandonment (no doubt deliberate) of all attempt at stately, and at the same time easy, musical, flow of language, than he has gained in adherence to the letter—to which, after all, neither he nor any man can adhere.

These last words may suggest that I claim graces which Dr. Leaf has not attained. I can make no such claim. All I claim is to have done my best towards making the less sanguinary parts of the *Iliad* interesting to English readers. The more sanguinary parts cannot be made interesting; indeed I doubt whether they can ever have been so, or even been intended to be so, to a highly cultivated audience. They had to be written, and they were written; but it is clear that Homer often wrote them with impatience, and that actual warfare was as distasteful to him as it was foreign to his experience. Happily there is much less fighting in the *Iliad* than people generally think.

One word more and I have done. I have burdened my translation with as few notes[1] as possible, intending to reserve what I have to say about the *Iliad* generally for another work to be undertaken when my complete translation of the *Odyssey* has been printed. Lastly, the reception of my recent book, *The Authoress of the Odyssey*, has convinced me that the general reader much prefers the Latinized names of gods and heroes to those which it has of late years been attempted to popularize: I have no hesitation, therefore, in adhering to the nomenclature to which Pope, Mr. Gladstone, and Lord Derby have long since familiarized the public.[2]

SAMUEL BUTLER
AUGUST 8, 1898

[1] Butler's sparse and not very helpful notes have been omitted.

[2] The names of gods and goddesses have been changed back to the Greek.

Principal Personages of *The Iliad*, Their Parentage, and Position

(The names by which they were known to Romans are in parentheses.)

Gods and Goddesses

ZEUS (Jove), son of Cronus (Saturn); king of the gods and ruler of the sky, arbiter of human destiny.

POSEIDON (Neptune), son of Cronus; king of the sea; favors the Greeks.

HADES, son of Cronus; ruler of the underworld of the dead.

HERA (Juno), daughter of Cronus and wife of Zeus; queen of the gods; favors the Greeks.

ATHENE (Minerva), daughter of Zeus; favors the Greeks.

APOLLO, son of Zeus and Leto; favors the Trojans.

ARTEMIS (Diana), daughter of Zeus and Leto; favors the Trojans.

APHRODITE (Venus), daughter of Zeus and Dione; favors the Trojans.

ARES (Mars), son of Zeus; favors the Trojans.

HEPHAESTUS (Vulcan), son of Zeus and Hera; favors the Greeks.

HERMES (Mercury), son of Zeus; favors the Trojans.

IRIS, messenger of the gods.

PAEËON, physician to the gods.

THETIS, a sea nymph, wedded to a mortal, Peleus; mother of Achilles.

GOD OF THE RIVER SCAMANDER, also called Xanthus; favors the Trojans.

Greeks, called by Homer Achaeans, Danaans, or Argives

AGAMEMNON, son of Atreus; king of Argos and Mycenae; leader of the host.

MENELAUS, son of Atreus and husband of Helen; king of Sparta, also called Lacedaemon.

ACHILLES, son of Peleus and the sea-nymph Thetis, grandson of Aeacus, son of Zeus; chief of the Myrmidons from Phthia and Hellas.

NESTOR, son of Neleus; aged king of Pylus and Dorium; father of Antilochus and Thrasymedes.

ODYSSEUS (Ulysses), son of Laertes and husband of Penelope; king of Ithaca and leader of the Cephallenians.

AJAX, son of Telamon; ruler of Salamis.

AJAX, son of Oïleus; ruler of Locris.

DIOMED, son of Tydeus and grandson of Oeneus; king of Middle Argos, Tiryns, and Aegina.

IDOMENEUS, son of Deucalion and grandson of Minos, king of Crete.

TLEPOLEMUS, son of Heracles; from Rhodes.

PATROCLUS, son of Menoetius; comrade and squire of Achilles.

PHOENIX, son of Amyntor; foster son of Achilles' father and old friend of Achilles; ruler of the Dolopians in Phthia.

STHENELUS, son of Capaneus; comrade of Diomed.

MERIONES, son of Molus; comrade and squire of Idomeneus

ANTILOCHUS, son of Nestor.

TEUCER, illegitimate son of Telamon, half brother of the first Ajax; a bowman.

CALCHAS, son of Thestor; seer and interpreter of omens.

MACHAON, son of the healer Asclepius; physician to the Greeks.

THERSITES, ugliest of the Greek soldiers; an endless talker.

ASCALAPHUS, leader of the Miniae; son of Ares.

TALTHYBIUS and EURYBATES, Greek heralds.

Trojans

PRIAM, son of Laomedon and descendant of Tros, the founder of Troy, and of Dardanus, son of Zeus; king of Troy.

PARIS, also called Alexander, son of Priam; seducer of Helen.

HECTOR, son of Priam; commander of the Trojan army.

HELENUS, son of Priam; soothsayer for the Trojans.

DEÏPHOBUS and LYCAON, sons of Priam.

ANTENOR, aged counselor to Priam and the Trojans.

SARPEDON, son of Zeus and Laodamia, grandson of Bellerophon; leader of the Lycians.

GLAUCUS, son of Hippolochus and grandson of Bellerophon; comrade and squire of Sarpedon.

AENEAS, son of Anchises and the goddess Aphrodite; leader of the Dardanians.

RHESUS, son of Eoneus; king of Thrace.

PANDARUS, son of Lycaon; chief of Telea, near Mount Ida.

POLYDAMAS, son of Panthoüs; Trojan warrior and councilor.

ARCHELOCHUS, LAODOCUS, and ACAMAS, sons of Antenor.

DOLON, son of Eumedes; scout for the Trojans.

IDAEUS, Trojan herald.

Women in Troy

HECUBA, wife of Priam; queen of Troy.

HELEN, daughter of Tyndareus and wife of the Greek king Menelaus; brought by Paris to Troy.

ANDROMACHE, daughter of Aëtion, king of Cilicia; wife of Hector and mother of his little son, Astyanax.

LAODICE, daughter of Priam and Hecuba; wife of Helicaon, son of Antenor.

CASSANDRA, daughter of Priam and Hecuba.

THEANO, daughter of Cisseus and wife of Antenor; priestess of Athene.

Scene of the Action

The plain before Troy, through which flows the river Scamander, also called Xanthus.

The camp of the Greeks around their black ships, which lie drawn up in a long row on the edge of the seashore.

The city of Troy, also called Ilium, on a height above the plain, with its citadel, called Pergamum.

The seat of the gods on Mount Olympus in northern Thessaly.

Book I

Agamemnon is compelled to restore the captive girl Chryseis to her father,
but in retaliation takes from Achilles the lovely Briseis. Achilles, enraged,
vows he will fight no more for Agamemnon and through his mother,
the sea nymph Thetis, secures the aid of Zeus for the Trojans.
This provokes the wrath of the goddess Hera.

SING, O GODDESS, THE ANGER OF ACHILLES, SON OF PELEUS, THAT brought countless ills upon the Achaeans. Many a brave soul did it send hurrying down to Hades, and many a hero did it yield a prey to dogs and vultures, for so were the counsels of Zeus fulfilled from the day on which the son of Atreus, king of men, and great Achilles first fell out with one another.

And which of the gods was it that set them on to quarrel? It was the son of Zeus and Leto; for he was angry with the king and sent a pestilence upon the host to plague the people, because the son of Atreus had dishonored Chryses, his priest. Now Chryses had come to the ships of the Achaeans to free his daughter and had brought with him a great ransom. Moreover, he bore in his hand the scepter of Apollo wreathed with a suppliant's wreath, and he besought the Achaeans, but most of all, the two sons of Atreus, who were their chiefs.

"Sons of Atreus," he cried, "and all other Achaeans, may the gods who dwell in Olympus grant you to sack the city of Priam and to reach your homes in safety; but free my daughter and accept a ransom for her, in reverence to Apollo, son of Zeus."

On this the rest of the Achaeans with one voice were for respecting the priest and taking the ransom that he offered; but not so Agamemnon, who spoke fiercely to him and sent him roughly away. "Old man," said he, "let me not find you tarrying about our ships, nor yet coming hereafter. Your scepter of the god and your wreath shall profit you nothing. I will not free her. She shall grow old in my house at Argos far from her own home, busying herself with her loom and visiting my couch. So go, and do not provoke me or it shall be the worse for you."

The old man feared him and obeyed. Not a word he spoke, but went by the shore of the sounding sea and prayed apart to King Apollo whom lovely Leto had borne. "Hear me," he cried, "O god of the silver bow; that protectest Chryse and holy Cilla and rulest Tenedos with thy might, hear me, O thou of Sminthe! If I have ever decked your temple with garlands, or burned your thighbones in fat of bulls or goats, grant my prayer and let your arrows avenge these my tears upon the Danaans."

Thus did he pray, and Apollo heard his prayer. He came down furious from the summits of Olympus, with his bow and his quiver upon his shoulder, and the arrows rattled on his back with the rage that trembled within him. He sat himself down away from the ships with a face as dark as night, and his silver bow rang death as he shot his arrow in the midst of them. First he smote their mules and their hounds, but presently he aimed his shafts at the people themselves, and all day long the pyres of the dead were burning.

For nine whole days he shot his arrows among the people, but upon the tenth day Achilles called them in assembly—moved thereto by Hera, who saw the Achaeans in their death throes and had compassion upon them. Then, when they were got together, he rose and spoke among them.

"Son of Atreus," said he, "I deem that we should now turn roving home if we would escape destruction, for we are being cut down by war and pestilence at once. Let us ask some priest or prophet, or some reader of dreams (for dreams, too, are of Zeus) who can tell us why Phoebus Apollo is so angry, and say whether it is for some vow that we have broken, or hecatomb that we have not offered, and whether he will accept the savor of lambs and goats without blemish, so as to take away the plague from us."

With these words he sat down, and Calchas, son of Thestor, wisest of augurs, who knew things past present and to come, rose to speak. He it was who had guided the Achaeans with their fleet to Ilium, through the prophesyings with which Phoebus Apollo had inspired him. With all sincerity and good will he addressed them thus:

"Achilles, loved of heaven, you bid me tell you about the anger of King Apollo; I will therefore do so; but consider first and swear that you will stand by me heartily in word and deed, for I know that I shall offend one who rules the Argives with might, and to whom all the Achaeans are in subjection. A plain man cannot stand against the anger of a king who, if he swallow his displeasure now, will yet nurse revenge till he has wreaked it. Consider, therefore, whether or no you will protect me."

And Achilles answered: "Fear not, but speak as it is borne in upon you from heaven, for by Apollo, Calchas, to whom you pray, and whose oracles you reveal to us, not a Danaan at our ships shall lay his hand upon you while I yet live to look upon the face of the earth—no, not though you name Agamemnon himself, who is by far the foremost of the Achaeans."

Thereon the seer spoke boldly. "The god," he said, "is angry neither about vow nor hecatomb, but for his priest's sake, whom Agamemnon has dishonored, in that he would not free his daughter nor take a ransom for her. Therefore has he sent these evils upon us and will yet send others. He will not deliver the Danaans from this pestilence till Agamemnon has restored the girl without fee or ransom to her father and has sent a holy hecatomb to Chryse. Thus we may perhaps appease him."

With these words he sat down, and Agamemnon rose in anger. His heart was black with rage, and his eyes flashed fire as he scowled on Calchas and said: "Seer of evil, you never yet prophesied smooth things concerning me, but have ever loved to foretell that which was evil. You have brought me neither comfort nor performance; and now you come seeing among the Danaans, and saying that Apollo has plagued us because I would not take a ransom for this girl, the daughter of Chryses. I have set my heart on keeping her in my own house, for I love her better even than my own wife, Clytemnestra, whose peer she is alike in form and feature, in understanding and accomplishments. Still I will give her up if I must, for I would have the people live, not die; but you must find me a prize instead, or I alone among the Argives shall be without one. This is not well; for you behold, all of you, that my prize is to go elsewhither."

And Achilles answered: "Most noble son of Atreus, covetous beyond all mankind, how shall the Achaeans find you another prize? We have no common store from which to take one. Those we took from the cities have been awarded; we cannot disallow the awards that have been made already. Give this girl, therefore, to the god, and if ever Zeus grants us to sack the city of Troy we will requite you three and fourfold."

Then Agamemnon said: "Achilles, valiant though you be, you shall not thus outwit me. You shall not overreach and you shall not persuade me. Are you to keep your own prize, while I sit tamely under my loss and give up the girl at your bidding? Let the Achaeans find me a prize in fair exchange to my liking, or I will come and take your own, or that of Ajax or of Odysseus; and he to whomsoever I may come shall rue my coming. But of this we will take thought hereafter; for the present, let us draw a ship into the sea, and find a crew for her expressly; let us put a hecatomb on board, and let us send Chryseis also. Further, let some chief man among us be in command, either Ajax, or Idomeneus, or yourself, son of Peleus, mighty warrior that you are, that we may offer sacrifice and appease the anger of the god."

Achilles scowled at him and answered: "You are steeped in insolence and lust of gain. With what heart can any of the Achaeans do your bidding, either on foray or in open fighting? I came not warring here for any ill the Trojans had done me. I have no quarrel with them. They have not raided my cattle or my horses, or cut down my harvests on the rich plains of Phthia; for between me and them there is a great space, both mountain and sounding sea. We have followed you, Sir Insolence! for your pleasure, not ours—to gain satisfaction from the Trojans for your shameless self and for Menelaus. You forget this, and threaten to rob me of the prize for which I have toiled, and which the sons of the Achaeans have given me. Never when the Achaeans sack any rich city of the Trojans do I receive so good a prize as you do, though it is my hands that do the better part of the fighting. When the sharing comes, your share is far the largest, and I, forsooth, must go back to my ships, take what I can get and be thankful, when my labor of fighting is done. Now, therefore, I shall go back to Phthia; it will be much better for me to return home with my ships, for I will not stay here dishonored to gather gold and substance for you."

And Agamemnon answered: "Fly if you will, I shall make you no prayers to stay you. I have others here who will do me honor, and above all Zeus, the lord of counsel. There is no king here so hateful to me as you are, for you are ever quarrelsome and ill-affected. What though you be brave? Was it not heaven that made you so? Go home, then, with your ships and comrades to lord it over the Myrmidons. I care neither for you nor for your anger; and thus will I do: since Phoebus Apollo is taking Chryseis from me, I shall send her with my ship and my followers, but I shall come to your tent and take your own prize Briseis, that you may learn how much stronger I am than you are, and that another may fear to set himself up as equal or comparable with me."

The son of Peleus was furious, and his heart within his shaggy breast was divided whether to draw his sword, push the others aside, and kill the son of Atreus, or to restrain himself and check his anger. While he was thus in two minds, and was drawing his mighty sword from its scabbard, Athene came down from heaven (for Hera had sent her in the love she bore to them both), and seized the son of Peleus by his yellow hair, visible to him alone, for of the others no man could see her. Achilles turned in amaze, and by the fire that flashed from her eyes at once knew that she was Athene. "Why are you here," said he, "daughter of aegis-bearing Zeus? To see the pride of Agamemnon, son of Atreus? Let me tell you—and it shall surely be—he shall pay for this insolence with his life."

And Athene said: "I come from heaven, if you will hear me, to bid you stay your anger. Hera has sent me, who cares for both of you alike. Cease, then, this brawling, and do not draw your sword. Rail at him if you will, and your railing will not be vain, for I tell you—and it shall surely be—that you shall hereafter receive gifts three times as splendid by reason of this present insult. Hold, therefore, and obey."

"Goddess," answered Achilles, "however angry a man may be, he must do as you two command him. This will be best, for the gods ever hear the prayers of him who has obeyed them."

He stayed his hand on the silver hilt of his sword, and thrust it back into the scabbard as Athene bade him. Then she went back to Olympus among the other gods, and to the house of aegis-bearing Zeus.

But the son of Peleus again began railing at the son of Atreus, for he was still in a rage. "Winebibber," he cried, "with the face of a dog and the heart of a hind, you never dare to go out with the host in fight, nor yet with our chosen men in ambuscade. You shun this as you do death itself. You had rather go round and rob his prizes from any man who contradicts you. You devour your people, for you are king over a feeble folk; otherwise, son of Atreus, henceforward you would insult no man. Therefore I say, and swear it with a great oath—nay, by this my scepter, which shall sprout neither leaf nor shoot, nor bud anew from the day on which it left its parent stem upon the mountains—for the ax stripped it of leaf and bark, and now the sons of the Achaeans bear it as judges and guardians of the decrees of heaven—so surely and solemnly do I swear that hereafter they shall look fondly for Achilles and shall not find him. In the day of your distress, when your men fall dying by the murderous hand of Hector, you shall not know how to help them and shall rend your heart with rage for the hour when you offered insult to the bravest of the Achaeans."

With this the son of Peleus dashed his gold-bestudded scepter on the ground and took his seat, while the son of Atreus was beginning fiercely from his place upon the other side. Then uprose smooth-tongued Nestor, the facile speaker of the Pylians, and the words fell from his lips sweeter than honey. Two generations of men born and bred in Pylos had passed away under his rule, and he was now reigning over the third. With all sincerity and good will, therefore, he addressed them thus:

"Of a truth," he said, "a great sorrow has befallen the Achaean land. Surely Priam with his sons would rejoice, and the Trojans be glad at heart if they could hear this quarrel between you two, who are so excellent in fight and counsel. I am older than either of you; therefore be guided by me. Moreover, I have been the familiar friend of men even greater than you are, and they did not disregard my counsels. Never again can I behold such men as Pirithoüs and Dryas, shepherd of his people, or as Caeneus, Exadius, godlike Polyphemus, and Theseus, son of Aegeus, peer of the immortals. These were the mightiest men ever born upon this earth—mightiest were they, and when they fought the fiercest tribes of mountain savages they utterly overthrew them. I came from distant Pylos and went about among them, for they would have me come, and I fought as it was in me to do. Not a man now living could withstand them, but they heard my words, and were persuaded by them. So be it also with yourselves, for this is the more excellent way. Therefore, Agamemnon, though you be strong, take not this girl away, for the sons of the Achaeans have already given her to Achilles; and you, Achilles, strive not further with the king, for no man who by the grace of Zeus wields a scepter has like honor with Agamemnon. You are strong and have a goddess for your mother, but Agamemnon is stronger than you, for he has more people under him. Son of

Atreus, check your anger, I implore you; end this quarrel with Achilles, who in the day of battle is a tower of strength to the Achaeans."

And Agamemnon answered: "Sir, all that you have said is true, but this fellow must needs become our lord and master: he must be lord of all, king of all, and captain of all, and this shall hardly be. Granted that the gods have made him a great warrior, have they also given him the right to speak with railing?"

Achilles interrupted him. "I should be a mean coward," he cried, "were I to give in to you in all things. Order other people about, not me, for I shall obey no longer. Furthermore I say—and lay my saying to your heart—I shall fight neither you nor any man about this girl, for those that take were those also that gave. But of all else that is at my ship you shall carry away nothing by force. Try, that others may see; if you do, my spear shall be reddened with your blood."

When they had quarreled thus angrily, they rose, and broke up the assembly at the ships of the Achaeans. The son of Peleus went back to his tents and ships with the son of Menoetius and his company, while Agamemnon drew a vessel into the water and chose a crew of twenty oarsmen. He escorted Chryseis on board and sent moreover a hecatomb for the god. And Odysseus went as captain.

These, then, went on board and sailed their ways over the sea. But the son of Atreus bade the people purify themselves; so they purified themselves and cast their filth into the sea. Then they offered hecatombs of bulls and goats without blemish on the seashore, and the smoke with the savor of their sacrifice rose curling up towards heaven.

Thus did they busy themselves throughout the host. But Agamemnon did not forget the threat that he had made Achilles and called his trusty messengers and squires, Talthybius and Eurybates. "Go," said he, "to the tent of Achilles, son of Peleus. Take Briseis by the hand and bring her hither; if he will not give her I shall come with others and take her—which will press him harder."

He charged them straightly further and dismissed them, whereon they went their way sorrowfully by the seaside, till they came to the tents and ships of the Myrmidons. They found Achilles sitting by his tent and his ships, and ill-pleased he was when he beheld them. They stood fearfully and reverently before him, and never a word did they speak, but he knew them and said: "Welcome, heralds, messengers of gods and men; draw near; my quarrel is not with you but with Agamemnon who has sent you for the girl Briseis. Therefore, Patroclus, bring her and give her to them, but let them be witnesses by the blessed gods, by mortal men, and by the fierceness of Agamemnon's anger, that if ever again there be need of me to save the people from ruin, they shall seek and they shall not find. Agamemnon is mad with rage and knows not how to look before and after that the Achaeans may fight by their ships in safety."

Patroclus did as his dear comrade had bidden him. He brought Briseis from the tent and gave her over to the heralds, who took her with them to the ships of the Achaeans—and the woman was loath to go. Then Achilles went all alone by the side of the hoar sea, weeping and looking out upon the boundless waste of waters. He raised his hands in prayer to his immortal mother. "Mother," he cried, "you bore me doomed to live but for a little season. Surely Zeus, who thunders from Olympus, might have made that little glorious. It is not so. Agamemnon, son of Atreus, has done me dishonor, and has robbed me of my prize by force."

As he spoke he wept aloud, and his mother heard him where she was sitting in the depths of the sea hard by the old man, her father. Forthwith she rose as it were a gray mist out of the waves, sat down before him as he stood weeping, caressed him with her hand, and said, "My son, why are you weeping? What is it that grieves you? Keep it not from me, but tell me, that we may know it together."

Achilles drew a deep sigh and said: "You know it; why tell you what you know well already? We went to Thebe, the strong city of Eëtion, sacked it, and brought hither the spoil. The sons of the Achaeans shared it duly among themselves, and chose lovely Chryseis as the meed of Agamemnon; but Chryses, priest of Apollo, came to the ships of the Achaeans to free his daughter, and brought with him a great ransom. Moreover, he bore in his hand the scepter of Apollo, wreathed with a suppliant's wreath, and he besought the Achaeans, but most of all the two sons of Atreus who were their chiefs.

"On this the rest of the Achaeans with one voice were for respecting the priest and taking the ransom that he offered; but not so Agamemnon, who spoke fiercely to him and sent him roughly away. So he went back in anger, and Apollo, who loved him dearly, heard his prayer. Then the god sent a deadly dart upon the Argives, and the people died thick on one another, for the arrows went everywhither among the wide host of the Achaeans. At last a seer in the fullness of his knowledge declared to us the oracles of Apollo, and I was myself first to say that we should appease him. Whereon the son of Atreus rose in anger, and threatened that which he has since done. The Achaeans are now taking the girl in a ship to Chryse, and sending gifts of sacrifice to the god; but the heralds have just taken from my tent the daughter of Briseus, whom the Achaeans had awarded to myself.

"Help your brave son, therefore, if you are able. Go to Olympus, and if you have ever done him service in word or deed, implore the aid of Zeus. Ofttimes in my father's house have I heard you glory in that you alone of the immortals saved the son of Cronus from ruin, when the others, with Hera, Poseidon, and Pallas Athene would have put him in bonds. It was you, goddess, who delivered him by calling to Olympus the hundred-handed monster whom gods call Briareus, but men Aegaeon, for he is stronger even than his father. When, therefore, he took his seat all-glorious beside the son of Cronus, the other gods were afraid, and did not bind him. Go, then, to him, remind him of all this, clasp his knees, and bid him give succor to the Trojans. Let the Achaeans be hemmed in at the sterns of their ships, and perish on the seashore, that they may reap what joy they may of their king, and that

Agamemnon may rue his blindness in offering insult to the foremost of the Achaeans."

Thetis wept and answered: "My son, woe is me that I should have borne or suckled you. Would indeed that you had lived your span free from all sorrow at your ships, for it is all too brief; alas, that you should be at once short of life and long of sorrow above your peers. Woe, therefore, was the hour in which I bore you. Nevertheless I will go to the snowy heights of Olympus, and tell this tale to Zeus, if he will hear our prayer. Meanwhile stay where you are with your ships, nurse your anger against the Achaeans, and hold aloof from fight. For Zeus went yesterday to Oceanus to a feast among the Ethiopians, and the other gods went with him. He will return to Olympus twelve days hence. I will then go to his mansion paved with bronze and will beseech him, nor do I doubt that I shall be able to persuade him."

On this she left him, still furious at the loss of her that had been taken from him. Meanwhile Odysseus reached Chryse with the hecatomb. When they had come inside the harbor they furled the sails and laid them in the ship's hold. They slackened the forestays, lowered the mast into its place, and rowed the ship to the place where they would have her lie. There they cast out their mooring stones and made fast the hawsers. They then got out upon the seashore and landed the hecatomb for Apollo; Chryseis also left the ship, and Odysseus led her to the altar to deliver her into the hands of her father. "Chryses," said he, "King Agamemnon has sent me to bring you back your child, and to offer sacrifice to Apollo on behalf of the Danaans, that we may propitiate the god, who has now brought much sorrow upon the Argives."

So saying he gave the girl over to her father, who received her gladly, and they ranged the holy hecatomb all orderly round the altar of the god. They washed their hands and took up the barley meal to sprinkle over the victims, while Chryses lifted up his hands and prayed aloud on their behalf. "Hear me," he cried, "O god of the silver bow, that protectest Chryse and holy Cilla, and rulest Tenedos with thy might! Even as thou didst hear me aforetime when I prayed, and didst press hardly upon the Achaeans, so hear me yet again, and stay this fearful pestilence from the Danaans."

Thus did he pray, and Apollo heard his prayer. When they had done praying and sprinkling the barley meal, they drew back the heads of the victims and killed and flayed them. They cut out the thighbones, wrapped them round in two layers of fat, set some pieces of raw meat on the top of them, and then Chryses laid them on the wood fire and poured wine over them, while the young men stood near him with five-pronged spits in their hands. When the thighbones were burned and they had tasted the inward meats, they cut the rest up small, put the pieces upon the spits, roasted them till they were done, and drew them off: then, when they had finished their work and the feast was ready, they ate it, and every man had his full share, so that all were satisfied. As soon as they had had enough to eat and drink, pages filled the mixing bowl with wine and water and handed it round, after giving every man his drink offering.

Thus all day long the young men worshiped the god with song, hymning him and chanting the joyous paean, and the god took pleasure in their voices; but when the sun went down and it came on dark, they laid themselves down to sleep by the stern cables of the ship, and when the child of morning, rosy-fingered Dawn, appeared they again set sail for the host of the Achaeans. Apollo sent them a fair wind, so they raised their mast and hoisted their white sails aloft. As the sail bellied with the wind the ship flew through the deep blue water, and the foam hissed against her bows as she sped onward. When they reached the wide-stretching host of the Achaeans, they drew the vessel ashore, high and dry upon the sands, set her strong props beneath her, and went their ways to their own tents and ships.

But Achilles abode at his ships and nursed his anger. He went not to the honorable assembly, and sallied not forth to fight, but gnawed at his own heart, pining for battle and the war cry.

Now after twelve days the immortal gods came back in a body to Olympus, and Zeus led the way. Thetis was not unmindful of the charge her son had laid upon her, so she rose from under the sea and went through great heaven with early morning to Olympus, where she found the mighty son of Cronus sitting all alone upon its topmost ridges. She sat herself down before him, and with her left hand seized his knees, while with her right she caught him under the chin, and besought him, saying:

"Father Zeus, if I ever did you service in word or deed among the immortals, hear my prayer, and do honor to my son, whose life is to be cut short so early. King Agamemnon has dishonored him by taking his prize and keeping her. Honor him then yourself, Olympian lord of counsel, and grant victory to the Trojans, till the Achaeans give my son his due and load him with riches in requital."

Zeus sat for a while silent, and without a word, but Thetis still kept firm hold of his knees, and besought him a second time. "Incline your head," said she, "and promise me surely, or else deny me—for you have nothing to fear— that I may learn how greatly you disdain me."

At this Zeus was much troubled and answered: "I shall have trouble if you set me quarreling with Hera, for she will provoke me with her taunting speeches; even now she is always railing at me before the other gods and accusing me of giving aid to the Trojans. Go back now, lest she should find out. I will consider the matter, and will bring it about as you wish. See, I incline my head that you may believe me. This is the most solemn token that I can give to any god. I never recall my word, or deceive, or fail to do what I say, when I have nodded my head."

As he spoke, the son of Cronus bowed his dark brows, and the ambrosial locks swayed on his immortal head, till vast Olympus reeled.

When the pair had thus laid their plans, they parted—Zeus to his own house, while the goddess quitted the splendor of Olympus, and plunged into the depths of the sea. The gods rose from their seats, before the coming of their sire. Not one of them dared to remain sitting, but all stood up as he came among them. There, then, he took his seat. But Hera, when she saw him, knew that he and the old merman's daughter, silver-footed Thetis, had been hatching mischief, so she at once began to upbraid him. "Trickster," she cried, "which of the gods have you been taking into your counsels now? You are always settling matters in secret behind my back, and have never yet told me, if you could help it, one word of your intentions."

"Hera," replied the sire of gods and men, "you must not expect to be informed of all my counsels. You are my wife, but you would find it hard to understand them. When it is proper for you to hear, there is no one, god or man, who will be told sooner, but when I mean to keep a matter to myself, you must not pry nor ask questions."

"Dread son of Cronus," answered Hera, "what are you talking about? I? Pry and ask questions? Never. I let you have your own way in everything. Still, I have a strong misgiving that the old merman's daughter Thetis has been talking you over, for she was with you and had hold of your knees this self-same morning. I believe, therefore, that you have been promising her to give glory to Achilles, and to kill much people at the ships of the Achaeans."

"Wife," said Zeus, "I can do nothing but you suspect me and find it out. You will take nothing by it, for I shall only dislike you the more, and it will go harder with you. Granted that it is as you say; I mean to have it so. Sit down and hold your tongue as I bid you, for if I once begin to lay my hands about you, though all heaven were on your side it would profit you nothing."

On this Hera was frightened, so she curbed her stubborn will and sat down in silence. But the heavenly beings were disquieted throughout the house of Zeus, till the cunning workman Hephaestus began to try and pacify his mother Hera. "It will be intolerable," said he, "if you two fall to wrangling and setting heaven in an uproar about a pack of mortals. If such ill counsels are to prevail, we shall have no pleasure at our banquet. Let me then advise my mother—and she must herself know that it will be better—to make friends with my dear father Zeus, lest he again scold her and disturb our feast. If the Olympian Thunderer wants to hurl us all from our seats, he can do so, for he is far the strongest, so give him fair words, and he will then soon be in a good humor with us."

As he spoke, he took a double cup of nectar and placed it in his mother's hand. "Cheer up, my dear mother," said he, "and make the best of it. I love you dearly, and should be very sorry to see you get a thrashing; however grieved I might be, I could not help you, for there is no standing against Zeus. Once before when I was trying to help you, he caught me by the foot and flung me from the heavenly threshold. All day long from morn till eve, was I falling, till at sunset I came to ground in the island of Lemnos, and there I lay, with very little life left in me, till the Sintians came and tended me."

Hera smiled at this, and as she smiled she took the cup from her son's hands. Then Hephaestus drew sweet nectar from the mixing bowl, and served it round among the gods, going from left to right; and the blessed gods laughed out a loud applause as they saw him bustling about the heavenly mansion.

Thus through the livelong day to the going down of the sun they feasted, and everyone had his full share, so that all were satisfied. Apollo struck his lyre, and the Muses lifted up their sweet voices, calling and answering one another. But when the sun's glorious light had faded, they went home to bed, each in his own abode, which lame Hephaestus with his consummate skill had fashioned for them. So Zeus, the Olympian lord of thunder, hied him to the bed in which he always slept; and when he had got on to it he went to sleep, with Hera of the golden throne by his side.

Book II

Zeus, keeping his promise, tricks Agamemnon with a false dream into imagining
he can capture Troy at once. Agamemnon craftily tests the spirit of his men by
telling them that Zeus has bidden him give up the siege. Athene, sent by Hera,
inspires Odysseus to oppose the plan, and with Nestor he incites the host to continue
the struggle. Both armies muster for battle. Their chiefs and forces are counted.

NOW THE OTHER GODS AND THE ARMED WARRIORS ON THE PLAIN slept soundly, but Zeus was wakeful, for he was thinking how to do honor to Achilles and destroy much people at the ships of the Achaeans. In the end he deemed it would be best to send a lying dream to King Agamemnon. So he called one to him and said to it: "Lying Dream, go to the ships of the Achaeans, into the tent of Agamemnon, and say to him word for word as I now bid you. Tell him to get the Achaeans instantly under arms, for he shall take Troy. There are no longer divided counsels among the gods. Hera has brought them to her own mind, and woe betides the Trojans."

The dream went when it had heard its message, and soon reached the ships of the Achaeans. It sought Agamemnon, son of Atreus, and found him in his tent, wrapped in a profound slumber. It hovered over his head in the likeness of Nestor, son of Neleus, whom Agamemnon honored above all his councilors, and said:

"You are sleeping, son of Atreus; one who has the welfare of his host and so much other care upon his shoulders should dock his sleep. Hear me at once, for

I come as a messenger from Zeus, who, though he be not near, yet takes thought for you and pities you. He bids you get the Achaeans instantly under arms, for you shall take Troy. There are no longer divided counsels among the gods; Hera has brought them over to her own mind, and woe betides the Trojans at the hands of Zeus. Remember this, and when you wake see that it does not escape you."

The dream then left him, and he thought of things that were surely not to be accomplished. He thought that on that same day he was to take the city of Priam, but he little knew what was in the mind of Zeus, who had many another hard-fought fight in store alike for Danaans and Trojans. Then presently he woke, with the divine message still ringing in his ears; so he sat upright, and put on his soft shirt so fair and new, and over this his heavy cloak. He bound his sandals on to his comely feet, and slung his silver-studded sword about his shoulders; then he took the imperishable staff of his father and sallied forth to the ships of the Achaeans.

The goddess Dawn now wended her way to vast Olympus that she might herald day to Zeus and to the other immortals, and Agamemnon sent the criers round to call the people in assembly; so they called them and the people gathered thereon. But first he summoned a meeting of the elders at the ship of Nestor, king of Pylos, and when they were assembled he laid a cunning counsel before them.

"My friends," said he, "I have had a dream from heaven in the dead of night, and its face and figure resembled none but Nestor's. It hovered over my head and said: 'You are sleeping, son of Atreus; one who has the welfare of his host and so much other care upon his shoulders should dock his sleep. Hear me at once, for I am a messenger from Zeus, who, though he be not near, yet takes thought for you and pities you. He bids you get the Achaeans instantly under arms, for you shall take Troy. There are no longer divided counsels among the gods; Hera has brought them over to her own mind, and woe betides the Trojans at the hands of Zeus. Remember this.' The dream then vanished and I awoke. Let us now, therefore, arm the sons of the Achaeans.

But it will be well that I should first sound them, and to this end I will tell them to fly with their ships; but do you others go about among the host and prevent their doing so."

He then sat down, and Nestor, the prince of Pylos, with all sincerity and good will addressed them thus: "My friends," said he, "princes and councilors of the Argives, if any other man of the Achaeans had told us of this dream we should have declared it false, and would have had nothing to do with it. But he who has seen it is the foremost man among us; we must therefore set about getting the people under arms."

With this he led the way from the assembly, and the other sceptered kings rose with him in obedience to the word of Agamemnon; but the people pressed forward to hear. They swarmed like bees that sally from some hollow cave and flit in countless throng among the spring flowers, bunched in knots and clusters; even so did the mighty multitude pour from ships and tents to the assembly, and range themselves upon the wide-watered shore, while among them ran Wildfire Rumor, messenger of Zeus, urging them ever to the fore. Thus they gathered in a pell-mell of mad confusion, and the earth groaned under the tramp of men as the people sought their places. Nine heralds went crying about among them to stay their tumult and bid them listen to the kings, till at last they were got into their several places and ceased their clamor. Then King Agamemnon rose, holding his scepter. This was the work of Hephaestus, who gave it to Zeus, the son of Cronus. Zeus gave it to Hermes, slayer of Argus, guide and guardian. King Hermes gave it to Pelops, the mighty charioteer, and Pelops to Atreus, shepherd of his people. Atreus, when he died, left it to Thyestes, rich in flocks, and Thyestes in his turn left it to be borne by Agamemnon, that he might be lord of all Argos and of the isles. Leaning, then, on his scepter, he addressed the Argives.

"My friends," he said, "heroes, servants of Ares, the hand of heaven has been laid heavily upon me. Cruel Zeus gave me his solemn promise that I should sack the city of Priam before returning, but he has played me false, and is now bidding me go ingloriously back to Argos with the loss of much people. Such is the will of Zeus, who has laid many a proud city in the dust, as he will yet lay others, for his power is above all. It will be a sorry tale hereafter that an Achaean host, at once so great and valiant, battled in vain against men fewer in number than themselves; but as yet the end is not in sight. Think that the Achaeans and Trojans have sworn to a solemn covenant, and that they have each been numbered—the Trojans by the roll of their householders, and we by companies of ten; think further that each of our companies desired to have a Trojan householder to pour out their wine; we are so greatly more in number that full many a company would have to go without its cupbearer. But they have in the town many allies from other places, and it is these that hinder me from being able to sack the rich city of Ilium. Nine of Zeus' years are gone. The timbers of our ships have rotted; their tackling is sound no longer. Our wives and little ones at home look anxiously for our coming, but the work that we came hither to do has not been done. Now, therefore, let us all do as I say: let us sail back to our own land, for we shall not take Troy."

With these words he moved the hearts of the multitude, so many of them as knew not the cunning counsel of Agamemnon. They surged to and fro like the waves of the Icarian Sea, when the east and south winds break from heaven's clouds to lash them; or as when the west wind sweeps over a field of corn and the ears bow beneath the blast, even so were they swayed as they flew with loud cries towards the ships, and the dust from under their feet rose heavenward. They cheered each other on to draw the ships into the sea; they cleared the channels in front of them; they began taking away the stays from underneath them, and the welkin rang with their glad cries, so eager were they to return.

Then surely the Argives would have returned after a fashion that was not fated. But Hera said to Athene, "Alas, daughter of aegis-bearing Zeus, unweariable, shall the Argives fly home to their own land over the broad sea, and leave Priam and the Trojans the glory of still keeping Helen, for whose sake so many of the Achaeans have died at Troy, far from their homes? Go about at once among the host, and speak fairly to them, man by man, that they draw not their ships into the sea."

Athene was not slack to do her bidding. Down she darted from the topmost summits of Olympus, and in a moment she was at the ships of the Achaeans. There she found Odysseus, peer of Zeus in counsel, standing alone. He had not as yet laid a hand upon his ship, for he was grieved and sorry; so she went close up to him and said, "Odysseus, noble son of Laertes, are you going to fling yourselves into your ships, and be off home to your own land in this way? Will you leave Priam and the Trojans the glory of still keeping Helen, for whose sake so many of the Achaeans have died at Troy, far from their homes? Go about at once among the host, and speak fairly to them, man by man, that they draw not their ships into the sea."

Odysseus knew the voice as that of the goddess: he flung his cloak from him and set off to run. His servant Eurybates, a man of Ithaca, who waited on him, took charge of the cloak, whereon Odysseus went straight up to Agamemnon and received from him his ancestral, imperishable staff. With this he went about among the ships of the Achaeans.

Whenever he met a king or chieftain, he stood by him and spoke him fairly. "Sir," said he, "this flight is cowardly and unworthy. Stand to your post, and bid your people also keep their places. You do not yet know the full mind of Agamemnon; he was sounding us, and ere long will visit the Achaeans with his displeasure. We were not all of us at the council to hear what he then said. See to it lest he be angry and do us a mischief; for the pride of kings is great, and the hand of Zeus is with them."

But when he came across any common man who was making a noise, he struck him with his staff and rebuked him, saying: "Sirrah, hold your peace, and listen to better men than yourself. You are a coward and no soldier; you are nobody either in fight or council; we cannot all be kings; it is not well that there should be many masters; one man must be supreme—one king to whom the son of scheming Cronus has given the scepter of sovereignty over you all."

Thus masterfully did he go about among the host, and the people hurried back to the council from their tents and ships with a sound as the thunder of surf when it comes crashing down upon the shore, and all the sea is in an uproar.

The rest now took their seats and kept to their own several places, but Thersites still went on wagging his unbridled tongue—a man of many words, and those unseemly; a monger of sedition, a railer against all who were in authority, who cared not what he said, so that he might set the Achaeans in a laugh. He was the ugliest man of all those that came before Troy—bandy-legged, lame of one foot, with his two shoulders rounded and hunched over his chest. His head ran up to a point, but there was little hair on the top of it. Achilles and Odysseus hated him worst of all, for it was with them that he was most wont to wrangle. Now, however, with a shrill squeaky voice he began heaping his abuse on Agamemnon. The Achaeans were angry and disgusted, yet nonetheless he kept on brawling and bawling at the son of Atreus.

"Agamemnon," he cried, "what ails you now, and what more do you want? Your tents are filled with bronze and with fair women, for whenever we take a town we give you the pick of them. Would you have yet more gold, which some Trojan is to give you as a ransom for his son, when I or another Achaean has taken him prisoner? Or is it some young girl to hide away and lie with? It is not well that you, the ruler of the Achaeans, should bring them into such misery. Weakling cowards, women rather than men, let us sail home, and leave this fellow here at Troy to stew in his own meeds of honor, and discover whether we were of any service to him or no. Achilles is a much better man than he is, and see how he has treated him—robbing him of his prize and keeping it himself. Achilles takes it meekly and shows no fight; if he did, son of Atreus, you would never again insult him."

Thus railed Thersites, but Odysseus at once went up to him and rebuked him sternly. "Check your glib tongue, Thersites," said he, "and babble not a word further. Chide not with princes when you have none to back you. There is no viler creature come before Troy with the sons of Atreus. Drop this chatter about kings, and neither revile them nor keep harping about going home. We do not yet know how things are going to be, nor whether the Achaeans are to return with good success or evil. How dare you gibe at Agamemnon because the Danaans have awarded him so many prizes? I tell you, therefore—and it shall surely be—that if I again catch you talking such nonsense, I will either forfeit my own head and be no more called father of Telemachus, or I will take you, strip you stark naked, and whip you out of the assembly till you go blubbering back to the ships."

On this he beat him with his staff about the back and shoulders till he dropped and fell a-weeping. The golden scepter raised a bloody weal on his back, so he sat down frightened and in pain, looking foolish as he wiped the tears from his eyes. The people were sorry for him, yet they laughed heartily, and one would turn to his neighbor, saying: "Odysseus has done many a good thing ere now in fight and council, but he never did the Argives a better turn than when he stopped this fellow's mouth from prating further. He will give the kings no more of his insolence."

Thus said the people. Then Odysseus rose, scepter in hand, and Athene in the likeness of a herald bade the people be still, that those who were far off might hear him and consider his counsel. He therefore with all sincerity and good will addressed them thus:

"King Agamemnon, the Achaeans are for making you a byword among all mankind. They forget the promise they made you when they set out from Argos, that you should not return till you had sacked the town of Troy, and, like children or widowed women, they murmur and would set off homeward. True it is that they have had toil enough to be disheartened. A man chafes at having to stay away from his wife even for a single month, when he is on shipboard, at the mercy of wind and sea, but it is now nine long years that we have been kept here. I cannot, therefore, blame the Achaeans if they turn restive.

Still we shall be shamed if we go home empty after so long a stay—therefore, my friends, be patient yet a little longer that we may learn whether the prophesyings of Calchas were false or true.

"All who have not since perished must remember as though it were yesterday or the day before, how the ships of the Achaeans were detained in Aulis when we were on our way hither to make war on Priam and the Trojans. We were ranged round about a fountain offering hecatombs to the gods upon their holy altars, and there was a fine plane tree from beneath which there welled a stream of pure water. Then we saw a prodigy; for Zeus sent a fearful serpent out of the ground, with blood-red stains upon its back, and it darted from under the altar on to the plane tree. Now there was a brood of young sparrows, quite small, upon the topmost bough, peeping out from under the leaves, eight in all, and their mother that hatched them made nine. The serpent ate the poor cheeping things, while the old bird flew about lamenting her little ones; but the serpent threw his coils about her and caught her by the wing as she was screaming. Then, when he had eaten both the sparrow and her young, the god who had sent him made him become a sign; for the son of scheming Cronus turned him into stone, and we stood there wondering at that which had come to pass. Seeing, then, that such a fearful portent had broken in upon our hecatombs, Calchas forthwith declared to us the oracles of heaven. 'Why, Achaeans,' said he, 'are you thus speechless? Zeus has sent us this sign, long in coming, and long ere it be fulfilled, though its fame shall last forever. As the serpent ate the eight fledglings and the sparrow that hatched them, which makes nine, so shall we fight nine years at Troy, but in the tenth shall take the town.' This was what he said, and now it is all coming true. Stay here, therefore, all of you, till we take the city of Priam."

On this the Argives raised a shout till the ships rang again with the uproar. Nestor, knight of Gerene, then addressed them. "Shame on you," he cried, "to stay talking here like children when you should fight like men. Where are our covenants now, and where the oaths that we have taken? Shall our counsels be flung into the fire, with our drink offerings and the right hands of fellowship wherein we have put our trust? We waste our time in words, and for all our talking here shall be no further forward. Stand, therefore, son of Atreus, by your own steadfast purpose. Lead the Argives on to battle, and leave this handful of men to rot, who scheme, and scheme in vain, to get back to Argos ere they have learned whether Zeus be true or a liar. For the mighty son of Cronus surely promised that we should succeed, when we Argives set sail to bring death and destruction upon the Trojans. He showed us favorable signs by flashing his lightning on our right hands. Therefore let none make haste to go till he has first lain with the wife of some Trojan and avenged the toil and sorrow that he has suffered for the sake of Helen. Nevertheless, if any man is in such haste to be at home again, let him lay his hand to his ship that he may meet his doom in the sight of all. But, O king, consider and give ear to my counsel, for the word that I say may not be neglected lightly. Divide your men, Agamemnon, into their several tribes and clans, that clans and tribes may stand by and help one another. If you do this, and if the Achaeans obey you, you will find out who, both chiefs and peoples, are brave, and who are cowards; for they will vie one against the other. Thus you shall also learn whether it is through the counsel of heaven or the cowardice of man that you shall fail to take the town."

And Agamemnon answered: "Nestor, you have again outdone the sons of the Achaeans in counsel. Would, by Father Zeus, Athene, and Apollo, that I had among them ten more such councilors, for the city of King Priam would then soon fall beneath our hands, and we should sack it. But the son of Cronus afflicts me with bootless wrangling and strife. Achilles and I are quarreling about this girl, in which matter I was the first to offend; if we can be of one mind again, the Trojans will not stave off destruction for a day. Now, therefore, get your morning meal, that our hosts may join in fight. Whet well your spears, see well to the ordering of your shields, give good feeds to your horses, and look your chariots carefully over, that we may do battle the livelong day;

for we shall have no rest, not for a moment, till night falls to part us. The bands that bear your shields shall be wet with the sweat upon your shoulders, your hands shall weary upon your spears, your horses shall steam in front of your chariots, and if I see any man shirking the fight, or trying to keep out of it at the ships, there shall be no help for him, but he shall be a prey to dogs and vultures."

Thus he spoke, and the Achaeans roared applause. As when the waves run high before the blast of the south wind and break on some lofty headland, dashing against it and buffeting it without ceasing as the storms from every quarter drive them, even so did the Achaeans rise and hurry in all directions to their ships. There they lighted their fires at their tents and got dinner, offering sacrifice every man to one or other of the gods, and praying each one of them that he might live to come out of the fight. Agamemnon, king of men, sacrificed a fat five-year-old bull to the mighty son of Cronus, and invited the princes and elders of his host. First he asked Nestor and King Idomeneus, then the two Ajaxes and the son of Tydeus, and sixthly, Odysseus, peer of gods in counsel; but Menelaus came of his own accord, for he knew how busy his brother then was. They stood round the bull with the barley meal in their hands, and Agamemnon prayed, saying: "Zeus, most glorious, supreme, that dwellest in heaven, and ridest upon the storm cloud, grant that the sun may not go down nor the night fall till the palace of Priam is laid low, and its gates are consumed with fire. Grant that my sword may pierce the shirt of Hector about his heart, and that full many of his comrades may bite the dust as they fall dying round him."

Thus he prayed, but the son of Cronus would not fulfill his prayer. He accepted the sacrifice, yet nonetheless increased their toil continually. When they had done praying and sprinkling the barley meal upon the victim, they drew back its head, killed it, and then flayed it. They cut out the thighbones, wrapped them round in two layers of fat, and set pieces of raw meat on the top of them. These they burned upon the split logs of firewood, but they spitted the inward meats and held them in the flames to cook. When the thighbones were burned, and they had tasted the inward meats, they cut the rest up small, put the pieces upon spits, roasted them till they were done, and drew them off; then, when they had finished their work and the feast was ready, they ate it, and every man had his full share, so that all were satisfied. As soon as they had had enough to eat and drink, Nestor, knight of Gerene, began to speak. "King Agamemnon," said he, "let us not stay talking here, nor be slack in the work that heaven has put into our hands. Let the heralds summon the people to gather at their several ships. We will then go about among the host, that we may begin fighting at once."

Thus did he speak, and Agamemnon heeded his words. He at once sent the criers round to call the people in assembly. So they called them, and the people gathered thereon. The chiefs about the son of Atreus chose their men and marshaled them, while Athene went among them holding her priceless aegis that knows neither age nor death. From it there waved a hundred tassels of pure gold, all deftly woven, and each one of them worth a hundred oxen. With this she darted furiously everywhere among the hosts of the Achaeans, urging them forward, and putting courage into the heart of each, so that he might fight and do battle without ceasing. Thus war became sweeter in their eyes even than returning home in their ships. As when some great forest fire is raging upon a mountain top and its light is seen afar, even so as they marched the gleam of their armor flashed up into the firmament of heaven.

They were like great flocks of geese, or cranes, or swans on the plain about the waters of Cayster, that wing their way hither and thither, glorying in the pride of flight, and crying as they settle till the fen is alive with their screaming. Even thus did their tribes pour from ships and tents on to the plain of the Scamander, and the ground rang as brass under the feet of men and horses. They stood as thick upon the flower-bespangled field as leaves that bloom in summer.

As countless swarms of flies buzz around a herdsman's homestead in the time of spring when the pails are drenched with milk, even so did the Achaeans swarm on to the plain to charge the Trojans and destroy them.

The chiefs disposed their men this way and that before the fight began, drafting them out as easily as goatherds draft their flocks when they have got mixed while feeding; and among them went King Agamemnon, with a head and face like Zeus, the lord of thunder, a waist like Ares, and a chest like that of Poseidon. As some great bull that lords it over the herds upon the plain, even so did Zeus make the son of Atreus stand peerless among the multitude of heroes.

And now, O Muses, dwellers in the mansions of Olympus, tell me—for you are goddesses and are in all places so that you see all things, while we know nothing but by report—who were the chiefs and princes of the Danaans? As for the common soldiers, they were so many that I could not name every single one of them though I had ten tongues, and though my voice failed not and my heart were of bronze within me, unless you, O Olympian Muses, daughters of aegis-bearing Zeus, were to recount them to me. Nevertheless, I will tell the captains of the ships and all the fleet together.

Peneleos, Leïtus, Arcesilaus, Prothoënor, and Clonius were captains of the Boeotians. These were they that dwelt in Hyria and rocky Aulis, and who held Schoenus, Scolus, and the highlands of Eteonus, with Thespeia, Graia, and the fair city of Mycalessus. They also held Harma, Eilesium, and Erythrae; and they had Eleon, Hyle, and Peteon; Ocalea and the strong fortress of Medeon; Copae, Eutresis, and Thisbe, the haunt of doves; Coronea, and the pastures of Haliartus; Plataea and Glisas; the fortress of Thebes the less; holy Onchestus with its famous grove of Neptune; Arne rich in vineyards; Midea, sacred Nisa, and Anthedon upon the sea. From these there came fifty ships, and in each there were a hundred and twenty young men of the Boeotians.

Ascalaphus and Ialmenus, sons of Ares, led the people that dwelt in Aspledon and Orchomenus, the realm of Minyas. Astyoche, a noble maiden, bore them in the house of Actor, son of Azeus; for she had gone with Ares secretly into an upper chamber, and he had lain with her. With these there came thirty ships.

The Phoceans were led by Schedius and Epistrophus, sons of mighty Iphitus, the son of Naubolus. These were they that held Cyparissus, rocky Pytho, holy Crisa, Daulis, and Panopeus; they also that dwelt in Anemorea and Hyampolis, and about the waters of the river Cephissus, and Lilaea by the springs of the Cephissus; with their chieftains came forty ships, and they marshaled the forces of the Phoceans, which were stationed next to the Boeotians, on their left.

Ajax, the fleet son of Oïleus, commanded the Locrians. He was not so great, nor nearly so great, as Ajax, the son of Telamon. He was a little man, and his breastplate was made of linen, but in use of the spear he excelled all the Hellenes and the Achaeans. These dwelt in Cynus, Opoüs, Calliarus, Bessa, Scarphe, fair Augeae, Tarphe, and Thronium about the river Boagrius. With him there came forty ships of the Locrians who dwell beyond Euboea.

The fierce Abantes held Euboea with its cities, Chalcis, Eretria, Histiaea, rich in vines, Cerinthus upon the sea, and the rock-perched town of Dium; with them were also the men of Carystus and Styra; Elephenor of the race of Ares was in command of these; he was son of Chalcodon, and chief over all the Abantes. With him they came, fleet of foot and wearing their hair long behind, brave warriors, who would ever strive to tear open the corslets of their foes with their long ashen spears. Of these there came fifty ships.

And they that held the strong city of Athens, the people of great Erechtheus, who was born of the soil itself, but Zeus' daughter, Athene, fostered him, and established him at Athens in her own rich sanctuary. There, year by year, the Athenian youths worship him with sacrifices of bulls and rams. These were commanded by Menestheus, son of Peteos. No man living could equal him in the marshaling of chariots and foot soldiers. Nestor could alone rival him, for he was older. With him there came fifty ships.

Ajax brought twelve ships from Salamis and stationed them alongside those of the Athenians.

The men of Argos, again, and those who held the walls of Tiryns, with Hermione, and Asine upon the gulf; Troezene, Eïonae, and the vineyard lands of Epidaurus; the Achaean youths, moreover, who came from Aegina, and Mases; these were led by Diomed of the loud battle cry, and Sthenelus, son of famed Capaneus. With them in command was Euryalus, son of king Mecisteus, son of Talaus; but Diomed was chief over them all. With these there came eighty ships.

Those who held the strong city of Mycenae, rich Corinth and Cleonae; Orneae, Araethyrea, and Sicyon, where Adrastus reigned of old; Hyperesia, high Gonoëssa, and Pellene; Aegium and all the coastland round about Helice. These sent a hundred ships under the command of King Agamemnon, son of Atreus. His force was far both finest and most numerous, and in their midst was the king himself, all glorious in his armor of gleaming bronze— foremost among the heroes, for he was the greatest king, and had most men under him.

And those that dwelt in Lacedaemon, lying low among the hills, Pharis, Sparta, with Messe, the haunt of doves; Bryseae, Augeae, Amyclae, and Helos upon the sea; Laas, moreover, and Oetylus. These were led by Menelaus of the loud battle cry, brother to Agamemnon, and of them there were sixty ships, drawn up apart from the others. Among them went Menelaus himself, strong in zeal, urging his men to fight; for he longed to avenge the toil and sorrow that he had suffered for the sake of Helen.

The men of Pylos and Arene, and Thryum where is the ford of the river Alpheus; strong Aipy, Cyparisseis, and Amphigenea; Pteleum, Helos, and Dorium, where the Muses met Thamyris, and stilled his minstrelsy forever. He was returning from Oechalia, where Eurytus lived and reigned, and boasted that he would surpass even the Muses, daughters of aegis-bearing Zeus, if they should sing against him; whereon they were angry, and maimed him. They robbed him of his divine power of song, and thenceforth he could strike the lyre no more. These were commanded by Nestor, knight of Gerene, and with him there came ninety ships.

And those that held Arcadia, under the high mountain of Cyllene, near the tomb of Aepytus, where the people fight hand to hand; the men of Pheneus also, and Orchomenus, rich in flocks; of Rhipae, Stratie, and bleak Enispe; of Tegea and fair Mantinea; of Stymphelus and Parrhasia; of these King Agapenor, son of Ancaeus, was commander, and they had sixty ships. Many Arcadians, good soldiers, came in each one of them, but Agamemnon found them the ships in which to cross the sea, for they were not a people that occupied their business upon the waters.

The men, moreover, of Buprasium and of Elis, so much of it as is enclosed between Hyrmine, Myrsinus upon the seashore, the rock Olene and Alesium. These had four leaders, and each of them had ten ships, with many Epeans on board. Their captains were Amphimachus and Thalpius—the one, son of Cteatus, and the other, of Eurytus—both of the race of Actor. The two others were Diores, son of Amarynces, and Polyxenus, son of King Agasthenes, son of Augeas.

And those of Dulichium with the sacred Echinean islands, who dwelt beyond the sea off Elis. These were led by Meges, peer of Ares, and the son of valiant Phyleus, dear to Zeus, who quarreled with his father, and went to settle in Dulichium. With him there came forty ships.

Odysseus led the brave Cephallenians, who held Ithaca, Neritum with its forests, Crocylea, rugged Aegilips, Samos and Zacynthus, with the mainland also that was over against the islands. These were led by Odysseus, peer of Zeus in counsel, and with him there came twelve ships.

Thoas, son of Andraemon, commanded the Aetolians, who dwelt in Pleuron, Olenus, Pylene, Chalcis by the sea, and rocky Calydon, for the great king Oeneus had now no sons living, and was himself dead, as was also golden-haired Meleager, who had been set over the Aetolians to be their king. And with Thoas there came forty ships.

The famous spearsman Idomeneus led the Cretans, who held Cnossus, and the well-walled city of Gortys; Lyctus also, Miletus and Lycastus that lies upon the chalk; the populous towns of Phaestus and Rhytium, with the other peoples that dwelt in the hundred cities of Crete. All these were led by Idomeneus, and by Meriones, peer of murderous Ares. And with these there came eighty ships.

Tlepolemus, son of Heracles, a man both brave and large of stature, brought nine ships of lordly warriors from Rhodes. These dwelt in Rhodes which is divided among the three cities of Lindus, Ielysus, and Cameirus, that lies upon the chalk. These were commanded by Tlepolemus, son of Heracles by Astyochea, whom he had carried off from Ephyra, on the river Selleïs, after sacking many cities of valiant warriors. When Tlepolemus grew up, he killed his father's uncle Licymnius, who had been a famous warrior in his time, but was then grown old. On this he built himself a fleet, gathered a great following, and fled beyond the sea, for he was menaced by the other sons and grandsons of Heracles. After a voyage, during which he suffered great hardship, he came to Rhodes, where the people divided into three communities, according to their tribes, and were dearly loved by Zeus, the lord of gods and men; wherefore the son of Cronus showered down great riches upon them.

And Nireus brought three ships from Syme—Nireus, who was the handsomest man that came up under Ilium of all the Danaans after the son of Peleus—but he was a man of no substance, and had but a small following.

And those that held Nisyrus, Crapathus, and Casus, with Cos, the city of Eurypylus, and the Calydnian islands, these were commanded by Pheidippus and Antiphus, two sons of King Thessalus, the son of Heracles. And with them there came thirty ships.

Those again who held Pelasgic Argos, Alos, Alope, and Trachis; and those of Phthia and Hellas, the land of fair women, who were called Myrmidons, Hellenes, and Achaeans; these had fifty ships, over which Achilles was in command. But they now took no part in the war, inasmuch as there was no one to marshal them; for Achilles stayed by his ships, furious about the loss of the girl Briseis, whom he had taken from Lyrnessus at his own great peril, when he had sacked Lyrnessus and Thebe, and had overthrown Mynes and Epistrophus, sons of king Evenor, son of Selepus. For her sake Achilles was still grieving, but ere long he was again to join them.

And those that held Phylace and the flowery meadows of Pyrasus, sanctuary of Demeter; Iton, mother of sheep; Antrum upon the sea, and Pteleum that lies upon the grasslands. Of these brave Protesilaus had been captain while he was yet alive, but he was now lying under the earth. He had left a wife behind him in Phylace to tear her cheeks in sorrow, and his house was only half finished, for he was slain by a Dardanian warrior while leaping foremost of the Achaeans upon the soil of Troy. Still, though his people mourned their chieftain, they were not without a leader, for Podarces, of the race of Ares, marshaled them; he was son of Iphiclus, rich in sheep, who was the son of Phylacus, and he was own brother to Protesilaus, only younger, Protesilaus being at once the elder and the more valiant. So the people were not without a leader, though they mourned him whom they had lost. With him there came forty ships.

And those that held Pherae by the Boebean lake, with Boebe, Glaphyrae, and the populous city of Iolcus, these with their eleven ships were led by Eumelus, son of Admetus, whom Alcestis bore to him, loveliest of the daughters of Pelias.

And those that held Methone and Thaumacia, with Meliboea and rugged Olizon, these were led by the skillful archer Philoctetes, and they had seven ships, each with fifty oarsmen all of them good archers; but Philoctetes was lying in great pain in the Island of Lemnos, where the sons of the Achaeans left him, for he had been bitten by a poisonous water snake. There he lay sick and sorry, and full soon did the Argives come to miss him. But his people, though they felt his loss, were not leaderless, for Medon, the bastard son of Oïleus by Rhene, set them in array.

Those, again, of Tricca and the stony region of Ithome, and they that held Oechalia, the city of Oechalian Eurytus, these were commanded by the two sons of Asclepius, skilled in the art of healing, Podalirius and Machaon. And with them there came thirty ships.

The men, moreover, of Ormenius, and by the fountain of Hypereia, with those that held Asterius, and the white crests of Titanus, these were led by Eurypylus, the son of Euaemon, and with them there came forty ships.

Those that held Argissa and Gyrtone, Orthe, Elone, and the white city of Oloösson, of these brave Polypoetes was leader. He was son of Pirithoüs, who was son of Zeus himself, for Hippodameia bore him to Pirithoüs on the day when he took his revenge on the shaggy mountain savages, and drove them from Mount Pelion to the Aithices. But Polypoetes was not sole in command, for with him was Leonteus, of the race of Ares, who was son of Coronus, the son of Caeneus. And with these there came forty ships.

Guneus brought two and twenty ships from Cyphus, and he was followed by the Enienes and the valiant Peraebi, who dwelt about wintry Dodona, and held the lands round the lovely river Titaresius, which sends its waters into the Peneus. They do not mingle with the silver eddies of the Peneus, but flow on the top of them like oil; for the Titaresius is a branch of dread Orcus and of the river Styx.

Of the Magnetes, Prothoüs, son of Tenthredon, was commander. They were they that dwelt about the river Peneus and Mount Pelion. Prothoüs, fleet of foot, was their leader, and with him there came forty ships.

Such were the chiefs and princes of the Danaans. Who, then, O Muse, was the foremost, whether man or horse, among those that followed after the sons of Atreus?

Of the horses, those of the son of Pheres were by far the finest. They were driven by Eumelus, and were as fleet as birds. They were of the same age and color, and perfectly matched in height. Apollo, of the silver bow, had bred them in Perea—both of them mares, and terrible as Ares in battle. Of the men, Ajax, son of Telamon, was much the foremost so long as Achilles' anger lasted, for Achilles excelled him greatly and he had also better horses; but

Achilles was now holding aloof at his ships by reason of his quarrel with Agamemnon, and his people passed their time upon the seashore, throwing discs or aiming with spears at a mark, and in archery. Their horses stood each by his own chariot, champing lotus and wild celery. The chariots were housed under cover, but their owners, for lack of leadership, wandered hither and thither about the host and went not forth to fight.

Thus marched the host like a consuming fire, and the earth groaned beneath them as when the lord of thunder is angry and lashes the land about Typhoeus among the Arimi, where they say Typhoeus lies. Even so did the earth groan beneath them as they sped over the plain.

And now Iris, fleet as the wind, was sent by Zeus to tell the bad news among the Trojans. They were gathered in assembly, old and young, at Priam's gates, and Iris came close up to Priam, speaking with the voice of Priam's son Polites, who, being fleet of foot, was stationed as watchman for the Trojans on the tomb of old Aesyetes, to look out for any sally of the Achaeans. In his likeness Iris spoke, saying: "Old man, you talk idly, as in time of peace, while war is at hand. I have been in many a battle, but never yet saw such a host as is now advancing. They are crossing the plain to attack the city as thick as leaves or as the sands of the sea. Hector, I charge you above all others, do as I say. There are many allies dispersed about the city of Priam from distant places and speaking divers tongues. Therefore, let each chief give orders to his own people, setting them severally in array and leading them forth to battle."

Thus she spoke, but Hector knew that it was the goddess, and at once broke up the assembly. The men flew to arms; all the gates were opened, and the people thronged through them, horse and foot, with the tramp as of a great multitude.

Now there is a high mound before the city, rising by itself upon the plain. Men call it Batieia, but the gods know that it is the tomb of lithe Myrine. Here the Trojans and their allies divided their forces.

Priam's son, great Hector of the gleaming helmet, commanded the Trojans, and with him were arrayed by far the greater number and most valiant of those who were longing for the fray.

The Dardanians were led by brave Aeneas, whom Aphrodite bore to Anchises, when she, goddess though she was, had lain with him upon the mountain slopes of Ida. He was not alone, for with him were the two sons of Antenor, Archilochus and Acamas, both skilled in all the arts of war.

They that dwelt in Zelea under the lowest spurs of Mount Ida, men of substance, who drink the limpid waters of the Aesepus, and are of Trojan blood—these were led by Pandarus, son of Lycaon, whom Apollo had taught to use the bow.

They that held Adresteia and the land of Apaesus, with Pityeia, and the high mountain of Tereia—these were led by Adrestus and Amphius, whose breastplate was of linen. These were the sons of Merops of Percote, who excelled in all kinds of divination. He told them not to take part in the war, but they gave him no heed, for fate lured them to destruction.

They that dwelt about Percote and Practius, with Sestos, Abydos, and Arisbe—these were led by Asius, son of Hyrtacus, a brave commander—Asius, the son of Hyrtacus, whom his powerful dark bay steeds, of the breed that comes from the river Selleïs, had brought from Arisbe.

Hippothoüs led the tribes of Pelasgian spearsmen, who dwelt in fertile Larisa—Hippothoüs, and Pylaeus of the race of Ares, two sons of the Pelasgian Lethus, son of Teutamus.

Acamas and the warrior Peiroüs commanded the Thracians and those that came from beyond the mighty stream of the Hellespont.

Euphemus, son of Troezenus, the son of Ceos, was captain of the Ciconian spearsmen.

Pyraechmes led the Paeonian archers from distant Amydon, by the broad waters of the river Axius, the fairest that flow upon the earth.

The Paphlagonians were commanded by stouthearted Pylaemenes from Enetae, where the mules run wild in herds. These were they that held Cytorus and the country round Sesamus, with the cities by the river Parthenius, Cromna, Aegialus, and lofty Erithini.

Odius and Epistrophus were captains over the Halizoni from distant Alybe, where there are mines of silver.

Chromis, and Ennomus, the augur, led the Mysians, but his skill in augury availed not to save him from destruction, for he fell by the hand of the fleet descendant of Aeacus in the river, where he slew others also of the Trojans.

Phorcys, again, and noble Ascanius led the Phrygians from the far country of Ascania, and both were eager for the fray.

Mesthles and Antiphus commanded the Meonians, sons of Talaemenes, born to him of the Gygaean lake. These led the Meonians, who dwelt under Mount Tmolus.

Nastes led the Carians, men of a strange speech. These held Miletus and the wooded mountain of Phthires, with the water of the river Maeander and the lofty crests of Mount Mycale. These were commanded by Nastes and Amphimachus, the brave sons of Nomion. He came into the fight with gold about him, like a girl; fool that he was, his gold was of no avail to save him, for he fell in the river by the hand of the fleet descendant of Aeacus, and Achilles bore away his gold.

Sarpedon and Glaucus led the Lycians from their distant land, by the eddying waters of the Xanthus.

Book III

Paris challenges Menelaus to single combat, to decide the war and the fate of Helen and her treasure. Priam and Agamemnon solemnize the agreement with oaths and sacrifices to Zeus. Helen mounts the Trojan battlements to watch the duel, and when Menelaus is getting the upper hand, Aphrodite rescues Paris, wafting him back to Troy in a cloud. Agamemnon demands that the Trojans keep their oath and surrender Helen.

WHEN THE COMPANIES WERE THUS ARRAYED, EACH UNDER ITS OWN captain, the Trojans advanced as a flight of wild fowl or cranes that scream overhead when rain and winter drive them over the flowing waters of Oceanus to bring death and destruction on the Pygmies, and they wrangle in the air as they fly; but the Achaeans marched silently, in high heart, and minded to stand by one another.

As when the south wind spreads a curtain of mist upon the mountain tops, bad for shepherds but better than night for thieves, and a man can see no further than he can throw a stone, even so rose the dust from under their feet as they made all speed over the plain.

When they were close up with one another, Paris came forward as champion on the Trojan side. On his shoulders he bore the skin of a panther, his bow, and his sword, and he brandished two spears shod with bronze as a challenge to the bravest of the Achaeans to meet him in single fight. Menelaus saw him thus stride out before the ranks, and was glad as a hungry lion that lights on the carcass of some goat or horned stag and devours

51

it there and then, though dogs and youths set upon him. Even thus was Menelaus glad when his eyes caught sight of Paris, for he deemed that now he should be revenged. He sprang, therefore, from his chariot, clad in his suit of armor.

Paris quailed as he saw Menelaus come forward, and shrank in fear of his life under cover of his men. As one who starts back affrighted, trembling and pale, when he comes suddenly upon a serpent in some mountain glade, even so did Paris plunge into the throng of Trojan warriors, terror-stricken at the sight of the son of Atreus.

Then Hector upbraided him. "Paris," said he, "evil-hearted Paris, fair to see, but woman-mad and false of tongue, would that you had never been born, or that you had died unwed. Better so, than live to be disgraced and looked askance at. Will not the Achaeans mock at us and say that we have sent one to champion us who is fair to see but who has neither wit nor courage? Did you not, such as you are, get your following together and sail beyond the seas? Did you not from a far country carry off a lovely woman wedded among a people of warriors—to bring sorrow upon your father, your city, and your whole country, but joy to your enemies, and hangdog shamefacedness to yourself? And now can you not dare face Menelaus and learn what manner of man he is whose wife you have stolen? Where indeed would be your lyre and your love tricks, your comely locks and your fair favor, when you were lying in the dust before him? The Trojans are a weak-kneed people, or ere this you would have had a shirt of stones for the wrongs you have done them."

And Paris answered: "Hector, your rebuke is just. You are hard as the ax which a shipwright wields at his work, and cleaves the timber to his liking. As the ax in his hand, so keen is the edge of your scorn. Still, taunt me not with the gifts that golden Aphrodite has given me; they are precious; let not a man disdain them, for the gods give them where they are minded, and none can have them for the asking. If you would have me do battle with Menelaus, bid the Trojans and Achaeans take their seats, while he and I fight in their midst for Helen and all her wealth. Let him who shall be victorious and prove to be the better man take the woman and all she has, to bear them to his home, but let the rest swear to a solemn covenant of peace whereby you Trojans shall stay here in Troy, while the others go home to Argos and the land of the Achaeans."

When Hector heard this he was glad and went about among the Trojan ranks, holding his spear by the middle to keep them back, and they all sat down at his bidding: but the Achaeans still aimed at him with stones and arrows, till Agamemnon shouted to them, saying, "Hold, Argives, shoot not, sons of the Achaeans. Hector desires to speak."

They ceased taking aim and were still, whereon Hector spoke. "Hear from my mouth," said he, "Trojans and Achaeans, the saying of Paris, through whom this quarrel has come about. He bids the Trojans and Achaeans lay their armor upon the ground, while he and Menelaus fight in the midst of you for Helen and all her wealth. Let him who shall be victorious and prove to be the better man take the woman and all she has, to bear them to his own home, but let the rest swear to a solemn covenant of peace."

Thus he spoke, and they all held their peace till Menelaus of the loud battle cry addressed them. "And now," he said, "hear me too, for it is I who am the most aggrieved. I deem that the parting of Achaeans and Trojans is at hand, as well it may be, seeing how much you have suffered for my quarrel with Paris and the wrong he did me. Let him who shall die, die, and let the others fight no more. Bring, then, two lambs, a white ram and a black ewe, for Earth and Sun, and we will bring a third for Zeus. Moreover, you shall bid Priam come, that he may swear to the covenant himself; for his sons are high-handed and ill to trust, and the oaths of Zeus must not be transgressed or taken in vain. Young men's minds are light as air, but when an old man comes he looks before and after, deeming that which shall be fairest upon both sides."

The Trojans and Achaeans were glad when they heard this, for they thought that they should now have rest. They backed their chariots toward the ranks, got out of them, and put off their armor, laying it down upon the ground; and the hosts were near to one another with a little space between them. Hector sent two messengers to the city to bring the lambs and to bid Priam come, while Agamemnon told Talthybius to fetch the other lamb from the ships, and he did as Agamemnon had said.

Meanwhile Iris went to Helen in the form of her sister-in-law, wife of the son of Antenor, for Helicaon, son of Antenor, had married Laodice, the fairest of Priam's daughters. She found her in her own room, working at a great web of purple linen, on which she was embroidering the battles between Trojans and Achaeans, that Ares had made them fight for her sake. Iris then came close up to her and said: "Come hither, child, and see the strange doings of the Trojans and Achaeans; till now they have been warring upon the plain, mad with lust of battle, but now they have left off fighting, and are leaning upon their shields, sitting still with their spears planted beside them. Paris and Menelaus are going to fight about yourself, and you are to be the wife of him who is the victor."

Thus spoke the goddess, and Helen's heart yearned after her former husband, her city, and her parents. She threw a white mantle over her head, and hurried from her room, weeping as she went, not alone, but attended by two of her handmaids, Aethra, daughter of Pittheus, and Clymene. And straightway they were at the Scaean gates.

The two sages, Ucalegon and Antenor, elders of the people, were seated by the Scaean gates, with Priam, Panthoüs, Thymoetes, Lampus, Clytius, and Hiketaon of the race of Ares. These were too old to fight, but they were fluent orators, and sat on the tower like cicadas that chirrup delicately from the boughs of some high tree in a wood. When they saw Helen coming towards the tower, they said softly to one another: "Small wonder that Trojans and Achaeans should endure so much and so long, for the sake of a woman so marvelously and divinely lovely. Still, fair though she be, let them take her and go, or she will breed sorrow for us and for our children after us."

But Priam bade her draw nigh. "My child," said he, "take your seat in front of me that you may see your former husband, your kinsmen, and your friends. I lay no blame upon you, it is the gods, not you, who are to blame. It is they that have brought about this terrible war with the Achaeans. Tell me, then, who is yonder huge hero so great and goodly? I have seen men taller by a head, but none so comely and so royal. Surely he must be a king."

"Sir," answered Helen, "father of my husband, dear and reverend in my eyes, would that I had chosen death rather than to have come here with your son, far from my bridal chamber, my friends, my darling daughter, and all the companions of my girlhood. But it was not to be, and my lot is one of tears and sorrow. As for your question, the hero of whom you ask is Agamemnon, son of Atreus, a good king and a brave soldier, brother-in-law as surely as that he lives, to my abhorred and miserable self."

The old man marveled at him, and said: "Happy son of Atreus, child of good fortune. I see that the Achaeans are subject to you in great multitudes. When I was in Phrygia I saw much horsemen, the people of Otreus and of Mygdon, who were camping upon the banks of the river Sangarius. I was their ally, and with them when the Amazons, peers of men, came up against them, but even they were not so many as the Achaeans."

The old man next looked upon Odysseus. 'Tell me," he said, "who is that other, shorter by a head than Agamemnon, but broader across the chest and shoulders? His armor is laid upon the ground, and he stalks in front of the ranks as it were some great woolly ram ordering his ewes."

And Helen answered: "He is Odysseus, a man of great craft, son of Laertes. He was born in rugged Ithaca, and excels in all manner of stratagems and subtle cunning."

On this Antenor said: "Madam, you have spoken truly. Odysseus once came here as envoy about yourself, and Menelaus with him. I received them in my own house, and therefore know both of them by sight and conversation. When they stood up in presence of the assembled Trojans, Menelaus was the broader-shouldered, but when both were seated Odysseus had the more royal presence. After a time they delivered their message, and the speech of Menelaus ran trippingly on the tongue. He did not say much, for he was a man of few words, but he spoke very clearly and to the point, though he was the younger man of the two. Odysseus, on the other hand, when he rose to speak was at first silent and kept his eyes fixed upon the ground. There was no play nor graceful movement of his scepter; he kept it straight and stiff like a man unpracticed in oratory—one might have taken him for a mere churl or simpleton; but when he raised his voice, and the words came driving from his deep chest like winter snow before the wind, then there was none to touch him, and no man thought further of what he looked like."

Priam then caught sight of Ajax and asked, "Who is that great and goodly warrior whose head and broad shoulders tower above the rest of the Argives?"

"That," answered Helen, "is huge Ajax, bulwark of the Achaeans, and on the other side of him, among the Cretans, stands Idomeneus looking like a god, and with the captains of the Cretans round him. Often did Menelaus receive him as a guest in our house when he came visiting us from Crete. I see, moreover, many other Achaeans whose names I could tell you, but there are two whom I can nowhere find, Castor, breaker of horses, and Pollux, the mighty boxer; they are children of my mother, and own brothers to myself. Either they have not left Lacedaemon, or else, though they have brought their ships, they will not show themselves in battle for the shame and disgrace that I have brought upon them."

She knew not that both these heroes were already lying under the earth in their own land of Lacedaemon.

Meanwhile the heralds were bringing the holy oath offerings through the city—two lambs and a goatskin of wine, the gift of earth; and Idaeus brought the mixing bowl and the cups of gold. He went up to Priam and said, "Son of Laomedon, the princes of the Trojans and Achaeans bid you come down on to the plain and swear to a solemn covenant. Paris and Menelaus are to fight for Helen in single combat, that she and all her wealth may go with him who is the victor. We are to swear to a solemn covenant of peace whereby we others shall dwell here in Troy, while the Achaeans return to Argos and the land of the Achaeans."

The old man trembled as he heard, but bade his followers yoke the horses, and they made all haste to do so. He mounted the chariot, gathered the reins in his hand, and Antenor took his seat beside him; they then drove through the Scaean gates on to the plain. When they reached the ranks of the Trojans and Achaeans they left the chariot and with measured pace advanced into the space between the hosts.

Agamemnon and Odysseus both rose to meet them. The attendants brought on the oath offerings and mixed the wine in the mixing bowls; they poured water over the hands of the chieftains, and the son of Atreus drew the dagger that hung by his sword, and cut wool from the lambs' heads; this the menservants gave about among the Trojan and Achaean princes, and the son of Atreus lifted up his hands in prayer. "Father Zeus," he cried, "that rulest in Ida, most glorious in power, and thou O Sun, that seest and givest ear to all things, Earth and Rivers, and ye who in the realms below chastise the soul of him that has broken his oath, witness these rites and guard them, that they be not vain. If Paris kills Menelaus, let him keep Helen and all her wealth, while we sail home with our ships; but if Menelaus kills Paris, let the Trojans give back Helen and all that she has; let them moreover pay such fine to the Achaeans as shall be agreed upon, in testimony among those that shall be born hereafter. And if Priam and his sons refuse such fine when Paris has fallen, then will I stay here and fight on till I have got satisfaction."

As he spoke he drew his knife across the throats of the victims, and laid them down gasping and dying upon the ground, for the knife had reft them of their strength. Then they poured wine from the mixing bowl into the cups, and prayed to the everlasting gods, saying, Trojans and Achaeans among one another, "Zeus, most great and glorious, and ye other everlasting gods, grant that the brains of them who shall first sin against their oaths—of them and their children—may be shed upon the ground even as this wine, and let their wives become the slaves of strangers."

Thus they prayed, but not as yet would Zeus grant them their prayer. Then Priam, descendant of Dardanus, spoke, saying: "Hear me, Trojans and Achaeans, I will now go back to the wind-beaten city of Ilium. I dare not with my own eyes witness this fight between my son and Menelaus, for Zeus and the other immortals alone know which shall fall."

On this he laid the two lambs on his chariot and took his seat. He gathered the reins in his hand, and Antenor sat beside him; the two then went back to Ilium. Hector and Odysseus measured the ground and cast lots from a helmet of bronze to see which should take aim first. Meanwhile the two hosts lifted up their hands and prayed, saying, "Father Zeus, that rulest from Ida, most glorious in power, grant that he who first brought about this war between us may die and enter the house of Hades, while we others remain at peace and abide by our oaths."

Great Hector now turned his head aside while he shook the helmet, and the lot of Paris flew out first. The others then took their several stations, each by his horses and the place where his arms were lying, while Paris, husband of lovely Helen, put on his goodly armor. First he greaved his legs with greaves of good make and fitted with ankle-clasps of silver; after this he donned the cuirass of his brother Lycaon, and fitted it to his own body. He hung his silver-studded sword of bronze about his shoulders, and then his mighty shield. On his comely head he set his helmet, well-wrought, with a crest of horsehair that nodded menacingly above it, and he grasped a redoubtable spear that suited his hands. In like fashion Menelaus also put on his armor.

When they had thus armed, each amid his own people, they strode fierce of aspect into the open space, and both Trojans and Achaeans were struck with awe as they beheld them. They stood near one another on the measured ground, brandishing their spears, and each furious against the other. Paris aimed first, and struck the round shield of the son of Atreus, but the spear did not pierce it, for the shield turned its point. Menelaus next took aim, praying to Father Zeus as he did so. "King Zeus," he said, "grant me revenge on Paris who has wronged me. Subdue him under my hand that in ages yet to come a man may shrink from doing ill deeds in the house of his host."

He poised his spear as he spoke and hurled it at the shield of Paris. Through shield and cuirass it went and tore the shirt by his flank, but Paris swerved aside, and thus saved his life. Then the son of Atreus drew his sword, and drove at the projecting part of his helmet, but the sword fell shivered in three or four pieces from his hand, and he cried, looking towards heaven, "Father Zeus, of all gods thou art the most despiteful; I made sure of my revenge, but the sword has broken in my hand, my spear has been hurled in vain, and I have not killed him."

With this he flew at Paris, caught him by the horsehair plume of his helmet, and began dragging him towards the Achaeans. The strap of the helmet that went under his chin was choking him, and Menelaus would have dragged him off to his own great glory had not Zeus' daughter Aphrodite been quick to mark and to break the strap of oxhide, so that the empty helmet came away in his hand. This he flung to his comrades among the Achaeans, and was again springing upon Paris to run him through with a spear, but Aphrodite snatched him up in a moment (as a god can do), hid him under a cloud of darkness, and conveyed him to his own bedchamber.

Then she went to call Helen, and found her on a high tower with the Trojan women crowding round her. She took the form of an old woman who used to dress wool for her when she was still in Lacedaemon, and of whom she was very fond. Thus disguised she plucked her by her perfumed robe, and said: "Come hither; Paris says you are to go to the house; he is on his bed in his own room, radiant with beauty and dressed in gorgeous apparel. No one would think he had just come from fighting, but rather that he was going to a dance, or had done dancing and was sitting down."

With these words she moved the heart of Helen to anger. When she marked the beautiful neck of the goddess, her lovely bosom, and sparkling eyes, she marveled at her and said: "Goddess, why do you thus beguile me? Are you going to send me afield still further to some man whom you have taken up in Phrygia or fair Meonia? Menelaus has just vanquished Paris, and is to take my hateful self back with him. You are come here to betray me. Go sit with Paris yourself; henceforth be goddess no longer; never let your feet carry you back to Olympus; worry about him and look after him till he make you his wife, or, for the matter of that, his slave—but me? I shall not go; I can garnish his bed no longer. I should be a byword among all the women of Troy. Besides, I have trouble on my mind."

Aphrodite was very angry, and said: "Bold hussy, do not provoke me; if you do, I shall leave you to your fate and hate you as much as I have loved you. I will stir up fierce hatred between Trojans and Achaeans, and you shall come to a bad end."

At this Helen was frightened. She wrapped her mantle about her and went in silence, following the goddess and unnoticed by the Trojan women.

When they came to the house of Paris the maidservants set about their work, but Helen went into her own room, and the laughter-loving goddess took a seat and set it for her facing Paris. On this Helen, daughter of aegis-bearing Zeus, sat down, and with eyes askance began to upbraid her husband.

"So you are come from the fight," said she; "would that you had fallen rather by the hand of that brave man who was my husband. You used to brag that you were a better man with your hands and spear than Menelaus; go, then, and challenge him again—but I should advise you not to do so, for if you are foolish enough to meet him in single combat, you will soon fall by his spear."

And Paris answered: "Wife, do not vex me with your reproaches. This time, with the help of Athene, Menelaus has vanquished me; another time I may myself be victor, for I too have gods that will stand by me. Come, let us lie down together and make friends. Never yet was I so passionately enamored of you as at this moment—not even when I first carried you off from Lacedaemon and sailed away with you—not even when I had converse with you upon the couch of love in the island of Cranaë was I so enthralled by my desire of you as now." On this he led her towards the bed, and his wife went with him.

Thus they laid themselves on the bed together; but the son of Atreus strode among the throng, looking everywhere for Paris, and no man, neither of the Trojans nor of the allies, could find him. If they had seen him they were in no mind to hide him, for they all of them hated him as they did death itself. Then Agamemnon, king of men, spoke, saying: "Hear me, Trojans, Dardanians, and allies. The victory has been with Menelaus. Therefore give back Helen with all her wealth, and pay such fine as shall be agreed upon, in testimony among them that shall be born hereafter."

Thus spoke the son of Atreus, and the Achaeans shouted in applause.

BOOK IV

On Olympus Zeus agrees that the Trojans should suffer for Paris' failure to fight his battle through. Athene goes down to the plain in disguise and persuades the Trojan Pandarus to shoot an arrow at the unsuspecting Menelaus, thereby breaking the solemn truce between the armies. Agamemnon, indignant, marshals his men for war.

NOW THE GODS WERE SITTING WITH ZEUS IN COUNCIL UPON THE GOLDEN floor while Hebe went round pouring out nectar for them to drink, and as they pledged one another in their cups of gold they looked down upon the town of Troy. The son of Cronus then began to tease Hera, talking at her so as to provoke her. "Menelaus," said he, "has two good friends among the goddesses, Hera of Argos, and Athene of Alalcomene, but they only sit still and look on, while Aphrodite keeps ever by Paris' side to defend him in any danger. Indeed she has just rescued him when he made sure that it was all over with him—for the victory really did lie with Menelaus. We must consider what we shall do about all this; shall we set them fighting anew or make peace between them? If you will agree to this last Menelaus can take back Helen and the city of Priam may remain still inhabited."

Athene and Hera muttered their discontent as they sat side by side hatching mischief for the Trojans. Athene scowled at her father, for she was in a furious passion with him, and said nothing, but Hera could not contain herself. "Dread son of Cronus," said she, "what, pray, is the meaning of all this? Is my trouble, then, to go for nothing, and the sweat that I have sweated, to say nothing of my horses, while getting the people together against Priam and his children? Do as you will, but we other gods shall not all of us approve your counsel."

Zeus was angry and answered: "My dear, what harm have Priam and his sons done you that you are so hotly bent on sacking the city of Ilium? Will nothing do for you but you must go within their walls and eat Priam raw, with his sons and all the other Trojans to boot? Have it your own way then; for I would not have this matter become a bone of contention between us. I say further, and lay my saying to your heart, if ever I want to sack a city belonging to friends of yours, you must not try to stop me; you will have to let me do it, for I am giving in to you sorely against my will. Of all inhabited cities under the sun and stars of heaven, there was none that I so much respected as Ilium with Priam and his whole people. Equitable feasts were never wanting about my altar, nor the savor of burning fat, which is the honor due to ourselves."

"My own three favorite cities," answered Hera, "are Argos, Sparta, and Mycenae. Sack them whenever you may be displeased with them. I shall not defend them and I shall not care. Even if I did, and tried to stay you, I should take nothing by it, for you are much stronger than I am, but I will not have my own work wasted. I too am a god and of the same race with yourself. I am Cronus' eldest daughter, and am honorable not on this ground only, but also because I am your wife and you are king over the gods. Let it be a case, then, of give-and-take between us, and the rest of the gods will follow our lead. Tell Athene to go and take part in the fight at once, and let her contrive that the Trojans shall be the first to break their oaths and set upon the Achaeans."

The sire of gods and men heeded her words and said to Athene, "Go at once into the Trojan and Achaean hosts, and contrive that the Trojans shall be the first to break their oaths and set upon the Achaeans."

This was what Athene was already eager to do, so down she darted from the topmost summits of Olympus. She shot through the sky as some brilliant meteor which the son of scheming Cronus has sent as a sign to mariners or to some great army, and a fiery train of light follows in its wake. The Trojans and

Achaeans were struck with awe as they beheld, and one would turn to his neighbor, saying, "Either we shall again have war and din of combat, or Zeus, the lord of battle, will now make peace between us."

Thus did they converse. Then Athene took the form of Laodocus, son of Antenor, and went through the ranks of the Trojans to find Pandarus, the redoubtable son of Lycaon. She found him standing among the stalwart heroes who had followed him from the banks of the Aesopus, so she went close up to him and said: "Brave son of Lycaon, will you do as I tell you? If you dare send an arrow at Menelaus you will win honor and thanks from all the Trojans, and especially from prince Paris—he would be the first to requite you very handsomely if he could see Menelaus mount his funeral pyre, slain by an arrow from your hand. Take your aim then, and pray to Lycian Apollo, the famous archer; vow that when you get home to your strong city of Zelea you will offer a hecatomb of firstling lambs in his honor."

His fool's heart was persuaded, and he took his bow from its case. This bow was made from the horns of a wild ibex which he had killed as it was bounding from a rock; he had stalked it, and it had fallen as the arrow struck it to the heart. Its horns were sixteen palms long, and a worker in horn had made them into a bow, smoothing them well down, and giving them tips of gold. When Pandarus had strung his bow he laid it carefully on the ground, and his brave followers held their shields before him lest the Achaeans should set upon him before he had shot Menelaus. Then he opened the lid of his quiver and took out a winged arrow that had never yet been shot, fraught with the pangs of death. He laid the arrow on the string and prayed to Lycian Apollo, the famous archer, vowing that when he got home to his strong city of Zelea he would offer a hecatomb of firstling lambs in his honor. He laid the notch of the arrow on the oxhide bowstring, and drew both notch and string to his breast till the arrowhead was near the bow; then when the bow was arched into a half circle, he let fly, and the bow twanged, and the string sang as the arrow flew gladly on over the heads of the throng.

But the blessed gods did not forget thee, O Menelaus, and Zeus' daughter, driver of the spoil, was the first to stand before thee and ward off the piercing arrow. She turned it from his skin as a mother whisks a fly from off her child when it is sleeping sweetly. She guided it to the part where the golden buckles of the belt that passed over his double cuirass were fastened, so the arrow struck the belt that went tightly round him. It went right through this and through the cuirass of cunning workmanship; it also pierced the belt beneath it, which he wore next his skin to keep out darts or arrows; it was this that served him in the best stead, nevertheless the arrow went through it and grazed the top of the skin, so that blood began flowing from the wound.

As when some woman of Meonia or Caria strains purple dye on to a piece of ivory that is to be the cheekpiece of a horse, and is to be laid up in a treasure house—many a knight is fain to bear it, but the king keeps it as an ornament of which both horse and driver may be proud—even so, O Menelaus, were your shapely thighs and your legs down to your fair ankles stained with blood.

When King Agamemnon saw the blood flowing from the wound he was afraid, and so was brave Menelaus himself till he saw that the barbs of the arrow and the thread that bound the arrowhead to the shaft were still outside the wound. Then he took heart, but Agamemnon heaved a deep sigh as he held Menelaus' hand in his own, and his comrades made moan in concert. "Dear brother," he cried, "I have been the death of you in pledging this covenant and letting you come forward as our champion. The Trojans have trampled on their oaths and have wounded you; nevertheless the oath, the blood of lambs, the drink offerings, and the right hands of fellowship in which we have put our trust shall not be vain. If he that rules Olympus fulfill it not here and now, he will yet fulfill it hereafter, and they shall pay dearly with their lives and with their wives and children. The day will surely come when mighty Ilium shall be laid low, with Priam and Priam's people, when the son of Cronus from his high throne shall overshadow them with his awful aegis in punishment of their present treachery. This shall surely be; but how, Menelaus, shall I mourn you, if it be your lot now to die? I should return to Argos as a byword, for the Achaeans will at once go home. We shall leave Priam and the Trojans the glory of still keeping Helen, and the earth will rot your bones as you lie here at Troy with your purpose not fulfilled. Then shall some braggart Trojan leap upon your tomb and say, 'Ever thus may Agamemnon wreak his vengeance. He brought his army in vain, he is gone home to his own land with empty ships, and has left Menelaus behind him.' Thus will one of them say, and may the earth then swallow me."

But Menelaus reassured him and said: "Take heart, and do not alarm the people; the arrow has not struck me in a mortal part, for my outer belt of burnished metal first stayed it, and under this my cuirass and the belt of mail which the bronze-smiths made me."

And Agamemnon answered: "I trust, dear Menelaus, that it may be even so, but the surgeon shall examine your wound and lay herbs upon it to relieve your pain."

He then said to Talthybius: "Talthybius, tell Machaon, son to the great physician Asclepius, to come and see Menelaus immediately. Some Trojan or Lycian archer has wounded him with an arrow to our dismay, and to his own great glory."

Talthybius did as he was told, and went about the host trying to find Machaon. Presently he found him standing amid the brave warriors who had followed him from Tricca; thereon he went up to him and said, "Son of Asclepius, King Agamemnon says you are to come and see Menelaus immediately. Some Trojan or Lycian archer has wounded him with an arrow to our dismay and to his own great glory."

Thus did he speak, and Machaon was moved to go. They passed through the spreading host of the Achaeans and went on till they came to the place where Menelaus had been wounded and was lying with the chieftains gathered in a circle round him. Machaon passed into the middle of the ring and at once drew the arrow from the belt, bending its barbs back through the force with which he pulled it out. He undid the burnished belt, and beneath this the cuirass and the belt of mail which the bronze-smiths had made; then, when he had seen the wound, he wiped away the blood and applied some soothing drugs which Chiron had given to Asclepius out of the good will he bore him.

While they were thus busy about Menelaus, the Trojans came forward against them, for they had put on their armor, and now renewed the fight.

You would not have then found Agamemnon asleep nor cowardly and unwilling to fight, but eager rather for the fray. He left his chariot rich with bronze and his panting steeds in charge of Eurymedon, son of Ptolemaeus, the son of Peiraeus, and bade him hold them in readiness against the time his limbs should weary of going about and giving orders to so many, for he went among the ranks on foot. When he saw men hasting to the front he stood by them and cheered them on. "Argives," said he, "slacken not one whit in your onset. Father Zeus will be no helper of liars. The Trojans have been the first to break their oaths and to attack us; therefore they shall be devoured of vultures. We shall take their city and carry off their wives and children in our ships."

But he angrily rebuked those whom he saw shirking and disinclined to fight. "Argives," he cried, "cowardly miserable creatures, have you no shame to stand here like frightened fawns who, when they can no longer scud over the plain, huddle together but show no fight? You are as dazed and spiritless as deer. Would you wait till the Trojans reach the stems of our ships as they lie on the shore, to see whether the son of Cronus will hold his hand over you to protect you?"

Thus did he go about giving his orders among the ranks. Passing through the crowd, he came presently on the Cretans, arming round Idomeneus, who was at their head, fierce as a wild boar, while Meriones was bringing up the battalions that were in the rear. Agamemnon was glad when he saw him, and spoke him fairly. "Idomeneus," said he, "I treat you with greater distinction than I do any other of the Achaeans, whether in war or in other things, or at table. When their princes are mixing my choicest wine in the mixing bowls, they have each of them a fixed allowance, but your cup is kept always full like my own, that you may drink whenever you are minded. Go, therefore, into battle, and show yourself the man you have been always proud to be."

Idomeneus answered: "I will be a trusty comrade, as I promised you from the first I would be. Urge on the other Achaeans, that we may join battle at once, for the Trojans have trampled upon their covenants. Death and destruction shall be theirs, seeing they have been the first to break their oaths and to attack us."

The son of Atreus went on, glad at heart, till he came upon the two Ajaxes arming themselves amid a host of foot soldiers. As when a goatherd from some high post watches a storm drive over the deep before the west wind— black as pitch is the offing and a mighty whirlwind draws towards him, so that he is afraid and drives his flock into a cave—even thus did the ranks of stalwart youths move in a dark mass to battle under the Ajaxes, horrid with shield and spear. Glad was King Agamemnon when he saw them. "No need," he cried, "to give orders to such leaders of the Argives as you are, for of your own selves you spur your men on to fight with might and main. Would, by father Zeus, Athene, and Apollo that all were so minded as you are, for the city of Priam would then soon fall beneath our hands, and we should sack it."

With this he left them and went onward to Nestor, the facile speaker of the Pylians, who was marshaling his men and urging them on, in company with Pelagon, Alastor, Chromius, Haemon, and Bias, shepherd of his people. He placed his knights with their chariots and horses in the front rank, while the foot soldiers, brave men and many, whom he could trust, were in the rear. The cowards he drove into the middle, that they might fight whether they would or no. He gave his orders to the knights first, bidding them hold their horses well in hand, so as to avoid confusion. "Let no man," he said, "relying on his strength or horsemanship, get before the others and engage singly with the Trojans, nor yet let him lag behind, or you will weaken your attack; but let each when he meets an enemy's chariot throw his spear from his own; this will be much the best. This is how the men of old took towns and strongholds; in this wise were they minded."

Thus did the old man charge them, for he had been in many a fight, and King Agamemnon was glad. "I wish," he said to him, "that your limbs were as supple and your strength as sure as your judgment is; but age, the common enemy of mankind, has laid his hand upon you; would that it had fallen upon some other, and that you were still young."

And Nestor, knight of Gerene, answered: "Son of Atreus, I too would gladly be the man I was when I slew mighty Ereuthalion; but the gods will not give us everything at one and the same time. I was then young and now I am old; still I can go with my knights and give them that counsel which old men have a right to give. The wielding of the spear I leave to those who are younger and stronger than myself."

Agamemnon went his way rejoicing, and presently found Menestheus, son of Peteos, tarrying in his place, and with him were the Athenians loud of tongue in battle. Near him also tarried cunning Odysseus, with his sturdy Cephallenians round him; they had not yet heard the battle cry, for the ranks of Trojans and Achaeans had only just begun to move, so they were standing still, waiting for some other columns of the Achaeans to attack the Trojans and begin the fighting. When he saw this Agamemnon rebuked them and said: "Son of Peteos, and you other, steeped in cunning, heart of guile, why stand you here cowering and waiting on others? You two should be of all men foremost when there is hard fighting to be done, for you are ever foremost to accept my invitation when we counselors of the Achaeans are holding feast. You are glad enough then to take your fill of roast meats and to drink wine as long as you please, whereas now you would not care though you saw ten columns of Achaeans engage the enemy in front of you."

Odysseus glared at him and answered: "Son of Atreus, what are you talking about? How can you say that we are slack? When the Achaeans are in full fight with the Trojans you shall see, if you care to do so, that the father of Telemachus will join battle with the foremost of them. You are talking idly."

When Agamemnon saw that Odysseus was angry, he smiled pleasantly at him and withdrew his words. "Odysseus," said he, "noble son of Laertes, excellent in all good counsel, I have neither fault to find nor orders to give you, for I know your heart is right, and that you and I are of a mind. Enough; I will make you amends for what I have said, and if any ill has now been spoken may the gods bring it to nothing."

He then left them and went on to others. Presently he saw the son of Tydeus, noble Diomed, standing by his chariot and horses with Sthenelus, the son of Capaneus, beside him; whereon he began to upbraid him. "Son of Tydeus," he said, "why stand you cowering here upon the brink of battle? Tydeus did not shrink thus, but was ever ahead of his men when leading them on against the foe—so, at least, say they that saw him in battle, for I never set eyes upon him myself. They say that there was no man like him. He came once to Mycenae, not as an enemy but as a guest, in company with Polynices to recruit his forces, for they were levying war against the strong city of Thebes and prayed our people for a body of picked men to help them. The men of Mycenae were willing to let them have one, but Zeus dissuaded them by showing them unfavorable omens. Tydeus, therefore, and Polynices went their way. When they had got as far as the deep-meadowed and rush-grown banks of the Aesopus, the Achaeans sent Tydeus as their envoy, and he found the Cadmeans gathered in great numbers to a banquet in the house of Eteocles. Stranger though he was, he knew no fear on finding himself single-handed among so many, but challenged them to contests of all kinds, and in each one of them was at once victorious, so mightily did Athene help him. The Cadmeans were incensed at his success, and set a force of fifty youths with two captains—the godlike hero Maeon, son of Haemon, and Polyphontes, son of Autophonus—at their head, to lie in wait for him on his return journey; but Tydeus slew every man of them, save only Maeon, whom he let go in obedience to heaven's omens. Such was Tydeus of Aetolia. His son can talk more glibly, but he cannot fight as his father did."

Diomed made no answer, for he was shamed by the rebuke of Agamemnon; but the son of Capaneus took up his words and said: "Son of Atreus, tell no lies, for you can speak truth if you will. We boast ourselves as even better men than our fathers; we took seven-gated Thebes, though the wall was stronger and our men were fewer in number, for we trusted in the omens of the gods and in the help of Zeus, whereas they perished through their own sheer folly; hold not, then, our fathers in like honor with us."

Diomed looked sternly at him and said, "Hold your peace, my friend, as I bid you. It is not amiss that Agamemnon should urge the Achaeans forward, for the glory will be his if we take the city, and his the shame if we are vanquished. Therefore let us acquit ourselves with valor."

As he spoke he sprang from his chariot, and his armor rang so fiercely about his body that even a brave man might well have been scared to hear it.

As when some mighty wave that thunders on the beach when the west wind has lashed it into fury—it has reared its head afar and now comes crashing down on the shore; it bows its arching crest high over the jagged rocks and spews its salt foam in all directions—even so did the serried phalanxes of the Danaans march steadfastly to battle. The chiefs gave orders each to his own people, but the men said never a word; no man would think it, for huge as the host was, it seemed as though there was not a tongue among them, so silent were they in their obedience; and as they marched the armor about their bodies glistened in the sun. But the clamor of the Trojan ranks was as that of many thousand ewes that stand waiting to be milked in the yards of some rich flockmaster, and bleat incessantly in answer to the bleating of their lambs; for they had not one speech nor language, but their tongues were diverse, and they came from many different places. These were inspired of Ares, but the others by Athene—and with them came Panic, Rout, and Strife whose fury never tires, sister and friend of murderous Ares, who, from being at first but low in stature, grows till she uprears her head to heaven, though her feet are still on earth. She it was that went about among them and flung down discord to the waxing of sorrow with even hand between them.

When they were got together in one place shield clashed with shield and spear with spear in the rage of battle. The bossed shields beat one upon another, and there was a tramp as of a great multitude—death cry and shout of triumph of slain and slayers, and the earth ran red with blood. As torrents swollen with rain course madly down their deep channels till the angry floods meet in some gorge, and the shepherd on the hillside hears their roaring from afar—even such was the toil and uproar of the hosts as they joined in battle.

First Antilochus slew an armed warrior of the Trojans, Echepolus, son of Thalysius, fighting in the foremost ranks. He struck at the projecting part of his helmet and drove the spear into his brow; the point of bronze pierced the bone, and darkness veiled his eyes; headlong as a tower he fell amid the press of the fight, and as he dropped King Elephenor, son of Chalcodon and captain of the proud Abantes, began dragging him out of reach of the darts that were falling around him, in haste to strip him of his armor. But his purpose was not for long; Agenor saw him haling the body away, and smote him in the side with his bronze-shod spear—for as he stooped his side was left unprotected by his shield—and thus he perished. Then the fight between Trojans and Achaeans grew furious over his body, and they flew upon each other like wolves, man and man crushing one upon the other.

Forthwith Ajax, son of Telamon, slew the fair youth Simoëisius, son of Anthemion, whom his mother bore by the banks of the Simois, as she was coming down from Mount Ida, where she had been with her parents to see their flocks. Therefore he was named Simoëisius, but he did not live to pay his parents for his rearing, for he was cut off untimely by the spear of mighty Ajax, who struck him in the breast by the right nipple as he was coming on among the foremost fighters; the spear went right through his shoulder, and he fell as a poplar that has grown straight and tall in a meadow by some mere, and its top is thick with branches. Then the wheelwright lays his ax to its roots that he may fashion a felly for the wheel of some goodly chariot, and it lies seasoning by the waterside. In such wise did Ajax fell to earth Simoëisius, son of Anthemion. Thereon Antiphus of the gleaming corslet, son of Priam, hurled a spear at Ajax from amid the crowd and missed him, but he hit Leucus, the brave comrade of Odysseus, in the groin, as he was dragging the body of Simoëisius over to the other side; so he fell upon the body and loosed his hold upon it. Odysseus was furious when he saw Leucus slain, and strode in full armor through the front ranks till he was quite close; then he glared round about him and took aim, and the Trojans fell back as he did so. His dart was not sped in vain, for it struck Democoön, the bastard son of Priam, who had come to him from Abydos, where he had charge of his father's mares. Odysseus, infuriated by the death of his comrade, hit him with his spear on one temple, and the bronze point came through on the other side of his forehead. Thereon darkness veiled his eyes, and his armor rang rattling round him as he fell heavily to the ground. Hector and they that were in front then gave ground while the Argives raised a shout and drew off the dead, pressing further forward as they did so. But Apollo looked down from Pergamus and called aloud to the Trojans, for he was displeased. "Trojans," he cried, "rush on the foe, and do not let yourselves be thus beaten by the Argives. Their skins are not stone nor iron that when you hit them you do them no harm. Moreover, Achilles, the son of lovely Thetis, is not fighting, but is nursing his anger at the ships."

Thus spoke the mighty god, crying to them from the city, while Zeus' redoubtable daughter, the Trito-born, went about among the host of the Achaeans, and urged them forward whenever she beheld them slackening.

Then fate fell upon Diores, son of Amarynceus, for he was struck by a jagged stone near the ankle of his right leg. He that hurled it was Peiroüs, son of Imbrasus, captain of the Thracians, who had come from Aenus; the bones and both the tendons were crushed by the pitiless stone. He fell to the ground on his back, and in his death throes stretched out his hands towards his comrades. But Peiroüs, who had wounded him, sprang on him and thrust a spear into his belly, so that his bowels came gushing out upon the ground, and darkness veiled his eyes. As he was leaving the body, Thoas of Aetolia struck him in the chest near the nipple, and the point fixed itself in his lungs. Thoas came close up to him, pulled the spear out of his chest, and then drawing his sword, smote him in the middle of the belly so that he died. But he did not strip him of his armor, for his Thracian comrades, men who wear their hair in a tuft at the top of their heads, stood round the body and kept him off with their long spears for all his great stature and valor; so he was driven back. Thus the two corpses lay stretched on earth near to one another, the one captain of the Thracians and the other of the Epeans; and many another fell round them.

And now no man would have made light of the fighting if he could have gone about among it scatheless and unwounded, with Athene leading him by the hand, and protecting him from the storm of spears and arrows. For many Trojans and Achaeans on that day lay stretched side by side face downwards upon the earth.

Book V

Diomed, guided by Athene, performs great exploits. Wounded by Pandarus, he rallies and kills him and later wounds Aeneas, who is snatched from death by his mother Aphrodite and healed by Apollo. Diomed then attacks and wounds Aphrodite, driving her from the field. The Trojans are spurred on by the god Ares and their leader Hector, but Athene shows Diomed how to drive Ares out of the fight and back to Olympus.

THEN PALLAS ATHENE PUT VALOR INTO THE HEART OF DIOMED, SON of Tydeus, that he might excel all the other Argives, and cover himself with glory. She made a stream of fire flare from his shield and helmet like the star that shines most brilliantly in summer after its bath in the waters of Oceanus—even such a fire did she kindle upon his head and shoulders as she bade him speed into the thickest hurly-burly of the fight.

Now there was a certain rich and honorable man among the Trojans, priest of Hephaestus, and his name was Dares. He had two sons, Phegeus and Idaeus, both of them skilled in all the arts of war. These two came forward from the main body of Trojans, and set upon Diomed, he being on foot, while they fought from their chariot. When they were close up to one another, Phegeus took aim first, but his spear went over Diomed's left shoulder without hitting him. Diomed then threw, and his spear sped not in vain, for it hit Phegeus on the breast near the nipple, and he fell from his chariot. Idaeus did not dare to bestride his brother's body, but sprang from the chariot and took to flight, or he would have shared his brother's fate; whereon Hephaestus saved him by wrapping him in a cloud of darkness, that his old father might not be utterly overwhelmed with grief; but the son of Tydeus drove off with the horses, and bade his followers take them to the ships. The Trojans were scared when they saw the two sons of Dares, one of them in flight and the other lying dead by his chariot. Athene, therefore, took Ares by the hand and said: "Ares, Ares, bane of men, bloodstained stormer of cities, may we not now leave the Trojans and Achaeans to fight it out, and see to which of the two Zeus will vouchsafe the victory? Let us go away, and thus avoid his anger."

So saying, she drew Ares out of the battle, and set him down upon the steep banks of the Scamander. Upon this the Danaans drove the Trojans back, and each one of their chieftains killed his man. First King Agamemnon flung mighty Odius, captain of the Halizoni, from his chariot. The spear of Agamemnon caught him on the broad of his back, just as he was turning in flight. It struck him between the shoulders and went right through his chest, and his armor rang rattling round him as he fell heavily to the ground.

Then Idomeneus killed Phaesus, son of Borus, the Meonian, who had come from Tarne. Mighty Idomeneus speared him on the right shoulder as he was mounting his chariot, and the darkness of death enshrouded him as he fell heavily from the car.

The squires of Idomeneus spoiled him of his armor, while Menelaus, son of Atreus, killed Scamandrius, the son of Strophius, a mighty huntsman and keen lover of the chase. Artemis herself had taught him how to kill every kind of wild creature that is bred in mountain forests, but neither she nor his famed skill in archery could now save him, for the spear of Menelaus struck him in the back as he was flying. It struck him between the shoulders and went right through his chest, so that he fell headlong and his armor rang rattling round him.

Meriones then killed Phereclus, the son of Tecton, who was the son of Harmon, a man whose hand was skilled in all manner of cunning workmanship, for Pallas Athene had dearly loved him. He it was that made the ships for Paris, which were the beginning of all mischief, and brought evil alike both on the Trojans and on Paris himself; for he heeded not the decrees of heaven. Meriones overtook him as he was flying, and struck him on the right buttock. The point of the spear went through the bone into the bladder, and death came upon him as he cried aloud and fell forward on his knees.

Meges, moreover, slew Pedaeus, son of Antenor, who, though he was a bastard, had been brought up by Theano as one of her own children, for the love she bore her husband. The son of Phyleus got close up to him and drove a spear into the nape of his neck: it went under his tongue all among his teeth, so he bit the cold bronze, and fell dead in the dust.

And Eurypylus, son of Euaemon, killed Hypsenor, the son of noble Dolopion, who had been made priest of the river Scamander, and was honored among the people as though he were a god. Eurypylus gave him chase as he was flying before him, smote him with his sword upon the arm, and lopped his strong hand from off it. The bloody hand fell to the ground, and the shades of death, with fate that no man can withstand, came over his eyes.

Thus furiously did the battle rage between them. As for the son of Tydeus, you could not say whether he was more among the Achaeans or the Trojans. He rushed across the plain like a winter torrent that has burst its barrier in full flood; no dykes, no walls of fruitful vineyards can embank it when it is swollen with rain from heaven, but in a moment it comes tearing onward, and lays many a field waste that many a strong man's hand has reclaimed—even so were the dense phalanxes of the Trojans driven in rout by the son of Tydeus, and many though they were, they dared not abide his onslaught.

Now when the son of Lycaon saw him scouring the plain and driving the Trojans pell-mell before him, he aimed an arrow and hit the front part of his cuirass near the shoulder. The arrow went right through the metal and pierced the flesh, so that the cuirass was covered with blood. On this the son of Lycaon shouted in triumph: "Knights Trojans, come on! The bravest of the

Achaeans is wounded, and he will not hold out much longer if King Apollo was indeed with me when I sped from Lycia hither."

Thus did he vaunt; but his arrow had not killed Diomed, who withdrew and made for the chariot and horses of Sthenelus, the son of Capaneus. "Dear son of Capaneus," said he, "come down from your chariot, and draw the arrow out of my shoulder."

Sthenelus sprang from his chariot, and drew the arrow from the wound, whereon the blood came spouting out through the hole that had been made in his shirt. Then Diomed prayed, saying: "Hear me, daughter of aegis-bearing Zeus, unwearyable! If ever you loved my father well and stood by him in the thick of a fight, do the like now by me; grant me to come within a spear's throw of that man and kill him. He has been too quick for me and has wounded me; and now he is boasting that I shall not see the light of the sun much longer."

Thus he prayed, and Pallas Athene heard him; she made his limbs supple and quickened his hands and his feet. Then she went close up to him and said, "Fear not, Diomed, to do battle with the Trojans, for I have set in your heart the spirit of your knightly father Tydeus. Moreover, I have withdrawn the veil from your eyes, that you may know gods and men apart. If, then, any other god comes here and offers you battle, do not fight him; but should Zeus' daughter Aphrodite come, strike her with your spear and wound her."

When she had said this Athene went away, and the son of Tydeus again took his place among the foremost fighters, three times more fierce even than he had been before. He was like a lion that some mountain shepherd has wounded, but not killed, as he is springing over the wall of a sheep yard to attack the sheep. The shepherd has roused the brute to fury but cannot defend his flock, so he takes shelter under cover of the buildings, while the sheep, panic-stricken on being deserted, are smothered in heaps one on top of the other, and the angry lion leaps out over the sheep yard wall. Even thus did Diomed go furiously about among the Trojans.

He killed Astynoüs and Hypeiron, shepherd of his people, the one with a thrust of his spear, which struck him above the nipple, the other with a sword cut on the collar bone, that severed his shoulder from his neck and back. He let both of them lie, and went in pursuit of Abas and Polyidus, sons of the old reader of dreams, Eurydamas. They never came back for him to read them any more dreams, for mighty Diomed made an end of them. He then gave chase to Xanthus and Thoön, the two sons of Phaenops, both of them very dear to him, for he was now worn out with age, and begat no more sons to inherit his possessions. But Diomed took both their lives and left their father sorrowing bitterly, for he nevermore saw them come home from battle alive, and his kinsmen divided his wealth among themselves.

Then he came upon two sons of Priam, Echemmon and Chromius, as they were both in one chariot. He sprang upon them as a lion fastens on the neck of some cow or heifer when the herd is feeding in a coppice. For all their vain struggles he flung them both from their chariot and stripped the armor from their bodies. Then he gave their horses to his comrades to take them back to the ships.

When Aeneas saw him thus making havoc among the ranks, he went through the fight amid the rain of spears to see if he could find Pandarus. When he had found the brave son of Lycaon, he said: "Pandarus, where is now your bow, your winged arrows, and your renown as an archer, in respect of which no man here can rival you nor is there any in Lycia that can beat you? Lift then your hands to Zeus and send an arrow at this fellow who is going so masterfully about, and has done such deadly work among the Trojans. He has killed many a brave man—unless indeed he is some god who is angry with the Trojans about their sacrifices, and has set his hand against them in his displeasure."

And the son of Lycaon answered: "Aeneas, I take him for none other than the son of Tydeus. I know him by his shield, the visor of his helmet, and by his horses. It is possible that he may be a god, but if he is the man I say he is, he is not making all this havoc without heaven's help, but has some god by his side who is shrouded in a cloud of darkness, and who turned my arrow aside when it had hit him. I have taken aim at him already and hit him on the right shoulder; my arrow went through the breastpiece of his cuirass; and I made sure I should send him hurrying to the world below, but it seems that I have not killed him. There must be a god who is angry with me. Moreover, I have neither horse nor chariot. In my father's stables there are eleven excellent chariots, fresh from the builder, quite new, with cloths spread over them; and by each of them there stand a pair of horses, champing barley and rye. My old father Lycaon urged me again and again when I was at home and on the point of starting to take chariots and horses with me that I might lead the Trojans in battle, but I would not listen to him. It would have been much better if I had done so, but I was thinking about the horses, which had been used to eat their fill, and I was afraid that in such a great gathering of men they might be ill-fed, so I left them at home and came on foot to Ilium armed only with my bow and arrows. These it seems, are of no use, for I have already hit two chieftains, the sons of Atreus and of Tydeus, and though I drew blood surely enough, I have only made them still more furious. I did ill to take my bow down from its peg on the day I led my band of Trojans to Ilium in Hector's service, and if ever I get home again to set eyes on my native place, my wife, and the greatness of my house, may someone cut my head off then and there if I do not break the bow and set it on a hot fire—such pranks as it plays me."

Aeneas answered: "Say no more. Things will not mend till we two go against this man with chariot and horses and bring him to a trial of arms. Mount my chariot, and note how cleverly the horses of Tros can speed hither and thither over the plain in pursuit or flight. If Zeus again vouchsafes glory to the son of Tydeus they will carry us safely back to the city. Take hold, then, of the whip and reins while I stand upon the car to fight, or else do you wait this man's onset while I look after the horses."

"Aeneas," replied the son of Lycaon, "take the reins and drive. If we have to fly before the son of Tydeus the horses will go better for their own driver.

If they miss the sound of your voice when they expect it they may be frightened, and refuse to take us out of the fight. The son of Tydeus will then kill both of us and take the horses. Therefore, drive them yourself and I will be ready for him with my spear."

They then mounted the chariot and drove full-speed towards the son of Tydeus. Sthenelus, son of Capaneus, saw them coming and said to Diomed: "Diomed, son of Tydeus, man after my own heart, I see two heroes speeding towards you, both of them men of might—the one a skillful archer, Pandarus, son of Lycaon, the other, Aeneas, whose sire is Anchises, while his mother is Aphrodite. Mount the chariot and let us retreat. Do not, I pray you, press so furiously forward, or you may get killed."

Diomed looked angrily at him and answered: "Talk not of flight, for I shall not listen to you: I am of a race that knows neither flight nor fear, and my limbs are as yet unwearied. I am in no mind to mount, but will go against them even as I am. Pallas Athene bids me be afraid of no man, and even though one of them escape, their steeds shall not take both back again. I say further, and lay my saying to your heart—if Athene sees fit to vouchsafe me the glory of killing both, stay your horses here and make the reins fast to the rim of the chariot; then be sure you spring upon Aeneas' horses and drive them from the Trojan to the Achaean ranks. They are of the stock that great Zeus gave to Tros in payment for his son Ganymede, and are the finest that live and move under the sun. King Anchises stole the blood by putting his mares to them without Laomedon's knowledge, and they bore him six foals. Four are still in his stables, but he gave the other two to Aeneas. We shall win great glory if we can take them."

Thus did they converse, but the other two had now driven close up to them, and the son of Lycaon spoke first. "Great and mighty son," said he, "of noble Tydeus, my arrow failed to lay you low, so I will now try with my spear."

He poised his spear as he spoke and hurled it from him. It struck the shield of the son of Tydeus; the bronze point pierced it and passed on till it reached the breastplate. Thereon the son of Lycaon shouted out and said, "You are hit clean through the belly; you will not stand out for long, and the glory of the fight is mine."

But Diomed all undismayed made answer, "You have missed, not hit, and before you two see the end of this matter one or other of you shall glut tough-shielded Ares with his blood."

With this he hurled his spear, and Athene guided it on to Pandarus' nose near the eye. It went crashing in among his white teeth. The bronze point cut through the root of his tongue, coming out under his chin, and his glistening armor rang rattling round him as he fell heavily to the ground. The horses started aside for fear, and he was reft of life and strength.

Aeneas sprang from his chariot armed with shield and spear, fearing lest the Achaeans should carry off the body. He bestrode it as a lion in the pride of strength, with shield and spear before him and a cry of battle on his lips—resolute to kill the first that should dare face him. But the son of Tydeus caught up a mighty stone, so huge and great that as men now are it would take two to lift it; nevertheless he bore it aloft with ease unaided, and with this he struck Aeneas on the groin where the hip turns in the joint that is called the "cup bone." The stone crushed this joint, and broke both the sinews, while its jagged edges tore away all the flesh. The hero fell on his knees, and propped himself with his hand resting on the ground till the darkness of night fell upon his eyes. And now Aeneas, king of men, would have perished then and there, had not his mother, Zeus' daughter Aphrodite, who had conceived him by Anchises when he was herding cattle, been quick to mark, and thrown her two white arms about the body of her dear son. She protected him by covering him with a fold of her own fair garment, lest some Danaan should drive a spear into his breast and kill him.

Thus, then, did she bear her dear son out of the fight. But the son of Capaneus was not unmindful of the orders that Diomed had given him. He made his own horses fast, away from the hurly-burly, by binding the reins to the rim of the chariot. Then he sprang upon Aeneas' horses and drove them from the Trojan to the Achaean ranks. When he had so done he gave them over to his chosen comrade Deipylus, whom he valued above all others as the one who was most like-minded with himself, to take them on to the ships. He then remounted his own chariot, seized the reins, and drove with all speed in search of the son of Tydeus.

Now the son of Tydeus was in pursuit of the Cyprian goddess, spear in hand, for he knew her to be feeble and not one of those goddesses that can lord it among men in battle like Athene, or Enyo, the waster of cities, and when at last after a long chase he caught her up, he flew at her and thrust his spear into the flesh of her delicate hand. The point tore through the ambrosial robe which the Graces had woven for her, and pierced the skin between her wrist and the palm of her hand, so that the immortal blood, or ichor, that flows in the veins of the blessed gods, came pouring from the wound; for the gods do not eat bread nor drink wine, hence they have no blood such as ours, and are immortal. Aphrodite screamed aloud, and let her son fall, but Phoebus Apollo caught him in his arms, and hid him in a cloud of darkness, lest some Danaan should drive a spear into his breast and kill him; and Diomed shouted out as he left her, "Daughter of Zeus, leave war and battle alone; can you not be contented with beguiling silly women? If you meddle with fighting you will get what will make you shudder at the very name of war."

The goddess went dazed and discomfited away, and Iris, fleet as the wind, drew her from the throng, in pain and with her fair skin all besmirched. She found fierce Ares waiting on the left of the battle, with his spear and his two fleet steeds resting on a cloud; whereon she fell on her knees before her brother and implored him to let her have his horses. "Dear brother," she cried, "save me, and give me your horses to take me to Olympus where the gods dwell. I am badly wounded by a mortal, the son of Tydeus, who would now fight even with father Zeus."

Thus she spoke, and Ares gave her his gold-bedizened steeds. She mounted the chariot sick and sorry at heart, while Iris sat beside her and took the reins in her hand. She lashed her horses on and they flew forward nothing loath, till in a trice they were at high Olympus, where the gods have their dwelling. There she stayed them, unloosed them from the chariot, and gave them their ambrosial forage; but Aphrodite flung herself on to the lap of her mother Dione, who threw her arms about her and caressed her, saying, "Which of the heavenly beings has been treating you in this way, as though you had been doing something wrong in the face of day?"

And laughter-loving Aphrodite answered: "Proud Diomed, the son of Tydeus, wounded me because I was bearing my dear son Aeneas, whom I love best of all mankind, out of the fight. The war is no longer one between Trojans and Achaeans, for the Danaans have now taken to fighting with the immortals."

"Bear it, my child," replied Dione, "and make the best of it. We dwellers in Olympus have to put up with much at the hands of men, and we lay much suffering on one another. Ares had to suffer when Otus and Ephialtes, children of Aloeus, bound him in cruel bonds, so that he lay thirteen months imprisoned in a vessel of bronze. Ares would have then perished had not fair Eëriboea, stepmother to the sons of Aloeus, told Hermes, who stole him away when he was already well-nigh worn out by the severity of his bondage. Hera again suffered when the mighty son of Amphitryon wounded her on the right breast with a three-barbed arrow, and nothing could assuage her pain. So, also, did huge Hades, when this same man, the son of aegis-bearing Zeus, hit him with an arrow even at the gates of hell and hurt him badly. Thereon Hades went to the house of Zeus on great Olympus, angry and full of pain; and the arrow in his brawny shoulder caused him great anguish till Paeëon healed him by spreading soothing herbs on the wound, for Hades was not of mortal mold. Daring, headstrong, evildoer who recked not of his sin in shooting the gods that dwell in Olympus. And now Athene has egged this son of

Tydeus on against yourself, fool that he is for not reflecting that no man who fights with gods will live long or hear his children prattling about his knees when he returns from battle. Let, then, the son of Tydeus see that he does not have to fight with one who is stronger than you are. Then shall his brave wife, Aegialeia, daughter of Adrestus, rouse her whole house from sleep, wailing for the loss of her wedded lord, Diomed, the bravest of the Achaeans."

So saying, she wiped the ichor from the wrist of her daughter with both hands, whereon the pain left her, and her hand was healed. But Athene and Hera, who were looking on, began to taunt Zeus with their mocking talk, and Athene was first to speak. "Father Zeus," said she, "do not be angry with me, but I think the Cyprian must have been persuading some one of the Achaean women to go with the Trojans of whom she is so very fond, and while caressing one or other of them she must have torn her delicate hand with the gold pin of the woman's brooch."

The sire of gods and men smiled, and called golden Aphrodite to his side. "My child," said he, "it has not been given you to be a warrior. Attend, henceforth, to your own delightful matrimonial duties, and leave all this fighting to Ares and to Athene."

Thus did they converse. But Diomed sprang upon Aeneas, though he knew him to be in the very arms of Apollo. Not one whit did he fear the mighty god, so set was he on killing Aeneas and stripping him of his armor. Thrice did he spring forward with might and main to slay him, and thrice did Apollo beat back his gleaming shield. When he was coming on for the fourth time, as though he were a god, Apollo shouted to him with an awful voice and said, "Take heed, son of Tydeus, and draw off. Think not to match yourself against gods, for men that walk the earth cannot hold their own with the immortals."

The son of Tydeus then gave way for a little space, to avoid the anger of the god, while Apollo took Aeneas out of the crowd and set him in sacred Pergamus, where his temple stood. There, within the mighty sanctuary,

Latona and Artemis healed him and made him glorious to behold, while Apollo of the silver bow fashioned a wraith in the likeness of Aeneas, and armed as he was. Round this the Trojans and Achaeans hacked at the bucklers about one another's breasts, hewing each other's round shields and light hide-covered targets. Then Phoebus Apollo said to Ares, "Ares, Ares, bane of men, bloodstained stormer of cities, can you not go to this man, the son of Tydeus, who would now fight even with father Zeus, and draw him out of the battle? He first went up to the Cyprian and wounded her in the hand near her wrist, and afterwards sprang upon me too, as though he were a god."

He then took his seat on the top of Pergamus, while murderous Ares went about among the ranks of the Trojans, cheering them on, in the likeness of fleet Acamas, chief of the Thracians. "Sons of Priam," said he, "how long will you let your people be thus slaughtered by the Achaeans? Would you wait till they are at the walls of Troy? Aeneas, the son of Anchises, has fallen, he whom we held in as high honor as Hector himself. Help me, then, to rescue our brave comrade from the stress of the fight."

With these words he put heart and soul into them all. Then Sarpedon rebuked Hector very sternly. "Hector," said he, "where is your prowess now? You used to say that though you had neither people nor allies you could hold the town alone with your brothers and brothers-in-law. I see not one of them here; they cower as hounds before a lion; it is we, your allies, who bear the brunt of the battle. I have come from afar, even from Lycia and the banks of the river Xanthus, where I have left my wife, my infant son, and much wealth to tempt whoever is needy. Nevertheless, I head my Lycian soldiers and stand my ground against any who would fight me though I have nothing here for the Achaeans to plunder, while you look on, without even bidding your men stand firm in defense of their wives. See that you fall not into the hands of your foes as men caught in the meshes of a net, and they sack your fair city forthwith. Keep this before your mind night and day, and beseech the captains of your allies to hold on without flinching, and thus put away their reproaches from you."

So spoke Sarpedon, and Hector smarted under his words. He sprang from his chariot clad in his suit of armor, and went about among the host brandishing his two spears, exhorting the men to fight and raising the terrible cry of battle. Then they rallied and again faced the Achaeans, but the Argives stood compact and firm, and were not driven back. As the breezes sport with the chaff upon some goodly threshing floor when men are winnowing—while yellow Demeter blows with the wind to sift the chaff from the grain, and the chaff heaps grow whiter and whiter—even so did the Achaeans whiten in the dust which the horses' hoofs raised to the firmament of heaven, as their drivers turned them back to battle, and they bore down with might upon the foe. Fierce Ares, to help the Trojans, covered them in a veil of darkness and went about everywhere among them, inasmuch as Phoebus Apollo had told him that when he saw Pallas Athene leave the fray he was to put courage into the hearts of the Trojans—for it was she who was helping the Danaans. Then Apollo sent Aeneas forth from his rich sanctuary, and filled his heart with valor, whereon he took his place among his comrades, who were overjoyed at seeing him alive, sound, and of a good courage; but they could not ask him how it had all happened, for they were too busy with the turmoil raised by Ares and by Strife, who raged insatiably in their midst.

The two Ajaxes, Odysseus, and Diomed cheered the Danaans on, fearless of the fury and onset of the Trojans. They stood as still as clouds which the son of Cronus has spread upon the mountain tops when there is no air and fierce Boreas sleeps with the other boisterous winds whose shrill blasts scatter the clouds in all directions—even so did the Danaans stand firm and unflinching against the Trojans. The son of Atreus went about among them and exhorted them. "My friends," said he, "quit yourselves like brave men, and shun dishonor in one another's eyes amid the stress of battle. They that shun dishonor more often live than get killed, but they that fly save neither life nor name."

As he spoke he hurled his spear and hit one of those who were in the front rank, the comrade of Aeneas, Deicoön, son of Pergasus, whom the Trojans held in no less honor than the sons of Priam, for he was ever quick to place himself among the foremost. The spear of King Agamemnon struck his shield and went right through it, for the shield stayed it not. It drove through his belt into the lower part of his belly, and his armor rang rattling round him as he fell heavily to the ground.

Then Aeneas killed two champions of the Danaans, Crethon and Orsilochus. Their father was a rich man who lived in the strong city of Phere and was descended from the river Alpheus, whose broad stream flows through the land of the Pylians. The river begat Orsilochus, who ruled over much people and was father to Diocles, who in his turn begat twin sons, Crethon and Orsilochus, well skilled in all the arts of war. These, when they grew up, went to Ilium with the Argive fleet in the cause of Menelaus and Agamemnon, sons of Atreus, and there they both of them fell. As two lions whom their dam has reared in the depths of some mountain forest to plunder homesteads and carry sheep and cattle till they get killed by the hand of man, so were these two vanquished by Aeneas, and fell like high pine trees to the ground.

Brave Menelaus pitied them in their fall, and made his way to the front, clad in gleaming bronze and brandishing his spear, for Ares egged him on to do so with intent that he should be killed by Aeneas; but Antilochus, the son of Nestor, saw him and sprang forward, fearing that the king might come to harm and thus bring all their labor to nothing; when, therefore, Aeneas and Menelaus were setting their hands and spears against one another eager to do battle, Antilochus placed himself by the side of Menelaus. Aeneas, bold though he was, drew back on seeing the two heroes side by side in front of him, so they drew the bodies of Credion and Orsilochus to the ranks of the Achaeans and committed the two poor fellows into the hands of their comrades. They then turned back and fought in the front ranks.

They killed Pylaemenes, peer of Ares, leader of the Paphlagonian warriors. Menelaus struck him on the collarbone, as he was standing on his chariot, while Antilochus hit his charioteer and squire Mydon, the son of Atymnius, who was turning his horses in flight. He hit him with a stone upon the elbow, and the reins, enriched with white ivory, fell from his hands into the dust. Antilochus rushed towards him and struck him on the temples with his sword, whereon he fell head first from the chariot to the ground. There he stood for a while with his head and shoulders buried deep in the dust—for he had fallen on sandy soil—till his horses kicked him and laid him flat on the ground, as Antilochus lashed them and drove them off to the host of the Achaeans.

But Hector marked them from across the ranks, and with a loud cry rushed towards them, followed by the strong battalions of the Trojans. Ares and dread Enyo led them on, she fraught with ruthless turmoil of battle, while Ares wielded a monstrous spear, and went about, now in front of Hector and now behind him.

Diomed shook with passion as he saw them. As a man crossing a wide plain is dismayed to find himself on the brink of some great river rolling swiftly to the sea—he sees its boiling waters and starts back in fear—even so did the son of Tydeus give ground. Then he said to his men: "My friends, how can we wonder that Hector wields the spear so well? Some god is ever by his side to protect him, and now Ares is with him in the likeness of mortal man. Keep your faces therefore towards the Trojans, but give ground backwards, for we dare not fight with gods."

As he spoke the Trojans drew close up, and Hector killed two men, both in one chariot, Menesthes and Anchialus, heroes well-versed in war. Ajax, son of Telamon, pitied them in their fall; he came close up and hurled his spear, hitting Amphius, the son of Selagus, a man of great wealth who lived in Paesus and owned much corn-growing land, but his lot had led him to come to the aid of Priam and his sons. Ajax struck him in the belt; the spear pierced the lower part of his belly, and he fell heavily to the ground. Then Ajax ran towards him to strip him of his armor, but the Trojans rained spears upon him, many of which fell upon his shield. He planted his heel upon the body and drew out his spear, but the darts pressed so heavily upon him that he could not strip the goodly armor from his shoulders. The Trojan chieftains, moreover, many and valiant, came about him with their spears, so that he dared not stay; great, brave, and valiant though he was, they drove him from them and he was beaten back.

Thus, then, did the battle rage between them. Presently the strong hand of fate impelled Tlepolemus, the son of Heracles, a man both brave and of great stature, to fight Sarpedon; so the two, son and grandson of great Zeus, drew near to one another, and Tlepolemus spoke first. "Sarpedon," said he, "councilor of the Lycians, why should you come skulking here—you who are a man of peace? They lie who call you son of aegis-bearing Zeus, for you are little like those who were of old his children. Far other was Heracles, my own brave and lion-hearted father, who came here for the horses of Laomedon, and though he had six ships only, and few men to follow him, sacked the city of Ilium and made a wilderness of her highways. You are a coward, and your people are falling from you. For all your strength, and all your coming from Lycia, you will be no help to the Trojans but will pass the gates of Hades vanquished by my hand."

And Sarpedon, captain of the Lycians, answered: "Tlepolemus, your father overthrew Ilium by reason of Laomedon's folly in refusing payment to one who had served him well. He would not give your father the horses which he had come so far to fetch. As for yourself, you shall meet death by my spear. You shall yield glory to myself, and your soul to Hades of the noble steeds."

Thus spoke Sarpedon and Tlepolemus upraised his spear. They threw at the same moment, and Sarpedon struck his foe in the middle of his throat;

the spear went right through, and the darkness of death fell upon his eyes. Tlepolemus' spear struck Sarpedon on the left thigh with such force that it tore through the flesh and grazed the bone, but his father as yet warded off destruction from him.

His comrades bore Sarpedon out of the fight, in great pain by the weight of the spear that was dragging from his wound. They were in such haste and stress as they bore him that no one thought of drawing the spear from his thigh so as to let him walk uprightly. Meanwhile the Achaeans carried off the body of Tlepolemus, whereon Odysseus was moved to pity, and panted for the fray as he beheld them. He doubted whether to pursue the son of Zeus or to make slaughter of the Lycian rank and file. It was not decreed, however, that he should slay the son of Zeus. Athene, therefore, turned him against the main body of the Lycians. He killed Coeranus, Alastor, Chromius, Alcandrus, Halius, Noëmon, and Prytanis, and would have slain yet more, had not great Hector marked him, and sped to the front of the fight clad in his suit of mail, filling the Danaans with terror. Sarpedon was glad when he saw him coming, and besought him, saying: "Son of Priam, let me not lie here to fall into the hands of the Danaans. Help me, and since I may not return home to gladden the hearts of my wife and of my infant son, let me die within the walls of your city."

Hector made him no answer, but rushed onward to fall at once upon the Achaeans and kill many among them. His comrades then bore Sarpedon away and laid him beneath Zeus' spreading oak tree. Pelagon his friend and comrade drew the spear out of his thigh, but Sarpedon fainted and a mist came over his eyes. Presently he came to himself again, for the breath of the north wind as it played upon him gave him new life, and brought him out of the deep swoon into which he had fallen.

Meanwhile the Argives were neither driven towards their ships by Ares and Hector, nor yet did they attack them; when they knew that Ares was with the Trojans they retreated, but kept their faces still turned towards the foe.

Who, then, was first and who last to be slain by Ares and Hector? They were valiant Teuthras, and Orestes, the renowned charioteer, Trechus, the Aetolian warrior, Oenomaus, Helenus, the son of Oenops, and Oresbius of the gleaming girdle, who was possessed of great wealth, and dwelt by the Cephisian lake with the other Boeotians who lived near him, owners of a fertile country.

Now when the goddess Hera saw the Argives thus falling, she said to Athene, "Alas, daughter of aegis-bearing Zeus, unweariable, the promise we made Menelaus that he should not return till he had sacked the city of Ilium will be of none effect if we let Ares rage thus furiously. Let us go into the fray at once."

Athene did not gainsay her. Thereon the august goddess, daughter of great Cronus, began to harness her gold-bedizened steeds. Hebe with all speed fitted on the eight-spoked wheels of bronze that were on either side of the iron axletree. The fellies of the wheels were of gold, imperishable, and over these there was a tire of bronze, wondrous to behold. The naves of the wheels were silver, turning round the axle upon either side. The car itself was made with plaited bands of gold and silver, and it had a double top rail running all round it. From the body of the car there went a pole of silver, on to the end of which she bound the golden yoke, with the bands of gold that were to go under the necks of the horses. Then Hera put her steeds under the yoke, eager for battle and the war cry.

Meanwhile Athene flung her richly embroidered vesture, made with her own hands, on to her father's threshold, and donned the shirt of Zeus, arming herself for battle. She threw her tasseled aegis about her shoulders, wreathed round with Rout as with a fringe, and on it were Strife, and Strength, and Panic whose blood runs cold; moreover there was the head of the dread monster Gorgon, grim and awful to behold, portent of aegis-bearing Zeus. On her head she set her helmet of gold, with four plumes, and coming to a peak both in front and behind—decked with the emblems of a hundred cities. Then she stepped into her flaming chariot and grasped the spear, so stout and sturdy and strong, with which she quells the ranks of heroes who have displeased her. Hera lashed the horses on, and the gates of heaven bellowed as they flew open of their own accord—gates over which the Hours preside, in whose hands are Heaven and Olympus, either to open the dense cloud that hides them, or to close it. Through these the goddesses drove their obedient steeds, and found the son of Cronus sitting all alone on the topmost ridges of Olympus. There Hera stayed her horses, and spoke to Zeus, the son of Cronus, lord of all. "Father Zeus," said she, "are you not angry with Ares for these high doings? See how great and goodly a host of the Achaeans he has destroyed to my great grief, and without either right or reason, while the Cyprian and Apollo are enjoying it all at their ease and setting this unrighteous madman on to do further mischief. I hope, Father Zeus, that you will not be angry if I hit Ares hard, and chase him out of the battle."

And Zeus answered, "Set Athene on to him, for she punishes him more often than anyone else does."

Hera did as he had said. She lashed her horses, and they flew forward nothing loath midway betwixt earth and sky. As far as a man can see when he looks out upon the sea from some high beacon, so far can the loud-neighing horses of the gods spring at a single bound. When they reached Troy and the place where its two flowing streams, Simois and Scamander, meet, there Hera stayed down and took them from the chariot. She hid them in a thick cloud, and Simois made ambrosia spring up for them to eat; the two goddesses then went on, flying like turtledoves in their eagerness to help the Argives. When they came to the part where the bravest and most in number were gathered about mighty Diomed, fighting like lions or wild boars of great strength and endurance, there Hera stood still and raised a shout like that of brazen-voiced Stentor, whose cry was as loud as that of fifty men together. "Argives," she cried; "shame on you, cowardly creatures, brave in semblance only! As long as Achilles was fighting his spear was so deadly that the Trojans dared not show themselves outside the Dardanian gates, but now they sally far from the city and fight even at your ships."

With these words she put heart and soul into them all, while Athene sprang to the side of the son of Tydeus whom she found near his chariot and horses, cooling the wound that Pandarus had given him. For the sweat caused by the band that bore the weight of his shield irritated the hurt: his arm was weary with pain, and he was lifting up the strap to wipe away the blood. The goddess laid her hand on the yoke of his horses, and said: "The son of Tydeus is not such another as his father. Tydeus was a little man, but he could fight, and rushed madly into the fray even when I told him not to do so. When he went all unattended as envoy to the city of Thebes among the Cadmeans, I bade him feast in their houses and be at peace; but with that high spirit which was ever present with him, he challenged the youth of the Cadmeans, and at once beat them in all that he attempted, so mightily did I help him. I stand by you too to protect you, and I bid you be instant in fighting the Trojans; but either you are tired out, or you are afraid and out of heart, and in that case I say that you are no true son of Tydeus, the son of Oeneus."

Diomed answered, "I know you, goddess, daughter of aegis-bearing Zeus, and will hide nothing from you. I am not afraid nor out of heart, nor is there any slackness in me. I am only following your own instructions; you told me not to fight any of the blessed gods, but if Zeus' daughter Aphrodite came into battle I was to wound her with my spear. Therefore I am retreating, and bidding the other Argives gather in this place, for I know that Ares is now lording it in the field."

"Diomed, son of Tydeus," replied Athene, "man after my own heart, fear neither Ares nor any other of the immortals, for I will befriend you. Nay, drive straight at Ares, and smite him in close combat. Fear not this raging madman, villain incarnate, first on one side and then on the other. But now he was holding talk with Hera and myself, saying he would help the Argives and attack the Trojans. Nevertheless, he is with the Trojans, and has forgotten the Argives."

With this she caught hold of Sthenelus and lifted him off the chariot on to the ground. In a second he was on the ground, whereupon the goddess mounted the car and placed herself by the side of Diomed. The oaken axle groaned aloud under the burden of the awful goddess and the hero; Pallas Athene took the whip and reins, and drove straight at Ares. He was in the act of stripping huge Periphas, son of Ochesius and bravest of the Aetolians. Bloody Ares was stripping him of his armor, and Athene donned the helmet of Hades, that he might not see her; when, therefore, he saw Diomed, he made straight for him and let Periphas lie where he had fallen. As soon as they were at close quarters he let fly with his bronze spear over the reins and yoke, thinking to take Diomed's life, but Athene caught the spear in her hand and made it fly harmlessly over the chariot. Diomed then threw, and Pallas Athene drove the spear into the pit of Ares' stomach where his under-girdle went round him. There Diomed wounded him, tearing his fair flesh and then drawing his spear out again. Ares roared as loudly as nine or ten thousand men in the thick of a fight, and the Achaeans and Trojans were struck with panic, so terrible was the cry he raised.

As a dark cloud in the sky when it comes on to blow after heat, even so did Diomed, son of Tydeus, see Ares ascend into the broad heavens. With all speed he reached high Olympus, home of the gods, and in great pain sat down beside Zeus, the son of Cronus. He showed Zeus the immortal blood that was flowing from his wound, and spoke piteously, saying: "Father Zeus, are you not angered by such doings? We gods are continually suffering in the most cruel manner at one another's hands while helping mortals; and we all owe you a grudge for having begotten that mad termagant of a daughter, who is always committing outrage of some kind. We other gods must all do as you bid us, but her you neither scold nor punish; you encourage her because the pestilent creature is your daughter. See how she has been inciting proud Diomed to vent his rage on the immortal gods. First he went up to the Cyprian and wounded her in the hand near her wrist, and then he sprang upon me too as though he were a god. Had I not run for it I must either have lain there for long enough in torments among the ghastly corpses, or have been beaten alive with spears till I had no more strength left in me."

Zeus looked angrily at him and said: "Do not come whining here, Sir Facing-both-ways. I hate you worst of all the gods in Olympus, for you are ever fighting and making mischief. You have the intolerable and stubborn spirit of your mother Hera: it is all I can do to manage her, and it is her doing that you are now in this plight: still, I cannot let you remain longer in such great pain; you are my own offspring, and it was by me that your mother conceived you. If, however, you had been the son of any other god, you are so destructive that by this time you should have been lying lower than the Titans."

He then bade Paeëon heal him, whereon Paeëon spread painkilling herbs upon his wound and cured him, for he was not of mortal mold. As the juice of the fig tree curdles milk, and thickens it in a moment though it is liquid, even so instantly did Paeëon cure fierce Ares. Then Hebe washed him and clothed him in goodly raiment, and he took his seat by his father Zeus all glorious to behold.

But Hera of Argos and Athene of Alalcomene, now that they had put a stop to the murderous doings of Ares, went back again to the house of Zeus.

Book VI

The tide of war surges back and forth across the plain. The Trojan Glaucus
challenges Diomed, only to discover that old ties of friendship prevent their
fighting one another. Hector, seeing his side hard-pressed, goes back to Troy
to order special sacrifices to Athene. Finding Paris with Helen, he
scornfully rebukes him. To his own wife, Andromache, and his baby son
he bids farewell. The two brothers then return together to the fray.

THE FIGHT BETWEEN TROJANS AND ACHAEANS WAS NOW LEFT TO RAGE
as it would, and the tide of war surged hither and thither over the
plain as they aimed their bronze-shod spears at one another between
the streams of Simois and Xanthus.

First, Ajax, son of Telamon, tower of strength to the Achaeans, broke a
phalanx of the Trojans, and came to the assistance of his comrades by killing
Acamas, son of Eussorus, the best man among the Thracians, being both
brave and of great stature. The spear struck the projecting peak of his helmet;
its bronze point then went through his forehead into the brain, and darkness
veiled his eyes.

Then Diomed killed Axylus, son of Teuthranus, a rich man who lived in
the strong city of Arisbe, and was beloved by all men; for he had a house by
the roadside, and entertained everyone who passed; howbeit not one of his
guests stood before him to save his life, and Diomed killed both him and his
squire Calesius, who was then his charioteer—so the pair passed beneath
the earth.

Euryalus killed Dresus and Opheltius, and then went in pursuit of Aesepus and Pedasus, whom the naiad nymph Abarbarea had borne to noble Bucolion. Bucolion was eldest son to Laomedon, but he was a bastard. While tending his sheep he had converse with the nymph, and she conceived twin sons. These the son of Mecisteus now slew, and he stripped the armor from their shoulders. Polypoetes then killed Astyalus, Ulysses Pidytes of Percote, and Teucer Aretaon. Ablerus fell by the spear of Nestor's son Antilochus, and Agamemnon, king of men, killed Elatus who dwelt in Pedasus by the banks of the river Satnioeis. Leïtus killed Phylacus as he was flying, and Eurypylus slew Melanthus.

Then Menelaus of the loud war cry took Adrestus alive, for his horses ran into a tamarisk bush, as they were flying wildly over the plain, and broke the pole from the car; they went on towards the city along with the others in full flight, but Adrestus rolled out, and fell in the dust flat on his face by the wheel of his chariot. Menelaus came up to him spear in hand, but Adrestus caught him by the knees begging for his life. "Take me alive," he cried, "son of Atreus, and you shall have a full ransom for me! My father is rich and has much treasure of gold, bronze, and wrought iron laid by in his house. From this store he will give you a large ransom should he hear of my being alive and at the ships of the Achaeans."

Thus did he plead, and Menelaus was for yielding and giving him to a squire to take to the ships of the Achaeans, but Agamemnon came running up to him and rebuked him. "My good Menelaus," said he, "this is no time for giving quarter. Has, then, your house fared so well at the hands of the Trojans? Let us not spare a single one of them—not even the child unborn and in its mother's womb; let not a man of them be left alive, but let all in Ilium perish, unheeded and forgotten."

Thus did he speak, and his brother was persuaded by him, for his words were just. Menelaus, therefore, thrust Adrestus from him, whereon King Agamemnon struck him in the flank, and he fell. Then the son of Atreus planted his foot upon his breast to draw his spear from the body.

Meanwhile Nestor shouted to the Argives, saying: "My friends, Danaan warriors, servants of Ares, let no man lag that he may spoil the dead, and bring back much booty to the ships. Let us kill as many as we can; the bodies will lie upon the plain, and you can despoil them later at your leisure."

With these words he put heart and soul into them all. And now the Trojans would have been routed and driven back into Ilium had not Priam's son Helenus, wisest of augurs, said to Hector and Aeneas: "Hector and Aeneas, you two are the mainstays of the Trojans and Lycians, for you are foremost at all times, alike in fight and counsel. Hold your ground here, and go about among the host to rally them in front of the gates, or they will fling themselves into the arms of their wives, to the great joy of our foes. Then, when you have put heart into all our companies, we will stand firm here and fight the Danaans however hard they press us, for there is nothing else to be done. Meanwhile do you, Hector, go to the city and tell our mother what is happening. Tell her to bid the matrons gather at the temple of Athene in the acropolis; let her then take her key and open the doors of the sacred building; there, upon the knees of Athene, let her lay the largest, fairest robe she has in her house—the one she sets most store by; let her, moreover, promise to sacrifice twelve yearling heifers that have never yet felt the goad, in the temple of the goddess, if she will take pity on the town, with the wives and little ones of the Trojans, and keep the son of Tydeus from falling on the goodly city of Ilium; for he fights with fury and fills men's souls with panic. I hold him mightiest of them all. We did not fear even their great champion Achilles, son of a goddess though he be, as we do this man. His rage is beyond all bounds, and there is none can vie with him in prowess."

Hector did as his brother bade him. He sprang from his chariot, and went about everywhere among the host, brandishing his spears, urging the men on to fight, and raising the dread cry of battle. Thereon they rallied and again faced the Achaeans, who gave ground and ceased their murderous onset, for they deemed that some one of the immortals had come down from starry heaven to help the Trojans, so strangely had they rallied. And Hector shouted to the Trojans, "Trojans and allies, be men, my friends, and fight with might and main, while I go to Ilium and tell the old men of our council and our wives to pray to the gods and vow hecatombs in their honor."

With this he went his way, and the black rim of hide that went round his shield beat against his neck and his ankles.

Then Glaucus, son of Hippolochus, and the son of Tydeus went into the open space between the hosts to fight in single combat. When they were close up to one another Diomed of the loud war cry was the first to speak. "Who, my good sir," said he, "who are you among men? I have never seen you in battle until now, but you are daring beyond all others if you abide my onset. Woe to those fathers whose sons face my might. If, however, you are one of the immortals and have come down from heaven, I will not fight you; for even valiant Lycurgus, son of Dryas, did not live long when he took to fighting with the gods. He it was that drove the nursing women who were in charge of frenzied Dionysus through the land of Nysa, and they flung their thyrsi on the ground as murderous Lycurgus beat them with his ox-goad. Dionysus himself plunged terror-stricken into the sea, and Thetis took him to her bosom to comfort him, for he was scared by the fury with which the man reviled him. Thereon the gods who live at ease were angry with Lycurgus and the son of Cronus struck him blind, nor did he live much longer after he had become hateful to the immortals. Therefore I will not fight with the blessed gods; but if you are of them that eat the fruit of the ground, draw near and meet your doom."

And the son of Hippolochus answered: "Mighty son of Tydeus, why ask me of my lineage? Men come and go as leaves year by year upon the trees. Those of autumn the wind sheds upon the ground, but when spring returns the forest buds forth with fresh ones. Even so is it with the generations of mankind, the new spring up as the old are passing away. If, then, you would learn my descent, it is one that is well known to many. There is a city in the heart of Argos, pastureland of horses, called Ephyra, where Sisyphus lived, who was the craftiest of all mankind. He was the son of Aeolus, and had a son named Glaucus, who was father to Bellerophon, whom heaven endowed with the most surpassing comeliness and beauty. But Proetus devised his ruin, and being stronger than he, drove him from the land of the Argives over which Zeus had made him ruler. For Antea, wife of Proetus, lusted after him, and would have had him lie with her in secret; but Bellerophon was an honorable man and would not, so she told lies about him to Proetus. 'Proetus,' said she, 'kill Bellerophon or die, for he would have had converse with me against my will.' The king was angered, but shrank from killing Bellerophon, so he sent him to Lycia with lying letters of introduction, written on a folded tablet, and containing much ill against the bearer. He bade Bellerophon show these letters to his father-in-law, to the end that he might thus perish. Bellerophon, therefore, went to Lycia, and the gods convoyed him safely.

"When he reached the river Xanthus, which is in Lycia, the king received him with all good will, feasted him nine days, and killed nine heifers in his honor, but when rosy-fingered morning appeared upon the tenth day, he questioned him and desired to see the letter from his son-in-law Proetus. When he had received the wicked letter he first commanded Bellerophon to kill that savage monster, the Chimaera, who was not a human being, but a goddess, for she had the head of a lion and the tail of a serpent, while her body was that of a goat, and she breathed forth flames of fire; but Bellerophon slew her, for he was guided by signs from heaven. He next fought the far-famed Solymi, and this, he said, was the hardest of all his battles. Thirdly, he killed the Amazons, women who were the peers of men, and as he was returning thence the king devised yet another plan for his destruction; he picked the bravest warriors in all Lycia and placed them in ambuscade, but not a man ever came back, for Bellerophon killed every one of them. Then the king knew that he must be the valiant offspring of a god, so he kept him in Lycia, gave him his daughter in marriage, and made him of equal honor in the kingdom with himself; and the Lycians gave him a piece of land, the best in all the country, fair with vineyards and tilled fields, to have and to hold.

"The king's daughter bore Bellerophon three children, Isander, Hippolochus, and Laodameia. Zeus, the lord of counsel, lay with Laodameia, and she bore him noble Sarpedon; but when Bellerophon came to be hated by all the gods, he wandered all desolate and dismayed upon the Alean plain, gnawing at his own heart, and shunning the path of man. Ares, insatiate of battle, killed his son Isander while he was fighting the Solymi; his daughter was killed by Artemis of the golden reins, for she was angered with her; but Hippolochus was father to myself, and when he sent me to Troy he urged me again and again to fight ever among the foremost and outvie my peers, so as not to shame the blood of my fathers who were the noblest in Ephyra and in all Lycia. This, then, is the descent I claim."

Thus did he speak, and the heart of Diomed was glad. He planted his spear in the ground, and spoke to him with friendly words. "Then," he said, "you are an old friend of my father's house. Great Oeneus once entertained Bellerophon for twenty days, and the two exchanged presents. Oeneus gave a belt rich with purple, and Bellerophon a double cup, which I left at home when I set out for Troy. I do not remember Tydeus, for he was taken from us while I was yet a child, when the army of the Achaeans was cut to pieces before Thebes. Henceforth, however, I must be your host in middle Argos, and you mine in Lycia, if I should ever go there; let us avoid one another's spears even during a general engagement. There are many noble Trojans and allies whom I can kill, if I overtake them and heaven delivers them into my hand; so again with yourself, there are many Achaeans whose lives you may take if you can; we two, then, will exchange armor, that all present may know of the old ties that subsist between us."

With these words they sprang from their chariots, grasped one another's hands, and plighted friendship. But the son of Cronus made Glaucus take leave of his wits, for he exchanged golden armor for bronze, the worth of a hundred head of cattle for the worth of nine.

Now when Hector reached the Scaean gates and the oak tree, the wives and daughters of the Trojans came running towards him to ask after their sons, brothers, kinsmen, and husbands; he told them to set about praying to the gods, and many were made sorrowful as they heard him.

Presently he reached the splendid palace of King Priam, adorned with colonnades of hewn stone. In it there were fifty bedchambers—all of hewn stone—built near one another, where the sons of Priam slept, each with his wedded wife. Opposite these, on the other side the courtyard, there were twelve upper rooms also of hewn stone for Priam's daughters, built near one another, where his sons-in-law slept with their wives. When Hector got there, his fond mother came up to him with Laodice, the fairest of her daughters. She took his hand within her own and said: "My son, why have you left the battle to come hither? Are the Achaeans, woe betide them, pressing you hard about the city that you have thought fit to come and uplift your hands to Zeus from the citadel? Wait till I can bring you wine that you may make offering to Zeus and to the other immortals, and may then drink and be refreshed. Wine gives a man fresh strength when he is wearied, as you now are with fighting on behalf of your kinsmen."

And Hector answered, "Honored mother, bring no wine, lest you unman me and I forget my strength. I dare not make a drink offering to Zeus with unwashed hands. One who is bespattered with blood and filth may not pray to the son of Cronus. Get the matrons together, and go with offerings to the temple of Athene, driver of the spoil; there, upon the knees of Athene, lay the largest and fairest robe you have in your house—the one you set most store by. Promise, moreover, to sacrifice twelve yearling heifers that have never yet felt the goad, in the temple of the goddess, if she will take pity on the town, with the wives and little ones of the Trojans, and keep the son of Tydeus from off the goodly city of Ilium, for he fights with fury, and fills men's souls with panic. Go, then, to the temple of Athene, while I seek Paris and exhort him, if he will hear my words. Would that the earth might open her jaws and swallow him, for Zeus bred him to be the bane of the Trojans, and of Priam and Priam's sons. Could I but see him go down into the house of Hades, my heart would forget its heaviness."

His mother went into the house and called her waiting-women who gathered the matrons throughout the city. She then went down into her fragrant storeroom, where her embroidered robes were kept, the work of Sidonian women, whom Paris had brought over from Sidon when he sailed the seas upon that voyage during which he carried off noble Helen. Hecuba took out the largest robe and the one that was most beautifully enriched with embroidery, as an offering to Athene: it glittered like a star and lay at the very bottom of the chest. With this she went on her way and many matrons with her.

When they reached the temple of Athene, lovely Theano, daughter of Cisseus and wife of Antenor, opened the doors, for the Trojans had made her priestess of Athene. The women lifted up their hands to the goddess with a loud cry, and Theano took the robe to lay it upon the knees of Athene, praying the while to the daughter of great Zeus. "Holy Athene," she cried, "protectress of our city, mighty goddess, break the spear of Diomed and lay him low before the Scaean gates. Do this, and we will sacrifice twelve heifers that have never yet known the goad, in your temple, if you will have pity upon the town, with the wives and little ones of the Trojans." Thus she prayed, but Pallas Athene granted not her prayer.

While they were thus praying to the daughter of great Zeus, Hector went to the fair house of Paris, which he had had built for him by the foremost builders in the land. They had built him his house, storehouse, and courtyard near those of Priam and Hector on the acropolis. Here Hector entered, with a spear eleven cubits long in his hand; the bronze point gleamed in front of him, and was fastened to the shaft of the spear by a ring of gold. He found Paris within the house, busied about his armor, his shield and cuirass, and handling his curved bow; there, too, sat Argive Helen with her women, setting them their several tasks; and as Hector saw him he rebuked him with words of scorn. "Sir," said he, "you do ill to nurse this rancor. The people perish fight-ing round this our town. You would yourself chide one whom you saw shirk-ing his part in the combat. Up then, or ere long the city will be in a blaze."

And Paris answered: "Hector, your rebuke is just; listen therefore, and believe me when I tell you that I am not here so much through rancor or ill will towards the Trojans, as from a desire to indulge my grief. My wife was even now gently urging me to battle, and I hold it better that I should go, for victory is ever fickle. Wait, then, while I put on my armor, or go first and I will follow. I shall be sure to overtake you."

Hector made no answer, but Helen tried to soothe him. "Brother," said she, "to my abhorred and sinful self, would that a whirlwind had caught me up on the day my mother brought me forth and had borne me to some moun-tain or to the waves of the roaring sea that should have swept me away ere this mischief had come about. But, since the gods have devised these evils, would, at any rate, that I had been wife to a better man—to one who could smart under dishonor and men's evil speeches. This fellow was never yet to be depended upon, nor never will be, and he will surely reap what he has sown. Still, brother, come in and rest upon this seat, for it is you who bear the brunt of that toil that has been caused by my hateful self and by the sin of Paris—both of whom Zeus has doomed to be a theme of song among those that shall be born hereafter."

And Hector answered: "Bid me not be seated, Helen, for all the good will you bear me. I cannot stay. I am in haste to help the Trojans, who miss me greatly when I am not among them; but urge your husband, and of his own self also let him make haste to overtake me before I am out of the city. I must go home to see my household, my wife and my little son, for I know not whether I shall ever again return to them, or whether the gods will cause me to fall by the hands of the Achaeans."

Then Hector left her, and forthwith was at his own house. He did not find Andromache, for she was on the wall with her child and one of her maids, weeping bitterly. Seeing, then, that she was not within, he stood on the threshold of the women's rooms and said: "Women, tell me, and tell me true, where did Andromache go when she left the house? Was it to my sisters or to my brothers' wives? Or is she at the temple of Athene where the other women are propitiating the awful goddess?"

His good housekeeper answered: "Hector, since you bid me tell you truly, she did not go to your sisters nor to your brothers' wives, nor yet to the temple of Athene, where the other women are propitiating the awful goddess, but she is on the high wall of Ilium, for she had heard the Trojans were being hard pressed, and that the Achaeans were in great force: therefore she went to the wall in frenzied haste, and the nurse went with her carrying the child."

Hector hurried from the house when she had done speaking, and went down the streets by the same way that he had come. When he had gone through the city and had reached the Scaean gates through which he would go out on to the plain, his wife came running towards him, Andromache, daughter of great Eëtion who ruled in Thebe under the wooded slopes of Mount Placus, and was king of the Cilicians. His daughter had married Hector, and now came to meet him with a nurse who carried his little child in her bosom—a mere babe, Hector's darling son, and lovely as a star. Hector had named him Scamandrius, but the people called him Astyanax ["king of the city"] for his father stood alone as chief guardian of Ilium.

Hector smiled as he looked upon the boy, but he did not speak, and Andromache stood by him weeping and taking his hand in her own. "Dear husband," said she, "your valor will bring you to destruction. Think on your infant son, and on my hapless self who ere long shall be your widow—for the Achaeans will set upon you in a body and kill you. It would be better for me, should I lose you, to lie dead and buried, for I shall have nothing left to comfort me when you are gone, save only sorrow. I have neither father nor mother now. Achilles slew my father when he sacked Thebe, the goodly city of the Cilicians. He slew him, but did not for very shame despoil him. When he had burned him in his wondrous armor, he raised a barrow over his ashes and the mountain nymphs, daughters of aegis-bearing Zeus, planted a grove of elms about his tomb. I had seven brothers in my father's house, but on the same day they all went within the house of Hades. Achilles killed them as they were with their sheep and cattle. My mother—her who had been queen of all the land under Mount Placus—he brought hither with the spoil, and freed her for a great sum, but the archer-queen Artemis took her in the house of your father. Nay—Hector—you who to me are father, mother, brother, and dear husband—have mercy upon me; stay here upon this wall; make not your child fatherless, and your wife a widow; as for the host, place them near the fig tree, where the city can be best scaled, and the wall is weakest. Thrice have the bravest of them come thither and assailed it, under the two Ajaxes, Idomeneus, the sons of Atreus, and the brave son of Tydeus, either of their own bidding, or because some soothsayer had told them."

And Hector answered: "Wife, I too have thought upon all this, but with what face should I look upon the Trojans, men or women, if I shirked battle like a coward? I cannot do so: I know nothing save to fight bravely in the forefront of the Trojan host and win renown alike for my father and myself. Well do I know that the day will surely come when mighty Ilium shall be destroyed with Priam and Priam's people, but I grieve for none of these—not even for Hecuba, nor King Priam, nor for my brothers many and brave who may fall in the dust before their foes—for none of these do I grieve as for yourself when the day shall come on which some one of the Achaeans shall rob you forever of your freedom, and bear you weeping away. It may be that you will have to ply the loom in Argos at the bidding of a mistress, or to fetch water from the springs Messeïs or Hypereia, treated brutally by some cruel taskmaster; then will one say who sees you weeping, 'She was wife to Hector, the bravest warrior among the Trojans during the war before Ilium.' On this your tears will break forth anew for him who would have put away the day of captivity from you. May I lie dead under the barrow that is heaped over my body ere I hear your cry as they carry you into bondage."

He stretched his arms towards his child, but the boy cried and nestled in his nurse's bosom, scared at the sight of his father's armor, and at the horse-hair plume that nodded fiercely from his helmet. His father and mother laughed to see him, but Hector took the helmet from his head and laid it all gleaming upon the ground. Then he took his darling child, kissed him, and dandled him in his arms, praying over him the while to Zeus and to all the gods. "Zeus," he cried, "grant that this my child may be even as myself, chief among the Trojans; let him be not less excellent in strength, and let him rule Ilium with his might. Then may one say of him as he comes from battle, 'The son is far better than the father.' May he bring back the bloodstained spoils of him whom he has laid low, and let his mother's heart be glad."

With this he laid the child again in the arms of his wife, who took him to her own soft bosom, smiling through her tears. As her husband watched her his heart yearned towards her and he caressed her fondly, saying: "My own wife, do not take these things too bitterly to heart. No one can hurry me down to Hades before my time, but if a man's hour is come, be he brave or be he coward, there is no escape for him when he has once been born. Go, then, within the house, and busy yourself with your daily duties, your loom, your distaff, and the ordering of your servants; for war is man's matter, and mine above all others of them that have been born in Ilium."

He took his plumed helmet from the ground, and his wife went back again to her house, weeping bitterly and often looking back towards him. When she reached her home she found her maidens within, and bade them all join in her lament; so they mourned Hector in his own house though he was yet alive, for they deemed that they should never see him return safe from battle, and from the furious hands of the Achaeans.

Paris did not remain long in his house. He donned his goodly armor over-laid with bronze, and hasted through the city as fast as his feet could take him.

As a horse, stabled and full-fed, breaks loose and gallops gloriously over the plain to the place where he is wont to bathe in the fair-flowing river—he holds his head high, and his mane streams upon his shoulders as he exults in his strength and flies like the wind to the haunts and feeding ground of the mares—even so went forth Paris from high Pergamus, gleaming like sunlight in his armor, and he laughed aloud as he sped swiftly on his way. Forthwith he came upon his brother Hector, who was then turning away from the place where he had held converse with his wife, and he was himself the first to speak. "Sir," said he, "I fear that I have kept you waiting when you are in haste, and have not come as quickly as you bade me."

"My good brother," answered Hector, "you fight bravely, and no man with any justice can make light of your doings in battle. But you are careless and willfully remiss. It grieves me to the heart to hear the ill that the Trojans speak about you, for they have suffered much on your account. Let us be going, and we will make things right hereafter, should Zeus vouchsafe us to set the cup of our deliverance before the ever-living gods of heaven in our own homes, when we have chased the Achaeans from Troy."

Book VII

*Paris and Hector raise such havoc that Athene and Apollo decide to stop
the bloodshed, while Hector and Ajax meet in single combat. The fall of
night stops the duel. A truce is agreed upon to allow both sides to bury their
dead, and the Greeks use this respite also to build a wall in front of their
ships. In Troy old Antenor proposes that Helen be returned to Menelaus
in accordance with the covenant, but Paris refuses.*

WITH THESE WORDS HECTOR PASSED THROUGH THE GATES, AND HIS
brother Paris with him, both eager for the fray. As when heaven
sends a breeze to sailors who have long looked for one in vain
and have labored at their oars till they are faint with toil, even so welcome was
the sight of these two heroes to the Trojans.

Thereon Paris killed Menesthius, the son of Areïthoüs. He lived in Arne
and was son of Areïthoüs, the Mace-man, and of Phylomedusa. Hector threw
a spear at Eioneus and struck him dead with a wound in the neck under the
bronze rim of his helmet. Glaucus, moreover, son of Hippolochus, captain of
the Lycians, in hard hand-to-hand fight smote Iphinöus, son of Dexius, on the
shoulder, as he was springing on to his chariot behind his fleet mares; so he
fell to earth from the car, and there was no life left in him.

When, therefore, Athene saw these men making havoc of the Argives, she
darted down to Ilium from the summits of Olympus, and Apollo, who was
looking on from Pergamus, went out to meet her; for he wanted the Trojans
to be victorious. The pair met by the oak tree, and King Apollo, son of Zeus,

was first to speak. "What would you have," said he, "daughter of great Zeus, that your proud spirit has sent you hither from Olympus? Have you no pity upon the Trojans, and would you incline the scales of victory in favor of the Danaans? Let me persuade you—for it will be better thus—stay the combat for today, but let them renew the fight hereafter till they compass the doom of Ilium, since you goddesses have made up your minds to destroy the city."

And Athene answered, "So be it, Far-darter; it was in this mind that I came down from Olympus to the Trojans and Achaeans. Tell me, then, how do you propose to end this present fighting?"

Apollo, son of Zeus, replied, "Let us incite great Hector to challenge some one of the Danaans in single combat; on this the Achaeans will be shamed into finding a man who will fight him."

Athene assented, and Helenus, son of Priam, divined the counsel of the gods. He therefore went up to Hector and said: "Hector, son of Priam, peer of gods in counsel, I am your brother, let me then persuade you. Bid the other Trojans and Achaeans all of them take their seats, and challenge the best man among the Achaeans to meet you in single combat. I have heard the voice of the ever-living gods, and the hour of your doom is not yet come."

Hector was glad when he heard this saying, and went in among the Trojans, grasping his spear by the middle to hold them back, and they all sat down. Agamemnon also bade the Achaeans be seated. But Athene and Apollo, in the likeness of vultures, perched on father Zeus' high oak tree, proud of their men; and the ranks sat close-ranged together, bristling with shield and helmet and spear. As when the rising west wind furs the face of the sea and the waters grow dark beneath it, so sat the companies of Trojans and Achaeans upon the plain. And Hector spoke thus:

"Hear me, Trojans and Achaeans, that I may speak even as I am minded. Zeus on his high throne has brought our oaths and covenants to nothing, and foreshadows ill for both of us, till you either take the towers of Troy, or are yourselves vanquished at your ships. The princes of the Achaeans are here present in the midst of you. Let him, then, that will fight me stand forward as your champion against Hector. Thus I say, and may Zeus be witness between us. If your champion slay me, let him strip me of my armor and take it to your ships, but let him send my body home that the Trojans and their wives may give me my dues of fire when I am dead. In like manner if Apollo vouchsafe me glory and I slay your champion, I will strip him of his armor and take it to the city of Ilium, where I will hang it in the temple of Apollo, but I will give up his body, that the Achaeans may bury him at their ships, and build him a mound by the wide waters of the Hellespont. Then will one say hereafter as he sails his ship over the sea, 'This is the monument of one who died long since—a champion who was slain by mighty Hector.' Thus will one say, and my fame shall not be lost."

Thus did he speak, but they all held their peace, ashamed to decline the challenge, yet fearing to accept it, till at last Menelaus rose and rebuked them, for he was angry. "Alas," he cried, "vain braggarts, women forsooth, not men, double-dyed indeed will be the stain upon us if no man of the Danaans will now face Hector! May you be turned every man of you into earth and water as you sit spiritless and inglorious in your places. I will myself go out against this man, but the upshot of the fight will be from on high in the hands of the immortal gods."

With these words he put on his armor; and then, O Menelaus, your life would have come to an end at the hands of Hector, for he was far the better man, had not the princes of the Achaeans sprung upon you and checked you. King Agamemnon caught him by the right hand and said: "Menelaus, you are mad; a truce to this folly. Be patient in spite of passion, do not think of fighting a man so much stronger than yourself as Hector, son of Priam, who is feared by many another as well as you. Even Achilles, who is far more doughty than you are, shrank from meeting him in battle. Sit down among your own people, and the Achaeans will send some other champion to fight Hector. Fearless and fond of battle though he be, I ween his knees will bend gladly under him if he comes out alive from the hurly-burly of this fight."

With these words of reasonable counsel he persuaded his brother, whereon his squires gladly stripped the armor from off his shoulders. Then Nestor rose and spoke. "Of a truth," said he, "the Achaean land is fallen upon evil times. The old knight Peleus, counselor and orator among the Myrmidons, loved when I was in his house to question me concerning the race and lineage of all the Argives. How would it not grieve him could he hear of them as now quailing before Hector? Many a time would he lift his hands in prayer that his soul might leave his body and go down within the house of Hades. Would, by father Zeus, Athene, and Apollo, that I were still young and strong as when the Pylians and Arcadians were gathered in fight by the rapid river Celadon under the walls of Pheia, and round about the waters of the river Iardanus. The godlike hero Ereuthalion stood forward as their champion, with the armor of King Areïthoüs upon his shoulders—Areïthoüs whom men and women had surnamed 'the Mace-man,' because he fought neither with bow nor spear, but broke the battalions of the foe with his iron mace. Lycurgus killed him, not in fair fight, but by entrapping him in a narrow way where his mace served him in no stead; for Lycurgus was too quick for him and speared him through the middle, so he fell to earth on his back. Lycurgus then spoiled him of the armor which Ares had given him, and bore it in battle thenceforward; but when he grew old and stayed at home, he gave it to his faithful squire Ereuthalion, who in this same armor challenged the foremost men among us. The others quaked and quailed, but my high spirit bade me fight him though none other would venture. I was the youngest man of them all, but when I fought him Athene vouchsafed me victory. He was the biggest and strongest man that ever I killed, and covered much ground as he lay sprawling upon the earth. Would that I were still young and strong as I then was, for the son of Priam would then soon find one who would face him. But you, foremost among the whole host though you be, have none of you any stomach for fighting Hector."

Thus did the old man rebuke them, and forthwith nine men started to their feet. Foremost of all uprose King Agamemnon, and after him brave

Diomed, the son of Tydeus. Next were the two Ajaxes, men clothed in valor as with a garment, and then Idomeneus, and Meriones his brother in arms. After these, Eurypylus, son of Euaemon, Thoas, the son of Andraemon, and Odysseus also rose. Then Nestor, knight of Gerene, again spoke, saying: "Cast lots among you to see who shall be chosen. If he come alive out of this fight he will have done good service alike to his own soul and to the Achaeans."

Thus he spoke, and when each of them had marked his lot, and had thrown it into the helmet of Agamemnon, son of Atreus, the people lifted their hands in prayer, and thus would one of them say as he looked into the vault of heaven, "Father Zeus, grant that the lot fall on Ajax, or on the son of Tydeus, or upon the king of rich Mycene himself."

As they were speaking, Nestor, knight of Gerene, shook the helmet, and from it there fell the very lot which they wanted—the lot of Ajax. The herald bore it about and showed it to all the chieftains of the Achaeans, going from left to right; but they none of them owned it. When, however, in due course he reached the man who had written upon it and had put it into the helmet, brave Ajax held out his hand, and the herald gave him the lot. When Ajax saw his mark he knew it and was glad; he threw it to the ground and said: "My friends, the lot is mine, and I rejoice, for I shall vanquish Hector. I will put on my armor; meanwhile, pray to King Zeus in silence among yourselves that the Trojans may not hear you—or aloud if you will, for we fear no man. None shall overcome me, neither by force nor cunning, for I was born and bred in Salamis, and can hold my own in all things."

With this they fell praying to King Zeus, the son of Cronus, and thus would one of them say as he looked into the vault of heaven, "Father Zeus that rulest from Ida, most glorious in power, vouchsafe victory to Ajax, and let him win great glory: but if you wish well to Hector also and would protect him, grant to each of them equal fame and prowess."

Thus they prayed, and Ajax armed himself in his suit of gleaming bronze. When he was in full array he sprang forward as monstrous Ares when he takes part among men whom Zeus has set fighting with one another—even so did huge Ajax, bulwark of the Achaeans, spring forward with a grim smile on his face as he brandished his long spear and strode onward. The Argives were elated as they beheld him, but the Trojans trembled in every limb, and the heart even of Hector beat quickly, but he could not now retreat and withdraw into the ranks behind him, for he had been the challenger. Ajax came up bearing his shield in front of him like a wall—a shield of bronze with seven folds of oxhide—the work of Tychius, who lived in Hyle and was by far the best worker in leather. He had made it with the hides of seven full-fed bulls, and over these he had set an eighth layer of bronze. Holding his shield before him, Ajax, son of Telamon, came close up to Hector and menaced him, saying: "Hector, you shall now learn, man to man, what kind of champions the Danaans have among them even besides lion-hearted Achilles, cleaver of the ranks of men. He now abides at the ships in anger with Agamemnon, shepherd of his people, but there are many of us who are well able to face you; therefore begin the fight."

And Hector answered: "Noble Ajax, son of Telamon, captain of the host, treat me not as though I were some puny boy or woman that cannot fight. I have been long used to the blood and butcheries of battle. I am quick to turn my leathern shield either to right or left, for this I deem the main thing in battle. I can charge among the chariots and horsemen, and in hand-to-hand fighting can delight the heart of Ares; howbeit I would not take such a man as you are off his guard—but I will smite you openly if I can."

He poised his spear as he spoke, and hurled it from him. It struck the sevenfold shield in its outermost layer—the eighth, which was of bronze—and went through six of the layers, but in the seventh hide it stayed. Then Ajax threw in his turn and struck the round shield of the son of Priam. The terrible spear went through his gleaming shield and pressed onward through his cuirass of cunning workmanship; it pierced the shirt against his side, but he swerved and thus saved his life. They then each of them drew out the spear from his shield and fell on one another like savage lions or wild boars of great strength and endurance. The son of Priam struck the middle of Ajax's shield, but the bronze did not break, and the point of his dart was turned. Ajax then sprang forward and pierced the shield of Hector; the spear went through it and staggered him as he was springing forward to attack. It gashed his neck and the blood came pouring from the wound, but even so Hector did not cease fighting. He gave ground, and with his brawny hand seized a stone, rugged and huge, that was lying upon the plain; with this he struck the shield of Ajax on the boss that was in its middle, so that the bronze rang again. But Ajax in turn caught up a far larger stone, swung it aloft, and hurled it with prodigious force. This millstone of a rock broke Hector's shield inwards and threw him down on his back with the shield crushing him under it, but Apollo raised him at once. Thereon they would have hacked at one another in close combat with their swords, had not heralds, messengers of gods and men, come forward, one from the Trojans and the other from the Achaeans—Talthybius and Idaeus, both of them honorable men; these parted them with their staves, and the good herald Idaeus said: "My sons, fight no longer, you are both of you valiant, and both are dear to Zeus; we know this; but night is now falling, and the behests of night may not be well gainsaid."

Ajax, son of Telamon, answered: "Idaeus, bid Hector say so, for it was he that challenged our princes. Let him speak first and I will accept his saying."

Then Hector said: "Ajax, heaven has vouchsafed you stature and strength, and judgment; and in wielding the spear you excel all others of the Achaeans. Let us for this day cease fighting; hereafter we will fight anew till heaven decide between us, and give victory to one or to the other; night is now falling, and the behests of night may not be well gainsaid. Gladden, then, the hearts of the Achaeans at your ships, and more especially those of your own followers and clansmen, while I, in the great city of King Priam, bring comfort to the Trojans and their women, who vie with one another in their prayers on my behalf. Let us, moreover, exchange presents, that it may be said among

Achaeans and Trojans, 'They fought with might and main, but were reconciled and parted in friendship.'"

On this he gave Ajax a silver-studded sword with its sheath and leathern baldric, and in return Ajax gave him a girdle dyed with purple. Thus they parted, the one going to the host of the Achaeans, and the other to that of the Trojans, who rejoiced when they saw their hero come to them safe and unharmed from the strong hands of mighty Ajax. They led him, therefore, to the city as one that had been saved beyond their hopes. On the other side the Achaeans brought Ajax elated with victory to Agamemnon.

When they reached the quarters of the son of Atreus, Agamemnon sacrificed for them a five-year-old bull in honor of Zeus, the son of Cronus. They flayed the carcass, made it ready, and divided it into joints. These they cut carefully up into smaller pieces, putting them on the spits, roasting them sufficiently, and then drawing them off. When they had done all this and had prepared the feast, they ate it, and every man had his full and equal share, so that all were satisfied, and King Agamemnon gave Ajax some slices cut lengthways down the loin, as a mark of special honor. As soon as they had had enough to eat and drink, old Nestor, whose counsel was ever truest, began to speak; with all sincerity and good will, therefore, he addressed them thus:

"Son of Atreus, and other chieftains, inasmuch as many of the Achaeans are now dead, whose blood Ares has shed by the banks of the Scamander, and their souls have gone down to the house of Hades, it will be well when morning comes that we should cease fighting; we will then wheel our dead together with oxen and mules and burn them not far from the ships, that when we sail hence we may take the bones of our comrades home to their children. Hard by the funeral pyre we will build a barrow that shall be raised from the plain for all in common; near this let us set about building a high wall, to shelter ourselves and our ships, and let it have well-made gates that there may be a way through them for our chariots. Close outside we will dig a deep trench all round it to keep off both horse and foot, that the Trojan chieftains may not bear hard upon us."

Thus he spoke, and the princes shouted in applause. Meanwhile the Trojans held a council, angry and full of discord, on the acropolis by the gates of King Priam's palace; and wise Antenor spoke. "Hear me," he said, "Trojans, Dardanians, and allies, that I may speak even as I am minded. Let us give up Argive Helen and her wealth to the sons of Atreus, for we are now fighting in violation of our solemn covenants, and shall not prosper till we have done as I say."

He then sat down and Paris, husband of lovely Helen, rose to speak. "Antenor," said he, "your words are not to my liking; you can find a better saying than this if you will. If, however, you have spoken in good earnest, then indeed has heaven robbed you of your reason. I will speak plainly, and hereby notify to the Trojans that I will not give up the woman; but the wealth that I brought home with her from Argos I will restore, and will add yet further of my own."

On this, when Paris had spoken and taken his seat, Priam of the race of Dardanus, peer of gods in counsel, rose and with all sincerity and good will addressed them thus: "Hear me, Trojans, Dardanians, and allies, that I may speak even as I am minded. Get your suppers now as hitherto throughout the city, but keep your watches and be wakeful. At daybreak let Idaeus go to the ships, and tell Agamemnon and Menelaus, sons of Atreus, the saying of Paris through whom this quarrel has come about; and let him also be instant with them that they now cease fighting till we burn our dead; hereafter we will fight anew, till heaven decide between us and give victory to one or to the other."

Thus did he speak, and they did even as he had said. They took supper in their companies and at daybreak Idaeus went his way to the ships. He found the Danaans, servants of Ares, in council at the stern of Agamemnon's ship, and took his place in the midst of them. "Son of Atreus," he said, "and princes of the Achaean host, Priam and the other noble Trojans have sent me to tell you the saying of Paris through whom this quarrel has come about, if so be that you may find it acceptable. All the treasure he took with him in his ships to Troy—would that he had sooner perished—he will restore, and will add yet further of his own, but he will not give up the wedded wife of Menelaus, though the Trojans would have him do so. Priam bade me inquire further if you will cease fighting till we burn our dead. Hereafter we will fight anew, till heaven decide between us and give victory to one or to the other."

They all held their peace, but presently Diomed of the loud war cry spoke, saying, "Let there be no taking, neither treasure, nor yet Helen, for even a child may see that the doom of the Trojans is at hand."

The sons of the Achaeans shouted applause at the words that Diomed had spoken, and thereon King Agamemnon said to Idaeus: "Idaeus, you have heard the answer the Achaeans make you—and I with them. But as concerning the dead, I give you leave to burn them, for when men are once dead there should be no grudging them the rites of fire. Let Zeus, the mighty husband of Hera, be witness to this covenant."

As he spoke he upheld his scepter in the sight of all the gods, and Idaeus went back to the strong city of Ilium. The Trojans and Dardanians were gathered in council waiting his return; when he came, he stood in their midst and delivered his message. As soon as they heard it they set about their twofold labor, some to gather the corpses, and others to bring in wood. The Argives on their part also hastened from their ships, some to gather the corpses, and others to bring in wood.

The sun was beginning to beat upon the fields, fresh risen into the vault of heaven from the slow still currents of deep Oceanus, when the two armies met. They could hardly recognize their dead, but they washed the clotted gore from off them, shed tears over them, and lifted them upon their wagons. Priam had forbidden the Trojans to wail aloud, so they heaped their dead sadly and silently upon the pyre, and having burned them went back to the city of Ilium. The Achaeans in like manner heaped their dead sadly and silently on the pyre, and having burned them went back to their ships.

Now in the twilight when it was not yet dawn, chosen bands of the Achaeans were gathered round the pyre and built one barrow that was raised in common for all, and hard by this they built a high wall to shelter themselves and their ships. They gave it strong gates that there might be a way through them for their chariots, and close outside it they dug a trench deep and wide, and they planted it within with stakes.

Thus did the Achaeans toil, and the gods, seated by the side of Zeus, the lord of lightning, marveled at their great work; but Poseidon, lord of the earthquake, spoke, saying, "Father Zeus, what mortal in the whole world will again take the gods into his counsel? See you not how the Achaeans have built a wall about their ships and driven a trench all round it, without offering hecatombs to the gods? The fame of this wall will reach as far as dawn itself, and men will no longer think anything of the one which Phoebus Apollo and myself built with so much labor for Laomedon."

Zeus was displeased and answered: "What, O shaker of the earth, are you talking about? A god less powerful than yourself might be alarmed at what they are doing, but your fame reaches as far as dawn itself. Surely when the Achaeans have gone home with their ships, you can shatter their wall and fling it into the sea; you can cover the beach with sand again, and the great wall of the Achaeans will then be utterly effaced."

Thus did they converse, and by sunset the work of the Achaeans was completed; they then slaughtered oxen at their tents and got their supper. Many ships had come with wine from Lemnos, sent by Euneüs, the son of Jason, born to him by Hypsipyle. The son of Jason freighted them with ten thousand measures of wine, which he sent specially to the sons of Atreus, Agamemnon and Menelaus. From this supply the Achaeans bought their wine, some with bronze, some with iron, some with hides, some with whole heifers, and some again with captives. They spread a goodly banquet and feasted the whole night through, as also did the Trojans and their allies in the city. But all the time Zeus boded them ill and roared with his portentous thunder. Pale fear got hold upon them, and they spilled the wine from their cups on to the ground, nor did any dare drink till he had made offerings to the most mighty son of Cronus. Then they laid themselves down to rest and enjoyed the boon of sleep.

Book VIII

In the morning, Zeus forbids further interference by the gods and goes down to Mount Ida to watch events. The advantage now goes to the Trojans. Nestor and Diomed drive together against Hector, but recoil as Zeus hurls flaming thunderbolts at them. Hera and Athene, who have started down from Olympus to aid the Greeks, are ordered back by Zeus. The Greeks are forced to retire behind their new wall and the Trojans bivouac confidently on the plain.

NOW WHEN MORNING, CLAD IN HER ROBE OF SAFFRON, HAD BEGUN to suffuse light over the earth, Zeus called the gods in council on the topmost crest of serrated Olympus. Then he spoke and all the other gods gave ear. "Hear me," said he, "gods and goddesses, that I may speak even as I am minded. Let none of you, neither goddess nor god, try to cross me, but obey me every one of you that I may bring this matter to an end. If I see anyone acting apart and helping either Trojans or Danaans, he shall be beaten inordinately ere he come back again to Olympus; or I will hurl him down into dark Tartarus far into the deepest pit under the earth, where the gates are iron and the floor bronze, as far beneath Hades as heaven is high above the earth, that you may learn how much the mightiest I am among you. Try me and find out for yourselves. Hang me a golden chain from heaven, and lay hold of it all of you, gods and goddesses together—tug as you will, you will not drag Zeus, the supreme counselor, from heaven to earth; but were I to pull at it myself I should draw you up with earth and sea into the bargain, then would I bind the chain about some pinnacle of

Olympus and leave you all dangling in the mid-firmament. So far am I above all others either of gods or men."

They were frightened and all of them held their peace, for he had spoken masterfully; but at last Athene answered: "Father, son of Cronus, king of kings, we all know that your might is not to be gainsaid, but we are also sorry for the Danaan warriors, who are perishing and coming to a bad end. We will, however, since you so bid us, refrain from actual fighting, but we will make serviceable suggestions to the Argives that they may not all of them perish in your displeasure."

Zeus smiled at her and answered, "Take heart, my child, Trito-born; I am not really in earnest, and I wish to be kind to you."

With this he yoked his fleet horses, with hoofs of bronze and manes of glittering gold. He girded himself also with gold about the body, seized his gold whip, and took his seat in his chariot. Thereon he lashed his horses and they flew forward nothing loath, midway twixt earth and starry heaven. After a while he reached many-fountained Ida, mother of wild beasts, and Gargarus, where are his grove and fragrant altar. There the father of gods and men stayed his horses, took them from the chariot, and hid them in a thick cloud. Then he took his seat all glorious upon the topmost crests, looking down upon the city of Troy and the ships of the Achaeans.

The Achaeans took their morning meal hastily at the ships, and afterwards put on their armor. The Trojans on the other hand likewise armed themselves throughout the city, fewer in numbers but nevertheless eager perforce to do battle for their wives and children. All the gates were flung wide open, and horse and foot sallied forth with the tramp as of a great multitude.

When they were got together in one place, shield clashed with shield, and spear with spear, in the conflict of mail-clad men. Mighty was the din as the bossed shields pressed hard on one another—death cry and shout of triumph of slain and slayers, and the earth ran red with blood.

Now so long as the day waxed and it was still morning their weapons beat against one another, and the people fell, but when the sun had reached mid-heaven, the sire of all balanced his golden scales and put two fates of death within them, one for the Trojans and the other for the Achaeans. He took the balance by the middle, and when he lifted it up the day of the Achaeans sank. The death-fraught scale of the Achaeans settled down upon the ground, while that of the Trojans rose heavenwards. Then he thundered aloud from Ida, and sent the glare of his lightning upon the Achaeans; when they saw this, pale fear fell upon them and they were sore afraid.

Idomeneus dared not stay nor yet Agamemnon, nor did the two Ajaxes, servants of Ares, hold their ground. Nestor, knight of Gerene, alone stood firm, bulwark of the Achaeans, not of his own will, but one of his horses was disabled. Paris, husband of lovely Helen, had hit it with an arrow just on the top of its head where the mane begins to grow away from the skull, a very deadly place. The horse bounded in his anguish as the arrow pierced his brain, and his struggles threw the others into confusion. The old man instantly began cutting the traces with his sword, but Hector's fleet horses bore down upon him through the rout with their bold charioteer, even Hector himself, and the old man would have perished there and then had not Diomed been quick to mark, and with a loud cry called Odysseus to help him.

"Odysseus," he cried, "noble son of Laertes, where are you flying to, with your back turned like a coward? See that you are not struck with a spear between the shoulders. Stay here and help me to defend Nestor from this man's furious onset."

Odysseus would not give ear, but sped onward to the ships of the Achaeans, and the son of Tydeus, flinging himself alone into the thick of the fight, took his stand before the horses of the son of Neleus. "Sir," said he, "these young warriors are pressing you hard, your force is spent, and age is heavy upon you, your squire is naught, and your horses are slow to move. Mount my chariot and see what the horses of Tros can do—how cleverly they can scud hither and thither over the plain either in flight or in pursuit. I took them from the hero Aeneas. Let our squires attend to your own steeds, but let us drive mine straight at the Trojans, that Hector may learn how furiously I too can wield my spear."

Nestor, knight of Gerene, hearkened to his words. Thereon the doughty squires, Sthenelus and kind-hearted Eurymedon, saw to Nestor's horses, while the two both mounted Diomed's chariot. Nestor took the reins in his hands and lashed the horses on. They were soon close up with Hector, and the son of Tydeus aimed a spear at him as he was charging full speed towards them. He missed him, but struck his charioteer and squire Eniopeus, son of noble Thebaeus, in the breast by the nipple while the reins were in his hands, so that he died there and then, and the horses swerved as he fell headlong from the chariot. Hector was greatly grieved at the loss of his charioteer, but let him lie for all his sorrow, while he went in quest of another driver; nor did his steeds have to go long without one, for he presently found brave Archeptolemus, the son of Iphitus, and made him get up behind the horses, giving the reins into his hand.

All had then been lost and no help for it, for they would have been penned up in Ilium like sheep, had not the sire of gods and men been quick to mark, and hurled a fiery flaming thunderbolt which fell just in front of Diomed's horses with a flare of burning brimstone. The horses were frightened and tried to back beneath the car, while the reins dropped from Nestor's hands. Then he was afraid and said to Diomed: "Son of Tydeus, turn your horses in flight. See you not that the hand of Zeus is against you? Today he vouchsafes victory to Hector; tomorrow, if it so please him, he will again grant it to ourselves. No man, however brave, may thwart the purpose of Zeus, for he is far stronger than any."

Diomed answered: "All that you have said is true; there is a grief however which pierces me to the very heart, for Hector will talk among the Trojans and say, 'The son of Tydeus fled before me to the ships.' This is the vaunt he will make, and may earth then swallow me."

"Son of Tydeus," replied Nestor, "what mean you?' Though Hector say that you are a coward the Trojans and Dardanians will not believe him, nor yet the wives of the mighty warriors whom you have laid low."

So saying he turned the horses back through the thick of the battle, and with a cry that rent the air the Trojans and Hector rained their darts after them. Hector shouted to him and said: "Son of Tydeus, the Danaans have done you honor hitherto as regards your place at table, the meals they give you, and the filling of your cup with wine. Henceforth they will despise you, for you are become no better than a woman. Be off, girl and coward that you are, you shall not scale our walls through any flinching on my part; neither shall you carry off our wives in your ships, for I shall kill you with my own hand."

The son of Tydeus was in two minds whether or no to turn his horses round again and fight him. Thrice did he doubt, and thrice did Zeus thunder from the heights of Ida in token to the Trojans that he would turn the battle in their favor. Hector then shouted to them and said: "Trojans, Lycians, and Dardanians, lovers of close fighting, be men, my friends, and fight with might and with main. I see that Zeus is minded to vouchsafe victory and great glory to myself, while he will deal destruction upon the Danaans. Fools, for having thought of building this weak and worthless wall. It shall not stay my fury; my horses will spring lightly over their trench, and when I am at their ships forget not to bring me fire that I may burn them, while I slaughter the Argives who will be all dazed and bewildered by the smoke."

Then he cried to his horses: "Xanthus and Podargus, and you Aethon and goodly Lampus, pay me for your keep now and for all the honey-sweet corn with which Andromache, daughter of great Eëtion, has fed you, and for the way in which she has mixed wine and water for you to drink whenever you would, before doing so even for me who am her own husband. Haste in pursuit, that we may take the shield of Nestor, the fame of which ascends to heaven, for it is of solid gold, arm-rods and all, and that we may strip from the shoulders of Diomed the cuirass which Hephaestus made him. Could we take these two things, the Achaeans would set sail in their ships this selfsame night."

Thus did he vaunt, but Queen Hera made high Olympus quake as she shook with rage upon her throne. Then said she to the mighty god Poseidon: "What now, wide-ruling lord of the earthquake? Can you find no compassion in your heart for the dying Danaans, who bring you many a welcome offering to Helice and to Aegae? Wish them well then. If all of us who are with the Danaans were to drive the Trojans back and keep Zeus from helping them, he would have to sit there sulking alone on Ida."

King Poseidon was greatly troubled and answered, "Hera, rash of tongue, what are you talking about? We other gods must not set ourselves against Zeus, for he is far stronger than we are."

Thus did they converse; but the whole space enclosed by the ditch, from the ships even to the wall, was filled with horses and warriors, who were pent up there by Hector, son of Priam, now that the hand of Zeus was with him. He would even have set fire to the ships and burned them had not Queen Hera put it into the mind of Agamemnon to bestir himself and to encourage the Achaeans. To this end he went round the ships and tents carrying a great purple cloak, and took his stand by the huge black hull of Odysseus' ship, which was middlemost of all. It was from this place that his voice would carry farthest, on the one hand towards the tents of Ajax, son of Telamon, and on the other towards those of Achilles—for these two heroes, well-assured of their own strength, had valorously drawn up their ships at the two ends of the line. From this spot then, with a voice that could be heard afar, he shouted to the Danaans, saying: "Argives, shame on you cowardly creatures, brave in semblance only! Where are now our vaunts that we should prove victorious—the vaunts we made so vaingloriously in Lemnos, when we ate the flesh of horned cattle and filled our mixing bowls to the brim? You vowed that you would each of you stand against a hundred or two hundred men, and now you prove no match even for one—for Hector, who will be ere long setting our ships in a blaze. Father Zeus, did you ever so ruin a great king and rob him so utterly of his greatness? Yet, when to my sorrow I was coming hither, I never let my ship pass your altars without offering the fat and thighbones of heifers upon every one of them, so eager was I to sack the city of Troy. Vouchsafe me then this prayer—suffer us to escape at any rate with our lives, and let not the Achaeans be so utterly vanquished by the Trojans."

Thus did he pray, and father Zeus pitying his tears vouchsafed him that his people should live, not die. Forthwith he sent them an eagle, most unfailingly portentous of all birds, with a young fawn in its talons; the eagle dropped the fawn by the altar on which the Achaeans sacrificed to Zeus the lord of omens. When, therefore, the people saw that the bird had come from Zeus, they sprang more fiercely upon the Trojans and fought more boldly.

There was no man of all the many Danaans who could then boast that he had driven his horses over the trench and gone forth to fight sooner than the son of Tydeus; long before anyone else could do so he slew an armed warrior of the Trojans, Agelaus, the son of Phradmon. He had turned his horses in flight, but the spear struck him in the back midway between his shoulders and went right through his chest, and his armor rang rattling round him as he fell forward from his chariot.

After him came Agamemnon and Menelaus, sons of Atreus, the two Ajaxes clothed in valor as with a garment, Idomeneus and his companion in arms, Meriones, peer of murderous Ares, and Eurypylus, the brave son of Euaemon. Ninth came Teucer with his bow, and took his place under cover of the shield of Ajax, son of Telamon. When Ajax lifted his shield Teucer would peer round, and when he had hit anyone in the throng, the man would fall dead; then Teucer would hie back to Ajax as a child to its mother, and again duck down under his shield.

Which of the Trojans did brave Teucer first kill? Orsilochus, and then Ormenus and Ophelestes, Daetor, Chromius, and godlike Lycophontes,

Amopaon, son of Polyaemon, and Melanippus. All these in turn did he lay low upon the earth, and King Agamemnon was glad when he saw him making havoc of the Trojans with his mighty bow. He went up to him and said: "Teucer, man after my own heart, son of Telamon, captain among the host, shoot on, and be at once the saving of the Danaans and the glory of your father Telamon, who brought you up and took care of you in his own house when you were a child, bastard though you were. Cover him with glory though he is far off. I will promise and I will assuredly perform; if aegis-bearing Zeus and Athene grant me to sack the city of Ilium, you shall have the next best meed of honor after my own—a tripod, or two horses with their chariot, or a woman who shall go up into your bed."

And Teucer answered: "Most noble son of Atreus, you need not urge me. From the moment we began to drive them back to Ilium, I have never ceased so far as in me lies to look out for men whom I can shoot and kill; I have shot eight barbed shafts, and all of them have been buried in the flesh of warlike youths, but this mad dog I cannot hit."

As he spoke he aimed another arrow straight at Hector, for he was bent on hitting him. Nevertheless he missed him, and the arrow hit Priam's brave son Gorgythion in the breast. His mother, fair Castianeira, lovely as a goddess, had been married from Aesyme, and now he bowed his head as a garden poppy in full bloom when it is weighed down by showers in spring—even thus heavily bowed his head beneath the weight of his helmet.

Again he aimed at Hector, for he was longing to hit him, and again his arrow missed, for Apollo turned it aside; but he hit Hector's brave charioteer Archeptolemus in the breast, by the nipple, as he was driving furiously into the fight. The horses swerved aside as he fell headlong from the chariot, and there was no life left in him. Hector was greatly grieved at the loss of his charioteer, but for all his sorrow he let him lie where he fell, and bade his brother Cebriones, who was hard by, take the reins. Cebriones did as he had said. Hector thereon with a loud cry sprang from his chariot to the ground and seizing a great stone made straight for Teucer with intent to kill him. Teucer had just taken an arrow from his quiver and had laid it upon the bowstring, but Hector struck him with the jagged stone as he was taking aim and drawing the string to his shoulder. He hit him just where the collarbone divides the neck from the chest, a very deadly place, and broke the sinew of his arm so that his wrist was powerless, and the bow dropped from his hand as he fell forward on his knees. Ajax saw that his brother had fallen, and running towards him bestrode him and sheltered him with his shield. Meanwhile his two trusty squires, Mecisteus, son of Echius, and Alastor, came up and bore him to the ships groaning in his great pain.

Zeus now again put heart into the Trojans, and they drove the Achaeans to their deep trench with Hector in all his glory at their head. As a hound grips a wild boar or lion in flank or buttock when he gives him chase, and watches warily for his wheeling, even so did Hector follow close upon the Achaeans, ever killing the hindmost as they rushed panic-stricken onwards. When they had fled through the set stakes and trench and many Achaeans had been laid low at the hands of the Trojans, they halted at their ships, calling upon one another and praying every man instantly as they lifted up their hands to the gods; but Hector wheeled his horses this way and that, his eyes glaring like those of Gorgo or murderous Ares.

Hera when she saw them had pity upon them, and at once said to Athene, "Alas, child of aegis-bearing Zeus, shall you and I take no more thought for the dying Danaans, though it be the last time we ever do so? See how they perish and come to a bad end before the onset of but a single man. Hector, the son of Priam, rages with intolerable fury, and has already done great mischief."

Athene answered: "Would, indeed, this fellow might die in his own land, and fall by the hands of the Achaeans; but my father Zeus is mad with spleen, ever foiling me, ever headstrong and unjust. He forgets how often I saved his son when he was worn out by the labors Eurystheus had laid on him. He would weep till his cry came up to heaven, and then Zeus would send me down to help him; if I had had the sense to foresee all this, when Eurystheus sent him to the house of Hades to fetch the hellhound from Erebus, he would never have come back alive out of the deep waters of the river Styx. And now Zeus hates me, while he lets Thetis have her way because she kissed his knees and took hold of his beard, when she was begging him to do honor to Achilles. I shall know what to do next time he begins calling me his gray-eyed darling. Get our horses ready, while I go within the house of aegis-bearing Zeus and put on my armor. We shall then find out whether Priam's son Hector will be glad to meet us in the highways of battle, or whether the Trojans will glut hounds and vultures with the fat of their flesh as they lie dead by the ships of the Achaeans."

Thus did she speak and white-armed Hera, daughter of great Cronus, obeyed her words; she set about harnessing her gold-bedizened steeds, while Athene, daughter of aegis-bearing Zeus, flung her richly embroidered vesture, made with her own hands, on to the threshold of her father, and donned the shirt of Zeus, arming herself for battle. Then she stepped into her flaming chariot, and grasped the spear so stout and sturdy and strong with which she quells the ranks of heroes who have displeased her. Hera lashed her horses, and the gates of heaven bellowed as they flew open of their own accord—gates over which the Hours preside, in whose hands are heaven and Olympus, either to open the dense cloud that hides them or to close it. Through these the goddesses drove their obedient steeds.

But father Zeus when he saw them from Ida was very angry, and sent winged Iris with a message to them. "Go," said he, "fleet Iris, turn them back and see that they do not come near me, for if we come to fighting there will be mischief. This is what I say and this is what I mean to do. I will lame their horses for them; I will hurl them from their chariot, and will break it in pieces. It will take them all ten years to heal the wounds my lightning shall inflict upon them; my gray-eyed daughter will then learn what quarreling with her father means. I am less surprised and angry with Hera, for whatever I say she always contradicts me."

With this Iris went her way, fleet as the wind, from the heights of Ida to the lofty summits of Olympus. She met the goddesses at the outer gates of its many valleys and gave them her message. "What," said she, "are you about? Are you mad? The son of Cronus forbids your going. This is what he says, and this is what he means to do: he will lame your horses for you, he will hurl you from your chariot, and will break it in pieces. It will take you all ten years to heal the wounds his lightning will inflict upon you, that you may learn, gray-eyed goddess, what quarreling with your father means. He is less hurt and angry with Hera, for whatever he says she always contradicts him—but you, bold hussy, will you really dare to raise your huge spear in defiance of Zeus?"

With this she left them, and Hera said to Athene, "Of a truth, child of aegis-bearing Zeus, I am not for fighting men's battles further in defiance of Zeus. Let them live or die as luck will have it, and let Zeus mete out his judgments upon the Trojans and Danaans according to his own pleasure."

She turned her steeds; the Hours presently unyoked them, made them fast to their ambrosial mangers, and leaned the chariot against the end wall of the courtyard. The two goddesses then sat down upon their golden thrones, amid the company of the other gods; but they were very angry.

Presently father Zeus drove his chariot to Olympus, and entered the assembly of gods. The mighty lord of the earthquake unyoked his horses for him, set the car upon its stand, and threw a cloth over it. Zeus then sat down upon his golden throne and Olympus reeled beneath him. Athene and Hera sat alone, apart from Zeus, and neither spoke nor asked him questions, but Zeus knew what they meant, and said, "Athene and Hera, why are you so angry? Are you fatigued with killing so many of your dear friends the Trojans? Be this as it may, such is the might of my hands that all the gods in Olympus cannot turn me. You were both of you trembling all over ere ever you saw the fight and its terrible doings. I tell you therefore—and it would have surely been—I should have struck you with lightning, and your chariots would never have brought you back again to Olympus."

Athene and Hera groaned in spirit as they sat side by side and brooded mischief for the Trojans. Athene sat silent without a word, for she was in a furious passion and bitterly incensed against her father; but Hera could not contain herself and said, "What, dread son of Cronus, are you talking about? We know how great your power is, nevertheless we have compassion upon the Danaan warriors who are perishing and coming to a bad end. We will, however, since you so bid us, refrain from actual fighting, but we will make serviceable suggestions to the Argives, that they may not all of them perish in your displeasure."

And Zeus answered: "Tomorrow morning, Hera, if you choose to do so, you will see the son of Cronus destroying large numbers of the Argives, for fierce Hector shall not cease fighting till he has roused the son of Peleus when they are fighting in dire straits at their ships' sterns about the body of Patroclus. Like it or no, this is how it is decreed. For aught I care, you may go to the lowest depths beneath earth and sea, where Iapetus and Cronus dwell in lone Tartarus with neither ray of light nor breath of wind to cheer them. You may go on and on till you get there, and I shall not care one whit for your displeasure; you are the greatest vixen living."

Hera made him no answer. The sun's glorious orb now sank into Oceanus and drew down night over the land. Sorry indeed were the Trojans when light failed them, but welcome and thrice prayed for did darkness fall upon the Achaeans.

Then Hector led the Trojans back from the ships, and held a council on the open space near the river, where there was a spot clear of corpses. They left their chariots and sat down on the ground to hear the speech he made them. He grasped a spear eleven cubits long, the bronze point of which gleamed in front of it, while the ring round the spearhead was of gold. Spear in hand he spoke.

"Hear me," said he, "Trojans, Dardanians, and allies. I deemed but now that I should destroy the ships and all the Achaeans with them ere I went back to Ilium, but darkness came on too soon. It was this alone that saved them and their ships upon the seashore. Now, therefore, let us obey the behests of night, and prepare our suppers. Take your horses out of their chariots and give them their feeds of corn; then make speed to bring sheep and cattle from the city; bring wine also and corn for your horses and gather much wood, that from dark till dawn we may burn watchfires whose flare may reach to heaven. For the Achaeans may try to fly beyond the sea by night, and they must not embark scatheless and unmolested; many a man among them must take a dart with him to nurse at home, hit with spear or arrow as he is leaping on board his ship, that others may fear to bring war and weeping upon the Trojans.

"Moreover, let the heralds tell it about the city that the growing youths and gray-bearded men are to camp upon its heaven-built walls. Let the women each of them light a great fire in her house, and let watch be safely kept lest the town be entered by surprise while the host is outside. See to it, brave Trojans, as I have said, and let this suffice for the moment; at daybreak I will instruct you further. I pray in hope to Zeus and to the gods that we may then drive those fate-sped hounds from our land, for 'tis the fates that have borne them and their ships hither. This night, therefore, let us keep watch, but with early morning let us put on our armor and rouse fierce war at the ships of the Achaeans; I shall then know whether brave Diomed, the son of Tydeus, will drive me back from the ships to the wall, or whether I shall myself slay him and carry off his bloodstained spoils. Tomorrow let him show his mettle, and abide my spear if he dare. I ween that at break of day, he shall be among the first to fall and many another of his comrades round him. Would that I were as sure of being immortal and never growing old, and of being worshiped like Athene and Apollo, as I am that this day will bring evil to the Argives."

Thus spoke Hector and the Trojans shouted applause. They took their sweating steeds from under the yoke and made them fast each by his own chariot. They made haste to bring sheep and cattle from the city, they brought wine also and corn from their houses and gathered much wood. They then offered unblemished hecatombs to the immortals, and the wind carried the sweet savor of sacrifice to heaven—but the blessed gods partook not thereof, for they bitterly hated Ilium with Priam and Priam's people. Thus high in hope they sat through the livelong night by the highways of war, and many a watchfire did they kindle. As when the stars shine clear, and the moon is bright—there is not a breath of air, not a peak nor a glade nor jutting headland but it stands out in the ineffable radiance that breaks from the serene of heaven; the stars can all of them be told and the heart of the shepherd is glad— even thus shone the watchfires of the Trojans before Ilium midway between the ships and the river Xanthus. A thousand campfires gleamed upon the plain, and in the glow of each there sat fifty men, while the horses, champing oats and corn beside their chariots, waited till dawn should come.

Book IX

*In despair of ever capturing Troy, Agamemnon calls his chiefs together
and proposes a return to Greece. Diomed and Nestor chide him for
cowardice, and also for his injustice to Achilles, which has lost them the help
of the bravest among them. Agamemnon admits his mistake and offers
full reparation if Achilles will fight. Odysseus, Ajax, and Phoenix are
dispatched as envoys, but Achilles rejects the offer.*

THUS DID THE TROJANS WATCH. BUT PANIC, COMRADE OF BLOODSTAINED Rout, had taken fast hold of the Achaeans, and their princes were all of them in despair. As when the two winds that blow from Thrace— the north and the northwest—spring up of a sudden and rouse the fury of the main—in a moment the dark waves uprear their heads and scatter their sea-wrack in all directions—even thus troubled were the hearts of the Achaeans.

The son of Atreus in dismay bade the heralds call the people to a council man by man, but not to cry the matter aloud; he made haste also himself to call them, and they sat sorry at heart in their assembly. Agamemnon shed tears as it were a running stream or cataract on the side of some sheer cliff; and thus, with many a heavy sigh he spoke to the Achaeans. "My friends," said he, "princes and councilors of the Argives, the hand of heaven has been laid heavily upon me. Cruel Zeus gave me his solemn promise that I should sack the city of Troy before returning, but he has played me false, and is now bidding me go ingloriously back to Argos with the loss of much people. Such is the will of Zeus, who has laid many a proud city in the dust as he will yet lay others, for his power is above all. Now, therefore, let us all do as I say and sail back to our own country, for we shall not take Troy."

Thus he spoke, and the sons of the Achaeans for a long while sat sorrowful there, but they all held their peace, till at last Diomed of the loud battle cry made answer, saying: "Son of Atreus, I will chide your folly, as is my right in council. Be not then aggrieved that I should do so. In the first place you attacked me before all the Danaans and said that I was a coward and no soldier. The Argives young and old know that you did so. But the son of scheming Cronus endowed you by halves only. He gave you honor as the chief ruler over us, but valor, which is the highest both right and might, he did not give you. Sir, think you that the sons of the Achaeans are indeed as unwarlike and cowardly as you say they are? If your own mind is set upon going home—go—the way is open to you: the many ships that followed you from Mycene stand ranged upon the seashore; but the rest of us will stay here till we have sacked Troy. Nay, though these too should turn homeward with their ships, Sthenelus and myself will still fight on till we reach the goal of Ilium, for heaven was with us when we came."

The sons of the Achaeans shouted applause at the words of Diomed, and presently Nestor rose to speak. "Son of Tydeus," said he, "in war your prowess is beyond question, and in counsel you excel all who are of your own years; no one of the Achaeans can make light of what you say nor gainsay it, but you have not yet come to the end of the whole matter. You are still young—you might be the youngest of my own children—still you have spoken wisely and have counseled the chief of the Achaeans not without discretion. Nevertheless, I am older than you and I will tell you everything. Therefore let no man, not even King Agamemnon, disregard my saying, for he that foments civil discord is a clanless, heartless outlaw.

"Now, however, let us obey the behests of night and get our suppers, but let the sentinels every man of them camp by the trench that is without the wall. I am giving these instructions to the young men. When they have been attended to, do you, son of Atreus, give your orders, for you are the most royal among us all. Prepare a feast for your councilors; it is right and reasonable that you should do so. There is abundance of wine in your tents, which the ships of the Achaeans bring from Thrace daily. You have everything at your disposal wherewith to entertain guests, and you have many subjects. When many are got together, you can be guided by him whose counsel is wisest—and sorely do we need shrewd and prudent counsel, for the foe has lit his watchfires hard by our ships. Who can be other than dismayed? This night will either be the ruin of our host, or save it."

Thus did he speak, and they did even as he had said. The sentinels went out in their armor under command of Nestor's son Thrasymedes, a captain of the host, and of the bold warriors Ascalaphus and Ialmenus. There were also Meriones, Aphareus and Deipyrus, and the son of Creion, noble Lycomedes. There were seven captains of the sentinels, and with each there went a hundred youths armed with long spears. They took their places midway between the trench and the wall, and when they had done so they lit their fires and got every man his supper.

The son of Atreus then bade many councilors of the Achaeans to his quarters and prepared a great feast in their honor. They laid their hands on the good things that were before them, and as soon as they had had enough to eat and drink, old Nestor, whose counsel was ever truest, was the first to lay his mind before them. He, therefore, with all sincerity and good will addressed them thus:

"With yourself, most noble son of Atreus, king of men, Agamemnon, will I both begin my speech and end it, for you are king over much people. Zeus, moreover, has vouchsafed you to wield the scepter and to uphold righteousness, that you may take thought for your people under you. Therefore, it behooves you above all others both to speak and to give ear, and to carry out the counsel of another who shall have been minded to speak wisely. All turns on you and on your commands, therefore I will say what I think will be best.

No man will be of a truer mind than that which has been mine from the hour when you, sir, angered Achilles by taking the girl Briseis from his tent against my judgment. I urged you not to do so, but you yielded to your own pride, and dishonored a hero whom heaven itself had honored—for you still hold the prize that had been awarded to him. Now, however, let us think how we may appease him, both with presents and fair speeches that may conciliate him."

And King Agamemnon answered: "Sir, you have reproved my folly justly. I was wrong. I own it. One whom heaven befriends is in himself a host, and Zeus has shown that he befriends this man by destroying much people of the Achaeans. I was blinded with passion and yielded to my worser mind; therefore I will make amends, and will give him great gifts by way of atonement. I will tell them in the presence of you all. I will give him seven tripods that have never yet been on the fire, and ten talents of gold. I will give him twenty iron cauldrons and twelve strong horses that have won races and carried off prizes. Rich, indeed, both in land and gold is he that has as many prizes as my horses have won me. I will give him seven excellent workwomen, Lesbians, whom I chose for myself when he took Lesbos—all of surpassing beauty. I will give him these, and with them her whom I erewhile took from him, the daughter of Briseus; and I swear a great oath that I never went up into her couch, nor have been with her after the manner of men and women.

"All these things will I give him now down, and if hereafter the gods vouchsafe me to sack the city of Priam, let him come when we Achaeans are dividing the spoil, and load his ship with gold and bronze to his liking. Furthermore let him take twenty Trojan women, the loveliest after Helen herself. Then, when we reach Achaean Argos, wealthiest of all lands, he shall be my son-in-law and I will show him like honor with my own dear son Orestes, who is being nurtured in all abundance. I have three daughters, Chrysothemis, Laodice, and Iphianassa: let him take the one of his choice, freely and without gifts of wooing, to the house of Peleus. I will add such dower to boot as no man ever yet gave his daughter, and will give him seven

well-established cities, Cardamyle, Enope, and Hire, where there is grass; holy
Pherae and the rich meadows of Anthea; Aepea also, and the vine-clad slopes
of Pedasus, all near the sea, and on the borders of sandy Pylos. The men that
dwell there are rich in cattle and sheep; they will honor him with gifts as
though he were a god, and be obedient to his comfortable ordinances. All this
will I do if he will now forgo his anger. Let him then yield—it is only Hades
who is utterly ruthless and unyielding—and hence he is of all gods the one
most hateful to mankind. Moreover, I am older and more royal than himself.
Therefore, let him now obey me."

Then Nestor answered: "Most noble son of Atreus, king of men,
Agamemnon. The gifts you offer are no small ones; let us then send chosen
messengers, who may go to the tent of Achilles, son of Peleus, without delay.
Let those go whom I shall name. Let Phoenix, dear to Zeus, lead the way; let
Ajax and Odysseus follow, and let the heralds Odius and Eurybates go with
them. Now bring water for our hands, and bid all keep silence while we pray
to Zeus, the son of Cronus, if so be that he may have mercy upon us."

Thus did he speak, and his saying pleased them well. Menservants poured
water over the hands of the guests, while pages filled the mixing bowls with
wine and water, and handed it round after giving every man his drink offer-
ing; then, when they had made their offerings, and had drunk each as much
as he was minded, the envoys set out from the tent of Agamemnon, son of
Atreus; and Nestor, looking first to one and then to another, but most espe-
cially at Odysseus, was insistent with them that they should prevail with the
noble son of Peleus.

They went their way by the shore of the sounding sea, and prayed ear-
nestly to earth-encircling Poseidon that the high spirit of the son of Aeacus
might incline favorably towards them. When they reached the ships and tents
of the Myrmidons, they found Achilles playing on a lyre, fair, of cunning
workmanship, and its cross-bar was of silver. It was part of the spoils which
he had taken when he sacked the city of Eëtion, and he was now diverting

himself with it and singing the feats of heroes. He was alone with Patroclus, who sat opposite to him and said nothing, waiting till he should cease singing. Odysseus and Ajax now came in—Odysseus leading the way—and stood before him. Achilles sprang from his seat with the lyre still in his hand, and Patroclus, when he saw the strangers, rose also. Achilles then greeted them, saying, "All hail and welcome! You must come upon some great matter, you, who for all my anger are still dearest to me of the Achaeans."

With this he led them forward, and bade them sit on seats covered with purple rugs; then he said to Patroclus, who was close by him, "Son of Menoetius, set a larger bowl upon the table, mix less water with the wine, and give every man his cup, for these are very dear friends, who are now under my roof."

Patroclus did as his comrade bade him; he set the chopping block in front of the fire, and on it he laid the loin of a sheep, the loin also of a goat, and the chine of a fat hog. Automedon held the meat while Achilles chopped it; he then sliced the pieces and put them on spits while the son of Menoetius made the fire burn high. When the flame had died down, he spread the embers, laid the spits on top of them, lifting them up and setting them upon the spit-racks; and he sprinkled them with salt. When the meat was roasted, he set it on platters, and handed bread round the table in fair baskets, while Achilles dealt them their portions. Then Achilles took his seat facing Odysseus against the opposite wall, and bade his comrade Patroclus offer sacrifice to the gods. So he cast the offerings into the fire, and they laid their hands upon the good things that were before them. As soon as they had had enough to eat and drink, Ajax made a sign to Phoenix, and when he saw this, Odysseus filled his cup with wine and pledged Achilles.

"Hail," said he, "Achilles, we have had no scant of good cheer, neither in the tent of Agamemnon, nor yet here; there has been plenty to eat and drink, but our thought turns upon no such matter. Sir, we are in the face of great disaster, and without your help know not whether we shall save our fleet or lose it. The Trojans and their allies have camped hard by our ships and by the wall; they have lit watchfires throughout their host and deem that nothing can now prevent them from falling on our fleet. Zeus, moreover, has sent his lightnings on their right. Hector, in all his glory, rages like a maniac. Confident that Zeus is with him he fears neither god nor man, but is gone raving mad, and prays for the approach of day. He vows that he will hew the high sterns of our ships in pieces, set fire to their hulls, and make havoc of the Achaeans while they are dazed and smothered in smoke. I much fear that heaven will make good his boasting, and it will prove our lot to perish at Troy far from our home in Argos. Up, then, and late though it be, save the sons of the Achaeans who faint before the fury of the Trojans. You will repent bitterly hereafter if you do not, for when the harm is done there will be no curing it; consider ere it be too late, and save the Danaans from destruction.

"My good friend, when your father Peleus sent you from Phthia to Agamemnon, did he not charge you saying, 'Son, Athene and Hera will make you strong if they choose, but check your high temper, for the better part is in good will. Eschew vain quarreling, and the Achaeans old and young will respect you more for doing so.' These were his words, but you have forgotten them. Even now, however, be appeased, and put away your anger from you. Agamemnon will make you great amends if you will forgive him. Listen, and I will tell you what he has said in his tent that he will give you. He will give you seven tripods that have never yet been on the fire, and ten talents of gold, twenty iron cauldrons, and twelve strong horses that have won races and carried off prizes. Rich indeed both in land and gold is he who has as many prizes as these horses have won for Agamemnon. Moreover, he will give you seven excellent workwomen, Lesbians, whom he chose for himself, when you took Lesbos—all of surpassing beauty. He will give you these, and with them her whom he ere while took from you, the daughter of Briseus, and he will swear a great oath, he has never gone up into her couch nor been with her after the manner of men and women. All these things will he give you now down, and if hereafter the gods vouchsafe him to sack the city of Priam, you can come when we Achaeans are dividing the spoil, and load your ship with gold and bronze to your liking. You can take twenty Trojan women, the loveliest after Helen herself.

"Then, when we reach Achaean Argos, wealthiest of all lands, you shall be his son-in-law, and he will show you like honor with his own dear son Orestes, who is being nurtured in all abundance. Agamemnon has three daughters, Chrysothemis, Laodice, and Iphianassa: you may take the one of your choice, freely and without gifts of wooing, to the house of Peleus. He will add such dower to boot as no man ever yet gave his daughter, and will give you seven well-established cities, Cardamyle, Enope, and Hire where there is grass; holy Pherae and the rich meadows of Anthea; Aepea also, and the vine-clad slopes of Pedasus, all near the sea, and on the borders of sandy Pylos. The men that dwell there are rich in cattle and sheep; they will honor you with gifts as though you were a god, and be obedient to your comfortable ordinances. All this will he do if you will forgo your anger.

"Moreover, though you hate both him and his gifts with all your heart, yet pity the rest of the Achaeans who are being harassed in all their host; they will honor you as a god, and you will earn great glory at their hands. You might even kill Hector; he will come within your reach, for he is infatuated, and declares that not a Danaan whom the ships have brought can hold his own against him."

Achilles answered: "Odysseus, noble son of Laertes, I should give you formal notice plainly and in all fixity of purpose that there be no more of this cajoling, from whatsoever quarter it may come. Him do I hate even as the gates of hell who says one thing while he hides another in his heart; therefore I will say what I mean. I will be appeased neither by Agamemnon, son of Atreus, nor by any other of the Danaans, for I see that I have no thanks for all my fighting. He that fights fares no better than he that does not. Coward and hero are held in equal honor, and death deals like measure to him who works and him who is idle. I have taken nothing by all my hardships—with my life ever in my hand. As a bird when she has found a morsel takes it to her nestlings and herself fares hardly, even so many a long night have I been wakeful, and many a bloody battle have I waged by day against those who were fighting for their women. With my ships I have taken twelve cities, and eleven round about Troy have I stormed with my men by land. I took great store of wealth from every one of them, but I gave all up to Agamemnon, son of Atreus. He stayed where he was by his ships, yet of what came to him he gave little, and kept much himself.

"Nevertheless, he did distribute some meeds of honor among the chieftains and kings, and these have them still; from me alone of the Achaeans did he take the woman in whom I delighted—let him keep her and sleep with her. Why, pray, must the Argives needs fight the Trojans? What made the son of Atreus gather the host and bring them? Was it not for the sake of Helen? Are the sons of Atreus the only men in the world who love their wives? Any man of common right feeling will love and cherish her who is his own, as I this woman, with my whole heart, though she was but a fruitling of my spear. Agamemnon has taken her from me; he has played me false; I know him; let him tempt me no further, for he shall not move me. Let him look to you, Odysseus, and to the other princes to save his ships from burning. He has done much without me already. He has built a wall, he has dug a trench deep and wide all round it, and he has planted it within with stakes; but even so he stays not the murderous might of Hector. So long as I fought among the Achaeans Hector suffered not the battle to range far from the city walls. He would come to the Scaean gates and to the oak tree, but no further. Once he stayed to meet me—and hardly did he escape my onset.

"Now, however, since I am in no mood to fight him, I will tomorrow offer sacrifice to Zeus and to all the gods; I will draw my ships into the water and then victual them duly; tomorrow morning, if you care to look, you will see my ships on the Hellespont, and my men rowing out to sea with might and main. If great Poseidon vouchsafes me a fair passage, in three days I shall be in Phthia. I have much there that I left behind me when I came here to my sorrow, and I shall bring back still further store of gold, of red copper, of fair women, and of iron, my share of the spoils that we have taken; but one prize, he who gave has insolently taken away. Tell him all as I now bid you, and tell him in public that the Achaeans may hate him and beware of him should he think that he can yet dupe others—for his effrontery never fails him.

"As for me, hound that he is, he dares not look me in the face. I will take no counsel with him, and will undertake nothing in common with him. He has wronged me and deceived me enough, he shall not cozen me further; let him go his own way, for Zeus has robbed him of his reason. I loathe his presents and for himself care not one straw. He may offer me ten or even twenty times what he has now done, nay—not though it be all that he has in the world, both now or ever shall have. He may promise me the wealth of Orchomenus or of Egyptian Thebes, which is the richest city in the whole world, for it has a hundred gates through each of which two hundred men may drive at once with their chariots and horses. He may offer me gifts as the sands of the sea or the dust of the plain in multitude, but even so he shall not move me till I have been revenged in full for the bitter wrong he has done me. I will not marry his daughter; she may be fair as Aphrodite, and skillful as Athene, but I will have none of her: let another take her, who may be a good match for her and who rules a larger kingdom. If the gods spare me to return home, Peleus will find me a wife; there are Achaean women in Hellas and Phthia, daughters of kings that have cities under them; of these I can take whom I will and marry her. Many a time was I minded when at home in Phthia to woo and wed a woman who would make me a suitable wife, and to enjoy the riches of my old father Peleus. My life is more to me than all the wealth of Ilium while it was yet at peace before the Achaeans went there, or than all the treasure that lies on the stone floor of Apollo's temple beneath the cliffs of Pytho. Cattle and sheep are to be had for harrying, and a man may buy both tripods and horses if he wants them, but when his life has once left him it can neither be bought nor harried back again.

"My mother Thetis tells me that there are two ways in which I may meet my end. If I stay here and fight, I shall not return alive but my name will live forever: whereas if I go home my name will die, but it will be long ere death shall take me. To the rest of you, then, I say, 'Go home, for you will not take Ilium.' Zeus has held his hand over her to protect her, and her people have taken heart. Go, therefore, as in duty bound, and tell the princes of the Achaeans the message that I have sent them. Tell them to find some other plan for the saving of their ships and people, for so long as my displeasure lasts the one that they have now hit upon may not be. As for Phoenix, let him sleep here that he may sail with me in the morning if he so will. But I will not take him by force."

They all held their peace, dismayed at the sternness with which he had denied them, till presently the old knight Phoenix in his great fear for the ships of the Achaeans, burst into tears and said: "Noble Achilles, if you are now minded to return, and in the fierceness of your anger will do nothing to save the ships from burning, how, my son, can I remain here without you? Your father Peleus bade me go with you when he sent you as a mere lad from Phthia to Agamemnon. You knew nothing neither of war nor of the arts whereby men make their mark in council, and he sent me with you to train you in all excellence of speech and action. Therefore, my son, I will not stay here without you—no, not though heaven itself vouchsafe to strip my years from off me, and make me young as I was when I first left Hellas, the land of fair women. I was then flying the anger of my father Amyntor, son of Ormenus, who was furious with me in the matter of his concubine, of whom he was enamored to the wronging of his wife my mother. My mother, therefore, prayed me without ceasing to lie with the woman myself, that so she might hate my father, and in the course of time I yielded.

"But my father soon came to know, and cursed me bitterly, calling the dread Erinyes to witness. He prayed that no son of mine might ever sit upon my knees—and the gods, Zeus of the world below and awful Proserpine, fulfilled his curse. I took counsel to kill him, but some god stayed my rashness and bade me think on men's evil tongues and how I should be branded as the murderer of my father. Nevertheless, I could not bear to stay in my father's house with him so bitter against me. My cousins and clansmen came about me, and pressed me sorely to remain. Many a sheep and many an ox did they slaughter, and many a fat hog did they set down to roast before the fire; many a jar, too, did they broach of my father's wine. Nine whole nights did they set a guard over me taking it in turns to watch, and they kept a fire always burning, both in the cloister of the outer court and in the inner court at the doors of the room wherein I lay. But when the darkness of the tenth night came, I broke through the closed doors of my room, and climbed the wall of the outer court after passing quickly and unperceived through the men on guard and the womenservants. I then fled through Hellas till I came to fertile Phthia, mother of sheep, and to King Peleus, who made me welcome and treated me as a father treats an only son who will be heir to all his wealth. He made me rich and set me over much people, establishing me on the borders of Phthia where I was chief ruler over the Dolopians.

"It was I, Achilles, who had the making of you; I loved you with all my heart: for you would eat neither at home nor when you had gone out elsewhere, till I had first set you upon my knees, cut up the dainty morsel that you were to eat, and held the wine cup to your lips. Many a time have you slobbered your wine in baby helplessness over my shirt. I had infinite trouble with you, but I knew that heaven had vouchsafed me no offspring of my own, and I made a son of you, Achilles, that in my hour of need you might protect me.

"Now, therefore, I say battle with your pride and beat it; cherish not your anger forever; the might and majesty of heaven are more than ours, but even heaven may be appeased; and if a man has sinned he prays the gods, and reconciles them to himself by his piteous cries and by frankincense, with drink offerings and the savor of burnt sacrifice. For prayers are as daughters to great Zeus; halt, wrinkled, with eyes askance, they follow in the footsteps of sin, who, being fierce and fleet of foot, leaves them far behind him, and ever baneful to mankind outstrips them even to the ends of the world; but, nevertheless, the prayers come hobbling and healing after. If a man has pity upon these daughters of Zeus when they draw near him, they will bless him and hear him too when he is praying; but if he deny them and will not listen to them, they go to Zeus, the son of Cronus, and pray that he may presently fall into sin—to his rueing bitterly hereafter.

"Therefore, Achilles, give these daughters of Zeus due reverence, and bow before them as all good men will bow. Were not the son of Atreus offering you gifts and promising others later—if he were still furious and implacable—I am not he that would bid you throw off your anger and help the Achaeans, no matter how great their need; but he is giving much now, and more hereafter. He has sent his captains to urge his suit, and has chosen those who of all the Argives are most acceptable to you; make not then their words and their coming to be of none effect. Your anger has been righteous so far. We have heard in song how heroes of old time quarreled when they were roused to fury, but still they could be won by gifts, and fair words could soothe them.

"I have an old story in my mind—a very old one—but you are all friends and I will tell it. The Curetes and the Aetolians were fighting and killing one another round Calydon—the Aetolians defending the city and the Curetes trying to destroy it. For Artemis of the golden throne was angry and did them hurt because Oeneus had not offered her his harvest first fruits. The other gods had all been feasted with hecatombs, but to the daughter of great Zeus alone he had made no sacrifice. He had forgotten her, or somehow or other it had escaped him, and this was a grievous sin. Thereon the archer goddess in her displeasure sent a prodigious creature against him—a savage wild boar with great white tusks that did much harm to his orchard lands, uprooting apple trees in full bloom and throwing them to the ground. But Meleager, son of Oeneus, got huntsmen and hounds from many cities and killed it—for it was so monstrous that not a few were needed, and many a man did it stretch upon his funeral pyre. On this the goddess set the Curetes and the Aetolians fighting furiously about the head and skin of the boar.

"So long as Meleager was in the field things went badly with the Curetes, and for all their numbers they could not hold their ground under the city walls; but in the course of time Meleager was angered as even a wise man will sometimes be. He was incensed with his mother Althaea, and therefore stayed at home with his wedded wife, fair Cleopatra, who was daughter of Marpessa, daughter of Euenus, and of Ides, the strongest man then living. He it was who took his bow and faced King Apollo himself for fair Marpessa's sake; her father and mother then named her Alcyone, because her mother had mourned with the plaintive strains of the halcyon-bird when Phoebus Apollo had carried her off. Meleager, then, stayed at home with Cleopatra, nursing the anger which he felt by reason of his mother's curses. His mother, grieving for the death of her brother, prayed the gods and beat the earth with her hands, calling upon Hades and on awful Proserpine. She went down upon her knees and her bosom was wet with tears as she prayed that they would kill her son—and Erinys that walks in darkness and knows no ruth heard her from Erebus.

"Then was heard the din of battle about the gates of Calydon, and the dull thump of the battering against their walls. Thereon the elders of the Aetolians besought Meleager. They sent the chiefest of their priests, and begged him to come out and help them, promising him a great reward. They bade him choose fifty plough-gates, the most fertile in the plain of Calydon, the one-half vineyard and the other open ploughland. The old warrior Oeneus implored him, standing at the threshold of his room and beating the doors in supplication. His sisters and his mother herself besought him sore, but he the more refused them. Those of his comrades who were nearest and dearest to him also prayed him, but they could not move him till the foe was battering at the very doors of his chamber, and the Curetes had scaled the walls and were setting fire to the city. Then at last his sorrowing wife detailed the horrors that befall those whose city is taken. She reminded him how the men are slain, and the city is given over to the flames, while the women and children are carried into captivity. When he heard all this, his heart was touched, and he donned his armor to go forth. Thus of his own inward motion he saved the city of the Aetolians, but they now gave him nothing of those rich rewards that they had offered earlier, and though he saved the city he took nothing by it. Be not then, my son, thus minded; let not heaven lure you into any such course. When the ships are burning it will be a harder matter to save them. Take the gifts, and go, for the Achaeans will then honor you as a god; whereas if you fight without taking them, you may beat the battle back, but you will not be held in like honor."

And Achilles answered: "Phoenix, old friend and father, I have no need of such honor. I have honor from Zeus himself, which will abide with me at my ships while I have breath in my body, and my limbs are strong. I say further—and lay my saying to your heart—vex me no more with this weeping and lamentation, all in the cause of the son of Atreus. Love him so well, and you may lose the love I bear you. You ought to help me rather in troubling those that trouble me. Be king as much as I am, and share like honor with myself. The others shall take my answer. Stay here yourself and sleep comfortably in your bed; at daybreak we will consider whether to remain or go."

On this he nodded quietly to Patroclus as a sign that he was to prepare a bed for Phoenix, and that the others should take their leave. Ajax, son of Telamon, then said: "Odysseus, noble son of Laertes, let us be gone, for I see that our journey is vain. We must now take our answer, unwelcome though it be, to the Danaans who are waiting to receive it. Achilles is savage and remorseless. He is cruel, and cares nothing for the love his comrades lavished upon him more than on all the others. He is implacable—and yet if a man's brother or son has been slain he will accept a fine by way of amends from him that killed him, and the wrongdoer having paid in full remains in peace among his own people; but as for you, Achilles, the gods have put a wicked unforgiving spirit in your heart, and this, all about one single girl, whereas we now offer you the seven best we have, and much else into the bargain. Be then of a more gracious mind, respect the hospitality of your own roof. We are with you as messengers from the host of the Danaans, and would fain be held nearest and dearest to yourself of all the Achaeans."

"Ajax," replied Achilles, "noble son of Telamon, you have spoken much to my liking, but my blood boils when I think it all over, and remember how the son of Atreus treated me with contumely as though I were some vile tramp, and that too in the presence of the Argives. Go, then, and deliver your message. Say that I will have no concern with fighting till Hector, son of noble Priam, reaches the tents of the Myrmidons in his murderous course, and flings fire upon their ships. For all his lust of battle, I take it he will be held in check when he is at my own tent and ship."

On this they took every man his double cup, made their drink offerings, and went back to the ships, Odysseus leading the way. But Patroclus told his men and the maidservants to make ready a comfortable bed for Phoenix; they therefore did so with sheepskins, a rug, and a sheet of fine linen. The old man then laid himself down and waited till morning came. But Achilles slept in an inner room, and beside him the daughter of Phorbas, lovely Diomedè, whom he had carried off from Lesbos. Patroclus lay on the other side of the room, and with him fair Iphis whom Achilles had given him when he took Scyros the city of Enyeüs.

When the envoys reached the tents of the son of Atreus, the Achaeans rose, pledged them in cups of gold, and began to question them. King Agamemnon was the first to do so. "Tell me, Odysseus," said he, "will he save the ships from burning, or did he refuse, and is he still furious?"

Odysseus answered: "Most noble son of Atreus, king of men, Agamemnon, Achilles will not be calmed, but is more fiercely angry than ever, and spurns both you and your gifts. He bids you take counsel with the Achaeans to save the ships and host as you best may; as for himself, he said that at daybreak he should draw his ships into the water. He said further that he should advise everyone to sail home likewise, for that you will not reach the goal of Ilium. 'Zeus,' he said, 'has laid his hand over the city to protect it, and the people have taken heart.' This is what he said, and the others who were with me can tell you the same story—Ajax and the two heralds, men, both of them, who may be trusted. The old man Phoenix stayed where he was to sleep, for so Achilles would have it, that he might go home with him in the morning if he so would; but he will not take him by force."

They all held their peace, sitting for a long time silent and dejected, by reason of the sternness with which Achilles had refused them, till presently Diomed said: "Most noble son of Atreus, king of men, Agamemnon, you ought not to have sued the son of Peleus nor offered him gifts. He is proud enough as it is, and you have encouraged him in his pride still further. Let him stay or go as he will. He will fight later when he is in the humor, and heaven puts it in his mind to do so. Now, therefore, let us all do as I say. We have eaten and drunk our fill, let us then take our rest, for in rest there is both strength and stay. But when fair rosy-fingered morn appears, forthwith bring out your host and your horsemen in front of the ships, urging them on, and yourself fighting among the foremost."

Thus he spoke, and the other chieftains approved his words. They then made their drink offerings and went every man to his own tent, where they lay down to rest and enjoyed the boon of sleep.

Book X

Later in the night, Agamemnon summons the Greek chiefs again.
Diomed and Odysseus are sent out to spy on the enemy's camp. From the
Trojan side Hector sends Dolon to spy on the Greeks. Diomed and Odysseus
capture Dolon, learn from him the disposition of the Trojan forces, and
kill him. They then surprise and kill Rhesus, the Thracian king, and drive
his fine horses back to their ships.

NOW THE OTHER PRINCES OF THE ACHAEANS SLEPT SOUNDLY THE whole night through, but Agamemnon, son of Atreus, was troubled, so that he could get no rest. As when fair Hera's lord flashes his lightning in token of great rain or hail or snow when the snowflakes whiten the ground, or again as a sign that he will open the wide jaws of hungry war, even so did Agamemnon heave many a heavy sigh, for his soul trembled within him. When he looked upon the plain of Troy he marveled at the many watchfires burning in front of Ilium, and at the sound of pipes and flutes and of the hum of men, but when presently he turned towards the ships and hosts of the Achaeans, he tore his hair by handfuls before Zeus on high, and groaned aloud for the very disquietness of his soul. In the end he deemed it best to go at once to Nestor, son of Neleus, and see if between them they could find any way of saving the Achaeans from destruction. He therefore rose, put on his shirt, bound his sandals about his comely feet, flung the skin of a huge tawny lion over his shoulders—a skin that reached his feet—and took his spear in his hand.

Neither could Menelaus sleep, for he too boded ill for the Argives who for his sake had sailed from far over the seas to fight the Trojans. He covered his broad back with the skin of a spotted panther, put a casque of bronze upon his head, and took his spear in his brawny hand. Then he went to rouse his brother, who was by far the most powerful of the Achaens, and was honored by the people as though he were a god. He found him by the stern of his ship already putting his goodly array about his shoulders, and right glad was he that his brother had come.

Menelaus spoke first. "Why," said he, "my dear brother, are you thus arming? Are you going to send any of our comrades to exploit the Trojans? I greatly fear that no one will do you this service, and spy upon the enemy alone in the dead of night. It will be a deed of great daring."

And King Agamemnon answered: "Menelaus, we both of us need shrewd counsel to save the Argives and our ships, for Zeus has changed his mind, and inclines towards Hector's sacrifices rather than ours. I never saw nor heard tell of any man as having wrought such ruin in one day as Hector has now wrought against the sons of the Achaeans—and that too of his own unaided self, for he is son neither to god nor goddess. The Argives will rue it long and deeply. Run, therefore, with all speed by the line of the ships and call Ajax and Idomeneus. Meanwhile I will go to Nestor, and bid him rise and go about among the companies of our sentinels to give them their instructions. They will listen to him sooner than to any man, for his own son, and Meriones, brother in arms to Idomeneus, are captains over them. It was to them more particularly that we gave this charge."

Menelaus replied: "How do I take your meaning? Am I to stay with them and wait your coming, or shall I return here as soon as I have given your orders?" "Wait," answered King Agamemnon, "for there are so many paths about the camp that we might miss one another. Call every man on your way, and bid him be stirring. Name him by his lineage and by his father's name, give each all titular observance, and stand not too much upon your own dignity. We must take our full share of toil, for at our birth Zeus laid this heavy burden upon us."

With these instructions he sent his brother on his way, and went on to Nestor, shepherd of his people. He found him sleeping in his tent hard by his own ship. His goodly armor lay beside him—his shield, his two spears, and his helmet; beside him also lay the gleaming girdle with which the old man girded himself when he armed to lead his people into battle—for his age stayed him not. He raised himself on his elbow and looked up at Agamemnon. "Who is it," said he, "that goes thus about the host and the ships alone and in the dead of night, when men are sleeping? Are you looking for one of your mules or for some comrade? Do not stand there and say nothing, but speak. What is your business?"

And Agamemnon answered: "Nestor, son of Neleus, honor to the Achaean name, it is I, Agamemnon, son of Atreus, on whom Zeus has laid labor and sorrow so long as there is breath in my body and my limbs carry me. I am thus abroad because sleep sits not upon my eyelids, but my heart is big with war and with the jeopardy of the Achaeans. I am in great fear for the Danaans. I am at sea, and without sure counsel; my heart beats as though it would leap out of my body, and my limbs fail me. If then you can do anything—for you too cannot sleep—let us go the round of the watch, and see whether they are drowsy with toil and sleeping to the neglect of their duty. The enemy is encamped hard by, and we know not but he may attack us by night."

Nestor replied: "Most noble son of Atreus, king of men, Agamemnon, Zeus will not do all for Hector that Hector thinks he will. He will have troubles yet in plenty if Achilles will lay aside his anger. I will go with you, and we will rouse others, either the son of Tydeus, or Odysseus, or fleet Ajax and the valiant son of Phyleus. Someone had also better go and call Ajax and King Idomeneus, for their ships are not near at hand but the farthest of all. I cannot however refrain from blaming Menelaus, much as I love him and respect him—and I will say so plainly, even at the risk of offending you—for sleeping and leaving all this trouble to yourself. He ought to be going about imploring aid from all the princes of the Achaeans, for we are in extreme danger."

And Agamemnon answered: "Sir, you may sometimes blame him justly, for he is often remiss and unwilling to exert himself—not indeed from sloth, nor yet heedlessness, but because he looks to me and expects me to take the lead. On this occasion, however, he was awake before I was, and came to me of his own accord. I have already sent him to call the very men whom you have named. And now let us be going. We shall find them with the watch outside the gates, for it was there I said that we would meet them."

"In that case," answered Nestor, "the Argives will not blame him nor disobey his orders when he urges them to fight or gives them instructions."

With this he put on his shirt, and bound his sandals about his comely feet. He buckled on his purple coat, of two thicknesses, large, and of a rough shaggy texture, grasped his redoubtable bronze-shod spear, and wended his way along the line of the Achaean ships. First he called loudly to Odysseus, peer of gods in counsel, and woke him, for he was soon roused by the sound of the battle cry. He came outside his tent and said: "Why do you go thus alone about the host, and along the line of the ships in the stillness of the night? What is it that you find so urgent?" And Nestor, knight of Gerene, answered: "Odysseus, noble son of Laertes, take it not amiss, for the Achaeans are in great straits. Come with me and let us wake some other, who may advise well with us whether we shall fight or fly."

On this Odysseus went at once into his tent, put his shield about his shoulders and came out with them. First they went to Diomed, son of Tydeus, and found him outside his tent clad in his armor with his comrades sleeping round him and using their shields as pillows; as for their spears, they stood upright on the spikes of their butts that were driven into the ground, and the burnished bronze flashed afar like the lightning of father Zeus. The hero was sleeping upon the skins of an ox, with a piece of fine carpet under his head. Nestor went up to him and stirred him with his heel to rouse him, upbraiding him and urging him to bestir himself. "Wake up," he exclaimed, "son of Tydeus. How can you sleep on in this way? Can you not see that the Trojans are encamped on the brow of the plain hard by our ships with but a little space between us and them?"

On these words Diomed leaped up instantly and said, "Old man, your heart is of iron; you rest not one moment from your labors. Are there no younger men among the Achaeans who could go about to rouse the princes? There is no tiring you."

And Nestor, knight of Gerene, made answer: "My son, all that you have said is true. I have good sons, and also much people who might call the chieftains, but the Achaeans are in the gravest danger. Life and death are balanced as it were on the edge of a razor. Go then, for you are younger than I, and of your courtesy rouse Ajax and the fleet son of Phyleus."

Diomed threw the skin of a great tawny lion about his shoulders—a skin that reached his feet—and grasped his spear. When he had roused the heroes, he brought them back with him; they then went the round of those who were on guard, and found the captains not sleeping at their posts but wakeful and sitting with their arms about them. As sheep dogs that watch their flocks when they are yarded, and hear a wild beast coming through the mountain forest towards them—forthwith there is a hue and cry of dogs and men, and slumber is broken—even so was sleep chased from the eyes of the Achaeans as they kept the watches of the wicked night, for they turned constantly towards the plain whenever they heard any stir among the Trojans. The old man was glad and bade them be of good cheer. "Watch on, my children," said he, "and let not sleep get hold upon you, lest our enemies triumph over us."

With this he passed the trench, and with him the other chiefs of the Achaeans who had been called to the council. Meriones and the brave son of Nestor went also, for the princes bade them. When they were beyond the trench that was dug round the wall they held their meeting on the open ground where there was a space clear of corpses, for it was here that when night fell Hector had turned back from his onslaught on the Argives. They sat down, therefore, and held debate with one another.

Nestor spoke first. "My friends," said he, "is there any man bold enough to venture among the Trojans, and cut off some straggler, or bring us news of what the enemy mean to do—whether they will stay here by the ships away from the city, or whether, now that they have worsted the Achaeans, they will retire within their walls. If he could learn all this and come back safely here, his fame would be high as heaven in the mouths of all men, and he would be rewarded richly; for the chiefs from all our ships would each of them give him a black ewe with her lamb—which is a present of surpassing value—and he would be asked as a guest to all feasts and clan gatherings."

They all held their peace, but Diomed of the loud war cry spoke saying: "Nestor, gladly will I visit the host of the Trojans over against us, but if another will go with me I shall do so in greater confidence and comfort. When two men are together, one of them may see some opportunity which the other has not caught sight of; if a man is alone he is less full of resources, and his wit is weaker."

On this several offered to go with Diomed. The two Ajaxes, servants of Ares, Meriones, and the son of Nestor all wanted to go, so did Menelaus, son of Atreus; Odysseus also wished to go among the host of the Trojans, for he was ever full of daring, and thereon Agamemnon, king of men, spoke thus: "Diomed," said he, "son of Tydeus, man after my own heart, choose your comrade for yourself—take the best man of those that have offered, for many would now go with you. Do not through delicacy reject the better man, and take the worst out of respect for his lineage, because he is of more royal blood."

He said this because he feared for Menelaus. Diomed answered: "If you bid me take the man of my own choice, how in that case can I fail to think of Odysseus, than whom there is no man more eager to face all kinds of danger—and Pallas Athene loves him well? If he were to go with me we should pass safely through fire itself, for he is quick to see and understand."

"Son of Tydeus," replied Odysseus, "say neither good nor ill about me, for you are among Argives who know me well. Let us be going, for the night wanes and dawn is at hand. The stars have gone forward, two-thirds of the night are already spent, and the third is alone left us."

They then put on their armor. Brave Thrasymedes provided the son of Tydeus with a sword and a shield (for he had left his own at his ship) and on his head he set a helmet of bull's hide without either peak or crest; it is called a skull-cap and is a common headgear. Meriones found a bow and quiver for Odysseus, and on his head he set a leathern helmet that was lined with a strong plaiting of leathern thongs, while on the outside it was thickly studded with boar's teeth, well and skillfully set into it; next the head there was an inner lining of felt. This helmet had been stolen by Autolycus out of Eleon when he broke into the house of Amyntor, son of Ormenus. He gave it to Amphidamas of Cythera to take to Scandea, and Amphidamas gave it as a guest-gift to Molus, who gave it to his son Meriones; and now it was set upon the head of Odysseus.

When the pair had armed, they set out, and left the other chieftains behind them. Pallas Athene sent them a heron by the wayside upon their right hands; they could not see it for the darkness, but they heard its cry. Odysseus was glad when he heard it and prayed to Athene: "Hear me," he cried, "daughter of aegis-bearing Zeus, you who spy out all my ways and who are with me in all my hardships! Befriend me in this mine hour, and grant that we may return to the ships covered with glory after having achieved some mighty exploit that shall bring sorrow to the Trojans."

. Then Diomed of the loud war cry also prayed: "Hear me too," said he, "daughter of Zeus, unweariable; be with me even as you were with my noble father Tydeus when he went to Thebes as envoy sent by the Achaeans. He left the Achaeans by the banks of the river Aesopus, and went to the city bearing a message of peace to the Cadmeians. On his return thence, with your help, goddess, he did great deeds of daring, for you were his ready helper. Even so guide me and guard me now, and in return I will offer you in sacrifice a broad-browed heifer of a year old, unbroken, and never yet brought by man under the yoke. I will gild her horns and will offer her up to you in sacrifice."

Thus they prayed, and Pallas Athene heard their prayer. When they had done praying to the daughter of great Zeus, they went their way like two lions prowling by night amid the armor and bloodstained bodies of them that had fallen.

Neither again did Hector let the Trojans sleep; for he too called the princes and councilors of the Trojans that he might set his counsel before them. "Is there one," said he, "who for a great reward will do me the service of which I will tell you? He shall be well paid if he will. I will give him a chariot and a couple of horses, the fleetest that can be found at the ships of the Achaeans, if he will dare this thing; and he will win infinite honor to boot. He must go to the ships and find out whether they are still guarded as heretofore, or whether now that we have beaten them the Achaeans design to fly, and through sheer exhaustion are neglecting to keep their watches."

They all held their peace; but there was among the Trojans a certain man named Dolon, son of Eumedes, the famous herald—a man rich in gold and bronze. He was ill-favored, but a good runner, and was an only son among five sisters. He it was that now addressed the Trojans. "I, Hector," said he, "will go to the ships and will exploit them. But first hold up your scepter and swear that you will give me the chariot, bedight with bronze, and the horses that now carry the noble son of Peleus. I will make you a good scout, and will not fail you. I will go through the host from one end to the other till I come to the ship of Agamemnon, where I take it the princes of the Achaeans are now consulting whether they shall fight or fly."

When he had done speaking Hector held up his scepter, and swore him his oath, saying, "May Zeus, the thundering husband of Hera, bear witness that no other Trojan but yourself shall mount those steeds, and that you shall have your will with them forever."

The oath he swore was bootless, but it made Dolon more keen on going. He hung his bow over his shoulder, and as an overall he wore the skin of a gray wolf, while on his head he set a cap of ferret skin. Then he took a pointed

javelin, and left the camp for the ships, but he was not to return with any news
for Hector. When he had left the horses and the troops behind him, he made
all speed on his way, but Odysseus perceived his coming and said to Diomed:
"Diomed, here is someone from the camp. I am not sure whether he is a spy,
or whether it is some thief who would plunder the bodies of the dead; let him
get a little past us, we can then spring upon him and take him. If, however, he
is too quick for us, go after him with your spear and hem him in towards the
ships away from the Trojan camp, to prevent his getting back to the town."

With this they turned out of their way and lay down among the corpses.
Dolon suspected nothing and soon passed them, but when he had got about as
far as the distance by which a mule-ploughed furrow exceeds one that has
been ploughed by oxen (for mules can plough fallow land quicker than oxen)
they ran after him, and when he heard their footsteps he stood still, for he
made sure they were friends from the Trojan camp come by Hector's order to
bid him return. When, however, they were only a spear's cast, or less, away
from him, he saw that they were enemies and ran away as fast as his legs could
take him. The others gave chase at once, and as a couple of well-trained
hounds press forward after a doe or hare that runs screaming in front of them,
even so did the son of Tydeus and Odysseus pursue Dolon and cut him off
from his own people. But when he had fled so far towards the ships that he
would soon have fallen in with the outposts, Athene infused fresh strength
into the son of Tydeus for fear some other of the Achaeans might have the
glory of being first to hit him, and he might himself be only second. He there-
fore sprang forward with his spear and said, "Stand, or I shall throw my spear,
and in that case I shall soon make an end of you."

He threw as he spoke, but missed his aim on purpose. The dart flew over
the man's right shoulder, and then stuck in the ground. He stood stock still,
trembling and in great fear; his teeth chattered, and he turned pale with fear.
The two came breathless up to him and seized his hands, whereon he began
to weep and said: 'Take me alive; I will ransom myself. We have great store

of gold, bronze, and wrought iron, and from this my father will satisfy you with a very large ransom, should he hear of my being alive at the ships of the Achaeans."

"Fear not," replied Odysseus, "let no thought of death be in your mind; but tell me, and tell me true, why are you thus going about alone in the dead of night away from your camp and towards the ships, while other men are sleeping? Is it to plunder the bodies of the slain, or did Hector send you to spy out what was going on at the ships? Or did you come here of your own mere notion?"

Dolon answered, his limbs trembling beneath him: "Hector, with his vain flattering promises, lured me from my better judgment. He said he would give me the horses of the noble son of Peleus and his bronze bedizened chariot; he bade me go through the darkness of the flying night, get close to the enemy, and find out whether the ships are still guarded as heretofore, or whether, now that we have beaten them, the Achaeans design to fly, and through sheer exhaustion are neglecting to keep their watches."

Odysseus smiled at him and answered: "You had indeed set your heart upon a great reward, but the horses of the descendant of Aeacus are hardly to be kept in hand or driven by any other mortal man than Achilles himself, whose mother was an immortal. But tell me, and tell me true, where did you leave Hector when you started? Where lies his armor and his horses? How, too, are the watches and sleeping ground of the Trojans ordered? What are their plans? Will they stay here by the ships and away from the city or, now that they have worsted the Achaeans, will they retire within their walls?"

And Dolon answered: "I will tell you truly all. Hector and the other councilors are now holding conference by the monument of great Ilus, away from the general tumult; as for the guards about which you ask me, there is no chosen watch to keep guard over the host. The Trojans have their watchfires, for they are bound to have them. They, therefore, are awake and keep each other to their duty as sentinels; but the allies who have come from other places are asleep and leave it to the Trojans to keep guard, for their wives and children are not here."

Odysseus then said: "Now tell me, are they sleeping among the Trojan troops, or do they lie apart? Explain this that I may understand it."

"I will tell you truly all," replied Dolon. 'To the seaward lie the Carians, the Paeonian bowmen, the Leleges, the Cauconians, and the noble Pelasgi. The Lysians and proud Mysians, with the Phrygians and Meonians, have their place on the side towards Thymbra; but why ask about all this? If you want to find your way into the host of the Trojans, there are the Thracians, who have lately come here and lie apart from the others at the far end of the camp; and they have Rhesus, son of Eïoneus, for their king. His horses are the finest and strongest that I have ever seen; they are whiter than snow and fleeter than any wind that blows. His chariot is bedight with silver and gold, and he has brought his marvelous golden armor, of the rarest workmanship—too splendid for any mortal man to carry, and meet only for the gods. Now, therefore, take me to the ships or bind me securely here, until you come back and have proved my words whether they be false or true."

Diomed looked sternly at him and answered: "Think not, Dolon, for all the good information you have given us, that you shall escape now you are in our hands, for if we ransom you or let you go, you will come some second time to the ships of the Achaeans either as a spy or as an open enemy, but if I kill you and make an end of you, you will give no more trouble."

On this Dolon would have caught him by the beard to beseech him further, but Diomed struck him in the middle of his neck with his sword and cut through both sinews so that his head fell rolling in the dust while he was yet speaking. They took the ferret-skin cap from his head, and also the wolf skin, the bow, and his long spear. Odysseus hung them up aloft in honor of Athene, the goddess of plunder, and prayed saying, "Accept these, goddess, for we give them to you in preference to all the gods in Olympus: therefore speed us still further towards the horses and sleeping ground of the Thracians."

With these words he took up the spoils and set them upon a tamarisk tree, and they marked the place by pulling up reeds and gathering boughs of tamarisk that they might not miss it as they came back through the flying hours of darkness. The two then went onwards amid the fallen armor and the blood, and came presently to the company of Thracian soldiers, who were sleeping, tired out with their day's toil. Their goodly armor was lying on the ground beside them all orderly in three rows, and each man had his yoke of horses beside him. Rhesus was sleeping in the middle, and hard by him his horses were made fast to the topmost rim of his chariot. Odysseus from some way off saw him and said: "This, Diomed, is the man, and these are the horses about which Dolon, whom we killed, told us. Do your very utmost; dally not about your armor, but loose the horses at once—or else kill the men yourself, while I see to the horses."

Thereon Athene put courage into the heart of Diomed, and he smote them right and left. They made a hideous groaning as they were being hacked about, and the earth was red with their blood. As a lion springs furiously upon a flock of sheep or goats when he finds them without their shepherd, so did the son of Tydeus set upon the Thracian soldiers till he had killed twelve. As he killed them Odysseus came and drew them aside by their feet one by one, that the horses might go forward freely without being frightened as they passed over the dead bodies, for they were not yet used to them. When the son of Tydeus came to the king, he killed him too (which made thirteen), as he was breathing hard, for by the counsel of Athene an evil dream, the seed of Oeneus, hovered that night over his head. Meanwhile Odysseus untied the horses, made them fast one to another and drove them off, striking them with his bow, for he had forgotten to take the whip from the chariot. Then he whistled as a sign to Diomed.

But Diomed stayed where he was, thinking what other daring deed he might accomplish. He was doubting whether to take the chariot in which the king's armor was lying, and draw it out by the pole, or to lift the armor out and carry it off; or whether again, he should not kill some more Thracians. While he was thus hesitating Athene came up to him and said, "Get back, Diomed, to the ships, or you may be driven thither, should some other god rouse the Trojans."

Diomed knew that it was the goddess, and at once sprang upon the horses. Odysseus beat them with his bow and they flew onward to the ships of the Achaeans.

But Apollo kept no blind lookout when he saw Athene with the son of Tydeus. He was angry with her, and coming to the host of the Trojans he roused Hippocoön, a counselor of the Thracians and a noble kinsman of Rhesus. He started up out of his sleep and saw that the horses were no longer in their place, and that the men were gasping in their death agony; on this he groaned aloud, and called upon his friend by name. Then the whole Trojan camp was in an uproar as the people kept hurrying together, and they marveled at the deeds of the heroes who had now got away towards the ships.

When they reached the place where they had killed Hector's scout, Odysseus stayed his horses, and the son of Tydeus, leaping to the ground, placed the bloodstained spoils in the hands of Odysseus and remounted: then he lashed the horses onwards, and they flew forward nothing loath towards the ships, as though of their own free will. Nestor was first to hear the tramp of their feet. "My friends," said he, "princes and counselors of the Argives, shall I guess right or wrong?—but I must say what I think: there is a sound in my ears as of the tramp of horses. I hope it may be Diomed and Odysseus driving in horses from the Trojans, but I much fear that the bravest of the Argives may have come to some harm at their hands."

He had hardly done speaking when the two men came in and dismounted, whereon the others shook hands right gladly with them and congratulated them. Nestor, knight of Gerene, was first to question them. "Tell me," said he, "renowned Odysseus, how did you two come by these horses? Did you steal in among the Trojan forces, or did some god meet you and give them to you?

They are like sunbeams. I am well conversant with the Trojans, for old warrior though I am I never hold back by the ships, but I never yet saw or heard of such horses as these are. Surely some god must have met you and given them to you, for you are both of you dear to Zeus, and to Zeus' daughter Athene."

And Odysseus answered, "Nestor, son of Neleus, honor to the Achaean name, heaven, if it so will, can give us even better horses than these, for the gods are far mightier than we are. These horses, however, about which you ask me, are freshly come from Thrace. Diomed killed their king with the twelve bravest of his companions. Hard by the ships we took a thirteenth man—a scout whom Hector and the other Trojans had sent as a spy upon our ships."

He laughed as he spoke and drove the horses over the ditch, while the other Achaeans followed him gladly. When they reached the strongly built quarters of the son of Tydeus, they tied the horses with thongs of leather to the manger, where the steeds of Diomed stood eating their sweet com, but Odysseus hung the bloodstained spoils of Dolon at the stern of his ship, that they might prepare a sacred offering to Athene. As for themselves, they went into the sea and washed the sweat from their bodies, and from their necks and thighs. When the sea water had taken all the sweat from off them, and had refreshed them, they went into the baths and washed themselves. After they had so done and had anointed themselves with oil, they sat down to table, and drawing from a full mixing bowl, made a drink offering of wine to Athene.

Book XI

*In the morning when the battle is resumed, Agamemnon is wounded and
retires to the ships. Hector, encouraged by Zeus, leads the Trojans forward.
Diomed attacks and stuns Hector, but is himself wounded by Paris and
leaves the field. Odysseus and the physician Machaon are also wounded.
Ajax tries to guard the Greek retreat while Nestor suggests to Achilles'
friend Patroclus that he fight in Achilles' armor to deceive the Trojans.*

AND NOW AS DAWN ROSE FROM HER COUCH BESIDE TITHONUS, HARBINGER
of light alike to mortals and immortals, Zeus sent fierce Discord
with the ensign of war in her hands to the ships of the Achaeans.
She took her stand by the huge black hull of Odysseus' ship which was middle-
most of all, so that her voice might carry furthest on either side, on the one
hand towards the tents of Ajax, son of Telamon, and on the other towards
those of Achilles—for these two heroes, well-assured of their own strength,
had valorously drawn up their ships at the two ends of the line. There she took
her stand, and raised a cry both loud and shrill that filled the Achaeans with
courage, giving them heart to fight resolutely and with all their might, so that
they had rather stay there and do battle than go home in their ships.

The son of Atreus shouted aloud and bade the Argives gird themselves for
battle while he put on his armor. First he girded his goodly greaves about his
legs, making them fast with ankle-clasps of silver; and about his chest he set
the breastplate which Cinyras had once given him as a guest-gift. It had been
noised abroad as far as Cyprus that the Achaeans were about to sail for Troy,

and therefore he gave it to the king. It had ten courses of dark cyanus, twelve of gold, and ten of tin. There were serpents of cyanus that reared themselves up towards the neck, three upon either side, like the rainbows which the son of Cronus has set in heaven as a sign to mortal men. About his shoulders he threw his sword, studded with bosses of gold; and the scabbard was of silver with a chain of gold wherewith to hang it. He took moreover the richly dight shield that covered his body when he was in battle—fair to see, with ten circles of bronze running all round it. On the body of the shield there were twenty bosses of white tin, with another of dark cyanus in the middle: this last was made to show a Gorgon's head, fierce and grim, with Rout and Panic on either side. The band for the arm to go through was of silver, on which there was a writhing snake of cyanus with three heads that sprang from a single neck, and went in and out among one another. On his head Agamemnon set a helmet, with a peak before and behind, and four plumes of horsehair that nodded menacingly above it. Then he grasped two redoubtable bronze-shod spears, and the gleam of his armor shot from him as a flame into the firmament, while Hera and Athene thundered in honor of the king of rich Mycenae.

Every man now left his horses in charge of his charioteer to hold them in readiness by the trench, while he went into battle on foot clad in full armor, and a mighty uproar rose on high into the dawning. The chiefs were armed and at the trench before the horses got there, but these came up presently. The son of Cronus sent a portent of evil sound about their host, and the dew fell red with blood, for he was about to send many a brave man hurrying down to Hades.

The Trojans, on the other side upon the rising slope of the plain, were gathered round great Hector, noble Polydamas, Aeneas who was honored by the Trojans like an immortal, and the three sons of Antenor, Polybus, Agenor, and young Acamas, beauteous as a god. Hector's round shield showed in the front rank, and as some baneful star that shines for a moment through a rent in the clouds and is again hidden beneath them; even so was Hector now seen in the front ranks and now again in the hindermost, and his bronze armor gleamed like the lightning of aegis-bearing Zeus.

And now as a band of reapers mow swathes of wheat or barley upon a rich man's land, and the sheaves fall thick before them, even so did the Trojans and Achaeans fall upon one another; they were in no mood for yielding but fought like wolves, and neither side got the better of the other. Discord was glad as she beheld them, for she was the only god that went among them; the others were not there, but stayed quietly each in his own home among the dells and valleys of Olympus. All of them blamed the son of Cronos for wanting to give victory to the Trojans, but father Zeus heeded them not: he held aloof from all, and sat apart in his all-glorious majesty, looking down upon the city of the Trojans, the ships of the Achaeans, the gleam of bronze, and alike upon the slayers and on the slain.

Now so long as the day waxed and it was still morning, their darts rained thick on one another and the people perished, but as the hour drew nigh when a woodman working in some mountain forest will get his midday meal—for he has felled till his hands are weary; he is tired out, and must now have food—then the Danaans with a cry that rang through all their ranks, broke the battalions of the enemy. Agamemnon led them on, and slew first Bienor, a leader of his people, and afterwards his comrade and charioteer Oïleus, who sprang from his chariot and was coming full towards him; but Agamemnon struck him on the forehead with his spear; his bronze vizor was of no avail against the weapon, which pierced both bronze and bone, so that his brains were battered in and he was killed in full fight.

Agamemnon stripped their shirts from off them and left them with their breasts all bare to lie where they had fallen. He then went on to kill Isus and Antiphus, two sons of Priam, the one a bastard, the other born in wedlock; they were in the same chariot—the bastard driving, while noble Antiphus fought beside him. Achilles had once taken both of them prisoners in the glades of Ida, and had bound them with fresh withes as they were shepherding, but he had taken a ransom for them; now, however, Agamemnon, son of Atreus, smote Isus in the chest above the nipple with his spear, while he struck Antiphus hard by the ear and threw him from his chariot. Forthwith he stripped their goodly armor from off them and recognized them, for he had already seen them at the ships when Achilles brought them in from Ida. As a lion fastens on the fawns of a hind and crushes them in his great jaws, robbing them of their tender life while he is on his way back to his lair—the hind can do nothing for them even though she be close by, for she is in an agony of fear, and flies through the thick forest, sweating, and at her utmost speed before the mighty monster—so, no man of the Trojans could help Isus and Antiphus, for they were themselves flying in panic before the Argives.

Then King Agamemnon took the two sons of Antimachus, Pisander and brave Hippolochus. It was Antimachus who had been foremost in preventing Helen's being restored to Menelaus, for he was largely bribed by Paris; and now Agamemnon took his two sons, both in the same chariot, trying to bring their horses to a stand—for they had lost hold of the reins and the horses were mad with fear. The son of Atreus sprang upon them like a lion, and the pair besought him from their chariot. "Take us alive," they cried, "son of Atreus, and you shall receive a great ransom for us. Our father Antimachus has great store of gold, bronze, and wrought iron, and from this he will satisfy you with a very large ransom should he hear of our being alive at the ships of the Achaeans."

With such piteous words and tears did they beseech the king, but they heard no pitiful answer in return. "If," said Agamemnon, "you are sons of Antimachus, who once at a council of Trojans proposed that Menelaus and Odysseus, who had come to you as envoys, should be killed and not suffered to return, you shall now pay for the foul iniquity of your father."

As he spoke he felled Pisander from his chariot to the earth, smiting him on the chest with his spear, so that he lay face uppermost upon the ground. Hippolochus fled, but him too did Agamemnon smite. He cut off his hands and his head—which he sent rolling in among the crowd as though it were a ball. There he let them both lie, and wherever the ranks were thickest thither he flew, while the other Achaeans followed. Foot soldiers drove the foot soldiers of the foe in rout before them, and slew them. Horsemen did the like by horsemen, and the thundering tramp of the horses raised a cloud of dust from off the plain. King Agamemnon followed after, ever slaying them and cheering on the Achaeans. As when some mighty forest is all ablaze—the eddying gusts whirl fire in all directions till the thickets shrivel and are consumed before the blast of the flame—even so fell the heads of the flying Trojans before Agamemnon, son of Atreus, and many a noble pair of steeds drew an empty chariot along the highways of war, for lack of drivers who were lying on the plain, more useful now to vultures than to their wives.

Zeus drew Hector away from the darts and dust, with the carnage and din of battle; but the son of Atreus sped onwards, calling out lustily to the Danaans. They flew on by the tomb of old Ilus, son of Dardanus, in the middle of the plain, and past the place of the wild fig tree making always for the city—the son of Atreus still shouting, and with hands all bedrabbled in gore; but when they had reached the Scaean gates and the oak tree, there they halted and waited for the others to come up. Meanwhile the Trojans kept on flying over the middle of the plain like a herd of cows maddened with fright when a lion has attacked them in the dead of night—he springs on one of them, seizes her neck in the grip of his strong teeth, and then laps up her blood and gorges himself upon her entrails—even so did King Agamemnon, son of Atreus, pursue the foe, ever slaughtering the hindmost as they fled pell-mell before him. Many a man was flung headlong from his chariot by the hand of the son of Atreus, for he wielded his spear with fury.

But when he was just about to reach the high wall and the city, the father of gods and men came down from heaven and took his seat, thunderbolt in hand, upon the crest of many-fountained Ida. He then told Iris of the golden wings to carry a message for him. "Go," said he, "fleet Iris, and speak thus to

Hector—say that so long as he sees Agamemnon heading his men and making havoc of the Trojan ranks, he is to keep aloof and bid the others bear the brunt of the battle, but when Agamemnon is wounded either by spear or arrow, and takes to his chariot, then will I vouchsafe him strength to slay till he reach the ships and night falls at the going down of the sun."

Iris hearkened and obeyed. Down she went to strong Ilium from the crests of Ida, and found Hector, son of Priam, standing by his chariot and horses. Then she said: "Hector, son of Priam, peer of gods in counsel, father Zeus has sent me to bear you this message—so long as you see Agamemnon heading his men and making havoc of the Trojan ranks, you are to keep aloof and bid the others bear the brunt of the battle, but when Agamemnon is wounded either by spear or arrow, and takes to his chariot, then will Zeus vouchsafe you strength to slay till you reach the ships, and till night falls at the going down of the sun."

When she had thus spoken Iris left him, and Hector sprang full-armed from his chariot to the ground, brandishing his spear as he went about everywhere among the host, cheering his men on to fight, and stirring the dread strife of battle. The Trojans then wheeled round, and again met the Achaeans, while the Argives on their part strengthened their battalions. The battle was now in array and they stood face to face with one another, Agamemnon ever pressing forward in his eagerness to be ahead of all others.

Tell me now, ye Muses that dwell in the mansions of Olympus, who, whether of the Trojans or of their allies, was first to face Agamemnon? It was Iphidamas, son of Antenor, a man both brave and of great stature, who was brought up in fertile Thrace, the mother of sheep. Cisses, his mother's father, brought him up in his own house when he was a child—Cisses, father to fair Theano. When he reached manhood, Cisses would have kept him there, and was for giving him his daughter in marriage, but as soon as he had married he set out to fight the Achaeans with twelve ships that followed him: these he had left at Percote and had come on by land to Ilium. He it was that now met

Agamemnon, son of Atreus. When they were close up with one another, the son of Atreus missed his aim, and Iphidamas hit him on the girdle below the cuirass and then flung himself upon him, trusting to his strength of arm. The girdle, however, was not pierced, nor nearly so, for the point of the spear struck against the silver and was turned aside as though it had been lead. King Agamemnon caught it from his hand, and drew it towards him with the fury of a lion. He then drew his sword and killed Iphidamas by striking him on the neck. So there the poor fellow lay, sleeping a sleep as it were of bronze, killed in the defense of his fellow citizens, far from his wedded wife, of whom he had had no joy though he had given much for her: he had given a hundred head of cattle down, and had promised later on to give a thousand sheep and goats mixed, from the countless flocks of which he was possessed. Agamemnon, son of Atreus, then despoiled him, and carried off his armor into the host of the Achaeans.

When noble Coön, Antenor's eldest son, saw this, sore indeed were his eyes at the sight of his fallen brother. Unseen by Agamemnon he got beside him, spear in hand, and wounded him in the middle of his arm below the elbow, the point of the spear going right through the arm. Agamemnon was convulsed with pain, but still not even for this did he leave off struggling and fighting, but grasped his spear that flew as fleet as the wind, and sprang upon Coön who was trying to drag off the body of his brother—his father's son—by the foot, and was crying for help to all the bravest of his comrades; but Agamemnon struck him with a bronze-shod spear and killed him as he was dragging the dead body through the press of men under cover of his shield: he then cut off his head, standing over the body of Iphidamas. Thus did the sons of Antenor meet their fate at the hands of the son of Atreus, and go down into the house of Hades.

As long as the blood still welled warm from his wound, Agamemnon went about attacking the ranks of the enemy with spear and sword and with great handfuls of stone, but when the blood had ceased to flow and the wound grew dry, the pain became great. As the sharp pangs which the Eilithuiae, goddesses of childbirth, daughters of Hera and dispensers of cruel pain, send upon a woman when she is in labor—even so sharp were the pangs of the son of Atreus. He sprang on to his chariot, and bade his charioteer drive to the ships, for he was in great agony. With a loud clear voice he shouted to the Danaans, "My friends, princes and counselors of the Argives, defend the ships yourselves, for Zeus has not suffered me to fight the whole day through against the Trojans."

With this the charioteer turned his horses towards the ships, and they flew forward nothing loath. Their chests were white with foam and their bellies with dust, as they drew the wounded king out of the battle.

When Hector saw Agamemnon quit the field, he shouted to the Trojans and Lycians, saying: "Trojans, Lycians, and Dardanian warriors, be men, my friends, and acquit yourselves in battle bravely. Their best man has left them, and Zeus has vouchsafed me a great triumph; charge the foe with your chariots that you may win still greater glory."

With these words he put heart and soul into them all, and as a huntsman hounds his dogs on against a lion or wild boar, even so did Hector, peer of Ares, hound the proud Trojans on against the Achaeans. Full of hope, he plunged in among the foremost, and fell on the fight like some fierce tempest that swoops down upon the sea and lashes its deep blue waters into fury.

What, then, is the full tale of those whom Hector, son of Priam, killed in the hour of triumph which Zeus then vouchsafed him? First Asaeus, Autonoüs, and Opites; Dolops, son of Clytius, Opheltius, and Agelaus; Aesymnus, Orus, and Hipponoüs, steadfast in battle. These chieftains of the Achaeans did Hector slay, and then he fell upon the rank and file. As when the west wind hustles the clouds of the white south and beats them down with the fierceness of its fury—the waves of the sea roll high, and the spray is flung aloft in the rage of the wandering wind—even so thick were the heads of them that fell by the hand of Hector.

All had then been lost and no help for it, and the Achaeans would have fled pell-mell to their ships, had not Odysseus cried out to Diomed, "Son of Tydeus, what has happened to us that we thus forget our prowess? Come, my good fellow, stand by my side and help me, we shall be shamed forever if Hector takes the ships."

And Diomed answered, "Come what may, I will stand firm; but we shall have scant joy of it, for Zeus is minded to give victory to the Trojans rather than to us."

With these words he struck Thymbraeus from his chariot to the ground, smiting him in the left breast with his spear, while Odysseus killed Molion who was his squire. These they let lie, now that they had stopped their fighting; the two heroes then went on playing havoc with the foe, like two wild boars that turn in fury and rend the hounds that hunt them. Thus did they turn upon the Trojans and slay them, and the Achaeans were thankful to have breathing time in their flight from Hector.

They then took two princes with their chariot, the two sons of Merops of Percote, who excelled all others in the arts of divination. He had forbidden his sons to go to the war, but they would not obey him, for fate lured them to their fall. Diomed, son of Tydeus, slew them both and stripped them of their armor, while Odysseus killed Hippodamus and Hypeirochus.

And now the son of Cronus as he looked down from Ida ordained that neither side should have the advantage, and they kept on killing one another. The son of Tydeus speared Agastrophus, son of Paeon, in the hip joint with his spear. His chariot was not at hand for him to fly with, so blindly confident had he been. His squire was in charge of it at some distance and he was fighting on foot among the foremost until he lost his life. Hector soon marked the havoc Diomed and Odysseus were making, and bore down upon them with a loud cry, followed by the Trojan ranks. Brave Diomed was dismayed when he saw them, and said to Odysseus who was beside him: "Great Hector is bearing down upon us and we shall be undone; let us stand firm and wait his onset."

He poised his spear as he spoke and hurled it, nor did he miss his mark. He had aimed at Hector's head near the top of his helmet, but bronze was turned by bronze, and Hector was untouched, for the spear was stayed by the vizored helm made with three plates of metal, which Phoebus Apollo had given him. Hector sprang back with a great bound under cover of the ranks. He fell on his knees and propped himself with his brawny hand leaning on the ground, for darkness had fallen on his eyes. The son of Tydeus, having thrown his spear, dashed in among the foremost fighters to the place where he had seen it strike the ground. Meanwhile Hector recovered himself and springing back into his chariot mingled with the crowd, by which means he saved his life. But Diomed made at him with his spear and said: "Dog, you have again got away though death was close on your heels. Phoebus Apollo, to whom I ween you pray ere you go into battle, has again saved you; nevertheless I will meet you and make an end of you hereafter, if there is any god who will stand by me too and be my helper. For the present I must pursue those whom I can lay hands on."

As he spoke he began stripping the spoils from the son of Paeon, but Paris, husband of lovely Helen, aimed an arrow at him, leaning against a pillar of the monument which men had raised to Ilus, son of Dardanus, a ruler in days of old. Diomed had taken the cuirass from off the breast of Agastrophus, his heavy helmet also, and the shield from off his shoulders, when Paris drew his bow and let fly an arrow that sped not from his hand in vain, but pierced the flat of Diomed's right foot, going right through it and fixing itself in the ground. Thereon Paris with a hearty laugh sprang forward from his hiding place, and taunted him saying: "You are wounded—my arrow has not been shot in vain. Would that it had hit you in the belly and killed you, for thus the Trojans, who fear you as goats fear a lion, would have had a truce from evil."

Diomed all undaunted answered: "Archer, you who without your bow are nothing, slanderer and seducer, if you were to be tried in single combat fighting in full armor, your bow and your arrows would serve you in little stead. Vain is your boast in that you have scratched the sole of my foot. I care no more than if a girl or some silly boy had hit me. A worthless coward can inflict but a light wound. When I wound a man, though I but graze his skin, it is another matter, for my weapon will lay him low. His wife will tear her cheeks for grief and his children will be fatherless: there will he rot, reddening the earth with his blood, and vultures, not women, will gather round him."

Thus he spoke, but Odysseus came up and stood over him. Under this cover he sat down to draw the arrow from his foot, and sharp was the pain he suffered as he did so. Then he sprang on to his chariot and bade the charioteer drive him to the ships, for he was sick at heart.

Odysseus was now alone; not one of the Argives stood by him, for they were all panic-stricken. "Alas," said he to himself in his dismay, "what will become of me? It is ill if I turn and fly before these odds, but it will be worse if I am left alone and taken prisoner, for the son of Cronus has struck the rest of the Danaans with panic. But why talk to myself in this way? Well do I know that though cowards quit the field, a hero, whether he wound or be wounded, must stand firm and hold his own."

While he was thus in two minds, the ranks of the Trojans advanced and hemmed him in, and bitterly did they come to rue it. As hounds and lusty youths set upon a wild boar that sallies from his lair whetting his white tusks—they attack him from every side and can hear the gnashing of his jaws, but for all his fierceness they still hold their ground—even so furiously did the Trojans attack Odysseus. First he sprang spear in hand upon Deïopites and wounded him on the shoulder with a downward blow; then he killed Thoön and Ennomus. After these he struck Chersidamas in the loins under his shield as he had just sprung down from his chariot; so he fell in the dust and clutched the earth in the hollow of his hand. These he let lie, and went on to wound Charops, son of Hippasus, own brother to noble Socus. Socus, hero that he was, made all speed to help him, and when he was close to Odysseus, he said, "Far-famed Odysseus, insatiable of craft and toil, this day you shall either boast of having killed both the sons of Hippasus and stripped them of their armor, or you shall fall before my spear."

With these words he struck the shield of Odysseus. The spear went through the shield and passed on through his richly wrought cuirass, tearing the flesh from his side, but Pallas Athene did not suffer it to pierce the entrails of the hero. Odysseus knew that his hour was not yet come, but he gave ground and said to Socus: "Wretch, you shall now surely die. You have stayed me from fighting further with the Trojans, but you shall now fall by my spear, yielding glory to myself, and your soul to Hades of the noble steeds."

Socus had turned in flight, but as he did so, the spear struck him in the back midway between the shoulders and went right through his chest. He fell heavily to the ground and Odysseus vaunted over him, saying: "O Socus, son of Hippasus, tamer of horses, death has been too quick for you and you have not escaped him. Poor wretch, not even in death shall your father and mother close your eyes, but the ravening vultures shall enshroud you with the flapping of their dark wings and devour you. Whereas even though I fall the Achaeans will give me my due rites of burial."

So saying he drew Socus' heavy spear out of his flesh and from his shield, and the blood welled forth when the spear was withdrawn so that he was much dismayed. When the Trojans saw that Odysseus was bleeding they raised a great shout and came on in a body towards him. He therefore gave ground, and called his comrades to come and help him. Thrice did he cry as loudly as man can cry, and thrice did brave Menelaus hear him. He turned, therefore, to Ajax who was close beside him and said: "Ajax, noble son of Telamon, captain of your people, the cry of Odysseus rings in my ears, as though the Trojans had cut him off and were worsting him while he is single-handed. Let us make our way through the throng; it will be well that we defend him. I fear he may come to harm for all his valor if he be left without support, and the Danaans would miss him sorely."

He led the way and mighty Ajax went with him. The Trojans had gathered round Odysseus like ravenous mountain jackals round the carcass of some horned stag that has been hit with an arrow—the stag has fled at full speed so long as his blood was warm and his strength has lasted, but when the arrow has overcome him, the savage jackals devour him in the shady glades of the forest. Then heaven sends a fierce lion thither, whereon the jackals fly in terror and the lion robs them of their prey—even so did Trojans many and brave gather round crafty Odysseus, but the hero stood at bay and kept them off with his spear. Ajax then came up with his shield before him like a wall and stood hard by, whereon the Trojans fled in all directions. Menelaus took Odysseus by the hand, and led him out of the press while his squire brought up his chariot, but Ajax rushed furiously on the Trojans and killed Doryclus, a bastard son of Priam; then he wounded Pandocus, Lysandrus, Pyrasus, and Pylartes. As some swollen torrent comes rushing in full flood from the mountains on to the plain, big with the rain of heaven—many a dry oak and many a pine does it engulf, and much mud does it bring down and cast into the sea—even so did brave Ajax chase the foe furiously over the plain, slaying both men and horses.

Hector did not yet know what Ajax was doing, for he was fighting on the extreme left of the battle by the banks of the river Scamander, where the carnage was thickest and the war cry loudest round Nestor and brave Idomeneus. Among these Hector was making great slaughter with his spear and furious driving, and was destroying the ranks that were opposed to him. Still the Achaeans would have given no ground, had not Paris, husband of lovely Helen, stayed the prowess of Machaon, shepherd of his people, by wounding him in the right shoulder with a triple-barbed arrow. The Achaeans were in great fear that as the fight had turned against them the Trojans might take him prisoner, and Idomeneus said to Nestor: "Nestor, son of Neleus, honor to the Achaean name, mount your chariot at once. Take Machaon with you and drive your horses to the ships as fast as you can. A physician is worth more than several other men put together, for he can cut out arrows and spread healing herbs."

Nestor, knight of Gerene, did as Idomeneus had counseled. He at once mounted his chariot, and Machaon, son of the famed physician Asclepius, went with him. He lashed his horses and they flew onward nothing loath towards the ships, as though of their own free will.

Then Cebriones, seeing the Trojans in confusion, said to Hector from his place beside him: "Hector, here are we two fighting on the extreme wing of the battle, while the other Trojans are in pell-mell rout, they and their horses. Ajax, son of Telamon, is driving them before him. I know him by the breadth of his shield. Let us turn our chariot and horses thither, where horse and foot are fighting most desperately, and where the cry of battle is loudest."

With this he lashed his goodly steeds, and when they felt the whip they drew the chariot full speed among the Achaeans and Trojans, over the bodies and shields of those that had fallen: the axle was bespattered with blood, and the rail round the car was covered with splashes both from the horses' hoofs and from the tires of the wheels. Hector tore his way through and flung himself into the thick of the fight, and his presence threw the Danaans into confusion, for his spear was not long idle. Nevertheless, though he went among the ranks with sword and spear and throwing great stones, he avoided Ajax, son of Telamon, for Zeus would have been angry with him if he had fought a better man than himself.

Then father Zeus from his high throne struck fear into the heart of Ajax, so that he stood there dazed and threw his shield behind him—looking fearfully at the throng of his foes as though he were some wild beast, and turning hither and thither but crouching slowly backwards. As peasants with their hounds chase a lion from their stockyard, and watch by night to prevent his carrying off the pick of their herd—he makes his greedy spring, but in vain, for the darts from many a strong hand fall thick around him, with burning brands that scare him for all his fury, and when morning comes he slinks foiled and angry away—even so did Ajax, sorely against his will, retreat angrily before the Trojans, fearing for the ships of the Achaeans. Or as some lazy ass that has had many a cudgel broken about his back, when he gets into a field begins eating the corn—boys beat him but he is too many for them, and though they lay about with their sticks they cannot hurt him; still, when he has had his fill they at last drive him from the field—even so did the Trojans and their allies pursue great Ajax, ever smiting the middle of his shield with their darts. Now and again he would turn and show fight, keeping back the battalions of the Trojans, and then he would again retreat; but he prevented any of them from making his way to the ships. Single-handed he stood midway between the Trojans and Achaeans. The spears that sped from their hands stuck some of them in his mighty shield, while many, though thirsting for his blood, fell to the ground ere they could reach him to the wounding of his fair flesh.

Now when Eurypylus, the brave son of Euaemon, saw that Ajax was being overpowered by the rain of arrows, he went up to him and hurled his spear. He struck Apisaon, son of Phausius, in the liver below the midriff, and laid him low. Eurypylus sprang upon him, and stripped the armor from his shoulders; but when Paris saw him, he aimed an arrow at him which struck him in the right thigh. The arrow broke, but the point that was left in the wound dragged on the thigh. He drew back, therefore, under cover of his comrades to save his life, shouting as he did so to the Danaans: "My friends, princes and counselors of the Argives, rally to the defense of Ajax who is being overpowered, and I doubt whether he will come out of the fight alive. Hither, then, to the rescue of great Ajax, son of Telamon."

Even so did he cry when he was wounded; thereon the others came near, and gathered round him, holding their shields upwards from their shoulders so as to give him cover. Ajax then made towards them, and turned round to stand at bay as soon as he had reached his men.

Thus then did they fight as it were a flaming fire. Meanwhile the mares of Neleus, all in a lather with sweat, were bearing Nestor out of the fight, and with him Machaon, shepherd of his people. Achilles saw and took note, for he was standing on the stem of his ship watching the hard stress and struggle of the fight. He called from the ship to his comrade Patroclus, who heard him in the tent and came out looking like Ares himself—here indeed was the beginning of the ill that presently befell him. "Why," said he, "Achilles, do you call me? What do you want with me?" And Achilles answered: "Noble son of Menoetius, man after my own heart, I take it that I shall now have the Achaeans praying at my knees, for they are in great straits. Go, Patroclus, and ask Nestor who it is that he is bearing away wounded from the field; from his back I should say it was Machaon, son of Asclepius, but I could not see his face for the horses went by me at full speed."

Patroclus did as his dear comrade had bidden him, and set off running by the ships and tents of the Achaeans.

When Nestor and Machaon had reached the tents of the son of Neleus, they dismounted, and an esquire, Eurymedon, took the horses from the chariot. The pair then stood in the breeze by the seaside to dry the sweat from their shirts, and when they had so done they came inside and took their seats. Fair Hecamedé, whom Nestor had had awarded to him from Tenedos when Achilles took it, mixed them a mess. She was daughter of wise Arsinoüs, and the Achaeans had given her to Nestor because he excelled all of them in counsel. First she set for them a fair and well-made table that had feet of cyanus. On it there was a vessel of bronze and an onion to give relish to the drink, with honey and cakes of barley meal. There was also a cup of rare workmanship which the old man had brought with him from home, studded with bosses of gold; it had four handles, on each of which there were two golden doves feeding, and it had two feet to stand on. Anyone else would hardly have been able to lift it from the table when it was full, but Nestor could do so quite easily. In this the woman, as fair as a goddess, mixed them a mess with Pramnian wine. She grated goat's-milk cheese into it with a bronze grater, threw in a handful of white barley meal, and having thus prepared the mess she bade them drink it.

When they had done so and had thus quenched their thirst, they fell talking with one another, and at this moment Patroclus appeared at the door.

When the old man saw him he sprang from his seat, seized his hand, led him into the tent, and bade him take his place among them; but Patroclus stood where he was and said, "Noble sir, I may not stay, you cannot persuade me to come in; he that sent me is not one to be trifled with, and he bade me ask who the wounded man was whom you were bearing away from the field. I can now see for myself that he is Machaon, shepherd of his people. I must go back and tell Achilles. You, sir, know what a terrible man he is, and how ready to blame even where no blame should lie."

And Nestor answered: "Why should Achilles care to know how many of the Achaeans may be wounded? He recks not of the dismay that reigns in our host; our most valiant chieftains lie disabled, brave Diomed, son of Tydeus, is wounded; so are Odysseus and Agamemnon; Eurypylus has been hit with an arrow in the thigh, and I have just been bringing this man from the field—he too wounded with an arrow. Nevertheless, Achilles, so valiant though he be, cares not and knows no ruth. Will he wait till the ships, do what we may, are in a blaze, and we perish one upon the other? As for me, I have no strength nor stay in me any longer; would that I were still young and strong as in the days when there was a fight between us and the men of Elis about some cattle raiding. I then killed Itymoneus, the valiant son of Hypeirochus, a dweller in Elis, as I was driving in the spoil; he was hit by a dart thrown by my hand while fighting in the front rank in defense of his cows, so he fell and the country people around him were in great fear. We drove off a vast quantity of booty from the plain, fifty herds of cattle and as many flocks of sheep; fifty droves also of pigs, and as many widespreading flocks of goats. Of horses, moreover, we seized a hundred and fifty, all of them mares, and many had foals running with them. All these did we drive by night to Pylus, the city of Neleus, taking them within the city; and the heart of Neleus was glad in that I had taken so much, though it was the first time I had ever been in the field. At daybreak the heralds went round crying that all in Elis to whom there was a debt owing should come, and the leading Pylians assembled to divide the spoils. There were many to whom the Epeans owed chattels, for we men of Pylus were few and had been oppressed with wrong. In former years Heracles had come, and had laid his hand heavy upon us, so that all our best men had perished. Neleus had had twelve sons, but I alone was left; the others had all been killed. The Epeans presuming upon all this had looked down upon us and had done us much evil. My father chose a herd of cattle and a great flock of sheep—three hundred in all—and he took their shepherds with him, for there was a great debt due to him in Elis, to wit four horses, winners of prizes. They and their chariots with them had gone to the games and were to run for a tripod, but King Augeas took them, and sent back their driver grieving for the loss of his horses. Neleus was angered by what he had both said and done, and took great value in return, but he divided the rest, that no man might have less than his full share.

"Thus did we order all things, and offer sacrifices to the gods throughout the city; but three days afterwards the Epeans came in a body, many in number, they and their chariots, in full array, and with them the two Moliones in their armor, though they were still lads and unused to fighting. Now there is a certain town, Thryoëssa, perched upon a rock on the river Alpheus, the border city of Pylos. This they would destroy, and pitched their camp about it, but when they had crossed their whole plain, Athene darted down by night from Olympus and bade us set ourselves in array; and she found willing soldiers in Pylos, for the men meant fighting. Neleus would not let me arm, and hid my horses, for he said that as yet I could know nothing about war. Nevertheless, Athene so ordered the fight that, all on foot as I was, I fought among our mounted forces and vied with the foremost of them. There is a river Minyeius that falls into the sea near Arene, and there they that were mounted (and I with them) waited till morning, when the companies of foot soldiers came up with us in force. Thence in full panoply and equipment we came towards noon to the sacred waters of the Alpheus, and there we offered victims to almighty Zeus, with a bull to Alpheus, another to Poseidon, and a herd-heifer to Athene. After this we took supper in our companies, and laid us down to rest each in his armor by the river.

"The Epeans were beleaguering the city and were determined to take it, but ere this might be there was a desperate fight in store for them. When the sun's rays began to fall upon the earth we joined battle, praying to Zeus and to Athene, and when the fight had begun, I was the first to kill my man and take his horses—to wit the warrior Mulius. He was son-in-law to Augeas, having married his eldest daughter, golden-haired Agamedé, who knew the virtues of every herb which grows upon the face of the earth. I speared him as he was coming towards me, and when he fell headlong in the dust, I sprang upon his chariot and took my place in the front ranks. The Epeans fled in all directions when they saw the captain of their horsemen (the best man they had) laid low, and I swept down on them like a whirlwind, taking fifty chariots— and in each of them two men bit the dust, slain by my spear. I should have even killed the two Moliones, sons of Actor, unless their real father, Poseidon, lord of the earthquake, had hidden them in a thick mist and borne them out of the fight. Thereon Zeus vouchsafed the Pylians a great victory, for we chased them far over the plain, killing the men and bringing in their armor, till we had brought our horses to Buprasium, rich in wheat, and to the Olenian rock, with the hill that is called Alision, at which point Athene turned the people back. There I slew the last man and left him; then the Achaeans drove their horses back from Buprasium to Pylos and gave thanks to Zeus among the gods, and among mortal men to Nestor.

"Such was I among my peers, as surely as ever was, but Achilles is for keeping all his valor for himself; bitterly will he rue it hereafter when the host is being cut to pieces. My good friend, did not Menoetius charge you thus, on the day when he sent you from Phthia to Agamemnon? Odysseus and I were in the house, inside, and heard all that he said to you; for we came to the fair house of Peleus while beating up recruits throughout all Achaea, and when we got there we found Menoetius and yourself, and Achilles with you. The old knight Peleus was in the outer court, roasting the fat thighbones of a heifer to Zeus, the lord of thunder; and he held a gold chalice in his hand from which he poured drink offerings of wine over the burning sacrifice. You two were busy cutting up the heifer, and at that moment we stood at the gates, whereon Achilles sprang to his feet, led us by the hand into the house, placed us at table, and set before us such hospitable entertainment as guests expect. When we had satisfied ourselves with meat and drink, I said my say and urged both of you to join us. You were ready enough to do so, and the two old men charged you much and straitly. Old Peleus bade his son Achilles fight ever among the foremost and outvie his peers, while Menoetius, the son of Actor, spoke thus to you: 'My son,' said he, 'Achilles is of nobler birth than you are, but you are older than he, though he is far the better man of the two. Counsel him wisely, guide him in the right way, and he will follow you to his own profit.' Thus did your father charge you, but you have forgotten. Nevertheless, even now, say all this to Achilles if he will listen to you. Who knows but with heaven's help you may talk him over, for it is good to take a friend's advice. If, however, he is fearful about some oracle, or if his mother has told him something from Zeus, then let him send you, and let the rest of the Myrmidons follow with you, if perchance you may bring light and saving to the Danaans. And let him send you into battle clad in his own armor, that the Trojans may mistake you for him and leave off fighting. The sons of the Achaeans may thus have time to get their breath, for they are hard pressed and there is little breathing time in battle. You, who are fresh, might easily drive a tired enemy back to his walls and away from the tents and ships."

With these words he moved the heart of Patroclus, who set off running by the line of the ships to Achilles, descendant of Aeacus. When he had got as far as the ships of Odysseus, where was their place of assembly and court of justice, with their altars dedicated to the gods, Eurypylus, son of Euaemon, met him, wounded in the thigh with an arrow, and limping out of the fight.

Sweat rained from his head and shoulders, and black blood welled from his cruel wound, but his mind did not wander. The son of Menoetius when he saw him had compassion upon him and spoke piteously, saying: "O unhappy princes and counselors of the Danaans, are you then doomed to feed the hounds of Troy with your fat, far from your friends and your native land? Say, noble Eurypylus, will the Achaeans be able to hold great Hector in check, or will they fall now before his spear?"

Wounded Eurypylus made answer: "Noble Patroclus, there is no hope left for the Achaeans but they will perish at their ships. All they that were princes among us are lying struck down and wounded at the hands of the Trojans, who are waxing stronger and stronger. But save me and take me to your ship. Cut out the arrow from my thigh, wash the black blood from off it with warm water, and lay upon it those gracious herbs which, so they say, have been shown you by Achilles, who was himself shown them by Chiron, most righteous of all the centaurs. For of the physicians Podalirius and Machaon, I hear that the one is lying wounded in his tent and is himself in need of healing, while the other is fighting the Trojans upon the plain."

"Hero Eurypylus," replied the brave son of Menoetius, "how may these things be? What can I do? I am on my way to bear a message to noble Achilles from Nestor of Gerene, bulwark of the Achaeans, but even so I will not be unmindful of your distress."

With this he clasped him round the middle and led him into the tent, and a servant, when he saw him, spread bullock skins on the ground for him to lie on. He laid him at full length and cut out the sharp arrow from his thigh; he washed the black blood from the wound with warm water; he then crushed a bitter herb, rubbing it between his hands, and spread it upon the wound. This was a virtuous herb which killed all pain, so the wound presently dried and the blood left off flowing.

Book XII

Led by Hector, the Trojans leave their horses and chariots and assail the
Greek wall on foot. The two Ajaxes head the Greek defense. Hector,
however, crashes through the gate and the Trojans behind him pour over
the wall, while the Greeks flee in panic to their ships.

S O THE SON OF MENOETIUS WAS ATTENDING TO THE HURT OF EURYPYLUS
within the tent, but the Argives and Trojans still fought desperately,
nor were the trench and the high wall above it to keep the Trojans in
check longer. They had built it to protect their ships and had dug the trench
all round it that it might safeguard both the ships and the rich spoils which
they had taken, but they had not offered hecatombs to the gods. It had been
built without the consent of the immortals, and therefore it did not last. So
long as Hector lived and Achilles nursed his anger and so long as the city of
Priam remained untaken, the great wall of the Achaeans stood firm; but
when the bravest of the Trojans were no more, and many also of the Argives,
though some were yet left alive—when, moreover, the city was sacked in
the tenth year, and the Argives had gone back with their ships to their own
country—then Poseidon and Apollo took counsel to destroy the wall, and
they turned on to it the streams of all the rivers from Mount Ida into the
sea, Rhesus, Heptaporus, Caresus, Rhodius, Grenicus, Aesopus, and goodly
Scamander, with Simois, where many a shield and helm had fallen, and many
a hero of the race of demigods had bitten the dust. Phoebus Apollo turned
the mouths of all these rivers together and made them flow for nine days

against the wall, while Zeus rained the whole time that he might wash it sooner into the sea. Poseidon himself, trident in hand, surveyed the work and threw into the sea all the foundations of beams and stones which the Achaeans had laid with so much toil. He made all level by the mighty stream of the Hellespont, and then when he had swept the wall away he spread a great beach of sand over the place where it had been. This done he turned the rivers back into their old courses.

This was what Poseidon and Apollo were to do in after time; but as yet battle and turmoil were still raging round the wall till its timbers rang under the blows that rained upon them. The Argives, cowed by the scourge of Zeus, were hemmed in at their ships in fear of Hector, the mighty minister of Rout, who as heretofore fought with the force and fury of a whirlwind. As a lion or wild boar turns fiercely on the dogs and men that attack him, while these form a solid wall and shower their javelins as they face him—his courage is all undaunted, but his high spirit will be the death of him. Many a time does he charge at his pursuers to scatter them, and they fall back as often as he does so—even so did Hector go about among the host exhorting his men and cheering them on to cross the trench.

But the horses dared not do so, and stood neighing upon its brink, for the width frightened them. They could neither jump it nor cross it, for it had overhanging banks all round upon either side, above which there were the sharp stakes that the sons of the Achaeans had planted so close and strong as a defense against all who would assail it. A horse, therefore, could not get into it and draw his chariot after him, but those who were on foot kept trying their very utmost. Then Polydamas went up to Hector and said: "Hector, and you other captains of the Trojans and allies, it is madness for us to try and drive our horses across the trench; it will be very hard to cross, for it is full of sharp stakes, and beyond these there is the wall. Our horses therefore cannot get down into it and would be of no use if they did; moreover, it is a narrow place and we should come to harm. If, indeed, great Zeus is minded to help the

Trojans and in his anger will utterly destroy the Achaeans, I would myself gladly see them perish now and here far from Argos; but if they should rally and we are driven back from the ships pell-mell into the trench there will be not so much as a man get back to the city to tell the tale. Now, therefore, let us all do as I say: let our squires hold our horses by the trench, but let us follow Hector in a body on foot, clad in full armor, and if the day of their doom is at hand the Achaeans will not be able to withstand us."

Thus spoke Polydamas and his saying pleased Hector, who sprang in full armor to the ground, and all the other Trojans, when they saw him do so, also left their chariots. Each man then gave his horses over to his charioteer in charge to hold them ready for him at the trench. Then they formed themselves into companies, made themselves ready, and in five bodies followed their leaders. Those that went with Hector and Polydamas were the bravest and most in number, and the most determined to break through the wall and fight at the ships. Cebriones was also joined with them as third in command, for Hector had left his chariot in charge of a less valiant soldier. The next company was led by Paris, Alcathoüs, and Agenor; the third by Helenus and Deïphobus, two sons of Priam, and with them was the hero Asius—Asius, the son of Hyrtacus, whose great black horses of the breed that comes from the river Selleis had brought him from Arisbe. Aeneas, the valiant son of Anchises, led the fourth; he and the two sons of Antenor, Archelochus and Acamas, men well-versed in all the arts of war. Sarpedon was captain over the allies, and took with him Glaucus and Asteropaeus whom he deemed most valiant after himself—for he was far the best man of them all. These helped to array one another in their oxhide shields, and then charged straight at the Danaans, for they felt sure that they would not hold out longer and that they should themselves now fall upon the ships.

The rest of the Trojans and their allies now followed the counsel of Polydamas, but Asius, son of Hyrtacus, would not leave his horses and his esquire behind him; in his foolhardiness he took them on with him towards the ships, nor did he fail to come by his end in consequence. Nevermore was he to return to wind-beaten Ilium, exulting in his chariot and his horses. Ere he could do so, death of ill-omened name had overshadowed him and he had fallen by the spear of Idomeneus, the noble son of Deucalion. He had driven towards the left wing of the ships, by which way the Achaeans used to return with their chariots and horses from the plain. Hither he drove and found the gates with their doors opened wide and the great bar down—for the gatemen kept them open so as to let those of their comrades enter who might be flying towards the ships. Hither of set purpose did he direct his horses, and his men followed him with a loud cry, for they felt sure that the Achaeans would not hold out longer and that they should now fall upon the ships. Little did they know that at the gates they should find two of the bravest chieftains, proud sons of the fighting Lapithae—the one, Polypoetes, mighty son of Pirithoüs, and the other Leonteus, peer of murderous Ares.

These stood before the gates like two high oak trees upon the mountains that tower from their widespreading roots and year after year battle with wind and rain—even so did these two men await the onset of great Asius confidently and without flinching. The Trojans led by him and by Iamenus, Orestes, Adamas, the son of Asius, Thoön, and Oenomaus, raised a loud cry of battle and made straight for the wall, holding their shields of dry oxhide above their heads; for a while the two defenders remained inside and cheered the Achaeans on to stand firm in the defense of their ships. When, however, they saw that the Trojans were attacking the wall, while the Danaans were crying out for help and being routed, they rushed outside and fought in front of the gates like two wild boars upon the mountains that abide the attack of men and dogs, and charging on either side break down the wood all around them tearing it up by the roots, and one can hear the clattering of their tusks, till someone hits them and makes an end of them—even so did the gleaming bronze rattle about their breasts as the weapons fell upon them; for they fought with great fury, trusting to their own prowess and to those who were on the wall above them. These threw great stones at their assailants in defense of themselves, their tents, and their ships. The stones fell thick as the flakes of snow which some fierce blast drives from the dark clouds and showers down in sheets upon the earth—even so fell the weapons from the hands alike of Trojans and Achaeans.

Helmet and shield rang out as the great stones rained upon them, and Asius, the son of Hyrtacus, in his dismay cried aloud and smote his two thighs. "Father Zeus," he cried, "of a truth you too are altogether given to lying. I made sure the Argive heroes could not withstand us, whereas like slim-waisted wasps, or bees that have their nests in the rocks by the wayside—they leave not the holes wherein they have built undefended, but fight for their little ones against all who would take them—even so these men, though they be but two, will not be driven from the gates, but stand firm either to slay or be slain." He spoke, but moved not the mind of Zeus, whose counsel it then was to give glory to Hector. Meanwhile the rest of the Trojans were fighting about the other gates. I, however, am no god to be able to tell about all these things, for the battle raged everywhere about the stone wall as it were a fiery furnace. The Argives, discomfited though they were, were forced to defend their ships, and all the gods who were defending the Achaeans were vexed in spirit; but the Lapithae kept on fighting with might and main.

Thereon Polypoetes, mighty son of Pirithoüs, hit Damasus with a spear upon his cheek-pierced helmet. The helmet did not protect him, for the point of the spear went through it and broke the bone, so that the brain inside was scattered about, and he died fighting. He then slew Pylon and Ormenus. Leonteus, of the race of Ares, killed Hippomachus, the son of Antimachus, by striking him with his spear upon the girdle. He then drew his sword and sprang first upon Antiphates whom he killed in close combat, and who fell face upwards on the earth. After him he killed Menon, Iamenus, and Orestes, and laid them low one after the other.

While they were busy stripping the armor from these heroes, the youths who were led on by Polydamas and Hector (and these were the greater part and the most valiant of those that were trying to break through the wall and fire the ships) were still standing by the trench, uncertain what they should do; for they had seen a sign from heaven when they had essayed to cross it— a soaring eagle that flew skirting the left wing of their host, with a monstrous blood-red snake in its talons still alive and struggling to escape. The snake was still bent on revenge, wriggling and twisting itself backwards till it struck the bird that held it, on the neck and breast; whereon the bird being in pain, let it fall, dropping it into the middle of the host, and then flew down the wind with a sharp cry. The Trojans were struck with terror when they saw the snake, portent of aegis-bearing Zeus, writhing in the midst of them, and Polydamas went up to Hector and said:

"Hector, at our councils of war you are ever given to rebuke me, even when I speak wisely, as though it were not well, forsooth, that one of the people should cross your will either in the field or at the council board; you would have them support you always. Nevertheless, I will say what I think will be best; let us not now go on to fight the Danaans at their ships, for I know what will happen if this soaring eagle which skirted the left wing of our host with a monstrous blood-red snake in its talons (the snake being still alive) was really sent as an omen to the Trojans on their essaying to cross the trench. The eagle let go her hold; she did not succeed in taking it home to her little ones, and so will it be with ourselves. Even though by a mighty effort we break through the gates and wall of the Achaeans, and they give way before us, still we shall not return in good order by the way we came, but shall leave many a man behind us whom the Achaeans will do to death in defense of their ships. Thus would any seer who was expert in these matters, and was trusted by the people, read the portent."

Hector looked fiercely at him and said: "Polydamas, I like not of your reading. You can find a better saying than this if you will. If, however, you have spoken in good earnest, then indeed has heaven robbed you of your reason. You would have me pay no heed to the counsels of Zeus, nor to the promises he made me"—and he bowed his head in confirmation; "you bid me be ruled rather by the flight of wild fowl. What care I whether they fly towards dawn or dark, and whether they be on my right hand or on my left? Let us put our trust rather in the counsel of great Zeus, king of mortals and immortals. There is one omen, and one only—that a man should fight for his country. Why are you so fearful? Though we be all of us slain at the ships of the Argives you are not likely to be killed yourself, for you are not steadfast nor coura- geous. If you will not fight, or would talk others over from doing so, you shall fall forthwith before my spear."

With these words he led the way, and the others followed after with a cry that rent the air. Then Zeus, the lord of thunder, sent the blast of a mighty wind from the mountains of Ida that bore the dust down towards the ships. He thus lulled the Achaeans into security, and gave victory to Hector and to the Trojans, who, trusting to their own might and to the signs he had shown them, essayed to break through the great wall of the Achaeans. They tore down the breastworks from the walls and overthrew the battlements. They upheaved the buttresses, which the Achaeans had set in front of the wall in order to support it; when they had pulled these down they made sure of breaking through the wall, but the Danaans still showed no sign of giving ground; they still fenced the battlements with their shields of oxhide and hurled their missiles down upon the foe as soon as any came below the wall.

The two Ajaxes went about everywhere on the walls cheering on the Achaeans, giving fair words to some while they spoke sharply to anyone whom they saw to be remiss. "My friends," they cried, "Argives one and all— good, bad, and indifferent, for there was never fight yet in which all were of equal prowess—there is now work enough, as you very well know, for all of you. See that you none of you turn in flight towards the ships, daunted by the shouting of the foe, but press forward and keep one another in heart, if it may so be that Olympian Zeus, the lord of lightning, will vouchsafe us to repel our foes, and drive them back towards the city."

Thus did the two go about shouting and cheering the Achaeans on. As the flakes that fall thick upon a winter's day, when Zeus is minded to snow and to display these his arrows to mankind—he lulls the wind to rest, and snows hour after hour till he has buried the tops of the high mountains, the headlands that jut into the sea, the grassy plains, and the tilled fields of men; the snow lies deep upon the forelands and havens of the gray sea, but the waves as they come rolling in stay it that it can come no further, though all else is wrapped as with a mantle, so heavy are the heavens with snow—even thus thickly did the stones fall on one side and on the other, some thrown at the Trojans, and some by the Trojans at the Achaeans; and the whole wall was in an uproar.

Still the Trojans and brave Hector would not yet have broken down the gates and the great bar, had not Zeus turned his son Sarpedon against the Argives as a lion against a herd of horned cattle. Before him he held his shield of hammered bronze, that the smith had beaten so fair and round, and had lined with oxhides which he had made fast with rivets of gold all round the shield. This he held in front of him, and brandishing his two spears came on like some lion of the wilderness, who has been long famished for want of meat and will dare break even into a well-fenced homestead to try and get at the sheep. He may find the shepherds keeping watch over their flocks with dogs and spears, but he is in no mind to be driven from the fold till he has had a try for it; he will either spring on a sheep and carry it off, or be hit by a spear from some strong hand—even so was Sarpedon fain to attack the wall and break down its battlements. Then he said to Glaucus, son of Hippolochus: "Glaucus, why in Lycia do we receive especial honor as regards our place at table? Why are the choicest portions served us and our cups kept brimming, and why do men look up to us as though we were gods? Moreover, we hold a large estate by the banks of the river Xanthus, fair with orchard lawns and wheat-growing land; it becomes us, therefore, to take our stand at the head of all the Lycians and bear the brunt of the fight, that one may say to another, 'Our princes in Lycia eat the fat of the land and drink the best of wine, but they are fine fellows; they fight well and are ever at the front in battle.' My good friend, if, when we were once out of this fight, we could escape old age and death thenceforward and forever, I should neither press forward myself nor bid you do so, but death in ten thousand shapes hangs ever over our heads, and no man can elude him. Therefore, let us go forward and either win glory for ourselves or yield it to another."

Glaucus heeded his saying, and the pair forthwith led on the host of Lycians. Menestheus, son of Peteos, was dismayed when he saw them, for it was against his part of the wall that they came—bringing destruction with them. He looked along the wall for some chieftain to support his comrades and saw the two Ajaxes, men ever eager for the fray, and Teucer, who had just come from his tent, standing near them; but he could not make his voice heard by shouting to them, so great an uproar was there from clashing shields and helmets and the battering of gates with a din which reached the skies. For all the gates had been closed, and the Trojans were hammering at them to try and break their way through them. Menestheus, therefore, sent Thoötes with a message to Ajax. "Run, good Thoötes," said he, "and call Ajax, or better still bid both come, for it will be all over with us here directly; the leaders of the Lycians are upon us, men who have ever fought desperately heretofore. But if the pair have too much on their hands to let them both come, at any rate let Ajax, son of Telamon, do so, and let Teucer, the famous bowman, come with him."

The messenger did as he was told, and set off running along the wall of the Achaeans. When he reached the Ajaxes he said to them: "Sirs, princes of the Argives, the son of noble Peteos bids you come to him for a while and help him. You had better both come if you can, or it will be all over with him directly. The leaders of the Lycians are upon him, men who have ever fought desperately heretofore. If you have too much on your hands to let both come, at any rate let Ajax, son of Telamon, do so, and let Teucer, the famous bowman, come with him."

Great Ajax, son of Telamon, heeded the message, and at once spoke to the son of Oïleus. "Ajax," said he, "do you two, yourself and brave Lycomedes, stay here and keep the Danaans in heart to fight their hardest. I will go over yonder, and bear my part in the fray, but I will come back here at once as soon as I have given them the help they need."

With this, Ajax, son of Telamon, set off, and Teucer, his brother by the same father, went also, with Pandion to carry Teucer's bow. They went along inside the wall, and when they came to the tower where Menestheus was (and hard-pressed indeed did they find him) the brave captains and leaders of the Lycians were storming the battlements as it were a thick dark cloud, fighting in close quarters, and raising the battle cry aloud.

First, Ajax, son of Telamon, killed brave Epicles, a comrade of Sarpedon, hitting him with a jagged stone that lay by the battlements at the very top of the wall. As men now are, even one who is in the bloom of youth could hardly lift it with his two hands, but Ajax raised it high aloft and flung it down, smashing Epicles' four-crested helmet so that the bones of his head were crushed to pieces, and he fell from the high wall as though he were diving, with no more life left in him. Then Teucer wounded Glaucus, the brave son of Hippolochus, as he was coming on to attack the wall. He saw his shoulder bare and aimed an arrow at it, which made Glaucus leave off fighting. Thereon he sprang covertly down for fear some of the Achaeans might see that he was wounded and taunt him. Sarpedon was stung with grief when he saw Glaucus leave him, still he did not leave off fighting, but aimed his spear at Alcmaon, the son of Thestor, and hit him. He drew his spear back again and Alcmaon came down headlong after it with his bronzed armor rattling round him. Then Sarpedon seized the battlement in his strong hands, and tugged at it till it all gave way together, and a breach was made through which many might pass.

Ajax and Teucer then both of them attacked him. Teucer hit him with an arrow on the band that bore the shield which covered his body, but Zeus saved his son from destruction that he might not fall by the ships' sterns. Meanwhile Ajax sprang on him and pierced his shield, but the spear did not go clean through, though it hustled him back that he could come on no further. He therefore retired a little space from the battlement, yet without losing all his ground, for he still thought to cover himself with glory. Then he turned round and shouted to the brave Lycians, saying: "Lycians, why do you thus fail me? For all my prowess I cannot break through the wall and open a way to the ships single-handed. Come close on behind me, for the more there are of us the better."

The Lycians, shamed by his rebuke, pressed closer round him who was their counselor and their king. The Argives on their part got their men in fighting order within the wall, and there was a deadly struggle between them. The Lycians could not break through the wall and force their way to the ships, nor could the Danaans drive the Lycians from the wall now that they had once reached it. As two men, measuring rods in hand, quarrel about their boundaries in a field that they own in common, and stickle for their rights though they be but in a mere strip, even so did the battlements now serve as a bone of contention, and they beat one another's round shields for their possession.

Many a man's body was wounded with the pitiless bronze as he turned round and bared his back to the foe, and many were struck clean through their shields. The wall and battlements were everywhere deluged with the blood alike of Trojans and of Achaeans. But even so the Trojans could not rout the Achaeans, who still held on; and as some honest hard-working woman weighs wool in her balance and sees that the scales be true, for she would gain some pitiful earnings for her little ones, even so was the fight balanced evenly between them till the time came when Zeus gave the greater glory to Hector, son of Priam, who was first to spring toward the walls of the Achaeans. As he did so, he cried aloud to the Trojans, "Up, Trojans, break the wall of the Argives, and fling fire upon their ships!"

Thus did he hound them on, and in one body they rushed straight at the wall as he had bidden them, and scaled the battlements with sharp spears in their hands. Hector laid hold of a stone that lay just outside the gates and was thick at one end but pointed at the other; two of the best men in a town, as men now are, could hardly raise it from the ground and put it on to a wagon, but Hector lifted it quite easily by himself, for the son of scheming Cronus made it light for him. As a shepherd picks up a ram's fleece with one hand and finds it no burden, so easily did Hector lift the great stone and drive it right at the doors that closed the gates so strong and so firmly set. These doors were double and high, and were kept closed by two crossbars to which there was but one key. When he had got close up to them, Hector strode towards them that his blow might gain in force and struck them in the middle, leaning his whole weight against them. He broke both hinges, and the stone fell inside by reason of its great weight. The portals reechoed with the sound, the bars held no longer, and the doors flew open, one one way, and the other the other, through the force of the blow. Then brave Hector leaped inside with a face as dark as that of flying night. The gleaming bronze flashed fiercely about his body and he had two spears in his hand. None but a god could have withstood him as he flung himself into the gateway, and his eyes glared like fire. Then he turned round towards the Trojans and called on them to scale the wall, and they did as he bade them—some of them at once climbing over the wall, while others passed through the gates. The Danaans then fled panic-stricken towards their ships, and all was uproar and confusion.

Book XIII

The sea-god Poseidon is angry with Zeus for showing such favor to the Trojans. In a series of disguises, he rallies the Greeks to stand against their onrushing enemies. The Cretan Idomeneus performs valorous deeds on the Greek side. Some Trojans retreat but Hector leads them on again.

NOW WHEN ZEUS HAD THUS BROUGHT HECTOR AND THE TROJANS TO the ships, he left them to their never-ending toil, and turned his keen eyes away, looking elsewhither towards the horse-breeders of Thrace, the Mysians, fighters at close quarters, the noble Hippemolgi, who live on milk, and the Abians, justest of mankind. He no longer turned so much as a glance towards Troy, for he did not think that any of the immortals would go and help either Trojans or Danaans.

But King Poseidon had kept no blind lookout; he had been looking admiringly on the battle from his seat on the topmost crests of wooded Samothrace, whence he could see all Ida, with the city of Priam and the ships of the Achaeans. He had come from under the sea and taken his place here, for he pitied the Achaeans who were being overcome by the Trojans; and he was furiously angry with Zeus.

Presently he came down from his post on the mountain top, and as he strode swiftly onwards the high hills and the forest quaked beneath the tread of his immortal feet. Three strides he took, and with the fourth he reached his goal—Aegae, where is his glittering golden palace, imperishable, in the depths of the sea. When he got there, he yoked his fleet brazen-footed steeds with their manes of gold all flying in the wind. He clothed himself in raiment of gold, grasped his gold whip, and took his stand upon his chariot. As he went his way over the waves the sea-monsters left their lairs, for they knew their lord, and came gamboling round him from every quarter of the deep, while the sea in her gladness opened a path before his chariot. So lightly did the horses fly that the bronze axle of the car was not even wet beneath it; and thus his bounding steeds took him to the ships of the Achaeans.

Now there is a certain huge cavern in the depths of the sea midway between Tenedos and rocky Imbrus. Here Poseidon, lord of the earthquake, stayed his horses, unyoked them, and set before them their ambrosial forage. He hobbled their feet with hobbles of gold which none could either unloose or break, so that they might stay there in that place until their lord should return. This done, he went his way to the host of the Achaeans.

Now the Trojans followed Hector, son of Priam, in close array like a storm cloud or flame of fire, fighting with might and main and raising the cry of battle; for they deemed that they should take the ships of the Achaeans and kill all their chiefest heroes then and there. Meanwhile, earth-encircling Poseidon, lord of the earthquake, cheered on the Argives, for he had come up out of the sea and had assumed the form and voice of Calchas.

First he spoke to the two Ajaxes, who were doing their best already, and said: "Ajaxes, you two can be the saving of the Achaeans if you will put out all your strength and not let yourselves be daunted. I am not afraid that the Trojans, who have got over the wall in force, will be victorious in any other part, for the Achaeans can hold all of them in check, but I much fear that some evil will befall us here where furious Hector, who boasts himself the son of great Zeus himself, is leading them on like a pillar of flame. May some god, then, put it into your hearts to make a firm stand here, and to incite others to do the like. In this case you will drive him from the ships even though he be inspired by Zeus himself."

As he spoke the earth-encircling lord of the earthquake struck both of them with his scepter and filled their hearts with daring. He made their legs light and active, as also their hands and their feet. Then, as the soaring falcon poises on the wing high above some sheer rock, and presently swoops down to chase some bird over the plain, even so did Poseidon, lord of the earthquake, wing his flight into the air and leave them. Of the two, swift Ajax, son of Oïleus, was the first to know who it was that had been speaking with them, and said to Ajax, son of Telamon: "Ajax, this is one of the gods that dwell on Olympus, who in the likeness of the prophet is bidding us fight hard by our ships. It was not Calchas, the seer and diviner of omens; I knew him at once by his feet and knees as he turned away, for the gods are soon recognized. Moreover I feel the lust of battle burn more fiercely within me, while my hands and my feet under me are more eager for the fray."

And Ajax, son of Telamon, answered: "I too feel my hands grasp my spear more firmly; my strength is greater, and my feet more nimble; I long, moreover, to meet furious Hector, son of Priam, even in single combat."

Thus did they converse, exulting in the hunger after battle with which the god had filled them. Meanwhile the earth-encircler roused the Achaeans, who were resting in the rear by the ships overcome at once by hard fighting and by grief at seeing that the Trojans had got over the wall in force. Tears began falling from their eyes as they beheld them, for they made sure that they should not escape destruction; but the lord of the earthquake passed lightly about among them and urged their battalions to the front.

First he went up to Teucer and Leïtus, the hero Peneleos, and Thoas and Deïpyrus; Meriones also and Antilochus, valiant warriors; all these did he exhort. "Shame on you, young Argives!" he cried. "It was on your prowess I relied for the saving of our ships; if you fight not with might and main, this very day will see us overcome by the Trojans. Of a truth my eyes behold a great and terrible portent which I had never thought to see—the Trojans at our ships—they, who heretofore were like panic-stricken hinds, the prey of jackals and wolves in a forest, with no strength but in flight for they cannot defend themselves. Hitherto the Trojans dared not for one moment face the attack of the Achaeans, but now they have sallied far from their city and are fighting at our very ships through the cowardice of our leader and the disaffection of the people themselves, who in their discontent care not to fight in defense of the ships but are being slaughtered near them. True, King Agamemnon, son of Atreus, is the cause of our disaster by having insulted the son of Peleus, still this is no reason why we should leave off fighting. Let us be quick to heal, for the hearts of the brave heal quickly. You do ill to be thus remiss, you, who are the finest soldiers in our whole army. I blame no man for keeping out of battle if he is a weakling, but I am indignant with such men as you are. My good friends, matters will soon become even worse through this slackness. Think, each one of you, of his own honor and credit, for the hazard of the fight is extreme. Great Hector is now fighting at our ships; he has broken through the gates and the strong bolt that held them."

Thus did the earth-encircler address the Achaeans and urge them on. Thereon round the two Ajaxes there gathered strong bands of men, of whom not even Ares nor Athene, marshaler of hosts, could make light if they went among them, for they were the picked men of all those who were now awaiting the onset of Hector and the Trojans. They made a living fence, spear to spear, shield to shield, buckler to buckler, helmet to helmet, and man to man. The horsehair crests on their gleaming helmets touched one another as they nodded forward, so closely serried were they; the spears they brandished in their strong hands were interlaced, and their hearts were set on battle.

The Trojans advanced in a dense body, with Hector at their head pressing right on as a rock that comes thundering down the side of some mountain from whose brow the winter torrents have torn it; the foundations of the dull thing have been loosened by floods of rain, and as it bounds headlong on its way it sets the whole forest in an uproar. It swerves neither to right nor left till it reaches level ground, but then for all its fury it can go no further—even so easily did Hector for a while seem as though he would career through the tents and ships of the Achaeans till he had reached the sea in his murderous course; but the closely serried battalions stayed him when he reached them, for the sons of the Achaeans thrust at him with swords and spears pointed at both ends, and drove him from them so that he staggered and gave ground. Thereon he shouted to the Trojans: "Trojans, Lycians, and Dardanians, fighters in close combat, stand firm! The Achaeans have set themselves as a wall against me, but they will not check me for long. They will give ground before me if the mightiest of the gods, the thundering spouse of Hera, has indeed inspired my onset."

With these words he put heart and soul into them all. Deïphobus, son of Priam, went about among them intent on deeds of daring with his round shield before him, under cover of which he strode quickly forward. Meriones took aim at him with a spear, nor did he fail to hit the broad orb of oxhide; but he was far from piercing it for the spear broke in two pieces long ere he could do so; moreover, Deïphobus had seen it coming and had held his shield well away from him. Meriones drew back under cover of his comrades, angry alike at having failed to vanquish Deïphobus and having broken his spear. He turned therefore towards the ships and tents to fetch a spear which he had left behind in his tent.

The others continued fighting, and the cry of battle rose up into the heavens. Teucer, son of Telamon, was the first to kill his man, to wit, the warrior Imbrius, son of Mentor, rich in horses. Until the Achaeans came he had lived in Pedaeum, and had married Medesicaste, a bastard daughter of Priam; but on the arrival of the Danaan fleet he had gone back to Ilium, and was a great man among the Trojans, dwelling near Priam himself, who gave him like honor with his own sons. The son of Telamon now struck him under the ear with a spear which he then drew back again, and Imbrius fell headlong as an ash tree when it is felled on the crest of some high mountain beacon, and its delicate green foliage comes toppling down to the ground. Thus did he fall with his bronze-dight armor ringing harshly round him, and Teucer sprang forward with intent to strip him of his armor; but as he was doing so, Hector took aim at him with a spear. Teucer saw the spear coming and swerved aside, whereon it hit Amphimachus, son of Cteatus, son of Actor, in the chest as he was coming into battle, and his armor rang rattling round him as he fell heavily to the ground. Hector sprang forward to take Amphimachus's helmet from off his temples, and in a moment Ajax threw a spear at him, but did not wound him, for he was encased all over in his terrible armor. Nevertheless, the spear struck the boss of his shield with such force as to drive him back from the two corpses, which the Achaeans then drew off. Stichius and Menestheus, captains of the Athenians, bore away Amphimachus to the host of the Achaeans, while the two brave and impetuous Ajaxes did the like by Imbrius. As two lions snatch a goat from the hounds that have it in their fangs, and bear it through thick brushwood high above the ground in their jaws, thus did the Ajaxes bear aloft the body of Imbrius, and strip it of its armor. Then the son of Oïleus severed the head from the neck in revenge for the death of Amphimachus, and sent it whirling over the crowd as though it had been a ball, till it fell in the dust at Hector's feet.

Poseidon was exceedingly angry that his grandson Amphimachus should have fallen. He therefore went to the tents and ships of the Achaeans to urge the Danaans still further, and to devise evil for the Trojans. Idomeneus met him, as he was taking leave of a comrade, who had just come to him from the fight, wounded in the knee. His fellow soldiers bore him off the field, and Idomeneus having given orders to the physicians went on to his tent, for he was still thirsting for battle. Poseidon spoke in the likeness and with the voice of Thoas, son of Andraemon, who ruled the Aetolians of all Pleuron and high Calydon, and was honored among his people as though he were a god. "Idomeneus," said he, "lawgiver to the Cretans, what has now become of the threats with which the sons of the Achaeans used to threaten the Trojans?"

And Idomeneus, chief among the Cretans, answered: "Thoas, no one, so far as I know, is in fault, for we can all fight. None are held back neither by fear nor slackness, but it seems to be the will of almighty Zeus that the Achaeans should perish ingloriously here far from Argos. You, Thoas, have been always staunch, and you keep others in heart if you see any fail in duty. Be not then remiss now, but exhort all to do their utmost."

To this Poseidon, lord of the earthquake, made answer: "Idomeneus, may he never return from Troy, but remain here for dogs to batten upon, who is this day willfully slack in fighting. Get your armor and go; we must make all haste together if we may be of any use, though we are only two. Even cowards gain courage from companionship, and we two can hold our own with the bravest."

Therewith the god went back into the thick of the fight, and Idomeneus when he had reached his tent donned his armor, grasped his two spears, and sallied forth. As the lightning which the son of Cronus brandishes from bright Olympus when he would show a sign to mortals, and its gleam flashes far and wide—even so did his armor gleam about him as he ran. Meriones, his sturdy squire, met him while he was still near his tent (for he was going to fetch his spear) and Idomeneus said:

"Meriones, fleet son of Molus, best of comrades, why have you left the field? Are you wounded, and is the point of the weapon hurting you? or have you been sent to fetch me? I want no fetching; I had far rather fight than stay in my tent."

"Idomeneus," answered Meriones, "I come for a spear, if I can find one in my tent. I have broken the one I had in throwing it at the shield of Deïphobus."

And Idomeneus, captain of the Cretans, answered: "You will find one spear, or twenty if you so please, standing up against the end wall of my tent. I have taken them from Trojans whom I have killed, for I am not one to keep my enemy at arm's length. Therefore I have spears, bossed shields, helmets, and burnished corslets."

Then Meriones said: "I too in my tent and at my ship have spoils taken from the Trojans, but they are not at hand. I have been at all times valorous, and wherever there has been hard fighting have held my own among the foremost. There may be those among the Achaeans who do not know how I fight, but you know it well enough yourself."

Idomeneus answered: "I know you for a brave man—you need not tell me. If the best men at the ships were being chosen to go on an ambush—and there is nothing like this for showing what a man is made of; it comes out then who is cowardly and who brave; the coward will change color at every touch and turn; he is full of fears, and keeps shifting his weight first on one knee and then on the other; his heart beats fast as he thinks of death, and one can hear the chattering of his teeth. Whereas the brave man will not change color nor be frightened on finding himself in ambush, but is all the time longing to go into action—if the best men were being chosen for such a service, no one could make light of your courage nor feats of arms. If you were struck by a dart or smitten in close combat, it would not be from behind, in your neck nor back, but the weapon would hit you in the chest or belly as you were pressing forward to a place in the front ranks. But let us no longer stay here talking like children, lest we be ill spoken of; go, fetch your spear from the tent at once."

On this Meriones, peer of Ares, went to the tent and got himself a spear of bronze. He then followed after Idomeneus, big with great deeds of valor. As when baneful Ares sallies forth to battle, and his son Panic so strong and dauntless goes with him, to strike terror even into the heart of a hero—the pair have gone from Thrace to arm themselves among the Ephyri or the brave Phlegyans, but they will not listen to both the contending hosts, and will give victory to one side or to the other—even so did Meriones and Idomeneus, captains of men, go out to battle clad in their bronze armor. Meriones was first to speak. "Son of Deucalion," said he, "where would you have us begin fighting? On the right wing of the host, in the center, or on the left wing, where I take it the Achaeans will be weakest?"

Idomeneus answered: "There are others to defend the center—the two Ajaxes and Teucer, who is the finest archer of all the Achaeans, and is good also in a hand-to-hand fight. These will give Hector, son of Priam, enough to do; fight as he may, he will find it hard to vanquish their indomitable fury, and fire the ships, unless the son of Cronus fling a firebrand upon them with his own hand. Great Ajax, son of Telamon, will yield to no man who is in mortal mold and eats the grain of Demeter, if bronze and great stones can overthrow him. He would not yield even to Achilles in hand-to-hand fight, and in fleetness of foot there is none to beat him; let us turn therefore towards the left wing, that we may know forthwith whether we are to give glory to some other, or he to us."

Meriones, peer of fleet Ares, then led the way till they came to the part of the host which Idomeneus had named.

Now when the Trojans saw Idomeneus coming on like a flame of fire, him and his squire clad in their richly wrought armor, they shouted and made towards him all in a body, and a furious hand-to-hand fight raged under the ships' sterns. Fierce as the shrill winds that whistle upon a day when dust lies deep on the roads, and the gusts raise it into a thick cloud—even such was the fury of the combat, and might and main did they hack at each other with spear and sword throughout the host. The field bristled with the long and deadly spears which they bore. Dazzling was the sheen of their gleaming helmets, their fresh-burnished breastplates, and glittering shields as they joined battle with one another. Iron indeed must be his courage who could take pleasure in the sight of such a turmoil, and look on it without being dismayed.

Thus did the two mighty sons of Cronus devise evil for mortal heroes. Zeus was minded to give victory to the Trojans and to Hector, so as to do honor to fleet Achilles, nevertheless he did not mean to utterly overthrow the Achaean host before Ilium, and only wanted to glorify Thetis and her valiant son. Poseidon on the other hand went about among the Argives to incite them, having come up from the gray sea in secret, for he was grieved at seeing them vanquished by the Trojans, and was furiously angry with Zeus. Both were of the same race and country, but Zeus was elder born and knew more, therefore Poseidon feared to defend the Argives openly, but in the likeness of man, he kept on encouraging them throughout their host. Thus, then, did these two devise a knot of war and battle, that none could unloose or break, and set both sides tugging at it, to the failing of men's knees beneath them.

And now Idomeneus, though his hair was already flecked with gray, called loud on the Danaans and spread panic among the Trojans as he leaped in among them. He slew Othryoneus from Cabesus, a sojourner, who had but lately come to take part in the war. He sought Cassandra, the fairest of Priam's daughters in marriage, but offered no gifts of wooing, for he promised a great thing, to wit, that he would drive the sons of the Achaeans willy nilly from Troy. Old King Priam had given his consent and promised her to him, whereon he fought on the strength of the promises thus made to him. Idomeneus aimed a spear, and hit him as he came striding on. His cuirass of bronze did not protect him, and the spear stuck in his belly, so that he fell heavily to the ground. Then Idomeneus vaunted over him saying: "Othryoneus, there is no one in the world whom I shall admire more than I do you, if you indeed perform what you have promised Priam, son of Dardanus, in return for his daughter. We two will make you an offer; we will give you the loveliest daughter of the son of Atreus, and will bring her from Argos for you to marry, if you will sack the goodly city of Ilium in company with ourselves. So come along with me, that we may make a covenant at the ships about the marriage, and we will not be hard upon you about gifts of wooing."

With this Idomeneus began dragging him by the foot through the thick of the fight, but Asius came up to protect the body, on foot, in front of his horses, which his esquire drove so close behind him that he could feel their breath upon his shoulder. He was longing to strike down Idomeneus, but ere he could do so Idomeneus smote him with his spear in the throat under the chin, and the bronze point went clean through it. He fell as an oak, or poplar, or pine which shipwrights have felled for ship's timber upon the mountains with whetted axes—even thus did he lie full length in front of his chariot and horses, grinding his teeth and clutching at the bloodstained dust. His charioteer was struck with panic and did not dare turn his horses round and escape. Thereupon Antilochus hit him in the middle of his body with a spear; his cuirass of bronze did not protect him, and the spear stuck in his belly. He fell gasping from his chariot and Antilochus, great Nestor's son, drove his horses from the Trojans to the Achaeans.

Deïphobus then came close up to Idomeneus to avenge Asius, and took aim at him with a spear, but Idomeneus was on the lookout and avoided it, for he was covered by the round shield he always wore—a shield of oxhide and bronze with two arm-rods on the inside. He crouched under cover of this, and the spear flew over him, but the shield rang out as the spear grazed it, and the weapon sped not in vain from the strong hand of Deïphobus, for it struck Hypsenor, son of Hippasus, shepherd of his people, in the liver under the midriff, and his limbs failed beneath him. Deïphobus vaunted over him and cried with a loud voice, saying, "Of a truth Asius has not fallen unavenged; he will be glad even while passing into the house of Hades, strong warden of the gate, that I have sent someone to escort him."

Thus did he vaunt, and the Argives were stung by his saying. Noble Antilochus was more angry than anyone, but grief did not make him forget his friend and comrade. He ran up to him, bestrode him, and covered him with his shield. Then two of his staunch comrades, Mecisteus, son of Echius, and Alastor, stooped down and bore him away groaning heavily to the ships. But Idomeneus ceased not his fury. He kept on striving continually either to enshroud some Trojan in the darkness of death, or himself to fall while warding off the evil day from the Achaeans. Then fell Alcathoüs, son of noble Aesyetes; he was son-in-law to Anchises, having married his eldest daughter Hippodameia, who was the darling of her father and mother and excelled all her generation in beauty, accomplishments, and understanding, wherefore the bravest man in all Troy had taken her to wife—him did Poseidon lay low by the hand of Idomeneus, blinding his bright eyes and binding his strong limbs in fetters so that he could neither go back nor to one side, but stood stock still like a pillar or lofty tree when Idomeneus struck him with a spear in the middle of his chest. The coat of mail that had hitherto protected his body was now broken and rang harshly as the spear tore through it. He fell heavily to the ground, and the spear stuck in his heart, which still beat, and made the butt end of the spear quiver till dread Ares put an end to his life. Idomeneus vaunted over him and cried with a loud voice, saying: "Deïphobus, since you are in a mood to vaunt, shall we cry quits now that we have killed three men to your one? Nay, sir, stand in fight with me yourself, that you may learn what manner of Zeus-begotten man am I that have come hither. Zeus first begot Minos chief ruler in Crete, and Minos in his turn begot a son, noble Deucalion. Deucalion begot me to be a ruler over many men in Crete, and my ships have now brought me hither, to be the bane of yourself, your father, and the Trojans."

Thus did he speak, and Deïphobus was in two minds, whether to go back and fetch some other Trojan to help him, or to take up the challenge single-handed. In the end, he deemed it best to go and fetch Aeneas, whom he found standing in the rear, for he had long been aggrieved with Priam because in spite of his brave deeds he did not give him his due share of honor. Deïphobus went up to him and said: "Aeneas, prince among the Trojans, if you know any ties of kinship, help me now to defend the body of your sister's husband. Come with me to the rescue of Alcathoüs, who being husband to your sister brought you up when you were a child in his house, and now Idomeneus has slain him."

With these words he moved the heart of Aeneas, and he went in pursuit of Idomeneus, big with great deeds of valor. But Idomeneus was not to be thus daunted as though he were a mere child. He held his ground as a wild boar at bay upon the mountains, who abides the coming of a great crowd of men in some lonely place—the bristles stand upright on his back, his eyes flash fire, and he whets his tusks in his eagerness to defend himself against hounds and men—even so did famed Idomeneus hold his ground and budge not at the coming of Aeneas. He cried aloud to his comrades, looking towards Ascalaphus, Aphareus, Deïpyrus, Meriones, and Antilochus, all of them brave soldiers. "Hither, my friends," he cried, "and leave me not single-handed—I go in great fear by fleet Aeneas, who is coming against me, and is a redoubtable dispenser of death in battle. Moreover, he is in the flower of youth when a man's strength is greatest. If I was of the same age as he is and in my present mind, either he or I should soon bear away the prize of victory."

On this, all of them as one man stood near him, shield on shoulder. Aeneas on the other side called to his comrades, looking towards Deïphobus, Paris, and Agenor, who were leaders of the Trojans along with himself, and the people followed them as sheep follow the ram when they go down to drink after they have been feeding, and the heart of the shepherd is glad—even so was the heart of Aeneas gladdened when he saw his people follow him.

Then they fought furiously in close combat about the body of Alcathoüs, wielding their long spears; and the bronze armor about their bodies rang fearfully as they took aim at one another in the press of the fight, while the two heroes, Aeneas and Idomeneus, peers of Ares, outvied everyone in their desire to hack at each other with sword and spear. Aeneas took aim first, but Idomeneus was on the lookout and avoided the spear, so that it sped from Aeneas' strong hand in vain and fell quivering in the ground. Idomeneus meanwhile smote Oenomaus in the middle of his belly and broke the plate of his corslet, whereon his bowels came gushing out and he clutched the earth in the palms of his hands as he fell sprawling in the dust. Idomeneus drew his spear out of the body, but could not strip him of the rest of his armor for the rain of darts that were showered upon him. Moreover, his strength was now beginning to fail him so that he could no longer charge, and could neither spring forward to recover his own weapon nor swerve aside to avoid one that was aimed at him. Therefore, though he still defended himself in hand-to-hand fight, his heavy feet could not bear him swiftly out of the battle. Deïphobus aimed a spear at him as he was retreating slowly from the field, for his bitterness against him was as fierce as ever, but again he missed him, and hit Ascalaphus, the son of Ares. The spear went through his shoulder, and he clutched the earth in the palms of his hands as he fell sprawling in the dust.

Grim Ares of awful voice did not yet know that his son had fallen, for he was sitting on the summits of Olympus under the golden clouds, by command of Zeus, where the other gods were also sitting, forbidden to take part in the battle. Meanwhile men fought furiously about the body. Deïphobus tore the helmet from off his head, but Meriones sprang upon him and struck him on the arm with a spear so that the visored helmet fell from his hand and came ringing down upon the ground. Thereon Meriones sprang upon him like a vulture, drew the spear from his shoulder, and fell back under cover of his men. Then Polites, own brother of Deïphobus, passed his arms around his waist, and bore him away from the battle till he got to his horses that were standing in the rear of the fight with the chariot and their driver. These took him towards the city groaning and in great pain, with the blood flowing from his arm.

The others still fought on, and the battle cry rose to heaven without ceasing. Aeneas sprang on Aphareus, son of Caletor, and struck him with a spear in his throat which was turned towards him; his head fell on one side, his helmet and shield came down along with him, and death, life's foe, was shed around him. Antilochus spied his chance, flew forward towards Thoön, and wounded him as he was turning round. He laid open the vein that runs all the way up the back to the neck; he cut this vein clean away throughout its whole course, and Thoön fell in the dust face upwards, stretching out his hands imploringly towards his comrades. Antilochus sprang upon him and stripped the armor from his shoulders, glaring round him fearfully as he did so. The Trojans came about him on every side and struck his broad and gleaming shield, but could not wound his body, for Poseidon stood guard over the son of Nestor, though the darts fell thickly round him. He was never clear of the foe, but was always in the thick of the fight; his spear was never idle; he poised and aimed it in every direction, so eager was he to hit someone from a distance or to fight him hand to hand.

As he was thus aiming among the crowd, he was seen by Adamas, son of Asius, who rushed towards him and struck him with a spear in the middle of his shield, but Poseidon made its point without effect, for he grudged him the life of Antilochus. One half, therefore, of the spear stuck fast like a charred stake in Antilochus's shield, while the other lay on the ground. Adamas then sought shelter under cover of his men, but Meriones followed after and hit him with a spear midway between the private parts and the navel, where a wound is particularly painful to wretched mortals. There did Meriones transfix him, and he writhed convulsively about the spear as some bull whom mountain herdsmen have bound with ropes of withes and are taking away perforce. Even so did he move convulsively for a while, but not for very long, till Meriones came up and drew the spear out of his body, and his eyes were veiled in darkness.

Helenus then struck Deïpyrus with a great Thracian sword, hitting him on the temple in close combat and tearing the helmet from his head. The helmet fell to the ground, and one of those who were fighting on the Achaean side took charge of it as it rolled at his feet, but the eyes of Deïpyrus were closed in the darkness of death.

On this Menelaus was grieved, and made menacingly towards Helenus, brandishing his spear; but Helenus drew his bow, and the two attacked one another at one and the same moment, the one with his spear, and the other with his bow and arrow. The son of Priam hit the breastplate of Menelaus' corslet, but the arrow glanced from off it. As black beans or pulse come pattering down on to a threshing floor from the broad winnowing-shovel, blown by shrill winds and shaken by the shovel—even so did the arrow glance off and recoil from the shield of Menelaus, who in his turn wounded the hand with which Helenus carried his bow. The spear went right through his hand and stuck in the bow itself, so that to save his life he retreated under cover of his men, with his hand dragging by his side—for the spear weighed it down till Agenor drew it out and bound the hand carefully up in a woolen sling which his esquire had with him.

Pisander then made straight at Menelaus—his evil destiny luring him on to his doom, for he was to fall in fight with you, O Menelaus. When the two were hard by one another the spear of the son of Atreus turned aside and he missed his aim. Pisander then struck the shield of brave Menelaus but could not pierce it, for the shield stayed the spear and broke the shaft. Nevertheless, he was glad and made sure of victory. Forthwith, however, the son of Atreus drew his sword and sprang upon him. Pisander then seized the bronze battle-ax with its long and polished handle of olive wood that hung by his side under his shield, and the two made at one another. Pisander struck the peak of Menelaus' crested helmet just under the crest itself, and Menelaus hit Pisander as he was coming towards him, on the forehead, just at the rise of his nose. The bones cracked and his two gore-bedrabbled eyes fell by his feet in the dust. He fell backwards to the ground, and Menelaus set his heel upon him, stripped him of his armor, and vaunted over him, saying:

"Even thus shall you Trojans leave the ships of the Achaeans, proud and insatiate of battle though you be, nor shall you lack any of the disgrace and shame which you have heaped upon myself. Cowardly she-wolves that you are, you feared not the anger of dread Zeus, avenger of violated hospitality, who will one day destroy your city. You stole my wedded wife and wickedly carried off much treasure when you were her guest, and now you would fling fire upon our ships and kill our heroes. A day will come when, rage as you may, you shall be stayed. O father Zeus, you, who they say art above all, both gods and men, in wisdom, and from whom all things that befall us do proceed, how can you thus favor the Trojans—men so proud and overweening that they are never tired of fighting? All things pall after a while—sleep, love, sweet song, and stately dance —still these are things of which a man would surely have his fill rather than of battle, whereas it is of battle that the Trojans are insatiate."

So saying, Menelaus stripped the bloodstained armor from the body of Pisander and handed it over to his men; then he again ranged himself among those who were in the front of the fight.

Harpalion, son of King Pylaemenes, then sprang upon him. He had come to fight at Troy along with his father, but he did not go home again. He struck the middle of Menelaus' shield with his spear but could not pierce it, and to save his life drew back under cover of his men, looking round him on every side lest he should be wounded. But Meriones aimed a bronze-tipped arrow at him as he was leaving the field, and hit him on the right buttock. The arrow pierced the bone through and through, and penetrated the bladder, so he sat down where he was and breathed his last in the arms of his comrades, stretched like a worm upon the ground and watering the earth with the blood that flowed from his wound. The brave Paphlagonians tended him with all due care; they raised him into his chariot, and bore him sadly off to the city of Troy. His father went also with him weeping bitterly, but there was no ransom that could bring his dead son to life again.

Paris was deeply grieved by the death of Harpalion, who was his host when he went among the Paphlagonians; he aimed an arrow, therefore, in order to avenge him. Now there was a certain man named Euchenor, son of Polyidus, the prophet, a brave man and wealthy, whose home was in Corinth. This Euchenor had set sail for Troy well knowing that it would be the death of him, for his good old father Polyidus had often told him that he must either stay at home and die of a terrible disease, or go with the Achaeans and perish at the hands of the Trojans. He chose, therefore, to avoid incurring the heavy fine the Achaeans would have laid upon him, and at the same time to escape the pain and suffering of disease. Paris now smote him on the jaw under his ear, whereon the life went out of him and he was enshrouded in the darkness of death.

Thus then did they fight as it were a flaming fire. But Hector had not yet heard, and did not know that the Argives were making havoc of his men on the left wing of the battle, where the Achaeans ere long would have triumphed over them, so vigorously did Poseidon cheer them on and help them. He therefore held on at the point where he had first forced his way through the gates and the wall, after breaking through the serried ranks of Danaan warriors. It was here that the ships of Ajax and Protesilaus were drawn up by the seashore. Here the wall was at its lowest, and the fight both of man and horse raged most fiercely. The Boeotians and the Ionians with their long tunics, the Locrians, the men of Phthia, and the famous force of the Epeans could hardly stay Hector as he rushed on towards the ships, nor could they drive him from them, for he was as a wall of fire. The chosen men of the Athenians were in the van, led by Menestheus, son of Peteos, with whom were also Pheidas, Stichius, and stalwart Bias; Meges, son of Phyleus, Amphion, and Dracius commanded the Epeans, while Medon and staunch Podarces led the men of Phthia. Of these, Medon was bastard son to Oïleus and brother of Ajax, but he lived in Phylace away from his own country, for he had killed the brother of his stepmother Eriopis, the wife of Oïleus. The other, Podarces, was the son of Iphiclus, son of Phylacus. These two stood in the van of the Phthians, and defended the ships along with the Boeotians.

Ajax, son of Oïleus, never for a moment left the side of Ajax, son of Telamon, but as two swart oxen both strain their utmost at the plow which they are drawing in a fallow field, and the sweat steams upwards from about the roots of their horns—nothing but the yoke divides them as they break up the ground till they reach the end of the field—even so did the two Ajaxes stand shoulder to shoulder by one another. Many and brave comrades followed the son of Telamon, to relieve him of his shield when he was overcome with sweat and toil, but the Locrians did not follow so close after the son of Oïleus, for they could not hold their own in a hand-to-hand fight. They had no bronze helmets with plumes of horsehair, neither had they shields nor ashen spears, but they had come to Troy armed with bows and with slings of twisted wool from which they showered their missiles to break the ranks of the Trojans. The others, therefore, with their heavy armor bore the brunt of the fight with the Trojans and with Hector, while the Locrians shot from behind, under their cover; and thus the Trojans began to lose heart, for the arrows threw them into confusion.

The Trojans would now have been driven in sorry plight from the ships and tents back to windy Ilium had not Polydamas presently said to Hector: "Hector, there is no persuading you to take advice. Because heaven has so richly endowed you with the arts of war, you think that you must therefore excel others in counsel; but you cannot thus claim preeminence in all things. Heaven has made one man an excellent soldier; of another it has made a dancer or a singer and player on the lyre; while yet in another Zeus has implanted a wise understanding of which men reap fruit to the saving of many, and he himself knows more about it than anyone; therefore I will say what I think will be best. The fight has hemmed you in as with a circle of fire, and even now that the Trojans are within the wall some of them stand aloof in full armor, while others are fighting scattered and outnumbered near the ships. Draw back, therefore, and call your chieftains round you, that we may advise together whether to fall now upon the ships in the hope that heaven may vouchsafe us victory, or to beat a retreat while we can yet safely do so. I greatly fear that the Achaeans will pay us their debt of yesterday in full, for there is one abiding at their ships who is never weary of battle, and who will not hold aloof much longer."

Thus spoke Polydamas, and his words pleased Hector well. He sprang in full armor from his chariot and said, "Polydamas, gather the chieftains here; I will go yonder into the fight, but will return at once when I have given them their orders."

He then sped onward, towering like a snowy mountain, and with a loud cry flew through the ranks of the Trojans and their allies. When they heard his voice they all hastened to gather round Polydamas, the excellent son of Panthoüs, but Hector kept on among the foremost, looking everywhere to find Deïphobus and prince Helenus, Adamas, son of Asius, and Asius, son of Hyrtacus; living, indeed, and scatheless he could no longer find them, for the two last were lying by the sterns of the Achaean ships, slain by the Argives, while the others had been also stricken and wounded by them; but upon the left wing of the dread battle he found Paris, husband of lovely Helen, cheering his men and urging them on to fight. He went up to him and upbraided him. "Paris," said he, "evil-hearted Paris, fair to see but woman-mad and false of tongue, where are Deïphobus and King Helenus? Where are Adamas, son of Asius, and Asius, son of Hyrtacus? Where too is Othryoneus? Ilium is undone and will now surely fall!"

Paris answered: "Hector, why find fault when there is no one to find fault with? I should hold aloof from battle on any day rather than this, for my mother bore me with nothing of the coward about me. From the moment when you set our men fighting about the ships we have been staying here and doing battle with the Danaans. Our comrades about whom you ask me are dead. Deïphobus and King Helenus alone have left the field, wounded both of them in the hand, but the son of Cronus saved them alive. Now, therefore, lead on where you would have us go, and we will follow with right good will. You shall not find us fail you in so far as our strength holds out, but no man can do more than in him lies, no matter how willing he may be."

With these words he satisfied his brother, and the two went towards the part of the battle where the fight was thickest, about Cebriones, brave Polydamas, Phalces, Orthaeus, godlike Polyphetes, Palmys, Ascanius, and Morys, son of Hippotion, who had come from fertile Ascania on the preceding day to relieve other troops. Then Zeus urged them on to fight. They flew forth like the blasts of some fierce wind that strike earth in the van of a thunderstorm—they buffet the salt sea into an uproar. Many and mighty are the great waves that come crashing in one after the other upon the shore with their arching heads all crested with foam—even so did rank behind rank of Trojans arrayed in gleaming armor follow their leaders onward. The way was led by Hector, son of Priam, peer of murderous Ares, with his round shield before him—his shield of oxhides covered with plates of bronze—and his gleaming helmet upon his temples. He kept stepping forward under cover of his shield in every direction, making trial of the ranks to see if they would give way before him, but he could not daunt the courage of the Achaeans. Ajax was the first to stride out and challenge him.

"Sir," he cried, "draw near! Why do you think thus vainly to dismay the Argives? We Achaeans are excellent soldiers, but the scourge of Zeus has fallen heavily upon us. Your heart, forsooth, is set on destroying our ships, but we too have hands that can keep you at bay, and your own fair town shall be sooner taken and sacked by ourselves. The time is near when you shall pray to Zeus and all the gods in your flight that your steeds may be swifter than hawks as they raise the dust on the plain and bear you back to your city."

As he was thus speaking a bird flew by upon his right hand, and the host of the Achaeans shouted, for they took heart at the omen. But Hector answered: "Ajax, braggart and false of tongue, would that I were as sure of being son forevermore to aegis-bearing Zeus, with Queen Hera for my mother, and of being held in like honor with Athene and Apollo, as I am that this day is big with the destruction of the Achaeans; and you shall fall among them if you dare abide my spear. It shall rend your fair body and bid you glut our hounds and birds of prey with your fat and your flesh, as you fall by the ships of the Achaeans."

With these words he led the way and the others followed after with a cry that rent the air, while the host shouted behind them. The Argives on their part raised a shout likewise, nor did they forget their prowess, but stood firm against the onslaught of the Trojan chieftains, and the cry from both the hosts rose up to heaven and to the brightness of Zeus' presence.

Book XIV

As the Greeks fall back, Agamemnon is again ready to take to the ships, but
Odysseus and Diomed declare that, shattered as their forces are, they will
return to the fray. Hera, plotting to distract the attention of Zeus, borrows
the magic girdle of Aphrodite, and entices her husband to love and slumber
on Mount Ida. While Zeus sleeps, the fortunes of battle change: Hector is
wounded by Ajax, and countless Trojans are slaughtered.

NESTOR WAS SITTING OVER HIS WINE, BUT THE CRY OF BATTLE DID
not escape him, and he said to the son of Asclepius: "What, noble
Machaon, is the meaning of all this? The shouts of men fighting
by our ships grow stronger and stronger. Stay here, therefore, and sit over
your wine, while fair Hecamedé heats you a bath and washes the clotted
blood from off you. I will go at once to the lookout station and see what it
is all about."

As he spoke he took up the shield of his son Thrasymedes that was lying in
his tent, all gleaming with bronze, for Thrasymedes had taken his father's
shield. He grasped his redoubtable bronze-shod spear, and as soon as he was
outside saw the disastrous rout of the Achaeans who, now that their wall was
overthrown, were flying pell-mell before the Trojans. As when there is a heavy
swell upon the sea, but the waves are dumb—they keep their eyes on the watch
for the quarter whence the fierce winds may spring upon them, but they stay
where they are and set neither this way nor that till some particular wind
sweeps down from heaven to determine them—even so did the old man pon-

der whether to make for the crowd of Danaans, or go in search of Agamemnon. In the end he deemed it best to go to the son of Atreus; but meanwhile the hosts were fighting and killing one another, and the hard bronze rattled on the bodies as they thrust at one another with their swords and spears.

The wounded kings, the son of Tydeus, Odysseus, and Agamemnon, son of Atreus, fell in with Nestor as they were coming up from their ships—for theirs were drawn up some way from where the fighting was going on, being on the shore itself, inasmuch as they had been beached first, while the wall had been built behind the hindermost. The stretch of the shore, wide though it was, did not afford room for all the ships, and the host was cramped for space; therefore they had placed the ships in rows one behind the other and had filled the whole opening of the bay between the two points that formed it. The kings, leaning on their spears, were coming out to survey the fight, being in great anxiety, and when old Nestor met them they were filled with dismay. Then King Agamemnon said to him: "Nestor, son of Neleus, honor to the Achaean name, why have you left the battle to come hither? I fear that what dread Hector said will come true, when he vaunted among the Trojans saying that he would not return to Ilium till he had fired our ships and killed us; this is what he said, and now it is all coming true. Alas! others of the Achaeans, like Achilles, are in anger with me that they refuse to fight by the sterns of our ships."

Then Nestor, knight of Gerene, answered: "It is indeed as you say; it is all coming true at this moment, and even Zeus who thunders from on high cannot prevent it. Fallen is the wall on which we relied as an impregnable bulwark both for us and our fleet. The Trojans are fighting stubbornly and without ceasing at the ships. Look where you may you cannot see from what quarter the rout of the Achaeans is coming; they are being killed in a confused mass and the battle cry ascends to heaven. Let us think, if counsel can be of any use, what we had better do; but I do not advise our going into battle ourselves, for a man cannot fight when he is wounded."

And King Agamemnon answered: "Nestor, if the Trojans are indeed fighting at the rear of our ships, and neither the wall nor the trench has served us—over which the Danaans toiled so hard, and which they deemed would be an impregnable bulwark both for us and our fleet—I see it must be the will of Zeus that the Achaeans should perish ingloriously here, far from Argos. I knew when Zeus was willing to defend us, and I know now that he is raising the Trojans to like honor with the gods, while us, on the other hand, he has bound hand and foot. Now, therefore, let us all do as I say. Let us bring down the ships that are on the beach and draw them into the water. Let us make them fast to their mooring-stones a little way out, against the fall of night—if even by night the Trojans will desist from fighting; we may then draw down the rest of the fleet. There is nothing wrong in flying ruin even by night: it is better for a man that he should fly and be saved than be caught and killed."

Odysseus looked fiercely at him and said: "Son of Atreus, what are you talking about? Wretch, you should have commanded some other and baser army, and not been ruler over us to whom Zeus has allotted a life of hard fighting from youth to old age, till we everyone of us perish. Is it thus that you would quit the city of Troy, to win which we have suffered so much hardship? Hold your peace, lest some other of the Achaeans hear you say what no man who knows how to give good counsel, no king over so great a host as that of the Argives should ever have let fall from his lips. I despise your judgment utterly for what you have been saying. Would you, then, have us draw down our ships into the water while the battle is raging and thus play further into the hands of the conquering Trojans? It would be ruin; the Achaeans will not go on fighting when they see the ships being drawn into the water, but will cease attacking and keep turning their eyes towards them; your counsel, therefore, sir captain, would be our destruction."

Agamemnon answered: "Odysseus, your rebuke has stung me to the heart. I am not, however, ordering the Achaeans to draw their ships into the sea whether they will or no. Someone, it may be, old or young, can offer us better counsel which I shall rejoice to hear."

Then said Diomed: "Such a one is at hand; he is not far to seek, if you will listen to me and not resent my speaking though I am younger than any of you. I am by lineage son to a noble sire, Tydeus, who lies buried at Thebes. For Portheus had three noble sons, two of whom, Agrius and Melas, abode in Pleuron and rocky Calydon. The third was the knight Oeneus, my father's father, and he was the most valiant of them all. Oeneus remained in his own country, but my father (as Zeus and the other gods ordained it) migrated to Argos. He married into the family of Adrastus, and his house was one of great abundance, for he had large estates of rich corn-growing land, with much orchard ground as well, and he had many sheep. Moreover, he excelled all the Argives in the use of the spear. You must yourselves have heard whether these things are true or no. Therefore when I say well, despise not my words as though I were a coward or of ignoble birth. I say, then, let us go to the fight as we needs must, wounded though we be. When there, we may keep out of the battle and beyond the range of the spears lest we get fresh wounds in addition to what we have already, but we can spur on others who have been indulging their spleen and holding aloof from battle hitherto."

Thus did he speak. Whereon they did even as he had said and set out, King Agamemnon leading the way.

Meanwhile Poseidon had kept no blind lookout and came up to them in the semblance of an old man. He took Agamemnon's right hand in his own and said: "Son of Atreus, I take it Achilles is glad now that he sees the Achaeans routed and slain, for he is utterly without remorse—may he come to a bad end and heaven confound him. As for yourself, the blessed gods are not yet so bitterly angry with you but that the princes and councilors of the Trojans shall again raise the dust upon the plain, and you shall see them flying from the ships and tents towards their city."

With this he raised a mighty cry of battle and sped forward to the plain. The voice that came from his deep chest was as that of nine or ten thousand men when they are shouting in the thick of a fight, and it put fresh courage into the hearts of the Achaeans to wage war and do battle without ceasing.

Hera of the golden throne looked down as she stood upon a peak of Olympus and her heart was gladdened at the sight of him who was at once her brother and her brother-in-law, hurrying hither and thither amid the fighting. Then she turned her eyes to Zeus as he sat on the topmost crests of many-fountained Ida, and loathed him. She set herself to think how she might hoodwink him, and in the end she deemed that it would be best for her to go to Ida and array herself in rich attire, in the hope that Zeus might become enamored of her, and wish to embrace her. While he was thus engaged a sweet and careless sleep might be made to steal over his eyes and senses.

She went, therefore, to the room which her son Hephaestus had made her, and the doors of which he had cunningly fastened by means of a secret key so that no other god could open them. Here she entered and closed the doors behind her. She cleansed all the dirt from her fair body with ambrosia, then she anointed herself with olive oil, ambrosial, very soft, and scented specially for herself—if it were so much as shaken in the bronze-floored house of Zeus, the scent pervaded the universe of heaven and earth. With this she anointed her delicate skin, and then she plaited the fair ambrosial locks that flowed in a stream of golden tresses from her immortal head. She put on the wondrous robe which Athene had worked for her with consummate art, and had embroidered with manifold devices. She fastened it about her bosom with golden clasps and she girded herself with a girdle that had a hundred tassels; then she fastened her earrings, three brilliant pendants that glistened most beautifully, through the pierced lobes of her ears, and threw a lovely new veil over her head. She bound her sandals on to her feet, and when she had arrayed herself perfectly to her satisfaction, she left her room and called Aphrodite to come aside and speak to her. "My dear child," said she, "will you do what I am going to ask of you, or will you refuse me because you are angry at my being on the Danaan side, while you are on the Trojan?"

Zeus' daughter Aphrodite answered, "Hera, august queen of goddesses, daughter of mighty Cronus, say what you want, and I will do it for you at once, if I can, and if it can be done at all."

Then Hera told her a lying tale and said: "I want you to endow me with some of those fascinating charms, the spells of which bring all things mortal and immortal to your feet. I am going to the world's end to visit Oceanus (from whom all we gods proceed) and mother Tethys: they received me in their house, took care of me, and brought me up, having taken me over from Rhaea when Zeus imprisoned great Cronus in the depths that are under earth and sea. I must go and see them that I may make peace between them; they have been quarreling, and are so angry that they have not slept with one another this long while. If I can bring them round and restore them to one another's embraces, they will be grateful to me and love me forever afterwards."

Thereon laughter-loving Aphrodite said, "I cannot and must not refuse you, for you sleep in the arms of Zeus who is our king."

As she spoke she loosed from her bosom the curiously embroidered girdle into which all her charms had been wrought—love, desire, and that sweet flattery which steals the judgment even of the most prudent. She gave the girdle to Hera and said, "Take this girdle wherein all my charms reside and lay it in your bosom. If you will wear it I promise you that your errand, be it what it may, will not be bootless."

When she heard this Hera smiled, and still smiling she laid the girdle in her bosom.

Aphrodite now went back into the house of Zeus, while Hera darted down from the summits of Olympus. She passed over Pieria and fair Emathia, and went on and on till she came to the snowy ranges of the Thracian horsemen, over whose topmost crests she sped without ever setting foot to ground.

When she came to Athos she went on over the waves of the sea till she reached Lemnos, the city of noble Thoas. There she met Sleep, own brother to Death, and caught him by the hand, saying: "Sleep, you who lord it alike over mortals and immortals, if you ever did me a service in times past, do one for me now, and I shall be grateful to you ever after. Close Zeus' keen eyes for me in slumber while I hold him clasped in my embrace, and I will give you a beautiful golden seat, that can never fall to pieces. My club-footed son Hephaestus shall make it for you, and he shall give it a footstool for you to rest your fair feet upon when you are at table."

Then Sleep answered: "Hera, great queen of goddesses, daughter of mighty Cronus, I would lull any other of the gods to sleep without compunction, not even excepting the waters of Oceanus from whom all of them proceed, but I dare not go near Zeus, nor send him to sleep unless he bids me. I have had one lesson already through doing what you asked me, on the day when Zeus' mighty son Heracles set sail from Ilium after having sacked the city of the Trojans. At your bidding I suffused my sweet self over the mind of aegis-bearing Zeus, and laid him to rest; meanwhile you hatched a plot against Heracles, and set the blasts of the angry winds beating upon the sea till you took him to the goodly city of Cos, away from all his friends. Zeus was furious when he awoke and began hurling the gods about all over the house. He was looking more particularly for myself, and would have flung me down through space into the sea where I should never have been heard of any more, had not Night who cows both men and gods protected me. I fled to her and Zeus left off looking for me in spite of his being so angry, for he did not dare do anything to displease Night. And now you are again asking me to do something on which I cannot venture."

And Hera said: "Sleep, why do you take such notions as those into your head? Do you think Zeus will be as anxious to help the Trojans as he was about his own son? Come, I will marry you to one of the youngest of the Graces, and she shall be your own—Pasithea, whom you have always wanted to marry."

Sleep was pleased when he heard this, and answered: "Then swear it to me by the dread waters of the river Styx. Lay one hand on the bounteous earth and the other on the sheen of the sea, so that all the gods who dwell down below with Saturn may be our witnesses, and see that you really do give me one of the youngest of the Graces, Pasithea, whom I have always wanted to marry."

Hera did as he had said. She swore, and invoked all the gods of the nether world, who are called Titans, to witness. When she had completed her oath, the two enshrouded themselves in a thick mist and sped lightly forward, leaving Lemnos and Imbrus behind them. Presently they reached many-fountained Ida, mother of wild beasts, and Lectum, where they left the sea to go on by land, and the tops of the trees of the forest soughed under the going of their feet. Here Sleep halted, and ere Zeus caught sight of him he climbed a lofty pine tree—the tallest that reared its head towards heaven on all Ida. He hid himself behind the branches and sat there in the semblance of the sweet-singing bird that haunts the mountains and is called Chalcis by the gods, but men call it Cymindis. Hera then went to Gargarus, the topmost peak of Ida, and Zeus, driver of the clouds, set eyes upon her. As soon as he did so he became inflamed with the same passionate desire for her that he had felt when they had first enjoyed each other's embraces, and slept with one another without their dear parents knowing anything about it. He went up to her and said, "What do you want that you have come hither from Olympus—and that too with neither chariot nor horses to convey you?"

Then Hera told him a lying tale and said: "I am going to the world's end, to visit Oceanus, from whom all we gods proceed, and mother Tethys; they received me into their house, took care of me, and brought me up. I must go and see them that I may make peace between them: they have been quarreling, and are so angry that they have not slept with one another this long time. The horses that will take me over land and sea are stationed on the lowermost spurs of many-fountained Ida, and I have come here from Olympus on purpose to consult you. I was afraid you might be angry with me later on, if I went to the house of Oceanus without letting you know."

And Zeus said: "Hera, you can choose some other time for paying your visit to Oceanus—for the present let us devote ourselves to love and to the enjoyment of one another. Never yet have I been so overpowered by passion neither for goddess nor mortal woman as I am at this moment for yourself—not even when I was in love with the wife of Ixion who bore me Pirithoüs, peer of gods in counsel, nor yet with Danaë, the daintily ankled daughter of Acrisius, who bore me the famed hero Perseus. Then there was the daughter of Phoenix, who bore me Minos and Rhadamanthus. There was Semele, and Alcmena in Thebes by whom I begot my lion-hearted son Heracles, while Semele became mother to Bacchus, the comforter of mankind. There was queen Demeter again, and lovely Leto, and yourself—but with none of these was I ever so much enamored as I now am with you."

Hera again answered him with a lying tale. "Most dread son of Cronus," she exclaimed, "what are you talking about? Would you have us enjoy one another here on the top of Mount Ida, where everything can be seen? What if one of the ever-living gods should see us sleeping together, and tell the others? It would be such a scandal that when I had risen from your embraces I could never show myself inside your house again; but if you are so minded, there is a room which your son Hephaestus has made me, and he has given it good strong doors; if you would so have it, let us go thither and lie down."

And Zeus answered, "Hera, you need not be afraid that either god or man will see you, for I will enshroud both of us in such a dense golden cloud, that the very sun for all his bright piercing beams shall not see through it."

With this the son of Cronus caught his wife in his embrace; whereon the earth sprouted them a cushion of young grass, with dew-bespangled lotus, crocus, and hyacinth, so soft and thick that it raised them well above the ground. Here they laid themselves down and overhead they were covered by a fair cloud of gold from which there fell glittering dewdrops.

Thus, then, did the sire of all things repose peacefully on the crest of Ida, overcome at once by sleep and love, and he held his spouse in his arms. Meanwhile Sleep made off to the ships of the Achaeans, to tell earth-encircling Poseidon, lord of the earthquake. When he had found him he said, "Now, Poseidon, you can help the Danaans with a will and give them victory, though it be only for a short time while Zeus is still sleeping. I have sent him into a sweet slumber, and Hera has beguiled him into going to bed with her."

Sleep now departed and went his ways to and fro among mankind, leaving Poseidon more eager than ever to help the Danaans. He darted forward among the first ranks and shouted, saying, "Argives, shall we let Hector, son of Priam, have the triumph of taking our ships and covering himself with glory? This is what he says that he shall now do, seeing that Achilles is still in dudgeon at his ships. We shall get on very well without him if we keep each other in heart and stand by one another. Now, therefore, let us all do as I say. Let us each take the best and largest shield we can lay hold of, put on our helmets, and sally forth with our longest spears in our hands. I will lead you on, and Hector, son of Priam, rage as he may, will not dare to hold out against us. If any good staunch soldier has only a small shield, let him hand it over to a worse man, and take a larger one for himself."

Thus did he speak, and they did even as he had said. The son of Tydeus, Odysseus, and Agamemnon, wounded though they were, set the others in array, and went about everywhere effecting the exchanges of armor; the most valiant took the best armor, and gave the worse to the worse man. When they had donned their bronze armor they marched on with Poseidon at their head. In his strong hand he grasped his terrible sword, keen of edge and flashing like lightning. Woe to him who comes across it in the day of battle; all men quake for fear and keep away from it.

Hector on the other side set the Trojans in array. Thereon Poseidon and Hector waged fierce war on one another—Hector on the Trojan and Poseidon on the Argive side. Mighty was the uproar as the two forces met; the sea came rolling in towards the ships and tents of the Achaeans, but waves do not thunder on the shore more loudly when driven before the blast of Boreas, nor do the flames of a forest fire roar more fiercely when it is well alight upon the mountains, nor does the wind bellow with ruder music as it tears on through the tops of the oaks when it is blowing its hardest, than the terrible shout which the Trojans and Achaeans raised as they sprang upon one another.

Hector first aimed his spear at Ajax, who was turned full towards him, nor did he miss his aim. The spear struck him where two bands passed over his chest—the band of his shield and that of his silver-studded sword—and these protected his body. Hector was angry that his spear should have been hurled in vain, and withdrew under cover of his men. As he was thus retreating, Ajax, son of Telamon, struck him with a stone, of which there were many lying about under the men's feet as they fought—brought there to give support to the ship's sides as they lay on the shore. Ajax caught up one of them and struck Hector above the rim of his shield close to his neck; the blow made him spin round like a top and reel in all directions. As an oak falls headlong when uprooted by the lightning flash of father Zeus, and there is a terrible smell of brimstone—no man can help being dismayed if he is standing near it, for a thunderbolt is a very awful thing—even so did Hector fall to earth and bite the dust. His spear fell from his hand, but his shield and helmet were made fast about his body, and his bronze armor rang about him.

The sons of the Achaeans came running with a loud cry towards him, hoping to drag him away, and they showered their darts on the Trojans, but none of them could wound him before he was surrounded and covered by the princes Polydamas, Aeneas, Agenor, Sarpedon, captain of the Lycians, and noble Glaucus. Of the others, too, there was not one who was unmindful of him, and they held their round shields over him to cover him. His comrades then lifted him off the ground and bore him away from the battle to the place where his horses stood waiting for him at the rear of the fight with their driver and the chariot. These then took him towards the city groaning and in great pain. When they reached the ford of the fair stream of Xanthus, begotten of immortal Zeus, they took him from off his chariot and laid him down on the ground. They poured water over him, and as they did so he breathed again and opened his eyes. Then kneeling on his knees he vomited blood, but soon fell back on to the ground, and his eyes were again closed in darkness for he was still stunned by the blow.

When the Argives saw Hector leaving the field, they took heart and set upon the Trojans yet more furiously. Ajax, fleet son of Oïleus, began by springing on Satnius, son of Enops, and wounding him with his spear. A fair naiad nymph had borne him to Enops as he was herding cattle by the banks of the river Satniöeis. The son of Oïleus came up to him and struck him in the flank so that he fell, and a fierce fight between Trojans and Danaans raged round his body. Polydamas, son of Panthoüs, drew near to avenge him, and wounded Prothoënor, son of Areïlycus, on the right shoulder. The terrible spear went right through his shoulder, and he clutched the earth as he fell in the dust. Polydamas vaunted loudly over him, saying: "Again I take it that the spear has not sped in vain from the strong hand of the son of Panthoüs. An Argive has caught it in his body, and it will serve him for a staff as he goes down into the house of Hades."

The Argives were maddened by this boasting. Ajax, son of Telamon, was more angry than any, for the man had fallen close beside him; so he aimed at Polydamas as he was retreating, but Polydamas saved himself by swerving aside and the spear struck Archelochus, son of Antenor, for heaven counseled his destruction. It struck him where the head springs from the neck at the top joint of the spine, and severed both the tendons at the back of the head. His head, mouth, and nostrils reached the ground long before his legs and knees could do so, and Ajax shouted to Polydamas, saying, "Think, Polydamas, and tell me truly whether this man is not as well worth killing as Prothoënor was: he seems rich, and of rich family, a brother, it may be, or son of the knight Antenor, for he is very like him."

But he knew well who it was, and the Trojans were greatly angered. Acamas then bestrode his brother's body and wounded Promachus the Boeotian with his spear, for he was trying to drag his brother's body away. Acamas vaunted loudly over him, saying: "Argive archers, braggarts that you are, toil and suffering shall not be for us only, but some of you too shall fall here as well as ourselves. See how Promachus now sleeps, vanquished by my spear. Payment for my brother's blood has not been long delayed; a man, therefore, may well be thankful if he leaves a kinsman in his house behind him to avenge his fall."

His taunts infuriated the Argives, and Peneleos was more enraged than any of them. He sprang towards Acamas, but Acamas did not stand his ground, and he killed Ilioneus, son of the rich flock-master Phorbas, whom Mercury had favored and endowed with greater wealth than any other of the Trojans. Ilioneus was his only son, and Peneleos now wounded him in the eye under his eyebrows, tearing the eyeball from its socket. The spear went right through the eye into the nape of the neck, and he fell, stretching out both hands before him. Peneleos then drew his sword and smote him on the neck, so that both head and helmet came tumbling down to the ground with the spear still sticking in the eye. He then held up the head as though it had been a poppy-head, and showed it to the Trojans, vaunting over them as he did so. "Trojans," he cried, "bid the father and mother of noble Ilioneus make moan for him in their house, for the wife also of Promachus, son of Alegenor, will never be gladdened by the coming of her dear husband when we Argives return with our ships from Troy."

As he spoke fear fell upon them, and every man looked round about to see whither he might fly for safety.

Tell me now, O Muses that dwell on Olympus, who was the first of the Argives to bear away bloodstained spoils after Poseidon, lord of the earthquake, had turned the fortune of war? Ajax, son of Telamon, was first to wound Hyrtius, son of Gyrtius, captain of the staunch Mysians. Antilochus killed Phalces and Mermerus, while Meriones slew Morys and Hippotion, Teucer also killed Prothoön and Periphetes. The son of Atreus then wounded Hyperenor, shepherd of his people, in the flank, and the bronze point made his entrails gush out as it tore in among them; on this his life came hurrying out of him at the place where he had been wounded, and his eyes were closed in darkness. Ajax, son of Oïleus, killed more than any other, for there was no man so fleet as he to pursue flying foes when Zeus had spread panic among them.

Book XV

*When Zeus discovers the guile of Hera, he tells her that the Greeks will
conquer Troy, but not until his promise to Thetis has been fulfilled.
Whereupon Hera returns sullenly to Olympus. Ares, who starts toward the
battlefield, is held back by Athene. Zeus orders Poseidon to stop aiding the
Greeks and Apollo to heal Hector's wound. Hector now leads another
assault over the Greek wall, calling on his men to set fire to the ships.
Patroclus tells Achilles of the Greek plight.*

BUT WHEN THEIR FLIGHT HAD TAKEN THEM PAST THE TRENCH AND THE SET stakes, and many had fallen by the hands of the Danaans, the Trojans made a halt on reaching their chariots, routed and pale with fear. Zeus now woke on the crests of Ida, where he was lying with golden-throned Hera by his side, and starting to his feet he saw the Trojans and Achaeans, the one thrown into confusion, and the others driving them pell-mell before them with King Poseidon in their midst. He saw Hector lying on the ground with his comrades gathered round him, gasping for breath, wandering in mind and vomiting blood, for it was not the feeblest of the Achaeans who struck him.

The sire of gods and men had pity on him, and looked fiercely on Hera. "I see, Hera," said he, "you mischief-making trickster, that your cunning has stayed Hector from fighting and has caused the rout of his host. I am in half a mind to thrash you, in which case you will be the first to reap the fruits of your scurvy knavery. Do you not remember how once upon a time I had you hanged? I fastened two anvils on to your feet, and bound your hands in a chain of gold which none might break, and you hung in midair among the clouds. All the gods in Olympus were in a fury, but they could not reach you to set you free. When I caught any one of them I gripped him and hurled him from the heavenly threshold till he came fainting down to earth. Yet even this did not relieve my mind from the incessant anxiety which I felt about noble Heracles whom you and Boreas had spitefully conveyed beyond the seas to Cos, after suborning the tempests; but I rescued him, and notwithstanding all his mighty labors I brought him back again to Argos. I would remind you of this that you may learn to leave off being so deceitful and discover how much you are likely to gain by the embraces out of which you have come here to trick me."

Hera trembled as he spoke, and said: "May heaven above and earth below be my witnesses, with the waters of the river Styx—and this is the most solemn oath that a blessed god can take—nay, I swear also by your own almighty head and by our bridal bed—things over which I could never possibly perjure myself—that Poseidon is not punishing Hector and the Trojans and helping the Achaeans through any doing of mine. It is all of his own mere motion because he was sorry to see the Achaeans hard-pressed at their ships: if I were advising him, I should tell him to do as you bid him."

The sire of gods and men smiled and answered: "If you, Hera, were always to support me when we sit in council of the gods, Poseidon, like it or no, would soon come round to your and my way of thinking. If, then, you are speaking the truth and mean what you say, go among the rank and file of the gods, and tell Iris and Apollo, lord of the bow, that I want them—Iris, that she may go to the Achaean host and tell Poseidon to leave off fighting and go home, and Apollo, that he may send Hector again into battle and give him fresh strength. He will thus forget his present sufferings, and drive the Achaeans back in confusion till they fall among the ships of Achilles, son of Peleus. Achilles will then send his comrade Patroclus into battle, and Hector will kill him in front of Ilium after he has slain many warriors, and among them my own noble son Sarpedon. Achilles will kill Hector to avenge Patroclus, and from that time I will bring it about that the Achaeans shall persistently drive the Trojans back till they fulfill the counsels of Athene and take Ilium. But I will not stay my anger, nor permit any god to help the Danaans till I have accomplished the desire of the son of Peleus, according to the promise I made ' by bowing my head on the day when Thetis touched my knees and besought me to give him honor."

Hera heeded his words and went from the heights of Ida to great Olympus. Swift as the thought of one whose fancy carries him over vast continents, and he says to himself, "Now I will be here, or there," and he would have all manner of things—even so swiftly did Hera wing her way till she came to high Olympus and went in among the gods who were gathered in the house of Zeus. When they saw her they all of them came up to her and held out their cups to her by way of greeting. She let the others be, but took the cup offered her by lovely Themis, who was first to come running up to her. "Hera," said she, "why are you here? And you seem troubled—has your husband, the son of Cronus, been frightening you?"

And Hera answered: "Themis, do not ask me about it. You know what a proud and cruel disposition my husband has. Lead the gods to table, where you and all the immortals can hear the wicked designs which he has avowed. Many a one, mortal and immortal, will be angered by them, however peaceably he may be feasting now."

On this Hera sat down, and the gods were troubled throughout the house of Zeus. Laughter sat on her lips, but her brow was furrowed with care, and she spoke up in a rage. "Fools that we are," she cried, "to be thus madly angry with Zeus. We keep on wanting to go up to him and stay him by force or by persuasion, but he sits aloof and cares for nobody, for he knows that he is much stronger than any other of the immortals. Make the best, therefore, of whatever ills he may choose to send each one of you. Ares, I take it, has had a taste of them already, for his son Ascalaphus has fallen in battle—the man whom of all others he loved most dearly and whose father he owns himself to be."

When he heard this Ares smote his two sturdy thighs with the flat of his hands, and said in anger, "Do not blame me, you gods that dwell in heaven, if I go to the ships of the Achaeans and avenge the death of my son, even though it end in my being struck by Zeus' lightning and lying in blood and dust among the corpses."

As he spoke he gave orders to yoke his horses Panic and Rout, while he put on his armor. On this, Zeus would have been roused to still more fierce and implacable enmity against the other immortals, had not Athene, alarmed for the safety of the gods, sprung from her seat and hurried outside. She tore the helmet from his head and the shield from his shoulders, and she took the bronze spear from his strong hand and set it on one side; then she said to Ares:

"Madman, you are undone; you have ears that hear not, or you have lost all judgment and understanding; have you not heard what Hera has said on coming straight from the presence of Olympian Zeus? Do you wish to go through all kinds of suffering before you are brought back sick and sorry to Olympus, after having caused infinite mischief to all us others? Zeus would instantly leave the Trojans and Achaeans to themselves; he would come to Olympus to punish us, and would grip us up one after another, guilty or not guilty. Therefore lay aside your anger for the death of your son. Better men than he have either been killed already or will fall hereafter, and one cannot protect everyone's whole family."

With these words she took Ares back to his seat. Meanwhile Hera called Apollo outside, with Iris the messenger of the gods. "Zeus," she said to them, "desires you to go to him at once on Mount Ida; when you have seen him you are to do as he may then bid you."

Thereon Hera left them and resumed her seat inside, while Iris and Apollo made all haste on their way. When they reached many-fountained Ida, mother of wild beasts, they found Zeus seated on topmost Gargarus with a fragrant cloud encircling his head as with a diadem. They stood before his presence, and he was pleased with them for having been so quick in obeying the orders his wife had given them.

He spoke to Iris first. "Go," said he, "fleet Iris, tell King Poseidon what I now bid you—and tell him true. Bid him leave off fighting, and either join the company of the gods, or go down into the sea. If he takes no heed and disobeys me, let him consider well whether he is strong enough to hold his own against me if I attack him. I am older and much stronger than he is; yet he is not afraid to set himself up as on a level with myself, of whom all the other gods stand in awe."

Iris, fleet as the wind, obeyed him, and as the cold hail or snowflakes that fly from out the clouds before the blast of Boreas, even so did she wing her way till she came close up to the great shaker of the earth. Then she said: "I have come, O dark-haired king that holds the world in his embrace, to bring you a message from Zeus. He bids you leave off fighting and either join the company of the gods or go down into the sea. If, however, you take no heed and disobey him, he says he will come down here and fight you. He would have you keep out of his reach, for he is older and much stronger than you are, and yet you are not afraid to set yourself up as on a level with himself, of whom all the other gods stand in awe."

Poseidon was very angry and said: "Great heavens! Strong as Zeus may be, he has said more than he can do if he has threatened violence against me, who am of like honor with himself. We were three brothers whom Rhea bore to Cronus—Zeus, myself, and Hades who rules the world below. Heaven and earth were divided into three parts, and each of us was to have an equal share. When we cast lots, it fell to me to have my dwelling in the sea forevermore. Hades took the darkness of the realms under the earth, while air and sky and clouds were the portion that fell to Zeus; but earth and great Olympus are the common property of all. Therefore I will not walk as Zeus would have me. For all his strength, let him keep to his own third share and be contented without threatening to lay hands upon me as though I were nobody. Let him keep his bragging talk for his own sons and daughters, who must perforce obey him."

Iris, fleet as the wind, then answered: "Am I really, Poseidon, to take this daring and unyielding message to Zeus, or will you reconsider your answer? Sensible people are open to argument, and you know that the Erinyes always range themselves on the side of the older person."

Poseidon answered: "Goddess Iris, your words have been spoken in season. It is well when a messenger shows so much discretion. Nevertheless, it cuts me to the very heart that anyone should rebuke so angrily another who is his own peer, and of like empire with himself. Now, however, I will give way in spite of my displeasure; furthermore let me tell you, and I mean what I say—if contrary to the desire of myself, Athene, driver of the spoil, Hera, Hermes, and King Hephaestus, Zeus spares steep Ilium, and will not let the Achaeans have the great triumph of sacking it, let him understand that he will incur our implacable resentment."

Poseidon now left the field to go down under the sea, and sorely did the Achaeans miss him. Then Zeus said to Apollo: "Go, dear Phoebus, to Hector, for Poseidon who holds the earth in his embrace has now gone down under the sea to avoid the severity of my displeasure. Had he not done so those gods who are below with Cronus would have come to hear of the fight between us. It is better for both of us that he should have curbed his anger and kept out of my reach, for I should have had much trouble with him. Take, then, your tasseled aegis, and shake it furiously, so as to set the Achaean heroes in a panic; take, moreover, brave Hector, O Far-darter, into your own care, and rouse him to deeds of daring, till the Achaeans are sent flying back to their ships and to the Hellespont. From that point I will think it well over, how the Achaeans may have a respite from their troubles."

Apollo obeyed his father's saying, and left the crests of Ida, flying like a falcon, bane of doves and swiftest of all birds. He found Hector no longer lying upon the ground, but sitting up, for he had just come to himself again.

He knew those who were about him, and the sweat and hard breathing had left him from the moment when the will of aegis-bearing Zeus had revived him. Apollo stood beside him and said, "Hector, son of Priam, why are you so faint, and why are you here away from the others? Has any mishap befallen you?"

Hector in a weak voice answered: "And which, kind sir, of the gods are you, who now ask me thus? Do you not know that Ajax struck me on the chest with a stone as I was killing his comrades at the ships of the Achaeans, and compelled me to leave off fighting? I made sure that this very day I should breathe my last and go down into the house of Hades."

Then King Apollo said to him: "Take heart; the son of Cronus has sent you a mighty helper from Ida to stand by you and defend you, even me, Phoebus Apollo of the golden sword, who have been guardian hitherto not only of yourself but of your city. Now, therefore, order your horsemen to drive their chariots to the ships in great multitudes. I will go before your horses to smooth the way for them, and will turn the Achaeans in flight."

As he spoke he infused great strength into the shepherd of his people. And as a horse, stabled and full-fed, breaks loose and gallops gloriously over the plain to the place where he is wont to take his bath in the river—he tosses his head, and his mane streams over his shoulders as in all the pride of his strength he flies full speed to the pastures where the mares are feeding—even so Hector, when he heard what the god said, urged his horsemen on, and sped forward as fast as his limbs could take him. As country peasants set their hounds on to a horned stag or wild goat—he has taken shelter under rock or thicket, and they cannot find him, but, lo, a bearded lion whom their shouts have roused stands in their path, and they are in no further humor for the chase—even so the Achaeans were still charging on in a body, using their swords and spears pointed at both ends, but when they saw Hector going about among his men they were afraid, and their hearts fell down into their feet.

Then spoke Thoas, son of Andraemon, leader of the Aetolians, a man who could throw a good throw, and who was staunch also in close fight, while few could surpass him in debate when opinions were divided. He then with all sincerity and good will addressed them thus: "What, in heaven's name, do I now see? Is it not Hector come to life again? Everyone made sure he had been killed by Ajax, son of Telamon, but it seems that one of the gods has again rescued him. He has killed many of us Danaans already, and I take it will yet do so, for the hand of Zeus must be with him or he would never dare show himself so masterful in the forefront of the battle. Now, therefore, let us all do as I say; let us order the main body of our forces to fall back upon the ships, but let those of us who profess to be the flower of the army stand firm, and see whether we cannot hold Hector back at the point of our spears as soon as he comes near us. I conceive that he will then think better of it before he tries to charge into the press of the Danaans."

Thus did he speak, and they did even as he had said. Those who were about Ajax and King Idomeneus, the followers moreover of Teucer, Meriones, and Meges, peer of Ares, called all their best men about them and sustained the fight against Hector and the Trojans, but the main body fell back upon the ships of the Achaeans.

The Trojans pressed forward in a dense body, with Hector striding on at their head. Before him went Phoebus Apollo, shrouded in cloud about his shoulders. He bore aloft the terrible aegis with its shaggy fringe, which Hephaestus, the smith, had given Zeus to strike terror into the hearts of men. With this in his hand he led on the Trojans.

The Argives held together and stood their ground. The cry of battle rose high from either side, and the arrows flew from the bowstrings. Many a spear sped from strong hands and fastened in the bodies of many a valiant warrior, while others fell to earth midway, before they could taste of man's fair flesh and glut themselves with blood. So long as Phoebus Apollo held his aegis quietly and without shaking it, the weapons on either side took effect and the people fell, but when he shook it straight in the face of the Danaans and raised his mighty battle cry their hearts fainted within them and they forgot their former prowess. As when two wild beasts spring in the dead of night on a herd of cattle or a large flock of sheep when the herdsman is not there—even so were the Danaans struck helpless, for Apollo filled them with panic and gave victory to Hector and the Trojans.

The fight then became more scattered and they killed one another where they best could. Hector killed Stichius and Arcesilaus, the one, leader of the Boeotians, and the other, friend and comrade of Menestheus. Aeneas killed Medon and Iasus. The first was bastard son to Oïleus, and brother to Ajax, but he lived in Phylace, away from his own country, for he had killed a man, a kinsman of his stepmother Eriopis, whom Oïleus had married. Iasus had become a leader of the Athenians, and was son of Sphelus, the son of Boucolos. Polydamas killed Mecisteus, and Polites Echius, in the front of the battle, while Agenor slew Clonius. Paris struck Deïochus from behind in the lower part of the shoulder as he was flying among the foremost, and the point of the spear went clean through him.

While they were spoiling these heroes of their armor, the Achaeans were flying pell-mell to the trench and the set stakes, and were forced back within their wall. Hector then cried out to the Trojans: "Forward to the ships, and let the spoils be! If I see any man keeping back on the other side of the wall away from the ships I will have him killed. His kinsmen and kinswomen shall not give him his dues of fire, but dogs shall tear him in pieces in front of our city."

As he spoke he laid his whip about his horses' shoulders and called to the Trojans throughout their ranks. The Trojans shouted with a cry that rent the air, and kept their horses neck and neck with his own. Phoebus Apollo went before, and kicked down the banks of the deep trench into its middle so as to make a great broad bridge, as broad as the throw of a spear when a man is trying his strength. The Trojan battalions poured over the bridge, and Apollo with his redoubtable aegis led the way. He kicked down the wall of the Achaeans as easily as a child who playing on the seashore has built a house of sand and then kicks it down again and destroys it—even so did you, O Apollo, shed toil and trouble upon the Argives, filling them with panic and confusion.

Thus then were the Achaeans hemmed in at their ships, calling out to one another and raising their hands with loud cries every man to heaven. Nestor of Gerene, tower of strength to the Achaeans, lifted up his hands to the starry firmament of heaven and prayed more fervently than any of them. "Father Zeus," said he, "if ever anyone in wheat-growing Argos burned you fat thigh-bones of sheep or heifer and prayed that he might return safely home, whereon you bowed your head to him in assent, bear it in mind now, and suffer not the Trojans to triumph thus over the Achaeans."

All-counseling Zeus thundered loudly in answer to the prayer of the aged son of Neleus. When the Trojans heard Zeus thunder they flung themselves yet more fiercely on the Achaeans. As a wave breaking over the bulwarks of a ship when the sea runs high before a gale—for it is the force of the wind that makes the waves so great—even so did the Trojans spring over the wall with a shout, and drive their chariots onwards. The two sides fought with their double-pointed spears in hand-to-hand encounter—the Trojans from their chariots, and the Achaeans climbing up into their ships and wielding the long pikes that were lying on the decks ready for use in a sea-fight, jointed and shod with bronze.

Now Patroclus, so long as the Achaeans and Trojans were fighting about the wall, but were not yet within it and at the ships, remained sitting in the tent of good Eurypylus, entertaining him with his conversation and spreading herbs over his wound to ease his pain. When, however, he saw the Trojans swarming through the breach in the wall, while the Achaeans were clamoring and struck with panic, he cried aloud, and smote his two thighs with the flat of his hands. "Eurypylus," said he in his dismay, "I know you want me badly, but I cannot stay with you any longer, for there is hard fighting going on. A servant shall take care of you now, for I must make all speed to Achilles, and induce him to fight if I can; who knows but with heaven's help I may persuade him. A man does well to listen to the advice of a friend."

When he had thus spoken he went his way. The Achaeans stood firm and resisted the attack of the Trojans, yet though these were fewer in number, they could not drive them back from the ships, neither could the Trojans break the Achaean ranks and make their way in among the tents and ships. As a carpenter's line gives a true edge to a piece of ship's timber, in the hand of some skilled workman whom Athene has instructed in all kinds of useful arts—even so level was the issue of the fight between the two sides as they fought, some round one ship and some round another.

Hector made straight for Ajax, and the two fought fiercely about the same ship. Hector could not force Ajax back and fire the ship, nor yet could Ajax drive Hector from the spot to which heaven had brought him.

Then Ajax struck Caletor, son of Clytius, in the chest with a spear as he was bringing fire towards the ship. He fell heavily to the ground and the torch dropped from his hand. When Hector saw his cousin fallen in front of the ship he shouted to the Trojans and Lycians, saying, "Trojans, Lycians, and Dardanians, good in close fight, bate not a jot, but rescue the son of Clytius, lest the Achaeans strip him of his armor now that he has fallen."

He then aimed a spear at Ajax, and missed him, but he hit Lycophron, a follower of Ajax, who came from Cythera, but was living with Ajax, inasmuch as he had killed a man among the Cythereans. Hector's spear struck him on the head below the ear, and he fell headlong from the ship's prow on to the ground with no life left in him. Ajax shook with rage and said to his brother: "Teucer, my good fellow, our trusty comrade, the son of Mastor, has fallen—he who came to live with us from Cythera and whom we honored as much as our own parents. Hector has just killed him; fetch your deadly arrows at once and the bow which Phoebus Apollo gave you."

Teucer heard him and hastened towards him with his bow and quiver in his hands. Forthwith he showered his arrows on the Trojans, and hit Cleitus, the son of Pisenor, comrade of Polydamas, the noble son of Panthoüs, with the reins in his hands as he was attending to his horses. He was in the middle of the very thickest part of the fight, doing good service to Hector and the Trojans, but evil had now come upon him, and not one of those who were fain to do so could avert it, for the arrow struck him on the back of the neck. He fell from his chariot and his horses shook the empty car as they swerved aside. King Polydamas saw what had happened, and was the first to come up to the horses. He gave them in charge to Astynoüs, son of Protiaon, and ordered him to look on, and to keep the horses near at hand. He then went back and took his place in the front ranks.

Teucer then aimed another arrow at Hector, and there would have been no more fighting at the ships if he had hit him and killed him then and there. Zeus, however, who kept watch over Hector, had his eyes on Teucer, and deprived him of his triumph by breaking his bowstring for him just as he was drawing it and about to take his aim; on this the arrow went astray and the bow fell from his hands. Teucer shook with anger and said to his brother, "Alas, see how heaven thwarts us in all we do; it has broken my bowstring and snatched the bow from my hand, though I strung it this selfsame morning that it might serve me for many an arrow."

Ajax, son of Telamon, answered: "My good fellow, let your bow and your arrows be, for Zeus has made them useless in order to spite the Danaans. Take your spear, lay your shield upon your shoulder, and both fight the Trojans yourself and urge others to do so. They may be successful for the moment, but if we fight as we ought they will find it a hard matter to take the ships."

Teucer then took his bow and put it by in his tent. He hung a shield four hides thick about his shoulders and on his comely head he set his helmet well wrought with a crest of horsehair that nodded menacingly above it; he grasped his redoubtable bronze-shod spear and forthwith he was by the side of Ajax.

When Hector saw that Teucer's bow was of no more use to him, he shouted out to the Trojans and Lycians: "Trojans, Lycians, and Dardanians good in close fight, be men, my friends, and show your mettle here at the ships, for I see the weapon of one of their chieftains made useless by the hand of Zeus. It is easy to see when Zeus is helping people and means to help them still further, or again when he is bringing them down and will do nothing for them. He is now on our side and is going against the Argives. Therefore swarm round the ships and fight. If any of you is struck by spear or sword and loses his life, let him die. He dies with honor who dies fighting for his country; and he will leave his wife and children safe behind him, with his house and allotment unplundered if only the Achaeans can be driven back to their own land, they and their ships."

With these words he put heart and soul into them all. Ajax on the other side exhorted his comrades, saying: "Shame on you, Argives, we are now utterly undone unless we can save ourselves by driving the enemy from our ships. Do you think, if Hector takes them, that you will be able to get home by land? Can you not hear him cheering on his whole host to fire our fleet and bidding them remember that they are not at a dance but in battle? Our only course is to fight them with might and main. We had better chance it, life or death, once for all, than fight long and without issue hemmed in at our ships by worse men than ourselves."

With these words he put life and soul into them all. Hector then killed Schedius, son of Perimedes, leader of the Phoceans, and Ajax killed Laodamas, captain of foot soldiers and son to Antenor. Polydamas killed Otus of Cyllene, a comrade of the son of Phyleus and chief of the proud Epeans. When Meges saw this he sprang upon him, but Polydamas crouched down, and he missed him, for Apollo would not suffer the son of Panthoüs to fall in battle; but the spear hit Croesmus in the middle of his chest, whereon he fell heavily to the ground, and Meges stripped him of his armor. At that moment the valiant soldier Dolops, son of Lampus, sprang upon him; Lampus was son of Laomedon and noted for his valor, while his son Dolops was versed in all the ways of war. He then struck the middle of the son of Phyleus' shield with his spear, setting on him at close quarters, but his good corslet made with plates of metal saved him. Phyleus had brought it from Ephyra and the river Selleïs, where his host, King Euphetes, had given it him to wear in battle and protect him. It now served to save the life of his son. Then Meges struck the topmost crest of Dolops' bronze helmet with his spear and tore away its plume of horsehair, so that all newly dyed with scarlet as it was it tumbled down into the dust.

While he was still fighting and confident of victory, Menelaus came up to help Meges, and got by the side of Dolops unperceived. He then speared him in the shoulder from behind, and the point, driven so furiously, went through into his chest, whereon he fell headlong. The two then made towards him to strip him of his armor, but Hector called on all his brothers for help, and he especially upbraided brave Melanippus, son of Hiketaon, who erewhile used to pasture his herds of cattle in Percote before the war broke out; but when the ships of the Danaans came, he went back to Ilium, where he was eminent among the Trojans, and lived near Priam who treated him as one of his own sons. Hector now rebuked him and said: "Why, Melanippus, are we thus remiss? Do you take no note of the death of your kinsman, and do you not see how they are trying to take Dolops' armor? Follow me; there must be no fighting the Argives from a distance now, but we must do so in close combat till either we kill them or they take the high wall of Ilium and slay her people."

He led on as he spoke, and the hero Melanippus followed after. Meanwhile Ajax, son of Telamon, was cheering on the Argives. "My friends," he cried, "be men, and fear dishonor! Quit yourselves in battle so as to win respect from one another. Men who respect each other's good opinion are less likely to be killed than those who do not, but in flight there is neither gain nor glory."

Thus did he exhort men who were already bent upon driving back the Trojans. They laid his words to heart and hedged the ships as with a wall of bronze, while Zeus urged on the Trojans. Menelaus of the loud battle cry urged Antilochus on. "Antilochus," said he, "you are young and there is none of the Achaeans more fleet of foot or more valiant than you are. See if you cannot spring upon some Trojan and kill him."

He hurried away when he had thus spurred Antilochus, who at once darted out from the front ranks and aimed a spear, after looking carefully round him. The Trojans fell back as he threw, and the dart did not speed from his hand without effect, for it struck Melanippus, the proud son of Hiketaon, in the breast by the nipple as he was coming forward, and his armor rang rattling round him as he fell heavily to the ground. Antilochus sprang upon him as a dog springs on a fawn which a hunter has hit as it was breaking away from its covert, and killed it. Even so, O Melanippus, did stalwart Antilochus spring upon you to strip you of your armor; but noble Hector marked him, and came running up to him through the thick of the battle. Antilochus, brave soldier though he was, would not stay to face him, but fled like some savage creature which knows it has done wrong, and flies, when it has killed a dog or a man who is herding his cattle, before a body of men can be gathered to attack it. Even so did the son of Nestor fly, and the Trojans and Hector, with a cry that rent the air, showered their weapons after him; nor did he turn round and stay his flight till he had reached his comrades.

The Trojans, fierce as lions, were still rushing on towards the ships in fulfillment of the behests of Zeus who kept spurring them on to new deeds of daring, while he deadened the courage of the Argives and defeated them by encouraging the Trojans. For he meant giving glory to Hector, son of Priam, and letting him throw fire upon the ships, till he had fulfilled the unrighteous prayer that Thetis had made him. Zeus, therefore, bided his time till he should see the glare of a blazing ship. From that hour he was about so to order it that the Trojans should be driven back from the ships and to vouchsafe glory to the Achaeans. With this purpose he inspired Hector, son of Priam, who was eager enough already, to assail the ships. His fury was as that of Ares, or as when a fire is raging in the glades of some dense forest upon the mountains. He foamed at the mouth, his eyes glared under his terrible eyebrows, and his helmet quivered on his temples by reason of the fury with which he fought. Zeus from heaven was with him, and though he was but one against many, vouchsafed him victory and glory; for he was doomed to an early death, and already Pallas Athene was hurrying on the hour of his destruction at the hands of the son of Peleus. Now, however, he kept trying to break the ranks of the enemy wherever he could see them thickest, and in the goodliest armor; but do what he might he could not break through them, for they stood as a tower foursquare, or as some high cliff rising from the gray sea that braves the anger of the gale, and of the waves that thunder up against it. He fell upon them like flames of fire from every quarter.

As when a wave, raised mountain high by wind and storm, breaks over a ship and covers it deep in foam, the fierce winds roar against the mast, the hearts of the sailors fail them for fear, and they are saved but by a very little from destruction—even so were the hearts of the Achaeans fainting within them. Or as a savage lion attacking a herd of cows while they are feeding by thousands in the low-lying meadows by some wide-watered shore—the herdsman is at his wits' end how to protect his herd and keeps going about now in the van and now in the rear of his cattle, while the lion springs into the thick of them and fastens on a cow so that they all tremble for fear—even so were the Achaeans utterly panic-stricken by Hector and father Zeus. Nevertheless, Hector only killed Periphetes of Mycenae; he was son of Copreus who was wont to take the orders of King Eurystheus to mighty Heracles, but the son was a far better man than the father in every way; he was fleet of foot, a valiant warrior, and in understanding ranked among the foremost men of Mycenae. He it was who then afforded Hector a triumph, for as he was turning back he stumbled against the rim of his shield which reached his feet, and served to keep the javelins off him. He tripped against this and fell face upward, his helmet ringing loudly about his head as he did so. Hector saw him fall and ran up to him; he then thrust a spear into his chest, and killed him close to his own comrades. These, for all their sorrow, could not help him for they were themselves terribly afraid of Hector.

They had now reached the ships and the prows of those that had been drawn up first were on every side of them, but the Trojans came pouring after them. The Argives were driven back from the first row of ships, but they made a stand by their tents without being broken up and scattered; shame and fear restrained them. They kept shouting incessantly to one another, and Nestor of Gerene, tower of strength to the Achaeans, was loudest in imploring every man by his parents, and beseeching him to stand firm.

"Be men, my friends," he cried, "and respect one another's good opinion! Think, all of you, on your children, your wives, your property, and your parents whether these be alive or dead. On their behalf though they are not here, I implore you to stand firm, and not to turn in flight."

With these words he put heart and soul into them all. Athene lifted the thick veil of darkness from their eyes, and much light fell upon them, alike on the side of the ships and on that where the fight was raging. They could see Hector and all his men, both those in the rear who were taking no part in the battle and those who were fighting by the ships.

Ajax could not bring himself to retreat along with the rest, but strode from deck to deck with a great sea-pike in his hands twelve cubits long and jointed with rings. As a man skilled in feats of horsemanship couples four horses together and comes tearing full speed along the public way from the country into some large town—many both men and women marvel as they see him for he keeps all the time changing his horse, springing from one to another without ever missing his feet while the horses are at a gallop—even so did Ajax go striding from one ship's deck to another, and his voice went up into the heavens. He kept on shouting his orders to the Danaans and exhorting them to defend their ships and tents; neither did Hector remain within the main body of the Trojan warriors, but as a dun eagle swoops down upon a flock of wild fowl feeding near a river—geese, it may be, or cranes, or long-necked swans—even so did Hector make straight for a dark-prowed ship, rushing right towards it; for Zeus with his mighty hand impelled him forward and roused his people to follow him.

And now the battle again raged furiously at the ships. You would have thought the men were coming on fresh and unwearied, so fiercely did they fight; and this was the mind in which they were—the Achaeans did not believe they should escape destruction, but thought themselves doomed, while there was not a Trojan but his heart beat high with the hope of firing the ships and putting the Achaean heroes to the sword.

Thus were the two sides minded. Then Hector seized the stern of the good ship that had brought Protesilaus to Troy, but never bore him back to his native land. Round this ship there raged a close hand-to-hand fight between Danaans and Trojans. They did not fight at a distance with bows and javelins, but with one mind hacked at one another in close combat with their mighty swords and spears pointed at both ends; they fought moreover with keen battle-axes and with hatchets. Many a good stout blade hiked and scabbarded with iron fell from hand or shoulder as they fought, and the earth ran red with blood. Hector, when he had seized the ship, would not loose his hold but held on to its curved stern and shouted to the Trojans: "Bring fire, and raise the battle cry all of you with a single voice. Now has Zeus vouchsafed us a day that will pay us for all the rest; this day we shall take the ships which came hither against heaven's will, and which have caused us such infinite suffering through the cowardice of our councilors, who when I would have done battle at the ships held me back and forbade the host to follow me; if Zeus did then indeed warp our judgments, himself now commands me and cheers me on."

As he spoke thus the Trojans sprang yet more fiercely on the Achaeans, and Ajax no longer held his ground, for he was overcome by the darts that were flung at him, and made sure that he was doomed. Therefore he left the raised deck at the stern, and stepped back on to the seven-foot bench of the oarsmen. Here he stood on the lookout, and with his spear held back any Trojan whom he saw bringing fire to the ships. All the time he kept on shouting at the top of his voice and exhorting the Danaans. "My friends," he cried, "Danaan heroes, servants of Ares, be men, my friends, and fight with might and with main. Can we hope to find helpers hereafter, or a wall to shield us more surely than the one we have? There is no strong city within reach whence we may draw fresh forces to turn the scales in our favor. We are on the plain of the armed Trojans with the sea behind us and far from our own country. Our salvation, therefore, is in the might of our hands and in hard fighting."

As he spoke he wielded his spear with still greater fury, and when any Trojan made towards the ships with fire at Hector's bidding, he would be on the lookout for him, and drive at him with his long spear. Twelve men did he thus kill in hand-to-hand fight before the ships.

Book XVI

*When Achilles hears that the situation is desperate, he tells Patroclus
to put on his armor, take his horses, and lead his Myrmidons into
the fight, charging him not to go beyond the Greek wall. The first ship is
set afire. At Patroclus' appearance, the Trojans take him for Achilles
and flee. Patroclus kills Sarpedon and drives the Trojans beyond the wall,
across the plain, and up to the city gates. Disabled by Apollo,
the hero falls before Hector's spear.*

T HUS DID THEY FIGHT ABOUT THE SHIP OF PROTESILAUS. THEN
Patroclus drew near to Achilles with tears welling from his eyes,
as from some spring whose crystal stream falls over the ledges
of a high precipice. When Achilles saw him thus weeping he was sorry
for him and said: "Why, Patroclus, do you stand there weeping like some silly
child that comes running to her mother, and begs to be taken up and car-
ried—she catches hold of her mother's dress to stay her, though she is in a
hurry, and looks tearfully up until her mother carries her—even such tears,
Patroclus, are you now shedding. Have you anything to say to the Myrmidons
or to myself? Or have you had news from Phthia which you alone know?
They tell me Menoetius, son of Actor, is still alive, as also Peleus, son of
Aeacus, among the Myrmidons—men whose loss we two should bitterly
deplore; or are you grieving about the Argives and the way in which they are
being killed at the ships, through their own high-handed doings? Do not hide
anything from me, but tell me that both of us may know about it."

Then, O knight Patroclus, with a deep sigh you answered: "Achilles, son of Peleus, foremost champion of the Achaeans, do not be angry, but I weep for the disaster that has now befallen the Argives. All those who have been their champions so far are lying at the ships, wounded by sword or spear. Brave Diomed, son of Tydeus, has been hit with a spear, while famed Odysseus and Agamemnon have received sword wounds; Eurypylus again has been struck with an arrow in the thigh; skilled apothecaries are attending to these heroes, and healing them of their wounds. Are you still, O Achilles, so inexorable? May it never be my lot to nurse such a passion as you have done, to the baning of your own good name. Who in future story will speak well of you unless you now save the Argives from ruin? You know no pity; knight Peleus was not your father nor Thetis your mother, but the gray sea bore you and the sheer cliffs begot you, so cruel and remorseless are you. If, however, you are kept back through knowledge of some oracle, or if your mother Thetis has told you something from the mouth of Zeus, at least send me and the Myrmidons with me, if I may bring deliverance to the Danaans. Let me, moreover, wear your armor. The Trojans may thus mistake me for you and quit the field, so that the hard-pressed sons of the Achaeans may have breathing time—which while they are fighting may hardly be. We who are fresh might soon drive tired men back from our ships and tents to their own city."

He knew not what he was asking, nor that he was suing for his own destruction. Achilles was deeply moved and answered: "What, noble Patroclus, are you saying? I know no prophesyings which I am heeding, nor has my mother told me anything from the mouth of Zeus, but I am cut to the very heart that one of my own rank should dare to rob me because he is more powerful than I am. This, after all that I have gone through, is more than I can endure. The girl whom the sons of the Achaeans chose for me, whom I won as the fruit of my spear on having sacked a city—her has King Agamemnon taken from me as though I were some common vagrant. Still, let bygones be bygones: no man may keep his anger forever. I said I would not relent till battle and the cry of war had reached my own ships. Nevertheless, now gird my armor about your shoulders, and lead the Myrmidons to battle, for the dark cloud of Trojans has burst furiously over our fleet. The Argives are driven back on to the beach, cooped within a narrow space, and the whole people of Troy has taken heart to sally out against them, because they see not the vizor of my helmet gleaming near them. Had they seen this, there would not have been a creek nor grip that had not been filled with their dead as they fled back again. And so it would have been, if only King Agamemnon had dealt fairly by me. As it is, the Trojans have beset our host. Diomed, son of Tydeus, no longer wields his spear to defend the Danaans, neither have I heard the voice of the son of Atreus coming from his hated head, whereas that of murderous Hector rings in my ears as he gives orders to the Trojans, who triumph over the Achaeans and fill the whole plain with their cry of battle. But even so, Patroclus, fall upon them and save the fleet, lest the Trojans fire it and prevent us from being able to return. Do, however, as I now bid you, that you may win me great honor from all the Danaans, and that they may restore the girl to me again and give me rich gifts into the bargain.

"When you have driven the Trojans from the ships, come back again. Though Hera's thundering husband should put triumph within your reach, do not fight the Trojans further in my absence, or you will rob me of glory that should be mine. And do not for lust of battle go on killing the Trojans nor lead the Achaeans on to Ilium, lest one of the ever-living gods from Olympus attack you—for Phoebus Apollo loves them well: return when you have freed the ships from peril, and let others wage war upon the plain. Would, by father Zeus, Athene, and Apollo, that not a single man of all the Trojans might be left alive, nor yet of the Argives, but that we two might be alone left to tear aside the mantle that veils the brow of Troy."

Thus did they converse. But Ajax could no longer hold his ground for the shower of darts that rained upon him. The will of Zeus and the javelins of the Trojans were too much for him; the helmet that gleamed about his temples rang with the continuous clatter of the missiles that kept pouring on to it and on to the cheek-pieces that protected his face. Moreover his left shoulder was tired with having held his shield so long; yet for all this, let fly at him as they would, they could not make him give ground. He could hardly draw his breath, the sweat rained from every pore of his body, he had not a moment's respite, and on all sides he was beset by danger upon danger.

And now, tell me, O Muses that hold your mansions on Olympus, how fire was thrown upon the ships of the Achaeans. Hector came close up and let drive with his great sword at the ashen spear of Ajax. He cut it clean in two just behind where the point was fastened on to the shaft of the spear. Ajax, therefore, had now nothing but a headless spear, while the bronze point flew some way off and came ringing down on to the ground. Ajax knew the hand of heaven in this, and was dismayed at seeing that Zeus had now left him utterly defenseless and was willing victory for the Trojans. Therefore he drew back, and the Trojans flung fire upon the ship which was at once wrapped in flame.

The fire was now flaring about the ship's stern, whereon Achilles smote his two thighs and said to Patroclus: "Up, noble knight, for I see the glare of hostile fire at our fleet; up, lest they destroy our ships, and there be no way by which we may retreat. Gird on your armor at once while I call our people together."

As he spoke Patroclus put on his armor. First he greaved his legs with greaves of good make, and fitted with ankle-clasps of silver; after this he donned the cuirass of the son of Aeacus, richly inlaid and studded. He hung his silver-studded sword of bronze about his shoulders, and then his mighty shield. On his comely head he set his helmet, well-wrought, with a crest of horsehair that nodded menacingly above it. He grasped two redoubtable spears that suited his hands, but he did not take the spear of noble Achilles, so stout and strong, for none other of the Achaeans could wield it, though Achilles could do so easily. This was the ashen spear from Mount Pelion, which Chiron had cut upon a mountain top and had given to Peleus, wherewith to deal out death among heroes. He bade Automedon yoke his horses with all speed, for he was the man whom he held in honor next after Achilles, and on whose support in battle he could rely most firmly. Automedon, therefore, yoked the fleet horses Xanthus and Balius, steeds that could fly like the wind. These were they whom the harpy Podarge bore to the west wind, as she was grazing in a meadow by the waters of the river Oceanus. In the side traces he set the noble horse Pedasus, whom Achilles had brought away with him when he sacked the city of Eëtion, and who, mortal steed though he was, could take his place along with those that were immortal.

Meanwhile Achilles went about everywhere among the tents, and bade his Myrmidons put on their armor. Even as fierce ravening wolves that are feasting upon a horned stag which they have killed upon the mountains, and their jaws are red with blood—they go in a pack to lap water from the clear spring with their long thin tongues, and they reek of blood and slaughter. They know not what fear is, for it is hunger drives them—even so did the leaders and councilors of the Myrmidons gather round the good squire of the fleet descendant of Aeacus, and among them stood Achilles himself cheering on both men and horses.

Fifty ships had noble Achilles brought to Troy, and in each there was a crew of fifty oarsmen. Over these he set five captains whom he could trust, while he was himself commander over them all. Menestheus of the gleaming corslet, son to the river Spercheius that streams from heaven, was captain of the first company. Fair Polydora, daughter of Peleus, bore him to ever-flowing Spercheius—a woman mated with a god—but he was called son of Borus, son of Perieres, with whom his mother was living as his wedded wife, and who gave great wealth to gain her. The second company was led by noble Eudorus, son to an unwedded woman. Polymele, daughter of Phylas, the graceful dancer, bore him. The mighty slayer of Argus was enamored of her as he saw her among the singing women at a dance held in honor of Artemis, the rushing huntress of the golden arrows; he therefore—Hermes, giver of all good—went with her into an upper chamber, and lay with her in secret, whereon she bore him a noble son Eudorus, singularly fleet of foot and in fight valiant. When Ilithuia, goddess of the pains of childbirth, brought him to the light of day, and he saw the face of the sun, mighty Echecles, son of Actor, took the mother to wife, and gave great wealth to gain her, but her father Phylas brought the child up, and took care of him, doting as fondly upon him as though he were his own son. The third company was led by Pisander, son of Maemalus, the finest spearman among all the Myrmidons next to Achilles' own comrade, Patroclus. The old knight Phoenix was captain of the fourth company, and Alcimedon, noble son of Laërceus, of the fifth.

When Achilles had chosen his men and had stationed them all with their captains, he charged them straitly, saying: "Myrmidons, remember your threats against the Trojans while you were at the ships in the time of my anger, and you were all complaining of me. 'Cruel son of Peleus,' you would say, 'your mother must have suckled you on gall, so ruthless are you. You keep us here at the ships against our will; if you are so relentless it were better we went home over the sea.' Often have you gathered and thus chided with me. The hour is now come for those high feats of arms that you have so long been pining for, therefore keep high hearts each one of you to do battle with the Trojans."

With these words he put heart and soul into them all, and they serried their companies yet more closely when they heard the words of their king. As the stones which a builder sets in the wall of some high house which is to give shelter from the winds—even so closely were the helmets and bossed shields set against one another. Shield pressed on shield, helm on helm, and man on man; so close were they that the horsehair plumes on the gleaming ridges of their helmets touched each other as they bent their heads.

In front of them all two men put on their armor—Patroclus and Automedon—two men, with but one mind to lead the Myrmidons. Then

Achilles went inside his tent and opened the lid of the strong chest which silver-footed Thetis had given him to take on board ship, and which she had filled with shirts, cloaks to keep out the cold, and good thick rugs. In this chest he had a cup of rare workmanship from which no man but himself might drink, nor would he make offering from it to any other god save only to father Zeus. He took the cup from the chest and cleansed it with sulfur. This done, he rinsed it in clean water, and after he had washed his hands he drew wine. Then he stood in the middle of the court and prayed, looking towards heaven, and making his drink offering of wine; nor was he unseen of Zeus whose joy is in thunder. "King Zeus," he cried, "lord of Dodona, god of the Pelasgi, who dwellest afar, you who hold wintry Dodona in your sway, where your prophets the Selli dwell around you with their feet unwashed and their couches made upon the ground—if you heard me when I prayed to you aforetime, and did me honor while you sent disaster on the Achaeans, vouchsafe me now the fulfillment of yet this further prayer. I shall stay here where my ships are lying, but I shall send my comrade into battle at the head of many Myrmidons. Grant, O all-seeing Zeus, that victory may go with him; put your courage into his heart that Hector may learn whether my squire is man enough to fight alone, or whether his might is only then so indomitable when I myself enter the turmoil of war. Afterwards when he has chased the fight and the cry of battle from the ships, grant that he may return unharmed, with his armor and his comrades, fighters in close combat."

Thus did he pray, and all-counseling Zeus heard his prayer. Part of it he did indeed vouchsafe him—but not the whole. He granted that Patroclus should thrust back war and battle from the ships, but refused to let him come safely out of the fight.

When he had made his drink offering and had thus prayed, Achilles went inside his tent and put back the cup into his chest. Then he again came out, for he still loved to look upon the fierce fight that raged between the Trojans and Achaeans.

Meanwhile the armed band that was about Patroclus marched on till they sprang high in hope upon the Trojans. They came swarming out like wasps whose nests are by the roadside and whom silly children love to tease, whereon anyone who happens to be passing may get stung—or again, if a wayfarer going along the road vexes them by accident, every wasp will come flying out in a fury to defend his little ones—even with such rage and courage did the Myrmidons swarm from their ships, and their cry of battle rose heavenwards. Patroclus called out to his men at the top of his voice: "Myrmidons, followers of Achilles, son of Peleus, be men, my friends, fight with might and with main, that we may win glory for the son of Peleus, who is far the foremost man at the ships of the Argives—he, and his close-fighting followers. The son of Atreus, King Agamemnon, will thus learn his folly in showing no respect to the bravest of the Achaeans."

With these words he put heart and soul into them all, and they fell in a body upon the Trojans. The ships rang again with the cry which the Achaeans raised, and when the Trojans saw the brave son of Menoetius and his squire all gleaming in their armor, they were daunted and their battalions were thrown into confusion, for they thought the fleet son of Peleus must now have put aside his anger, and have been reconciled to Agamemnon. Everyone, therefore, looked round about to see whither he might fly for safety.

Patroclus first aimed a spear into the middle of the press where men were packed most closely by the stern of the ship of Protesilaus. He hit Pyraechmes who had led his Paeonian horsemen from the Amydon and the broad waters of the river Axius. The spear struck him on the right shoulder, and with a groan he fell backwards in the dust. On this his men were thrown into confusion, for by killing their leader, who was the finest soldier among them, Patroclus struck panic into them all. He thus drove them from the ship and quenched the fire that was then blazing—leaving the half-burnt ship to lie where it was. The Trojans were now driven back with a shout that rent the skies, while the Danaans poured after them from their ships, shouting also without ceasing. As when Zeus, gatherer of the thundercloud, spreads a dense canopy on the top of some lofty mountain, and all the peaks, the jutting head-lands, and forest glades show out in the great light that flashes from the burst-ing heavens, even so when the Danaans had now driven back the fire from their ships, they took breath for a little while; but the fury of the fight was not yet over, for the Trojans were not driven back in utter rout, but still gave bat-tle, and were ousted from their ground only by sheer fighting.

The fight then became more scattered, and the chieftains killed one another when and how they could. The valiant son of Menoetius first drove his spear into the thigh of Areïlycus just as he was turning round. The point went clean through and broke the bone so that he fell forward. Meanwhile Menelaus struck Thoas in the chest, where it was exposed near the rim of his shield, and he fell dead. The son of Phyleus saw Amphiclus about to attack him, and ere he could do so took aim at the upper part of his thigh, where the muscles are thicker than in any other part. The spear tore through all the sin-ews of the leg, and his eyes were closed in darkness. Of the sons of Nestor one, Antilochus, speared Atymnius, driving the point of the spear through his throat, and down he fell. Maris then sprang on Antilochus in hand-to-hand fight to avenge his brother and bestrode the body spear in hand. But valiant Thrasymedes was too quick for him, and in a moment had struck him in the shoulder ere he could deal his blow. His aim was true, and the spear severed all the muscles at the root of his arm, and tore them right down to the bone, so he fell heavily to the ground and his eyes were closed in darkness. Thus did these two noble comrades of Sarpedon go down to Erebus, slain by the two sons of Nestor; they were the warrior sons of Amisodorus, who had reared the invincible Chimaera, to the bane of many. Ajax, son of Oïleus, sprang on Cleobulus and took him alive as he was entangled in the crush; but he killed him then and there by a sword blow on the neck. The sword reeked with his blood, while dark death and the strong hand of fate gripped him and closed his eyes.

Peneleos and Lycon now met in close fight, for they had missed each other with their spears. They had both thrown without effect, so now they drew their swords. Lycon struck the plumed crest of Peneleos' helmet but his sword broke at the hilt, while Peneleos smote Lycon on the neck under the ear. The blade sank so deep that the head was held on by nothing but the skin, and there was no more life left in him. Meriones gave chase to Acamas on foot and caught him up just as he was about to mount his chariot. He drove a spear through his right shoulder so that he fell headlong from the car, and his eyes were closed in darkness. Idomeneus speared Erymas in the mouth. The bronze point of the spear went clean through it beneath the brain, crashing in among the white bones and smashing them up. His teeth were all of them knocked out and the blood came gushing in a stream from both his eyes; it also came gurgling up from his mouth and nostrils, and the darkness of death enfolded him round about.

Thus did these chieftains of the Danaans each of them kill his man. As ravening wolves seize on kids or lambs, fastening on them when they are alone on the hillsides and have strayed from the main flock through the carelessness of the shepherd—and when the wolves see this they pounce upon them at once because they cannot defend themselves—even so did the Danaans now fall on the Trojans, who fled with ill-omened cries in their panic and had no more fight left in them.

Meanwhile great Ajax kept on trying to drive a spear into Hector, but Hector was so skillful that he held his broad shoulders well under cover of his oxhide shield, ever on the lookout for the whizzing of the arrows and the heavy thud of the spears. He well knew that the fortunes of the day had changed, but still stood his ground and tried to protect his comrades.

As when a cloud goes up into heaven from Olympus, rising out of a clear sky when Zeus is brewing a gale—even with such panic-stricken rout did the Trojans now fly, and there was no order in their going. Hector's fleet horses bore him and his armor out of the fight, and he left the Trojan host penned in by the deep trench against their will. Many a yoke of horses snapped the pole of their chariots in the trench and left their master's car behind them. Patroclus gave chase, calling impetuously on the Danaans and full of fury against the Trojans, who, being now no longer in a body, filled all the ways with their cries of panic and rout. The air was darkened with the clouds of dust they raised, and the horses strained every nerve in their flight from the tents and ships towards the city.

Patroclus kept on heading his horses wherever he saw most men flying in confusion, cheering on his men the while. Chariots were being smashed in all directions, and many a man came tumbling down from his own car to fall beneath the wheels of that of Patroclus whose immortal steeds, given by the gods to Peleus, sprang over the trench at a bound as they sped onward. He was intent on trying to get near Hector, for he had set his heart on spearing him, but Hector's horses were now hurrying him away. As the whole dark earth bows before some tempest on an autumn day when Zeus rains his hardest to punish men for giving crooked judgment in their courts and driving justice therefrom without heed to the decrees of heaven—all the rivers run full and the torrents tear many a new channel as they roar headlong from the mountains to the dark sea, and it fares ill with the works of men—even such was the stress and strain of the Trojan horses in their flight.

Patroclus now cut off the battalions that were nearest to him and drove them back to the ships. They were doing their best to reach the city, but he would not let them, and bore down on them between the river and the ships and wall. Many a fallen comrade did he then avenge. First he hit Pronoüs with a spear on the chest where it was exposed near the rim of his shield, and he fell heavily to the ground. Next he sprang on Thestor, son of Enops, who was sitting all huddled up in his chariot, for he had lost his head and the reins had been torn out of his hands. Patroclus went up to him and drove a spear into his right jaw; he thus hooked him by the teeth and the spear pulled him over the rim of his car, as one who sits at the end of some jutting rock and draws a strong fish out of the sea with a hook and a line—even so with his spear did he pull Thestor all gaping from his chariot; he then threw him down on his face and he died while falling. On this, as Erylaus was coming on to attack him, he struck him full on the head with a stone, and his brains were all battered inside his helmet, whereon he fell headlong to the ground and the pangs of death took hold upon him. Then he laid low, one after the other, Erymas, Amphoterus, Epaltes, Tlepolemus, Echius, son of Damastor, Pyris, Ipheus, Euippus, and Polymelus, son of Argeas.

Now when Sarpedon saw his comrades, men who wore ungirdled tunics, being overcome by Patroclus, son of Menoetius, he rebuked the Lycians, saying: "Shame on you, where are you flying to? Show your mettle. I will myself meet this man in fight and learn who it is that is so masterful; he has done us much hurt, and has stretched many a brave man upon the ground."

He sprang from his chariot as he spoke, and Patroclus, when he saw this, leaped on to the ground also. The two then rushed at one another with loud cries like eagle-beaked crook-taloned vultures that scream and tear at one another in some high mountain fastness.

The son of scheming Cronus looked down upon them in pity and said to Hera who was his wife and sister: "Alas, that it should be the lot of Sarpedon whom I love so dearly to perish by the hand of Patroclus! I am in two minds whether to catch him up out of the fight and set him down safe and sound in the fertile land of Lycia, or to let him now fall by the hand of the son of Menoetius."

And Hera answered: "Most dread son of Cronus, what is this that you are saying? Would you snatch a mortal man, whose doom has long been fated, out of the jaws of death? Do as you will, but we shall not all of us be of your mind. I say further, and lay my saying to your heart, that if you send Sarpedon safely to his own home, some other of the gods will be also wanting to escort his son out of battle, for there are many sons of gods fighting round the city of Troy, and you will make everyone jealous. If, however, you are fond of him and pity him, let him indeed fall by the hand of Patroclus, but as soon as the life is gone out of him, send Death and sweet Sleep to bear him off the field and take him to the broad lands of Lycia, where his brothers and his kinsmen will bury him with mound and pillar, in due honor to the dead."

The sire of gods and men assented, but he shed a rain of blood upon the earth in honor of his son whom Patroclus was about to kill on the rich plain of Troy far from his home.

When they were now come close to one another, Patroclus struck Thrasydemus, the brave squire of Sarpedon, in the lower part of the belly, and killed him. Sarpedon then aimed a spear at Patroclus and missed him, but he struck the horse Pedasus in the right shoulder, and it screamed aloud as it lay, groaning in the dust until the life went out of it. The other two horses began to plunge; the pole of the chariot cracked, and they got entangled in the reins through the fall of the horse that was yoked along with them. But Automedon knew what to do; without the loss of a moment he drew the keen blade that hung by his sturdy thigh and cut the third horse adrift; whereon the other two righted themselves, and pulling hard at the reins again went together into battle.

Sarpedon now took a second aim at Patroclus, and again missed him; the point of the spear passed over his left shoulder without hitting him. Patroclus then aimed in his turn, and the spear sped not from his hand in vain, for he hit Sarpedon just where the midriff surrounds the ever-beating heart. He fell like some oak or silver poplar or tall pine to which woodmen have laid their axes upon the mountains to make timber for ship-building— even so did he he stretched at full length in front of his chariot and horses, moaning and clutching at the bloodstained dust. As when a lion springs with a bound upon a herd of cattle and fastens on a great black bull which dies bellowing in its clutches—even so did the leader of the Lycian warriors struggle in death as he fell by the hand of Patroclus. He called on his trusty comrade and said: "Glaucus, my brother, hero among heroes, put forth all your strength, fight with might and main, now if ever quit yourself like a valiant soldier. First go about among the Lycian captains and bid them fight for Sarpedon; then yourself also do battle to save my armor from being taken. My name will haunt you henceforth and forever if the Achaeans rob me of my armor, now that I have fallen at their ships. Do your very utmost and call all my people together."

Death closed his eyes as he spoke. Patroclus planted his heel on his breast whereon his senses came out along with it, and he drew out both spear point and Sarpedon's soul at the same time. Hard by the Myrmidons held his snorting steeds, who were wild with panic at finding themselves deserted by their lords.

Glaucus was overcome with grief when he heard what Sarpedon said, for he could not help him. He had to support his arm with his other hand, being in great pain through the wound which Teucer's arrow had given him when Teucer was defending the wall as he, Glaucus, was assailing it. Therefore he prayed to far-darting Apollo, saying: "Hear me, O king, from your seat, may be in the rich land of Lycia, or may be in Troy, for in all places you can hear the prayer of one who is in distress, as I now am. I have a grievous wound; my hand is aching with pain, there is no staunching the blood, and my whole arm drags by reason of my hurt, so that I cannot grasp my sword nor go among my foes and fight them, though our prince, Zeus' son Sarpedon, is slain. Zeus defended not his son, do you, therefore, O king, heal me of my wound, ease my pain and grant me strength both to cheer on the Lycians and to fight along with them round the body of him who has fallen."

Thus did he pray, and Apollo heard his prayer. He eased his pain, stanched the black blood from the wound, and gave him new strength. Glaucus perceived this, and was thankful that the mighty god had answered his prayer; forthwith, therefore, he went among the Lycian captains, and bade them come to fight about the body of Sarpedon. From these he strode on among the Trojans to Polydamas, son of Panthoüs, and Agenor; he then went in search of Aeneas and Hector, and when he had found them he said: "Hector, you have utterly forgotten your allies, who languish here for your sake far from friends and home while you do nothing to support them? Sarpedon, leader of the Lycian warriors, has fallen—he who was at once the right and might of Lycia; Ares has laid him low by the spear of Patroclus. Stand by him, my friends, and suffer not the Myrmidons to strip him of his armor, nor to treat his body with contumely in revenge for all the Danaans whom we have speared at the ships."

As he spoke the Trojans were plunged in extreme and ungovernable grief; for Sarpedon, alien though he was, had been one of the mainstays of their city, both as having much people with him, and as himself the foremost among them all. Led by Hector, who was infuriated by the fall of Sarpedon, they made instantly for the Danaans with all their might, while the undaunted spirit of Patroclus, son of Menoetius, cheered on the Achaeans. First he spoke to the two Ajaxes, men who needed no bidding. "Ajaxes," said he, "may it now please you to show yourselves the men you always have been, or even better—Sarpedon is fallen—he who was first to overleap the wall of the Achaeans; let us take the body and outrage it; let us strip the armor from his shoulders, and kill his comrades if they try to rescue his body."

He spoke to men who of themselves were full eager; both sides, therefore, the Trojans and Lycians on the one hand, and the Myrmidons and Achaeans on the other, strengthened their battalions and fought desperately about the body of Sarpedon, shouting fiercely the while. Mighty was the din of their armor as they came together, and Zeus shed a thick darkness over the fight, to increase the fury of the battle over the body of his son.

At first the Trojans made some headway against the Achaeans, for one of the best men among the Myrmidons was killed, Epeigeus, son of noble Agacles who had erewhile been king in the good city of Budeum; but presently, having killed a valiant kinsman of his own, he took refuge with Peleus and Thetis, who sent him to Ilium, the land of noble steeds, to fight the Trojans under Achilles. Hector now struck him on the head with a stone just as he had caught hold of the body, and his brains inside his helmet were all battered in, so that he fell face foremost upon the body of Sarpedon, and there died. Patroclus was enraged by the death of his comrade, and sped through the front ranks as swiftly as a hawk that swoops down on a flock of daws or starlings. Even so swiftly, O noble knight Patroclus, did you make straight for the Lycians and Trojans to avenge your comrade! Forthwith he struck Sthenelaus, the son of Ithaemenes, on the neck with a stone, and broke the tendons that join it to the head and spine. On this Hector and the front rank of his men gave ground. As far as a man can throw a javelin when competing for some prize, or even in battle—so far did, the Trojans now retreat before the Achaeans. Glaucus, captain of the Lycians, was the first to rally them, by killing Bathycles, son of Chalcon, who lived in Hellas and was the richest man among the Myrmidons. Glaucus turned round suddenly, just as Bathycles who was pursuing him was about to lay hold of him, and drove his spear right into the middle of his chest, whereon he fell heavily to the ground, and the fall of so good a man filled the Achaeans with dismay, while the Trojans were exultant, and came up in a body round the corpse. Nevertheless the Achaeans, mindful of their prowess, bore straight down upon them.

Meriones then killed a helmed warrior of the Trojans, Laogonus, son of Onetor, who was priest of Zeus of Mount Ida, and was honored by the people as though he were a god. Meriones struck him under the jaw and ear, so that life went out of him and the darkness of death laid hold upon him. Aeneas then aimed a spear at Meriones, hoping to hit him under the shield as he was advancing, but Meriones saw it coming and stooped forward to avoid it, whereon the spear flew past him and the point stuck in the ground, while the butt end went on quivering till Ares robbed it of its force. The spear, therefore, sped from Aeneas' hand in vain and fell quivering to the ground. Aeneas was angry and said, "Meriones, you are a good dancer, but if I had hit you my spear would soon have made an end of you."

And Meriones answered: "Aeneas, for all your bravery, you will not be able to make an end of everyone who comes against you. You are only a mortal like myself, and if I were to hit you in the middle of your shield with my spear, however strong and self-confident you may be, I should soon vanquish you, and you would yield your life to Hades of the noble steeds."

On this the son of Menoetius rebuked him and said: "Meriones, hero though you be, you should not speak thus. Taunting speeches, my good friend, will not make the Trojans draw away from the dead body. Some of them must go under ground first; blows for battle, and words for counsel; fight, therefore, and say nothing."

He led the way as he spoke and the hero went forward with him. As the sound of woodcutters in some forest glade upon the mountains—and the thud of their axes is heard afar—even such a din now rose from earth—clash of bronze armor and of good oxhide shields, as men smote each other with their swords and spears pointed at both ends. A man had need of good eyesight now to know Sarpedon, so covered was he from head to foot with spears and blood and dust. Men swarmed about the body, as flies that buzz round the full milk-pails in spring when they are brimming with milk—even so did they gather round Sarpedon. Nor did Zeus turn his keen eyes away for one moment from the fight, but kept looking at it all the time, for he was settling how best to kill Patroclus, and considering whether Hector should be allowed to end him now in the fight round the body of Sarpedon, and strip him of his armor, or whether he should let him give yet further trouble to the Trojans. In the end, he deemed it best that the brave squire of Achilles, son of Peleus, should drive Hector and the Trojans back towards the city and take the lives of many. First, therefore, he made Hector turn fainthearted, whereon he mounted his chariot and fled, bidding the other Trojans fly also, for he saw that the scales of Zeus had turned against him. Neither would the brave Lycians stand firm: they were dismayed when they saw their king lying struck to the heart amid a heap of corpses—for when the son of Cronus made the fight wax hot many had fallen above him. The Achaeans, therefore, stripped the gleaming armor from his shoulders and the brave son of Menoetius gave it to his men to take to the ships. Then Zeus, lord of the storm cloud, said to Apollo: "Dear Phoebus, go, I pray you, and take Sarpedon out of range of the weapons. Cleanse the black blood from off him, and then bear him a long way off where you may wash him in the river, anoint him with ambrosia, and clothe him in immortal raiment; this done, commit him to the arms of the two fleet messengers, Death and Sleep, who will carry him straightway to the rich land of Lycia, where his brothers and kinsmen will inter him and will raise both mound and pillar to his memory, in due honor to the dead."

Thus he spoke. Apollo obeyed his father's saying and came down from the heights of Ida into the thick of the fight. Forthwith he took Sarpedon out of range of the weapons, and then bore him a long way off, where he washed him in the river, anointed him with ambrosia, and clothed him in immortal raiment. This done, he committed him to the arms of the two fleet messengers, Death and Sleep, who presently set him down in the rich land of Lycia.

Meanwhile Patroclus, with many a shout to his horses and to Automedon, pursued the Trojans and Lycians in the pride and foolishness of his heart. Had he but obeyed the bidding of the son of Peleus, he would have escaped death and have been scatheless; but the counsels of Zeus pass man's understanding; he will put even a brave man to flight and snatch victory from his grasp, or again he will set him on to fight, as he now did when he put a high spirit into the heart of Patroclus.

Who then first, and who last, was slain by you, O Patroclus, when the gods had now called you to meet your doom? First Adrestus, Autonoüs, Echeclus, Perimus, the son of Megas, Epistor and Melanippus; after these he killed Elasus, Mulius, and Pylartes. These he slew, but the rest saved themselves by flight.

The sons of the Achaeans would now have taken Troy by the hands of Patroclus, for his spear flew in all directions, had not Phoebus Apollo taken his stand upon the wall to defeat his purpose and to aid the Trojans. Thrice did Patroclus charge at an angle of the high wall, and thrice did Apollo beat him back, striking his shield with his own immortal hands. When Patroclus was coming on like a god for yet a fourth time, Apollo shouted to him with an awful voice and said: "Draw back, noble Patroclus, it is not your lot to sack the city of the Trojan chieftains, nor yet will it be that of Achilles who is a far better man than you are." On hearing this, Patroclus withdrew to some distance and avoided the anger of Apollo.

Meanwhile Hector was waiting with his horses inside the Scaean gates, in doubt whether to drive out again and go on fighting, or to call the army inside the gates. As he was thus doubting, Phoebus Apollo drew near him in the likeness of a young and lusty warrior Asius, who was Hector's uncle, being own brother to Hecuba and son of Dymas who lived in Phrygia by the waters of the river Sangarius. In his likeness Zeus' son Apollo now spoke to Hector, saying: "Hector, why have you left off fighting? It is ill done of you. If I were as much better a man than you, as I am worse, you should soon rue your slackness. Drive straight towards Patroclus, if so be that Apollo may grant you a triumph over him, and you may kill him."

With this the god went back into the hurly-burly, and Hector bade Cebriones drive again into the fight. Apollo passed in among them, and struck panic into the Argives, while he gave triumph to Hector and the Trojans. Hector let the other Danaans alone and killed no man, but drove straight at Patroclus. Patroclus then sprang from his chariot to the ground, with a spear in his left hand, and in his right a jagged stone as large as his hand could hold. He stood still and threw it, nor did it go far without hitting someone. The cast was not in vain, for the stone struck Cebriones, Hector's charioteer, a bastard son of Priam, as he held the reins in his hands. The stone hit him on the forehead and drove his brows into his head, for the bone was smashed, and his eyes fell to the ground at his feet. He dropped dead from his chariot as though he were diving, and there was no more life left in him. Over him did you then vaunt, O knight Patroclus, saying: "Bless my heart, how active he is, and how well he dives. If we had been at sea this fellow would have dived from the ship's side and brought up as many oysters as the whole crew could stomach, even in rough water, for he has dived beautifully off his chariot on to the ground. It seems, then, that there are divers also among the Trojans."

As he spoke, he flung himself on Cebriones with the spring, as it were, of a lion that while attacking a stockyard is himself struck in the chest, and his courage is his own bane—even so furiously, O Patroclus, did you then spring upon Cebriones. Hector sprang also from his chariot to the ground. The pair then fought over the body of Cebriones. As two famished lions fight fiercely on some high mountain over the body of a stag that they have killed, even so did these two mighty warriors, Patroclus, son of Menoetius, and brave Hector, hack and hew at one another over the corpse of Cebriones. Hector would not let him go when he had once got him by the head, while Patroclus kept fast hold of his feet, and a fierce fight raged between the other Danaans and Trojans. As the east and south wind buffet one another when they beat upon some dense forest on the mountains—there is beech and ash and spreading cornel; the tops of the trees roar as they beat on one another, and one can hear the boughs cracking and breaking—even so did the Trojans and Achaeans spring upon one another and lay about each other, and neither side would give way. Many a pointed spear fell to ground and many a winged arrow sped from its bowstring about the body of Cebriones. Many a great stone, moreover, beat on many a shield as they fought around his body, but there he lay in the whirling clouds of dust, all huge and hugely, heedless of his driving now.

So long as the sun was still high in midheaven the weapons of either side were alike deadly, and the people fell; but when he went down towards the time when men loose their oxen, the Achaeans proved to be beyond all forecast stronger, so that they drew Cebriones out of range of the darts and tumult of the Trojans, and stripped the armor from his shoulders. Then Patroclus sprang like Ares with fierce intent and a terrific shout upon the Trojans, and thrice did he kill nine men; but as he was coming on like a god for a fourth time, then, O Patroclus, was the hour of your end approaching, for Phoebus fought you in fell earnest. Patroclus did not see him as he moved about in the crush, for he was enshrouded in thick darkness, and the god struck him from behind on his back and his broad shoulders with the flat of his hand, so that his eyes turned dizzy. Phoebus Apollo beat the helmet from off his head, and it rolled rattling off under the horses' feet, where its horsehair plumes were all begrimed with dust and blood. Never indeed had that helmet fared so before, for it had served to protect the head and comely forehead of the godlike hero Achilles. Now, however, Zeus delivered it over to be worn by Hector. Nevertheless, the end of Hector also was near. The bronze-shod spear, so great and so strong, was broken in the hand of Patroclus, while his shield that covered him from head to foot fell to the ground as did also the band that held it, and Apollo undid the fastenings of his corslet.

On this his mind became clouded; his limbs failed him, and he stood as one dazed; whereon Euphorbus, son of Panthoüs, a Dardanian, the best spearman of his time, as also the finest horseman and fleetest runner, came behind him and struck him in the back with a spear, midway between the shoulders. This man as soon as ever he had come up with his chariot had dismounted twenty men, so proficient was he in all the arts of war—he it was, O knight Patroclus, that first drove a weapon into you, but he did not quite overpower you. Euphorbus then ran back into the crowd, after drawing his ashen spear out of the wound; he would not stand firm and wait for Patroclus, unarmed though he now was, to attack him; but Patroclus, unnerved, alike by the blow the god had given him and by the spear wound, drew back under cover of his men in fear for his life. Hector on this, seeing him to be wounded and giving ground, forced his way through the ranks, and when close up with him struck him in the lower part of the belly with a spear, driving the bronze point right through it, so that he fell heavily to the ground to the great grief of the Achaeans. As when a lion has fought some fierce wild boar and worsted him—the two fight furiously upon the mountains over some little fountain at which they would both drink, and the lion has beaten the boar till he can hardly breathe—even so did Hector, son of Priam, take the life of the brave son of Menoetius, who had killed so many, striking him from close at hand and vaunting over him the while. "Patroclus," said he, "you deemed that you should sack our city, rob our Trojan women of their freedom, and carry them off in your ships to your own country. Fool! Hector and his fleet horses were ever straining their utmost to defend them. I am foremost of all the Trojan warriors to stave the day of bondage from off them. As for you, vultures shall devour you here. Poor wretch, Achilles with all his bravery availed you nothing; and yet I ween when you left him he charged you straitly, saying, 'Come not back to the ships, knight Patroclus, till you have rent the bloodstained shirt of murderous Hector about his body.' Thus I ween did he charge you, and your fool's heart answered him 'yea' within you."

Then, as the life ebbed out of you, you answered, O knight Patroclus: "Hector, vaunt as you will, for Zeus, the son of Cronus, and Apollo have vouchsafed you victory; it is they who have vanquished me so easily, and they who have stripped the armor from my shoulders; had twenty such men as you attacked me, all of them would have fallen before my spear. Fate and the son of Leto have overpowered me, and among mortal men Euphorbus; you are yourself third only in the killing of me. I say further, and lay my saying to your heart, you too shall live but for a little season. Death and the day of your doom are close upon you, and they will lay you low by the hand of Achilles, son of Aeacus."

When he had thus spoken his eyes were closed in death, his soul left his body and flitted down to the house of Hades, mourning its sad fate and bidding farewell to the youth and vigor of its manhood. Dead though he was, Hector still spoke to him, saying, "Patroclus, why should you thus foretell my doom? Who knows but Achilles, son of lovely Thetis, may be smitten by my spear and die before me?"

As he spoke he drew the bronze spear from the wound, planting his foot upon the body, which he thrust off and let lie on its back. He then went spear in hand after Automedon, squire of the fleet descendant of Aeacus, for he longed to lay him low, but the immortal steeds which the gods had given as a rich gift to Peleus bore him swiftly from the field.

Book XVII

*A struggle rages over the body of Patroclus, which Hector strips of its armor.
Menelaus, assisted by Ajax, tries to rescue the body. Apollo aids the
Trojans, Athene the Greeks. Achilles' horses stand mourning their driver's
death. Menelaus sends word to Achilles of what has happened, and the
Greeks, bearing Patroclus' body, push slowly toward the ships.*

BRAVE MENELAUS, SON OF ATREUS, NOW CAME TO KNOW THAT PATROCLUS had fallen, and made his way through the front ranks clad in full armor to bestride him. As a cow stands lowing over her first calf, even so did yellow-haired Menelaus bestride Patroclus. He held his round shield and his spear in front of him, resolute to kill any who should dare face him. But the son of Panthoüs had also noted the body, and came up to Menelaus, saying: "Menelaus, son of Atreus, draw back, leave the body, and let the blood-stained spoils be. I was first of the Trojans and their brave allies to drive my spear into Patroclus, let me, therefore, have my full glory among the Trojans, or I will take aim and kill you."

To this Menelaus answered in great anger: "By father Zeus, boasting is an ill thing. The pard is not more bold, nor the lion nor savage wild boar, which is fiercest and most dauntless of all creatures, than are the proud sons of Panthoüs. Yet Hyperenor did not see out the days of his youth when he made light of me and withstood me, deeming me the meanest soldier among the Danaans. His own feet never bore him back to gladden his wife and parents. Even so shall I make an end of you too, if you withstand me. Get you back into the crowd and do not face me, or it shall be worse for you. Even a fool may be wise after the event."

Euphorbus would not listen and said: "Now indeed, Menelaus, shall you pay for the death of my brother over whom you vaunted, and whose wife you widowed in her bridal chamber while you brought grief unspeakable on his parents. I shall comfort these poor people if I bring your head and armor and place them in the hands of Panthoüs and noble Phrontis. The time is come when this matter shall be fought out and settled, for me or against me."

As he spoke he struck Menelaus full on the shield, but the spear did not go through, for the shield turned its point. Menelaus then took aim, praying to father Zeus as he did so. Euphorbus was drawing back, and Menelaus struck him about the roots of his throat, leaning his whole weight on the spear, so as to drive it home. The point went clean through his neck, and his armor rang rattling round him as he fell heavily to the ground. His hair, which was like that of the Graces, and his locks so deftly bound in bands of silver and gold were all bedrabbled with blood. As one who has grown a fine young olive tree in a clear space where there is abundance of water—the plant is full of promise, and though the winds beat upon it from every quarter it puts forth its white blossoms till the blasts of some fierce hurricane sweep down upon it and level it with the ground—even so did Menelaus strip the fair youth Euphorbus of his armor after he had slain him. Or as some fierce lion upon the mountains in the pride of his strength fastens on the finest heifer in a herd as it is feeding—first he breaks her neck with his strong jaws and then gorges on her blood and entrails. Dogs and shepherds raise a hue and cry against him, but they stand aloof and will not come close to him, for they are pale with fear—even so no one had the courage to face valiant Menelaus. The son of Atreus would have then carried off the armor of the son of Panthoüs with ease had not Phoebus Apollo been angry and in the guise of Mentes, chief of the Cicons, incited Hector to attack him. "Hector," said he, "you are now going after the horses of the noble son of Aeacus, but you will not take them.

They cannot be kept in hand and driven by mortal man, save only by Achilles, who is son to an immortal mother. Meanwhile, Menelaus, son of Atreus, has bestridden the body of Patroclus and killed the noblest of the Trojans, Euphorbus, son of Panthoüs, so that he can fight no more."

The god then went back into the toil and turmoil, but the soul of Hector was darkened with a cloud of grief; he looked along the ranks and saw Euphorbus lying on the ground with the blood still flowing from his wound, and Menelaus stripping him of his armor. On this he made his way to the front like a flame of fire, clad in his gleaming armor, and crying with a loud voice. When the son of Atreus heard him, he said to himself in his dismay: "Alas! what shall I do? I may not let the Trojans take the armor of Patroclus who has fallen fighting on my behalf, lest some Danaan who sees me should cry shame upon me. Still if for my honor's sake I fight Hector and the Trojans single-handed, they will prove too many for me, for Hector is bringing them up in force. Why, however, should I thus hesitate? When a man fights in despite of heaven with one whom a god befriends, he will soon rue it. Let no Danaan think ill of me if I give place to Hector, for the hand of heaven is with him. Yet, if I could find Ajax, the two of us would fight Hector and heaven too, if we might only save the body of Patroclus for Achilles, son of Peleus. This, of many evils, would be the least."

While he was thus in two minds, the Trojans came up to him with Hector at their head; he therefore drew back and left the body, turning about like some bearded lion who is being chased by dogs and men from a stockyard with spears and hue and cry, whereon he is daunted and slinks sulkily off—even so did Menelaus, son of Atreus, turn and leave the body of Patroclus. When among the body of his men, he looked around for mighty Ajax, son of Telamon, and presently saw him on the extreme left of the fight, cheering on his men and exhorting them to keep on fighting, for Phoebus Apollo had spread a great panic among them. He ran up to him and said, "Ajax, my good friend, come with me at once to dead Patroclus, if so be that we may take the body to Achilles—as for his armor, Hector already has it."

These words stirred the heart of Ajax, and he made his way among the front ranks, Menelaus going with him. Hector had stripped Patroclus of his armor, and was dragging him away to cut off his head and take the body to fling before the dogs of Troy. But Ajax came up with his shield like a wall before him, on which Hector withdrew under shelter of his men, and sprang on to his chariot, giving the armor over to the Trojans to take to the city, as a great trophy for himself. Ajax, therefore, covered the body of Patroclus with his broad shield and bestrode him; as a lion stands over his whelps if hunters have come upon him in a forest when he is with his little ones—in the pride and fierceness of his strength he draws his knit brows down till they cover his eyes—even so did Ajax bestride the body of Patroclus, and by his side stood Menelaus, son of Atreus, nursing great sorrow in his heart.

Then Glaucus, son of Hippolochus, looked fiercely at Hector and rebuked him sternly. "Hector," said he, "you make a brave show, but in fight you are sadly wanting. A runaway like yourself has no claim to so great a reputation. Think how you may now save your town and citadel by the hands of your own people born in Ilium; for you will get no Lycians to fight for you, seeing what thanks they have had for their incessant hardships. Are you likely, sir, to do anything to help a man of less note, after leaving Sarpedon, who was at once your guest and comrade in arms, to be the spoil and prey of the Danaans? So long as he lived he did good service both to your city and yourself. Yet you had no stomach to save his body from the dogs. If the Lycians will listen to me, they will go home and leave Troy to its fate. If the Trojans had any of that daring fearless spirit which lays hold of men who are fighting for their country and harassing those who would attack it, we should soon bear off Patroclus into Ilium. Could we get this dead man away and bring him into the city of Priam, the Argives would readily give up the armor of Sarpedon, and we should get his body to boot.

For he whose squire has been now killed is the foremost man at the ships of the Achaeans—he and his close-fighting followers. Nevertheless, you dared not make a stand against Ajax, nor face him, eye to eye, with battle all round you, for he is a braver man than you are."

Hector scowled at him and answered: "Glaucus, you should know better. I have held you so far as a man of more understanding than any in all Lycia, but now I despise you for saying that I am afraid of Ajax. I fear neither battle nor the din of chariots, but Zeus' will is stronger than ours. Zeus at one time makes even a strong man draw back and snatches victory from his grasp, while at another he will set him on to fight. Come hither then, my friend, stand by me and see indeed whether I shall play the coward the whole day through as you say, or whether I shall not stay some even of the boldest Danaans from fighting round the body of Patroclus."

As he spoke he called loudly on the Trojans, saying, "Trojans, Lycians, and Dardanians, fighters in close combat, be men, my friends, and fight might and main, while I put on the goodly armor of Achilles, which I took when I killed Patroclus."

With this Hector left the fight, and ran full speed after his men who were taking the armor of Achilles to Troy, but had not yet got far. Standing for a while apart from the woeful fight, he changed his armor. His own he sent to the strong city of Ilium and to the Trojans, while he put on the immortal armor of the son of Peleus, which the gods had given to Peleus, who in his age gave it to his son; but the son did not grow old in his father's armor.

When Zeus, lord of the storm cloud, saw Hector standing aloof and arming himself in the armor of the son of Peleus, he wagged his head and muttered to himself, saying: "Alas! poor wretch, you arm in the armor of a hero before whom many another trembles, and you reck nothing of the doom that is already close upon you. You have killed his comrade so brave and strong, but it was not well that you should strip the armor from his head and shoulders. I do indeed endow you with great might now, but as against this you shall not return from battle to lay the armor of the son of Peleus before Andromache."

The son of Cronus bowed his portentous brows, and Hector fitted the armor to his body, while terrible Ares entered into him and filled his whole body with might and valor. With a shout he strode in among the allies, and his armor flashed about him so that he seemed to all of them like the great son of Peleus himself. He went about among them and cheered them on—Mesthles, Glaucus, Medon, Thersilochus, Asteropaeus, Deisenor, Hippothoüs, Phorcys, Chromius, and Ennomus, the augur. All these did he exhort, saying: "Hear me, allies from other cities who are here in your thousands, it was not in order to have a crowd about me that I called you hither each from his several city, but that with heart and soul you might defend the wives and little ones of the Trojans from the fierce Achaeans. For this do I oppress my people with your food and the presents that make you rich. Therefore turn, and charge at the foe, to stand or fall as is the game of war. Whoever shall bring Patroclus, dead though he be, into the hands of the Trojans, and shall make Ajax give way before him, I will give him one half of the spoils while I keep the other. He will thus share like honor with myself."

When he had thus spoken they charged full weight upon the Danaans with their spears held out before them, and the hopes of each ran high that he should force Ajax, son of Telamon, to yield up the body—fools that they were, for he was about to take the lives of many. Then Ajax said to Menelaus: "My good friend Menelaus, you and I shall hardly come out of this fight alive. I am less concerned for the body of Patroclus, who will shortly become meat for the dogs and vultures of Troy, than for the safety of my own head and yours. Hector has wrapped us round in a storm of battle from every quarter, and our destruction seems now certain. Call then upon the princes of the Danaans if there is any who can hear us."

Menelaus did as he said, and shouted to the Danaans for help at the top of his voice. "My friends," he cried, "princes and counselors of the Argives, all you who with Agamemnon and Menelaus drink at the public cost, and give orders each to his own people as Zeus vouchsafes him power and glory, the fight is so thick about me that I cannot distinguish you severally. Come on, therefore, every man unbidden, and think it shame that Patroclus should become meat and morsel for Trojan hounds."

Fleet Ajax, son of Oïleus, heard him and was first to force his way through the fight and run to help him. Next came Idomeneus and Meriones, his esquire, peer of murderous Ares. As for the others that came into the fight after these, who of his own self could name them?

The Trojans with Hector at their head charged in a body. As a great wave that comes thundering in at the mouth of some heaven-born river, and the rocks that jut into the sea ring with the roar of the breakers that beat and buffet them—even with such a roar did the Trojans come on; but the Achaeans in singleness of heart stood firm about the son of Menoetius and fenced him with their bronze shields. Zeus, moreover, hid the brightness of their helmets in a thick cloud, for he had borne no grudge against the son of Menoetius while he was still alive and squire to the descendant of Aeacus. Therefore he was loath to let him fall a prey to the dogs of his foes, the Trojans, and urged his comrades on to defend him.

At first the Trojans drove the Achaeans back, and they withdrew from the dead man daunted. The Trojans did not succeed in killing anyone, nevertheless they drew the body away. But the Achaeans did not lose it long, for Ajax, foremost of all the Danaans after the son of Peleus alike in stature and prowess, quickly rallied them and made towards the front like a wild boar upon the mountains when he stands at bay in the forest glades and routs the hounds and lusty youths that have attacked him—even so did Ajax, son of Telamon, passing easily in among the phalanxes of the Trojans, disperse those who had bestridden Patroclus and were most bent on winning glory by dragging him off to their city. At this moment Hippothoüs, brave son of the Pelasgian Lethus, in his zeal for Hector and the Trojans, was dragging the body off by the foot through the press of the fight, having bound a strap round the sinews near the ankle; but a mischief scon befell him from which none of those could save him who would have gladly done so, for the son of Telamon sprang forward and smote him on his bronze-cheeked helmet. The plumed headpiece broke about the point of the weapon, struck at once by the spear and by the strong hand of Ajax, so that the bloody brain came oozing out through the crest-socket. His strength then failed him and he let Patroclus' foot drop from his hand, as he fell full length dead upon the body. Thus he died far from the fertile land of Larisa and never repaid his parents the cost of bringing him up, for his life was cut short early by the spear of mighty Ajax. Hector then took aim at Ajax with a spear, but he saw it coming and just managed to avoid it. The spear passed on and struck Schedius, son of noble Iphitus, captain of the Phoceans, who dwelt in famed Panopeus and reigned over much people. It struck him under the middle of the collarbone; the bronze point went right through him, coming out at the bottom of his shoulder blade, and his armor rang rattling round him as he fell heavily to the ground. Ajax in his turn struck noble Phorcys, son of Phaenops, in the middle of the belly as he was bestriding Hippothoüs, and broke the plate of his cuirass; whereon the spear tore out his entrails and he clutched the ground in his palm as he fell to earth. Hector and those who were in the front rank then gave ground, while the Argives raised a loud cry of triumph and drew off the bodies of Phorcys and Hippothoüs, which they stripped presently of their armor.

The Trojans would now have been worsted by the brave Achaeans and driven back to Ilium through their own cowardice, while the Argives, so great was their courage and endurance, would have achieved a triumph even against the will of Zeus, if Apollo had not roused Aeneas, in the likeness of Periphas, son of Epytus, an attendant who had grown old in the service of Aeneas' aged father and was at all times devoted to him. In his likeness, then, Apollo said: "Aeneas, can you not manage, even though heaven be against us, to save high Ilium? I have known men, whose numbers, courage, and self-reliance have saved their people in spite of Zeus, whereas in this case he would much rather give victory to us than to the Danaans, if you would only fight instead of being so terribly afraid."

Aeneas knew Apollo when he looked straight at him, and shouted to Hector, saying: "Hector and all other Trojans and allies, shame on us if we are beaten by the Achaeans and driven back to Ilium through our own cowardice. A god has just come up to me and told me that Zeus the supreme disposer will be with us. Therefore, let us make for the Danaans, that it may go hard with them ere they bear away dead Patroclus to the ships."

As he spoke he sprang out far in front of the others, who then rallied and again faced the Achaeans. Aeneas speared Leiocritus, son of Arisbas, a valiant follower of Lycomedes, and Lycomedes was moved with pity as he saw him fall. He therefore went close up, and speared Apisaon, son of Hippasus, shepherd of his people, in the liver under the midriff, so that he died. He had come from fertile Paeonia and was the best man of them all after Asteropaeus. Asteropaeus flew forward to avenge him and attack the Danaans, but this might no longer be, inasmuch as those about Patroclus were well-covered by their shields, and held their spears in front of them, for Ajax had given them strict orders that no man was either to give ground, or to stand out before the others, but all were to hold well together about the body and fight hand to hand. Thus did huge Ajax bid them, and the earth ran red with blood as the corpses fell thick on one another alike on the side of the Trojans and allies, and on that of the Danaans; for these last, too, fought no bloodless fight though many fewer of them perished, through the care they took to defend and stand by one another.

Thus did they fight as it were a flaming fire. It seemed as though it had gone hard even with the sun and moon, for they were hidden over all that part where the bravest heroes were fighting about the dead son of Menoetius, whereas the other Danaans and Achaeans fought at their ease in full daylight with brilliant sunshine all round them, and there was not a cloud to be seen neither on plain nor mountain. These last, moreover, would rest for a while and leave off fighting, for they were some distance apart and beyond the range of one another's weapons, whereas those who were in the thick of the fray suffered both from battle and darkness. All the best of them were being worn out by the great weight of their armor, but the two valiant heroes, Thrasymedes and Antilochus, had not yet heard of the death of Patroclus, and believed him to be still alive and leading the van against the Trojans. They were keeping themselves in reserve against the death or rout of their own comrades, for so Nestor had ordered when he sent them from the ships into battle.

Thus through the livelong day did they wage fierce war, and the sweat of their toil rained ever on their legs under them, and on their hands and eyes, as they fought over the squire of the fleet son of Peleus. It was as when a man gives a great oxhide all drenched in fat to his men, and bids them stretch it; whereon they stand round it in a ring and tug till the moisture leaves it, and the fat soaks in for the many that pull at it, and it is well-stretched—even so did the two sides tug the dead body hither and thither within the compass of but a little space—the Trojans steadfastly set on dragging it into Ilium, while the Achaeans were no less so on taking it to their ships; and fierce was the fight between them. Not Ares, himself, the lord of hosts, nor yet Athene, even in their fullest fury could make light of such a battle.

Such fearful turmoil of men and horses did Zeus on that day ordain round the body of Patroclus. Meanwhile Achilles did not know that he had fallen, for the fight was under the wall of Troy, a long way off the ships. He had no idea, therefore, that Patroclus was dead, and deemed that he would return alive as soon as he had gone close up to the gates. He knew that he was not to sack the city neither with nor without himself, for his mother had often told him this when he had sat alone with her, and she had informed him of the counsels of great Zeus. Now, however, she had not told him how great a disaster had befallen him in the death of the one who was far dearest to him of all his comrades.

The others still kept on charging one another round the body with their pointed spears and killing each other. Then would one say, "My friends, we can never again show our faces at the ships—better, and greatly better, that earth should open and swallow us here in this place, than that we should let the Trojans have the triumph of bearing off Patroclus to their city." The Trojans also on their part spoke to one another, saying: "Friends, though we fall to a man beside this body, let none shrink from fighting." With such words did they exhort each other. They fought and fought, and an iron clank rose through the void air to the brazen vault of heaven.

The horses of the descendant of Aeacus stood out of the fight and wept when they heard that their driver had been laid low by the hand of murderous Hector. Automedon, valiant son of Diores, lashed them again and again. Many a time did he speak kindly to them, and many a time did he upbraid them, but they would neither go back to the ships by the waters of the broad Hellespont, nor yet into battle among the Achaeans. They stood with their chariot stock still, as a pillar set over the tomb of some dead man or woman, and bowed their heads to the ground. Hot tears fell from their eyes as they mourned the loss of their charioteer, and their noble manes drooped all wet from under the yoke-straps on either side the yoke.

The son of Cronus saw them and took pity upon their sorrow. He wagged his head and muttered to himself, saying: "Poor things, why did we give you to King Peleus who is a mortal, while you are yourselves ageless and immortal? Was it that you might share the sorrows that befall mankind? For of all creatures that live and move upon the earth there is none so pitiable as he is—still, Hector, son of Priam, shall drive neither you nor your chariot. I will not have it. It is enough that he should have the armor over which he vaunts so vainly. Furthermore, I will give you strength of heart and limb to bear Automedon safely to the ships from battle, for I shall let the Trojans triumph still further and go on killing till they reach the ships; whereon night shall fall and darkness overshadow the land."

As he spoke he breathed heart and strength into the horses so that they shook the dust from out of their manes and bore their chariot swiftly into the fight that raged between Trojans and Achaeans. Behind them fought Automedon, full of sorrow for his comrade, as a vulture amid a flock of geese. In and out and here and there, full speed he dashed amid the throng of the Trojans, but for all the fury of his pursuit he killed no man, for he could not wield his spear and keep his horses in hand when alone in the chariot. At last, however, a comrade, Alcimedon, son of Laerces, son of Haemon, caught sight of him and came up behind his chariot. "Automedon," said he, "what god has put this folly into your heart and robbed you of your right mind, that you fight the Trojans in the front rank single-handed? He who was your comrade is slain, and Hector plumes himself on being armed in the armor of the descendant of Aeacus."

Automedon, son of Diores, answered: "Alcimedon, there is no one else who can control and guide the immortal steeds so well as you can, save only Patroclus—while he was alive—peer of gods in counsel. Take then the whip and reins, while I go down from the car and fight."

Alcimedon sprang on to the chariot and caught up the whip and reins, while Automedon leaped from off the car. When Hector saw him he said to Aeneas, who was near him: "Aeneas, counselor of the mail-clad Trojans, I see the steeds of the fleet son of Aeacus come into battle with weak hands to drive them. I am sure, if you think well, that we might take them; they will not dare face us if we both attack them."

The valiant son of Anchises was of the same mind, and the pair went right on, with their shoulders covered under shields of tough dry oxhide, overlaid with much bronze. Chromius and Arenas went also with them, and their hearts beat high with hope that they might kill the men and capture the horses—fools that they were, for they were not to return scatheless from their meeting with Automedon, who prayed to father Zeus and was forthwith filled with courage and strength abounding. He turned to his trusty comrade Alcimedon and said: "Alcimedon, keep your horses so close up that I may feel their breath upon my back. I doubt that we shall not stay Hector, son of Priam, till he has killed us and mounted behind the horses; he will then either spread panic among the ranks of the Achaeans, or himself be killed among the foremost."

On this he cried out to the two Ajaxes and Menelaus: "Ajaxes, captains of the Argives, and Menelaus, give the dead body over to them that are best able to defend it, and come to the rescue of us living; for Hector and Aeneas, who are the two best men among the Trojans, are pressing us hard in the full tide of war. Nevertheless, the issue lies on the lap of heaven. I will therefore hurl my spear and leave the rest to Zeus."

He poised and hurled as he spoke, whereon the spear struck the round shield of Aretus, and went right through it for the shield stayed it not, so that it was driven through his belt into the lower part of his belly. As when some sturdy youth, ax in hand, deals his blow behind the horns of an ox and severs the tendons at the back of its neck so that it springs forward and then drops, even so did Aretus give one bound and then fall on his back—the spear quivering in his body till it made an end of him. Hector then aimed a spear at Automedon but he saw it coming and stooped forward to avoid it, so that it flew past him and the point stuck in the ground, while the butt end went on quivering till Ares robbed it of its force. They would then have fought hand to hand with swords had not the two Ajaxes forced their way through the crowd when they heard their comrade calling, and parted them for all their fury—for Hector, Aeneas, and Chromius were afraid and drew back, leaving Aretus to lie there struck to the heart. Automedon, peer of fleet Ares, then stripped him of his armor and vaunted over him, saying: "I have done little to assuage my sorrow for the son of Menoetius, for the man I have killed is not so good as he was."

As he spoke he took the bloodstained spoils and laid them upon his chariot; then he mounted the car with his hands and feet all steeped in gore as a lion that has been gorging upon a bull.

And now the fierce groanful fight again raged about Patroclus, for Athene came down from heaven and roused its fury by the command of far-seeing

Zeus, who had changed his mind and sent her to encourage the Danaans. As when Zeus bends his bright bow in heaven in token to mankind either of war or of the chill storms that stay men from their labor and plague the flocks— even so, wrapped in such radiant raiment, did Athene go in among the host and speak man by man to each. First she took the form and voice of Phoenix and spoke to Menelaus, son of Atreus, who was standing near her. "Menelaus," said she, "it will be shame and dishonor to you if dogs tear the noble comrade of Achilles under the walls of Troy. Therefore be staunch and urge your men to be so also."

Menelaus answered: "Phoenix, my good old friend, may Athene vouch-safe me strength and keep the darts from off me, for so shall I stand by Patroclus and defend him. His death has gone to my heart, but Hector is as a raging fire and deals his blows without ceasing, for Zeus is now granting him a time of triumph."

Athene was pleased at his having named herself before any of the other gods. Therefore she put strength into his knees and shoulders and made him as bold as a fly, which, though driven off will yet come again and bite if it can, so dearly does it love man's blood—even so bold as this did she make him as he stood over Patroclus and threw his spear. Now there was among the Trojans a man named Podes, son of Eëtion, who was both rich and valiant. Hector held him in the highest honor for he was his comrade and boon companion. The spear of Menelaus struck this man in the girdle just as he had turned in flight, and went right through him. Whereon he fell heavily forward, and Menelaus, son of Atreus, drew off his body from the Trojans into the ranks of his own people.

Apollo then went up to Hector and spurred him on to fight, in the like-ness of Phaenops, son of Asius, who lived in Abydos and was the most favored of all Hector's guests. In his likeness Apollo said: "Hector, who of the Achaeans will fear you henceforward now that you have quailed before Menelaus, who has ever been rated poorly as a soldier? Yet he has now got a corpse away from the Trojans single-handed, and has slain your own true comrade, a man brave among the foremost, Podes, son of Eëtion."

A dark cloud of grief fell upon Hector as he heard, and he made his way to the front clad in full armor. Thereon the son of Cronus seized his bright-tasseled aegis and veiled Ida in cloud. He sent forth his lightnings and his thunders, and as he shook his aegis he gave victory to the Trojans and routed the Achaeans.

The panic was begun by Peneleos, the Boeotian, for while keeping his face turned ever towards the foe he had been hit with a spear on the upper part of the shoulder. A spear thrown by Polydamas had grazed the top of the bone, for Polydamas had come up to him and struck him from close at hand. Then Hector in close combat struck Leïtus, son of noble Alectryon, in the hand by the wrist, and disabled him from fighting further. He looked about him in dismay, knowing that never again should he wield spear in battle with the Trojans. While Hector was in pursuit of Leïtus, Idomeneus struck him on the breastplate over his chest near the nipple, but the spear broke in the shaft, and the Trojans cheered aloud. Hector then aimed at Idomeneus, son of Deucalion, as he was standing on his chariot, and very narrowly missed him, but the spear hit Coiranus, a follower and charioteer of Meriones who had come with him from Lyctus. Idomeneus had left the ships on foot and would have afforded a great triumph to the Trojans if Coiranus had not driven quickly up to him; he therefore brought life and rescue to Idomeneus, but himself fell by the hand of murderous Hector. For Hector hit him on the jaw under the ear; the end of the spear drove out his teeth and cut his tongue in two pieces, so that he fell from his chariot and let the reins fall to the ground. Meriones gathered them up from the ground and took them into his own hands, then he said to Idomeneus, "Lay on, till you get back to the ships, for you must see that the day is no longer ours." On this Idomeneus lashed the horses to the ships, for fear had taken hold upon him.

Ajax and Menelaus noted how Zeus had turned the scale in favor of the Trojans, and Ajax was first to speak. "Alas," said he, "even a fool may see that father Zeus is helping the Trojans. All their weapons strike home; no matter whether it be a brave man or a coward that hurls them, Zeus speeds all alike, whereas ours fall each one of them without effect. What, then, will be best both as regards rescuing the body, and our return to the joy of our friends who will be grieving as they look hitherwards? For they will make sure that nothing can now check the terrible hands of Hector, and that he will fling himself upon our ships. I wish that someone would go and tell the son of Peleus at once, for I do not think he can have yet heard the sad news that the dearest of his friends has fallen. But I can see not a man among the Achaeans to send, for they and their chariots are alike hidden in darkness. O father Zeus, lift this cloud from over the sons of the Achaeans! Make heaven serene, and let us see; if you will that we perish, let us fall, at any rate, by daylight."

Father Zeus heard him and had compassion upon his tears. Forthwith he chased away the cloud of darkness, so that the sun shone out and all the fighting was revealed. Ajax then said to Menelaus, "Look, Menelaus, and if Antilochus, son of Nestor, be still living, send him at once to tell Achilles that by far the dearest to him of all his comrades has fallen."

Menelaus heeded his words and went his way as a lion from a stockyard—the lion is tired of attacking the men and hounds, who keep watch the whole night through and will not let him feast on the fat of their herd. In his lust of meat he makes straight at them but in vain, for darts from strong hands assail him, and burning brands which daunt him for all his hunger, so in the morning he slinks sulkily away—even so did Menelaus sorely against his will leave Patroclus, in great fear lest the Achaeans should be driven back in rout and let him fall into the hands of the foe. He charged Meriones and the two Ajaxes straitly, saying, "Ajaxes and Meriones, leaders of the Argives, now indeed remember how good Patroclus was; he was ever courteous while alive, bear it in mind now that he is dead."

With this Menelaus left them, looking round him as keenly as an eagle, whose sight they say is keener than that of any other bird—however high he may be in the heavens, not a hare that runs can escape him by crouching under bush or thicket, for he will swoop down upon it and make an end of it—even so, O Menelaus, did your keen eyes range round the mighty host of your followers to see if you could find the son of Nestor still alive? Presently Menelaus saw him on the extreme left of the battle, cheering on his men and exhorting them to fight boldly. Menelaus went up to him and said: "Antilochus, come here and listen to sad news, which I would indeed were untrue. You must see with your own eyes that heaven is heaping calamity upon the Danaans, and giving victory to the Trojans. Patroclus has fallen, who was the bravest of the Achaeans, and sorely will the Danaans miss him. Run instantly to the ships and tell Achilles, that he may come to rescue the body and bear it to the ships. As for the armor, Hector already has it."

Antilochus was struck with horror. For a long time he was speechless. His eyes filled with tears and he could find no utterance, but he did as Menelaus had said, and set off running as soon as he had given his armor to a comrade, Laodocus, who was wheeling his horses round, close beside him.

Thus, then, did he run weeping from the field, to carry the bad news to Achilles, son of Peleus. Nor were you, O Menelaus, minded to succor his harassed comrades, when Antilochus had left the Pylians—and greatly did they miss him—but he sent them noble Thrasymedes, and himself went back to Patroclus. He came running up to the two Ajaxes and said: "I have sent Antilochus to the ships to tell Achilles, but rage against Hector as he may, he cannot come, for he cannot fight without armor. What then will be our best plan both as regards rescuing the dead and our own escape from death amid the battle cries of the Trojans?"

Ajax answered: "Menelaus, you have said well: do you, then, and Meriones stoop down, raise the body, and bear it out of the fray, while we two behind you keep off Hector and the Trojans, one in heart as in name, and long used to fighting side by side with one another."

On this Menelaus and Meriones took the dead man in their arms and lifted him high aloft with a great effort. The Trojan host raised a hue and cry behind them when they saw the Achaeans bearing the body away, and flew after them like hounds attacking a wounded boar at the loo of a band of young huntsmen. For a while the hounds fly at him as though they would tear him in pieces, but now and again he turns on them in a fury, scaring and scattering them in all directions—even so did the Trojans for a while charge in a body, striking with sword and with spears pointed at both the ends, but when the two Ajaxes faced them and stood at bay, they would turn pale and no man dared press on to fight further about the dead.

In this wise did the two heroes strain every nerve to bear the body to the ships out of the fight. The battle raged round them like fierce flames that when once kindled spread like wildfire over a city and the houses fall in the glare of its burning—even such was the roar and tramp of men and horses that pursued them as they bore Patroclus from the field. Or as mules that put forth all their strength to draw some beam or great piece of ship's timber down a rough mountain track, and they pant and sweat as they go—even so did Menelaus and Meriones pant and sweat as they bore the body of Patroclus. Behind them the two Ajaxes held stoutly out. As some wooded mountain spur that stretches across a plain will turn water and check the flow even of a great river, nor is there any stream strong enough to break through it—even so did the two Ajaxes face the Trojans and stem the tide of their fighting though they kept pouring on towards them—and foremost among them all was Aeneas, son of Anchises, with valiant Hector. As a flock of daws or starlings fall to screaming and chattering when they see a falcon, foe to all small birds, come soaring near them, even so did the Achaean youth raise a babel of cries as they fled before Aeneas and Hector, unmindful of their former prowess. In the rout of the Danaans much goodly armor fell round about the trench, and of fighting there was no end.

Book XVIII

Thetis promises Achilles, grief-stricken at Patroclus' death, to get him new armor. Achilles shows himself on the wall, shouting encouragement, and the Trojans fall back in terror. Patroclus' body is borne into the camp. In view of Achilles' reappearance, Polydamas advises Hector to draw the Trojans back to the shelter of the city walls. Hector refuses. The god Hephaestus forges magnificent new armor for Achilles.

THUS THEN DID THEY FIGHT AS IT WERE A FLAMING FIRE. MEANWHILE, the fleet runner Antilochus, who had been sent as messenger, reached Achilles, and found him sitting by his tall ships and boding that which was indeed too surely true. "Alas," said he to himself in the heaviness of his heart, "why are the Achaeans again scouring the plain and flocking towards the ships? Heaven grant the gods be not now bringing that sorrow upon me of which my mother Thetis spoke, saying that while I was yet alive the bravest of the Myrmidons should fall before the Trojans and see the light of the sun no longer. I fear the brave son of Menoetius has fallen through his own daring—and yet I bade him return to the ships as soon as he had driven back those that were bringing fire against them, and not join battle with Hector."

As he was thus pondering, the son of Nestor came up to him and told his sad tale, weeping bitterly the while. "Alas," he cried, "son of noble Peleus, I bring you bad tidings! Would indeed that they were untrue. Patroclus has fallen, and a fight is raging about his naked body—for Hector holds his armor."

A dark cloud of grief fell upon Achilles as he listened. He filled both hands with dust from off the ground and poured it over his head, disfiguring his comely face and letting the refuse settle over his shirt so fair and new. He flung himself down all huge and hugely at full length and tore his hair with his hands. The bondswomen whom Achilles and Patroclus had taken captive screamed aloud for grief, beating their breasts, and with their limbs failing them for sorrow. Antilochus bent over him the while, weeping and holding both his hands as he lay groaning, for he feared that he might plunge a knife into his own throat.

Then Achilles gave a loud cry and his mother heard him as she was sitting in the depths of the sea by the old man her father, whereon she screamed, and all the goddesses, daughters of Nereus that dwelt at the bottom of the sea, came gathering round her. There were Glauce, Thalia and Cymodoce, Nesaia, Speo, Thoë and darkeyed Halië, Cymothoë, Actaea and Limnorea, Melite, Iaera, Amphithoë and Agave, Doto and Proto, Pherusa and Dynamene, Dexamene, Amphinome and Callianeira, Doris, Panope, and the famous sea-nymph Galatea, Nemertes, Apseudes, and Callianassa. There were also Clymene, Ianeira and Ianassa, Maera, Oreithuia and Amatheia of the lovely locks, with other Nereids who dwell in the depths of the sea. The crystal cave was filled with their multitude and they all beat their breasts while Thetis led them in their lament.

"Listen," she cried, "sisters, daughters of Nereus, that you may hear the burden of my sorrows! Alas, woe is me, woe in that I have borne the most glorious of offspring. I bore him fair and strong, hero among heroes, and he shot up as a sapling. I tended him as a plant in a goodly garden, and sent him with his ships to Ilium to fight the Trojans, but never shall I welcome him back to the house of Peleus. So long as he lives to look upon the light of the sun he is in heaviness, and though I go to him I cannot help him. Nevertheless, I will go, that I may see my dear son and learn what sorrow has befallen him though he is still holding aloof from battle."

She left the cave as she spoke, while the others followed weeping after, and the waves opened a path before them. When they reached the rich plain of Troy, they came up out of the sea in a long line on to the sands, at the place where the ships of the Myrmidons were drawn up in close order round the tents of Achilles. His mother went up to him as he lay groaning; she laid her hand upon his head and spoke piteously, saying: "My son, why are you thus weeping? What sorrow has now befallen you? Tell me; hide it not from me. Surely Zeus has granted you the prayer you made him, when you lifted up your hands and besought him that the Achaeans might all of them be pent up at their ships, and rue it bitterly in that you were no longer with them."

Achilles groaned and answered: "Mother, Olympian Zeus has indeed vouchsafed me the fulfillment of my prayer, but what boots it to me, seeing that my dear comrade Patroclus has fallen—he whom I valued more than all others and loved as dearly as my own life? I have lost him; aye, and Hector when he had killed him stripped him of the wondrous armor, so glorious to behold, which the gods gave to Peleus when they laid you in the couch of a mortal man. Would that you were still dwelling among the immortal sea-nymphs, and that Peleus had taken to himself some mortal bride. For now you shall have grief infinite by reason of the death of that son whom you can never welcome home—nay, I will not live nor go about among mankind unless Hector fall by my spear, and thus pay me for having slain Patroclus, son of Menoetius."

Thetis wept and answered, "Then, my son, is your end near at hand—for your own death awaits you full soon after that of Hector."

Then said Achilles in his great grief: "I would die here and now, in that I could not save my comrade. He has fallen far from home, and in his hour of need my hand was not there to help him. What is there for me? Return to my own land I shall not, and I have brought no saving neither to Patroclus nor to my other comrades of whom so many have been slain by mighty Hector. I stay here by my ships a bootless burden upon the earth, I, who in fight have no peer among the Achaeans, though in counsel there are better than I.

Therefore, perish strife both from among gods and men, and anger, wherein even a righteous man will harden his heart—which rises up in the soul of a man like smoke, and the taste thereof is sweeter than drops of honey. Even so has Agamemnon angered me. And yet—so be it, for it is over; I will force my soul into subjection as I needs must; I will go; I will pursue Hector, who has slain him whom I loved so dearly, and will then abide my doom when it may please Zeus and the other gods to send it. Even Heracles, the best loved of Zeus—even he could not escape the hand of death, but fate and Hera's fierce anger laid him low, as I too shall lie when I am dead if a like doom awaits me. Till then I will win fame and will bid Trojan and Dardanian women wring tears from their tender cheeks with both their hands in the grievousness of their great sorrow; thus shall they know that he who has held aloof so long will hold aloof no longer. Hold me not back, therefore, in the love you bear me, for you shall not move me."

Then silver-footed Thetis answered: "My son, what you have said is true. It is well to save your comrades from destruction, but your armor is in the hands of the Trojans. Hector bears it in triumph upon his own shoulders. Full well I know that his vaunt shall not be lasting, for his end is close at hand. Go not, however, into the press of battle till you see me return hither; tomorrow at break of day I shall be here, and will bring you goodly armor from King Hephaestus."

On this she left her brave son, and as she turned away she said to the sea-nymphs, her sisters: "Dive into the bosom of the sea and go to the house of the old sea-god, my father. Tell him everything; as for me, I will go to the cunning workman Hephaestus on high Olympus, and ask him to provide my son with a suit of splendid armor."

When she had so said, they dived forthwith beneath the waves, while silver-footed Thetis went her way that she might bring the armor for her son.

Thus, then, did her feet bear the goddess to Olympus, and meanwhile the Achaeans were flying with loud cries before murderous Hector till they reached the ships and the Hellespont, and they could not draw the body of Ares' servant Patroclus out of reach of the weapons that were showered upon him, for Hector, son of Priam, with his host and horsemen had again caught up to him like the flame of a fiery furnace; thrice did brave Hector seize him by the feet, striving with might and main to draw him away and calling loudly on the Trojans, and thrice did the two Ajaxes, clothed in valor as with a garment, beat him from off the body; but all undaunted he would now charge into the thick of the fight, and now again he would stand still and cry aloud, but he would give no ground. As upland shepherds that cannot chase some famished lion from a carcass, even so could not the two Ajaxes scare Hector, son of Priam, from the body of Patroclus.

And now he would even have dragged it off and have won imperishable glory had not Iris, fleet as the wind, winged her way as messenger from Olympus to the son of Peleus and bidden him arm. She came secretly without the knowledge of Zeus and of the other gods, for Hera sent her, and when she had got close to him she said: "Up, son of Peleus, mightiest of all mankind! Rescue Patroclus about whom this fearful fight is now raging by the ships. Men are killing one another, the Danaans in defense of the dead body, while the Trojans are trying to hale it away, and take it to windy Ilium; Hector is the most furious of them all; he is for cutting the head from the body and fixing it on the stakes of the wall. Up, then, and bide here no longer; shrink from the thought that Patroclus may become meat for the dogs of Troy. Shame on you, should his body suffer any kind of outrage."

And Achilles said, "Iris, which of the gods was it that sent you to me?"

Iris answered, "It was Hera, the royal spouse of Zeus, but the son of Cronus does not know of my coming, nor yet does any other of the immortals who dwell on the snowy summits of Olympus."

Then fleet Achilles answered her, saying: "How can I go up into the battle? They have my armor. My mother forbade me to arm till I should see her come, for she promised to bring me goodly armor from Hephaestus; I know no man whose arms I can put on, save only the shield of Ajax, son of Telamon, and he surely must be fighting in the front rank and wielding his spear about the body of dead Patroclus."

Iris said: "We know that your armor has been taken, but go as you are; go to the deep trench and show yourself before the Trojans, that they may fear you and cease fighting. Thus will the fainting sons of the Achaeans gain some brief breathing time, which in battle may hardly be."

Iris left him when she had so spoken. But Achilles, dear to Zeus, arose, and Athene flung her tasseled aegis round his strong shoulders; she crowned his head with a halo of golden cloud from which she kindled a glow of gleaming fire. As the smoke that goes up into heaven from some city that is being beleaguered on an island far out at sea—all day long do men sally from the city and fight their hardest, and at the going down of the sun the line of beacon fires blazes forth, flaring high for those that dwell near them to behold, if so be that they may come with their ships and succor them—even so did the light flare from the head of Achilles, as he stood by the trench, going beyond the wall—but he did not join the Achaeans, for he heeded the charge which his mother laid upon him.

There did he stand and shout aloud. Athene also raised her voice from afar and spread terror unspeakable among the Trojans. Ringing as the note of a trumpet that sounds alarm when the foe is at the gates of a city, even so brazen was the voice of the son of Aeacus, and when the Trojans heard its clarion tones they were dismayed. The horses turned back with their chariots for they boded mischief, and their drivers were awes truck by the steady flame which the gray-eyed goddess had kindled above the head of the great son of Peleus.

Thrice did Achilles raise his loud cry as he stood by the trench, and thrice were the Trojans and their brave allies thrown into confusion; whereon twelve of their noblest champions fell beneath the wheels of their chariots and perished by their own spears. The Achaeans to their great joy then drew Patroclus out of reach of the weapons and laid him on a litter. His comrades stood mourning round him, and among them fleet Achilles who wept bitterly as he saw his true comrade lying dead upon his bier. He had sent him out with horses and chariots into battle, but his return he was not to welcome.

Then Hera sent the busy sun, loath though he was, into the waters of Oceanus; so he set, and the Achaeans had rest from the tug and turmoil of war.

Now the Trojans, when they had come out of the fight, unyoked their horses and gathered in assembly before preparing their supper. They kept their feet, nor would any dare to sit down, for fear had fallen upon them all because Achilles had shown himself after having held aloof so long from battle. Polydamas, son of Panthoüs, was first to speak, a man of judgment, who alone among them could look both before and after. He was comrade to Hector, and they had been born upon the same night. With all sincerity and good will, therefore, he addressed them thus:

"Look to it well, my friends; I would urge you to go back now to your city and not wait here by the ships till morning, for we are far from our walls. So long as this man was at enmity with Agamemnon the Achaeans were easier to deal with, and I would have gladly camped by the ships in the hope of taking them. But now I go in great fear of the fleet son of Peleus. He is so daring that he will never bide here on the plain whereon the Trojans and Achaeans fight with equal valor, but he will try to storm our city and carry off our women. Do then as I say, and let us retreat. For this is what will happen. The darkness of night will for a time stay the son of Peleus, but if he find us here in the morning when he sallies forth in full armor, we shall have knowledge of him in good earnest. Glad indeed will he be who can escape and get back to Ilium, and many a Trojan will become meat for dogs and vultures—may I never live to hear it. If we do as I say, little though we may like it, we shall have strength in counsel during the night, and the great gates with the doors that close them will protect the city. At dawn we can arm and take our stand on the walls. He will then rue it if he sallies from the ships to fight us. He will go back when he has given his horses their fill of being driven all whithers under our walls, and will be in no mind to try and force his way into the city. Neither will he ever sack it; dogs shall devour him ere he do so."

Hector looked fiercely at him and answered: "Polydamas, your words are not to my liking in that you bid us go back and be pent within the city. Have you not had enough of being cooped up behind walls? In the old days the city of Priam was famous the whole world over for its wealth of gold and bronze, but our treasures are wasted out of our houses, and much goods have been sold away to Phrygia and fair Meonia, for the hand of Zeus has been laid heavily upon us. Now, therefore, that the son of scheming Cronus has vouchsafed me to win glory here and to hem the Achaeans in at their ships, prate no more in this fool's wise among the people. You will have no man with you; it shall not be; do all of you as I now say; take your suppers in your companies throughout the host, and keep your watches and be wakeful every man of you. If any Trojan is uneasy about his possessions, let him gather them and give them out among the people. Better let these, rather than the Achaeans, have them. At daybreak we will arm and fight about the ships. Granted that Achilles has again come forward to defend them, let it be as he will, but it shall go hard with him. I shall not shun him, but will fight him, to fall or conquer. The god of war deals out like measure to all, and the slayer may yet be slain."

Thus spoke Hector, and the Trojans, fools that they were, shouted in applause, for Pallas Athene had robbed them of their understanding. They gave ear to Hector with his evil counsel, but the wise words of Polydamas no man would heed. They took their supper throughout the host, and meanwhile through the whole night the Achaeans mourned Patroclus, and the son of Peleus led them in their lament. He laid his murderous hands upon the breast of his comrade, groaning again and again as a bearded lion when a man who was chasing deer has robbed him of his young in some dense forest. When the lion comes back he is furious, and searches dingle and dell to track the hunter if he can find him, for he is mad with rage—even so with many a sigh did Achilles speak among the Myrmidons, saying: "Alas! vain were the words with which I cheered the hero Menoetius in his own house; I said that I would bring his brave son back again to Opöeis after he had sacked Ilium and taken his share of the spoils—but Zeus does not give all men their heart's desire. The same soil shall be reddened here at Troy by the blood of us both, for I too shall never be welcomed home by the old knight Peleus, nor by my mother Thetis, but even in this place shall the earth cover me. Nevertheless, O Patroclus, now that I am left behind you, I will not bury you till I have brought hither the head and armor of mighty Hector who has slain you. Twelve noble sons of Trojans will I behead before your bier to avenge you; till I have done so you shall lie as you are by the ships, and fair women of Troy and Dardanus, whom we have taken with spear and strength of arm when we sacked men's goodly cities, shall weep over you both night and day."

Then Achilles told his men to set a large tripod upon the fire that they might wash the clotted gore from off Patroclus. Thereon they set a tripod full of bath water on to a clear fire; they threw sticks on to it to make a blaze, and the water became hot as the flame played about the belly of the tripod. When the water in the cauldron was boiling they washed the body, anointed it with oil, and closed its wounds with ointment that had been kept nine years. Then they laid it on a bier and covered it with a linen cloth from head to foot, and over this they laid a fair white robe. Thus all night long did the Myrmidons gather round Achilles to mourn Patroclus.

Then Zeus said to Hera, his sister-wife: "So, Queen Hera, you have gained your end, and have roused fleet Achilles. One would think that the Achaeans were of your own flesh and blood."

And Hera answered: "Dread son of Cronus, why should you say this thing? May not a man though he be only mortal and knows less than we do, do what he can for another person? And shall not I—foremost of all goddesses both by descent and as wife to you who reign in heaven—devise evil for the Trojans if I am angry with them?"

Thus did they converse. Meanwhile Thetis came to the house of Hephaestus, imperishable, star-bespangled, fairest of the abodes in heaven, a house of bronze wrought by the lame god's own hands. She found him busy with his bellows, sweating and hard at work, for he was making twenty tripods that were to stand by the wall of his house, and he set wheels of gold under them all that they might go of their own selves to the assemblies of the gods, and come back again—marvels indeed to see. They were finished all but the ears of cunning workmanship which yet remained to be fixed to them; these he was now fixing, and he was hammering at the rivets. While he was thus at work, silver-footed Thetis came to the house. Charis, of graceful head-dress, wife to the far-famed lame god, came towards her as soon as she saw her and took her hand in her own, saying: "Why have you come to our house, Thetis, honored and ever welcomed? for you do not visit us often. Come inside and let me set refreshment before you."

The goddess led the way as she spoke and bade Thetis sit on a richly decorated seat inlaid with silver; there was a footstool also under her feet. Then she called Hephaestus and said, "Hephaestus, come here, Thetis wants you"; and the far-famed lame god answered: "Then it is indeed an august and honored goddess who has come here; she it was that took care of me when I was suffering from the heavy fall which I had through my cruel mother's anger—for she would have got rid of me because I was lame. It would have gone hardly with me had not Eurynome, daughter of the ever-encircling waters of Oceanus, and Thetis taken me to their bosom. Nine years did I stay with them, and many beautiful works in bronze, brooches, spiral armlets, cups, and chains did I make for them in their cave, with the roaring waters of Oceanus foaming as they rushed ever past it; and no one knew, neither of gods nor men, save only Thetis and Eurynome who took care of me. If, then, Thetis has come to my house I must make her due requital for having saved me. Entertain her, therefore, with all hospitality, while I put by my bellows and all my tools."

On this the mighty monster hobbled off from his anvil, his thin legs plying lustily under him. He set the bellows away from the fire and gathered his tools into a silver chest. Then he took a sponge and washed his face and hands, his shaggy chest and brawny neck; he donned his shirt, grasped his strong staff, and limped towards the door. There were golden handmaids also who worked for him and were like real young women, with sense and reason, voice also and strength, and all the learning of the immortals. These busied themselves as the king bade them, while he drew near to Thetis, seated her upon a goodly seat, and took her hand in his own, saying: "Why have you come to our house, Thetis honored and ever welcome?—for you do not visit us often. Say what you want, and I will do it for you at once if I can, and if it can be done at all."

Thetis wept and answered: "Hephaestus, is there another goddess in Olympus whom the son of Cronus has been pleased to try with so much affliction as he has me? Me alone of the marine goddesses did he make subject to a mortal husband, Peleus, son of Aeacus, and sorely against my will did I submit to the embraces of one who was but mortal, and who now stays at home worn out with age. Neither is this all. Heaven vouchsafed me a son, hero among heroes, and he shot up as a sapling. I tended him as a plant in a goodly garden and sent him with his ships to Ilium to fight the Trojans, but never shall I welcome him back to the house of Peleus. So long as he lives to look upon the light of the sun, he is in heaviness, and though I go to him I cannot help him. King Agamemnon has made him give up the maiden whom the sons of the Achaeans had awarded him, and he wastes with sorrow for her sake.

"Then the Trojans hemmed the Achaeans in at their ships' sterns and would not let them come forth. The elders, therefore, of the Argives besought Achilles and offered him great treasure, whereon he refused to bring deliverance to them himself, but put his own armor on Patroclus and sent him into the fight with much people after him. All day long they fought by the Scaean gates and would have taken the city there and then had not Apollo vouchsafed glory to Hector and slain the valiant son of Menoetius after he had done the Trojans much evil. Therefore I am suppliant at your knees if haply you may be pleased to provide my son, whose end is near at hand, with helmet and shield, with goodly greaves fitted with ankle-clasps, and with a breastplate, for he lost his own when his true comrade fell at the hands of the Trojans, and he now lies stretched on earth in the bitterness of his soul."

And Hephaestus answered: "Take heart, and be no more disquieted about this matter. Would that I could hide him from death's sight when his hour is come, so surely as I can find him armor that shall amaze the eyes of all who behold it."

When he had so said he left her and went to his bellows, turning them towards the fire and bidding them do their office. Twenty bellows blew upon the melting pots, and they blew blasts of every kind, some fierce to help him when he had need of them, and others less strong as Hephaestus willed it in the course of his work. He threw tough copper into the fire, and tin, with silver and gold. He set his great anvil on its block, and with one hand grasped his mighty hammer while he took the tongs in the other.

First he shaped the shield so great and strong, adorning it all over and binding it round with a gleaming circuit in three layers; and the baldric was made of silver. He made the shield in five thicknesses, and with many a wonder did his cunning hand enrich it.

He wrought the earth, the heavens, and the sea; the moon also at her full and the untiring sun, with all the signs that glorify the face of heaven—the Pleiades, the Hyades, huge Orion, and the Bear, which men also call the Wain and which turns round ever in one place, facing Orion, and alone never dips into the stream of Oceanus.

He wrought also two cities, fair to see and busy with the hum of men. In the one were weddings and wedding feasts, and they were going about the city with brides whom they were escorting by torchlight from their chambers. Loud rose the cry of Hymen, and the youths danced to the music of flute and lyre, while the women stood each at her house door to see them.

Meanwhile the people were gathered in assembly, for there was a quarrel, and two men were wrangling about the blood money for a man who had been killed, the one saying before the people that he had paid damages in full and the other that he had not been paid. Each was trying to make his own case good, and the people took sides, each man backing the side that he had taken; but the heralds kept them back, and the elders sate on their seats of stone in a solemn circle, holding the staves which the heralds had put into their hands. Then they rose and each in his turn gave judgment, and there were two talents laid down, to be given to him whose judgment should be deemed the fairest.

About the other city there lay encamped two hosts in gleaming armor, and they were divided whether to sack it, or to spare it and accept the half of what it contained. But the men of the city would not yet consent, and armed themselves for a surprise; their wives and little children kept guard upon the walls, and with them were the men who were past fighting through age; but the others sallied forth with Ares and Pallas Athene at their head— both of them wrought in gold and clad in golden raiment, great and fair with their armor as befitting gods, while they that followed were smaller. When they reached the place where they would lay their ambush, it was on a riverbed to which livestock of all kinds would come from far and near to water. Here, then, they lay concealed, clad in full armor. Some way off them there were two scouts who were on the lookout for the coming of sheep or cattle, which presently came, followed by two shepherds who were playing on their pipes, and had not so much as a thought of danger. When those who were in ambush saw this, they cut off the flocks and herds and killed the shepherds.

Meanwhile the besiegers, when they heard much noise among the cattle as they sat in council, sprang to their horses, and made with all speed towards them. When they reached them they set battle in array by the banks of the river, and the hosts aimed their bronze-shod spears at one another. With them were Strife and Riot, and fell Fate who was dragging three men after her, one with a fresh wound, and the other unwounded, while the third was dead, and she was dragging him along by his heel: and her robe was bedrabbled in men's blood. They went in and out with one another and fought as though they were living people haling away one another's dead.

He wrought also a fair fallow field, large and thrice ploughed already. Many men were working at the plough within it, turning their oxen to and fro, furrow after furrow. Each time that they turned on reaching the head-land a man would come up to them and give them a cup of wine, and they would go back to their furrows looking forward to the time when they should again reach the headland. The part that they had ploughed was dark behind them, so that the field, though it was of gold, still looked as if it were being ploughed—very curious to behold.

He wrought also a field of harvest corn, and the reapers were reaping with sharp sickles in their hands. Swathe after swathe fell to the ground in a straight line behind them, and the binders bound them in bands of twisted straw. There were three binders, and behind them there were boys who gathered the cut corn in armfuls and kept on bringing them to be bound. Among them all the owner of the land stood by in silence and was glad. The servants were getting a meal ready under an oak, for they had sacrificed a great ox and were busy cutting him up while the women were making a porridge of much white barley for the laborers' dinner.

He wrought also a vineyard, golden and fair to see, and the vines were loaded with grapes. The bunches overhead were black, but the vines were trained on poles of silver. He ran a ditch of dark metal all round it and fenced it with a fence of tin; there was only one path to it, and by this the vintagers went when they would gather the vintage. Youths and maidens all blithe and full of glee carried the luscious fruit in plaited baskets, and with them there went a boy who made sweet music with his lyre and sang the Linus-song with his clear boyish voice.

He wrought also a herd of horned cattle. He made the cows of gold and tin, and they lowed as they came full speed out of the yards to go and feed among the waving reeds that grow by the banks of the river. Along with the cattle there went four shepherds, all of them in gold, and their nine fleet dogs went with them. Two terrible lions had fastened on a bellowing bull that was with the foremost cows, and bellow as he might they haled him, while the dogs and men gave chase. The lions tore through the bull's thick hide and were gorging on his blood and bowels, but the herdsmen were afraid to do anything, and only hounded on their dogs; the dogs dared not fasten on the lions but stood by barking and keeping out of harm's way.

The god wrought also a pasture in a fair mountain dell, and a large flock of sheep, with a homestead and huts, and sheltered sheepfolds.

Furthermore, he wrought a green, like that which Daedalus once made in Cnossus for lovely Ariadne. Hereon there danced youths and maidens whom all would woo, with their hands on one another's wrists. The maidens wore robes of light linen, and the youths well-woven shirts that were slightly oiled. The girls were crowned with garlands, while the young men had daggers of gold that hung by silver baldrics. Sometimes they would dance deftly in a ring with merry twinkling feet, as it were a potter sitting at his work and making trial of his wheel to see whether it will run, and sometimes they would go all in line with one another, and much people were gathered joyously about the green. There was a bard also to sing to them and play his lyre, while two tumblers went about performing in the midst of them when the man struck up with his tune.

All round the outermost rim of the shield he set the mighty stream of the river Oceanus.

Then when he had fashioned the shield so great and strong, he made a breastplate also that shone brighter than fire. He made a helmet, close fitting to the brow, and richly worked, with a golden plume overhanging it; and he made greaves also of beaten tin.

Lastly, when the famed lame god had made all the armor, he took it and set it before the mother of Achilles; whereon she darted like a falcon from the snowy summits of Olympus and bore away the gleaming armor from the house of Hephaestus.

Book XIX

*With the morning Thetis brings new armor to Achilles, who calls all the
Greeks to an assembly on the beach and is reconciled to Agamemnon.
Agamemnon expresses regret for his folly, and sends the girl Briseis with
rich gifts back to Achilles' tent. The Greek army eats and prepares for battle.
As Achilles dons his armor and springs into his chariot, his horse Xanthus
warns him of his own approaching death.*

NOW WHEN DAWN IN ROBE OF SAFFRON WAS HASTING FROM THE
streams of Oceanus, to bring light to mortals and immortals,
Thetis reached the ships with the armor that the god had
given her. She found her son fallen about the body of Patroclus and
weeping bitterly. Many also of his followers were weeping round him, but
when the goddess came among them she clasped his hand in her own,
saying, "My son, grieve as we may we must let this man lie, for it is by
heaven's will that he has fallen; now, therefore, accept from Hephaestus
this rich and goodly armor, which no man has ever yet borne upon
his shoulders."

As she spoke she set the armor before Achilles, and it rang out bravely as
she did so. The Myrmidons were struck with awe, and none dared look full at
it, for they were afraid; but Achilles was roused to still greater fury, and his
eyes gleamed with a fierce light, for he was glad when he handled the splendid
present which the god had made him. Then, as soon as he had satisfied him-
self with looking at it, he said to his mother: "Mother, the god has given me

armor, meet handiwork for an immortal and such as no man living could have fashioned. I will now arm, but I much fear that flies will settle upon the son of Menoetius and breed worms about his wounds, so that his body, now he is dead, will be disfigured and the flesh will rot."

Silver-footed Thetis answered: "My son, be not disquieted about this matter. I will find means to protect him from the swarms of noisome flies that prey on the bodies of men who have been killed in battle. He may lie for a whole year, and his flesh shall still be as sound as ever, or even sounder. Call, therefore, the Achaean heroes in assembly. Unsay your anger against Agamemnon. Arm at once, and fight with might and main."

As she spoke she put strength and courage into his heart, and she then dropped ambrosia and red nectar into the wounds of Patroclus, that his body might suffer no change.

Then Achilles went out upon the seashore, and with a loud cry called on the Achaean heroes. On this even those who as yet had stayed always at the ships, the pilots and helmsmen, and even the stewards who were about the ships and served out rations, all came to the place of assembly because Achilles had shown himself after having held aloof so long from fighting. Two sons of Ares, Odysseus and the son of Tydeus, came limping, for their wounds still pained them; nevertheless they came, and took their seats in the front row of the assembly. Last of all came Agamemnon, king of men, he too wounded, for Coön, son of Antenor, had struck him with a spear in battle.

When the Achaeans were got together Achilles rose and said: "Son of Atreus, surely it would have been better alike for both you and me, when we two were in such high anger about Briseis, surely it would have been better had Artemis' arrow slain her at the ships on the day when I took her after having sacked Lyrnessus. For so, many an Achaean the less would have bitten dust before the foe in the days of my anger. It has been well for Hector and the Trojans, but the Achaeans will long indeed remember our quarrel. Now, however, let it be, for it is over. If we have been angry, necessity has schooled our anger. I put it from me: I dare not nurse it forever. Therefore, bid the Achaeans arm forthwith that I may go out against the Trojans, and learn whether they will be in a mind to sleep by the ships or no. Glad, I ween, will he be to rest his knees who may fly my spear when I wield it."

Thus did he speak, and the Achaeans rejoiced in that he had put away his anger.

Then Agamemnon spoke, rising in his place, and not going into the middle of the assembly. "Danaan heroes," said he, "servants of Ares, it is well to listen when a man stands up to speak, and it is not seemly to interrupt him, or it will go hard even with a practiced speaker. Who can either hear or speak in an uproar? Even the finest orator will be disconcerted by it. I will expound to the son of Peleus, and do you other Achaeans heed me and mark me well. Often have the Achaeans spoken to me of this matter and upbraided me, but it was not I that did it: Zeus, and Fate, and Erinys that walks in darkness struck me mad when we were assembled on the day that I took from Achilles the meed that had been awarded to him. What could I do? All things are in the hand of heaven, and Folly, eldest of Zeus' daughters, shuts men's eyes to their destruction. She walks delicately, not on the solid earth, but hovers over the heads of men to make them stumble or to ensnare them.

"Time was when she fooled Zeus himself, who, they say, is greatest whether of gods or men; for Hera, woman though she was, beguiled him on the day when Alcmena was to bring forth mighty Heracles in the fair city of Thebes. He told it out among the gods, saying, 'Hear me all gods and goddesses, that I may speak even as I am minded; this day shall an Ilithuia, helper of women who are in labor, bring a man child into the world who shall be lord over all that dwell about him who are of my blood and lineage.' Then said Hera, all crafty and full of guile, 'You will play false, and will not hold to your word. Swear me, O Olympian, swear me a great oath that he who shall this day fall between the feet of a woman shall be lord over all that dwell about him who are of your blood and lineage.'

"Thus she spoke, and Zeus suspected her not, but swore the great oath, to his much ruing thereafter. For Hera darted down from the high summit of Olympus and went in haste to Achaean Argos where she knew that the noble wife of Sthenelus, son of Perseus, then was. She being with child and in her seventh month, Hera brought the child to birth though there was a month still wanting, but she stayed the offspring of Alcmena and kept back the Ilithuiae. Then she went to tell Zeus, the son of Cronus, and said, 'Father Zeus, lord of the lightning—I have a word for your ear. There is a fine child born this day, Eurystheus, son to Sthenelus, the son of Perseus. He is of your lineage; it is well, therefore, that he should reign over the Argives.'

"On this Zeus was stung to the very quick, and in his rage he caught Folly by the hair, and swore a great oath that never should she again invade starry heaven and Olympus, for she was the bane of all. Then he whirled her round with a twist of his hand and flung her down from heaven so that she fell on to the fields of mortal men; and he was ever angry with her when he saw his son groaning under the cruel labors that Eurystheus laid upon him. Even so did I grieve when mighty Hector was killing the Argives at their ships, and all the time I kept thinking of Folly who had so baned me. I was blind, and Zeus robbed me of my reason. I will now make atonement, and will add much treasure by way of amends. Go, therefore, into battle, you and your people with you. I will give you all that Odysseus offered you yesterday in your tents; or, if it so please you, wait, though you would fain fight at once, and my squires shall bring the gifts from my ship, that you may see whether what I give you is enough."

And Achilles answered: "Son of Atreus, king of men, Agamemnon, you can give such gifts as you think proper, or you can withhold them: it is in your own hands. Let us now set battle in array. It is not well to tarry talking about trifles, for there is a deed which is as yet to do. Achilles shall again be seen fighting among the foremost, and laying low the ranks of the Trojans: bear this in mind each one of you when he is fighting."

Then Odysseus said: "Achilles, godlike and brave, send not the Achaeans thus against Ilium to fight the Trojans fasting, for the battle will be no brief one, when it is once begun, and heaven has filled both sides with fury; bid them first take food, both bread and wine, by the ships, for in this there is strength and stay. No man can do battle the livelong day to the going down of the sun if he is without food. However much he may want to fight his strength will fail him before he knows it; hunger and thirst will find him out, and his limbs will grow weary under him. But a man can fight all day if he is full fed with meat and wine; his heart beats high, and his strength will stay till he has routed all his foes. Therefore, send the people away and bid them prepare their meal. King Agamemnon will bring out the gifts in presence of the assembly, that all may see them and you may be satisfied. Moreover, let him swear on oath before the Argives that he has never gone up into the couch of Briseis, nor been with her after the manner of men and women; and do you, too, show yourself of a gracious mind. Let Agamemnon entertain you in his tents with a feast of reconciliation, that so you may have had your dues in full. As for you, son of Atreus, treat people more righteously in future. It is no disgrace even to a king that he should make amends if he was wrong in the first instance."

And King Agamemnon answered: "Son of Laertes, your words please me well, for throughout you have spoken wisely. I will swear as you would have me do; I do so of my own free will, neither shall I take the name of heaven in vain. Let, then, Achilles wait, though he would fain fight at once, and do you others wait also, till the gifts come from my tent and we ratify the oath with sacrifice. Thus, then, do I charge you: take some noble young Achaeans with you, and bring from my tents the gifts that I promised yesterday to Achilles, and bring the women also. Furthermore, let Talthybius find me a boar from those that are with the host, and make it ready for sacrifice to Zeus and to the sun."

Then said Achilles: "Son of Atreus, king of men, Agamemnon, see to these matters at some other season, when there is breathing time and when

I am calmer. Would you have men eat while the bodies of those whom Hector, son of Priam, slew are still lying mangled upon the plain? Let the sons of the Achaeans, say I, fight fasting and without food, till we have avenged them; afterwards at the going down of the sun let them eat their fill. As for me, Patroclus is lying dead in my tent, all hacked and hewn, with his feet to the door, and his comrades are mourning round him. Therefore I can take thought of nothing save only slaughter and blood and the rattle in the throat of the dying."

Odysseus answered: "Achilles, son of Peleus, mightiest of all the Achaeans, in battle you are better than I, and that more than a little, but in counsel I am much before you, for I am older and of greater knowledge. Therefore be patient under my words. Fighting is a thing of which men soon surfeit, and when Zeus, who is war's steward, weighs the upshot, it may well prove that the straw which our sickles have reaped is far heavier than the grain. It may not be that the Achaeans should mourn the dead with their bellies; day by day men fall thick and threefold continually. When should we have respite from our sorrow? Let us mourn our dead for a day and bury them out of sight and mind, but let those of us who are left eat and drink that we may arm and fight our foes more fiercely. In that hour let no man hold back, waiting for a second summons; such summons shall bode ill for him who is found lagging behind at our ships. Let us rather sally as one man and loose the fury of war upon the Trojans."

When he had thus spoken he took with him the sons of Nestor, with Meges, son of Phyleus, Thoas, Meriones, Lycomedes, son of Creontes and Melanippus, and went to the tent of Agamemnon, son of Atreus. The word was not sooner said than the deed was done. They brought out the seven tripods which Agamemnon had promised, with the twenty metal cauldrons and the twelve horses; they also brought the women skilled in useful arts, seven in number, with Briseis, which made eight. Odysseus weighed out the ten talents of gold and then led the way back, while the young

Achaeans brought the rest of the gifts and laid them in the middle of the assembly.

Agamemnon then rose, and Talthybius, whose voice was like that of a god, came up to him with the boar. The son of Atreus drew the knife which he wore by the scabbard of his mighty sword, and began by cutting off some bristles from the boar, lifting up his hands in prayer as he did so. The other Achaeans sat where they were all silent and orderly to hear the king, and Agamemnon looked into the vault of heaven and prayed, saying: "I call Zeus, the first and mightiest of all gods, to witness, I call also Earth and Sun and the Erinyes who dwell below and take vengeance on him who shall swear falsely, that I have laid no hand upon the girl Briseis, neither to take her to my bed nor otherwise, but that she has remained in my tents inviolate. If I swear falsely may heaven visit me with all the penalties which it metes out to those who perjure themselves."

He cut the boar's throat as he spoke, whereon Talthybius whirled it round his head, and flung it into the wide sea to feed the fishes. Then Achilles also rose and said to the Argives: "Father Zeus, of a truth you blind men's eyes and bane them. The son of Atreus had not else stirred me to so fierce an anger, nor so stubbornly taken Briseis from me against my will. Surely Zeus must have counseled the destruction of many an Argive. Go, now, and take your food that we may begin fighting."

On this he broke up the assembly, and every man went back to his own ship. The Myrmidons attended to the presents and took them away to the ship of Achilles. They placed them in his tents, while the stablemen drove the horses in among the others.

Briseis, fair as Aphrodite, when she saw the mangled body of Patroclus, flung herself upon it and cried aloud, tearing her breast, her neck, and her lovely face with both her hands. Beautiful as a goddess she wept and said: "Patroclus, dearest friend, when I went hence I left you living; I return, O prince, to find you dead; thus do fresh sorrows multiply upon me one after the other. I saw him to whom my father and mother married me cut down before our city, and my three own dear brothers perished with him on the selfsame day; but you, Patroclus, even when Achilles slew my husband and sacked the city of noble Mynes, told me that I was not to weep, for you said you would make Achilles marry me, and take me back with him to Phthia, where we should have a wedding feast among the Myrmidons. You were always kind to me and I shall never cease to grieve for you."

She wept as she spoke, and the women joined in her lament—making as though their tears were for Patroclus, but in truth each was weeping for her own sorrows. The elders of the Achaeans gathered round Achilles and prayed him to take food, but he groaned and would not do so. "I pray you," said he, "if any comrade will hear me, bid me neither eat nor drink, for I am in great heaviness, and will stay fasting even to the going down of the sun."

On this he sent the other princes away, save only the two sons of Atreus, Odysseus, Nestor, Idomeneus, and the old knight Phoenix, who stayed behind and tried to comfort him in the bitterness of his sorrow; but he would not be comforted till he should have flung himself into the jaws of battle, and he fetched sigh on sigh, thinking ever of Patroclus. Then he said:

"Hapless and dearest comrade, you it was who would get a good dinner ready for me at once and without delay when the Achaeans were hasting to fight the Trojans; now, therefore, though I have meat and drink in my tents, yet will I fast for sorrow. Grief greater than this I could not know, not even though I were to hear of the death of my father, who is now in Phthia weeping for the loss of me his son, who am here fighting the Trojans in a strange land for the accursed sake of Helen, nor yet though I should hear that my son is no more—he who is being brought up in Scyros—if indeed Neoptolemus is still living. Till now I made sure that I alone was to fall here at Troy away from Argos, while you were to return to Phthia, bring back my son with you in your own ship, and show him all my property, my bondsmen, and the greatness of my house—for Peleus must surely be either dead, or what little life remains to him is oppressed alike with the infirmities of age and ever-present fear lest he should hear the sad tidings of my death."

He wept as he spoke, and the elders sighed in concert as each thought on what he had left at home behind him. The son of Cronus looked down with pity upon them, and said presently to Athene: "My child, you have quite deserted your hero. Is he then gone so clean out of your recollection? There he sits by the ships all desolate for the loss of his dear comrade, and though the others are gone to their dinner he will neither eat nor drink. Go then and drop nectar and ambrosia into his breast, that he may know no hunger."

With these words he urged Athene, who was already of the same mind. She darted down from heaven into the air like some falcon sailing on his broad wings and screaming. Meanwhile the Achaeans were arming throughout the host, and when Athene had dropped nectar and ambrosia into Achilles so that no cruel hunger should cause his limbs to fail him, she went back to the house of her mighty father. Thick as the chill snowflakes shed from the hand of Zeus and borne on the keen blasts of the north wind, even so thick did the gleaming helmets, the bossed shields, the strongly plated breastplates, and the ashen spears stream from the ships. The sheen pierced the sky, the whole land was radiant with their flashing armor, and the sound of the tramp of their treading rose from under their feet. In the midst of them all Achilles put on his armor. He gnashed his teeth, his eyes gleamed like fire, for his grief was greater than he could bear. Thus, then, full of fury against the Trojans, did he don the gift of the god, the armor that Hephaestus had made him.

First he put on the goodly greaves fitted with ankle-clasps, and next he did on the breastplate about his chest. He slung the silver-studded sword of bronze about his shoulders, and then took up the shield so great and strong that shone afar with a splendor as of the moon. As the light seen by sailors from out at sea, when men have lit a fire in their homestead high up among the mountains, but the sailors are carried out to sea by wind and storm far from the haven where they would be—even so did the gleam of Achilles' wondrous shield strike up into the heavens. He lifted the redoubtable helmet, and set it upon his head, from whence it shone like a star, and the golden plumes which Hephaestus had set thick about the ridge of the helmet waved all around it. Then Achilles made trial of himself in his armor to see whether it fitted him, so that his limbs could play freely under it, and it seemed to buoy him up as though it had been wings.

He also drew his father's spear out of the spear stand, a spear so great and heavy and strong that none of the Achaeans save only Achilles had strength to wield it. This was the spear of Pelian ash from the topmost ridges of Mount Pelion, which Chiron had once given to Peleus, fraught with the death of heroes. Automedon and Alcimus busied themselves with the harnessing of his horses; they made the bands fast about them, and put the bit in their mouths, drawing the reins back towards the chariot. Automedon, whip in hand, sprang up behind the horses, and after him Achilles mounted in full armor, resplendent as the sun-god Hyperion. Then with a loud voice he chided with his father's horses, saying, "Xanthus and Balius, famed offspring of Podarge— this time when we have done fighting be sure and bring your driver safely back to the host of the Achaeans, and do not leave him dead on the plain as you did Patroclus."

Then fleet Xanthus answered from under the yoke—for white-armed Hera had endowed him with human speech—and he bowed his head till his mane touched the ground as it hung down from under the yoke-band. "Dread Achilles," said he, "we will indeed save you now, but the day of your death is near, and the blame will not be ours, for it will be heaven and stern fate that will destroy you. Neither was it through any sloth or slackness on our part that the Trojans stripped Patroclus of his armor. It was the mighty god whom lovely Leto bore that slew him as he fought among the foremost, and vouchsafed a triumph to Hector. We two can fly as swiftly as Zephyrus who they say is fleetest of all winds; nevertheless it is your doom to fall by the hand of a man and of a god."

When he had thus said the Erinyes stayed his speech, and Achilles answered him in great sadness, saying, "Why, O Xanthus, do you thus foretell my death? You need not do so, for I well know that I am to fall here, far from my dear father and mother; none the more, however, shall I stay my hand till I have given the Trojans their fill of fighting."

So saying, with a loud cry he drove his horses to the front.

Book XX

Zeus informs the gods that they are now free to take what part they please in the conflict. Apollo incites Aeneas to attack Achilles, but Poseidon intervenes and carries Aeneas off to safety. Apollo delivers Hector from quick death at Achilles' hands. Achilles rages over the field and kills many Trojans.

THUS, THEN, DID THE ACHAEANS ARM BY THEIR SHIPS ROUND YOU, O son of Peleus, who were hungering for battle; while the Trojans over against them armed upon the rise of the plain.

Meanwhile Zeus, from the top of many-delled Olympus, bade Themis gather the gods in council, whereon she went about and called them to the house of Zeus. There was not a river absent except Oceanus, nor a single one of the nymphs that haunt fair groves, or springs of rivers and meadows of green grass. When they reached the house of cloud-compelling Zeus, they took their seats in the arcades of polished marble which Hephaestus with his consummate skill had made for father Zeus.

In such wise, therefore, did they gather in the house of Zeus. Poseidon also, lord of the earthquake, obeyed the call of the goddess, and came up out of the sea to join them. There, sitting in the midst of them, he asked what Zeus' purpose might be. "Why," said he, "wielder of the lightning, have you called the gods in council? Are you considering some matter that concerns the Trojans and Achaeans—for the blaze of battle is on the point of being kindled between them?"

And Zeus answered: "You know my purpose, shaker of earth, and wherefore I have called you hither. I take thought for them even in their destruction. For my own part I shall stay here seated on Mount Olympus and look on in peace, but do you others go about among Trojans and Achaeans and help either side as you may be severally disposed. If Achilles fights the Trojans without hindrance they will make no stand against him. They have ever trembled at the sight of him, and now that he is roused to such fury about his comrade, he will override fate itself and storm their city."

Thus spoke Zeus and gave the word for war, whereon the gods took their several sides and went into battle. Hera, Pallas Athene, earth-encircling Poseidon, Hermes, bringer of good luck and excellent in all cunning—all these joined the host that came from the ships; with them also came Hephaestus in all his glory, limping, but yet with his thin legs plying lustily under him. Ares of gleaming helmet joined the Trojans, and with him Apollo of locks unshorn, and the archer-goddess Artemis, Leto, Xanthus, and laughter-loving Aphrodite.

So long as the gods held themselves aloof from mortal warriors the Achaeans were triumphant, for Achilles who had long refused to fight was now with them. There was not a Trojan but his limbs failed him for fear as he beheld the fleet son of Peleus all glorious in his armor, and looking like Ares himself. When, however, the Olympians came to take their part among men, forthwith uprose strong Strife, rouser of hosts, and Athene raised her loud voice, now standing by the deep trench that ran outside the wall and now shouting with all her might upon the shore of the sounding sea. Ares also bellowed out upon the other side, dark as some black thundercloud, and called on the Trojans at the top of his voice, now from the acropolis and now speeding up the side of the river Simois, till he came to the hill Callicolone.

Thus did the gods spur on both hosts to fight, and rouse fierce contention also among themselves. The sire of gods and men thundered from heaven above, while from beneath Poseidon shook the vast earth, and bade the high hills tremble. The spurs and crests of many-fountained Ida quaked, as also the city of the Trojans and the ships of the Achaeans. Hades, king of the realms below, was struck with fear; he sprang panic-stricken from his throne and cried aloud in terror lest Poseidon, lord of the earthquake, should crack the ground over his head, and lay bare his moldy mansions to the sight of mortals and immortals—mansions so ghastly grim that even the gods shudder to think of them. Such was the uproar as the gods came together in battle. Apollo with his arrows took his stand to face King Poseidon, while Athene took hers against the god of war; the archer goddess Artemis with her golden arrows, sister of far-darting Apollo, stood to face Hera; Hermes, the lusty bringer of good luck, faced Leto, while the mighty eddying river whom men call Scamander, but gods Xanthus, matched himself against Hephaestus.

The gods, then, were thus ranged against one another. But the heart of Achilles was set on meeting Hector, son of Priam, for it was with his blood that he longed above all things else to glut the stubborn lord of battle. Meanwhile, Apollo set Aeneas on to attack the son of Peleus, and put courage into his heart, speaking with the voice of Lycaon, son of Priam. In his likeness, therefore, he said to Aeneas, "Aeneas, counselor of the Trojans, where are now the brave words with which you vaunted over your wine before the Trojan princes, saying that you would fight Achilles, son of Peleus, in single combat?"

And Aeneas answered: "Why do you thus bid me fight the proud son of Peleus, when I am in no mind to do so? Were I to face him now, it would not be for the first time. His spear has already put me to flight from Ida, when he attacked our cattle and sacked Lyrnessus and Pedasus. Zeus indeed saved me in that he vouchsafed me strength to fly, else had I fallen by the hands of Achilles and Athene, who went before him to protect him and urged him to fall upon the Lelegae and Trojans. No man may fight Achilles, for one of the gods is always with him as his guardian angel, and even were it not so, his weapon flies ever straight, and fails not to pierce the flesh of him who is against him. If heaven would let me fight him on even terms he should not soon overcome me, though he boasts that he is made of bronze."

Then said King Apollo, son to Zeus: "Nay, hero, pray to the ever-living gods, for men say that you were born of Zeus' daughter Aphrodite, whereas Achilles is son to a goddess of inferior rank. Aphrodite is child to Zeus, while Thetis is but daughter to the old man of the sea. Bring, therefore, your spear to bear upon him, and let him not scare you with his taunts and menaces."

As he spoke he put courage into the heart of the shepherd of his people, and he strode in full armor among the ranks of the foremost fighters. Nor did the son of Anchises escape the notice of white-armed Hera, as he went forth into the throng to meet Achilles. She called the gods about her, and said: "Look to it, you two, Poseidon and Athene, and consider how this shall be; Phoebus Apollo has been sending Aeneas clad in full armor to fight Achilles. Shall we turn him back at once, or shall one of us stand by Achilles and endow him with strength so that his heart fail not, and he may learn that the chiefs of the immortals are on his side, while the others who have all along been defending the Trojans are but vain helpers? Let us all come down from Olympus and join in the fight, that this day he may take no hurt at the hands of the Trojans. Hereafter let him suffer whatever fate may have spun out for him when he was begotten and his mother bore him. If Achilles be not thus assured by the voice of a god, he may come to fear presently when one of us meets him in battle, for the gods are terrible if they are seen face to face."

Poseidon, lord of the earthquake, answered her, saying: "Hera, restrain your fury; it is not well. I am not in favor of forcing the other gods to fight us, for the advantage is too greatly on our own side. Let us take our places on some hill out of the beaten track, and let mortals fight it out among themselves. If Ares or Phoebus Apollo begin fighting, or keep Achilles in check so that he cannot fight, we, too, will at once raise the cry of battle, and in that case they will soon leave the field and go back vanquished to Olympus among the other gods."

With these words the dark-haired god led the way to the high earth-barrow of Heracles, built round solid masonry, and made by the Trojans and Pallas Athene for him to fly to when the sea-monster was chasing him from the shore on to the plain. Here Poseidon and those that were with him took their seats, wrapped in a thick cloud of darkness; but the other gods seated themselves on the brow of Callicolone round you, O Phoebus, and Ares, the waster of cities.

Thus did the gods sit apart and form their plans, but neither side was willing to begin battle with the other, and Zeus from his seat on high was in command over them all. Meanwhile the whole plain was alive with men and horses, and blazing with the gleam of armor. The earth rang again under the tramp of their feet as they rushed towards each other, and two champions, by far the foremost of them all, met between the hosts to fight—to wit, Aeneas, son of Anchises, and noble Achilles.

Aeneas was first to stride forward in attack, his doughty helmet tossing defiance as he came on. He held his strong shield before his breast, and brandished his bronze spear. The son of Peleus from the other side sprang forth to meet him, like some fierce lion that the whole countryside has met to hunt and kill—at first he bodes no ill, but when some daring youth has struck him with a spear, he crouches open-mouthed, his jaws foam, he roars with fury, he lashes his tail from side to side about his ribs and loins, and glares as he springs straight before him, to find out whether he is to slay, or be slain among the foremost of his foes—even with such fury did Achilles burn to spring upon Aeneas.

When they were now close up with one another Achilles was first to speak. "Aeneas," said he, "why do you stand thus out before the host to fight me? Is it that you hope to reign over the Trojans in the seat of Priam? Nay, though you kill me Priam will not hand his kingdom over to you. He is a man of sound judgment, and he has sons of his own. Or have the Trojans been allotting you a demesne of passing richness, fair with orchard lawns and corn lands, if you should slay me? This you shall hardly do. I have discomfited you once already. Have you forgotten how when you were alone I chased you from your herds helter-skelter down the slopes of Ida? You did not turn round to look behind you; you took refuge in Lyrnessus, but I attacked the city, and with the help of Athene and father Zeus I sacked it and carried its women into captivity, though Zeus and the other gods rescued you. You think they will protect you now, but they will not do so. Therefore, I say go back into the host, and do not face me, or you will rue it. Even a fool may be wise after the event."

Then Aeneas answered: "Son of Peleus, think not that your words can scare me as though I were a child. I too, if I will, can brag and talk unseemly. We know one another's race and parentage as matters of common fame, though neither have you ever seen my parents nor I yours. Men say that you are son to noble Peleus, and that your mother is Thetis, fair-haired daughter of the sea. I have noble Anchises for my father, and Aphrodite for my mother. The parents of one or other of us shall this day mourn a son, for it will be more than silly talk that shall part us when the fight is over. Learn, then, my lineage if you will—and it is known to many.

"In the beginning Dardanus was the son of Zeus, and founded Dardania, for Ilium was not yet established on the plain for men to dwell in, and her people still abode on the spurs of many-fountained Ida. Dardanus had a son, King Erichthonius, who was wealthiest of all men living. He had three thousand mares that fed by the water meadows, they and their foals with them. Boreas was enamored of them as they were feeding, and covered them in the semblance of a dark-maned stallion. Twelve filly foals did they conceive and bear him, and these, as they sped over the rich plain, would go bounding on over the ripe ears of corn and not break them; or again when they would disport themselves on the broad back of Ocean they could gallop on the crest of a breaker. Erichthonius begat Tros, king of the Trojans, and Tros had three noble sons, Ilus, Assaracus, and Ganymede who was comeliest of mortal men.

Wherefore the gods carried him off to be Zeus' cupbearer, for his beauty's sake, that he might dwell among the immortals. Ilus begat Laomedon, and Laomedon begat Tithonus, Priam, Lampus, Clytius, and Hiketaon of the stock of Ares. But Assaracus was father to Capys, and Capys to Anchises, who was my father, while Hector is son to Priam.

"Such do I declare my blood and lineage, but as for valor, Zeus gives it or takes it as he will, for he is lord of all. And now let there be no more of this prating in midbattle as though we were children. We could fling taunts without end at one another; a hundred-oared galley would not hold them. The tongue can run all whithers and talk all wise. It can go here and there, and as a man says, so shall he be gainsaid. What is the use of our bandying hard words, like women who when they fall foul of one another go out and wrangle in the streets, one half true and the other lies, as rage inspires them? No words of yours shall turn me now that I am fain to fight—therefore let us make trial of one another with our spears."

As he spoke he drove his spear at the great and terrible shield of Achilles, which rang out as the point struck it. The son of Peleus held the shield before him with his strong hand and he was afraid, for he deemed that Aeneas' spear would go through it quite easily, not reflecting that the god's glorious gifts were little likely to yield before the blows of mortal men; and indeed Aeneas' spear did not pierce the shield, for the layer of gold, gift of the god, stayed the point. It went through two layers, but the god had made the shield in five, two of bronze, the two innermost ones of tin, and one of gold; it was in this that the spear was stayed.

Achilles in his turn threw, and struck the round shield of Aeneas at the very edge, where the bronze was thinnest. The spear of Pelian ash went clean through, and the shield rang under the blow. Aeneas was afraid, and crouched backwards, holding the shield away from him; the spear, however, flew over his back, and stuck quivering in the ground, after having gone through both circles of the sheltering shield. Aeneas, though he had avoided the spear, stood still, blinded with fear and grief because the weapon had gone so near him; then Achilles sprang furiously upon him, with a cry as of death and with his keen blade drawn, and Aeneas seized a great stone, so huge that two men, as men now are, would be unable to lift it, but Aeneas wielded it quite easily.

Aeneas would then have struck Achilles as he was springing towards him, either on the helmet or on the shield that covered him, and Achilles would have closed with him and despatched him with his sword had not Poseidon, lord of the earthquake, been quick to mark, and said forthwith to the immortals: "Alas, I am sorry for great Aeneas, who will now go down to the house of Hades, vanquished by the son of Peleus. Fool that he was to give ear to the counsel of Apollo. Apollo will never save him from destruction. Why should this man suffer when he is guiltless, to no purpose, and in another's quarrel? Has he not at all times offered acceptable sacrifice to the gods that dwell in heaven? Let us then snatch him from death's jaws, lest the son of Cronus be angry should Achilles slay him. It is fated, moreover, that he should escape and that the race of Dardanus, whom Zeus loved above all the sons born to him of mortal women, shall not perish utterly without seed or sign. For now indeed has Zeus hated the blood of Priam, while Aeneas shall reign over the Trojans, he and his children's children that shall be born hereafter."

Then answered Hera: "Earth-shaker, look to this matter yourself, and consider concerning Aeneas, whether you will save him, or suffer him, brave though he be, to fall by the hand of Achilles, son of Peleus. For of a truth we two, I and Pallas Athene, have sworn full many a time before all the immortals, that never would we shield Trojans from destruction, not even when all Troy is burning in the flames that the Achaeans shall kindle."

When earth-encircling Poseidon heard this he went into the battle amid the clash of spears and came to the place where Achilles and Aeneas were. Forthwith he shed a darkness before the eyes of the son of Peleus, drew the bronze-headed ashen spear from the shield of Aeneas, and laid it at the feet of Achilles. Then he lifted Aeneas on high from off the earth and hurried him away. Over the heads of many a band of warriors both horse and foot did he soar as the god's hand sped him, till he came to the very fringe of the battle where the Cauconians were arming themselves for fight. Poseidon, shaker of the earth, then came near to him and said: "Aeneas, what god has egged you on to this folly in fighting the son of Peleus, who is both a mightier man of valor and more beloved of heaven than you are? Give way before him whensoever you meet him, lest you go down to the house of Hades even though fate would have it otherwise. When Achilles is dead you may then fight among the foremost undaunted, for none other of the Achaeans shall slay you."

The god left him when he had given him these instructions, and at once removed the darkness from before the eyes of Achilles, who opened them wide indeed and said in great anger: "Alas! what marvel am I now beholding? Here is my spear upon the ground, but I see not him whom I meant to kill when I hurled it. Of a truth Aeneas also must be under heaven's protection, although I had thought his boasting was idle. Let him go hang. He will be in no mood to fight me further, seeing how narrowly he has missed being killed. I will now give my orders to the Danaans and attack some other of the Trojans."

He sprang forward along the line and cheered his men on as he did so. "Let not the Trojans," he cried, "keep you at arm's length, Achaeans, but go for them and fight them man for man. However valiant I may be, I cannot give chase to so many and fight all of them. Even Ares, who is an immortal, or Athene, would shrink from flinging himself into the jaws of such a fight and laying about him. Nevertheless, so far as in me lies I will show no slackness of hand or foot nor want of endurance, not even for a moment. I will utterly break their ranks, and woe to the Trojan who shall venture within reach of my spear."

Thus did he exhort them. Meanwhile Hector called upon the Trojans and declared that he would fight Achilles. "Be not afraid, proud Trojans," said he, "to face the son of Peleus. I could fight gods myself if the battle were one of words only, but they would be more than a match for me, if we had to use our spears. Even so, the deed of Achilles will fall somewhat short of his word; he will do in part, and the other part he will clip short. I will go up against him though his hands be as fire—though his hands be fire and his strength iron."

Thus urged, the Trojans lifted up their spears against the Achaeans and raised the cry of battle as they flung themselves into the midst of their ranks. But Phoebus Apollo came up to Hector and said, "Hector, on no account must you challenge Achilles to single combat. Keep a lookout for him while you are under cover of the others and away from the thick of the fight; otherwise he will either hit you with a spear or cut you down at close quarters."

Thus he spoke, and Hector drew back within the crowd, for he was afraid when he heard what the god had said to him. Achilles then sprang upon the Trojans with a terrible cry, clothed in valor as with a garment. First he killed Iphition, son of Otrynteus, a leader of much people whom a naiad nymph had borne to Otrynteus, waster of cities, in the land of Hyde under the snowy heights of Mount Tmolus. Achilles struck him full on the head as he was coming on towards him, and split it clean in two. Whereon he fell heavily to the ground, and Achilles vaunted over him, saying, "You lie low, son of Otrynteus, mighty hero; your death is here, but your lineage is on the Gygaean lake where your father's estate lies, by Hyllus, rich in fish, and the eddying waters of Hermus."

Thus did he vaunt, but darkness closed the eyes of the other. The chariots of the Achaeans cut him up as their wheels passed over him in the front of the battle, and after him Achilles killed Demoleon, a valiant man of war and son to Antenor. He struck him on the temple through his bronze-cheeked helmet. The helmet did not stay the spear, but it went right on, crushing the bone so that the brain inside was shed in all directions, and his lust of fighting was ended. Then he struck Hippodamas in the midriff as he was springing down from his chariot in front of him, and trying to escape. He breathed his last, bellowing like a bull bellows when young men are dragging him to offer him in sacrifice to the King of Helice, and the heart of the earth-shaker is glad: even so did he bellow as he lay dying. Achilles then went in pursuit of Polydorus, son of Priam, whom his father had always forbidden to fight because he was the youngest of his sons, the one he loved best, and the fastest runner. He, in his folly and showing off the fleetness of his feet, was rushing about among the front ranks until he lost his life, for Achilles struck him in the middle of the back as he was darting past him—he struck him just at the golden fastenings of his belt and where the two pieces of the double breast-plate overlapped. The point of the spear pierced him through and came out by the navel, whereon he fell groaning on to his knees and a cloud of darkness overshadowed him as he sank, holding his entrails in his hands.

When Hector saw his brother Polydorus with his entrails in his hands and sinking down upon the ground, a mist came over his eyes, and he could not bear to keep longer at a distance. He therefore poised his spear and darted towards Achilles like a flame of fire. When Achilles saw him he bounded for-ward and vaunted, saying: "This is he that has wounded my heart most deeply and has slain my beloved comrade. Not for long shall we two quail before one another on the highways of war."

He looked fiercely on Hector and said, "Draw near, that you may meet your doom the sooner." Hector feared him not and answered: "Son of Peleus, think not that your words can scare me as though I were a child; I too if I will can brag and talk unseemly. I know that you are a mighty warrior, mightier by far than I. Nevertheless, the issue lies in the lap of heaven whether I, worse man though I be, may not slay you with my spear, for this too has been found keen ere now."

He hurled his spear as he spoke, but Athene breathed upon it, and though she breathed but very lightly she turned it back from going towards Achilles, so that it returned to Hector and lay at his feet in front of him. Achilles then sprang furiously on him with a loud cry, bent on killing him, but Apollo caught him up easily as a god can, and hid him in a thick darkness. Thrice did

Achilles spring towards him spear in hand, and thrice did he waste his blow upon the air. When he rushed forward for the fourth time as though he were a god, he shouted aloud, saying: "Hound, this time too you have escaped death—but of a truth it came exceedingly near you. Phoebus Apollo, to whom it seems you pray before you go into battle, has again saved you; but if I too have any friend among the gods I will surely make an end of you when I come across you at some other time. Now, however, I will pursue and overtake other Trojans."

On this he struck Dryops with his spear, about the middle of his neck, and he fell headlong at his feet. There he let him lie and stayed Demouchus, son of Philetor, a man both brave and of great stature, by hitting him on the knee with a spear. Then he smote him with his sword and killed him. After this, he sprang on Laogonus and Dardanus, sons of Bias, and threw them from their chariot, the one with a blow from a thrown spear, while the other he cut down in hand-to-hand fight. There was also Tros, the son of Alastor—he came up to Achilles and clasped his knees in the hope that he would spare him and not kill him but let him go, because they were both of the same age. Fool, he might have known that he should not prevail with him, for the man was in no mood for pity or forbearance but was in grim earnest. Therefore when Tros laid hold of his knees and sought a hearing for his prayers, Achilles drove his sword into his liver, and the liver came rolling out, while his bosom was all covered with the black blood that welled from the wound. Thus did death close his eyes as he lay lifeless.

Achilles then went up to Mulius and struck him on the ear with a spear, and the bronze spearhead came right out at the other ear. He also struck Echeclus, son of Agenor, on the head with his sword, which became warm with the blood, while death and stern fate closed the eyes of Echeclus. Next in order the bronze point of his spear wounded Deucalion in the forearm where the sinews of the elbow are united, whereon he waited Achilles' onset with his arm hanging down and death staring him in the face. Achilles cut his head off with a blow from his sword and flung it helmet and all away from him, and the marrow came oozing out of his backbone as he lay. He then went in pursuit of Rhigmus, noble son of Peires, who had come from fertile Thrace, and struck him through the middle with a spear which fixed itself in his belly, so that he fell headlong from his chariot. He also speared Areïthoüs, squire to Rhigmus, in the back as he was turning his horses in flight, and thrust him from his chariot, while the horses were struck with panic.

As a fire raging in some mountain glen after long drought—and the dense forest is in a blaze, while the wind carries great tongues of fire in every direction—even so furiously did Achilles rage, wielding his spear as though he were a god and giving chase to those whom he would slay, till the dark earth ran with blood. Or as one who yokes broad-browed oxen that they may tread barley in a threshing floor—and it is soon bruised small under the feet of the lowing cattle—even so did the horses of Achilles trample on the shields and bodies of the slain. The axle underneath and the railing that ran round the car were bespattered with clots of blood thrown up by the horses' hoofs and from the tires of the wheels; but the son of Peleus pressed on to win still further glory, and his hands were bedrabbled with gore.

Book XXI

Achilles, storming forward, cuts the Trojan army in two. At the river Scamander, he kills until the stream runs red. The river god, angry at this carnage, rises to overwhelm Achilles, but Hera calls on Hephaestus to scorch the river with his fiery blasts. On the plain, Athene and Hera fight Ares, Aphrodite, and Artemis. Meanwhile, the routed Trojans take refuge within the city walls.

NOW WHEN THEY CAME TO THE FORD OF THE FULL-FLOWING RIVER Xanthus, begotten of immortal Zeus, Achilles cut their forces in two: one half he chased over the plain towards the city by the same way that the Achaeans had taken when flying panic-stricken on the preceding day with Hector in full triumph. This way did they fly pell-mell, and Hera sent down a thick mist in front of them to stay them. The other half were hemmed in by the deep silver-eddying stream, and fell into it with a great uproar. The waters resounded, and the banks rang again, as they swam hither and thither with loud cries amid the whirling eddies. As locusts flying to a river before the blast of a grass fire—the flame comes on and on till at last it overtakes them and they huddle into the water—even so was the eddying stream of Xanthus filled with the uproar of men and horses, all struggling in confusion before Achilles.

Forthwith the hero left his spear upon the bank, leaning it against a tamarisk bush, and plunged into the river like a god, armed with his sword only. Fell was his purpose as he hewed the Trojans down on every side. Their dying groans rose hideous as the sword smote them, and the river ran red with blood. As when fish fly scared before a huge dolphin, and fill every nook and corner of some fair haven—for he is sure to eat all he can catch—even so did the Trojans cower under the banks of the mighty river, and when Achilles' arms grew weary with killing them, he drew twelve youths alive out of the water, to sacrifice in revenge for Patroclus, son of Menoetius. He drew them out like dazed fawns, bound their hands behind them with the girdles of their own shirts, and gave them over to his men to take back to the ships. Then he sprang into the river, thirsting for still further blood.

There he found Lycaon, son of Priam, seed of Dardanus, as he was escaping out of the water. He it was whom he had once taken prisoner when he was in his father's vineyard, having set upon him by night, as he was cutting young shoots from a wild fig tree to make the wicker sides of a chariot. Achilles then caught him to his sorrow unawares, and sent him by sea to Lemnos, where the son of Jason bought him. But a guest-friend, Eëtion of Imbros, freed him with a great sum, and sent him to Arisbe, whence he had escaped and returned to his father's house. He had spent eleven days happily with his friends after he had come from Lemnos, but on the twelfth heaven again delivered him into the hands of Achilles, who was to send him to the house of Hades sorely against his will. He was unarmed when Achilles caught sight of him, and had neither helmet nor shield; nor yet had he any spear, for he had thrown all his armor from him on to the bank, and was sweating with his struggles to get out of the river, so that his strength was now failing him.

Then Achilles said to himself in his surprise: "What marvel do I see here? If this man can come back alive after having been sold over into Lemnos, I shall have the Trojans also whom I have slain rising from the world below. Could not even the waters of the gray sea imprison him, as they do many another whether he will or no? This time let him taste my spear, that I may know for certain whether mother earth, who can keep even a strong man down, will be able to hold him, or whether thence too he will return."

Thus did he pause and ponder. But Lycaon came up to him dazed and trying hard to embrace his knees, for he would fain live, not die. Achilles thrust at him with his spear, meaning to kill him, but Lycaon ran crouching up to him and caught his knees, whereby the spear passed over his back and stuck in the ground, hungering though it was for blood. With one hand he caught Achilles' knees as he besought him and with the other he clutched the spear and would not let it go. Then he said: "Achilles, have mercy upon me and spare me, for I am your suppliant. It was in your tents that I first broke bread on the day when you took me prisoner in the vineyard; after which you sold me away to Lemnos far from my father and my friends, and I brought you the price of a hundred oxen. I have paid three times as much to gain my freedom. It is but twelve days that I have come to Ilium after much suffering, and now cruel fate has again thrown me into your hands. Surely father Zeus must hate me, that he has given me over to you a second time. Short of life indeed did my mother Laothoë bear me, daughter of aged Altes—of Altes who reigns over the warlike Lelegae and holds steep Pedasus on the river Satniöeis. Priam married his daughter along with many other women and two sons were born of her, both of whom you will have slain. Your spear slew noble Polydorus as he was fighting in the front ranks, and now evil will here befall me, for I fear that I shall not escape you since heaven has delivered me over to you. Furthermore I say, and lay my saying to your heart, spare me, for I am not of the same womb as Hector who slew your brave and noble comrade."

With such words did the princely son of Priam beseech Achilles, but Achilles answered him sternly. "Idiot," said he, "talk not to me of ransom. Until Patroclus fell I preferred to give the Trojans quarter, and sold beyond the sea many of those whom I had taken alive; but now not a man shall live of those whom heaven delivers into my hands before the city of Ilium—and of all Trojans it shall fare hardest with the sons of Priam. Therefore, my friend, you too shall die. Why should you whine in this way? Patroclus fell, and he was a better man than you are. I too—see you not how I am great and goodly?

I am son to a noble father and have a goddess for my mother, but the hands of doom and death overshadow me all as surely. The day will come, either at dawn or dark, or at the noontide, when one shall take my life also in battle, either with his spear, or with an arrow sped from his bow."

Thus did he speak, and Lycaon's heart sank within him. He loosed his hold of the spear and held out both hands before him, but Achilles drew his keen blade and struck him by the collarbone on his neck. He plunged his two-edged sword into him to the very hilt, whereon he lay at full length on the ground with the dark blood welling from him till the earth was soaked. Then Achilles caught him by the foot and flung him into the river to go downstream, vaunting over him the while and saying:

"Lie there among the fishes, who will lick the blood from your wound and gloat over it. Your mother shall not lay you on any bier to mourn you, but the eddies of Scamander shall bear you into the broad bosom of the sea. There shall the fishes feed on the fat of Lycaon as they dart under the dark ripple of the waters—so perish all of you till we reach the citadel of strong Ilium—you in flight, and I following after to destroy you. The river with its broad silver stream shall serve you in no stead, for all the bulls you offered him and all the horses that you flung living into his waters. None the less miserably shall you perish till there is not a man of you but has paid in full for the death of Patroclus and the havoc you wrought among the Achaeans whom you have slain while I held aloof from battle."

So spoke Achilles, but the river grew more and more angry, and pondered within himself how he should stay the hand of Achilles and save the Trojans from disaster. Meanwhile the son of Peleus, spear in hand, sprang upon Asteropaeus, son of Pelegon, to kill him. He was son to the broad river Axius and Periboea, eldest daughter of Acessamenus; for the river had lain with her. Asteropaeus stood up out of the water to face him with a spear in either hand, and Xanthus filled him with courage, being angry for the death of the youths whom Achilles was slaying ruthlessly within his waters. When they were close up with one another, Achilles was first to speak. "Who and whence are you," said he, "who dare to face me? Woe to the parents whose son stands up against me." And the son of Pelegon answered: "Great son of Peleus, why should you ask my lineage? I am from the fertile land of far Paeonia, captain of the Paeonians, and it is now eleven days that I am at Ilium. I am of the blood of the river Axius—of Axius that is the fairest of all rivers that run. He begot the famed warrior Pelegon, whose son men call me. Let us now fight, Achilles."

Thus did he defy him, and Achilles raised his spear of Pelian ash. Asteropaeus failed with both his spears, for he could use both hands alike. With the one spear he struck Achilles' shield, but did not pierce it, for the layer of gold, gift of the god, stayed the point; with the other spear he grazed the elbow of Achilles' right arm, drawing dark blood, but the spear itself went by him and fixed itself in the ground, foiled of its bloody banquet. Then Achilles, fain to kill him, hurled his spear at Asteropaeus, but failed to hit him and struck the steep bank of the river, driving the spear half its length into the earth. The son of Peleus then drew his sword and sprang furiously upon him. Asteropaeus vainly tried to draw Achilles' spear out of the bank by main force. Thrice did he tug at it, trying with all his might to draw it out, and thrice he had to leave off trying; the fourth time he tried to bend and break it, but ere he could do so Achilles smote him with his sword and killed him. He struck him in the belly near the navel, so that all his bowels came gushing out on to the ground, and the darkness of death came over him as he lay gasping. Then Achilles set his foot on his chest and spoiled him of his armor, vaunting over him and saying:

"Lie there—begotten of a river though you be, it is hard for you to strive with the offspring of Cronus' son. You declare yourself sprung from the blood of a broad river, but I am of the seed of mighty Zeus. My father is Peleus, son of Aeacus, ruler over the many Myrmidons, and Aeacus was the son of Zeus. Therefore as Zeus is mightier than any river that flows into the sea, so are his children stronger than those of any river whatsoever. Moreover, you have a great river hard by if he can be of any use to you, but there is no fighting against Zeus, the son of Cronus, with whom not even King Achelous can compare, nor the mighty stream of deep-flowing Oceanus, from whom all rivers and seas with all springs and deep wells proceed. Even Oceanus fears the lightnings of great Zeus and his thunder that comes crashing out of heaven."

With this he drew his bronze spear out of the bank, and now that he had killed Asteropaeus, he let him lie where he was on the sand with the dark water flowing over him and the eels and fishes busy nibbling and gnawing the fat that was about his kidneys. Then he went in chase of the Paeonians, who were flying along the bank of the river in panic when they saw their leader slain by the hands of the son of Peleus. Therein he slew Thersilochus, Mydon, Astypylus, Mnesus, Thrasius, Oeneus, and Ophelestes, and he would have slain yet others, had not the river in anger taken human form, and spoken to him from out the deep waters, saying: "Achilles, if you excel all in strength, so do you also in wickedness, for the gods are ever with you to protect you. If, then, the son of Cronus has vouchsafed it to you to destroy all the Trojans, at any rate drive them out of my stream, and do your grim work on land. My fair waters are now filled with corpses, nor can I find any channel by which I may pour myself into the sea for I am choked with dead, and yet you go on mercilessly slaying. I am in despair; therefore, O captain of your host, trouble me no further."

Achilles answered: "So be it, Scamander, Zeus-descended; but I will never cease dealing out death among the Trojans till I have pent them up in their city and made trial of Hector face to face, that I may learn whether he is to vanquish me, or I him."

As he spoke he set upon the Trojans with a fury like that of the gods. But the river said to Apollo: "Surely, son of Zeus, lord of the silver bow, you are not obeying the commands of Zeus who charged you straitly that you should stand by the Trojans and defend them till twilight fades and darkness is over all the earth."

Meanwhile Achilles sprang from the bank into midstream, whereon the river raised a high wave and attacked him. He swelled his stream into a torrent and swept away the many dead whom Achilles had slain and left within his waters. These he cast out on to the land, bellowing like a bull the while, but the living he saved alive, hiding them in his mighty eddies. The great and terrible wave gathered about Achilles, falling upon him and beating on his shield, so that he could not keep his feet. He caught hold of a great elm tree, but it came up by the roots and tore away the bank, damming the stream with its thick branches and bridging it all across; whereby Achilles struggled out of the stream and fled full speed over the plain, for he was afraid.

But the mighty god ceased not in his pursuit and sprang upon him with a dark-crested wave, to stay his hands and save the Trojans from destruction. The son of Peleus darted away a spear's throw from him; swift as the swoop of a black hunter-eagle which is the strongest and fleetest of all birds, even so did he spring forward, and the armor rang loudly about his breast. He fled on in front, but the river with a loud roar came tearing after. As one who would water his garden leads a stream from some fountain over his plants, and all his ground—spade in hand he clears away the dams to free the channels, and the little stones run rolling round and round with the water as it goes merrily down the bank faster than the man can follow—even so did the river keep catching up with Achilles albeit he was a fleet runner, for the gods are stronger than men. As often as he would strive to stand his ground, and see whether or no all the gods in heaven were in league against him, so often would the mighty wave come beating down upon his shoulders, and he would have to keep flying on and on in great dismay; for the angry flood was tiring him out as it flowed past him and ate the ground from under his feet.

Then the son of Peleus lifted up his voice to heaven, saying: "Father Zeus, is there none of the gods who will take pity upon me, and save me from the river? I do not care what may happen to me afterwards. I blame none of the other dwellers on Olympus so severely as I do my dear mother, who has beguiled and tricked me. She told me I was to fall under the walls of Troy by the flying arrows of Apollo. Would that Hector, the best man among the Trojans, might there slay me; then should I fall a hero by the hand of a hero. Whereas now it seems that I shall come to a most pitiable end, trapped in this river as though I were some swineherd's boy, who gets carried down a torrent while trying to cross it during a storm."

As soon as he had spoken thus, Poseidon and Athene came up to him in the likeness of two men and took him by the hand to reassure him. Poseidon spoke first. "Son of Peleus," said he, "be not so exceeding fearful; we are two gods, come with Zeus' sanction to assist you, I, and Pallas Athene. It is not your fate to perish in this river. He will abate presently as you will see. Moreover, we strongly advise you, if you will be guided by us, not to stay your hand from fighting till you have pent the Trojan host within the famed walls of Ilium—as many of them as may escape. Then kill Hector and go back to the ships, for we will vouchsafe you a triumph over him."

When they had so said they went back to the other immortals, but Achilles strove onward over the plain, encouraged by the charge the gods had laid upon him. All was now covered with the flood of waters, and much goodly armor of the youths that had been slain was drifting about, as also many corpses, but he forced his way against the stream, speeding right onwards, nor could the broad waters stay him, for Athene had endowed him with great strength. Nevertheless Scamander did not slacken in his pursuit, but was still more furious with the son of Peleus. He lifted his waters into a high crest and cried aloud to Simois, saying:

"Dear brother, let the two of us unite to stay this man, or he will sack the mighty city of King Priam, and the Trojans will not hold out against him. Help me at once. Fill your streams with water from their sources, rouse all your torrents to a fury; raise your wave on high and let snags and stones come thundering down you that we may make an end of this savage creature who is now lording it as though he were a god. Nothing shall serve him longer, not strength nor comeliness, nor his fine armor, which forsooth shall soon be lying low in the deep waters covered over with mud. I will wrap him in sand, and pour tons of shingle round him, so that the Achaeans shall not know how to gather his bones for the silt in which I shall have hidden him, and when they celebrate his funeral they need build no barrow."

On this he upraised his tumultuous flood high against Achilles, seething as it was with foam and blood and the bodies of the dead. The dark waters of the river stood upright and would have overwhelmed the son of Peleus, but Hera, trembling lest Achilles should be swept away in the mighty torrent, lifted her voice on high and called out to Hephaestus, her son. "Crook-foot," she cried, "my child, be up and doing, for I deem it is with you that Xanthus is fain to fight. Help us at once; kindle a fierce fire. I will then bring up the west and the white south wind in a mighty hurricane from the sea that shall bear the flames against the heads and armor of the Trojans and consume them, while you go along the banks of Xanthus burning his trees and wrapping him round with fire. Let him not turn you back neither by fair words nor foul and slacken not till I shout and tell you. Then you may stay your flames."

On this Hephaestus kindled a fierce fire, which broke out first upon the plain and burned the many dead whom Achilles had killed and whose bodies were lying about in great numbers; by this means the plain was dried and the flood stayed. As the north wind, blowing on an orchard that has been sodden with autumn rain, soon dries it, and the heart of the owner is glad—even so the whole plain was dried and the dead bodies were consumed. Then he turned tongues of fire on to the river. He burned the elms, the willows, and the tamarisks, the lotus also, with the rushes and marshy herbage that grew abundantly by the banks of the river. The eels and fishes that go darting about everywhere in the water, these, too, were sorely harassed by the flames that cunning Hephaestus had kindled, and the river himself was scalded, so that he spoke, saying: "Hephaestus, there is no god can hold his own against you. I cannot fight you when you flare out your flames in this way; strive with me no longer. Let Achilles drive the Trojans out of their city immediately. What have I to do with quarreling and helping people?"

He was boiling as he spoke, and all his waters were seething. As a cauldron upon a large fire boils when it is melting the lard of some fatted hog, and the lard keeps bubbling up all over when the dry faggots blaze under it—even so were the goodly waters of Xanthus heated with the fire till they were boiling. He could flow no longer but stayed his stream, so afflicted was he by the blasts of fire which cunning Hephaestus had raised. Then he prayed to Hera and besought her, saying, "Hera, why should your son vex my stream with such especial fury? I am not so much to blame as all the others are who have been helping the Trojans. I will leave off, since you so desire it, and let your son leave off also. Furthermore I swear that never again will I do anything to save the Trojans from destruction, not even when all Troy is burning in the flames which the Achaeans will kindle."

As soon as Hera heard this she said to her son Hephaestus: "Son Hephaestus, hold now your flames; we ought not to use such violence against a god for the sake of mortals."

When she had thus spoken Hephaestus quenched his flames, and the river went back once more into his own fair bed.

Xanthus was now beaten, so these two left off fighting, for Hera stayed them though she was still angry; but a furious quarrel broke out among the other gods, for they were of divided counsels. They fell on one another with a mighty uproar—earth groaned, and the spacious firmament rang out as with a blare of trumpets. Zeus heard as he was sitting on Olympus and laughed for joy when he saw the gods coming to blows among themselves. They were not long about beginning, and Ares, piercer of shields, opened the battle. Sword in hand, he sprang at once upon Athene and reviled her. "Why, vixen," said he, "have you again set the gods by the ears in the pride and haughtiness of your heart? Have you forgotten how you set Diomed, son of Tydeus, on to wound me, and yourself took visible spear and drove it into me to the hurt of my fair body? You shall now suffer for what you then did to me."

As he spoke he struck her on the terrible tasseled aegis—so terrible that not even can Zeus' lightning pierce it. Here did murderous Ares strike her with his great spear. She drew back and with her strong hand seized a stone that was lying on the plain—great and rugged and black—which men of old had set for the boundary of a field. With this she struck Ares on the neck and brought him down. Nine roods did he cover in his fall, and his hair was all soiled in the dust, while his armor rang rattling round him. But Athene laughed and vaunted over him, saying: "Idiot, have you not learned how far stronger I am than you, but you must still match yourself against me? Thus do your mother's curses now roost upon you, for she is angry and would do you mischief because you have deserted the Achaeans and are helping the Trojans."

She then turned her two piercing eyes elsewhere, whereon Zeus' daughter Aphrodite took Ares by the hand and led him away, groaning all the time, for it was only with great difficulty that he had come to himself again. When Queen Hera saw her, she said to Athene, "Look, daughter of aegis-bearing Zeus, unweariable, that vixen Aphrodite is again taking Ares through the crowd out of the battle; go after her at once."

Thus she spoke. Athene sped after Aphrodite with a will, and made at her, striking her on the bosom with her strong hand so that she fell fainting to the ground, and there they both lay stretched at full length. Then Athene vaunted over her, saying: "May all who help the Trojans against the Argives prove just as redoubtable and stalwart as Aphrodite did when she came across me while she was helping Ares. Had this been so, we should long since have ended the war by sacking the strong city of Ilium."

Hera smiled as she listened. Meanwhile King Poseidon turned to Apollo, saying: "Phoebus, why should we keep each other at arm's length? It is not well, now that the others have begun fighting; it will be disgraceful to us if we return to Zeus' bronze-floored mansion on Olympus without having fought each other. Therefore come on, you are the younger of the two, and I ought not to attack you, for I am older and have had more experience. Idiot, you have no sense, and forget how we two alone of all the gods fared hardly round about Ilium when we came from Zeus' house and worked for Laomedon a whole year at a stated wage and he gave us his orders. I built the Trojans the wall about their city, so wide and fair that it might be impregnable, while you, Phoebus, herded cattle for him in the dales of many-valleyed Ida. When, however, the glad hours brought round the time of payment, mighty Laomedon robbed us of all our hire and sent us off with nothing but abuse. He threatened to bind us hand and foot and sell us over into some distant island. He tried, moreover, to cut off the ears of both of us, so we went away in a rage, furious about the payment he had promised us, and yet withheld. In spite of all this, you are now showing favor to his people and will not join us in compassing the utter ruin of the proud Trojans with their wives and children."

And King Apollo answered: "Lord of the earthquake, you would have no respect for me if I were to fight you about a pack of miserable mortals, who come out like leaves in summer and eat the fruit of the field and presently fall lifeless to the ground. Let us stay this fighting at once and let them settle it among themselves."

He turned away as he spoke, for he would lay no hand on the brother of his own father. But his sister, the huntress Artemis, patroness of wild beasts, was very angry with him and said: "So you would fly, Far-darter, and hand victory over to Poseidon with a cheap vaunt to boot. Baby, why keep your bow thus idle? Never let me again hear you bragging in my father's house, as you often have done in the presence of the immortals, that you would stand up and fight with Poseidon."

Apollo made her no answer, but Zeus' august queen was angry and upbraided her bitterly. "Bold vixen," she cried, "how dare you cross me thus?

For all your bow you will find it hard to hold your own against me. Zeus made you as a lion among women, and lets you kill them whenever you choose. You will find it better to chase wild beasts and deer upon the mountains than to fight those who are stronger than you are. If you would try war, do so, and find out by pitting yourself against me how far stronger I am than you are."

She caught both Artemis' wrists with her left hand as she spoke and with her right she took the bow from her shoulders, and laughed as she beat her with it about the ears while Artemis wriggled and writhed under her blows. Her swift arrows were shed upon the ground, and she fled weeping from under Hera's hand as a dove that flies before a falcon to the cleft of some hollow rock, when it is her good fortune to escape. Even so did she fly weeping away, leaving her bow and arrows behind her.

Then the slayer of Argus, guide and guardian, said to Leto: "Leto, I shall not fight you; it is ill to come to blows with any of Zeus' wives. Therefore, boast as you will among the immortals that you worsted me in fair fight."

Leto then gathered up Artemis' bow and arrows that had fallen about amid the whirling dust, and when she had got them she made all haste after her daughter. Artemis had now reached Zeus' bronze-floored mansion on Olympus and sat herself down with many tears on the knees of her father, while her ambrosial raiment was quivering all about her. The son of Cronus drew her towards him, and laughing pleasantly the while began to question her, saying: "Which of the heavenly beings, my dear child, has been treating you in this cruel manner, as though you had been misconducting yourself in the face of everybody?" And the fair-crowned goddess of the chase answered: "It was your wife Hera, father, who has been beating me; it is always her doing when there is any quarreling among the immortals."

Thus did they converse, and meanwhile Phoebus Apollo entered the strong city of Ilium, for he was uneasy lest the wall should not hold out and the Danaans should take the city then and there, before its hour had come; but the rest of the ever-living gods went back, some angry and some triumphant, to Olympus, where they took their seats beside Zeus, lord of the storm cloud, while Achilles still kept on dealing out death alike on the Trojans and on their horses. As when the smoke from some burning city ascends to heaven when the anger of the gods has kindled it—there is then toil for all, and sorrow for not a few—even so did Achilles bring toil and sorrow on the Trojans.

Old King Priam stood on a high tower of the wall looking down on huge Achilles as the Trojans fled panic-stricken before him, and there was none to help them. Presently he came down from off the tower and with many a groan went along the wall to give orders to the brave warders of the gate. "Keep the gates," said he, "wide open till the people come flying into the city, for Achilles is hard by and is driving them in rout before him. I see we are in great peril. As soon as our people are inside and in safety, close the strong gates, for I fear lest that terrible man should come bounding inside along with the others."

As he spoke they drew back the bolts and opened the gates, and when these were opened there was a haven of refuge for the Trojans. Apollo then came full speed out of the city to meet them and protect them. Right for the city and the high wall, parched with thirst and grimy with dust, still they fled on, with Achilles wielding his spear furiously behind them. For he was as one possessed and was thirsting after glory.

Then had the sons of the Achaeans taken the lofty gates of Troy if Apollo had not spurred on Agenor, valiant and noble son to Antenor. He put courage into his heart and stood by his side to guard him, leaning against a beech tree and shrouded in thick darkness. When Agenor saw Achilles he stood still and his heart was clouded with care. "Alas," said he to himself in his dismay, "if I fly before mighty Achilles and go where all the others are being driven in rout, he will nonetheless catch me and kill me for a coward. How would it be were I to let Achilles drive the others before him, and then fly from the wall to the plain that is behind Ilium till I reach the spurs of Ida and can hide in the underwood that is thereon? I could then wash the sweat from off me in the river and in the evening return to Ilium. But why commune with myself in this way? Like enough he would see me as I am hurrying from the city over the plain and would speed after me till he had caught me—I should stand no chance against him, for he is mightiest of all mankind. What, then, if I go out and meet him in front of the city? His flesh too, I take it, can be pierced by pointed bronze. Life is the same in one and all, and men say that he is but mortal despite the triumph that Zeus, son of Cronus, vouchsafes him."

So saying he stood on his guard and awaited Achilles, for he was now fain to fight him. As a leopardess that bounds from out a thick covert to attack a hunter—she knows no fear and is not dismayed by the baying of the hounds; even though the man be too quick for her and wound her either with thrust or spear, still, though the spear has pierced her she will not give in till she has either caught him in her grip or been killed outright—even so did noble Agenor, son of Antenor, refuse to fly till he had made trial of Achilles, and took aim at him with his spear, holding his round shield before him and crying with a loud voice. "Of a truth," said he, "noble Achilles, you deem that you shall this day sack the city of the proud Trojans. Fool, there will be trouble enough yet before it, for there is many a brave man of us still inside who will stand in front of our dear parents with our wives and children, to defend Ilium. Here, therefore, huge and mighty warrior though you be, here shall you die."

As he spoke his strong hand hurled his javelin from him, and the spear struck Achilles on the leg beneath the knee. The greave of newly wrought tin rang loudly, but the spear recoiled from the body of him whom it had struck, and did not pierce it, for the god's gift stayed it. Achilles in his turn attacked noble Agenor, but Apollo would not vouchsafe him glory, for he snatched Agenor away and hid him in a thick mist, sending him out of the battle unmolested. Then he craftily drew the son of Peleus away from going after the host, for he put on the semblance of Agenor and stood in front of Achilles, who ran towards him to give him chase and pursued him over the corn lands of the plain, turning him towards the deep waters of the river Scamander. Apollo ran but a little way before him and beguiled Achilles by making him think all the time that he was on the point of overtaking him. Meanwhile the rabble of routed Trojans was thankful to crowd within the city till their numbers thronged it. No longer did they dare wait for one another outside the city walls to learn who had escaped and who were fallen in fight, but all whose feet and knees could still carry them poured pell-mell into the town.

Book XXII

*Outside the gates of Troy, Hector stands alone to face the oncoming Achilles,
deaf to the entreaties of his parents on the wall above him. As Achilles draws
near, Hector's courage gives way. He turns and runs, Achilles after him,
three times around the city. At length, tricked by Athene, he turns, fights,
and is slain. Achilles lashes his body to his chariot, and drags it away, trailing
in the dust. Priam, Hecuba, and Andromache bewail Hector's end.*

THUS THE TROJANS IN THE CITY, SCARED LIKE FAWNS, WIPED THE SWEAT
from off them and drank to quench their thirst, leaning against the
goodly battlements, while the Achaeans with their shields laid upon
their shoulders drew close up to the walls. But stern fate bade Hector stay where
he was before Ilium and the Scaean gates. Then Phoebus Apollo spoke to the son
of Peleus, saying: "Why, son of Peleus, do you, who are but man, give chase to
me who am immortal? Have you not yet found out that it is a god whom you
pursue so furiously? You did not harass the Trojans whom you had routed, and
now they are within their walls, while you have been decoyed hither away from
them. Me you cannot kill, for death can take no hold upon me."

Achilles was greatly angered and said: "You have balked me, Far-darter,
most malicious of all gods, and have drawn me away from the wall, where
many another man would have bitten the dust ere he got within Ilium. You
have robbed me of great glory and have saved the Trojans at no risk to your-
self, for you have nothing to fear, but I would indeed have my revenge if it
were in my power to do so."

On this, with fell intent he made towards the city, and as the winning horse in a chariot race strains every nerve when he is flying over the plain, even so fast and furiously did the limbs of Achilles bear him onwards. King Priam was first to note him as he scoured the plain, all radiant as the star which men call Orion's Hound, and whose beams blaze forth in time of harvest more brilliantly than those of any other that shines by night; brightest of them all though he be, he yet bodes ill for mortals, for he brings fire and fever in his train—even so did Achilles' armor gleam on his breast as he sped onwards. Priam raised a cry and beat his head with his hands as he lifted them up and shouted out to his dear son, imploring him to return; but Hector still stayed before the gates, for his heart was set upon doing battle with Achilles.

The old man reached out his arms towards him and bade him for pity's sake come within the walls. "Hector," he cried, "my son, stay not to face this man alone and unsupported, or you will meet death at the hands of the son of Peleus, for he is mightier than you. Monster that he is; would indeed that the gods loved him no better than I do, for so, dogs and vultures would soon devour him as he lay stretched on earth, and a load of grief would be lifted from my heart, for many a brave son has he reft from me, either by killing them or selling them away in the islands that are beyond the sea. Even now I miss two sons from among the Trojans who have thronged within the city, Lycaon and Polydorus, whom Laothoë, peeress among women, bore me. Should they be still alive and in the hands of the Achaeans, we will ransom them with gold and bronze, of which we have store, for the old man Altes endowed his daughter richly; but if they are already dead and in the house of Hades, sorrow will it be to us two who were their parents; albeit the grief of others will be more short-lived unless you too perish at the hands of Achilles. Come, then, my son, within the city, to be the guardian of Trojan men and Trojan women, or you will both lose your own life and afford a mighty triumph to the son of Peleus. Have pity also on your unhappy father while life yet remains to him—on me, whom the son of Cronus will destroy by a terrible doom on the threshold of old age, after I have seen my sons slain and my daughters haled away as captives, my bridal chambers pillaged, little children dashed to earth amid the rage of battle, and my sons' wives dragged away by the cruel hands of the Achaeans. In the end fierce hounds will tear me in pieces at my own gates after someone has beaten the life out of my body with sword or spear—hounds that I myself reared and fed at my own table to guard my gates, but who will yet lap my blood and then lie all distraught at my doors. When a young man falls by the sword in battle, he may lie where he is and there is nothing unseemly; let what will be seen, all is honorable in death, but when an old man is slain there is nothing in this world more pitiable than that dogs should defile his gray hair and beard and all that men hide for shame."

The old man tore his gray hair as he spoke, but he moved not the heart of Hector. His mother hard by wept and moaned aloud as she bared her bosom and pointed to the breast which had suckled him. "Hector," she cried, weeping bitterly the while, "Hector, my son, spurn not this breast, but have pity upon me too! If I have ever given you comfort from my own bosom, think on it now, dear son, and come within the wall to protect us from this man; stand not without to meet him. Should the wretch kill you, neither I nor your richly dowered wife shall ever weep, dear offshoot of myself, over the bed on which you lie, for dogs will devour you at the ships of the Achaeans."

Thus did the two with many tears implore their son, but they moved not the heart of Hector, and he stood his ground awaiting huge Achilles as he drew nearer towards him. As a serpent in its den upon the mountains, full-fed with deadly poisons, waits for the approach of man—he is filled with fury and his eyes glare terribly as he goes writhing round his den—even so Hector leaned his shield against a tower that jutted out from the wall and stood where he was, undaunted.

"Alas," said he to himself in the heaviness of his heart, "if I go within the gates, Polydamas will be the first to heap reproach upon me, for it was he that urged me to lead the Trojans back to the city on that awful night when Achilles again came forth against us. I would not listen, but it would have been indeed better if I had done so. Now that my folly has destroyed the host, I dare not look Trojan men and Trojan women in the face, lest a worse man should say, 'Hector has ruined us by his self-confidence.' Surely it would be better for me to return after having fought Achilles and slain him, or to die gloriously here before the city. What, again, if I were to lay down my shield and helmet, lean my spear against the wall and go straight up to noble Achilles? What if I were to promise to give up Helen, who was the fountainhead of all this war, and all the treasure that Paris brought with him in his ships to Troy, aye, and to let the Achaeans divide the half of everything that the city contains among themselves? I might make the Trojans, by the mouths of their princes, take a solemn oath that they would hide nothing, but would divide into two shares all that is within the city—but why argue with myself in this way? Were I to go up to him he would show me no kind of mercy; he would kill me then and there as easily as though I were a woman, when I had put off my armor. There is no parleying with him from some rock or oak tree as young men and maidens prattle with one another. Better fight him at once, and learn to which of us Zeus will vouchsafe victory."

Thus did he stand and ponder, but Achilles came up to him as it were Ares himself, plumed lord of battle. From his right shoulder he brandished his terrible spear of Pelian ash, and the bronze gleamed around him like flashing fire or the rays of the rising sun. Fear fell upon Hector as he beheld him and he dared not stay longer where he was, but fled in dismay from before the gates, while Achilles darted after him at his utmost speed. As a mountain falcon, swiftest of all birds, swoops down upon some cowering dove—the dove flies before him but the falcon with a shrill scream follows close after, resolved to have her—even so did Achilles make straight for Hector with all his might, while Hector fled under the Trojan wall as fast as his limbs could take him.

On they flew along the wagon-road that ran hard by under the wall, past the lookout station, and past the weather-beaten wild fig tree, till they came to two fair springs which feed the river Scamander. One of these two springs is warm, and steam rises from it as smoke from a burning fire, but the other even in summer is as cold as hail or snow, or the ice that forms on water. Here, hard by the springs, are the goodly washing troughs of stone, where in the time of peace before the coming of the Achaeans the wives and fair daughters of the Trojans used to wash their clothes. Past these did they fly, the one in front and the other giving chase behind him: good was the man that fled, but better far was he that followed after, and swiftly indeed did they run, for the prize was no mere beast for sacrifice or bullock's hide, as it might be for a common foot race, but they ran for the life of Hector. As horses in a chariot race speed round the turning posts when they are running for some great prize—a tripod or a woman—at the games in honor of some dead hero, so did these two run full speed three times round the city of Priam. All the gods watched them, and the sire of gods and men was the first to speak.

"Alas," said he, "my eyes behold a man who is dear to me being pursued round the walls of Troy. My heart is full of pity for Hector, who has burned the thighbones of many a heifer in my honor, at one while on the crests of many-valleyed Ida, and again on the citadel of Troy; and now I see noble Achilles in full pursuit of him round the city of Priam. What say you? Consider among yourselves and decide whether we shall now save him or let him fall, valiant though he be, before Achilles, son of Peleus."

Then Athene said, "Father, wielder of the lightning, lord of cloud and storm, what mean you? Would you pluck this mortal whose doom has long been decreed out of the jaws of death? Do as you will, but we others shall not be of a mind with you."

And Zeus answered, "My child, Trito-born, take heart. I did not speak in full earnest, and I will let you have your way. Do without let or hindrance as you are minded."

Thus did he urge Athene who was already eager, and down she darted from the topmost summits of Olympus.

Achilles was still in full pursuit of Hector, as a hound chasing a fawn which he has started from its covert on the mountains, and hunts through glade and thicket. The fawn may try to elude him by crouching under cover of a bush, but he will scent her out and follow her up until he gets her—even so there was no escape for Hector from the fleet son of Peleus. Whenever he made a set to get near the Dardanian gates and under the walls, that his people might help him by showering down weapons from above, Achilles would gain on him and head him back towards the plain, keeping himself always on the city side. As a man in a dream who fails to lay hands upon another whom he is pursuing—the one cannot escape nor the other overtake—even so neither could Achilles come up with Hector, nor Hector break away from Achilles. Nevertheless, he might even yet have escaped death had not the time come when Apollo, who thus far had sustained his strength and nerved his running, was now no longer to stay by him. Achilles made signs to the Achaean host and shook his head to show that no man was to aim a dart at Hector, lest another might win the glory of having hit him and he might himself come in second. Then, at last, as they were nearing the fountains for the fourth time, the father of all balanced his golden scales and placed a doom in each of them, one for Achilles and the other for Hector. As he held the scales by the middle, the doom of Hector fell down deep into the house of Hades—and then Phoebus Apollo left him. Thereon Athene went close up to the son of Peleus and said: "Noble Achilles, favored of heaven, we two shall surely take back to the ships a triumph for the Achaeans by slaying Hector, for all his lust of battle. Do what Apollo may as he lies groveling before his father, aegis-bearing Zeus, Hector cannot escape us longer. Stay here and take breath, while I go up to him and persuade him to make a stand and fight you."

Thus spoke Athene. Achilles obeyed her gladly and stood still, leaning on his bronze-pointed ashen spear, while Athene left him and went after Hector in the form and with the voice of Deïphobus. She came close up to him and said, "Dear brother, I see you are hard-pressed by Achilles who is chasing you at full speed round the city of Priam; let us await his onset and stand on our defense."

And Hector answered, "Deïphobus, you have always been dearest to me of all my brothers, children of Hecuba and Priam, but henceforth I shall rate you yet more highly, inasmuch as you have ventured outside the wall for my sake when all the others remain inside."

Then Athene said: "Dear brother, my father and mother went down on their knees and implored me, as did all my comrades, to remain inside, so great a fear has fallen upon them all; but I was in an agony of grief when I beheld you. Now, therefore, let us two make a stand and fight, and let there be no keeping our spears in reserve, that we may learn whether Achilles shall kill us and bear off our spoils to the ships, or whether he shall fall before you."

Thus did Athene inveigle him by her cunning, and when the two were now close to one another great Hector was first to speak. "I will no longer fly you, son of Peleus," said he, "as I have been doing hitherto. Three times have I fled round the mighty city of Priam, without daring to withstand you, but now, let me either slay or be slain, for I am in the mind to face you. Let us, then, give pledges to one another by our gods, who are the fittest witnesses and guardians of all covenants; let it be agreed between us that if Zeus vouchsafes me the longer stay and I take your life, I am not to treat your dead body in any unseemly fashion, but when I have stripped you of your armor, I am to give up your body to the Achaeans. And do you likewise."

Achilles glared at him and answered: "Fool, prate not to me about covenants. There can be no covenants between men and lions; wolves and lambs can never be of one mind, but hate each other out and out all through. Therefore there can be no understanding between you and me, nor may there be any covenants between us, till one or other shall fall and glut grim Ares with his life's blood. Put forth all your strength; you have need now to prove yourself indeed a bold soldier and man of war. You have no more chance, and Pallas Athene will forthwith vanquish you by my spear: you shall now pay me in full for the grief you have caused me on account of my comrades whom you have killed in battle."

He poised his spear as he spoke and hurled it. Hector saw it coming and avoided it; he watched it and crouched down so that it flew over his head and stuck in the ground beyond; Athene then snatched it up and gave it back to Achilles without Hector's seeing her; Hector thereon said to the son of Peleus: "You have missed your aim, Achilles, peer of the gods, and Zeus has not yet revealed to you the hour of my doom, though you made sure that he had done so. You were a false-tongued liar when you deemed that I should forget my valor and quail before you. You shall not drive your spear into the back of a runaway—drive it, should heaven so grant you power, drive it into me as I make straight towards you; and now for your own part avoid my spear if you can—would that you might receive the whole of it into your body. If you were once dead the Trojans would find the war an easier matter, for it is you who have harmed them most."

He poised his spear as he spoke and hurled it. His aim was true for he hit the middle of Achilles' shield, but the spear rebounded from it, and did not pierce it. Hector was angry when he saw that the weapon had sped from his hand in vain, and stood there in dismay for he had no second spear. With a loud cry he called Deïphobus and asked him for one, but there was no man; then he saw the truth and said to himself, "Alas! the gods have lured me on to my destruction. I deemed that the hero Deïphobus was by my side, but he is within the wall, and Athene has inveigled me; death is now indeed exceedingly near at hand and there is no way out of it—for so Zeus and his son Apollo, the far-darter, have willed it, though heretofore they have been ever ready to protect me. My doom has come upon me; let me not then die ingloriously and without a struggle, but let me first do some great thing that shall be told among men hereafter."

As he spoke he drew the keen blade that hung so great and strong by his side, and gathering himself together he sprang on Achilles like a soaring eagle which swoops down from the clouds on to some lamb or timid hare—even so did Hector brandish his sword and spring upon Achilles. Achilles, mad with rage, darted towards him, with his wondrous shield before his breast, and his gleaming helmet, made with four layers of metal, nodding fiercely forward. The thick tresses of gold with which Hephaestus had crested the helmet floated round it, and as the evening star that shines brighter than all others through the stillness of night, even such was the gleam of the spear which Achilles poised in his right hand, fraught with the death of noble Hector. He eyed his fair flesh over and over to see where he could best wound it, but all was protected by the goodly armor of which Hector had spoiled Patroclus after he had slain him, save only the throat where the collarbones divide the neck from the shoulders, and this is a most deadly place. Here then did Achilles strike him as he was coming on towards him, and the point of his spear went right through the fleshy part of the neck, but it did not sever his windpipe so that he could still speak.

Hector fell headlong, and Achilles vaunted over him, saying: "Hector, you deemed that you should come off scatheless when you were spoiling Patroclus, and recked not of myself who was not with him. Fool that you were: for I, his comrade, mightier far than he, was still left behind him at the ships, and now I have laid you low. The Achaeans shall give him all due funeral rites, while dogs and vultures shall work their will upon yourself."

Then Hector said, as the life ebbed out of him, "I pray you by your life and knees, and by your parents, let not dogs devour me at the ships of the Achaeans, but accept the rich treasure of gold and bronze which my father and mother will offer you, and send my body home, that the Trojans and their wives may give me my dues of fire when I am dead."

Achilles glared at him and answered: "Dog, talk not to me neither of knees nor parents; would that I could be as sure of being able to cut your flesh into pieces and eat it raw, for the ill you have done me, as I am that nothing shall save you from the dogs—it shall not be, though they bring ten or twenty-fold ransom and weigh it out for me on the spot, with promise of yet more hereafter. Though Priam, son of Dardanus, should bid them offer me your weight in gold, even so your mother shall never lay you out and make lament over the son she bore, but dogs and vultures shall eat you utterly up."

Hector with his dying breath then said: "I know you what you are, and was sure that I should not move you, for your heart is hard as iron; look to it that I bring not heaven's anger upon you on the day when Paris and Phoebus Apollo, valiant though you be, shall slay you at the Scaean gates."

When he had thus said the shrouds of death enfolded him, whereon his soul went out of him and flew down to the house of Hades, lamenting its sad fate that it should enjoy youth and strength no longer. But Achilles said, speaking to the dead body, "Die; for my part I will accept my fate whensoever Zeus and the other gods see fit to send it."

As he spoke he drew his spear from the body and set it on one side; then he stripped the bloodstained armor from Hector's shoulders while the other Achaeans came running up to view his wondrous strength and beauty; and no one came near him without giving him a fresh wound. Then would one turn to his neighbor and say, "It is easier to handle Hector now than when he was flinging fire on to our ships"—and as he spoke he would thrust his spear into him anew.

When Achilles had done spoiling Hector of his armor, he stood among the Argives and said: "My friends, princes and counselors of the Argives, now that heaven has vouchsafed us to overcome this man, who has done us more hurt than all the others together, consider whether we should not attack the city in force, and discover in what mind the Trojans may be. We should thus learn whether they will desert their city now that Hector has fallen, or will still hold out even though he is no longer living. But why argue with myself in this way, while Patroclus is still lying at the ships unburied, and unmourned—he whom I can never forget so long as I am alive and my strength fails not? Though men forget their dead when once they are within the house of Hades, yet not even there will I forget the comrade whom I have lost. Now, therefore, Achaean youths, let us raise the song of victory and go back to the ships taking this man along with us; for we have achieved a mighty triumph and have slain noble Hector to whom the Trojans prayed throughout their city as though he were a god."

On this he treated the body of Hector with contumely: he pierced the sinews at the back of both his feet from heel to ankle and passed thongs of oxhide through the slits he had made: thus he made the body fast to his chariot, letting the head trail upon the ground. Then when he had put the goodly armor on the chariot and had himself mounted, he lashed his horses on and they flew forward nothing loath. The dust rose from Hector as he was being dragged along, his dark hair flew all abroad, and his head once so comely was laid low on earth, for Zeus had now delivered him into the hands of his foes to do him outrage in his own land.

Thus was the head of Hector being dishonored in the dust. His mother tore her hair, and flung her veil from her with a loud cry as she looked upon her son. His father made piteous moan, and throughout the city the people fell to weeping and wailing. It was as though the whole of frowning Ilium was being smirched with fire. Hardly could the people hold Priam back in his hot haste to rush without the gates of the city. He groveled in the mire and besought them, calling each one of them by his name. "Let be, my friends," he cried, "and for all your sorrow, suffer me to go single-handed to the ships of the Achaeans. Let me beseech this cruel and terrible man, if maybe he will respect the feeling of his fellow men, and have compassion on my old age. His own father is even such another as myself—Peleus, who bred him and reared him to be the bane of us Trojans, and of myself more than of all others. Many a son of mine has he slain in the flower of his youth, and yet, grieve for these as I may, I do so for one—Hector—more than for them all, and the bitterness of my sorrow will bring me down to the house of Hades. Would that he had died in my arms, for so both his ill-starred mother who bore him and myself should have had the comfort of weeping and mourning over him."

Thus did he speak with many tears, and all the people of the city joined in his lament. Hecuba then raised the cry of wailing among the Trojans. "Alas, my son," she cried, "what have I left to live for now that you are no more? Night and day did I glory in you throughout the city, for you were a tower of strength to all in Troy, and both men and women alike hailed you as a god. So long as you lived you were their pride, but now death and destruction have fallen upon you."

Hector's wife had as yet heard nothing, for no one had come to tell her that her husband had remained without the gates. She was at her loom in an inner part of the house, weaving a double purple web, and embroidering it with many flowers. She told her maids to set a large tripod on the fire, so as to have a warm bath ready for Hector when he came out of battle; poor woman, she knew not that he was now beyond the reach of baths, and that Athene had laid him low by the hands of Achilles. She heard the cry coming as from the wall, and trembled in every limb. The shuttle fell from her hands, and again she spoke to her waiting-women. "Two of you," she said, "come with me that I may learn what it is that has befallen. I heard the voice of my husband's honored mother. My own heart beats as though it would come into my mouth and my limbs refuse to carry me; some great misfortune for Priam's children must be at hand. May I never live to hear it, but I greatly fear that Achilles has cut off the retreat of brave Hector and has chased him on to the plain where he was single-handed; I fear he may have put an end to the reckless daring which possessed my husband, who would never remain with the body of his men, but would dash on far in front, foremost of them all in valor."

Her heart beat fast, and as she spoke she flew from the house like a maniac, with her waiting-women following after. When she reached the battlements and the crowd of people, she stood looking out upon the wall, and saw Hector being borne away in front of the city—the horses dragging him without heed or care over the ground towards the ships of the Achaeans. Her eyes were then shrouded as with the darkness of night and she fell fainting backwards. She tore the tiring from her head and flung it from her, the frontlet and net with its plaited band, and the veil which golden Aphrodite had given her on the day when Hector took her with him from the house of Eëtion, after having given countless gifts of wooing for her sake. Her husband's sisters and the wives of his brothers crowded round her and supported her, for she was fain to die in her distraction. When she again presently breathed and came to herself, she sobbed and made lament among the Trojans, saying:

"Woe is me, O Hector! Woe, indeed, that to share a common lot we were born, you at Troy in the house of Priam, and I at Thebes under the wooded mountain of Placus in the house of Eëtion who brought me up when I was a child—ill-starred sire of an ill-starred daughter—would that he had never begotten me. You are now going into the house of Hades under the secret places of the earth, and you leave me a sorrowing widow in your house. The child of whom you and I are the unhappy parents is as yet a mere infant. Now that you are gone, O Hector, you can do nothing for him nor he for you. Even though he escape the horrors of this woeful war with the Achaeans, yet shall his life henceforth be one of labor and sorrow, for others will seize his lands. The day that robs a child of his parents severs him from his own kind. His head is bowed, his cheeks are wet with tears, and he will go about destitute among the friends of his father, plucking one by the cloak and another by the shirt. Some one or other of these may so far pity him as to hold the cup for a moment towards him and let him moisten his lips, but he must not drink enough to wet the roof of his mouth; then one whose parents are alive will drive him from the table with blows and angry words. 'Out with you,' he will say, 'you have no father here,' and the child will go crying back to his widowed mother—he, Astyanax, who erewhile would sit upon his father's knees, and have none but the daintiest and choicest morsels set before him. When he had played till he was tired and went to sleep, he would lie in a bed, in the arms of his nurse, on a soft couch, knowing neither want nor care, whereas now that he has lost his father his lot will be full of hardship—he, whom the Trojans name Astyanax, because you, O Hector, were the only defense of their gates and battlements. The wriggling writhing worms will now eat you at the ships, far from your parents, when the dogs have glutted themselves upon you. You will lie naked, although in your house you have fine and goodly raiment made by the hands of women. This will I now burn; it is of no use to you, for you can never again wear it, and thus you will have respect shown you by the Trojans both men and women."

In such wise did she cry aloud amid her tears, and the women joined in her lament.

Book XXIII

Achilles brings Hector's corpse into the Greek camp and gives orders for the funeral of Patroclus, whose spirit visits him in the night. In the morning the funeral pyre is built and all day sacrifices are offered and the rites of honor celebrated to comfort the hero's spirit. The following day Patroclus' ashes are laid in a tomb, and Achilles presides over splendid funeral games.

THUS DID THEY MAKE THEIR MOAN THROUGHOUT THE CITY, WHILE THE Achaeans when they reached the Hellespont went back every man to his own ship. But Achilles would not let the Myrmidons go, and spoke to his brave comrades, saying: "Myrmidons, famed horsemen and my own trusted friends, not yet, forsooth, let us unyoke, but with horse and chariot draw near to the body and mourn Patroclus, in due honor to the dead. When we have had full comfort of lamentation we will unyoke our horses and take supper all of us here."

On this they all joined in a cry of wailing and Achilles led them in their lament. Thrice did they drive their chariots all sorrowing round the body, and Thetis stirred within them a still deeper yearning. The sands of the seashore and the men's armor were wet with their weeping, so great a minister of fear was he whom they had lost. Chief in all their mourning was the son of Peleus: he laid his bloodstained hand on the breast of his friend. "Farewell," he cried, "Patroclus, even in the house of Hades. I will now do all that I erewhile promised you; I will drag Hector hither and let dogs devour him raw; twelve noble sons of Trojans will I also slay before your pyre to avenge you."

As he spoke he treated the body of noble Hector with contumely, laying it at full length in the dust beside the bier of Patroclus. The others then put off every man his armor, took the horses from their chariots, and seated themselves in great multitude by the ship of the fleet descendant of Aeacus, who thereon feasted them with an abundant funeral banquet. Many a goodly ox, with many a sheep and bleating goat, did they butcher and cut up; many a tusked boar, moreover, fat and well-fed, did they singe and set to roast in the flames of Hephaestus; and rivulets of blood flowed all round the place where the body was lying.

Then the princes of the Achaeans took the son of Peleus to Agamemnon, but hardly could they persuade him to come with them, so wroth was he for the death of his comrade. As soon as they reached Agamemnon's tent they told the servingmen to set a large tripod over the fire, in case they might persuade the son of Peleus to wash the clotted gore from his body, but he denied them sternly, and swore it with a solemn oath, saying, "Nay, by King Zeus, first and mightiest of all gods, it is not meet that water should touch my body, till I have laid Patroclus on the flames, have built him a barrow, and shaved my head—for so long as I live no such second sorrow shall ever draw nigh me. Now, therefore, let us do all that this sad festival demands, but at break of day, King Agamemnon, bid your men bring wood, and provide all else that the dead may duly take into the realm of darkness; the fire shall thus burn him out of our sight the sooner, and the people shall turn again to their own labors."

Thus did he speak, and they did even as he had said. They made haste to prepare the meal, they ate, and every man had his full share so that all were satisfied. As soon as they had had enough to eat and drink, the others went to their rest each in his own tent, but the son of Peleus lay grieving among his Myrmidons by the shore of the sounding sea, in an open place where the waves came surging in one after another. Here a very deep slumber took hold upon him and eased the burden of his sorrows, for his limbs were weary with chasing Hector round windy Ilium. Presently the sad spirit of Patroclus drew near him, like what he had been in stature, voice, and the light of his beaming eyes, clad, too, as he had been clad in life. The spirit hovered over his head and said:

"You sleep, Achilles, and have forgotten me. You loved me living, but now that I am dead you think for me no further. Bury me with all speed that I may pass the gates of Hades. The ghosts, vain shadows of men that can labor no more, drive me away from them. They will not yet suffer me to join those that are beyond the river, and I wander all desolate by the wide gates of the house of Hades. Give me now your hand I pray you, for when you have once given me my dues of fire, never shall I again come forth out of the house of Hades. Nevermore shall we sit apart and take sweet counsel among the living; the cruel fate which was my birthright has yawned its wide jaws around me—nay, you too Achilles, peer of gods, are doomed to die beneath the wall of the noble Trojans.

"One prayer more will I make you, if you will grant it. Let not my bones be laid apart from yours, Achilles, but with them. Even as we were brought up together in your own home, what time Menoetius brought me to you as a child from Opöeis because by a sad spite I had killed the son of Amphidamas—not of set purpose, but in childish quarrel over the dice. The knight Peleus took me into his house, entreated me kindly, and named me to be your squire. Therefore let our bones lie in but a single urn, the two-handled golden vase given to you by your mother."

And Achilles answered: "Why, true heart, are you come hither to lay these charges upon me? I will of my own self do all as you have bidden me. Draw closer to me, let us once more throw our arms around one another, and find sad comfort in the sharing of our sorrows."

He opened his arms towards him as he spoke and would have clasped him in them, but there was nothing, and the spirit vanished as a vapor, gibbering and whining into the earth. Achilles sprang to his feet, smote his two hands, and made lamentation, saying: "Of a truth, even in the house of Hades there are ghosts and phantoms that have no life in them. All night long the sad spirit of Patroclus has hovered over my head making piteous moan, telling me what I am to do for him, and looking wondrously like himself."

Thus did he speak and his words set them all weeping and mourning about the poor dumb dead, till rosy-fingered morn appeared. Then King Agamemnon sent men and mules from all parts of the camp to bring wood, and Meriones, squire to Idomeneus, was in charge over them. They went out with woodmen's axes and strong ropes in their hands, and before them went the mules. Up hill and down dale did they go, by straight ways and crooked, and when they reached the heights of many-fountained Ida, they laid their axes to the roots of many a tall branching oak that came thundering down as they felled it. They split the trees and bound them behind the mules, which then wended their way as they best could through the thick brushwood on to the plain. All who had been cutting wood bore logs, for so Meriones, squire to Idomeneus, had bidden them, and they threw them down in a line upon the seashore at the place where Achilles would make a mighty monument for Patroclus and for himself.

When they had thrown down their great logs of wood over the whole ground, they stayed all of them where they were, but Achilles ordered his brave Myrmidons to gird on their armor, and to yoke each man his horses; they therefore rose, girded on their armor, and mounted each his chariot— they and their charioteers with them. The chariots went before, and they that were on foot followed as a cloud in their tens of thousands after. In the midst of them his comrades bore Patroclus and covered him with the locks of their hair which they cut off and threw upon his body. Last came Achilles with his head bowed for sorrow, so noble a comrade was he taking to the house of Hades.

When they came to the place of which Achilles had told them, they laid the body down and built up the wood. Achilles then bethought him of another matter. He went a space away from the pyre, and cut off the yellow lock which he had let grow for the river Spercheius. He looked all sorrowfully out upon the dark sea and said, "Spercheius, in vain did my father Peleus vow to you that when I returned home to my loved native land I should cut off this lock and offer you a holy hecatomb; fifty he-goats was I to sacrifice to you there at your springs, where is your grove and your altar fragrant with burnt offerings. Thus did my father vow, but you have not fulfilled his prayer; now, therefore, that I shall see my home no more, I give this lock as a keepsake to the hero Patroclus."

As he spoke he placed the lock in the hands of his dear comrade, and all who stood by were filled with yearning and lamentation. The sun would have gone down upon their mourning had not Achilles presently said to Agamemnon: "Son of Atreus, for it is to you that the people will give ear; there is a time to mourn and a time to cease from mourning; bid the people now leave the pyre and set about getting their dinners. We, to whom the dead is dearest, will see to what is wanted here, and let the other princes also stay by me."

When King Agamemnon heard this he dismissed the people to their ships, but those who were about the dead heaped up wood and built a pyre a hundred feet this way and that; then they laid the dead all sorrowfully upon the top of it. They flayed and dressed many fat sheep and oxen before the pyre, and Achilles took fat from all of them and wrapped the body therein from head to foot, heaping the flayed carcasses all round it. Against the bier he leaned two-handled jars of honey and unguents; four proud horses did he then cast upon the pyre, groaning the while he did so. The dead hero had had nine house dogs; two of them did Achilles slay and throw upon the pyre; he also put twelve brave sons of noble Trojans to the sword and laid them with the rest, for he was full of bitterness and fury. Then he committed all to the resistless and devouring might of the fire. He groaned aloud and called on his dead comrade by name. "Farewell," he cried, "Patroclus, even in the house of Hades. I am now doing all that I have promised you. Twelve brave sons of noble Trojans shall the flames consume along with yourself, but dogs, not fire, shall devour the flesh of Hector, son of Priam."

Thus did he vaunt, but the dogs came not about the body of Hector, for Zeus' daughter Aphrodite kept them off him night and day, and anointed him with ambrosial oil of roses that his flesh might not be torn when Achilles was dragging him about. Phoebus Apollo moreover sent a dark cloud from heaven to earth, which gave shade to the whole place where Hector lay, that the heat of the sun might not parch his body.

Now the pyre about dead Patroclus would not kindle. Achilles therefore bethought him of another matter; he went apart and prayed to the two winds Boreas and Zephyrus, vowing them goodly offerings. He made them many drink offerings from his golden cup, and besought them to come and help him that the wood might make haste to kindle and the dead bodies be consumed. Fleet Iris heard him praying and started off to fetch the winds. They were holding high feast in the house of boisterous Zephyrus when Iris came running up to the stone threshold of the house and stood there, but as soon as they set eyes on her they all came towards her and each of them called her to him, but Iris would not sit down. "I cannot stay," she said, "I must go back to the streams of Oceanus and the land of the Ethiopians who are offering hecatombs to the immortals, and I would have my share; but Achilles prays that Boreas and shrill Zephyrus will come to him, and he vows them goodly offerings; he would have you blow upon the pyre of Patroclus for whom all the Achaeans are lamenting."

With this she left them, and the two winds rose with a cry that rent the air and swept the clouds before them. They blew on and on until they came to the sea, and the waves rose high beneath them, but when they reached Troy they fell upon the pyre till the mighty flames roared under the blast that they blew. All night long did they blow hard and beat upon the fire, and all night long did Achilles grasp his double cup, drawing wine from a mixing bowl of gold, and calling upon the spirit of dead Patroclus as he poured it upon the ground until the earth was drenched. As a father mourns when he is burning the bones of his bridegroom son whose death has wrung the hearts of his parents, even so did Achilles mourn while burning the body of his comrade, pacing round the bier with piteous groaning and lamentation.

At length as the morning star was beginning to herald the light which saffron-mantled Dawn was soon to suffuse over the sea, the flames fell and the fire began to die. The winds then went home beyond the Thracian sea, which roared and boiled as they swept over it. The son of Peleus now turned away from the pyre and lay down, overcome with toil, till he fell into a sweet slumber. Presently they who were about the son of Atreus drew near in a body, and roused him with the noise and tramp of their coming. He sate upright and said: "Son of Atreus, and all other princes of the Achaeans, first pour red wine everywhere upon the fire and quench it. Let us then gather the bones of Patroclus, son of Menoetius, singling them out with care; they are easily found, for they lie in the middle of the pyre, while all else, both men and horses, has been thrown in a heap and burned at the outer edge. We will lay the bones in a golden urn, in two layers of fat, against the time when I shall myself go down into the house of Hades. As for the barrow, labor not to raise a great one now, but such as is reasonable. Afterwards, let those Achaeans who may be left at the ships when I am gone build it both broad and high."

Thus he spoke and they obeyed the word of the son of Peleus. First they poured red wine upon the thick layer of ashes and quenched the fire. With many tears they singled out the whitened bones of their loved comrade and laid them within a golden urn in two layers of fat: they then covered the urn with a linen cloth and took it inside the tent. They marked off the circle where the barrow should be, made a foundation for it about the pyre, and forthwith heaped up the earth. When they had thus raised a mound they were going away, but Achilles stayed the people and made them sit in assembly. He brought prizes from the ships—cauldrons, tripods, horses and mules, noble oxen, women with fair girdles, and swart iron.

The first prize he offered was for the chariot races—a woman skilled in all useful arts, and a three-legged cauldron that had ears for handles, and would hold twenty-two measures. This was for the man who came in first. For the second there was a six-year-old mare, unbroken, and in foal to a he-ass. The third was to have a goodly cauldron that had never yet been on the fire; it was still bright as when it left the maker, and would hold four measures. The fourth prize was two talents of gold, and the fifth a two-handled urn as yet unsoiled by smoke. Then he stood up and spoke among the Argives, saying:

"Son of Atreus, and all other Achaeans, these are the prizes that lie waiting the winners of the chariot races. At any other time I should carry off the first prize and take it to my own tent. You know how far my steeds excel all others—for they are immortal. Poseidon gave them to my father Peleus, who in his turn gave them to myself; but I shall hold aloof, I and my steeds that have lost their brave and kind driver, who many a time has washed them in clear water and anointed their manes with oil. See how they stand weeping here, with their manes trailing on the ground in the extremity of their sorrow. But do you others set yourselves in order throughout the host, whosoever has confidence in his horses and in the strength of his chariot."

Thus spoke the son of Peleus and the drivers of chariots bestirred themselves. First among them all uprose Eumelus, king of men, son of Admetus, a man excellent in horsemanship. Next to him rose mighty Diomed, son of Tydeus; he yoked the Trojan horses which he had taken from Aeneas, when Apollo bore him out of the fight. Next to him, yellow-haired Menelaus, son of Atreus, rose and yoked his fleet horses, Agamemnon's mare Aethe, and his own horse Podargus. The mare had been given to Agamemnon by Echepolus, son of Anchises, that he might not have to follow him to Ilium, but might stay at home and take his ease; for Zeus had endowed him with great wealth and he lived in spacious Sicyon. This mare, all eager for the race, did Menelaus put under the yoke.

Fourth in order, Antilochus, son to noble Nestor, son of Neleus, made ready his horses. These were bred in Pylos, and his father came up to him to give him good advice of which, however, he stood in but little need.

"Antilochus," said Nestor, "you are young, but Zeus and Poseidon have loved you well, and have made you an excellent horseman. I need not therefore say much by way of instruction. You are skillful at wheeling your horses round the post, but the horses themselves are very slow, and it is this that will, I fear, mar your chances. The odaer drivers know less than you do, but their horses are fleeter; therefore, my dear son, see if you cannot hit upon some artifice whereby you may ensure that the prize shall not slip through your fingers. The woodman does more by skill than by brute force; by skill the pilot guides his storm-tossed bark over the sea, and so by skill one driver can beat another. If a man leaves all to his horses, they will go wide in rounding the posts at either end of the course. He has no command over them and cannot keep them from swerving this way and that, whereas a man who knows what he is doing may have worse horses, but he will keep them well in hand when he sees the doubling-post. He knows the precise moment at which to pull the rein and keeps his eye well on the man in front of him. I will give you this certain token which cannot escape your notice. There is a stump of a dead tree—oak or pine as it may be—some six feet above the ground, and not yet rotted away by rain; it stands at the fork of the road; it has two white stones set one on each side, and there is a clear course all round it. It may have been a monument to someone long since dead, or it may have been used as a doubling-post in days gone by. Now, however, it has been fixed on by Achilles as the mark round which the chariots shall turn; hug it as close as you can, but as you stand in your chariot lean over a little to the left; urge on your right-hand horse with voice and lash, and give him a loose rein, but let the left-hand horse keep so close in, that the nave of your wheel shall almost graze the post; but mind the stone, or you will wound your horses and break your chariot in pieces, which would be sport for others but confusion for yourself. Therefore, my dear son, mind well what you are about, for if you can be first to round the post there is no chance of anyone giving you the go-by later, not even though you had Adrestus' horse Arion behind you—a horse which is of divine race—or those of Laomedon, which are the noblest in this country."

When Nestor had made an end of counseling his son he sat down in his place, and fifth in order, Meriones got ready his horses. They then all mounted their chariots and cast lots. Achilles shook the helmet, and the lot of Antilochus, son of Nestor, fell out first; next came that of King Eumelus, and after his, those of Menelaus, son of Atreus, and of Meriones. The last place fell to the lot of Diomed, son of Tydeus, who was the best man of them all. They took their places in line. Achilles showed them the doubling-post round which they were to turn, some way off upon the plain. Here he stationed his father's follower Phoenix as umpire, to note the running and report truly.

At the same instant they all of them lashed their horses, struck them with the reins, and shouted at them with all their might. They flew full speed over the plain away from the ships, the dust rose from under them as it were a cloud or whirlwind, and their manes were all flying in the wind. At one moment the chariots seemed to touch the ground, and then again they bounded into the air. The drivers stood erect, and their hearts beat fast and furious in their lust of victory. Each kept calling on his horses, and the horses scoured the plain amid the clouds of dust that they raised.

It was when they were doing the last part of the course on their way back towards the sea that their pace was strained to the utmost and it was seen what each could do. The horses of the descendant of Pheres now took the lead, and close behind them came the Trojan stallions of Diomed. They seemed as if about to mount Eumelus' chariot, and he could feel their warm breath on his back and on his broad shoulders, for their heads were close to him as they flew over the course. Diomed would have now passed him, or there would have been a dead heat, but Phoebus Apollo to spite him made him drop his whip. Tears of anger fell from his eyes as he saw the mares going on faster than ever, while his own horses lost ground through his having no whip. Athene saw the trick which Apollo had played the son of Tydeus, so she brought him his whip and put spirit into his horses. Moreover, she went after the son of Admetus in a rage and broke his yoke for him. The mares went one to one side the course, and the other to the other, and the pole was broken against the ground. Eumelus was thrown from his chariot close to the wheel, his elbows, mouth, and nostrils were all torn, and his forehead was bruised above his eyebrows. His eyes filled with tears and he could find no utterance. But the son of Tydeus turned his horses aside and shot far ahead, for Athene put fresh strength into them and covered Diomed himself with glory.

Menelaus, son of Atreus, came next behind him, but Antilochus called to his father's horses. "On with you both," he cried, "and do your very utmost. I do not bid you try to beat the steeds of the son of Tydeus, for Athene has put running into them and has covered Diomed with glory; but you must over-take the horses of the son of Atreus and not be left behind, or Aethe who is so fleet will taunt you. Why, my good fellows, are you lagging? I tell you, and it shall surely be—Nestor will keep neither of you, but will put both of you to the sword, if we win any the worse a prize through your carelessness. Hie after them at your utmost speed; I will hit on a plan for passing them in a nar-row part of the way, and it shall not fail me."

They feared the rebuke of their master, and for a short space went quicker. Presently Antilochus saw a narrow place where the road had sunk. The ground was broken, for the winter's rain had gathered and had worn the road so that the whole place was deepened. Menelaus was making towards it so as to get there first, for fear of a foul, but Antilochus turned his horses out of the way, and followed him a little on one side. The son of Atreus was afraid and shouted out: "Antilochus, you are driving recklessly; rein in your horses; the road is too narrow here, it will be wider soon, and you can pass me then; if you foul my chariot you may bring both of us to a mischief."

But Antilochus plied his whip, and drove faster, as though he had not heard him. They went side by side for about as far as a young man can hurl a disc from his shoulder when he is trying his strength, and then Menelaus' mares drew behind, for he left off driving for fear the horses should foul one another and upset the chariots; thus, while pressing on in quest of victory, they might both come headlong to the ground. Menelaus then upbraided Antilochus and said: "There is no greater trickster living than you are. Go, and bad luck go with you. The Achaeans say not well that you have understanding, and come what may you shall not bear away the prize without sworn protest on my part."

Then he called on his horses and said to them: "Keep your pace, and slacken not. The limbs of the other horses will weary sooner than yours, for they are neither of them young."

The horses feared the rebuke of their master and went faster, so that they were soon nearly up with the others.

Meanwhile the Achaeans from their seats were watching how the horses went, as they scoured the plain amid clouds of their own dust. Idomeneus, captain of the Cretans, was first to make out the running, for he was not in the thick of the crowd, but stood on the most commanding part of the ground. The driver was a long way off, but Idomeneus could hear him shouting, and could see the foremost horse quite plainly—a chestnut with a round white star, like the moon, on its forehead. He stood up and said among the Argives: "My friends, princes and counselors of the Argives, can you see the running as well as I can? There seems to be another pair in front now, and another driver. Those that led off at the start must have been disabled out on the plain. I saw them at first making their way round the doubling-post, but now, though I search the plain of Troy, I cannot find them. Perhaps the reins fell from the driver's hand so that he lost command of his horses at the doubling-post, and could not turn it. I suppose he must have been thrown out there, and broken his chariot, while his mares have left the course and gone off wildly in a panic. Come up and see for yourselves, I cannot make out for certain, but the driver seems an Aetolian by descent, ruler over the Argives, brave Diomed, the son of Tydeus."

Ajax, the son of Oïleus, took him up rudely and said: "Idomeneus, why should you be in such a hurry to tell us all about it, when the mares are still so far out upon the plain? You are none of the youngest, nor your eyes none of the sharpest, but you are always laying down the law. You have no right to do so, for there are better men here than you are. Eumelus' horses are in front now, as they always have been, and he is on the chariot holding the reins."

The captain of the Cretans was angry, and answered, "Ajax, you are an excellent railer, but you have no judgment, and are wanting in much else as well, for you have a vile temper. I will wager you a tripod or cauldron, and Agamemnon, son of Atreus, shall decide whose horses are first. You will then know to your cost."

Ajax, son of Oïleus, was for making him an angry answer, and there would have been yet further brawling between them had not Achilles risen in his place and said: "Cease your railing, Ajax and Idomeneus. It is not seemly; you would be scandalized if you saw anyone else do the like: sit down and keep your eyes on the horses. They are speeding towards the winning post and will be here directly. You will then both of you know whose horses are first, and whose come after."

As he was speaking, the son of Tydeus came driving in, plying his whip lustily from his shoulder, and his horses stepping high as they flew over the course. The sand and grit rained thick on the driver, and the chariot inlaid with gold and tin ran close behind his fleet horses. There was little trace of wheel marks in the fine dust, and the horses came flying in at their utmost speed. Diomed stayed them in the middle of the crowd, and the sweat from their manes and chests fell in streams on to the ground. Forthwith he sprang from his goodly chariot, and leaned his whip against his horses' yoke. Brave Sthenelus now lost no time, but at once brought on the prize, and gave the woman and the ear-handled cauldron to his comrades to take away. Then he unyoked the horses.

Next after him came in Antilochus of the race of Neleus, who had passed Menelaus by a trick and not by the fleetness of his horses; but even so Menelaus came in as close behind him as the wheel is to the horse that draws both the chariot and its master. The end hairs of a horse's tail touch the tire of the wheel, and there is never much space between wheel and horse when the chariot is going. Menelaus was no further than this behind Antilochus, though at first he had been a full disc's throw behind him. He had soon caught him up again, for Agamemnon's mare Aethe kept pulling stronger and stronger, so that if the course had been longer he would have passed him, and there would not even have been a dead heat. Idomeneus' brave squire Meriones was about a spear's cast behind Menelaus. His horses were slowest of all, and he was the worst driver. Last of them all came the son of Admetus, dragging his chariot and driving his horses on in front. When Achilles saw him he was sorry, and stood up among the Argives, saying, "The best man is coming in last. Let us give him a prize for it is reasonable. He shall have the second, but the first must go to the son of Tydeus."

Thus did he speak and the others all of them applauded his saying, and were for doing as he had said, but Nestor's son Antilochus stood up and claimed his rights from the son of Peleus. "Achilles," said he, "I shall take it much amiss if you do this thing. You would rob me of my prize because you think Eumelus' chariot and horses were thrown out, and himself too, good man that he is. He should have prayed duly to the immortals: he would not have come in last if he had done so. If you are sorry for him and so choose, you have much gold in your tents, with bronze, sheep, cattle, and horses. Take something from this store if you would have the Achaeans speak well of you, and give him a better prize even than that which you have now offered; but I will not give up the mare, and he that will fight me for her, let him come on."

Achilles smiled as he heard this and was pleased with Antilochus, who was one of his dearest comrades. So he said:

"Antilochus, if you would have me find Eumelus another prize, I will give him the bronze breastplate with a rim of tin running all round it which I took from Asteropaeus. It will be worth much money to him."

He bade his comrade Automedon bring the breastplate from his tent, and he did so. Achilles then gave it over to Eumelus, who received it gladly. But Menelaus got up in a rage, furiously angry with Antilochus. An attendant placed his staff in his hands and bade the Argives keep silence. The hero then addressed them. "Antilochus," said he, "what is this—from you who have been so far blameless? You have made me cut a poor figure and balked my horses by flinging your own in front of them, though yours are much worse than mine are. Therefore, O princes and counselors of the Argives, judge between us and show no favor, lest one of the Achaeans say, 'Menelaus has got the mare through lying and corruption; his horses were far inferior to Antilochus', but he has greater weight and influence.' Nay, I will determine the matter myself, and no man will blame me, for I shall do what is just. Come here, Antilochus, and stand, as our custom is, whip in hand before your chariot and horses. Lay your hand on your steeds, and swear by earth-encircling Poseidon that you did not purposely and guilefully get in the way of my horses."

And Antilochus answered: "Forgive me; I am much younger, King Menelaus, than you are. You stand higher than I do and are the better man of the two. You know how easily young men are betrayed into indiscretion; their tempers are more hasty and they have less judgment. Make due allowances, therefore, and bear with me. I will of my own accord give up the mare that I have won, and if you claim any further chattel from my own possessions, I would rather yield it to you at once than fall from your good graces henceforth, and do wrong in the sight of heaven."

The son of Nestor then took the mare and gave her over to Menelaus, whose anger was thus appeased; as when dew falls upon a field of ripening corn, and the lands are bristling with the harvest—even so, O Menelaus, was your heart made glad within you. He turned to Antilochus and said: "Now, Antilochus, angry though I have been, I can give way to you of my own free will; you have never been headstrong nor ill-disposed hitherto, but this time your youth has got the better of your judgment. Be careful how you out-wit your betters in future. No one else could have brought me round so easily, but your good father, your brother, and yourself have all of you had infinite trouble on my behalf. I therefore yield to your entreaty, and will give up the mare to you, mine though it indeed be; the people will thus see that I am nei-ther harsh nor vindictive."

With this he gave the mare over to Antilochus' comrade Noëmon and then took the cauldron. Meriones, who had come in fourth, carried off the two talents of gold, and the fifth prize, the two-handled urn, being unawarded, Achilles gave it to Nestor, going up to him among the assembled Argives and saying: "Take this, my good old friend, as an heirloom and memorial of the funeral of Patroclus—for you shall see him no more among the Argives. I give you this prize though you cannot win one. You can now neither wrestle nor fight, and cannot enter for the javelin match nor foot races, for the hand of age has been laid heavily upon you."

So saying he gave the urn over to Nestor, who received it gladly and answered: "My son, all that you have said is true. There is no strength now in my legs and feet, nor can I hit out with my hands from either shoulder. Would that I were still young and strong as when the Epeans were burying King Amarynceus in Buprasium, and his sons offered prizes in his honor. There was then none that could vie with me, neither of the Epeans nor the Pylians themselves nor the Aetolians. In boxing I overcame Clytomedes, son of Enops, and in wrestling, Ancaeus of Pleuron who had come forward against me. Iphiclus was a good runner, but I beat him, and threw further with my spear than either Phyleus or Polydorus. In chariot racing alone did the two sons of Actor surpass me by crowding their horses in front of me, for they were angry at the way victory had gone, and at the greater part of the prizes remaining in the place in which they had been offered. They were twins, and the one kept on holding the reins, and holding the reins, while the other plied the whip. Such was I then, but now I must leave these matters to younger men. I must bow before the weight of years, but in those days I was eminent among heroes. And now, sir, go on with the funeral contests in honor of your comrade. Gladly do I accept this urn, and my heart rejoices that you do not forget me but are ever mindful of my good will towards you and of the respect due to me from the Achaeans. For all which may the grace of heaven be vouchsafed you in great abundance."

Thereon the son of Peleus, when he had listened to all the thanks of Nestor, went about among the concourse of the Achaeans, and presently offered prizes for skill in the painful art of boxing. He brought out a strong mule and made it fast in the middle of the crowd—a she-mule never yet broken, but six years old—when it is hardest of all to break them: this was for the victor, and for the vanquished he offered a double cup. Then he stood up and said among the Argives: "Son of Atreus, and all other Achaeans, I invite our two champion boxers to lay about them lustily and compete for these prizes. He to whom Apollo vouchsafes the greater endurance, and whom the Achaeans acknowledge as victor, shall take the mule back with him to his own tent, while he that is vanquished shall have the double cup."

As he spoke there stood up a champion both brave and of great stature, a skillful boxer, Epeüs, son of Panopeus. He laid his hand on the mule and said, "Let the man who is to have the cup come hither, for none but myself will take the mule. I am the best boxer of all here present, and none can beat me. Is it not enough that I should fall short of you in actual fighting? Still, no man can be good at everything. I tell you plainly, and it shall come true, if any man will box with me I will bruise his body and break his bones. Therefore let his friends stay here in a body and be at hand to take him away when I have done with him."

They all held their peace, and no man rose save Euryalus, son of Mecisteus, who was son of Talaüs. Mecisteus went once to Thebes after the fall of Oedipus, to attend his funeral, and he beat all the people of Cadmus. The son of Tydeus was Euryalus' second, cheering him on and hoping heartily that he would win. First he put a waistband round him and then he gave him some well-cut thongs of oxhide. The two men being now girt went into the middle of the ring and immediately fell to. Heavily indeed did they punish one another and lay about them with their brawny fists. One could hear the horrid crashing of their jaws, and they sweated from every pore of their skin. Presently Epeüs came on and gave Euryalus a blow on the jaw as he was looking round. Euryalus could not keep his legs; they gave way under him in a moment and he sprang up with a bound, as a fish leaps into the air near some shore that is all bestrewn with sea-wrack, when Boreas furs the top of the waves, and then falls back into deep water. But noble Epeüs caught hold of him and raised him up; his comrades also came round him and led him from the ring, unsteady in his gait, his head hanging on one side, and spitting great clots of gore. They set him down in a swoon and then went to fetch the double cup.

The son of Peleus now brought out the prizes for the third contest and showed them to the Argives. These were for the painful art of wrestling. For the winner there was a great tripod ready for setting upon the fire, and the Achaeans valued it among themselves at twelve oxen. For the loser he brought out a woman skilled in all manner of arts, and they valued her at four oxen. He rose and said among the Argives, "Stand forward, you who will essay this contest."

Forthwith uprose great Ajax, the son of Telamon, and crafty Odysseus, full of wiles, rose also. The two girded themselves and went into the middle of the ring. They gripped each other in their strong hands like the rafters which some master builder frames for the roof of a high house to keep the wind out. Their backbones cracked as they tugged at one another with their mighty arms—and sweat rained from them in torrents. Many a bloody weal sprang up on their sides and shoulders, but they kept on striving with might and main for victory and to win the tripod. Odysseus could not throw Ajax, nor Ajax him. Odysseus was too strong for him, but when the Achaeans began to tire of watching them, Ajax said to Odysseus, "Odysseus, noble son of Laertes, you shall either lift me, or I you, and let Zeus settle it between us."

He lifted him from the ground as he spoke, but Odysseus did not forget his cunning. He hit Ajax in the hollow at the back of his knee, so that he could not keep his feet, but fell on his back with Odysseus lying upon his chest, and all who saw it marveled. Then Odysseus in turn lifted Ajax and stirred him a little from the ground but could not lift him right off it, his knee sank under him, and the two fell side by side on the ground and were all begrimed with dust. They now sprang towards one another and were for wrestling yet a third time, but Achilles rose and stayed them. "Put not each other further," said he, "to such cruel suffering. The victory is with both alike, take each of you an equal prize, and let the other Achaeans now compete."

Thus did he speak and they did even as he had said, and put on their shirts again after wiping the dust from off their bodies.

The son of Peleus then offered prizes for speed in running—a mixing bowl beautifully wrought, of pure silver. It would hold six measures, and far exceeded all others in the whole world for beauty. It was the work of cunning artificers in Sidon and had been brought into port by Phoenicians from beyond the sea, who had made a present of it to Thoas. Eueneus, son of Jason, had given it to Patroclus in ransom of Priam's son Lycaon, and Achilles now offered it as a prize in honor of his comrade to him who should be the swiftest runner. For the second prize he offered a large ox, well-fattened, while for the last there was to be half a talent of gold. He then rose and said among the Argives, "Stand forward, you who will essay this contest."

Forthwith uprose fleet Ajax, son of Oïleus, with cunning Odysseus, and Nestor's son Antilochus, the fastest runner among all the youth of his time. They stood side by side and Achilles showed them the goal. The course was set out for them from the starting post, and the son of Oïleus took the lead at once, with Odysseus as close behind him as the shuttle is to a woman's bosom when she throws the woof across the warp and holds it close up to her; even so close behind him was Odysseus—treading in his footprints before the dust could settle there, and Ajax could feel his breath on the back of his head as he ran swiftly on. The Achaeans all shouted applause as they saw him straining his utmost, and cheered him as he shot past them; but when they were now nearing the end of the course Odysseus prayed inwardly to Athene. "Hear me," he cried, "and help my feet, O goddess!"

Thus did he pray, and Pallas Athene heard his prayer. She made his hands and his feet feel light, and when the runners were at the point of pouncing upon the prize, Ajax, through Athene's spite slipped upon some offal that was lying there from the cattle which Achilles had slaughtered in honor of Patroclus, and his mouth and nostrils were all filled with cow dung. Odysseus therefore carried off the mixing bowl, for he got before Ajax and came in first. But Ajax took the ox and stood with his hand on one of its horns, spitting the dung out of his mouth. Then he said to the Argives: "Alas, the goddess has spoiled my running; she watches over Odysseus and stands by him as though she were his own mother." Thus did he speak and they all of them laughed heartily.

Antilochus carried off the last prize and smiled as he said to the bystanders: "You all see, my friends, that now too the gods have shown their respect for seniority. Ajax is somewhat older than I am, and as for Odysseus, he belongs to an earlier generation, but he is hale in spite of his years, and no man of the Achaeans can run against him save only Achilles."

He said this to pay a compliment to the son of Peleus, and Achilles answered, "Antilochus, you shall not have praised me to no purpose; I shall give you an additional half talent of gold." He then gave the half talent to Antilochus, who received it gladly.

Then the son of Peleus brought out the spear, helmet, and shield that had been borne by Sarpedon, and were taken from him by Patroclus. He stood up and said among the Argives: "We bid two champions put on their armor, take their keen blades, and make trial of one another in the presence of the multitude.

Whichever of them can first wound the flesh of the other, cut through his armor, and draw blood, to him will I give this goodly Thracian sword inlaid with silver, which I took from Asteropaeus, but the armor let both hold in partnership, and I will give each of them a hearty meal in my own tent."

Forthwith uprose great Ajax, the son of Telamon, as also mighty Diomed, son of Tydeus. When they had put on their armor each on his own side of the ring, they both went into the middle eager to engage, and with fire flashing from their eyes. The Achaeans marveled as they beheld them, and when the two were now close up with one another, thrice did they spring forward and thrice try to strike each other in close combat. Ajax pierced Diomed's round shield, but did not draw blood, for the cuirass beneath the shield protected him. Thereon the son of Tydeus from over his huge shield kept aiming continually at Ajax's neck with the point of his spear, and the Achaeans alarmed for his safety bade them leave off fighting and divide the prize between them. Achilles then gave the great sword to the son of Tydeus, with its scabbard and the leathern belt with which to hang it.

Achilles next offered the massive iron quoit which mighty Eëtion had erewhile been used to hurl, until Achilles had slain him and carried it off in his ships along with other spoils. He stood up and said among the Argives: "Stand forward, you who would essay this contest. He who wins it will have a store of iron that will last him five years as they go rolling round, and if his fair fields lie far from a town his shepherd or plowman will not have to make a journey to buy iron, for he will have a stock of it on his own premises."

Then uprose the two mighty men, Polypoetes and Leonteus, with Ajax, son of Telamon, and noble Epeus. They stood up one after the other and Epeus took the quoit, whirled it, and flung it from him, which set all the Achaeans laughing. After him threw Leonteus of the race of Ares. Ajax, son of Telamon, threw third, sending the quoit beyond any mark that had been made yet, but when mighty Polypoetes took the quoit he hurled it as though it had been a stockman's stick which he sends flying about among his cattle when he is driving them, so far did his throw outdistance those of the others. All who saw it roared applause, and his comrades carried the prize for him and set it on board his ship.

Achilles next offered a prize of iron for archery—ten double-edged axes and ten with single edges. He set up a ship's mast, some way off upon the sands, and with a fine string tied a pigeon to it by the foot: this was what they were to aim at. "Whoever," he said, "can hit the pigeon shall have all the axes and take them away with him; he who hits the string without hitting the bird will have taken a worse aim and shall have the single-edged axes."

Then uprose King Teucer, and Meriones, the stalwart squire of Idomeneus, rose also. They cast lots in a bronze helmet and the lot of Teucer fell first. He let fly with his arrow forthwith, but he did not promise hecatombs of firstling lambs to King Apollo, and missed his bird, for Apollo foiled his aim, but he hit the string with which the bird was tied, near its foot. The arrow cut the string clean through so that it hung down towards the ground, while the bird flew up into the sky, and the Achaeans shouted applause. Meriones, who had his arrow ready while Teucer was aiming, snatched the bow out of his hand, and at once promised that he would sacrifice a hecatomb of firstling lambs to Apollo, lord of the bow. Then espying the pigeon high up under the clouds, he hit her in the middle of the wing as she was circling upwards; the arrow went clean through the wing and fixed itself in the ground at Meriones' feet, but the bird perched on the ship's mast hanging her head and with all her feathers drooping; the life went out of her, and she fell heavily from the mast. Meriones, therefore, took all ten double-edged axes, while Teucer bore off the single-edged ones to his ships.

Then the son of Peleus brought in a spear and a cauldron that had never been on the fire. It was worth an ox, and was chased with a pattern of flowers. And those that would throw the javelin stood up—to wit, the son of Atreus, king of men, Agamemnon, and Meriones, stalwart squire of Idomeneus. But

Achilles spoke, saying: "Son of Atreus, we know how far you excel all others both in power and in throwing the javelin. Take the cauldron back with you to your ships, but if it so please you, let us give the spear to Meriones. This at least is what I should myself wish."

King Agamemnon assented. So he gave the bronze spear to Meriones, and handed the goodly cauldron to Talthybius, his esquire.

Book XXIV

*Achilles drags Hector's body around Patroclus' tomb. At Apollo's protests,
Thetis is sent to tell her son to allow Priam to ransom Hector's body.
Guided by Hermes, Priam goes to Achilles, who is moved to pity and
restores Hector's body, promising an eleven days' truce. Hermes conducts
Priam back to Troy. Andromache, Hecuba, and Helen raise the dirge for
Hector. His funeral is celebrated fittingly.*

THE ASSEMBLY NOW BROKE UP AND THE PEOPLE WENT THEIR WAYS EACH
to his own ship. There they made ready their supper, and then
bethought them of the blessed boon of sleep; but Achilles still wept
for thinking of his dear comrade, and sleep, before whom all things bow,
could take no hold upon him. This way and that did he turn as he yearned
after the might and manfulness of Patroclus; he thought of all they had done
together, and all they had gone through both on the field of battle and on
the waves of the weary sea. As he dwelt on these things he wept bitterly and
lay now on his side, now on his back, and now face downwards, till at last
he rose and went out as one distraught to wander upon the seashore. Then,
when he saw dawn breaking over beach and sea, he yoked his horses to his
chariot, and bound the body of Hector behind it that he might drag it about.
Thrice did he drag it round the tomb of the son of Menoetius, and then went
back into his tent, leaving the body on the ground full length and with its
face downwards. But Apollo would not suffer it to be disfigured, for he pitied
the man, dead though he now was. Therefore, he shielded him with his

387

golden aegis continually, that he might take no hurt while Achilles was dragging him.

Thus shamefully did Achilles in his fury dishonor Hector; but the blessed gods looked down in pity from heaven, and urged Hermes, slayer of Argus, to steal the body. All were of this mind save only Hera, Poseidon, and Zeus' gray-eyed daughter, who persisted in the hate which they had ever borne towards Ilium with Priam and his people; for they forgave not the wrong done them by Paris in disdaining the goddesses who came to him when he was in his sheepyards, and preferring her who had offered him a wanton to his ruin.

When, therefore, the morning of the twelfth day had now come, Phoebus Apollo spoke among the immortals, saying: "You gods ought to be ashamed of yourselves; you are cruel and hard-hearted. Did not Hector burn you thigh-bones of heifers and of unblemished goats? And now dare you not rescue even his dead body, for his wife to look upon, with his mother and child, his father Priam, and his people, who would forthwith commit him to the flames and give him his due funeral rites? So, then, you would all be on the side of mad Achilles, who knows neither right nor ruth? He is like some savage lion that in the pride of his great strength and daring springs upon men's flocks and gorges on them. Even so has Achilles flung aside all pity, and all that conscience which at once so greatly banes yet greatly boons him that will heed it. A man may lose one far dearer than Achilles has lost—a son, it may be, or a brother born from his own mother's womb; yet when he has mourned him and wept over him he will let him bide, for it takes much sorrow to kill a man; whereas Achilles, now that he has slain noble Hector, drags him behind his chariot round the tomb of his comrade. It were better of him, and for him, that he should not do so, for brave though he be we gods may take it ill that he should vent his fury upon dead clay."

Hera spoke up in a rage. "This were well," she cried, "O lord of the silver bow, if you would give like honor to Hector and to Achilles; but Hector was mortal and suckled at a woman's breast, whereas Achilles is the offspring of a goddess whom I myself reared and brought up. I married her to Peleus, who is above measure dear to the immortals. You gods came all of you to her wedding; you feasted along with them yourself and brought your lyre—false, and fond of low company, that you have ever been."

Then said Zeus: "Hera, be not so bitter. Their honor shall not be equal, but of all that dwell in Ilium, Hector was dearest to the gods, as also to myself, for his offerings never failed me. Never was my altar stinted of its dues, nor of the drink offerings and savor of sacrifice which we claim of right. I shall therefore permit the body of mighty Hector to be stolen; and yet this may hardly be without Achilles coming to know it, for his mother keeps night and day beside him. Let some one of you, therefore, send Thetis to me, and I will impart my counsel to her, namely that Achilles is to accept a ransom from Priam and give up the body."

On this Iris, fleet as the wind, went forth to carry his message. Down she plunged into the dark sea midway between Samos and rocky Imbrus. The waters hissed as they closed over her, and she sank into the bottom as the lead at the end of an ox-horn that is sped to carry death to fishes. She found Thetis sitting in a great cave with the other sea-goddesses gathered round her; there she sat in the midst of them weeping for her noble son who was to fall far from his own land, on the rich plains of Troy. Iris went up to her and said, "Rise, Thetis. Zeus, whose counsels fail not, bids you come to him." And Thetis answered: "Why does the mighty god so bid me? I am in great grief, and shrink from going in and out among the immortals. Still, I will go, and the word that he may speak shall not be spoken in vain."

The goddess took her dark veil, than which there can be no robe more somber, and went forth with fleet Iris leading the way before her. The waves of the sea opened them a path, and when they reached the shore they flew up into the heavens, where they found the all-seeing son of Cronus with the blessed gods that live forever assembled near him. Athene gave up her seat to her, and she sat down by the side of father Zeus. Hera then placed a fair golden cup in her hand, and spoke to her in words of comfort, whereon Thetis drank and gave her back the cup; and the sire of gods and men was the first to speak.

"So, goddess," said he, "for all your sorrow, and the grief that I well know reigns ever in your heart, you have come hither to Olympus, and I will tell you why I have sent for you. This nine days past the immortals have been quarreling about Achilles, waster of cities, and the body of Hector. The gods would have Hermes, slayer of Argus, steal the body, but in furtherance of our peace and amity henceforward, I will concede such honor to your son as I will now tell you. Go, then, to the host and lay these commands upon him. Say that the gods are angry with him, and that I am myself more angry than them all, in that he keeps Hector at the ships and will not give him up. He may thus fear me and let the body go. At the same time I will send Iris to great Priam to bid him go to the ships of the Achaeans, and ransom his son, taking with him such gifts for Achilles as may give him satisfaction."

Silver-footed Thetis did as the god had told her, and forthwith down she darted from the topmost summits of Olympus. She went to her son's tents where she found him grieving bitterly, while his trusty comrades round him were busy preparing their morning meal, for which they had killed a great woolly sheep. His mother sat down beside him and caressed him with her hand, saying: "My son, how long will you keep on thus grieving and making moan? You are gnawing at your own heart, and think neither of food nor of woman's embraces; and yet these too were well, for you have no long time to live, and death with the strong hand of fate is already close beside you. Now, therefore, heed what I say, for I come as a messenger from Zeus. He says that the gods are angry with you, and himself more angry than them all, in that you keep Hector at the ships and will not give him up. Therefore let him go, and accept a ransom for his body."

And Achilles answered: "So be it. If Olympian Zeus of his own motion thus commands me, let him that brings the ransom bear the body away."

Thus did mother and son talk together at the ships in long discourse with one another. Meanwhile, the son of Cronus sent Iris to the strong city of Ilium. "Go," said he, "fleet Iris, from the mansions of Olympus, and tell King Priam in Ilium that he is to go to the ships of the Achaeans and free the body of his dear son. He is to take such gifts with him as shall give satisfaction to Achilles, and he is to go alone, with no other Trojan, save only some honored servant who may drive his mules and wagon, and bring back the body of him whom noble Achilles has slain. Let him have no thought nor fear of death in his heart, for we will send the slayer of Argus to escort him, and bring him within the tent of Achilles. Achilles will not kill him nor let another do so, for he will take heed to his ways and sin not, and he will entreat a suppliant with all honorable courtesy."

On this Iris, fleet as the wind, sped forth to deliver her message. She went to Priam's house, and found weeping and lamentation therein. His sons were seated round their father in the outer courtyard, and their raiment was wet with tears. The old man sat in the midst of them with his mantle wrapped close about his body, and his head and neck all covered with the filth which he had clutched as he lay groveling in the mire. His daughters and his sons' wives went wailing about the house, as they thought of the many and brave men who lay dead, slain by the Argives. The messenger of Zeus stood by Priam and spoke softly to him, but fear fell upon him as she did so.

"Take heart," she said, "Priam, offspring of Dardanus, take heart and fear not. I bring no evil tidings, but am minded well towards you. I come as a messenger from Zeus, who though he be not near, takes thought for you and pities you. The lord of Olympus bids you go and ransom noble Hector, and take with you such gifts as shall give satisfaction to Achilles. You are to go alone, with no other Trojan, save only some honored servant who may drive your mules and wagon, and bring back to the city the body of him whom noble Achilles has slain. You are to have no thought, nor fear of death, for Zeus will send the slayer of Argus to escort you. When he has brought you within Achilles' tent, Achilles will not kill you nor let another do so, for he will take heed to his ways and sin not, and he will treat a suppliant with all honorable courtesy."

Iris went her way when she had thus spoken, and Priam told his sons to get a mule-wagon ready, and to make the body of the wagon fast upon the top of its bed. Then he went down into his fragrant storeroom, high-vaulted, and made of cedarwood, where his many treasures were kept, and he called Hecuba, his wife. "Wife," said he, "a messenger has come to me from Olympus, and has told me to go to the ships of the Achaeans to ransom my dear son, taking with me such gifts as shall give satisfaction to Achilles. What think you of this matter? For my own part, I am greatly moved to pass through the host of the Achaeans and go to their ships."

His wife cried aloud as she heard him, and said: "Alas, what has become of that judgment for which you have been ever famous both among strangers and your own people? How can you venture alone to the ships of the Achaeans, and look into the face of him who has slain so many of your brave sons? You must have iron courage, for if the cruel savage sees you and lays hold on you, he will know neither respect nor pity. Let us then weep Hector from afar here in our own house, for when I gave him birth the threads of overruling fate were spun for him that dogs should eat his flesh far from his parents, in the house of that terrible man on whose liver I would fain fasten and devour it. Thus would I avenge my son, who showed no cowardice when Achilles slew him, and thought neither of flight nor of avoiding battle as he stood in defense of Trojan men and Trojan women."

Then Priam said: "I would go; do not, therefore, stay me nor be as a bird of ill omen in my house, for you will not move me. Had it been some mortal man who had sent me—some prophet or priest who divines from sacrifice—I should have deemed him false and have given him no heed; but now I have heard the goddess and seen her face to face; therefore I will go and her saying shall not be in vain. If it be my fate to die at the ships of the Achaeans even so would I have it. Let Achilles slay me, if I may but first have taken my son in my arms and mourned him to my heart's comforting."

So saying he lifted the lids of his chests, and took out twelve goodly vestments. He took also twelve cloaks of single fold, twelve rugs, twelve fair mantles, and an equal number of shirts. He weighed out ten talents of gold, and brought moreover two burnished tripods, four cauldrons, and a very beautiful cup which the Thracians had given him when he had gone to them on an embassy. It was very precious, but he grudged not even this, so eager was he to ransom the body of his son. Then he chased all the Trojans from the court and rebuked them with words of anger. "Out," he cried, "shame and disgrace to me that you are! Have you no grief in your own homes that you are come to plague me here? Is it a small thing, think you, that the son of Cronus has sent this sorrow upon me, to lose the bravest of my sons? Nay, you shall prove it in person, for now he is gone the Achaeans will have easier work in killing you. As for me, let me go down within the house of Hades, ere mine eyes behold the sacking and wasting of the city."

He drove the men away with his staff, and they went forth as the old man sped them. Then he called to his sons, upbraiding Helenus, Paris, noble Agathon, Pammon, Antiphonus, Polites of the loud battle cry, Deïphobus, Hippothoüs, and Dius. These nine did the old man call near him. "Come to me at once," he cried, "worthless sons who do me shame! Would that you had all been killed at the ships rather than Hector. Miserable man that I am, I have had the bravest sons in all Troy—noble Mestor, Troïlus, the dauntless charioteer, and Hector who was a god among men, so that one would have thought he was son to an immortal—yet there is not one of them left. Ares has slain them and those of whom I am ashamed are alone left me. Liars, and light of foot, heroes of the dance, robbers of lambs and kids from your own people, why do you not get a wagon ready for me at once, and put all these things upon it that I may set out on my way?"

Thus did he speak, and they feared the rebuke of their father. They brought out a strong mule-wagon, newly made, and set the body of the wagon fast on its bed. They took the mule-yoke from the peg on which it hung, a yoke of boxwood with a knob on the top of it and rings for the reins to go through. Then they brought a yoke-band eleven cubits long, to bind the yoke to the pole. They bound it on at the far end of the pole and put the ring over the upright pin, making it fast with three turns of the band on either side the knob and bending the thong of the yoke beneath it. This done, they brought from the store-chamber the rich ransom that was to purchase the body of Hector, and they set it all orderly on the wagon. Then they yoked the strong harness-mules which the Mysians had on a time given as a goodly present to Priam; but for Priam himself they yoked horses which the old king had bred, and kept for his own use.

Thus heedfully did Priam and his servant see to the yoking of their cars at the palace. Then Hecuba came to them all sorrowful, with a golden goblet of wine in her right hand, that they might make a drink offering before they set out. She stood in front of the horses and said: 'Take this, make a drink offering to father Zeus, and since you are minded to go to the ships in spite of me, pray that you may come safely back from the hands of your enemies. Pray to the son of Cronus, lord of the whirlwind, who sits on Ida and looks down over all Troy, pray him to send his swift messenger on your right hand, the bird of omen which is strongest and most dear to him of all birds, that you may see it with your own eyes and trust it as you go forth to the ships of the Danaans. If all-seeing Zeus will not send you this messenger, however set upon it you may be, I would not have you go to the ships of the Argives."

And Priam answered, "Wife, I will do as you desire me; it is well to lift hands in prayer to Zeus, if so be he may have mercy upon me."

With this the old man bade the servingwoman pour pure water over his hands, and the woman came, bearing the water in a bowl. He washed his hands and took the cup from his wife; then he made the drink offering and prayed, standing in the middle of the courtyard and turning his eyes to heaven. "Father Zeus," he said, "that rulest from Ida, most glorious and most great, grant that I may be received kindly and compassionately in the tents of Achilles; and send your swift messenger upon my right hand, the bird of omen which is strongest and most dear to you of all birds, that I may see it with my own eyes and trust it as I go forth to the ships of the Danaans."

So did he pray, and Zeus, the lord of counsel, heard his prayer. Forthwith he sent an eagle, the most unerring portent of all birds that fly, the dusky hunter that men also call the Black Eagle. His wings were spread abroad on either side as wide as the well-made and well-bolted door of a rich man's chamber. He came to them flying over the city upon their right hands, and when they saw him they were glad and their hearts took comfort within them. The old man made haste to mount his chariot, and drove out through the inner gateway and under the echoing gatehouse of the outer court. Before him went the mules drawing the four-wheeled wagon, and driven by wise Idaeus; behind these were the horses, which the old man lashed with his whip and drove swiftly through the city, while his friends followed after, wailing and lamenting for him as though he were on his road to death. As soon as they had come down from the city and had reached the plain, his sons and sons-in-law who had followed him went back to Ilium.

But Priam and Idaeus as they showed out upon the plain did not escape the ken of all-seeing Zeus, who looked down upon the old man and pitied him; then he spoke to his son Hermes and said, "Hermes, for it is you who are the most disposed to escort men on their way, and to hear those whom you will hear, go, and so conduct Priam to the ships of the Achaeans that no other of the Danaans shall see him nor take note of him until he reach the son of Peleus."

Thus he spoke and Hermes, guide and guardian, slayer of Argus, did as he was told. Forthwith he bound on his glittering golden sandals with which he could fly like the wind over land and sea; he took the wand with which he seals men's eyes in sleep, or wakes them just as he pleases, and flew holding it in his hand till he came to Troy and to the Hellespont. To look at, he was like a young man of noble birth in the heyday of his youth and beauty with the down just coming upon his face.

Now when Priam and Idaeus had driven past the great tomb of Ilus, they stayed their mules and horses that they might drink in the river, for the shades of night were falling; when, therefore, Idaeus saw Hermes standing near them he said to Priam: "Take heed, descendant of Dardanus; here is matter which demands consideration. I see a man who I think will presently fall upon us. Let us fly with our horses, or at least embrace his knees and implore him to take compassion upon us."

When he heard this the old man's heart failed him, and he was in great fear. He stayed where he was as one dazed, and the hair stood on end over his whole body; but the bringer of good luck came up to him and took him by the hand, saying: "Whither, father, are you thus driving your mules and horses in the dead of night when other men are asleep? Are you not afraid of the fierce Achaeans who are hard by you, so cruel and relentless? Should some one of them see you bearing so much treasure through the darkness of the flying night, what would not your state then be? You are no longer young, and he who is with you is too old to protect you from those who would attack you. For myself, I will do you no harm, and I will defend you from anyone else, for you remind me of my own father."

And Priam answered: "It is indeed as you say, my dear son. Nevertheless, some god has held his hand over me, in that he has sent such a wayfarer as yourself to meet me so opportunely; you are so comely in mien and figure, and your judgment is so excellent that you must come of blessed parents."

Then said the slayer of Argus, guide and guardian: "Sir, all that you have said is right; but tell me and tell me true, are you taking this rich treasure to send it to a foreign people where it may be safe, or are you all leaving strong

Ilium in dismay now that your son has fallen who was the bravest man among you and was never lacking in battle with the Achaeans?"

And Priam said: "Who are you, my friend, and who are your parents, that you speak so truly about the fate of my unhappy son?"

The slayer of Argus, guide and guardian, answered him: "Sir, you would prove me, that you question me about noble Hector. Many a time have I set eyes upon him in battle when he was driving the Argives to their ships and putting them to the sword. We stood still and marveled, for Achilles in his anger with the son of Atreus suffered us not to fight. I am his squire and came with him in the same ship. I am a Myrmidon, and my father's name is Polyctor; he is a rich man and about as old as you are; he has six sons besides myself, and I am the seventh. We cast lots, and it fell upon me to sail hither with Achilles. I am now come from the ships on to the plain, for with daybreak the Achaeans will set battle in array about the city. They chafe at doing nothing, and are so eager that their princes cannot hold them back."

Then answered Priam: "If you are indeed the squire of Achilles, son of Peleus, tell me now the whole truth. Is my son still at the ships, or has Achilles hewn him limb from limb and given him to his hounds?"

"Sir," replied the slayer of Argus, guide and guardian, "neither hounds nor vultures have yet devoured him. He is still just lying at the tents by the ship of Achilles, and though it is now twelve days that he has lain there, his flesh is not wasted nor have the worms eaten him, although they feed on warriors. At daybreak Achilles drags him cruelly round the sepulcher of his dear comrade, but it does him no hurt. You should come yourself and see how he lies fresh as dew, with the blood all washed away, and his wounds every one of them closed though many pierced him with their spears. Such care have the blessed gods taken of your brave son, for he was dear to them beyond all measure."

The old man was comforted as he heard him and said: "My son, see what a good thing it is to have made due offerings to the immortals; for, as sure as that he was born, my son never forgot the gods that hold Olympus, and now they requite it to him even in death. Accept, therefore, at my hands this goodly chalice. Guard me and with heaven's help guide me till I come to the tent of the son of Peleus."

Then answered the slayer of Argus, guide and guardian: "Sir, you are tempting me and playing upon my youth, but you shall not move me, for you are offering me presents without the knowledge of Achilles whom I fear and hold it great guiltiness to defraud, lest some evil presently befall me; but as your guide I would go with you even to Argos itself, and would guard you so carefully whether by sea or land that no one should attack you through making light of him who was with you."

The bringer of good luck then sprang on to the chariot, and seizing the whip and reins he breathed fresh spirit into the mules and horses. When they reached the trench and the wall that was before the ships, those who were on guard had just been getting their suppers, and the slayer of Argus threw them all into a deep sleep. Then he drew back the bolts to open the gates, and took Priam inside with the treasure he had upon his wagon. Ere long they came to the lofty dwelling of the son of Peleus for which the Myrmidons had cut pine and which they had built for their king. When they had built it they thatched it with coarse tussock-grass which they had mown out on the plain, and all round it they made a large courtyard, which was fenced with stakes set close together. The gate was barred with a single bolt of pine which it took three men to force into its place, and three to draw back so as to open the gate, but Achilles could draw it by himself. Hermes opened the gate for the old man, and brought in the treasure that he was taking with him for the son of Peleus. Then he sprang from the chariot on to the ground and said: "Sir, it is I, immortal Hermes, that am come with you, for my father sent me to escort you. I will now leave you, and will not enter into the presence of Achilles, for it might anger him that a god should befriend mortal men thus openly. Go you within, and embrace the knees of the son of Peleus. Beseech him by his father, his lovely mother, and his son; thus you may move him."

With these words Hermes went back to high Olympus. Priam sprang from his chariot to the ground, leaving Idaeus where he was, in charge of the mules and horses. The old man went straight into the house where Achilles, loved of the gods, was sitting. There he found him with his men seated at a distance from him: only two, the hero Automedon, and Alcimus of the race of Ares, were busy in attendance about his person, for he had but just done eating and drinking, and the table was still there. King Priam entered without their seeing him, and going right up to Achilles he clasped his knees and kissed the dread murderous hands that had slain so many of his sons.

As when some cruel spite has befallen a man that he should have killed someone in his own country, and must fly to a great man's protection in a land of strangers, and all marvel who see him, even so did Achilles marvel as he beheld Priam. The others looked one to another and marveled also, but Priam besought Achilles, saying, "Think of your father, O Achilles like unto the gods, who is such even as I am, on the sad threshold of old age. It may be that those who dwell near him harass him, and there is none to keep war and ruin from him. Yet when he hears of you as being still alive, he is glad, and his days are full of hope that he shall see his dear son come home to him from Troy; but I, wretched man that I am, had the bravest in all Troy for my sons, and there is not one of them left. I had fifty sons when the Achaeans came here; nineteen of them were from a single womb, and the others were borne to me by the women of my household. The greater part of them has fierce Ares laid low, and Hector, him who was alone left, him who was the guardian of our city and ourselves, him have you lately slain. Therefore I am now come to the ships of the Achaeans to ransom his body from you with a great ransom. Fear, O Achilles, the wrath of heaven! Think on your own father and have compassion upon me, who am the more pitiable, for I have steeled myself as no man has ever yet steeled himself before me, and have raised to my lips the hand of him who slew my son."

Thus spoke Priam, and the heart of Achilles yearned as he bethought him of his father. He took the old man's hand and moved him gently away. The two wept bitterly—Priam, as he lay at Achilles' feet, weeping for Hector, and Achilles, now for his father and now for Patroclus, till the house was filled with their lamentation. But when Achilles was now sated with grief and had unburdened the bitterness of his sorrow, he left his seat and raised the old man by the hand, in pity for his white hair and beard. Then he said: "Unhappy man, you have indeed been greatly daring. How could you venture to come alone to the ships of the Achaeans and enter the presence of him who has slain so many of your brave sons? You must have iron courage. Sit now upon this seat, and for all our grief we will hide our sorrows in our hearts, for weeping will not avail us. The immortals know no care, yet the lot they spin for man is full of sorrow. On the floor of Zeus' palace there stand two urns, the one filled with evil gifts, and the other with good ones. He for whom Zeus, the lord of thunder, mixes the gifts he sends, will meet now with good and now with evil fortune; but he to whom Zeus sends none but evil gifts will be pointed at by the finger of scorn, the hand of famine will pursue him to the ends of the world, and he will go up and down the face of the earth, respected neither by gods nor men. Even so did it befall Peleus; the gods endowed him with all good things from his birth upwards, for he reigned over the Myrmidons, excelling all men in prosperity and wealth, and mortal though he was they gave him a goddess for his bride. But even on him too did heaven send misfortune, for there is no race of royal children born to him in his house, save one son who is doomed to die all untimely; nor may I take care of him now that he is growing old, for I must stay here at Troy to be the bane of you and of your children.

"And you too, O Priam, I have heard that you were aforetime happy. They say that in wealth and plenitude of offspring you surpassed all that is in Lesbos, the realm of Makar to the northward, Phrygia that is more inland, and those that dwell upon the great Hellespont; but from the day when the dwellers in heaven sent this evil upon you, war and slaughter have been about your city continually. Bear up against it, and let there be some intervals in your sorrow. Mourn as you may for your brave son, you will take nothing by it. You cannot raise him from the dead; ere you do so yet another sorrow shall befall you."

And Priam answered: "O king, bid me not be seated, while Hector is still lying uncared for in your tents, but accept the great ransom which I have brought you, and give him to me at once that I may look upon him. May you prosper with the ransom and reach your own land in safety, seeing that you have suffered me to live and to look upon the light of the sun."

Achilles looked at him sternly and said: "Vex me, sir, no longer; I am of myself minded to give up the body of Hector. My mother, daughter of the old man of the sea, came to me from Zeus to bid me deliver it to you. Moreover, I know well, O Priam, and you cannot hide it, that some god has brought you to the ships of the Achaeans, for else, no man however strong and in his prime would dare to come to our host. He could neither pass our guard unseen, nor draw the bolt of my gates thus easily. Therefore, provoke me no further, lest I sin against the word of Zeus, and suffer you not, suppliant though you are, within my tents."

The old man feared him and obeyed. Then the son of Peleus sprang like a lion through the door of his house, not alone, but with him went his two squires, Automedon and Alcimus, who were closer to him than any others of his comrades now that Patroclus was no more. These unyoked the horses and mules, and bade Priam's herald and attendant be seated within the house. They lifted the ransom for Hector's body from the wagon, but they left two mantles and a goodly shirt, that Achilles might wrap the body in them when he gave it to be taken home. Then he called to his servants and ordered them to wash the body and anoint it, but he first took it to a place where Priam should not see it, lest if he did so, he should break out in the bitterness of his grief, and enrage Achilles, who might then kill him and sin against the word of Zeus. When the servants had washed the body and anointed it, and had wrapped it in a fair shirt and mantle, Achilles himself lifted it onto a bier, and he and his men then laid it on the wagon. He cried aloud as he did so and called on the name of his dear comrade. "Be not angry with me, Patroclus," he said, "if you hear even in the house of Hades that I have given Hector to his father for a ransom. It has been no unworthy one, and I will share it equitably with you."

Achilles then went back into the tent and took his place on the richly inlaid seat from which he had risen, by the wall that was at right angles to the one against which Priam was sitting. "Sir," he said, "your son is now laid upon his bier and is ransomed according to your desire. You shall look upon him when you take him away at daybreak; for the present let us prepare our supper. Even lovely Niobe had to think about eating, though her twelve children—six daughters and six lusty sons—had been all slain in her house. Apollo killed the sons with arrows from his silver bow, to punish Niobe, and Artemis slew the daughters, because Niobe had vaunted herself against Leto. She said Leto had borne two children only, whereas she had herself borne many—whereon the two killed the many. Nine days did they lie weltering, and there was none to bury them, for the son of Cronus turned the people into stone; but on the tenth day the gods in heaven themselves buried them, and Niobe then took food, being worn out with weeping. They say that somewhere among the rocks on the mountain pastures of Sipylus, where the nymphs live that haunt the river Acheloüs, there, they say, she lives in stone and still nurses the sorrows sent upon her by the hand of heaven. Therefore, noble sir, let us two now take food; you can weep for your dear son hereafter as you are bearing him back to Ilium—and many a tear will he cost you."

With this Achilles sprang from his seat and killed a sheep of silvery whiteness, which his followers skinned and made ready all in due order. They cut the meat carefully up into smaller pieces, spitted them, and drew them off again when they were well-roasted. Automedon brought bread in fair baskets and served it round the table, while Achilles dealt out the meat, and they laid their hands on the good things that were before them. As soon as they had

had enough to eat and drink, Priam, descendant of Dardanus, marveled at the strength and beauty of Achilles for he was as a god to see, and Achilles marveled at Priam as he listened to him and looked upon his noble presence. When they had gazed their fill Priam spoke first. "And now, O king," he said, "take me to my couch that we may lie down and enjoy the blessed boon of sleep. Never once have my eyes been closed from the day your hands took the life of my son; I have groveled without ceasing in the mire of my stableyard, making moan and brooding over my countless sorrows. Now, moreover, I have eaten bread and drunk wine; hitherto I have tasted nothing."

As he spoke Achilles told his men and the womenservants to set beds in the room that was in the gatehouse, and make them with good red rugs, and spread coverlets on the top of them with woolen cloaks for Priam and Idaeus to wear. So the maids went out carrying a torch and got the two beds ready in all haste. Then Achilles said laughingly to Priam: "Dear sir, you shall lie outside, lest some counselor of those who in due course keep coming to advise with me should see you here in the darkness of the flying night, and tell it to Agamemnon. This might cause delay in the delivery of the body. And now tell me and tell me true, for how many days would you celebrate the funeral rites of noble Hector? Tell me, that I may hold aloof from war and restrain the host."

And Priam answered: "Since, then, you suffer me to bury my noble son with all due rites, do thus, Achilles, and I shall be grateful. You know how we are pent up within our city. It is far for us to fetch wood from the mountain, and the people live in fear. Nine days, therefore, will we mourn Hector in my house; on the tenth day we will bury him and there shall be a public feast in his honor; on the eleventh we will build a mound over his ashes, and on the twelfth, if there be need, we will fight."

And Achilles answered: "All, King Priam, shall be as you have said. I will stay our fighting for as long a time as you have named."

As he spoke he laid his hand on the old man's right wrist, in token that he should have no fear; thus then did Priam and his attendant sleep there in the forecourt, full of thought, while Achilles lay in an inner room of the house, with fair Briseis by his side.

And now both gods and mortals were fast asleep through the livelong night, but upon Hermes alone, the bringer of good luck, sleep could take no hold for he was thinking all the time how to get King Priam away from the ships without his being seen by the strong force of sentinels. He hovered therefore over Priam's head and said: "Sir, now that Achilles has spared your life, you seem to have no fear about sleeping in the thick of your foes. You have paid a great ransom, and have received the body of your son. Were you still alive and a prisoner the sons whom you have left at home would have to give three times as much to free you; and so it would be if Agamemnon and the other Achaeans were to know of your being here."

When he heard this the old man was afraid and roused his servant. Hermes then yoked their horses and mules and drove them quickly through the host so that no man perceived them. When they came to the ford of eddying Xanthus, begotten of immortal Zeus, Hermes went back to high Olympus, and dawn in robe of saffron began to break over all the land. Priam and Idaeus then drove on towards the city lamenting and making moan, and the mules drew the body of Hector. No one neither man nor woman saw them, till Cassandra, fair as golden Aphrodite standing on Pergamus, caught sight of her dear father in his chariot, and his servant that was the city's herald with him. Then she saw him that was lying upon the bier, drawn by the mules, and with a loud cry she went about the city, saying, "Come hither, Trojans, men and women, and look on Hector. If ever you rejoiced to see him coming from battle when he was alive, look now on him that was the glory of our city and all our people."

At this there was not man nor woman left in the city, so great a sorrow had possessed them. Hard by the gates they met Priam as he was bringing in the body. Hector's wife and his mother were the first to mourn him: they flew towards the wagon and laid their hands upon his head, while the crowd stood weeping round them. They would have stayed before the gates, weeping and lamenting the livelong day to the going down of the sun, had not Priam spoken to them from the chariot and said, "Make way for the mules to pass you. Afterwards, when I have taken the body home, you shall have your fill of weeping."

On this the people stood asunder and made a way for the wagon. When they had borne the body within the house they laid it upon a bed and seated minstrels round it to lead the dirge, whereon the women joined in the sad music of their lament. Foremost among them all Andromache led their wailing as she clasped the head of mighty Hector in her embrace. "Husband," she cried, "you have died young, and leave me in your house a widow. He of whom we are the ill-starred parents is still a mere child, and I fear he may not reach manhood. Ere he can do so our city will be razed and overthrown, for you who watched over it are no more—you who were its savior, the guardian of our wives and children. Our women will be carried away captives to the ships, and I among them, while you, my child, who will be with me will be put to some unseemly tasks, working for a cruel master. Or, may be, some Achaean will hurl you (O miserable death) from our walls to avenge some brother, son, or father whom Hector slew. Many of them have indeed bitten the dust at his hands, for your father's hand in battle was no light one. Therefore do the people mourn him. You have left, O Hector, sorrow unutterable to your parents, and my own grief is greatest of all, for you did not stretch forth your arms and embrace me as you lay dying, nor say to me any words that might have lived with me in my tears night and day forevermore."

Bitterly did she weep the while, and the women joined in her lament. Hecuba in her turn took up the strains of woe. "Hector," she cried, "dearest to me of all my children! So long as you were alive the gods loved you well, and even in death they have not been utterly unmindful of you; for when Achilles took any other of my sons, he would sell him beyond the seas, to Samos Imbrus or rugged Lemnos. And when he had slain you too with his sword, many a time did he drag you round the sepulcher of his comrade—though this could not give him life—yet here you lie all fresh as dew and comely as one whom Apollo has slain with his painless shafts."

Thus did she too speak through her tears with bitter moan, and then Helen for a third time took up the strain of lamentation. "Hector," said she, "dearest of all my brothers-in-law—for I am wife to Paris who brought me hither to Troy—would that I had died ere he did so—twenty years are come and gone since I left my home and came from over the sea, but I have never heard one word of insult or unkindness from you. When another would chide with me, as it might be one of your brothers or sisters or of your brothers' wives, or my mother-in-law—for Priam was as kind to me as though he were my own father—you would rebuke and check them with words of gentleness and good will. Therefore my tears flow both for you and for my unhappy self, for there is no one else in Troy who is kind to me, but all shrink and shudder as they go by me."

She wept as she spoke and the vast crowd that was gathered round her joined in her lament. Then King Priam spoke to them, saying, "Bring wood, O Trojans, to the city, and fear no cunning ambush of the Argives, for Achilles when he dismissed me from the ships gave me his word that they should not attack us until the morning of the twelfth day."

Forthwith they yoked their oxen and mules and gathered together before the city. Nine days long did they bring in great heaps of wood, and on the morning of the tenth day with many tears they took brave Hector forth, laid his dead body upon the summit of the pile, and set the fire thereto. Then when the child of morning, rosy-fingered dawn, appeared on the eleventh day, the people again assembled round the pyre of mighty Hector. When they were got together, they first quenched the fire with wine wherever it was burning, and then his brothers and comrades with many a bitter tear gathered his white bones, wrapped them in soft robes of purple, and laid them in a golden urn, which they placed in a grave and covered over with large stones set close together. Then they built a barrow hurriedly over it keeping guard on every side lest the Achaeans should attack them before they had finished. When they had heaped up the barrow they went back again into the city, and being well assembled they held high feast in the house of Priam, their king.

Thus, then, did they celebrate the funeral of Hector, tamer of horses.

THE END

THE
ODYSSEY

CONTENTS

Preface

T his translation is intended to supplement a work entitled *The Authoress of the Odyssey*, which I published in 1897. I could not give the whole *Odyssey* in that book without making it unwieldy, I therefore epitomized my translation, which was already completed and which I now publish in full.

I shall not here argue the two main points dealt with in the work just mentioned; I have nothing either to add to, or to withdraw from, what I have there written. The points in question are:

(1) that the *Odyssey* was written entirely at, and drawn entirely from, the place now called Trapani on the west coast of Sicily, alike as regards the Phaeacian and the Ithaca scenes; while the voyages of Ulysses,[1] when once he is within easy reach of Sicily, resolve themselves into a periplus of the island, practically from Trapani back to Trapani, via the Lipari islands, the Straits of Messina, and the island of Pantellaria;

(2) that the poem was entirely written by a very young woman, who lived at the place now called Trapani, and introduced herself into her work under the name of Nausicaa.

The main arguments on which I base the first of these somewhat startling contentions, have been prominently and repeatedly before the English and Italian public ever since they appeared (without rejoinder) in the *Athenaeum* for 30th January and 20th February 1892. Both contentions were urged (also without rejoinder) in the Johnian *Eagle* for the Lent and October Terms of the same year. Nothing to which I should reply has reached me from any quarter,

---

[1] In this edition of Butler's translation the name Ulysses has been restored to its Greek form, Odysseus.

and knowing how anxiously I have endeavored to learn the existence of any flaws in my argument, I begin to feel some confidence that, did such flaws exist, I should have heard, at any rate about some of them, before now. Without, therefore, for a moment pretending to think that scholars generally acquiesce in my conclusions, I shall act as thinking them little likely so to gainsay me as that it will be incumbent upon me to reply, and shall confine myself to translating the *Odyssey* for English readers, with such notes as I think will be found useful. . . . .

In the preface to my translation of the *Iliad*[2] I have given my views as to the main principles by which a translator should be guided, and need not repeat them here, beyond pointing out that the initial liberty of translating poetry into prose involves the continual taking of more or less liberty throughout the translation; for much that is right in poetry is wrong in prose, and the exigencies of readable prose are the first things to be considered in a prose translation. That the reader, however, may see how far I have departed from strict construe, I will print here Messrs. Butcher and Lang's translation of the first lines of the *Odyssey*. Their translation runs:

"Tell me, Muse, of that man, so ready at need, who wandered far and wide, after he had sacked the sacred citadel of Troy, and many were the men whose towns he saw and whose mind he learnt, yea, and many the woes he suffered in his heart on the deep, striving to win his own life and the return of his company. Nay, but even so he saved not his company, though he desired it sore. For through the blindness of their own hearts they perished, fools, who devoured the oxen of Helios Hyperion: but the god took from them their days of returning. Of these things, goddess, daughter of Zeus, whencesoever thou hast heard thereof, declare thou even unto us.

"Now all the rest, as many as fled from sheer destruction, were at home, and had escaped both war and sea, but Odysseus only, craving for his wife and for his homeward path, the lady nymph Calypso held, that fair goddess, in

[2] See Classics Club *Iliad*, xxix.

her hollow caves, longing to have him for her lord. But when now the year had come in the courses of the seasons, wherein the gods had ordained that he should return home to Ithaca, not even there was he quit of labours, not even among his own; but all the gods had pity on him save Poseidon, who raged continually against god-like Odysseus, till he came to his own country. Howbeit Poseidon had now departed for the distant Ethiopians, the Ethiopians that are sundered in twain, the uttermost of men, abiding some where Hyperion sinks and some where he rises. There he looked to receive his hecatomb of bulls and rams, there he made merry, sitting at the feast, but the other gods were gathered in the halls of Olympian Zeus. Then among them the father of men and gods began to speak, for he bethought him in his heart of noble Aegisthus, whom the son of Agamemnon, far-famed Orestes, slew. Thinking upon him he spake out among the Immortals:

" 'Lo you now, how vainly mortal men do blame the gods! For of us they say comes evil, whereas they even of themselves, through the blindness of their own hearts, have sorrows beyond that which is ordained. Even as of late Aegisthus, beyond that which was ordained, took to him the wedded wife of the son of Atreus and killed her lord on his return, and that with sheer doom before his eyes, since we had warned him by the embassy of Hermes the keen-sighted, the slayer of Argos, that he should neither kill the man, nor woo his wife. . . .' "

The *Odyssey* (as everyone knows) abounds in passages borrowed from the *Iliad;* I had wished to print these in a slightly different type, with marginal references to the *Iliad,* and had marked them to this end in my MS. I found, however, that the translation would be thus hopelessly scholasticized, and abandoned my intention. I would nevertheless again urge on those who have the management of our University presses, that they would render a great service to students if they would publish a Greek text of the *Odyssey* with the Iliadic passages printed in a different type, and with marginal references. I have given the British Museum a copy of the *Odyssey* with the Iliadic passages underlined and referred to in MS.; I have also given an *Iliad* marked with all the Odyssean passages, and their references; but copies of both the *Iliad* and *Odyssey* so marked ought to be within easy reach of all students.

Anyone who at the present day discusses the questions that have arisen round the *Iliad* since Wolf's[3] time, without keeping it well before his reader's mind that the *Odyssey* was demonstrably written from one single neighborhood, and hence (even though nothing else pointed to this conclusion) presumably by one person only—that it was written certainly before 750, and in all probability before 1000 B.C.—that the writer of this very early poem was demonstrably familiar with the *Iliad* as we now have it, borrowing as freely from those books whose genuineness has been most impugned, as from those which are admitted to be by Homer—anyone who fails to keep these points well before his readers, is hardly dealing equitably by them. Anyone, on the other hand, who will mark his *Iliad* and his *Odyssey* from the copies in the British Museum above referred to, and who will draw the only inference that common sense can draw from the presence of so many identical passages in both poems, will, I believe, find no difficulty in assigning their proper value to a large number of books here and on the Continent that at present enjoy considerable reputations. Furthermore, and this perhaps is an advantage better worth securing, he will find many puzzles of the *Odyssey* cease to puzzle him on the discovery that they arise from oversaturation with the *Iliad*.

Other difficulties will also disappear as soon as the development of the poem in the writer's mind is understood. I have dealt with this at some length in *The Authoress of the Odyssey*. Briefly, the *Odyssey* consists of two distinct poems: (1) The Return of Ulysses, which alone the Muse is asked to sing in the opening lines of the poem. This poem includes the Phaeacian episode, and

---

[3] The German scholar, Wolf, was the founder of a school of modern higher critics who denied that Homer was the author of the *Iliad* and the *Odyssey*. He broke both poems up into separate folk lays, which he claimed had been composed at different times and only at a much later period united as we have them.

the account of Ulysses' adventures as told by himself in Books IX–XII. It consists of lines 1–79 (roughly) of Book I, of line 28 of Book V, and thence without intermission to the middle of line 187 of Book XIII, at which point the original scheme was abandoned.

(2) The story of Penelope and the suitors, with the episode of Telemachus' voyage to Pylos. This poem begins with line 80 (roughly) of Book I, is continued to the end of Book IV, and not resumed till Ulysses wakes in the middle of line 187, Book XIII, from whence it continues to the end of Book XXIV.

In *The Authoress of the Odyssey* I wrote:

"The introduction of lines xi, 115–137, and of line IX, 535, with the writing a new council of the gods at the beginning of Book V, to take the place of the one that was removed to Book I, 1–79, were the only things that were done to give even a semblance of unity to the old scheme and the new, and to conceal the fact that the Muse, after being asked to sing of one subject, spent two-thirds of her time in singing a very different one, with a climax for which no one has asked her. For roughly the Return occupies eight books, and Penelope and the Suitors sixteen."

I believe this to be substantially correct.

SAMUEL BUTLER
JULY 25, 1900

Principal Personages of *The Odyssey*, Their Parentage, and Position

(The names by which they were known to the Romans, when different from the Greek, are given in parentheses.)

Gods and Goddesses

ZEUS (Jupiter, Jove), son of Cronus (Saturn); king of the gods and ruler of the sky.

POSEIDON (Neptune), son of Cronus; king of the sea.

HADES, son of Cronus; ruler of the house of the dead.

ATHENE (Minerva), daughter of Zeus; goddess of skill and intelligence.

APOLLO, son of Zeus and Leto; archer god of light.

ARTEMIS (Diana), daughter of Zeus and Leto; huntress goddess of the woods.

APHRODITE (Venus), daughter of Zeus and Dione; goddess of love.

ARES (Mars), son of Zeus; god of war.

HEPHAESTUS (Vulcan), son of Zeus and Hera; god of metalworking and handicraft.

HERMES (Mercury), son of Zeus; messenger of the gods.

PERSEPHONE (Proserpina), daughter of Demeter; wife of Hades and queen of the underworld.

Lesser Divinities

PROTEUS, old man of the sea, one of the gods deposed by Zeus.

EIDOTHEA, daughter of Proteus; sea-nymph.

CALYPSO, daughter of Atlas; island nymph of Ogygia.

AEOLUS, son of Hippotas; keeper of the winds.

CIRCE, daughter of the sun; goddess of the wild, enchantress.

Family and Household of Odysseus

ODYSSEUS (Ulysses), son of Laertes; king of Ithaca.

LAERTES, son of Arceisius; aged father of Odysseus.

PENELOPE, daughter of Icarius; wife of Odysseus.

TELEMACHUS, son of Odysseus and Penelope.

MENTOR, friend and steward of Odysseus.

PHEMIUS, son of Terpes; minstrel in the house.

MEDON, herald.

EUMAEUS, son of Ctesius; keeper of Odysseus' swine.

MELANTHIUS, son of Dolius; keeper of the goats.

PHILOETIUS, keeper of the cattle.

DOLIUS, aged gardener and field worker.

EURYCLEA, daughter of Ops; old nurse of Odysseus and
Telemachus.

EURYNOME, head maid and housekeeper.

MELANTHO, daughter of Dolius; favored maid of Penelope.

EURYLOCHUS, husband of Odysseus' sister; sailor with Odysseus.

ELPENOR, youngest sailor with Odysseus.

Men of Ithaca and Suitors for the Hand of Penelope

AEGYPTIUS, aged lord in Ithaca.

HALITHERSES, son of Mastor; seer and prophet.

NOEMON, son of Phronius; shipowner.

PIRAEUS, son of Clytius; trusty friend of Telemachus.

EUPEITHES, lord in Ithaca.

IRUS, town beggar.

ANTINOUS, son of Eupeithes; leader of the suitors.

EURYMACHUS, son of Polybus;

LEIOCRITUS, son of Evenor;

AGELAUS, son of Damastor;

AMPHIMEDON, son of Melanus;

} suitors from Ithaca.

CTESIPPUS, son of Polytherses; suitor from Same.

AMPHINOMUS, son of Nisus; suitor from Dulichium.

LEIODES, son of Oenops; soothsayer for the suitors.

Persons met by Telemachus on his Trip to the Mainland

NESTOR, son of Neleus; aged king of Pylos, returned from Troy.

PISISTRATUS, son of Nestor.

MENELAUS, son of Atreus; king of Sparta, returned from Troy.

HELEN, daughter of Zeus and Leda; wife of Menelaus, brought back from Troy.

THEOCLYMENUS, son of Polypheides; fugitive seer from Argos, received by Telemachus.

Dwellers in the Land of the Phaeacians

ALCINOUS, son of Nausithous; king of the Phaeacians in Scheria.

ARETE, daughter of Rhexenor; wife of Alcinous and queen of the Phaeacians.

LAODAMAS, eldest son of Alcinous and Arete.

NAUSICAA, young daughter of Alcinous and Arete.

DEMODOCUS, blind bard at Alcinous' court.

EURYALUS, son of Naubolus; Phaeacian noble.

Monsters and Other Inhuman Beings

POLYPHEMUS, son of Poseidon; giant Cyclops and ogre.

ANTIPHATES, king of the cannibal Laestrygonians.

TWO SIRENS, fatal beguilers of men with their singing.

SCYLLA, daughter of Crataiis; six-headed monster and man-eater.

CHARYBDIS, a whirlpool which draws vessels to their doom.

Spirits of the Dead in the House of Hades

TEIRESIAS, blind prophet of Thebes.

ANTICLEIA, daughter of Autolycus; wife of Laertes and mother of Odysseus.

TYRO, daughter of Salmoneus; mother by Poseidon of Pelias and Neleus.

EPICASTE, also called Jocasta, mother and wife of Oedipus, king of Thebes.

AGAMEMNON, son of Atreus; king of the Greeks at Troy.

ACHILLES, son of Peleus; hero of the *Iliad.*

PATROCLUS, son of Menoetius; comrade of Achilles.

AJAX, son of Telamon; great warrior at Troy.

TITYUS
TANTALUS } spirits tormented in punishment.
SISYPHUS

SHADE OF HERACLES (Hercules), son of Zeus; heroic laborer for mankind.

NEW ARRIVALS, spirits of Elpenor and of the suitors.

Scene of Action

Island of Ithaca.

Nestor's home at Pylos.

Palace of Menelaus in Sparta.

Calypso's island of Ogygia in the West.

River mouth in Scheria, land of the Phaeacians, and palace of the king, Alcinous.

> *The names of the gods and goddesses and of the hero Odysseus, which our translator, Samuel Butler, turned into Latin forms, have in this edition been restored to the Greek.*

BOOK I

The gods in council agree that the time has come for Odysseus to be brought home to avenge himself on Penelope's suitors and to recover his kingdom. Hermes is sent to Calypso's isle to bid her release the captive Odysseus. Athene, disguised as Mentes, appears to Telemachus, advising him to call an assembly of the men of Ithaca, to complain of the behavior of the suitors; then to go himself in quest of his father to Pylos and Sparta.

TELL ME, O MUSE, OF THAT INGENIOUS HERO WHO TRAVELED FAR and wide after he had sacked the famous town of Troy. Many cities did he visit, and many were the nations with whose manners and customs he was acquainted; moreover he suffered much by sea while trying to save his own life and bring his men safely home; but do what he might he could not have his men, for they perished through their own sheer folly in eating the cattle of the Sun-god Hyperion; so the god prevented them from ever reaching home. Tell me, too, about all these things, O daughter of Zeus, from whatsoever source you may know them.

So now all who escaped death in battle or by shipwreck had got safely home except Odysseus, and he, though he was longing to return to his wife and country, was detained by the goddess Calypso, who had got him into a large cave and wanted to marry him. But as years went by, there came a time when the gods settled that he should go back to Ithaca; even then, however, when he was among his own people, his troubles were not yet over. Nevertheless, all the gods had now begun to pity him except Poseidon, who still persecuted him without ceasing and would not let him go home.

Now Poseidon had gone off to the Ethiopians, who are at the world's end, and lie in two halves, the one looking west and the other east.[1] He had gone there to accept a hecatomb of sheep and oxen, and was enjoying himself at his festival; but the other gods met in the house of Olympian Zeus, and the sire of gods and men spoke first. At that moment he was thinking of Aegisthus, who had been killed by Agamemnon's son Orestes;[2] so he said to the other gods:

"See now, how men lay blame upon us gods for what is after all nothing but their own folly. Look at Aegisthus; he must needs make love to Agamemnon's wife unrighteously and then kill Agamemnon, though he knew it would be the death of him; for I sent Hermes to warn him not to do either of these things, inasmuch as Orestes would be sure to take his revenge when he grew up and wanted to return home. Hermes told him this in all good will but he would not listen, and now he has paid for everything in full."

Then Athene said: "Father, son of Cronus, king of kings, it served Aegisthus right, and so it would anyone else who does as he did; but Aegisthus is neither here nor there; it is for Odysseus that my heart bleeds, when I think of his sufferings in that lonely sea-girt island, far away, poor man, from all his friends. It is an island covered with forest, in the very middle of the sea, and a goddess lives there, daughter of the magician Atlas, who looks after the bottom of the ocean, and carries the great columns that keep heaven and earth

---

[1] Black races are evidently known to the writer as stretching all across Africa, one half looking west on to the Atlantic, and the other east on to the Indian Ocean. (B.)

[2] Zeus refers here to the terrible homecoming of Agamemnon, king of Argos and chief of the Greeks at Troy, and his murder by the slave Aegisthus, whom Queen Clytemnestra had taken as her lover. Since then Agamemnon's and Clytemnestra's son, Orestes, had killed both his mother and Aegisthus to avenge his father's death. For fuller accounts of the same dreadful deed, see Books III, IV, and XI.

asunder. This daughter of Atlas has got hold of poor unhappy Odysseus, and keeps trying by every kind of blandishment to make him forget his home, so that he is tired of life, and thinks of nothing but how he may once more see the smoke of his own chimneys. You, sir, take no heed of this, and yet when Odysseus was before Troy did he not propitiate you with many a burnt sacrifice? Why then should you keep on being so angry with him?"

And Zeus said: "My child, what are you talking about? How can I forget Odysseus than whom there is no more capable man on earth, nor more liberal in his offerings to the immortal gods that live in heaven? Bear in mind, however, that Poseidon is still furious with Odysseus for having blinded an eye of Polyphemus, king of the Cyclopes. Polyphemus is son to Poseidon by the nymph Thoosa, daughter to the sea-king Phorcys; therefore though he will not kill Odysseus outright, he torments him by preventing him from getting home. Still, let us lay our heads together and see how we can help him to return; Poseidon will then be pacified, for if we are all of a mind he can hardly stand out against us."

And Athene said: "Father, son of Cronus, king of kings, if, then, the gods now mean that Odysseus should get home, we should first send Hermes to the Ogygian island to tell Calypso that we have made up our minds and that he is to return. In the meantime I will go to Ithaca, to put heart into Odysseus' son Telemachus; I will embolden him to call the Achaeans in assembly, and speak out to the suitors of his mother Penelope, who persist in eating up any number of his sheep and oxen; I will also conduct him to Sparta and to Pylos, to see if he can hear anything about the return of his dear father—for this will make people speak well of him."

So saying she bound on her glittering golden sandals, imperishable, with which she can fly like the wind over land or sea; she grasped the redoubtable bronze-shod spear, so stout and sturdy and strong, wherewith she quells the ranks of heroes who have displeased her, and down she darted from the topmost summits of Olympus, whereon forthwith she was in Ithaca, at the gateway of Odysseus' house, disguised as a visitor, Mentes, chief of the Taphians, and she held a bronze spear in her hand. There she found the lordly suitors seated on hides of the oxen which they had killed and eaten, and playing draughts in front of the house. Menservants and pages were bustling about to wait upon them, some mixing wine with water in the mixing bowls, some cleaning down the tables with wet sponges and laying them out again, and some cutting up great quantities of meat.

Telemachus saw her long before anyone else did. He was sitting moodily among the suitors thinking about his brave father, and how he would send them flying out of the house, if he were to come to his own again and be honored as in days gone by. Thus brooding as he sat among them, he caught sight of Athene and went straight to the gate, for he was vexed that a stranger should be kept waiting for admittance. He took her right hand in his own, and bade her give him her spear. "Welcome," said he, "to our house, and when you have partaken of food you shall tell us what you have come for."

He led the way as he spoke, and Athene followed him. When they were within he took her spear and set it in the spear-stand against a strong bearing-post along with the many other spears of his unhappy father, and he conducted her to a richly decorated seat under which he threw a cloth of damask. There was a footstool also for her feet,[3] and he set another seat near her for himself, away from the suitors, that she might not be annoyed while eating by their noise and insolence, and that he might ask her more freely about his father.

A maidservant then brought them water in a beautiful golden ewer and poured it into a silver basin for them to wash their hands, and she drew a clean table beside them. An upper servant brought them bread, and offered them many good things of what there was in the house, the carver fetched them plates of all manner of meats and set cups of gold by their side, and a manservant brought them wine and poured it out for them.

[3] The original use of the footstool was probably less to test the feet than to keep them (especially when bare) from a floor which was often wet and dirty. (B.)

Then the suitors came in and took their places on the benches and seats. Forthwith menservants poured water over their hands, maids went round with the bread-baskets, pages filled the mixing bowls with wine and water, and they laid their hands upon the good things that were before them. As soon as they had had enough to eat and drink they wanted music and dancing, which are the crowning embellishments of a banquet, so a servant brought a lyre to Phemius, whom they compelled perforce to sing to them. As soon as he touched his lyre and began to sing, Telemachus spoke low to Athene, with his head close to hers that no man might hear.

"I hope, sir," said he, "that you will not be offended with what I am going to say. Singing comes cheap to those who do not pay for it, and all this is done at the cost of one whose bones lie rotting in some wilderness or grinding to powder in the surf. If these men were to see my father come back to Ithaca they would pray for longer legs rather than a longer purse, for money would not serve them; but he, alas, has fallen on an ill fate, and even when people do sometimes say that he is coming, we no longer heed them; we shall never see him again. And now, sir, tell me and tell me true, who you are and where you come from. Tell me of your town and parents, what manner of ship you came in, how your crew brought you to Ithaca, and of what nation they declared themselves to be—for you cannot have come by land. Tell me also truly, for I want to know, are you a stranger to this house, or have you been here in my father's time? In the old days we had many visitors for my father went about much himself."

And Athene answered: "I will tell you truly and particularly all about it. I am Mentes son of Anchialus, and I am king of the Taphians. I have come here with my ship and crew, on a voyage to men of a foreign tongue being bound for Temesa[4] with a cargo of iron, and I shall bring back copper. As for my ship, it lies over yonder off the open country away from the town, in the

---

[4] Temesa was on the West Coast of the toe of Italy, in what is now the gulf of Sta Eufemia. It was famous in remote times for its copper mines. (B.)

harbor Rheithron under the wooded mountain Neritum. Our fathers were friends before us, as old Laertes will tell you, if you will go and ask him. They say, however, that he never comes to town now, and lives by himself in the country, faring hardly, with an old woman to look after him and get his dinner for him, when he comes in tired from pottering about his vineyard. They told me your father was at home again, and that was why I came, but it seems the gods are still keeping him back, for he is not dead yet—not on the mainland. It is more likely he is on some sea-girt island in midocean, or a prisoner among savages who are detaining him against his will. I am no prophet, and know very little about omens, but I speak as it is borne in upon me from heaven, and assure you that he will not be away much longer; for he is a man of such resource that even though he were in chains of iron he would find some means of getting home again. But tell me, and tell me true, can Odysseus really have such a fine-looking fellow for a son? You are indeed wonderfully like him about the head and eyes, for we were close friends before he set sail for Troy where the flower of all the Argives went also. Since that time we have never either of us seen the other."

"My mother," answered Telemachus, "tells me I am son to Odysseus, but it is a wise child that knows his own father. Would that I were son to one who had grown old upon his own estates, for, since you ask me, there is no more ill-starred man under heaven than he who they tell me is my father."

And Athene said: "There is no fear of your race dying out yet, while Penelope has such a fine son as you are. But tell me, and tell me true, what is the meaning of all this feasting, and who are these people? What is it all about? Have you some banquet, or is there a wedding in the family—for no one seems to be bringing any provisions of his own? And the guests—how atrociously they are behaving; what riot they make over the whole house; it is enough to disgust any respectable person who comes near them."

"Sir," said Telemachus, "as regards your question, so long as my father was here it was well with us and with the house, but the gods in their displeasure have willed it otherwise, and have hidden him away more closely than mortal man was ever yet hidden. I could have borne it better even though he were dead, if he had fallen with his men before Troy, or had died with friends around him when the days of his fighting were done; for then the Achaeans would have built a mound over his ashes, and I should myself have been heir to his renown; but now the storm winds have spirited him away we know not whither; he is gone without leaving so much as a trace behind him, and I inherit nothing but dismay. Nor does the matter end simply with grief for the loss of my father; heaven has laid sorrows upon me of yet another kind; for the chiefs from all our islands, Dulichium, Same, and the woodland island of Zacynthus, as also all the principal men of Ithaca itself, are eating up my house under the pretext of paying their court to my mother, who will neither point-blank say that she will not marry, nor yet bring matters to an end; so they are making havoc of my estate, and before long will do so also with myself."

"Is that so?" exclaimed Athene. "Then you do indeed want Odysseus home again. Give him his helmet, shield, and a couple of lances, and if he is the man he was when I first knew him in our house, drinking and making merry, he would soon lay his hands about these rascally suitors, were he to stand once more upon his own threshold. He was then coming from Ephyra, where he had been to beg poison for his arrows from Ilus son of Mermerus. Ilus feared the ever-living gods and would not give him any, but my father let him have some, for he was very fond of him. If Odysseus is the man he then was, these suitors will have a short shrift and a sorry wedding.

"But there! It rests with heaven to determine whether he is to return, and take his revenge in his own house or no; I would, however, urge you to set about trying to get rid of these suitors at once. Take my advice, call the Achaean heroes in assembly tomorrow morning—lay your case before them, and call heaven to bear you witness. Bid the suitors take themselves off, each to his own place, and if your mother's mind is set on marrying again, let her go back to her father, who will find her a husband and provide her with all the marriage gifts that so dear a daughter may expect. As for yourself, let me prevail upon you to take the best ship you can get, with a crew of twenty men, and go in quest of your father who has so long been missing. Someone may tell you something, or (and people often hear things in this way) some heaven-sent message may direct you. First go to Pylos and ask Nestor; thence go on to Sparta and visit Menelaus, for he got home last of all the Achaeans; if you hear that your father is alive and on his way home, you can put up with the waste these suitors will make for yet another twelve months. If on the other hand you hear of his death, come home at once, celebrate his funeral rites with all due pomp, build a barrow to his memory, and make your mother marry again. Then, having done all this, think it well over in your mind how, by fair means or foul, you may kill these suitors in your own house. You are too old to plead infancy any longer; have you not heard how people are singing Orestes' praises for having killed his father's murderer Aegisthus? You are a fine, smart-looking fellow; show your mettle, then, and make yourself a name in story. Now, however, I must go back to my ship and to my crew, who will be impatient if I keep them waiting longer, think the matter over for yourself, and remember what I have said to you."

"Sir," answered Telemachus, "it has been very kind of you to talk to me in this way, as though I were your own son, and I will do all you tell me. I know you want to be getting on with your voyage, but stay a little longer till you have taken a bath and refreshed yourself. I will then give you a present, and you shall go on your way rejoicing; I will give you one of great beauty and value—a keepsake such as only dear friends give to one another."

Athene answered, "Do not try to keep me, for I would be on my way at once. As for any present you may be disposed to make me, keep it till I come again, and I will take it home with me. You shall give me a very good one, and I will give you one of no less value in return."

With these words she flew away like a bird into the air, but she had given Telemachus courage, and had made him think more than ever about his father. He felt the change, wondered at it, and knew that the stranger had been a god, so he went straight to where the suitors were sitting.

Phemius was still singing, and his hearers sat rapt in silence as he told the sad tale of the return from Troy, and the ills Athene had laid upon the Achaeans. Penelope daughter of Icarius heard his song from her room upstairs, and came down by the great staircase, not alone, but attended by two of her handmaids. When she reached the suitors she stood by one of the bearingposts that supported the roof of the cloisters,[5] with a staid maiden on either side of her. She held a veil, moreover, before her face, and was weeping bitterly.

"Phemius," she cried, "you know many another feat of gods and heroes, such as poets love to celebrate. Sing the suitors some one of these, and let them drink their wine in silence, but cease this sad tale, for it breaks my sorrowful heart, and reminds me of my lost husband whom I mourn ever without ceasing, and whose name was great over all Hellas and middle Argos."

"Mother," answered Telemachus, "let the bard sing what he has a mind to; bards do not make the ills they sing of; it is Zeus, not they, who makes them, and who sends weal or woe upon mankind according to his own good pleasure. This fellow means no harm by singing the ill-fated return of the Danaans, for people always applaud the latest songs most warmly. Make up your mind to it and bear it; Odysseus is not the only man who never came back from Troy, but many another went down as well as he. Go, then, within the house and busy yourself with your daily duties, your loom, your distaff, and the ordering of your servants; for speech is man's matter, and mine above all others—for it is I who am master here."

She went wondering back into the house, and laid her son's saying in her heart. Then, going upstairs with her handmaids into her room, she mourned her dear husband till Athene shed sweet sleep over her eyes. But the suitors

---

[5] See note on these cloisters. Book XVIII.

were clamorous throughout the covered cloisters,[6] and prayed each one that he might be her bedfellow.

Then Telemachus spoke. "Shameless," he cried, "and insolent suitors, let us feast at our pleasure now, and let there be no brawling, for it is a rare thing to hear a man with such a divine voice as Phemius has; but in the morning meet me in full assembly that I may give you formal notice to depart, and feast at one another's houses, turn and turn about, at your own cost. If, on the other hand, you choose to persist in sponging upon one man, heaven help me, but Zeus shall reckon with you in full, and when you fall in my father's house there shall be no man to avenge you."

The suitors bit their lips as they heard him, and marveled at the boldness of his speech. Then, Antinous son of Eupeithes said, "The gods seem to have given you lessons in bluster and tall talking; may Zeus never grant you to be chief in Ithaca as your father was before you."

Telemachus answered: "Antinous, do not chide with me, but, god willing, I will be chief too if I can. Is this the worst fate you can think of for me? It is no bad thing to be a chief, for it brings both riches and honor. Still, now that Odysseus is dead there are many great men in Ithaca both old and young, and some other may take the lead among them. Nevertheless, I will be chief in my own house, and will rule those whom Odysseus has won for me."

Then Eurymachus son of Polybus answered: "It rests with heaven to decide who shall be chief among us, but you shall be master in your own house and over your own possessions; while there is a man in Ithaca no one shall do you violence or rob you. And now, my good fellow, I want to know about this stranger. What country does he come from? Of what family is he, and where is his estate? Has he brought you news about the return of your

---

[6] The whole inner court that made the forepart off the house had a covered cloister running around it. This covered part was distinguished by being called "shady" or "shadow-giving." It was in this part that the tables for the suitors were laid. The arrangement is still common in Sicily and the Greek islands.

father, or was he on business of his own? He seemed a well-to-do man, but he hurried off so suddenly that he was gone in a moment before we could get to know him."

"My father is dead and gone," answered Telemachus, "and even if some rumor reaches me I put no more faith in it now. My mother does indeed sometimes send for a soothsayer and question him, but I give his prophesyings no heed. As for the stranger, he was Mentes son of Anchialus, chief of the Taphians, an old friend of my father's." But in his heart he knew that it had been the goddess.

The suitors then returned to their singing and dancing until the evening; but when night fell upon their pleasuring they went home to bed each in his own abode.[7] Telemachus' room was high up in a tower that looked on to the outer court; hither, then, he hied, brooding and full of thought. A good old woman, Euryclea, daughter of Ops the son of Pisenor, went before him with a couple of blazing torches. Laertes had bought her with his own money when she was quite young; he gave the worth of twenty oxen for her, and showed as much respect to her in his household as he did to his own wedded wife, but he did not take her to his bed for he feared his wife's resentment. She it was who now lighted Telemachus to his room, and she loved him better than any of the other women in the house did, for she had nursed him when he was a baby. He opened the door of his bedroom and sat down upon the bed; as he took off his shirt he gave it to the good old woman, who folded it tidily up, and hung it for him over a peg by his bedside, after which she went out, pulled the door to by a silver catch, and drew the bolt home by means of the strap. But Telemachus as he lay covered with a woolen fleece kept thinking all night through of his intended voyage and of the counsel that Athene had given him.

[7] The reader will note that none of the suitors were allowed to sleep in Odysseus' house. (B.)

Book II

*Telemachus manfully calls an assembly and presents his grievances,
appealing to the suitors to stop wasting his substance and to quit his house.
Disregarding his appeal, the suitors taunt him. Telemachus prays to Athene
and hastens his preparations for the journey, aided by the goddess and the old
nurse Euryclea. At nightfall Athene causes the suitors to fall into a deep
slumber, and herself sets sail with Telemachus for Pylos.*

NOW WHEN THE CHILD OF MORNING, ROSY-FINGERED DAWN, APPEARED, Telemachus rose and dressed himself. He bound his sandals on to his comely feet, girded his sword about his shoulder, and left his room looking like an immortal god. He at once sent the criers round to call the people in assembly, so they called them and the people gathered thereon. Then, when they were got together, he went to the place of assembly spear in hand—not alone, for his two hounds went with him. Athene endowed him with a presence of such divine comeliness that all marveled at him as he went by, and when he took his place in his father's seat even the oldest councilors made way for him.

Aegyptius, a man bent double with age, and of infinite experience, was the first to speak. His son Antiphus had gone with Odysseus to Ilium, land of noble steeds, but the savage Cyclops had killed him when they were all shut up in the cave, and had cooked his last dinner for him.[1] He had three

---

[1] Aegyptius cannot of course know of the fate Antiphus had met with, for there had as yet been no news of or from Odysseus. (B.)

sons left, of whom two still worked on their father's land, while the third, Eurynomus, was one of the suitors. Nevertheless, their father could not get over the loss of Antiphus, and was still weeping for him when he began his speech.

"Men of Ithaca," he said, "hear my words. From the day Odysseus left us there has been no meeting of our councilors until now. Who then can it be, whether old or young, that finds it so necessary to convene us? Has he got wind of some host approaching, and does he wish to warn us, or would he speak upon some other matter of public moment? I am sure he is an excellent person, and I hope Zeus will grant him his heart's desire."

Telemachus took this speech as of good omen and rose at once, for he was bursting with what he had to say. He stood in the middle of the assembly and the good herald Pisenor brought him his staff. Then, turning to Aegyptius, "Sir," said he, "it is I, as you will shortly learn, who have convened you, for it is I who am the most aggrieved. I have not got wind of any host approaching about which I would warn you, nor is there any matter of public moment on which I would speak. My grievance is purely personal, and turns on two great misfortunes which have fallen upon my house. The first of these is the loss of my excellent father, who was chief among all you here present, and was like a father to every one of you; the second is much more serious, and ere long will be the utter ruin of my estate. The sons of all the chief men among you are pestering my mother to marry them against her will. They are afraid to go to her father Icarius, asking him to choose the one he likes best, and to provide marriage gifts for his daughter, but day by day they keep hanging about my father's house, sacrificing our oxen, sheep, and fat goats for their banquets, and never giving so much as a thought to the quantity of wine they drink. No estate can stand such recklessness. We have now no Odysseus to ward off harm from our doors, and I cannot hold my own against them. I shall never all my days be as good a man as he was; still I would indeed defend myself if I had power to do so, for I cannot stand such treatment any longer; my house is being disgraced and ruined. Have respect, therefore, to your own consciences and to public opinion. Fear, too, the wrath of heaven, lest the gods should be displeased and turn upon you. I pray you by Zeus and Themis, who is the beginning and the end of counsels, do not hold back, my friends, and leave me singlehanded—unless it be that my brave father Odysseus did some wrong to the Achaeans which you would now avenge on me, by aiding and abetting these suitors. Moreover, if I am to be eaten out of house and home at all, I had rather you did the eating yourselves, for I could then take action against you to some purpose, and serve you with notices from house to house till I got paid in full, whereas now I have no remedy."[2]

With this Telemachus dashed his staff to the ground and burst into tears. Everyone was very sorry for him, but they all sat still and no one ventured to make him an angry answer, save only Antinous, who spoke thus:

"Telemachus, insolent braggart that you are, how dare you try to throw the blame upon us suitors? It is your mother's fault, not ours, for she is a very artful woman. This three years past, and close on four, she has been driving us out of our minds by encouraging each one of us, and sending him messages without meaning one word of what she says. And then there was that other trick she played us. She set up a great tambour frame in her room, and began to work on an enormous piece of fine needlework. 'Sweet hearts,' said she, 'Odysseus is indeed dead, still do not press me to marry again immediately, wait—for I would not have my skill in needlework perish unrecorded—till I have completed a pall for the hero Laertes, to be in readiness against the time when death shall take him. He is very rich, and the women of the place will talk if he is laid out without a pall.'

"This was what she said, and we assented; whereon we could see her working on her great web all day long, but at night she would unpick the stitches again by torchlight. She fooled us in this way for three years and we

---

[2] That is, you have money, and could pay when I got judgment, whereas the suitors are men of straw. (B.)

never found her out, but as time wore on and she was now in her fourth year, one of her maids who knew what she was doing told us, and we caught her in the act of undoing her work, so she had to finish it whether she would or no. The suitors, therefore, make you this answer, that both you and the Achaeans may understand: 'Send your mother away, and bid her marry the man of her own and of her father's choice'; for I do not know what will happen if she goes on plaguing us much longer with the airs she gives herself on the score of the accomplishments Athene has taught her, and because she is so clever. We never yet heard of such a woman; we know all about Tyro, Alcmena, Mycene, and the famous women of old, but they were nothing to your mother, any one of them. It was not fair of her to treat us in that way, and as long as she continues in the mind with which heaven has now endowed her, so long shall we go on eating up your estate; and I do not see why she should change, for she gets all the honor and glory, and it is you who pay for it, not she. Understand, then, that we will not go back to our lands, neither here nor elsewhere, till she has made her choice and married some one or other of us."

Telemachus answered: "Antinous, how can I drive the mother who bore me from my father's house? My father is abroad and we do not know whether he is alive or dead. It will be hard on me if I have to pay Icarius the large sum which I must give him if I insist on sending his daughter back to him. Not only will he deal rigorously with me, but heaven will also punish me; for my mother when she leaves the house will call on the Furies to avenge her; besides, it would not be a creditable thing to do, and I will have nothing to say to it. If you choose to take offense at this, leave the house and feast elsewhere at one another's house at your own cost, turn and turn about. If, on the other hand, you elect to persist in sponging upon one man, heaven help me, but Zeus shall reckon with you in full, and when you fall in my father's house there shall be no man to avenge you."

As he spoke Zeus sent two eagles from the top of the mountain, and they flew on and on with the wind, sailing side by side in their own lordly flight.

When they were right over the middle of the assembly they wheeled and circled about, beating the air with their wings and glaring death into the eyes of them that were below; then, fighting fiercely and tearing at one another, they flew off towards the right over the town. The people wondered as they saw them, and asked each other what all this might be; whereon Halitherses, who was the best prophet and reader of omens among them, spoke to them plainly and in all honesty, saying:

"Hear me, men of Ithaca, and I speak more particularly to the suitors, for I see mischief brewing for them. Odysseus is not going to be away much longer; indeed he is close at hand to deal out death and destruction, not on them alone, but on many another of us who live in Ithaca. Let us then be wise in time, and put a stop to this wickedness before he comes. Let the suitors do so of their own accord; it will be better for them, for I am not prophesying without due knowledge; everything has happened to Odysseus as I foretold when the Argives set out for Troy, and he with them. I said that after going through much hardship and losing all his men he should come home again in the twentieth year and that no one would know him; and now all this is coming true."

Eurymachus son of Polybus then said: "Go home, old man, and prophesy to your own children, or it may be worse for them. I can read these omens myself much better than you can; birds are always flying about in the sunshine somewhere or other, but they seldom mean anything. Odysseus has died in a far country, and it is a pity you are not dead along with him, instead of prating here about omens and adding fuel to the anger of Telemachus which is fierce enough as it is. I suppose you think he will give you something for your family, but I tell you—and it shall surely be—when an old man like you, who should know better, talks a young one over till he becomes troublesome, in the first place his young friend will only fare so much the worse—he will take nothing by it, for the suitors will prevent this—and in the next, we will lay a heavier fine, sir, upon yourself than you will at all like paying, for it will bear hardly upon you. As for Telemachus, I warn him in the presence of you all to send his mother back to her father, who will find her a husband and provide her with all the marriage gifts so dear a daughter may expect. Till then we shall go on harassing him with our suit; for we fear no man, and care neither for him, with all his fine speeches, nor for any fortune-telling of yours. You may preach as much as you please, but we shall only hate you the more. We shall go back and continue to eat up Telemachus' estate without paying him, till such time as his mother leaves off tormenting us by keeping us day after day on the tiptoe of expectation, each vying with the other in his suit for a prize of such rare perfection. Besides, we cannot go after the other women whom we should marry in due course, but for the way in which she treats us."

Then Telemachus said: "Eurymachus, and you other suitors, I shall say no more, and entreat you no further, for the gods and the people of Ithaca now know my story. Give me, then, a ship and a crew of twenty men to take me hither and thither, and I will go to Sparta and to Pylos in quest of my father who has so long been missing. Someone may tell me something, or (and people often hear things in this way) some heaven-sent message may direct me. If I can hear of him as alive and on his way home I will put up with the waste you suitors will make for yet another twelve months. If, on the other hand, I hear of his death, I will return at once, celebrate his funeral rites with all due pomp, build a barrow to his memory, and make my mother marry again."

With these words he sat down, and Mentor, who had been a friend of Odysseus and had been left in charge of everything with full authority over the servants, rose to speak. He, then, plainly and in all honesty addressed them thus:

"Hear me, men of Ithaca, I hope that you may never have a kind and well-disposed ruler any more, nor one who will govern you equitably; I hope that all your chiefs henceforward may be cruel and unjust, for there is not one of you but has forgotten Odysseus, who ruled you as though he were your father.

I am not half so angry with the suitors, for if they choose to do violence in the naughtiness of their hearts, and wager their heads that Odysseus will not return, they can take the high hand and eat up his estate, but as for you others I am shocked at the way in which you all sit still without even trying to stop such scandalous goings on—which you could do if you chose, for you are many and they are few."

Leiocritus son of Evenor answered him, saying: "Mentor, what folly is all this, that you should set the people to stay us? It is a hard thing for one man to fight with many about his victuals. Even though Odysseus himself were to set upon us while we are feasting in his house and do his best to oust us, his wife, who wants him back so very badly, would have small cause for rejoicing, and his blood would be upon his own head if he fought against such great odds. There is no sense in what you have been saying. Now, therefore, do you people go about your business, and let his father's old friends, Mentor and Halitherses, speed this boy on his journey, if he goes at all—which I do not think he will, for he is more likely to stay where he is till someone comes and tells him something."

On this he broke up the assembly, and every man went back to his own abode, while the suitors returned to the house of Odysseus.

Then Telemachus went all alone by the seaside, washed his hands in the gray waves, and prayed to Athene.

"Hear me," he cried, "you god who visited me yesterday, and bade me sail the seas in search of my father who has so long been missing. I would obey you, but the Achaeans, and more particularly the wicked suitors, are hindering me that I cannot do so."

As he thus prayed, Athene came close up to him in the likeness and with the voice of Mentor. "Telemachus," said she, "if you are made of the same stuff as your father, you will be neither fool nor coward henceforward, for Odysseus never broke his word nor left his work half done. If, then, you take after him, your voyage will not be fruitless, but unless you have the blood of Odysseus and of Penelope in your veins I see no likelihood of your succeeding. Sons are seldom as good men as their fathers; they are generally worse, not better. Still, as you are not going to be either fool or coward henceforward, and are not entirely without some share of your father's wise discernment, I look with hope upon your undertaking. But mind you never make common cause with any of those foolish suitors, for they have neither sense nor virtue, and give no thought to death and to the doom that will shortly fall on one and all of them, so that they shall perish on the same day. As for your voyage, it shall not be long delayed. Your father was such an old friend of mine that I will find you a ship and will come with you myself. Now, however, return home, and go about among the suitors; begin getting provisions ready for your voyage; see everything well-stowed, the wine in jars, and the barley meal, which is the staff of life, in leathern bags, while I go round the town and beat up volunteers at once. There are many ships in Ithaca both old and new; I will run my eye over them for you and will choose the best; we will get her ready and will put out to sea without delay."

Thus spoke Athene daughter of Zeus, and Telemachus lost no time in doing as the goddess told him. He went moodily home, and found the suitors flaying goats and singeing pigs in the outer court.[3] Antinous came up to him at once and laughed as he took his hand in his own, saying, "Telemachus, my fine fire-eater, bear no more ill blood neither in word nor deed, but eat and drink with us as you used to do. The Achaeans will supply you with everything—a ship and a picked crew to boot—so that you can set sail for Pylos at once and get news of your noble father."

"Antinous," answered Telemachus, "I cannot eat in peace, nor take pleasure of any kind with such men as you are. Was it not enough that you should

---

[3] The walled outer court, closed by a great gateway, formed the approach to the house. Around it stood the barns, storehouses, and other outbuildings, and in the center a large altar.

waste so much good property of mine while I was yet a boy? Now that I am older and know about it, I am also stronger, and whether here among this people, or by going to Pylos, I will do you all the harm I can. I shall go, and my going will not be in vain—though, thanks to you suitors, I have neither ship nor crew of my own, and must be passenger not captain."

As he spoke he snatched his hand from that of Antinous. Meanwhile the others went on getting dinner ready about the buildings, jeering at him tauntingly as they did so.

"Telemachus," said one youngster, "means to be the death of us. I suppose he thinks he can bring friends to help him from Pylos, or again from Sparta, where he seems bent on going. Or will he go to Ephyra as well, for poison to put in our wine and kill us?"

Another said: "Perhaps if Telemachus goes on board ship, he will be like his father and perish far from his friends. In this case we should have plenty to do, for we could then divide up his property among us. As for the house, we can let his mother and the man who marries her have that."

This was how they talked. But Telemachus went down into the lofty and spacious storeroom where his father's treasure of gold and bronze lay heaped up upon the floor, and where the linen and spare clothes were kept in oaken chests. Here, too, there was a store of fragrant olive oil, while casks of old well-ripened wine, unblended and fit for a god to drink, were ranged against the wall in case Odysseus should come home again after all. The room was closed with well-made doors opening in the middle; moreover, the faithful old housekeeper Euryclea, daughter of Ops the son of Pisenor, was in charge of everything both night and day. Telemachus called her to the storeroom and said:

"Nurse, draw me off some of the best wine you have, after what you are keeping for my father's own drinking, in case, poor man, he should escape death, and find his way home again after all. Let me have twelve jars, and see that they all have lids; also fill me some well-sewn leathern bags with barley meal—about twenty measures in all. Get these things put together at once, and say nothing about it. I will take everything away this evening as soon as my mother has gone upstairs for the night. I am going to Sparta and to Pylos to see if I can hear anything about the return of my dear father."

When Euryclea heard this she began to cry, and spoke fondly to him, saying: "My dear child, whatever can have put such a notion as that into your head? Where in the world do you want to go to—you, who are the one hope of the house? Your poor father is dead and gone in some foreign country nobody knows where, and as soon as your back is turned these wicked ones here will be scheming to get you put out of the way, and will share all your possessions among themselves; stay where you are among your own people, and do not go wandering and worrying your life out on the barren ocean."

"Fear not, nurse," answered Telemachus, "my scheme is not without heaven's sanction; but swear that you will say nothing about all this to my mother, till I have been away some ten or twelve days, unless she hears of my having gone, and asks you; for I do not want her to spoil her beauty by crying."

The old woman swore most solemnly that she would not, and when she had completed her oath, she began drawing off the wine into jars, and getting the barley meal into the bags, while Telemachus went back to the suitors.

Then Athene bethought her of another matter. She took his shape, and went round the town to each one of the crew, telling them to meet at the ship by sundown. She went also to Noemon son of Phronius, and asked him to let her have a ship—which he was very ready to do. When the sun had set and darkness was over all the land, she got the ship into the water, put all the tackle on board her that ships generally carry, and stationed her at the end of the harbor. Presently the crew came up, and the goddess spoke encouragingly to each of them.

Furthermore, she went to the house of Odysseus, and threw the suitors into a deep slumber. She caused their drink to fuddle them, and made them drop their cups from their hands, so that instead of sitting over their wine, they went back into the town to sleep, with their eyes heavy and full of drowsiness. Then she took the form and voice of Mentor, and called Telemachus to come outside.

"Telemachus," said she, "the men are on board and at their oars, waiting for you to give your orders, so make haste and let us be off."

On this she led the way, while Telemachus followed in her steps. When they got to the ship they found the crew waiting by the water side, and Telemachus said, "Now my men, help me to get the stores on board; they are all put together in the cloister, and my mother does not know anything about it, nor any of the maidservants except one."

With these words he led the way and the others followed after. When they had brought the things as he told them, Telemachus went on board, Athene going before him and taking her seat in the stern of the vessel, while Telemachus sat beside her. Then the men loosed the hawsers and took their places on the benches. Athene sent them a fair wind from the west that whistled over the deep blue waves, whereon Telemachus told them to catch hold of the ropes and hoist sail, and they did as he told them. They set the mast in its socket in the cross plank, raised it, and made it fast with the forestays; then they hoisted their white sails aloft with ropes of twisted oxhide. As the sail bellied out with the wind, the ship flew through the deep blue water, and the foam hissed against her bows as she sped onward. Then they made all fast throughout the ship, filled the mixing bowls to the brim, and made drink offerings to the immortal gods that are from everlasting, but more particularly to the gray-eyed daughter of Zeus.

Thus, then, the ship sped on her way through the watches of the night from dark till dawn.

Book III

*Telemachus is warmly welcomed by Nestor in Pylos and joins in celebrating
the festival of Poseidon. Nestor tells stories of the return of himself and the
other heroes from Troy, but knows nothing of the fate of Odysseus. The next
day sacrifices are offered for Telemachus' success. Nestor sends his son
Pisistratus with Telemachus, as he continues his journey to Sparta by land.*

A S THE SUN WAS RISING FROM THE FAIR SEA INTO THE FIRMAMENT OF
heaven to shed light on mortals and immortals, they reached
Pylos, the city of Neleus. Now the people of Pylos were gathered
on the seashore to offer sacrifice of black bulls to Poseidon lord of the earth-
quake. There were nine guilds with five hundred men in each, and there
were nine bulls to each guild. As they were eating the inward meats[1] and
burning the thighbones [on the embers] in the name of Poseidon, Telemachus
and his crew arrived, furled their sails, brought their ship to anchor, and
went ashore.

Athene led the way and Telemachus followed her. Presently she said,
"Telemachus, you must not be in the least shy or nervous. You have taken this
voyage to try and find out where your father is buried and how he came by his
end; so go straight up to Nestor that we may see what he has got to tell us. Beg
of him to speak the truth, and he will tell no lies, for he is an excellent person."

---

[1] The heart, liver, lights, kidneys, etc., were taken out from the inside and eaten first as being
more readily cooked: the bone meat was cooking while the inward meats were being eaten.
I imagine that the thighbones made a kind of gridiron, while at the same time the marrow
inside them got cooked. (B.)

"But how, Mentor," replied Telemachus, "dare I go up to Nestor, and how am I to address him? I have never yet been used to holding long conversations with people, and am ashamed to begin questioning one who is so much older than myself."

"Some things, Telemachus," answered Athene, "will be suggested to you by your own instinct, and heaven will prompt you further; for I am assured that the gods have been with you from the time of your birth until now."

She then went quickly on, and Telemachus followed in her steps till they reached the place where the guilds of the Pylian people were assembled. There they found Nestor sitting with his sons, while his company round him were busy getting dinner ready, and putting pieces of meat on to the spits[2] while other pieces were cooking. When they saw the strangers they crowded round them, took them by the hand, and bade them take their places. Nestor's son Pisistratus at once offered his hand to each of them, and seated them on some soft sheep skins that were lying on the sands near his father and his brother Thrasymedes. Then he gave them their portions of the inward meats and poured wine for them into a golden cup, handing it to Athene first, and saluting her at the same time.

"Offer a prayer, sir," said he, "to King Poseidon, for it is his feast that you are joining. When you have duly prayed and made your drink offering, pass the cup to your friend that he may do so also. I doubt not that he too lifts his hands in prayer, for man cannot live without God in the world. Still he is younger than you are, and is much of an age with myself, so I will give you the precedence."

As he spoke he handed her the cup. Athene thought it very right and proper of him to have given it to herself first; she accordingly began praying

---

[2] The meat would be pierced with the skewer, and laid over the ashes to grill—the two ends of the skewer being supported in whatever way might be found convenient. Meat so cooking may be seen in any eating house in Smyrna, or any Eastern town. When I rode across the Troad from the Dardanelles to Hissarlik and Mount Ida, I noticed that my dragoman and his men did all our outdoor cooking exactly in the Odyssean and Iliadic fashion. (B.)

heartily to Poseidon. "O thou," she cried, "that encirclest the earth, vouchsafe to grant the prayers of thy servants that call upon thee. More especially we pray thee send down thy grace on Nestor and on his sons; thereafter also make the rest of the Pylian people some handsome return for the goodly hecatomb they are offering you. Lastly, grant Telemachus and myself a happy issue, in respect of the matter that has brought us in our ship to Pylos."

When she had thus made an end of praying, she handed the cup to Telemachus and he prayed likewise. By and by, when the outer meats were roasted and had been taken off the spits, the carvers gave every man his portion and they all made an excellent dinner. As soon as they had had enough to eat and drink, Nestor, knight of Gerene, began to speak.

"Now," said he, "that our guests have done their dinner, it will be best to ask them who they are. Who, then, sir strangers, are you, and from what port have you sailed? Are you traders? or do you sail the seas as rovers with your hand against every man, and every man's hand against you?"

Telemachus answered boldly, for Athene had given him courage to ask about his father and get himself a good name.

"Nestor," said he, "son of Neleus, honor to the Achaean name, you ask whence we come, and I will tell you. We come from Ithaca under Neritum, and the matter about which I would speak is of private not public import. I seek news of my unhappy father Odysseus, who is said to have sacked the town of Troy in company with yourself. We know what fate befell each one of the other heroes who fought at Troy, but as regards Odysseus heaven has hidden from us the knowledge even that he is dead at all, for no one can certify us in what place he perished, nor say whether he fell in battle on the mainland or was lost at sea amid the waves of Amphitrite. Therefore I am suppliant at your knees, if haply you may be pleased to tell me of his melancholy end, whether you saw it with your own eyes, or heard it from some other traveler, for he was a man born to trouble. Do not soften things out of any pity for me, but tell me in all plainness exactly what you saw. If my brave father Odysseus ever did you loyal service, either by word or deed, when you Achaeans were harassed among the Trojans, bear it in mind now as in my favor and tell me truly all."

"My friend," answered Nestor, "you recall a time of much sorrow to my mind, for the brave Achaeans suffered much both at sea, while privateering under Achilles, and when fighting before the great city of King Priam. Our best men all of them fell there—Ajax, Achilles, Patroclus, peer of gods in counsel, and my own dear son Antilochus, a man singularly fleet of foot and in fight valiant. But we suffered much more than this; what mortal tongue indeed could tell the whole story? Though you were to stay here and question me for five years, or even six, I could not tell you all that the Achaeans suffered, and you would turn homeward weary of my tale before it ended. Nine long years did we try every kind of stratagem, but the hand of heaven was against us; during all this time there was no one who could compare with your father in subtlety—if indeed you are his son—I can hardly believe my eyes—and you talk just like him too—no one would say that people of such different ages could speak so much alike. He and I never had any kind of difference from first to last neither in camp nor council, but in singleness of heart and purpose we advised the Argives how all might be ordered for the best.

"When, however, we had sacked the city of Priam, and were setting sail in our ships as heaven had dispersed us, then Zeus saw fit to vex the Argives on their homeward voyage; for they had not all been either wise or understanding, and hence many came to a bad end through the displeasure of Zeus' daughter Athene, who brought about a quarrel between the two sons of Atreus.[3]

"The sons of Atreus called a meeting which was not as it should be, for it was sunset and the Achaeans were heavy with wine. When they explained why they had called the people together, it seemed that Menelaus was for sailing homeward at once, and this displeased Agamemnon, who thought that we should wait till we had offered hecatombs to appease the anger of Athene. Fool

---

[3] That is, the brothers, Agamemnon and Menelaus.

that he was, he might have known that he would not prevail with her, for when the gods have made up their minds they do not change them lightly. So the two stood bandying hard words, whereon the Achaeans sprang to their feet with a cry that rent the air, and were of two minds as to what they should do.

"That night we rested and nursed our anger, for Zeus was hatching mischief against us. But in the morning some of us drew our ships into the water and put our goods with our women on board, while the rest, about half in number, stayed behind with Agamemnon. We—the other half—embarked and sailed; and the ships went well, for heaven had smoothed the sea. When we reached Tenedos we offered sacrifices to the gods, for we were longing to get home. Cruel Zeus, however, did not yet mean that we should do so, and raised a second quarrel in the course of which some among us turned their ships back again, and sailed away under Odysseus to make their peace with Agamemnon; but I and all the ships that were with me pressed forward, for I saw that mischief was brewing. The son of Tydeus[4] went on also with me, and his crews with him. Later on Menelaus joined us at Lesbos, and found us making up our minds about our course—for we did not know whether to go outside Chios by the island of Psyra, keeping this to our left, or inside Chios, over against the stormy headland of Mimas. So we asked heaven for a sign, and were shown one to the effect that we should be soonest out of danger if we headed our ships across the open sea to Euboea. This we therefore did, and a fair wind sprang up which gave us a quick passage during the night to Geraestus, where we offered many sacrifices to Poseidon for having helped us so far on our way. Four days later Diomed and his men stationed their ships in Argos, but I held on for Pylos, and the wind never fell light from the day when heaven first made it fair for me.

"Therefore, my dear young friend, I returned without hearing anything about the others. I know neither who got home safely nor who were lost but, as in duty bound, I will give you without reserve the reports that have reached

[4] Diomed.

me since I have been here in my own house. They say the Myrmidons returned home safely under Achilles' son Neoptolemus; so also did the valiant son of Poias, Philoctetes. Idomeneus, again, lost no men at sea, and all his followers who escaped death in the field got safe home with him to Crete. No matter how far out of the world you live, you will have heard of Agamemnon and the bad end he came to at the hands of Aegisthus—and a fearful reckoning did Aegisthus presently pay. See what a good thing it is for a man to leave a son behind him to do as Orestes did, who killed false Aegisthus, the murderer of his noble father. You too, then—for you are a tall, smart-looking fellow—show your mettle and make yourself a name in story."

"Nestor son of Neleus," answered Telemachus, "honor to the Achaean name, the Achaeans applaud Orestes and his name will live through all time for he has avenged his father nobly. Would that heaven might grant me to do like vengeance on the insolence of the wicked suitors who are ill-treating me and plotting my ruin; but the gods have no such happiness in store for me and for my father, so we must bear it as best we may."

"My friend," said Nestor, "now that you remind me, I remember to have heard that your mother has many suitors, who are ill-disposed towards you and are making havoc of your estate. Do you submit to this tamely, or are public feeling and the voice of heaven against you? Who knows but what Odysseus may come back after all, and pay these scoundrels in full, either single-handed or with a force of Achaeans behind him? If Athene were to take as great a liking to you as she did to Odysseus when we were fighting before Troy (for I never yet saw the gods so openly fond of anyone as Athene then was of your father), if she would take as good care of you as she did of him, these wooers would soon some of them forget their wooing."

Telemachus answered: "I can expect nothing of the kind; it would be far too much to hope for. I dare not let myself think of it. Even though the gods themselves willed it no such good fortune could befall me."

On this Athene said: "Telemachus, what are you talking about? Heaven has a long arm if it is minded to save a man; and if it were me, I should not care how much I suffered before getting home, provided I could be safe when I was once there. I would rather this than get home quickly, and then be killed in my own house as Agamemnon was by the treachery of Aegisthus and his wife. Still, death is certain, and when a man's hour is come, not even the gods can save him, no matter how fond they are of him."

"Mentor," answered Telemachus, "do not let us talk about it any more. There is no chance of my father's ever coming back; the gods have long since counseled his destruction. There is something else, however, about which I should like to ask Nestor, for he knows much more than anyone else does. They say he has reigned for three generations so that it is like talking to an immortal. Tell me, therefore, Nestor, and tell me true, how did Agamemnon come to die in that way? What was Menelaus doing? And how came false Aegisthus to kill so far better a man than himself? Was Menelaus away from Achaean Argos, voyaging elsewhither among mankind, that Aegisthus took heart and killed Agamemnon?"

"I will tell you truly," answered Nestor, "and indeed you have yourself divined how it all happened. If Menelaus when he got back from Troy had found Aegisthus still alive in his house, there would have been no barrow heaped up for him, not even when he was dead, but he would have been thrown outside the city to dogs and vultures, and not a woman would have mourned him, for he had done a deed of great wickedness. But we were over there, fighting hard at Troy, while Aegisthus, who was taking his ease quietly in the heart of Argos, cajoled Agamemnon's wife Clytemnestra with incessant flattery.

"At first she would have nothing to do with his wicked scheme, for she was of a good natural disposition; moreover there was a bard with her, to whom Agamemnon had given strict orders on setting out for Troy, that he was to keep guard over his wife; but when heaven had counseled her destruction, Aegisthus carried this bard off to a desert island, and left him there for crows and seagulls to batten upon—after which she went willingly enough to the house of Aegisthus. Then he offered many burnt sacrifices to the gods, and decorated many temples with tapestries and gilding, for he had succeeded far beyond his expectations.

"Meanwhile Menelaus and I were on our way home from Troy, on good terms with one another. When we got to Sunium, which is the point of Athens, Apollo with his painless shafts killed Phrontis, the steersman of Menelaus' ship (and never man knew better how to handle a vessel in rough weather), so that he died then and there with the helm in his hand, and Menelaus, though very anxious to press forward, had to wait in order to bury his comrade and give him his due funeral rites. Presently, when he too could put to sea again, and had sailed on as far as the Malean heads, Zeus counseled evil against him and made it blow hard till the waves ran mountains high. Here he divided his fleet and took the one half towards Crete where the Cydonians dwell round about the waters of the river Iardanus. There is a high headland hereabouts stretching out into the sea from a place called Gortyn, and all along this part of the coast as far as Phaestus the sea runs high when there is a south wind blowing, but after Phaestus the coast is more protected, for a small headland can make a great shelter. Here this part of the fleet was driven on to the rocks and wrecked; but the crews just managed to save themselves. As for the other five ships, they were taken by winds and seas to Egypt, where Menelaus gathered much gold and substance among people of an alien speech. Meanwhile Aegisthus here at home plotted his evil deed. For seven years after he had killed Agamemnon he ruled in Mycene, and the people were obedient under him, but in the eighth year Orestes came back from Athens to be his bane, and killed the murderer of his father. Then he celebrated the funeral rites of his mother and of false Aegisthus by a banquet to the people of Argos, and on that very day Menelaus came home with as much treasure as his ships could carry.

"Take my advice then, and do not go traveling about for long so far from home, nor leave your property with such dangerous people in your house; they will eat up everything you have among them, and you will have been on a fool's errand. Still, I should advise you by all means to go and visit Menelaus, who has lately come off a voyage among such distant peoples as no man could ever hope to get back from, when the winds had once carried him so far out of his reckoning; even birds cannot fly the distance in a twelvemonth, so vast and terrible are the seas that they must cross. Go to him, therefore, by sea, and take your own men with you; or if you would rather travel by land you can have a chariot, you can have horses, and here are my sons who can escort you to Sparta where Menelaus lives. Beg of him to speak the truth, and he will tell you no lies, for he is an excellent person."

As he spoke the sun set and it came on dark, whereon Athene said: "Sir, all that you have said is well; now, however, order the tongues of the victims to be cut, and mix wine that we may make drink offerings to Poseidon and the other immortals, and then go to bed, for it is bedtime. People should go away early and not keep late hours at a religious festival."

Thus spoke the daughter of Zeus, and they obeyed her saying. Menservants poured water over the hands of the guests, while pages filled the mixing bowls with wine and water, and handed it round after giving every man his drink offering; then they threw the tongues of the victims into the fire, and stood up to make their drink offerings. When they had made their offerings and had drunk each as much as he was minded, Athene and Telemachus were for going on board their ship, but Nestor caught them up at once and stayed them.

"Heaven and the immortal gods," he exclaimed, "forbid that you should leave my house to go on board of a ship! Do you think I am so poor and short of clothes, or that I have so few cloaks and rugs as to be unable to find comfortable beds both for myself and for my guests? Let me tell you I have store both of rugs and cloaks, and shall not permit the son of my old friend Odysseus to camp down on the deck of a ship—not while I live—nor yet will my sons after me, but they will keep open house as I have done."

Then Athene answered: "Sir, you have spoken well, and it will be much better that Telemachus should do as you have said. He, therefore, shall return with you and sleep at your house, but I must go back to give orders to my crew, and keep them in good heart. I am the only older person among them. The rest are all young men of Telemachus' own age, who have taken this voyage out of friendship; so I must return to the ship and sleep there. Moreover tomorrow I must go to the Cauconians where I have a large sum of money long owing to me. As for Telemachus, now that he is your guest, send him to Sparta in a chariot, and let one of your sons go with him. Be pleased also to provide him with your best and fleetest horses."

When she had thus spoken, she flew away in the form of an eagle, and all marveled as they beheld it. Nestor was astonished, and took Telemachus by the hand. "My friend," said he, "I see that you are going to be a great hero someday, since the gods wait upon you thus while you are still so young. This can have been none other of those who dwell in heaven than Zeus' redoubtable daughter, the Trito-born, who showed such favor towards your brave father among the Argives. Holy queen," he continued, "vouchsafe to send down thy grace upon myself, my good wife, and my children. In return, I will offer you in sacrifice a broad-browed heifer of a year old, unbroken, and never yet brought by man under the yoke. I will gild her horns, and will offer her up to you in sacrifice."

Thus did he pray, and Athene heard his prayer. He then led the way to his own house, followed by his sons and sons-in-law. When they had got there and had taken their places on the benches and seats, he mixed them a bowl of sweet wine that was eleven years old when the housekeeper took the lid off the jar that held it. As he mixed the wine, he prayed much and made drink offerings to Athene, daughter of aegis-bearing Zeus. Then, when they had made their drink offerings and had drunk each as much as he was minded, the

others went home to bed each in his own abode; but Nestor put Telemachus
to sleep in the room that was over the gateway along with Pisistratus, who
was the only unmarried son now left him. As for himself, he slept in an inner
room of the house, with the queen his wife by his side.

Now when the child of morning, rosy-fingered Dawn, appeared, Nestor
left his couch and took his seat on the benches of white and polished marble
that stood in front of his house. Here aforetime sat Neleus, peer of gods in
counsel, but he was now dead, and had gone to the house of Hades; so Nestor
sat in his seat, scepter in hand, as guardian of the public weal. His sons as they
left their rooms gathered round him, Echephron, Stratius, Perseus, Aretus,
and Thrasymedes; the sixth son was Pisistratus, and when Telemachus joined
them they made him sit with them. Nestor then addressed them.

"My sons," said he, "make haste to do as I shall bid you. I wish first and
foremost to propitiate the great goddess Athene, who manifested herself visi-
bly to me during yesterday's festivities. Go, then, one or other of you to the
plain, tell the stockman to look me out a heifer, and come on here with it at
once. Another must go to Telemachus' ship, and invite all the crew, leaving
two men only in charge of the vessel. Someone else will run and fetch Laerceus
the goldsmith to gild the horns of the heifer. The rest, stay all of you where
you are; tell the maids in the house to prepare an excellent dinner, and to fetch
seats, and logs of wood for a burnt offering. Tell them also to bring me some
clear spring water."

On this they hurried off on their several errands. The heifer was brought
in from the plain, and Telemachus' crew came from the ship. The goldsmith
brought the anvil, hammer, and tongs with which he worked his gold, and
Athene herself came to accept the sacrifice. Nestor gave out the gold, and the
smith gilded the horns of the heifer that the goddess might have pleasure in
their beauty. Then Stratius and Echephron brought her in by the horns; Aretus
fetched water from the house in a ewer that had a flower pattern on it, and in
his other hand he held a basket of barley meal; sturdy Thrasymedes stood by

with a sharp axe, ready to strike the heifer, while Perseus held a bucket. Then Nestor began with washing his hands and sprinkling the barley meal, and he offered many a prayer to Athene as he threw a lock from the heifer's head upon the fire.

When they had done praying and sprinkling the barley meal Thrasymedes dealt his blow, and brought the heifer down with a stroke that cut through the tendons at the base of her neck, whereon the daughters and daughters-in-law of Nestor, and his venerable wife Eurydice (she was eldest daughter to Clymenus) screamed with delight. Then they lifted the heifer's head from off the ground, and Pisistratus cut her throat. When she had done bleeding and was quite dead, they cut her up. They cut out the thighbones all in due course, wrapped them round in two layers of fat, and set some pieces of raw meat on the top of them; then Nestor laid them upon the wood fire and poured wine over them, while the young men stood near him with five-pronged spits in their hands. When the thighs were burned and they had tasted the inward meats, they cut the rest of the meat up small, put the pieces on the spits and toasted them over the fire.

Meanwhile lovely Polycaste, Nestor's youngest daughter, washed Telemachus. When she had washed him and anointed him with oil, she brought him a fair mantle and shirt, and he looked like a god as he came from the bath and took his seat by the side of Nestor. When the outer meats were done they drew them off the spits and sat down to dinner where they were waited upon by some worthy henchmen, who kept pouring them out their wine in cups of gold. As soon as they had had enough to eat and drink Nestor said, "Sons, put Telemachus' horses to the chariot that he may start at once."

Thus did he speak, and they did even as he had said, and yoked the fleet horses to the chariot. The housekeeper packed them up a provision of bread, wine, and sweetmeats fit for the sons of princes. Then Telemachus got into the chariot, while Pisistratus gathered up the reins and took his seat beside him. He lashed the horses on and they flew forward nothing loath into the open country, leaving the high citadel of Pylos behind them. All that day did they travel, swaying the yoke upon their necks till the sun went down and darkness was over all the land. Then they reached Pherae where Diocles lived, who was son to Ortilochus and grandson to Alpheus. Here they passed the night and Dicoles entertained them hospitably. When the child of morning, rosy-fingered Dawn, appeared, they again yoked their horses and drove out through the gateway under the echoing gatehouse. Pisistratus lashed the horses on and they flew forward nothing loth. Presently they came to the corn lands of the open country, and in the course of time completed their journey, so well did their steeds take them.

Book IV

*At Sparta Telemachus is joyfully received by Menelaus and Helen, who recount
stories of Odysseus. Menelaus describes their own many adventures on the return
from Troy. He reveals that the god Proteus has told him that Odysseus is a
prisoner on Calypso's isle. Back in Ithaca, the suitors, learning of Telemachus'
journey, plan to murder him. Penelope hears of it and is terrified. Athene sends a
vision to Penelope to assure her that her son will come back safely.*

NOW WHEN THE SUN HAD SET AND DARKENSS WAS OVER THE LAND,
they reached the low-lying city of Sparta, where they drove
straight to the abode of Menelaus and found him in his own
house, feasting with his many clansmen in honor of the wedding of his son,
and also of his daughter, whom he was marrying to the son of that valiant warrior Achilles. He had given his consent and promised her to him while he was
still at Troy, and now the gods were bringing the marriage about; so he was
sending her with chariots and horses to the city of the Myrmidons over whom
Achilles' son was reigning. For his only son he had found a bride from Sparta,
the daughter of Alector. This son, Megapenthes, was born to him of a bondwoman, for heaven vouchsafed Helen no more children after she had borne
Hermione, who was fair as golden Aphrodite herself.

So the neighbors and kinsmen of Menelaus were feasting and making
merry in his house. There was a bard also to sing to them and play his lyre,
while two tumblers went about performing in the midst of them when the
man struck up with his tune.

Telemachus and the son of Nestor stayed their horses at the gate, whereon Eteoneus, servant to Menelaus, came out, and as soon as he saw them ran hurrying back into the house to tell his master. He went close up to him and said, "Menelaus, there are some strangers come here, two men, who look like sons of Zeus. What are we to do? Shall we take their horses out, or tell them to find friends elsewhere as they best can?"

Menelaus was very angry and said: "Eteoneus son of Boethous, you never used to be a fool, but now you talk like a simpleton. Take their horses out, of course, and show the strangers in that they may have supper. You and I have stayed often enough at other people's houses before we got back here, where heaven grant that we may rest in peace henceforward."

So Eteoneus bustled back and bade the other servants come with him. They took their sweating steeds from under the yoke, made them fast to the mangers, and gave them a feed of oats and barley mixed. Then they leaned the chariot against the end wall of the courtyard, and led the way into the house. Telemachus and Pisistratus were astonished when they saw it, for its splendor was as that of the sun and moon; then, when they had admired everything to their heart's content, they went into the bathroom and washed themselves.

When the servants had washed them and anointed them with oil, they brought them woolen cloaks and shirts, and the two took their seats by the side of Menelaus. A maidservant brought them water in a beautiful golden ewer, and poured it into a silver basin for them to wash their hands; and she drew a clean table beside them. An upper servant brought them bread, and offered them many good things of what there was in the house, while the carver fetched them plates of all manner of meats and set cups of gold by their side.

Menelaus then greeted them, saying: "Fall to, and welcome. When you have done supper, I shall ask who you are, for the lineage of such men as you cannot have been lost. You must be descended from a line of scepter-bearing kings, for poor people do not have such sons as you are."

On this he handed them a piece of fat roast loin, which had been set near him as being a prime part, and they laid their hands on the good things that were before them. As soon as they had had enough to eat and drink, Telemachus said to the son of Nestor, with his head so close that no one might hear, "Look, Pisistratus, man after my own heart, see the gleam of bronze and gold—of amber,[1] ivory, and silver. Everything is so splendid that it is like seeing the palace of Olympian Zeus. I am lost in admiration."

Menelaus overheard him and said: "No one, my sons, can hold his own with Zeus, for his house and everything about him is immortal; but among mortal men—well, there may be another who has as much wealth as I have, or there may not. But at all events I have traveled much and have undergone much hardship, for it was nearly eight years before I could get home with my fleet. I went to Cyprus, Phoenicia, and the Egyptians; I went also to the Ethiopians, the Sidonians, and the Erembians, and to Libya where the lambs have horns as soon as they are born, and the sheep lamb down three times a year. Everyone in that country, whether master or man, has plenty of cheese, meat, and good milk, for the ewes yield all the year round. But while I was traveling and getting great riches among these people, my brother was secretly and shockingly murdered through the perfidy of his wicked wife, so that I have no pleasure in being lord of all this wealth.

"Whoever your parents may be, they must have told you about all this, and of my heavy loss in the ruin[2] of a stately mansion fully and magnificently furnished. Would that I had only a third of what I now have so that I had stayed at home, and all those were living who perished on the plain of Troy, far from Argos. I often grieve, as I sit here in my house, for one and all of them. At times I cry aloud for sorrow, but presently I leave off again, for cry-

---

[1] Amber is never mentioned in the *Iliad*. Sicily was probably the only amber-producing country known in the Odyssean age. (B.)

[2] This no doubt refers to the story, told in the lost poem of the Cypria, of how Paris and Helen robbed Menelaus of the greater part of his treasures, when they sailed together for Troy. (B.)

ing is cold comfort and one soon tires of it. Yet grieve for these as I may, I do so for one man more than for them all. I cannot even think of him without loathing both food and sleep, so miserable does he make me, for no one of all the Achaeans worked so hard or risked so much as he did. He took nothing by it, and has left a legacy of sorrow to myself, for he has been gone a long time, and we know not whether he is alive or dead. His old father, his long-suffering wife Penelope, and his son Telemachus, whom he left behind him an infant in arms, are plunged in grief on his account."

Thus spoke Menelaus, and the heart of Telemachus yearned as he bethought him of his father. Tears fell from his eyes as he heard him thus mentioned, so that he held his cloak before his face with both hands. When Menelaus saw this he doubted whether to let him choose his own time for speaking, or to ask him at once and find what it was all about.

While he was thus in two minds, Helen came down from her high-vaulted and perfumed room, looking as lovely as Artemis herself. Adraste brought her a seat, Alcippe a soft woolen rug, while Phylo fetched her the silver work-box which Alcandra wife of Polybus had given her. Polybus lived in Egyptian Thebes, which is the richest city in the whole world; he gave Menelaus two baths, both of pure silver, two tripods, and ten talents of gold; besides all this, his wife gave Helen some beautiful presents, to wit, a golden distaff, and a silver work-box that ran on wheels, with a gold band round the top of it. Phylo now placed this by her side, full of fine spun yarn, and a distaff charged with violet-colored wool was laid upon the top of it. Then Helen took her seat, put her feet upon the footstool, and began to question her husband.

"Do we know, Menelaus," said she, "the names of these strangers who have come to visit us? Shall I guess right or wrong?—but I cannot help saying what I think. Never yet have I seen either man or woman so like somebody else (indeed when I look at him I hardly know what to think) as this young man is like Telemachus, whom Odysseus left as a baby behind him, when you Achaeans went to Troy with battle in your hearts, on account of my most shameless self."

"My dear wife," replied Menelaus, "I see the likeness just as you do. His hands and feet are just like Odysseus'; so is his hair, with the shape of his head and the expression of his eyes. Moreover, when I was talking about Odysseus, and saying how much he had suffered on my account, tears fell from his eyes, and he hid his face in his mantle."

Then Pisistratus said: "Menelaus son of Atreus, you are right in thinking that this young man is Telemachus, but he is very modest, and is ashamed to come here and begin opening up discourse with one whose conversation is so divinely interesting as your own. My father, Nestor, sent me to escort him hither, for he wanted to know whether you could give him any counsel or suggestion. A son has always trouble at home when his father has gone away leaving him without supporters; and this is how Telemachus is now placed, for his father is absent, and there is no one among his own people to stand by him."

"Bless my heart," replied Menelaus, "then I am receiving a visit from the son of a very dear friend, who suffered much hardship for my sake. I had always hoped to entertain him with most marked distinction when heaven had granted us a safe return from beyond the seas. I should have founded a city for him in Argos, and built him a house. I should have made him leave Ithaca, with his goods, his son, and all his people, and should have sacked for them some one of the neighboring cities that are subject to me. We should thus have seen one another continually, and nothing but death could have interrupted so close and happy an intercourse. I suppose, however, that heaven grudged us such great good fortune, for it has prevented the poor fellow from ever getting home at all."

Thus did he speak, and his words set them all a-weeping. Helen wept, Telemachus wept, and so did Menelaus, nor could Pisistratus keep his eyes from filling, when he remembered his dear brother Antilochus whom the son of bright Dawn had killed. Thereon he said to Menelaus:

"Sir, my father Nestor, when we used to talk about you at home, told me you were a person of rare and excellent understanding. If, then, it be possible, do as I would urge you. I am not fond of crying while I am getting my supper. Morning will come in due course, and in the forenoon I care not how much I cry for those that are dead and gone. This is all we can do for the poor things. We can only shave our heads for them and wring the tears from our cheeks. I had a brother who died at Troy; he was by no means the worst man there; you are sure to have known him—his name was Antilochus. I never set eyes upon him myself, but they say that he was singularly fleet of foot and in fight valiant."

"Your discretion, my friend," answered Menelaus, "is beyond your years. It is plain you take after your father. One can soon see when a man is son to one whom heaven has blessed both as regards wife and offspring—and it has blessed Nestor from first to last all his days, giving him a green old age in his own house, with sons about him who are both well-disposed and valiant. We will put an end therefore to all this weeping, and attend to our supper again. Let water be poured over our hands. Telemachus and I can talk with one another fully in the morning."

On this Asphalion, one of the servants, poured water over their hands and they laid their hands on the good things that were before them.

Then Zeus' daughter Helen bethought her of another matter. She drugged the wine with an herb that banishes all care, sorrow, and ill humor. Whoever drinks wine thus drugged cannot shed a single tear all the rest of the day, not even though his father and mother both of them drop down dead, or he sees a brother or a son hewn in pieces before his very eyes. This drug, of such sovereign power and virtue, had been given to Helen by Polydamna wife of Thon, a woman of Egypt, where there grow all sorts of herbs, some good to put into the mixing bowl and others poisonous. Moreover, everyone in the whole country is a skilled physician, for they are of the race of Paeeon.[3] When Helen had put this drug in the bowl and had told the servants to serve the wine round, she said:

---

[3] Physician to the gods, whose healing skill is described in the *Iliad*.

"Menelaus son of Atreus, and you my good friends, sons of honorable men (which is as Zeus wills, for he is the giver both of good and evil, and can do what he chooses), feast here as you will, and listen while I tell you a tale in season. I cannot indeed name every single one of the exploits of Odysseus, but I can say what he did when he was before Troy, and you Achaeans were in all sorts of difficulties. He covered himself with wounds and bruises, dressed himself all in rags, and entered the enemy's city looking like a menial or a beggar, and quite different from what he did when he was among his own people. In this disguise he entered the city of Troy, and no one said anything to him. I alone recognized him and began to question him, but he was too cunning for me. When, however, I had washed and anointed him and had given him clothes, and after I had sworn a solemn oath not to betray him to the Trojans till he had got safely back to his own camp and to the ships, he told me all that the Achaeans meant to do. He killed many Trojans and got much information before he reached the Argive camp, for all which things the Trojan women made lamentation, but for my own part I was glad, for my heart was beginning to yearn after my home, and I was unhappy about the wrong that Aphrodite had done me in taking me over there, away from my country, my little girl, and my lawful wedded husband, who is indeed by no means deficient either in person or understanding."

Then Menelaus said: "All that you have been saying, my dear wife, is true. I have traveled much, and have had much to do with heroes, but I have never seen such another man as Odysseus. What endurance too, and what courage he displayed within the wooden horse, wherein all the bravest of the Argives were lying in wait to bring death and destruction upon the Trojans.[4] At that moment you came up to us; some god who wished well to the Trojans must

[4]In the Italian insurrection of 1848, eight young men who were being hotly pursued by the Austrian police hid themselves inside Donatello's colossal wooden horse in the Salone at Padua, and remained there for a week, being fed by their confederates. In 1898 the last survivor was carried round Padua in triumph. (B.)

have set you on to it and you had Deïphobus with you. Three times did you go all around our hiding place and pat it; you called our chiefs each by his own name, and mimicked all our wives. Diomed, Odysseus, and I from our seats inside heard what a noise you made. Diomed and I could not make up our minds whether to spring out then and there, or to answer you from inside, but Odysseus held us all in check, so we sat quite still, all except Anticlus, who was beginning to answer you, when Odysseus clapped his two brawny hands over his mouth, and kept them there. It was this that saved us all, for he muzzled Anticlus till Athene took you away again."

"How sad," exclaimed Telemachus, "that all this was of no avail to save him, nor yet his own iron courage. But now, sir, be pleased to send us all to bed, that we may lie down and enjoy the blessed boon of sleep."

On this Helen told the maidservants to set beds in the room that was in the gatehouse, and to make them with good red rugs, and spread coverlets on the top of them with woolen cloaks for the guests to wear. So the maids went out, carrying a torch, and made the beds, to which a manservant presently conducted the strangers. Thus, then, did Telemachus and Pisistratus sleep there in the forecourt, while the son of Atreus lay in an inner room with lovely Helen by his side.

When the child of morning, rosy-fingered Dawn, appeared, Menelaus rose and dressed himself. He bound his sandals on to his comely feet, girded his sword about his shoulders, and left his room looking like an immortal god. Then, taking a seat near Telemachus, he said:

"And what, Telemachus, has led you to take this long sea-voyage to Sparta? Are you on public or private business? Tell me all about it."

"I have come, sir," replied Telemachus, "to see if you can tell me anything about my father. I am being eaten out of house and home; my fair estate is being wasted, and my house is full of miscreants who keep killing great numbers of my sheep and oxen, on the pretense of paying their addresses to my mother. Therefore, I am suppliant at your knees if haply you may tell me about my father's melancholy end, whether you saw it with your own eyes, or heard it from some other traveler, for he was a man born to trouble. Do not soften things out of any pity for myself, but tell me in all plainness exactly what you saw. If my brave father Odysseus ever did you loyal service either by word or deed, when you Achaeans were harassed by the Trojans, bear it in mind now as in my favor and tell me truly all."

Menelaus on hearing this was very much shocked. "So," he exclaimed, "these cowards would usurp a brave man's bed? A hind might as well lay her newborn young in the lair of a lion, and then go off to feed in the forest or in some grassy dell; the lion when he comes back to his lair will make short work with the pair of them—and so will Odysseus with these suitors. By father Zeus, Athene, and Apollo, if Odysseus is still the man that he was when he wrestled with Philomeleides in Lesbos, and threw him so heavily that all the Achaeans cheered him—if he is still such and were to come near these suitors, they would have a short shrift and a sorry wedding. As regards your questions, however, I will not prevaricate or deceive you, but will tell you without concealment all that the old man of the sea told me.

"I was trying to come on here, but the gods detained me in Egypt, for my hecatombs had not given them full satisfaction, and the gods are very strict about having their dues. Now off Egypt, about as far as a ship can sail in a day with a good stiff breeze behind her, there is an island called Pharos. It has a good harbor from which vessels can get out into open sea when they have taken in water—and here the gods becalmed me twenty days without so much as a breath of fair wind to help me forward. We should have run clean out of provisions and my men would have starved, if a goddess had not taken pity upon me and saved me in the person of Idothea, daughter to Proteus, the old man of the sea, for she had taken a great fancy to me.

"She came to me one day when I was by myself, as I often was, for the men used to go with their barbed hooks all over the island in the hope of catching a fish or two to save them from the pangs of hunger. 'Stranger,' said she, 'it seems to me that you like starving in this way—at any rate it does not greatly trouble you, for you stick here day after day, without even trying to get away though your men are dying by inches.'

" 'Let me tell you,' said I, 'whichever of the goddesses you may happen to be, that I am not staying here of my own accord, but must have offended the gods that live in heaven. Tell me, therefore, for the gods know everything, which of the immortals it is that is hindering me in this way, and tell me also how I may sail the sea so as to reach my home.'

" 'Stranger,' replied she,' I will make it all quite clear to you. There is an old immortal who lives under the sea hereabouts and whose name is Proteus. He is an Egyptian, and people say he is my father. He is Poseidon's head man and knows every inch of ground all over the bottom of the sea. If you can snare him and hold him tight, he will tell you about your voyage, what courses you are to take, and how you are to sail the sea so as to reach your home. He will also tell you, if you so will, all that has been going on at your house both good and bad, while you have been away on your long and dangerous journey.'

" 'Can you show me,' said I, 'some stratagem by means of which I may catch this old god without his suspecting it and finding me out? For a god is not easily caught—not by a mortal man.'

" 'Stranger,' said she, 'I will make it all quite clear to you. About the time when the sun shall have reached midheaven, the old man of the sea comes up from under the waves, heralded by the west wind that furs the water over his head. As soon as he has come up he lies down, and goes to sleep in a great sea-cave, where the seals—Halosydne's chickens as they call them—come up also from the gray sea, and go to sleep in shoals all round him; and a very strong and fishlike smell do they bring with them. Early tomorrow morning I will take you to this place and will lay you in ambush. Pick out, therefore, the three best men you have in your fleet, and I will tell you all the tricks that the old man will play you.

" 'First he will look over all his seals, and count them; then, when he has seen them and tallied them on his five fingers, he will go to sleep among them, as a shepherd among his sheep. The moment you see that he is asleep, seize him; put forth all your strength and hold him fast, for he will do his very utmost to get away from you. He will turn himself into every kind of creature that goes upon the earth, and will become also both fire and water; but you must hold him fast and grip him tighter and tighter, till he begins to talk to you and comes back to what he was when you saw him go to sleep. Then you may slacken your hold and let him go; and you can ask him which of the gods it is that is angry with you, and what you must do to reach your home over the seas.'

"Having so said, she dived under the waves, whereon I turned back to the place where my ships were ranged upon the shore; and my heart was clouded with care as I went along. When I reached my ship we got supper ready, for night was falling, and camped down upon the beach.

"When the child of morning, rosy-fingered Dawn, appeared, I took the three men on whose prowess of all kinds I could most rely, and went along by the seaside, praying heartily to heaven. Meanwhile the goddess fetched me up four sealskins from the bottom of the sea, all of them just skinned, for she meant playing a trick upon her father. Then she dug four pits for us to lie in, and sat down to wait till we should come up. When we were close to her, she made us lie down in the pits one after the other, and threw a sealskin over each of us. Our ambuscade would have been intolerable, for the stench of the fishy seals was most distressing—who would go to bed with a sea-monster if he could help it?—but here, too, the goddess helped us, and thought of something that gave us great relief, for she put some ambrosia under each man's nostrils, which was so fragrant that it killed the smell of the seals.

"We waited the whole morning and made the best of it, watching the seals come up in hundreds to bask upon the seashore, till at noon the old man of the sea came up too, and when he had found his fat seals he went over them and counted them. We were among the first he counted, and he never suspected any guile, but laid himself down to sleep as soon as he had done counting. Then we rushed upon him with a shout and seized him; on which he began at once with his old tricks, and changed himself first into a lion with a great mane; then all of a sudden he became a dragon, a leopard, a wild boar; the next moment he was running water, and then again directly he was a tree, but we stuck to him and never lost hold, till at last the cunning old creature became distressed, and said, 'Which of the gods was it, son of Atreus, that hatched this plot with you for snaring me and seizing me against my will? What do you want?'

" 'You know that yourself, old man,' I answered, 'you will gain nothing by trying to put me off. It is because I have been kept so long in this island, and see no sign of my being able to get away. I am losing all heart. Tell me, then, for you gods know everything, which of the immortals it is that is hindering me, and tell me also how I may sail the sea so as to reach my home.'

" 'Then,' he said, 'if you would finish your voyage and get home quickly, you must offer sacrifices to Zeus and to the rest of the gods before embarking; for it is decreed that you shall not get back to your friends and to your own house, till you have returned to the heaven-fed stream of Egypt, and offered holy hecatombs to the immortal gods that reign in heaven. When you have done this they will let you finish your voyage.'

"I was brokenhearted when I heard that I must go back all that long and terrible voyage to Egypt. Nevertheless, I answered, 'I will do all, old man, that you have laid upon me; but now tell me, and tell me true, whether all the Achaeans whom Nestor and I left behind us when we set sail from Troy have got home safely, or whether any one of them came to a bad end, either on board his own ship or among his friends when the days of his fighting were done.'

" 'Son of Atreus,' he answered, 'why ask me? You had better not know what I can tell you, for your eyes will surely fill when you have heard my story. Many of those about whom you ask are dead and gone, but many still remain, and only two of the chief men among the Achaeans perished during their return home. As for what happened on the field of battle—you were there yourself. A third Achaean leader is still at sea, alive, but hindered from returning. Ajax was wrecked, for Poseidon drove him on to the great rocks of Gyrae; nevertheless, he let him get safe out of the water, and in spite of all Athene's hatred he would have escaped death if he had not ruined himself by boasting. He said the gods could not drown him even though they had tried to do so, and when Poseidon heard this large talk, he seized his trident in his two brawny hands, and split the rock of Gyrae in two pieces. The base remained where it was, but the part on which Ajax was sitting fell headlong into the sea and carried Ajax with it; so he drank salt water and was drowned.

" 'Your brother and his ships escaped, for Hera protected him, but when he was just about to reach the high promontory of Malea, he was caught by a heavy gale, which carried him out to sea again sorely against his will, and drove him to the foreland where Thyestes used to dwell, but where Aegisthus was then living. By and by, however, it seemed as though he was to return safely after all, for the gods backed the wind into its old quarter and they reached home; whereon Agamemnon kissed his native soil, and shed tears of joy at finding himself again in his own country.

" 'Now there was a watchman whom Aegisthus kept always on the watch, and to whom he had promised two talents of gold. This man had been looking out for a whole year to make sure that Agamemnon did not give him the slip and prepare war; when, therefore, this man saw Agamemnon go by, he went and told Aegisthus, who at once began to lay a plot for him. He picked twenty of his bravest warriors and placed them in ambuscade on one side of the cloister, while on the opposite side he prepared a banquet. Then he sent his chariots and horsemen to Agamemnon, and invited him to the feast, but he meant foul play. He got him there, all unsuspicious of the doom that was awaiting him, and killed him when the banquet was over as though he were butchering an ox in the shambles; not one of Agamemnon's followers was left alive, nor yet one of Aegisthus', but they were all killed there in the cloisters.'

"Thus spoke Proteus, and I was brokenhearted as I heard him. I sat down upon the sands and wept; I felt as though I could no longer bear to live nor look upon the light of the sun. Presently, when I had had my fill of weeping and writhing upon the ground, the old man of the sea said, 'Son of Atreus, do not waste any more time in crying so bitterly; it can do no manner of good; find your way home as fast as ever you can, for Aegisthus may be still alive, and even though Orestes has been beforehand with you in killing him, you may yet come in for his funeral.'

"On this I took comfort in spite of all my sorrow, and said, 'I know, then, about these two. Tell me, therefore, about the third man of whom you spoke; is he still alive, but at sea, and unable to get home? or is he dead? Tell me, no matter how much it may grieve me.'

" 'The third man,' he answered, 'is Odysseus who dwells in Ithaca. I can see him in an island sorrowing bitterly in the house of the nymph Calypso, who is keeping him prisoner, and he cannot reach his home for he has no ships or sailors to take him over the sea. As for your own end, Menelaus, you shall not die in Argos, but the gods will take you to the Elysian plain, which is at the ends of the world. There fair-haired Rhadamanthus reigns, and men lead an easier life than anywhere else in the world, for in Elysium there falls not rain, nor hail, nor snow, but Oceanus breathes ever with a west wind that sings softly from the sea, and gives fresh life to all men. This will happen to you because you have married Helen, and are Zeus' son-in-law.'

"As he spoke he dived under the waves, whereon I turned back to the ships with my companions, and my heart was clouded with care as I went along. When we reached the ships we got supper ready, for night was falling, and camped down upon the beach. When the child of morning, rosy-fingered Dawn, appeared, we drew our ships into the water, and put our masts and sails within them; then we went on board ourselves, took our seats on the benches, and smote the gray sea with our oars. I again stationed my ships in the heaven-fed stream of Egypt, and offered hecatombs that were full and sufficient. When I had thus appeased heaven's anger, I raised a barrow to the memory of Agamemnon that his name might live forever, after which I had a quick passage home, for the gods sent me a fair wind.

"And now for yourself—stay here some ten or twelve days longer, and I will then speed you on your way. I will make you a noble present of a chariot and three horses. I will also give you a beautiful chalice, that so long as you live you may think of me whenever you make a drink offering to the immortal gods."

"Son of Atreus," replied Telemachus, "do not press me to stay longer; I should be contented to remain with you for another twelve months. I find your conversation so delightful that I should never once wish myself at home with my parents; but my crew whom I have left at Pylos are already impatient, and you are detaining me from them. As for any present you may be disposed to make me, I had rather that it should be a piece of plate. I will take no horses back with me to Ithaca, but will leave them to adorn your own stables, for you have much flat ground in your kingdom, where lotus thrives, and also meadow-sweet and wheat and barley, and oats with their white and spreading ears; whereas in Ithaca we have neither open fields nor racecourses, and the country is more fit for goats than horses, and I like it the better for that. None of our islands have much level ground, suitable for horses, and Ithaca least of all."

Menelaus smiled and took Telemachus' hand within his own. "What you say," said he, "shows that you come of good family. I both can, and will, make this exchange for you, by giving you the finest and most precious piece of plate in all my house. It is a mixing bowl by Hephaestus' own hand, of pure silver, except the rim, which is inlaid with gold. Phaedimus, king of the Sidonians, gave it me in the course of a visit which I paid him when I returned thither on my homeward journey. I will make you a present of it."

Thus did they converse while guests kept coming to the king's house. They brought sheep and wine, while their wives had put up bread for them to take with them; so they were busy cooking their dinners in the courts.

Meanwhile [in Ithaca] the suitors were throwing discs or aiming with spears at a mark on the leveled ground in front of Odysseus' house, and were behaving with all their old insolence. Antinous and Eurymachus, who were their ringleaders and much the foremost among them all, were sitting together when Noemon son of Phronius came up and said to Antinous:

"Have we any idea, Antinous, on what day Telemachus returns from Pylos? He has a ship of mine, and I want it, to cross over to Elis. I have twelve brood mares there with yearling mule foals by their side not yet broken in, and I want to bring one of them over here and break him."

They were astounded when they heard this, for they had made sure that Telemachus had not gone to the city of Neleus. They thought he was only away somewhere on the farms, and was with the sheep, or with the swineherd; so Antinous said, "When did he go? Tell me truly, and what young men did he take with him? Were they freemen or his own bondsmen—for he might manage that too? Tell me also, did you let him have the ship of your own free will because he asked you, or did he take it without your leave?"

"I lent it him," answered Noemon. "What else could I do when a man of his position said he was in a difficulty, and asked me to oblige him? I could not possibly refuse. As for those who went with him, they were the best young men we have, and I saw Mentor go on board as captain—or some god who was exactly like him. I cannot understand it, for I saw Mentor here myself yesterday morning, and yet he was then setting out for Pylos."

Noemon then went back to his father's house, but Antinous and Eurymachus were very angry. They told the others to leave off playing, and to come and sit down along with themselves. When they came, Antinous son of Eupeithes spoke in anger. His heart was black with rage, and his eyes flashed fire as he said:

"Good heavens, this voyage of Telemachus is a very serious matter! We had made sure that it would come to nothing, but the young fellow has got away in spite of us, and with a picked crew too. He will be giving us trouble presently; may Zeus take him before he is full grown. Find me a ship, therefore, with a crew of twenty men, and I will lie in wait for him in the straits between Ithaca and Same. He will then rue the day that he set out to try and get news of his father."

Thus did he speak, and the others applauded his saying; they then all of them went inside the buildings.

It was not long ere Penelope came to know what the suitors were plotting; for a manservant, Medon, overheard them from outside the outer court as they were laying their schemes within, and went to tell his mistress. As he crossed the threshold of her room, Penelope said: "Medon, what have the suitors sent you here for? Is it to tell the maids to leave their master's business and cook dinner for them? I wish they may neither woo nor dine henceforward, neither here nor anywhere else, but let this be the very last time, for the waste you all make of my son's estate. Did not your fathers tell you when you were children how good Odysseus had been to them—never doing anything high-handed, nor speaking harshly to anybody? Kings may say things sometimes, and they may take a fancy to one man and dislike another, but Odysseus never did an unjust thing by anybody—which shows what bad hearts you have, and that there is no such thing as gratitude left in this world."

Then Medon said: "I wish, madam, that this were all; but they are plotting something much more dreadful now—may heaven frustrate their design! They are going to try and murder Telemachus as he is coming home from Pylos and Sparta, where he has been to get news of his father."

Then Penelope's heart sank within her, and for a long time she was speechless; her eyes filled with tears, and she could find no utterance. At last, however, she said, "Why did my son leave me? What business had he to go sailing off in ships that make long voyages over the ocean like sea-horses? Does he want to die without leaving anyone behind him to keep up his name?"

"I do not know," answered Medon, "whether some god set him on to it, or whether he went on his own impulse to see if he could find out if his father was dead, or alive and on his way home."

Then he went downstairs again,[5] leaving Penelope in an agony of grief. There were plenty of seats in the house, but she had no heart for sitting on any one of them; she could only fling herself on the floor of her own room and cry; whereon all the maids in the house, both old and young, gathered round her and began to cry too, till at last in a transport of sorrow she exclaimed:

"My dears, heaven has been pleased to try me with more affliction than any other woman of my age and country. First I lost my brave and lion-hearted husband, who had every good quality under heaven, and whose name was great over all Hellas and middle Argos, and now my darling son is at the mercy of the winds and waves, without my having heard one word about his leaving home. You hussies, there was not one of you would so much as think of giving me a call out of my bed, though you all of you very well knew when he was starting! If I had known he meant taking this voyage, he would have had to give it up, no matter how much he was bent upon it, or leave me a corpse behind him—one or other. Now, however, go some of you and call old Dolius, who was given me by my father on my marriage, and who is my gardener. Bid him go at once and tell everything to Laertes, who may be able to hit on some plan for enlisting public sympathy on our side, as against those who are trying to exterminate his own race and that of Odysseus."

Then the dear old nurse Euryclea said: "You may kill me, madam, or let me live on in your house, whichever you please, but I will tell you the real truth. I knew all about it, and gave him everything he wanted in the way of bread and wine, but he made me take my solemn oath that I would not tell you anything for some ten or twelve days, unless you asked or happened to hear of his having gone, for he did not want you to spoil your beauty by

---

[5] The rampart or body of the house was two stories high. It contained among other things the women's apartments and the storeroom for valuable treasure.

crying. And now, madam, wash your face, change your dress, and go upstairs with your maids to offer prayers to Athene, daughter of aegis-bearing Zeus, for she can save him even though he be in the jaws of death. Do not trouble Laertes: he has trouble enough already. Besides, I cannot think that the gods hate the race of the son of Arceisius so much, but there will be a son left to come up after him, and inherit both the house and the fair fields that lie far all round it."

With these words she made her mistress leave off crying, and dried the tears from her eyes. Penelope washed her face, changed her dress, and went upstairs with her maids. She then put some bruised barley into a basket and began praying to Athene.

"Hear me," she cried, "daughter of aegis-bearing Zeus, unweariable. If ever Odysseus while he was here burned you fat thighbones of sheep or heifer, bear it in mind now as in my favor, and save my darling son from the villainy of the suitors."

She cried aloud as she spoke, and the goddess heard her prayer. Meanwhile the suitors were clamorous throughout the covered cloister, and one of them said:

"The queen is preparing for her marriage with one or other of us. Little does she dream that her son has now been doomed to die."

This was what they said, but they did not know what was going to happen. Then Antinous said, "Comrades, let there be no loud talking, lest some of it get carried inside. Let us be up and do that in silence, about which we are all of a mind."

He then chose twenty men, and they went down to their ship and to the seaside. They drew the vessel into the water and got her mast and sails inside her; they bound the oars to the thole-pins with twisted thongs of leather, all in due course, and spread the white sails aloft, while their fine servants brought them their armor. Then they made the ship fast a little way out, came on shore again, got their suppers, and waited until night should fall.

But Penelope lay in her own room upstairs unable to eat or drink, and wondering whether her brave son would escape, or be overpowered by the wicked suitors. Like a lioness caught in the toils with huntsmen hemming her in on every side, she thought and thought till she sank into a slumber, and lay on her bed bereft of thought and motion.

Then Athene bethought her of another matter, and made a vision in the likeness of Penelope's sister Iphthime, daughter of Icarius, who had married Eumelus and lived in Pherae. She told the vision to go to the house of Odysseus, and to make Penelope leave off crying. So it came into her room by the hole through which the thong went for pulling the door to, and hovered over her head, saying,

"You are asleep, Penelope. The gods who live at ease will not suffer you to weep and be so sad. Your son has done them no wrong, so he will yet come back to you."

Penelope, who was sleeping sweetly at the gates of dreamland, answered: "Sister, why have you come here? You do not come very often, but I suppose that is because you live such a long way off. Am I, then, to leave off crying and refrain from all the sad thoughts that torture me? I, who have lost my brave and lion-hearted husband, who had every good quality under heaven, and whose name was great over all Hellas and middle Argos; and now my darling son has gone off on board of a ship—a foolish fellow who has never been used to roughing it, or to going about among gatherings of men. I am even more anxious about him than about my husband. I am all in a tremble when I think of him, lest something should happen to him, either from the people among whom he has gone, or by sea, for he has many enemies who are plotting against him, and are bent on killing him before he can return home."

Then the vision said: "Take heart, and be not so much dismayed. There is one gone with him whom many a man would be glad enough to have stand by his side, I mean Athene; it is she who has compassion upon you, and who has sent me to bear you this message."

"Then," said Penelope, "if you are a god or have been sent here by divine commission, tell me also about that other unhappy one—is he still alive, or is he already dead and in the house of Hades?"

And the vision said, "I shall not tell you for certain whether he is alive or dead, and there is no use in idle conversation."

Then it vanished through the thong-hole of the door and was dissipated into thin air; but Penelope rose from her sleep refreshed and comforted, so vivid had been her dream.

Meantime the suitors went on board and sailed their ways over the sea, intent on murdering Telemachus. Now there is a rocky islet called Asteris, of no great size, in midchannel between Ithaca and Same, and there is a harbor on either side of it where a ship can lie. Here then the Achaeans placed themselves in ambush.

BOOK V

Hermes, bidden by Zeus, flies to Calypso's isle to charge her to let Odysseus go. Obeying the god, Calypso helps her captive to build a raft and set sail. But after seventeen days of smooth sailing, the raft is wrecked in a storm summoned by Poseidon. Odysseus battles the waves bravely and at length reaches shore on the land of the Phaeacians. Exhausted and naked, he finds shelter in a wood and sleeps.

AND NOW, AS DAWN ROSE FROM HER COUCH BESIDE TITHONUS— harbinger of light alike to mortals and immortals—the gods met in council and with them, Zeus the lord of thunder, who is their king. Thereon Athene began to tell them of the many sufferings of Odysseus, for she pitied him away there in the house of the nymph Calypso.

"Father Zeus," said she, "and all you other gods that live in everlasting bliss, I hope there may never be such a thing as a kind and well-disposed ruler anymore, nor one who will govern equitably. I hope they will be all henceforth cruel and unjust, for there is not one of his subjects but has forgotten Odysseus, who ruled them as though he were their father. There he is, lying in great pain in an island where dwells the nymph Calypso, who will not let him go; and he cannot get back to his own country, for he can find neither ships nor sailors to take him over the sea. Furthermore, wicked people are now trying to murder his only son Telemachus, who is coming home from Pylos and Sparta, where he has been to see if he can get news of his father."

"What, my dear, are you talking about?" replied her father. "Did you not send him there yourself, because you thought it would help Odysseus to get home and punish the suitors? Besides, you are perfectly able to protect Telemachus, and to see him safely home again, while the suitors have to come hurry-skurrying back without having killed him."

When he had thus spoken, he said to his son Hermes, "Hermes, you are our messenger, go therefore and tell Calypso we have decreed that poor Odysseus is to return home. He is to be convoyed neither by gods nor men, but after a perilous voyage of twenty days upon a raft he is to reach fertile Scheria, the land of the Phaecians, who are near of kin to the gods, and will honor him as though he were one of ourselves. They will send him in a ship to his own country, and will give him more bronze and gold and raiment than he would have brought back from Troy, if he had had all his prize money and had got home without disaster. This is how we have settled that he shall return to his country and his friends."

Thus he spoke, and Hermes, guide and guardian, slayer of Argus, did as he was told. Forthwith he bound on his glittering golden sandals with which he could fly like the wind over land and sea. He took the wand with which he seals men's eyes in sleep or wakes them just as he pleases, and flew holding it in his hand over Pieria. Then he swooped down through the firmament till he reached the level of the sea, whose waves he skimmed like a cormorant that flies fishing every hole and corner of the ocean, and drenching its thick plumage in the spray. He flew and flew over many a weary wave, but when at last he got to the island which was his journey's end, he left the sea and went on by land till he came to the cave where the nymph Calypso lived.

He found her at home. There was a large fire burning on the hearth, and one could smell from far the fragrant reek of burning cedar and sandalwood. As for herself, she was busy at her loom, shooting her golden shuttle through the warp and singing beautifully. Round her cave there was a thick wood of alder, poplar, and sweet-smelling cypress trees, wherein all kinds of great birds had built their nests—owls, hawks, and chattering sea-crows that occupy their business in the waters. A vine loaded with grapes was trained and grew luxuriantly about the mouth of the cave; there were also four running rills of water in channels cut pretty close together, and turned hither and thither so as to irrigate the beds of violets and luscious herbage over which they flowed. Even a god could not help being charmed with such a lovely spot, so Hermes stood still and looked at it; but when he had admired it sufficiently he went inside the cave.

Calypso knew him at once—for the gods all know each other, no matter how far they live from one another—but Odysseus was not within; he was on the seashore as usual, looking out upon the barren ocean with tears in his eyes, groaning and breaking his heart for sorrow. Calypso gave Hermes a seat and said: "Why have you come to see me, Hermes—honored, and ever welcome—for you do not visit me often? Say what you want; I will do it for you at once if I can, and if it can be done at all. But come inside, and let me set refreshment before you."

As she spoke she drew a table loaded with ambrosia beside him and mixed him some red nectar, so Hermes ate and drank till he had had enough, and then said:

"We are speaking god and goddess to one another, and you ask me why I have come here, and I will tell you truly as you would have me do. Zeus sent me; it was no doing of mine. Who could possibly want to come all this way over the sea where there are no cities full of people to offer me sacrifices or choice hecatombs? Nevertheless, I had to come, for none of us other gods can cross Zeus, or transgress his orders. He says that you have here the most ill-starred of all those who fought nine years before the city of King Priam and sailed home in the tenth year after having sacked it. On their way home they sinned against Athene, who raised both wind and waves against them, so that all his brave companions perished, and he alone was carried hither by wind and tide. Zeus says that you are to let this man go at once, for it is decreed that he shall not perish here, far from his own people, but shall return to his house and country and see his friends again."

Calypso trembled with rage when she heard this. "You gods," she exclaimed, "ought to be ashamed of yourselves! You are always jealous, and hate seeing a goddess take a fancy to a mortal man, and live with him in open matrimony. So when rosy-fingered Dawn made love to Orion, you precious gods were all of you furious till Artemis went and killed him in Ortygia. So again when Demeter fell in love with Iasion, and yielded to him in a thrice-ploughed fallow field, Zeus came to hear of it before so very long and killed Iasion with his thunderbolts. And now you are angry with me too because I have a man here. I found the poor creature sitting, all alone astride of a keel, for Zeus had struck his ship with lightning and sunk it in midocean, so that all his crew were drowned, while he himself was driven by wind and waves on to my island. I got fond of him and cherished him, and had set my heart on making him immortal, so that he should never grow old all his days. Still I cannot cross Zeus, or bring his counsels to nothing; therefore, if he insists upon it, let the man go beyond the seas again. But I cannot send him anywhere myself, for I have neither ships nor men who can take him. Nevertheless, I will readily give him such advice, in all good faith, as will be likely to bring him safely to his own country."

"Then send him away," said Hermes, "or Zeus will be angry with you and punish you."

On this he took his leave, and Calypso went out to look for Odysseus, for she had heard Zeus' message. She found him sitting upon the beach with his eyes ever filled with tears, and dying of sheer homesickness; for he had got tired of Calypso, and though he was forced to sleep with her in the cave by night, it was she, not he, that would have it so. As for the daytime, he spent it on the rocks and on the seashore, weeping, crying aloud for his despair, and always looking out upon the sea. Calypso then went close up to him and said:

"My poor fellow, you shall not stay here grieving and fretting your life out any longer. I am going to send you away of my own free will; so go, cut some beams of wood, and make yourself a large raft with an upper deck, that it may carry you safely over the sea. I will put bread, wine, and water on board to save you from starving. I will also give you clothes, and will send you a fair wind to take you home, if the gods in heaven so will it—for they know more about these things, and can settle them better than I can."

Odysseus shuddered as he heard her. "Now, goddess," he answered, "there is something behind all this; you cannot be really meaning to help me home when you bid me do such a dreadful thing as put to sea on a raft. Not even a well-found ship with a fair wind could venture on such a distant voyage: nothing that you can say or do shall make me go on board a raft unless you first solemnly swear that you mean me no mischief."

Calypso smiled at this, and caressed him with her hand. "You know a great deal," said she, "but you are quite wrong here. May heaven above and earth below be my witnesses, with the waters of the river Styx—and this is the most solemn oath which a blessed god can take—that I mean you no sort of harm, and am only advising you to do exactly what I should do myself in your place. I am dealing with you quite straightforwardly; my heart is not made of iron, and I am very sorry for you."

When she had thus spoken she led the way rapidly before him, and Odysseus followed in her steps; so the pair, goddess and man, went on and on till they came to Calypso's cave, where Odysseus took the seat that Hermes had just left. Calypso set meat and drink before him of the food that mortals eat; but her maids brought ambrosia and nectar for herself, and they laid their hands on the good things that were before them. When they had satisfied themselves with meat and drink, Calypso spoke, saying:

"Odysseus, noble son of Laertes, so you would start home to your own land at once? Good luck go with you, but if you could only know how much suffering is in store for you before you get back to your own country, you would stay where you are, keep house along with me, and let me make you immortal, no matter how anxious you may be to see this wife of yours, of whom you are thinking all the time day after day. Yet I flatter myself that I am no whit less tall or well-looking than she is, for it is not to be expected that a mortal woman should compare in beauty with an immortal."

"Goddess," replied Odysseus, "do not be angry with me about this. I am quite aware that my wife Penelope is nothing like so tall or so beautiful as yourself. She is only a woman, whereas you are an immortal. Nevertheless, I want to get home, and can think of nothing else. If some god wrecks me when I am on the sea, I will bear it and make the best of it. I have had infinite trouble both by land and sea already, so let this go with the rest."

Presently the sun set and it became dark, whereon the pair retired into the inner part of the cave and went to bed.

When the child of morning, rosy-fingered Dawn, appeared, Odysseus put on his shirt and cloak, while the goddess wore a dress of a light gossamer fabric, very fine and graceful, with a beautiful golden girdle about her waist and a veil to cover her head. She at once set herself to think how she could speed Odysseus on his way. So she gave him a great bronze ax that suited his hands; it was sharpened on both sides, and had a beautiful olive-wood handle fitted firmly on to it. She also gave him a sharp adze, and then led the way to the far end of the island where the largest trees grew—alder, poplar, and pine, that reached the sky—very dry and well-seasoned, so as to sail light for him in the water. Then, when she had shown him where the best trees grew, Calypso went home, leaving him to cut them, which he soon finished doing. He cut down twenty trees in all and adzed them smooth, squaring them by rule in good workmanlike fashion. Meanwhile Calypso came back with some augers, so he bored holes with them and fitted the timbers together with bolts and rivets. He made the raft as broad as a skilled shipwright makes the beam of a large vessel, and he fixed a deck on top of the ribs, and ran a gunwale all around it. He also made a mast with a yard arm, and a rudder to steer with.

He fenced the raft all round with wicker hurdles as a protection against the waves, and then he threw on a quantity of wood. By and by Calypso brought him some linen to make the sails, and he made these too, excellently, making them fast with braces and sheets. Last of all, with the help of levers, he drew the raft down into the water.

In four days he had completed the whole work, and on the fifth Calypso sent him from the island after washing him and giving him some clean clothes. She gave him a goat skin full of black wine,[1] and another larger one of water; she also gave him a wallet full of provisions, and supplied him with much good meat. Moreover, she made the wind fair and warm for him, and gladly did Odysseus spread his sail before it, while he sat and guided the raft skillfully by means of the rudder. He never closed his eyes, but kept them fixed on the Pleiads, on late-setting Bootes, and on the Bear—which men also call the wain, and which turns round and round where it is, facing Orion, and alone never dipping into the stream of Oceanus—for Calypso had told him to keep this to his left. Days seven and ten did he sail over the sea, and on the eighteenth the dim outlines of the mountains on the nearest part of the Phaeacian coast appeared, rising like a shield on the horizon.

But King Poseidon, who was returning from the Ethiopians, caught sight of Odysseus a long way off, from the mountains of the Solymi. He could see him sailing upon the sea, and it made him very angry, so he wagged his head and muttered to himself, saying, "Good heavens, so the gods have been changing their minds about Odysseus while I was away in Ethiopia, and now he is close to the land of the Phaeacians, where it is decreed that he shall escape from the calamities that have befallen him. Still, he shall have plenty of hardship yet before he has done with it."

Thereon he gathered his clouds together, grasped his trident, stirred it round in the sea, and roused the rage of every wind that blows till earth, sea,

---

[1] That is, very deep red like some of the present Sicilian wines that look more black than anything else. (B.)

and sky were hidden in cloud, and night sprang forth out of the heavens. Winds from east, south, north, and west fell upon him all at the same time, and a tremendous sea got up, so that Odysseus' heart began to fail him. "Alas," he said to himself in his dismay, "what ever will become of me? I am afraid Calypso was right when she said I should have trouble by sea before I got back home. It is all coming true. How black is Zeus making heaven with his clouds, and what a sea the winds are raising from every quarter at once. I am now safe to perish. Blest and thrice blest were those Danaans who fell before Troy in the cause of the sons of Atreus. Would that I had been killed on the day when the Trojans were pressing me so sorely about the dead body of Achilles, for then I should have had due burial and the Achaeans would have honored my name; but now it seems that I shall come to a most pitiable end."

As he spoke a sea broke over him with such terrific fury that the raft reeled again, and he was carried overboard a long way off. He let go the helm, and the force of the hurricane was so great that it broke the mast halfway up, and both sail and yard went over into the sea. For a long time Odysseus was under water, and it was all he could do to rise to the surface again, for the clothes Calypso had given him weighed him down; but at last he got his head above water and spat out the bitter brine that was running down his face in streams. In spite of all this, however, he did not lose sight of his raft, but swam as fast as he could towards it, got hold of it, and climbed on board again so as to escape drowning. The sea took the raft and tossed it about as autumn winds whirl thistledown round and round upon a road. It was as though the south, north, east, and west winds were all playing battledore and shuttlecock with it at once.

When he was in this plight, Ino daughter of Cadmus, also called Leucothea, saw him. She had formerly been a mere mortal, but had been since raised to the rank of a marine goddess. Seeing in what great distress Odysseus now was, she had compassion upon him, and, rising like a seagull from the waves, took her seat upon the raft.

"My poor good man," said she, "why is Poseidon so furiously angry with you? He is giving you a great deal of trouble, but for all his bluster he will not kill you. You seem to be a sensible person, do then as I bid you; strip, leave your raft to drive before the wind, and swim to the Phaeacian coast where better luck awaits you. And here, take my veil and put it round your chest; it is enchanted, and you can come to no harm so long as you wear it. As soon as you touch land take it off, throw it back as far as you can into the sea, and then go away again." With these words she took off her veil and gave it him. Then she dived down again like a seagull and vanished beneath the dark blue waters.

But Odysseus did not know what to think. "Alas," he said to himself in his dismay, "this is only some one or other of the gods who is luring me to ruin by advising me to quit my raft. At any rate I will not do so at present, for the land where she said I should be quit of all my troubles seems to be still a good way off. I know what I will do—I am sure it will be best—no matter what happens, I will stick to the raft as long as her timbers hold together, but when the sea breaks her up I will swim for it. I do not see how I can do any better than this."

While he was thus in two minds, Poseidon sent a terrible great wave that seemed to rear itself above his head till it broke right over the raft, which then went to pieces as though it were a heap of dry chaff tossed about by a whirlwind. Odysseus got astride of one plank and rode upon it as if he were on horseback. He then took off the clothes Calypso had given him, bound Ino's veil under his arms, and plunged into the sea—meaning to swim on shore. King Poseidon watched him as he did so, and wagged his head, muttering to himself and saying, "There now, swim up and down as you best can till you fall in with well-to-do people. I do not think you will be able to say that I have let you off too lightly." On this he lashed his horses and drove to Aegae where his palace is.

But Athene resolved to help Odysseus, so she bound the ways of all the winds except one, and made them lie quite still; but she roused a good stiff breeze from the north that should lay the waters till Odysseus reached the land of the Phaeacians where he would be safe.

Thereon he floated about for two nights and two days in the water, with a heavy swell on the sea and death staring him in the face; but when the third day broke, the wind fell and there was a dead calm without so much as a breath of air stirring. As he rose on the swell, he looked eagerly ahead, and could see land quite near. Then, as children rejoice when their dear father begins to get better after having for a long time borne sore affliction sent him by some angry spirit, but the gods deliver him from evil, so was Odysseus thankful when he again saw land and trees, and swam on with all his strength that he might once more set foot upon dry ground. When, however, he got within earshot, he began to hear the surf thundering up against the rocks, for the swell still broke against them with a terrific roar. Everything was enveloped in spray; there were no harbors where a ship might ride, or shelter of any kind, but only headlands, low-lying rocks, and mountain tops.

Odysseus' heart now began to fail him, and he said despairingly to himself: "Alas, Zeus has let me see land after swimming so far that I had given up all hope, but I can find no landing place, for the coast is rocky and surf-beaten, the rocks are smooth and rise sheer from the sea, with deep water close under them so that I cannot climb out for want of foothold. I am afraid some great wave will lift me off my legs and dash me against the rocks as I leave the water—which would give me a sorry landing. If, on the other hand, I swim further in search of some shelving beach or harbor, a hurricane may carry me out to sea again sorely against my will, or heaven may send some great monster of the deep to attack me; for Amphitrite breeds many such, and I know that Poseidon is very angry with me."

While he was thus in two minds a wave caught him and took him with such force against the rocks that he would have been smashed and torn to pieces if Athene had not shown him what to do. He caught hold of the rock with both hands and clung to it groaning with pain till the wave retired, so he was saved that time; but presently the wave came on again and carried him back with it far into the sea—tearing his hands as the suckers of a polypus are torn when someone plucks it from its bed, and the stones come up along with it—even so did the rocks tear the skin from his strong hands, and then the wave drew him deep down under the water.

Here poor Odysseus would have certainly perished, even in spite of his own destiny, if Athene had not helped him to keep his wits about him. He swam seaward again, beyond reach of the surf that was beating against the land, and at the same time he kept looking towards the shore to see if he could find some haven, or a spit that should take the waves aslant. By and by, as he swam on, he came to the mouth of a river, and here he thought would be the best place, for there were no rocks, and it afforded shelter from the wind. He felt that there was a current, so he prayed inwardly and said:

"Hear me, O king, whoever you may be, and save me from the anger of the sea-god Poseidon, for I approach you prayerfully. Anyone who has lost his way has at all times a claim even upon the gods, wherefore in my distress I draw near to your stream, and cling to the knees of your riverhood. Have mercy upon me, O king, for I declare myself your suppliant."

Then the god stayed his stream and stilled the waves, making all calm before him, and bringing him safely into the mouth of the river. Here at last Odysseus' knees and strong hands failed him, for the sea had completely broken him. His body was all swollen, and his mouth and nostrils ran down like a river with sea-water, so that he could neither breathe nor speak, and lay swooning from sheer exhaustion. Presently, when he had got his breath and came to himself again, he took off the scarf that Ino had given him and threw it back into the salt[2] stream of the river, whereon Ino received it into her hands from the wave that bore it towards her. Then he left the river, laid himself down among the rushes, and kissed the bounteous earth.

---

[2] The reader will note that the river was flowing with salt water, that is, that it was tidal.

"Alas," he cried to himself in his dismay, "what ever will become of me, and how is it all to end? If I stay here upon the riverbed through the long watches of the night, I am so exhausted that the bitter cold and damp may make an end of me—for towards sunrise there will be a keen wind blowing from off the river. If, on the other hand, I climb the hillside, find shelter in the woods, and sleep in some thicket, I may escape the cold and have a good night's rest, but some savage beast may take advantage of me and devour me."

In the end he deemed it best to take to the woods, and he found one upon some high ground not far from the water. There he crept beneath two shoots of olive that grew from a single stock—the one an ungrafted sucker, while the other had been grafted. No wind, however squally, could break through the cover they afforded, nor could the sun's rays pierce them, nor the rain get through them, so closely did they grow into one another. Odysseus crept under these and began to make himself a bed to lie on, for there was a great litter of dead leaves lying about—enough to make a covering for two or three men even in hard winter weather. He was glad enough to see this, so he laid himself down and heaped the leaves all round him. Then, as one who lives alone in the country, far from any neighbor, hides a brand as fire-seed in the ashes to save himself from having to get a light elsewhere, even so did Odysseus cover himself up with leaves; and Athene shed a sweet sleep upon his eyes, closed his eyelids, and made him lose all memory of his sorrows.

Book VI

Nausicaa, daughter of Alcinous, king of the Phaeacians, drives with her maidens to the washing pools by the seashore, near where Odysseus lies sleeping. Awakened, Odysseus appeals to Nausicaa for aid, who, undaunted by his savage appearance, generously gives him food and clothing and invites him to her father's house. She and her maidens precede him into the town.

S O HERE ODYSSEUS SLEPT, OVERCOME BY SLEEP AND TOIL; BUT ATHENE went off to the country and city of the Phaeacians, a people who used to live in the fair town of Hypereia, near the lawless Cyclopes. Now the Cyclopes were stronger than they and plundered them, so their king Nausithous moved them thence and settled them in Scheria, far from all other people. He surrounded the city with a wall, built houses and temples, and divided the lands among his people; but he was dead and gone to the house of Hades, and King Alcinous, whose counsels were inspired of heaven, was now reigning. To his house, then, did Athene hie in furtherance of the return of Odysseus.

She went straight to the beautifully decorated bedroom in which there slept a girl who was as lovely as a goddess, Nausicaa, daughter to King Alcinous. Two maidservants were sleeping near her, both very pretty, one on either side of the doorway, which was closed with well-made folding doors. Athene took the form of the famous sea captain Dymas' daughter, who was a bosom friend of Nausicaa and just her own age; then, coming up to the girl's bedside like a breath of wind, she hovered over her head and said:

"Nausicaa, what can your mother have been about, to have such a lazy daughter? Here are your clothes all lying in disorder, yet you are going to be married almost immediately, and should not only be well-dressed yourself, but should find good clothes for those who attend you. This is the way to get yourself a good name, and to make your father and mother proud of you. Suppose, then, that we make tomorrow a washing day, and start at daybreak. I will come and help you so that you may have everything ready as soon as possible, for all the best young men among your own people are courting you, and you are not going to remain a maid much longer. Ask your father, therefore, to have a wagon and mules ready for us at daybreak, to take the rugs, robes, and girdles; and you can ride, too, which will be much pleasanter for you than walking, for the washing cisterns are some way from the town."

When she had said this Athene went away to Olympus, which they say is the everlasting home of the gods. Here no wind beats roughly, and neither rain nor snow can fall; but it abides in everlasting sunshine and in a great peacefulness of light, wherein the blessed gods are illumined for ever and ever. This was the place to which the goddess went when she had given instructions to the girl.

By and by morning came and woke Nausicaa, who began wondering about her dream; she therefore went to the other end of the house to tell her father and mother all about it, and found them in their own room. Her mother was sitting by the fireside spinning her purple yarn with her maids around her, and she happened to catch her father just as he was going out to attend a meeting of the town council, which the Phaeacian aldermen had convened. She stopped him and said:

"Papa dear, could you manage to let me have a good big wagon? I want to take all our dirty clothes to the river and wash them. You are the chief man here, so it is only right that you should have a clean shirt when you attend meetings of the council. Moreover, you have five sons at home, two of them married, while the other three are good-looking bachelors; you know they always like to have clean linen when they go to a dance, and I have been thinking about all this."

She did not say a word about her own wedding, for she did not like to, but her father knew and said, "You shall have the mules, my love, and whatever else you have a mind for. Be off with you, and the men shall get you a good strong wagon with a body to it that will hold all your clothes."

On this he gave his orders to the servants, who got the wagon out, harnessed the mules, and put them to, while the girl brought the clothes down from the linen room and placed them on the wagon. Her mother prepared her a basket of provisions; with all sorts of good things, and a goat skin full of wine. The girl now got into the wagon, and her mother gave her also a golden cruse of oil, that she and her women might anoint themselves. Then she took the whip and reins and lashed the mules on, whereon they set off, and their hoofs clattered on the road. They pulled without flagging, and carried not only Nausicaa and her wash of clothes but the maids also who were with her.

When they reached the waterside they went to the washing cisterns, through which there ran at all times enough pure water to wash any quantity of linen, no matter how dirty. Here they unharnessed the mules and turned them out to feed on the sweet juicy herbage that grew by the waterside. They took the clothes out of the wagon, put them in the water, and vied with one another in treading them in the pits to get the dirt out. After they had washed them and got them quite clean, they laid them out by the seaside, where the waves had raised a high beach of shingle, and set about washing themselves and anointing themselves with olive oil. Then they got their dinner by the side of the stream, and waited for the sun to finish drying the clothes. When they had done dinner they threw off the veils that covered their heads and began to play at ball, while Nausicaa sang for them. As the huntress Artemis goes forth upon the mountains of Taygetus or Erymanthus to hunt wild boars or deer, and the wood-nymphs, daughters of aegis-bearing Zeus, take their sport along with her (then is Leto[1] proud at seeing her daughter stand a full head taller than the others, and eclipse the

---

[1] Mother of the goddess Artemis by Zeus.

loveliest amid a whole bevy of beauties), even so did the girl outshine her handmaids.

When it was time for them to start home, and they were folding the clothes and putting them into the wagon, Athene began to consider how Odysseus should wake up and see the handsome girl who was to conduct him to the city of the Phaeacians. The girl, therefore, threw a ball at one of the maids, which missed her and fell into deep water. On this they all shouted, and the noise they made woke Odysseus, who sat up in his bed of leaves and began to wonder what it might all be.

"Alas," said he to himself, "what kind of people have I come among? Are they cruel, savage, and uncivilized, or hospitable and humane? I seem to hear the voices of young women, and they sound like those of the nymphs that haunt mountain tops, or springs of rivers and meadows of green grass. At any rate I am among a race of men and women. Let me try if I cannot manage to get a look at them."

As he said this he crept from under his bush, and broke off a bough covered with thick leaves to hide his nakedness. He looked like some lion of the wilderness that stalks about exulting in his strength and defying both wind and rain; his eyes glare as he prowls in quest of oxen, sheep, or deer, for he is famished, and will dare break even into a well-fenced homestead, trying to get at the sheep—even such did Odysseus seem to the young women, as he drew near to them all naked as he was, for he was in great want. On seeing one so unkempt and so begrimed with salt water, the others scampered off along the spits that jutted out into the sea, but the daughter of Alcinous stood firm, for Athene put courage into her heart and took away all fear from her. She stood right in front of Odysseus, and he doubted whether he should go up to her, throw himself at her feet, and embrace her knees as a suppliant, or stay where he was and entreat her to give him some clothes and show him the way to the town. In the end he deemed it best to entreat her from a distance, in case the girl should take offense at his coming near enough to clasp her knees, so he addressed her in honeyed and persuasive language.

"O queen," he said, "I implore your aid—but tell me, are you a goddess or are you a mortal woman? If you are a goddess and dwell in heaven, I can only conjecture that you are Zeus' daughter Artemis, for your face and figure resemble none but hers; if, on the other hand, you are a mortal and live on earth, thrice happy are your father and mother—thrice happy, too, are your brothers and sisters. How proud and delighted they must feel when they see so fair a scion as yourself going out to a dance! Most happy, however, of all will he be whose wedding gifts have been the richest, and who takes you to his own home. I never yet saw anyone so beautiful, neither man nor woman, and am lost in admiration as I behold you. I can only compare you to a young palm tree which I saw when I was at Delos growing near the altar of Apollo— for I was there, too, with much people after me, when I was on that journey which has been the source of all my troubles. Never yet did such a young plant shoot out of the ground as that was, and I admired and wondered at it exactly as I now admire and wonder at yourself. I dare not clasp your knees, but I am in great distress; yesterday made the twentieth day that I had been tossing about upon the sea. The winds and waves have taken me all the way from the Ogygian island, and now fate has flung me upon this coast that I may endure still further suffering; for I do not think that I have yet come to the end of it, but rather that heaven has still much evil in store for me.

"And now, O queen, have pity upon me, for you are the first person I have met, and I know no one else in this country. Show me the way to your town, and let me have anything that you may have brought hither to wrap your clothes in. May heaven grant you in all things your heart's desire—husband, house, and a happy, peaceful home; for there is nothing better in this world than that man and wife should be of one mind in a house. It discomfits their enemies, makes the hearts of their friends glad, and they themselves know more about it than anyone."

To this Nausicaa answered: "Stranger, you appear to be a sensible, well-disposed person. There is no accounting for luck; Zeus gives prosperity to rich and poor just as he chooses, so you must take what he has seen fit to send you, and make the best of it. Now, however, that you have come to this our country, you shall not want for clothes or for anything else that a foreigner in distress may reasonably look for. I will show you the way to the town, and will tell you the name of our people. We are called Phaeacians, and I am daughter to Alcinous, in whom the whole power of the state is vested."

Then she called her maids and said: "Stay where you are, you girls. Can you not see a man without running away from him? Do you take him for a robber or a murderer? Neither he nor anyone else can come here to do us Phaeacians any harm, for we are dear to the gods, and live apart on a land's end that juts into the sounding sea, and have nothing to do with any other people. This is only some poor man who has lost his way, and we must be kind to him, for strangers and foreigners in distress are under Zeus' protection, and will take what they can get and be thankful. So, girls, give the poor fellow something to eat and drink, and wash him in the stream at some place that is sheltered from the wind."

On this the maids left off running away and began calling one another back. They made Odysseus sit down in the shelter as Nausicaa had told them, and brought him a shirt and cloak. They also brought him the little golden cruse of oil, and told him to go and wash in the stream. But Odysseus said, "Young women, please to stand a little on one side that I may wash the brine from my shoulders and anoint myself with oil, for it is long enough since my skin has had a drop of oil upon it. I cannot wash as long as you all keep standing there. I am ashamed to strip before a number of good-looking young women."

Then they stood on one side and went to tell the girl, while Odysseus washed himself in the stream and scrubbed the brine from his back and from his broad shoulders. When he had thoroughly washed himself, and had got the brine out of his hair, he anointed himself with oil, and put on the clothes which the girl had given him. Athene then made him look taller and stronger than before; she also made the hair grow thick on the top of his head, and flow down in curls like hyacinth blossoms. She glorified him about the head and shoulders as a skillful workman who has studied art of all kinds under Hephaestus and Athene enriches a piece of silver plate by gilding it—and his work is full of beauty. Then he went and sat down a little way off upon the beach, looking quite young and handsome, and the girl gazed on him with admiration; then she said to her maids:

"Hush, my dears, for I want to say something. I believe the gods who live in heaven have sent this man to the Phaeacians. When I first saw him I thought him plain, but now his appearance is like that of the gods who dwell in heaven. I should like my future husband to be just such another as he is, if he would only stay here and not want to go away. However, give him something to eat and drink."

They did as they were told, and set food before Odysseus, who ate and drank ravenously, for it was long since he had had food of any kind. Meanwhile, Nausicaa bethought her of another matter. She got the linen folded and placed in the wagon, she then yoked the mules, and, as she took her seat, she called Odysseus:

"Stranger," said she, "rise and let us be going back to the town; I will introduce you at the house of my excellent father, where I can tell you that you will meet all the best people among the Phaeacians. But be sure and do as I bid you, for you seem to be a sensible person. As long as we are going past the fields and farm lands, follow briskly behind the wagon along with the maids and I will lead the way myself. Presently, however, we shall come to the town, where you will find a high wall running all round it, and a good harbor on either side with a narrow entrance into the city, and the ships will be drawn up by the roadside, for everyone has a place where his own ship can lie. You will see the marketplace with a temple of Poseidon in the middle of it, and paved with large stones bedded in the earth. Here people deal in ship's gear of all kinds, such as cables and sails, and here, too, are the places where oars are made; for the Phaeacians are not a nation of archers—they know nothing about bows and arrows, but are a seafaring folk, and pride themselves on their masts, oars, and ships, with which they travel far over the sea.

"I am afraid of the gossip and scandal that may be set on foot against me later on; for the people here are very ill-natured, and some low fellow, if he met us, might say, 'Who is this fine-looking stranger that is going about with Nausicaa? Where did she find him? I suppose she is going to marry him. Perhaps he is a vagabond sailor whom she has taken from some foreign vessel, for we have no neighbors; or some god has at last come down from heaven in answer to her prayers, and she is going to live with him all the rest of her life. It would be a good thing if she would take herself off and find a husband somewhere else, for she will not look at one of the many excellent young Phaeacians who are in love with her.' This is the kind of disparaging remark that would be made about me, and I could not complain, for I should myself be scandalized at seeing any other girl do the like, and go about with men in spite of everybody, while her father and mother were still alive, and without having been married in the face of all the world.

"If, therefore, you want my father to give you an escort and to help you home, do as I bid you. You will see a beautiful grove of poplars by the roadside dedicated to Athene; it has a well in it and a meadow all round it. Here my father has a field of rich garden ground, about as far from the town as a man's voice will carry. Sit down there and wait for a while till the rest of us can get into the town and reach my father's house. Then, when you think we must have done this, come into the town and ask the way to the house of my father Alcinous. You will have no difficulty in finding it; any child will point it out to you, for no one else in the whole town has anything like such a fine house as he has. When you have got past the gates and through the outer court, go right across the inner court till you come to my mother. You will find her sitting by the fire and spinning her purple wool by firelight. It is a fine sight to see her as she leans back against one of the bearing-posts with her maids all ranged behind her. Close to her seat stands that of my father, on which he sits and topes like an immortal god. Never mind him, but go up to my mother and lay your hands upon her knees, if you would get home quickly. If you can gain her over, you may hope to see your own country again, no matter how distant it may be."

So saying she lashed the mules with her whip and they left the river. The mules drew well, and their hoofs went up and down upon the road. She was careful not to go too fast for Odysseus and the maids who were following on foot along with the wagon, so she plied her whip with judgment. As the sun was going down they came to the sacred grove of Athene, and there Odysseus sat down and prayed to the mighty daughter of Zeus.

"Hear me," he cried, "daughter of aegis-bearing Zeus, unweariable, hear me now, for you gave no heed to my prayers when Poseidon was wrecking me. Now, therefore, have pity upon me and grant that I may find friends and be hospitably received by the Phaeacians."

Thus did he pray, and Athene heard his prayer, but she would not show herself to him openly, for she was afraid of her uncle Poseidon, who was still furious in his endeavors to prevent Odysseus from getting home.

Book VII

Athene guides Odysseus to the splendid palace of King Alcinous and Queen Arete. They welcome him kindly and listen while he explains his arrival on their shores and appearance at the palace. Moved by his tale, they promise to send him safely back to his home.

THUS, THEN, DID ODYSSEUS WAIT AND PRAY, BUT THE GIRL DROVE ON TO the town. When she reached her father's house she drew up at the gateway, and her brothers—comely as the gods—gathered round her, took the mules out of the wagon, and carried the clothes into the house, while she went to her own room, where an old servant, Eurymedusa of Apeira, lit the fire for her. This old woman had been brought by sea from Apeira, and had been chosen as a prize for Alcinous because he was king over the Phaeacians, and the people obeyed him as though he were a god. She had been nurse to Nausicaa, and had now lit the fire for her, and brought her supper for her into her own room.

Presently Odysseus got up to go towards the town, and Athene shed a thick mist all round him to hide him, in case any of the proud Phaeacians who met him should be rude to him or ask him who he was. Then, as he was just entering the town, she came towards him in the likeness of a little girl carrying a pitcher. She stood right in front of him, and Odysseus said:

"My dear, will you be so kind as to show me the house of King Alcinous? I am an unfortunate foreigner in distress, and do not know anyone in your town and country."

Then Athene said: "Yes, father stranger, I will show you the house you want, for Alcinous lives quite close to my own father. I will go before you and show the way, but say not a word as you go, and do not look at any man, or ask him questions; for the people here cannot abide strangers and do not like men who come from some other place. They are a seafaring folk, and sail the seas by the grace of Poseidon in ships that glide along like thought, or as a bird in the air."

On this she led the way, and Odysseus followed in her steps; but not one of the Phaeacians could see him as he passed through the city in the midst of them, for the great goddess Athene in her good will towards him had hidden him in a thick cloud of darkness. He admired their harbors, ships, places of assembly, and the lofty walls of the city, which, with the palisade on top of them, were very striking, and when they reached the king's house Athene said:

"This is the house, father stranger, which you would have me show you. You will find a number of great people sitting at table, but do not be afraid. Go straight in, for the bolder a man is the more likely he is to carry his point, even though he a stranger. First find the queen. Her name is Arete, and she comes of the same family as her husband Alcinous. They both descend originally from Poseidon, who was father to Nausithous by Periboea, a woman of great beauty. Periboea was the youngest daughter of Eurymedon, who at one time reigned over the giants, but he ruined his ill-fated people and lost his own life to boot.

"Poseidon, however, lay with his daughter, and she had a son by him, the great Nausithous, who reigned over the Phaeacians. Nausithous had two sons, Rhexenor and Alcinous,[1] Apollo killed the first of them while he was still a bridegroom and without male issue, but he left a daughter Arete, whom Alcinous married, and honors as no other woman is honored of all those that keep house along with their husbands.

---

[1] Polyphemus was also son to Poseidon, see Book IX. He was therefore half-brother to Nausithous, half-uncle to King Alcinous, and half-great-uncle to Nausicaa.

"Thus she both was, and still is, respected beyond measure by her children, by Alcinous himself, and by the whole people, who look upon her as a goddess, and greet her whenever she goes about the city. For she is a thoroughly good woman both in head and heart, and when any women are friends of hers, she will help their husbands also to settle their disputes. If you can gain her good will, you may have every hope of seeing your friends again, and getting safely back to your home and country."

Then Athene left Scheria and went away over the sea. She went to Marathon and to the spacious streets of Athens, where she entered the abode of Erechtheus; but Odysseus went on to the house of Alcinous, and he pondered much as he paused a while before reaching the threshold of bronze, for the splendor of the palace was like that of the sun or moon. The walls on either side were of bronze from end to end, and the cornice was of blue enamel. The doors were gold, and hung on pillars of silver that rose from a floor of bronze, while the lintel was silver and the hook of the door was of gold.

On either side there stood gold and silver mastiffs which Hephaestus, with his consummate skill, had fashioned expressly to keep watch over the palace of King Alcinous; so they were immortal and could never grow old. Seats were ranged all along the wall, here and there from one end to the other, with coverings of fine woven work which the women of the house had made. Here the chief persons of the Phaeacians used to sit and eat and drink, for there was abundance at all seasons; and there were golden figures of young men with lighted torches in their hands, raised on pedestals, to give light by night to those who were at table. There are fifty maidservants in the house, some of whom are always grinding rich yellow grain at the mill, while others work at the loom, or sit and spin, and their shuttles go backwards and forwards like the fluttering of aspen leaves, while the linen is so closely woven that it will turn oil. As the Phaeacians are the best sailors in the world, so their women excel all others in weaving, for Athene has taught them all manner of useful arts, and they are very intelligent.

Outside the gate of the outer court there is a large garden of about four acres with a wall all round it. It is full of beautiful trees—pears, pomegranates, and the most delicious apples. There are luscious figs also, and olives in full growth. The fruits never rot nor fail all the year round, neither winter nor summer, for the air is so soft that a new crop ripens before the old has dropped. Pear grows on pear, apple on apple, and fig on fig, and so also with the grapes, for there is an excellent vineyard. On the level ground of a part of this, the grapes are being made into raisins; in another part they are being gathered; some are being trodden in the wine tubs, others further on have shed their blossom and are beginning to show fruit, others again are just changing color. In the furthest part of the ground there are beautifully arranged beds of flowers that are in bloom all the year round. Two streams go through it, the one turned in ducts throughout the whole garden, while the other is carried under the ground of the outer court to the house itself, and the townspeople draw water from it. Such, then, were the splendors with which the gods had endowed the house of King Alcinous.

So here Odysseus stood for a while and looked about him, but when he had looked long enough he crossed the threshold and went within the precincts of the house. There he found all the chief people among the Phaeacians making their drink offerings to Hermes, which they always did the last thing before going away for the night. He went straight through the court, still hidden by the cloak of darkness in which Athene had enveloped him, till he reached Arete and King Alcinous; then he laid his hands upon the knees of the queen, and at that moment the miraculous darkness fell away from him and he became visible. Everyone was speechless with surprise at seeing a man there, but Odysseus began at once with his petition.

"Queen Arete," he exclaimed, "daughter of great Rhexenor, in my distress I humbly pray you, as also your husband and these your guests (whom may heaven prosper with long life and happiness, and may they leave their possessions to their children, and all the honor conferred upon them by the state) to help me home to my own country as soon as possible; for I have been long in trouble and away from my friends."

Then he sat down on the hearth among the ashes[2] and they all held their peace, till presently the old hero Echeneus, who was an excellent speaker and an elder among the Phaeacians, plainly and in all honesty addressed them thus:

"Alcinous," said he, "it is not creditable to you that a stranger should be seen sitting among the ashes of your hearth; everyone is waiting to hear what you are about to say. Tell him, then, to rise and take a seat on a stool inlaid with silver, and bid your servants mix some wine and water that we may make a drink offering to Zeus, the lord of thunder, who takes all well-disposed suppliants under his protection; and let the housekeeper give him some supper, of whatever there may be in the house."

When Alcinous heard this, he took Odysseus by the hand, raised him from the hearth, and bade him take the seat of Laodamas, who had been sitting beside him, and was his favorite son. A maidservant then brought him water in a beautiful golden ewer and poured it into a silver basin for him to wash his hands, and she drew a clean table beside him; an upper servant brought him bread and offered him many good things of what there was in the house, and Odysseus ate and drank. Then Alcinous said to one of the servants, "Pontonous, mix a cup of wine and hand it round that we may make drink offerings to Zeus, the lord of thunder, who is the protector of all well-disposed suppliants."

Pontonous then mixed wine and water, and handed it round after giving every man his drink offering. When they had made their offerings, and had drunk each as much as he was minded, Alcinous said:

"Aldermen and town councilors of the Phaeacians, hear my words. You have had your supper, so now go home to bed. Tomorrow morning I shall invite a still larger number of aldermen, and will give a sacrificial banquet in

[2] The humble place, where any Greek suppliant for mercy and help would sit.

honor of our guest. We can then discuss the question of his escort, and consider how we may at once send him back rejoicing to his own country without trouble or inconvenience to himself, no matter how distant it may be. We must see that he comes to no harm while on his homeward journey, but when he is once at home he will have to take the luck he was born with, for better or worse, like other people. It is possible, however, that the stranger is one of the immortals who has come down from heaven to visit us; but in this case the gods are departing from their usual practice, for hitherto they have made themselves perfectly clear to us when we have been offering them hecatombs. They come and sit at our feasts just like one of our selves, and if any solitary wayfarer happens to stumble upon some one or other of them, they effect no concealment, for we are as near of kin to the gods as the Cyclopes and the savage giants are."

Then Odysseus said: "Pray, Alcinous, do not take any such notion into your head. I have nothing of the immortal about me, neither in body nor mind, and most resemble those among you who are the most afflicted. Indeed, were I to tell you all that heaven has seen fit to lay upon me, you would say that I was still worse off than they are. Nevertheless, let me sup in spite of sorrow, for an empty stomach is a very importunate thing, and thrusts itself on a man's notice no matter how dire is his distress. I am in great trouble, yet it insists that I shall eat and drink, bids me lay aside all memory of my sorrows and dwell only on the due replenishing of itself. As for yourselves, do as you propose, and at break of day set about helping me to get home. I shall be content to die if I may first once more behold my property, my bondsmen, and all the greatness of my house."

Thus did he speak. Everyone approved his saying, and agreed that he should have his escort, inasmuch as he had spoken reasonably. Then when they had made their drink offerings, and had drunk each as much as he was minded, they went home to bed, every man in his own abode, leaving Odysseus in the cloister with Arete and Alcinous while the servants were taking the things away after supper. Arete was the first to speak, for she recognized the shirt, cloak, and good clothes that Odysseus was wearing, as the work of herself and of her maids; so she said, "Stranger, before we go any further, there is a question I should like to ask you. Who, and whence are you, and who gave you those clothes? Did you not say you had come here from beyond the sea?"

And Odysseus answered: "It would be a long story, madam, were I to relate in full the tale of my misfortunes, for the hand of heaven has been laid heavy upon me; but as regards your question, there is an island far away in the sea which is called the Ogygian. Here dwells the cunning and powerful goddess Calypso, daughter of Atlas. She lives by herself far from all neighbors, human or divine. Fortune, however, brought me to her hearth all desolate and alone, for Zeus struck my ship with his thunderbolts, and broke it up in midocean. My brave comrades were drowned, every man of them, but I stuck to the keel and was carried hither and thither for the space of nine days, till at last during the darkness of the tenth night the gods brought me to the Ogygian island where the great goddess Calypso lives. She took me in and treated me with the utmost kindness; indeed she wanted to make me immortal that I might never grow old, but she could not persuade me to let her do so.

"I stayed with Calypso seven years straight on end, and watered the good clothes she gave me with my tears during the whole time; but at last when the eighth year came round she bade me depart of her own free will, either because Zeus had told her she must, or because she had changed her mind. She sent me from her island on a raft, which she provisioned with abundance of bread and wine. Moreover she gave me good stout clothing, and sent me a wind that blew both warm and fair. Days seven and ten did I sail over the sea, and on the eighteenth I caught sight of the first outlines of the mountains upon your coast—and glad indeed was I to set eyes upon them. Nevertheless, there was still much trouble in store for me, for at this point Poseidon would let me go no further, and raised a great storm against me. The sea was so terribly high that I could no longer keep to my raft, which went to pieces under the fury of the gale, and I had to swim for it, till wind and current brought me to your shores.

"There I tried to land, but could not, for it was a bad place and the waves dashed me against the rocks, so I again took to the sea and swam on till I came to a river that seemed the most likely landing place, for there were no rocks and it was sheltered from the wind. Here, then, I got out of the water and gathered my senses together again. Night was coming on, so I left the river and went into a thicket, where I covered myself all over with leaves, and presently heaven sent me off into a very deep sleep. Sick and sorry as I was I slept among the leaves all night, and through the next day till afternoon, when I woke as the sun was westering, and saw your daughter's maidservants playing upon the beach, and your daughter among them looking like a goddess. I besought her aid, and she proved to be of an excellent disposition, much more so than could be expected from so young a person—for young people are apt to be thoughtless. She gave me plenty of bread and wine, and when she had had me washed in the river she also gave me the clothes in which you see me. Now, therefore, though it has pained me to do so, I have told you the whole truth."

Then Alcinous said, "Stranger, it was very wrong of my daughter not to bring you on at once to my house along with the maids, seeing that she was the first person whose aid you asked."

"Pray do not scold her," replied Odysseus; "she is not to blame. She did tell me to follow along with the maids, but I was ashamed and afraid, for I thought you might perhaps be displeased if you saw me. Every human being is sometimes a little suspicious and irritable."

"Stranger," replied Alcinous, "I am not the kind of man to get angry about nothing; it is always better to be reasonable. But by Father Zeus, Athene, and Apollo, now that I see what kind of person you are, and how much you think as I do, I wish you would stay here, marry my daughter, and become my son-in-law. If you will stay I will give you a house and an estate; but no one (heaven forbid) shall keep you here against your own wish, and that you may be sure of this, I will attend tomorrow to the matter of your escort. You can sleep during the whole voyage if you like, and the men shall sail you over smooth waters either to your own home, or wherever you please, even though it be a long way further off than Euboea, which those of my people who saw it, when they took yellow-haired Rhadamanthus to see Tityus the son of Gaia, tell me is the furthest of any place. And yet they did the whole voyage in a single day without distressing themselves, and came back again afterwards. You will thus see how much my ships excel all others, and what magnificent oarsmen my sailors are."

Then was Odysseus glad and prayed aloud, saying, "Father Zeus, grant that Alcinous may do all as he has said, for so he will win an imperishable name among mankind, and at the same time I shall return to my own country."

Thus did they converse. Then Arete told her maids to set a bed in the room that was in the gatehouse, and make it with good red rugs, and to spread coverlets on the top of them with woolen cloaks for Odysseus to wear. The maids thereon went out with torches in their hands, and when they had made the bed they came up to Odysseus and said, "Rise, sir stranger, and come with us for your bed is ready," and glad indeed was he to go to his rest.

So Odysseus slept in a bed placed in a room over the echoing gateway; but Alcinous lay in the inner part of the house, with the queen his wife by his side.

Book VIII

The next day King Alcinous orders a ship made ready for Odysseus and gives a magnificent banquet to the Phaeacians. The blind bard Demodocus sings, and afterward there are games of prowess. Odysseus, challenged to take part, excels in disc-throwing. The Phaeacians dance, and the chiefs bestow gifts on Odysseus. Demodocus sings of the Trojan War, Odysseus weeps, and the king begs him to declare who he is.

NOW WHEN THE CHILD OF MORNING, ROSY-FINGERED DAWN, APPEARED, Alcinous and Odysseus both rose, and Alcinous led the way to the Phaeacian place of assembly, which was near the ships. When they got there they sat down side by side on a seat of polished stone, while Athene took the form of one of Alcinous' servants, and went round the town in order to help Odysseus to get home. She went up to the citizens, man by man, and said: "Aldermen and town councilors of the Phaeacians, come to the assembly all of you and listen to the stranger who has just come off a long voyage to the house of King Alcinous. He looks like an immortal god."

With these words she made them all want to come, and they flocked to the assembly till seats and standing room were alike crowded. Everyone was struck with the appearance of Odysseus, for Athene had beautified him about the head and shoulders, making him look taller and stouter than he really was, that he might impress the Phaeacians favorably as being a very remarkable man, and might come off well in the many trials of skill to which they would challenge him. Then, when they were got together, Alcinous spoke:

"Hear me," said he, "aldermen and town councilors of the Phaeacians, that I may speak even as I am minded. This stranger, whoever he may be, has found his way to my house from somewhere or other either east or west. He wants an escort and wishes to have the matter settled. Let us then get one ready for him, as we have done for others before him. Indeed, no one who ever yet came to my house has been able to complain of me for not speeding him on his way soon enough. Let us draw a ship into the sea—one that has never yet made a voyage—and man her with two and fifty of our smartest young sailors. Then when you have made fast your oars each by his own seat, leave the ship and come to my house to prepare a feast.[1] I will supply you with everything. I am giving these instructions to the young men who will form the crew. As regards you aldermen and town councilors, you will join me in entertaining our guest in the cloisters. I can take no excuses, and we will have Demodocus to sing to us; for there is no bard like him, whatever he may choose to sing about."

Alcinous then led the way, and the others followed after, while a servant went to fetch Demodocus. The fifty-two picked oarsmen went to the seashore as they had been told, and when they got there they drew the ship into the water, got her mast and sails inside her, bound the oars to the thole-pins with twisted thongs of leather, all in due course, and spread the white sails aloft. They moored the vessel a little way out from land, and then came on shore and went to the house of King Alcinous. The outhouses, yards, and all the precincts were filled with crowds of men in great multitudes both old and young; and Alcinous killed them a dozen sheep, eight full grown pigs, and two oxen. These they skinned and dressed so as to provide a magnificent banquet.

A servant presently led in the famous bard Demodocus, whom the muse had dearly loved, but to whom she had given both good and evil, for though

---

[1] There were two classes—the lower who were given provisions which they had to cook for themselves in the yards and outer precincts, where they would also eat—and the upper who would eat in the cloisters of the inner court, and have their cooking done for them. (B.)

she had endowed him with a divine gift of song, she had robbed him of his eyesight. Pontonous set a seat for him among the guests, leaning it up against a bearing-post. He hung the lyre for him on a peg over his head, and showed him where he was to feel for it with his hands. He also set a fair table with a basket of victuals by his side, and a cup of wine from which he might drink whenever he was so disposed.

The company then laid their hands upon the good things that were before them, but as soon as they had had enough to eat and drink, the muse inspired Demodocus to sing the feats of heroes, and more especially a matter that was then in the mouths of all men, to wit, the quarrel between Odysseus and Achilles, and the fierce words that they heaped on one another as they sat together at a banquet.[2] But Agamemnon was glad when he heard his chieftains quarreling with one another, for Apollo had foretold him this at Pytho when he crossed the stone floor to consult the oracle. Here was the beginning of the evil that by the will of Zeus fell both upon Danaans and Trojans.

Thus sang the bard, but Odysseus drew his purple mantle over his head and covered his face, for he was ashamed to let the Phaeacians see that he was weeping. When the bard left off singing, he wiped the tears from his eyes, uncovered his face, and, taking his cup, made a drink offering to the gods; but when the Phaeacians pressed Demodocus to sing further, for they delighted in his lays, then Odysseus again drew his mantle over his head and wept bitterly. No one noticed his distress except Alcinous, who was sitting near him, and heard the heavy sighs that he was heaving. So he at once said, "Aldermen and town councilors of the Phaeacians, we have had enough now, both of the feast and of the minstrelsy that is its due accompaniment. Let us proceed therefore to the athletic sports, so that out guest on his return home may be able to tell his friends how much we surpass all other nations as boxers, wrestlers, jumpers, and runners."

---

[2] No account of this quarrel by any Greek poet has come down to us.

With these words he led the way, and the others followed after. A servant hung Demodocus' lyre on its peg for him, led him out of the cloister, and set him on the same way as that along which all the chief men of the Phaeacians were going to see the sports; a crowd of several thousands of people followed them, and there were many excellent competitors for all the prizes. Acroneos, Ocyalus, Elatreus, Nauteus, Prymneus, Anchialus, Eretmeus, Ponteus, Proreus, Thoon, Anabesineus, and Amphialus son of Polyneus son of Tecton. There was also Euryalus son of Naubolus, who was like Ares himself, and was the best-looking man among the Phaeacians except Laodamas. Three sons of Alcinous—Laodamas, Halios, and Clytoneus—competed also.

The foot races came first. The course was set out for them from the starting post, and they raised a dust upon the plain as they all flew forward at the same moment. Clytoneus came in first by a long way; he left everyone else behind him by the length of the furrow that a couple of mules can plow in a fallow field. They then turned to the painful art of wrestling, and here Euryalus proved to be the best man. Amphialus excelled all the others in jumping, while at throwing the disc there was no one who could approach Elatreus. Alcinous' son Laodamas was the best boxer, and he it was who presently said, when they had all been diverted with the games, "Let us ask the stranger whether he excels in any of these sports. He seems very powerfully built; his thighs, calves, hands, and neck are of prodigious strength, nor is he at all old, but he has suffered much lately, and there is nothing like the sea for making havoc with a man, no matter how strong he is."

"You are quite right, Laodamas," replied Euryalus, "go up to your guest and speak to him about it yourself."

When Laodamas heard this he made his way into the middle of the crowd and said to Odysseus, "I hope, sir, that you will enter yourself for some one or other of our competitions if you are skilled in any of them—and you must have gone in for many a one before now. There is nothing that does anyone so much credit all his life long as the showing himself a proper man with his hands and feet. Have a try therefore at something, and banish all sorrow from your mind. Your return home will not be long delayed, for the ship is already drawn into the water, and the crew is found."

Odysseus answered, "Laodamas, why do you taunt me in this way? My mind is set rather on cares than contests; I have been through infinite trouble, and am come among you now as a suppliant, praying your king and people to further me on my return home."

Then Euryalus reviled him outright and said: "I gather, then, that you are unskilled in any of the many sports that men generally delight in. I suppose you are one of those grasping traders that go about in ships as captains or merchants, and who think of nothing but of their outward freights and home-ward cargoes. There does not seem to be much of the athlete about you."

"For shame, sir!" answered Odysseus, fiercely. "You are an insolent fellow—so true is it that the gods do not grace all men alike in speech, person, and understanding. One man may be of weak presence, but heaven has adorned him with such a good conversation that he charms everyone who sees him; his honeyed moderation carries his hearers with him so that he is leader in all assemblies of his fellows, and wherever he goes he is looked up to. Another may be as handsome as a god, but his good looks are not crowned with discretion. This is your case. No god could make a finer-looking fellow than you are, but you are a fool. Your ill-judged remarks have made me exceedingly angry, and you are quite mistaken, for I excel in a great many athletic exercises. Indeed, so long as I had youth and strength, I was among the first athletes of the age. Now, however, I am worn out by labor and sorrow, for I have gone through much both on the field of battle and by the waves of the weary sea. Still, in spite of all this I will compete, for your taunts have stung me to the quick."

So he hurried up without even taking his cloak off, and seized a disc, larger, more massive, and much heavier than those used by the Phaeacians when disc-throwing among themselves. Then, swinging it back, he threw it from his brawny hand, and it made a humming sound in the air as he did so. The Phaeacians quailed beneath the rushing of its flight as it sped gracefully from his hand, and flew beyond any mark that had been made yet. Athene, in the form of a man, came and marked the place where it had fallen. "A blind man, sir," said she, "could easily tell your mark by groping for it—it is so far ahead of any other. You may make your mind easy about this contest, for no Phaeacian can come near to such a throw as yours."

Odysseus was glad when he found he had a friend among the lookers-on, so he began to speak more pleasantly. "Young men," said he, "come up to that throw if you can, and I will throw another disc as heavy or even heavier. If anyone wants to have a bout with me let him come on, for I am exceedingly angry. I will box, wrestle, or run, I do not care what it is, with any man of you all except Laodamas, but not with him because I am his guest, and one cannot compete with one's own personal friend. At least I do not think it a prudent or a sensible thing for a guest to challenge his host's family at any game, especially when he is in a foreign country. He will cut the ground from under his own feet if he does. But I make no exception as regards anyone else, for I want to have the matter out and know which is the best man.

"I am a good hand at every kind of athletic sport known among mankind. I am an excellent archer. In battle I am always the first to bring a man down with my arrow, no matter how many more are taking aim at him alongside of me. Philoctetes was the only man who could shoot better than I could when we Achaeans were before Troy and in practice. I far excel everyone else in the whole world, of those who still eat bread upon the face of the earth, but I should not like to shoot against the mighty dead, such as Heracles, or Eurytus the Oechalian—men who could shoot against the gods themselves. This in fact was how Eurytus came prematurely by his end, for Apollo was angry with him and killed him because he challenged him as an archer. I can throw a dart further than anyone else can shoot an arrow. Running is the only point in respect of which I am afraid some of the Phaeacians might beat me, for

I have been brought down very low at sea; my provisions ran short, and therefore I am still weak."

They all held their peace except King Alcinous, who began: "Sir, we have had much pleasure in hearing all that you have told us, from which I understand that you are willing to show your prowess, as having been displeased with some insolent remarks that have been made to you by one of our athletes, and which could never have been uttered by anyone who knows how to talk with propriety. I hope you will apprehend my meaning, and will explain to any one of your chief men who may be dining with yourself and your family when you get home, that we have an hereditary aptitude for accomplishments of all kinds. We are not particularly remarkable for our boxing, nor yet as wrestlers, but we are singularly fleet of foot and are excellent sailors. We are extremely fond of good dinners, music, and dancing; we also like frequent changes of linen, warm baths, and good beds. So now, please, some of you who are the best dancers set about dancing, that our guest on his return home may be able to tell his friends how much we surpass all other nations as sailors, runners, dancers, and minstrels. Demodocus has left his lyre at my house, so run some one or other of you and fetch it for him."

On this a servant hurried off to bring the lyre from the king's house, and the nine men who had been chosen as stewards stood forward. It was their business to manage everything connected with the sports, so they made the ground smooth and marked a wide space for the dancers. Presently the servant came back with Demodocus' lyre, and he took his place in the midst of them, whereon the best young dancers in the town began to foot and trip it so nimbly that Odysseus was delighted with the merry twinkling of their feet.

Meanwhile the bard began to sing the loves of Ares and Aphrodite, and how they first began their intrigue in the house of Hephaestus. Ares made Aphrodite many presents, and defiled King Hephaestus' marriage bed, so the sun, who saw what they were about, told Hephaestus. Hephaestus was very angry when he heard such dreadful news, so he went to his smithy brooding mischief, got his great anvil into its place, and began to forge some chains which none could either unloose or break, so that they might stay there in that place. When he had finished his snare he went into his bedroom and festooned the bed-posts all over with chains like cobwebs; he also let many hang down from the great beam of the ceiling. Not even a god could see them, so fine and subtle were they. As soon as he had spread the chains all over the bed, he made as though he were setting out for the fair state of Lemnos, which of all places in the world was the one he was most fond of. But Ares kept no blind lookout, and as soon as he saw him start, hurried off to his house, burning with love for Aphrodite.

Now Aphrodite was just come in from a visit to her father Zeus, and was about sitting down when Ares came inside the house, and said as he took her hand in his own, "Let us go to the couch of Hephaestus: he is not at home, but is gone off to Lemnos among the Sintians, whose speech is barbarous."

She was nothing loath, so they went to the couch to take their rest, whereon they were caught in the toils which cunning Hephaestus had spread for them, and could neither get up nor stir hand or foot, but found too late that they were in a trap. Then Hephaestus came up to them, for he had turned back before reaching Lemnos, when his scout the sun told him what was going on. He was in a furious passion, and stood in the vestibule making a dreadful noise as he shouted to all the gods.

"Father Zeus," he cried, "and all you other blessed gods who live forever, come here and see the ridiculous and disgraceful sight that I will show you. Zeus' daughter Aphrodite is always dishonoring me because I am lame. She is in love with Ares, who is handsome and clean built, whereas I am a cripple—but my parents are to blame for that, not I; they ought never to have begotten me. Come and see the pair together asleep on my bed. It makes me furious to look at them. They are very fond of one another, but I do not think they will lie there longer than they can help, nor do I think that they will sleep much. There, however, they shall stay till her father has repaid me the sum I gave him for his baggage of a daughter, who is fair but not honest."

On this the gods gathered to the house of Hephaestus. Earth-encircling Poseidon came, and Hermes, the bringer of luck, and King Apollo, but the goddesses stayed at home all of them for shame. Then the givers of all good things stood in the doorway, and the blessed gods roared with inextinguishable laughter, as they saw how cunning Hephaestus had been, whereon one would turn towards his neighbor, saying:

"Ill deeds do not prosper, and the weak confound the strong. See how limping Hephaestus, lame as he is, has caught Ares, who is the fleetest god in heaven; and now Ares will be cast in heavy damages."

Thus did they converse, but King Apollo said to Hermes, "Messenger Hermes, giver of good things, you would not care how strong the chains were, would you, if you could sleep with Aphrodite?"

"King Apollo," answered Hermes, "I only wish I might get the chance, though there were three times as many chains—and you might look on, all of you, gods and goddesses, but I would sleep with her if I could."

The immortal gods burst out laughing as they heard him, but Poseidon took it all seriously, and kept on imploring Hephaestus to set Ares free again. "Let him go," he cried, "and I will undertake, as you require, that he shall pay you all the damages that are held reasonable among the immortal gods."

"Do not," replied Hephaestus, "ask me to do this; a bad man's bond is bad security. What remedy could I enforce against you if Ares should go away and leave his debts behind him along with his chains?"

"Hephaestus," said Poseidon, "if Ares goes away without paying his damages, I will pay you myself." So Hephaestus answered, "In this case I cannot and must not refuse you."

Thereon he loosed the bonds that bound them, and as soon as they were free they scampered off, Ares to Thrace and laughter-loving Aphrodite to Cyprus and to Paphos, where is her grove and her altar fragrant with burnt offerings. Here the Graces bathed her, and anointed her with oil of ambrosia such as the immortal gods make use of, and they clothed her in raiment of the most enchanting beauty.

Thus sang the bard, and both Odysseus and the seafaring Phaeacians were charmed as they heard him.

Then Alcinous told Laodamas and Halius to dance alone, for there was no one to compete with them. So they took a red ball which Polybus had made for them, and one of them bent himself backwards and threw it up towards the clouds, while the other jumped from off the ground and caught it with ease before it came down again. When they had done throwing the ball straight up into the air they began to dance, and at the same time kept on throwing it backwards and forwards to one another, while all the young men in the ring applauded and made a great stamping with their feet. Then Odysseus said:

"King Alcinous, you said your people were the nimblest dancers in the world, and indeed they have proved themselves to be so. I was astonished as I saw them."

The king was delighted at this, and exclaimed to the Phaeacians: "Aldermen and town councilors, our guest seems to be a person of singular judgment. Let us give him such proof of our hospitality as he may reasonably expect. There are twelve chief men among you, and counting myself there are thirteen; contribute, each of you, a clean cloak, a shirt, and a talent of fine gold; let us give him all this in a lump down at once, so that when he gets his supper he may do so with a light heart. As for Euryalus, he will have to make a formal apology and a present too, for he has been rude."

Thus did he speak. The others all of them applauded his saying, and sent their servants to fetch the presents. Then Euryalus said: "King Alcinous, I will give the stranger all the satisfaction you require. He shall have my sword, which is of bronze, all but the hilt, which is of silver. I will also give him the scabbard of newly sawn ivory into which it fits. It will be worth a great deal to him."

As he spoke he placed the sword in the hands of Odysseus and said: "Good luck to you, father stranger. If anything has been said amiss, may the winds blow it away with them, and may heaven grant you a safe return, for I understand you have been long away from home and have gone through much hardship."

To which Odysseus answered: "Good luck to you too, my friend, and may the gods grant you every happiness. I hope you will not miss the sword you have given me along with your apology."

With these words he girded the sword about his shoulders and towards sundown the presents began to make their appearance, as the servants of the donors kept bringing them to the house of King Alcinous; here his sons received them, and placed them under their mother's charge. Then Alcinous led the way to the house and bade his guests take their seats.

"Wife," said he, turning to Queen Arete, "go, fetch the best chest we have, and put a clean cloak and shirt in it. Also, set a copper on the fire and heat some water; our guest will take a warm bath. See also to the careful packing of the presents that the noble Phaeacians have made him; he will thus better enjoy both his supper and the singing that will follow. I shall myself give him this golden goblet, which is of exquisite workmanship, that he may be reminded of me for the rest of his life whenever he makes a drink offering to Zeus, or to any of the gods."

Then Arete told her maids to set a large tripod upon the fire as fast as they could, whereon they set a tripod full of bath water on to a clear fire. They threw on sticks to make it blaze, and the water became hot as the flame played about the belly of the tripod. Meanwhile Arete brought a magnificent chest from her own room, and inside it she packed all the beautiful presents of gold and raiment which the Phaeacians had brought. Lastly she added a cloak and a good shirt from Alcinous, and said to Odysseus:

"See to the lid yourself, and have the whole bound round at once, for fear anyone should rob you by the way when you are asleep in your ship."

When Odysseus heard this he put the lid on the chest and made it fast with a bond that Circe had taught him. He had hardly done so before an upper servant told him to come to the bath and wash himself. He was very glad of a warm bath, for he had had no one to wait upon him ever since he left the house of Calypso, who as long as he remained with her had taken as good care of him as though he had been a god. When the servants had done washing and anointing him with oil and had given him a clean cloak and shirt, he left the bathroom and joined the guests who were sitting over their wine. Lovely Nausicaa stood by one of the bearing-posts supporting the roof of the cloister, and admired him as she saw him pass. "Farewell, stranger," said she, "do not forget me when you are safe at home again, for it is to me first that you owe a ransom for having saved your life."

And Odysseus said, "Nausicaa, daughter of great Alcinous, may Zeus the mighty husband of Hera grant that I may reach my home; so shall I bless you as my guardian angel all my days, for it was you who saved me."

When he had said this, he seated himself beside Alcinous. Supper was then served, and the wine was mixed for drinking. A servant led in the favorite bard Demodocus, and set him in the midst of the company, near one of the bearing-posts supporting the cloister, that he might lean against it. Then Odysseus cut off a piece of roast pork with plenty of fat (for there was abundance left on the joint) and said to a servant, "Take this piece of pork over to Demodocus and tell him to eat it; for all the pain his lays may cause me I will salute him none the less; bards are honored and respected throughout the world, for the muse teaches them their songs and loves them."

The servant carried the pork in his fingers over to Demodocus, who took it and was very much pleased. They then laid their hands on the good things that were before them, and as soon as they had had enough to eat and drink, Odysseus said to Demodocus: "Demodocus, there is no one in the world whom I admire more than I do you. You must have studied under the muse, Zeus' daughter, and under Apollo, so accurately do you sing the return of the

Achaeans with all their sufferings and adventures. If you were not there your-self, you must have heard it all from someone who was. Now, however, change your song and tell us of the wooden horse which Epeus made with the assis-tance of Athene, and which Odysseus got by stratagem into the fort of Troy after freighting it with the men who afterwards sacked the city. If you will sing this tale aright, I will tell all the world how magnificently heaven has endowed you."

The bard inspired of heaven took up the story at the point where some of the Argives set fire to their tents and sailed away while others, hidden within the horse, were waiting with Odysseus in the Trojan place of assem-bly. For the Trojans themselves had drawn the horse into their fortress, and it stood there while they sat in council round it, and were in three minds as to what they should do. Some were for breaking it up then and there; others would have it dragged to the top of the rock on which the fortress stood, and then thrown down the precipice; while yet others were for letting it remain as an offering and propitiation for the gods. And this was how they settled it in the end, for the city was doomed when it took in that horse, within which were all the bravest of the Argives waiting to bring death and destruction on the Trojans. Anon he sang how the sons of the Achaeans issued from the horse, and sacked the town, breaking out from their ambuscade. He sang how they overran the city hither and thither and ravaged it, and how Odysseus went raging like Ares along with Menelaus to the house of Deïphobus. It was there that the fight raged most furiously, nevertheless by Athene's help he was victorious.

All this he told, but Odysseus was overcome as he heard him, and his cheeks were wet with tears. He wept as a woman weeps when she throws herself on the body of her husband who has fallen before his own city and people, fighting bravely in defense of his home and children. She screams aloud and flings her arms about him as he lies gasping for breath and dying, but her enemies beat her from behind about the back and shoulders, and carry her off into slavery, to a life of labor and sorrow, and the beauty fades from her cheeks. Even so piteously did Odysseus weep, but none of those present perceived his tears except Alcinous, who was sitting near him, and could hear the sobs and sighs that he was heaving. The king, therefore, at once rose and said:

"Aldermen and town councilors of the Phaeacians, let Demodocus cease his song, for there are those present who do not seem to like it. From the moment that we had done supper and Demodocus began to sing, our guest has been all the time groaning and lamenting. He is evidently in great trouble, so let the bard leave off, that we may all enjoy ourselves, hosts and guests alike. This will be much more as it should be, for all these festivities, with the escort and the presents that we are making with so much good will, are wholly in his honor, and anyone with even a moderate amount of right feeling knows that he ought to treat a guest and a suppliant as though he were his own brother.

"Therefore, sir, do you on your part affect no more concealment or reserve in the matter about which I shall ask you; it will be more polite in you to give me a plain answer. Tell me the name by which your father and mother over yonder used to call you, and by which you were known among your neighbors and fellow citizens. There is no one, either rich or poor, who is absolutely without any name whatever, for people's fathers and mothers give them names as soon as they are born. Tell me also your country, nation, and city, that our ships may shape their purpose accordingly and take you there. For the Phaeacians have no pilots; their vessels have no rudders as those of other nations have, but the ships themselves understand what it is that we are thinking about and want; they know all the cities and countries in the whole world, and can traverse the sea just as well even when it is covered with mist and clouds, so that there is no danger of being wrecked or coming to any harm. Still I do remember hearing my father say that Poseidon was angry with us for being too easygoing in the matter of giving people escorts. He said that one of these days he should wreck a ship of ours as it was returning from having escorted someone,[3] and bury our city under a high mountain. This is what my father used to say, but whether the god will carry out his threat or no is a matter which he will decide for himself.

"And now, tell me and tell me true. Where have you been wandering, and in what countries have you traveled? Tell us of the peoples themselves, and of their cities—who were hostile, savage, and uncivilized, and who, on the other hand, hospitable and humane. Tell us also why you are made so unhappy on hearing about the return of the Argive Danaans from Troy. The gods arranged all this, and sent them their misfortunes in order that future generations might have something to sing about. Did you lose some brave kinsman of your wife's when you were before Troy—a son-in-law or father-in-law, which are the nearest relations a man has outside his own flesh and blood? Or was it some brave and kindly-natured comrade—for a good friend is as dear to a man as his own brother?"

[3] The reader will find this threat fulfilled in Book XIII.

Book IX

Odysseus now tells his name and begins the long chronicle of his adventures since leaving Troy. With twelve ships he sailed first to Ismarus, where he sacked a city. Thence he was driven by tempests to the far-off land of the Lotus-eaters. Setting sail again, he reached the land of the Cyclopes. Trapped in the cave of the monster Polyphemus, Odysseus and six of his men escaped through a clever stratagem, but six others were killed.

AND ODYSSEUS ANSWERED, "KING ALCINOUS, IT IS A GOOD THING TO hear a bard with such a divine voice as this man has. There is nothing better or more delightful than when a whole people make merry together, with the guests sitting orderly to listen, while the table is loaded with bread and meats, and the cupbearer draws wine and fills his cup for every man. This is indeed as fair a sight as a man can see. Now, however, since you are inclined to ask the story of my sorrows, and rekindle my own sad memories in respect of them, I do not know how to begin, nor yet how to continue and conclude my tale, for the hand of heaven has been laid heavily upon me.

"Firstly, then, I will tell you my name that you too may know it, and one day, if I outlive this time of sorrow, may become my guests though I live so far away from all of you. I am Odysseus son of Laertes, renowned among mankind for all manner of subtlety, so that my fame ascends to heaven. I live in Ithaca, where there is a high mountain called Neritum, covered with forests; and not far from it there is a group of islands very near to one another—Dulichium,

Same, and the wooded island of Zacynthus. It lies squat on the horizon, all highest up in the sea towards the sunset, while the others lie away from it towards dawn. It is a rugged island, but it breeds brave men, and my eyes know none that they better love to look upon. The goddess Calypso kept me with her in her cave, and wanted me to marry her, as did also the cunning Aeaean goddess Circe; but they could neither of them persuade me, for there is nothing dearer to a man than his own country and his parents, and however splendid a home he may have in a foreign country, if it be far from father or mother, he does not care about it. Now, however, I will tell you of the many hazardous adventures which by Zeus' will I met with on my return from Troy.

"When I had set sail thence the wind took me first to Ismarus, which is the city of the Cicones. There I sacked the town and put the people to the sword. We took their wives and also much booty, which we divided equitably among us, so that none might have reason to complain. I then said that we had better make off at once, but my men very foolishly would not obey me, so they stayed there drinking much wine and killing great numbers of sheep and oxen on the seashore. Meanwhile the Cicones cried out for help to other Cicones who lived inland. These were more in number, and stronger, and they were more skilled in the art of war, for they could fight, either from chariots or on foot as the occasion served. In the morning, therefore, they came as thick as leaves and bloom in summer, and the hand of heaven was against us, so that we were hard-pressed. They set the battle in array near the ships, and the hosts aimed their bronze-shod spears at one another. So long as the day waxed and it was still morning, we held our own against them, though they were more in number than we; but as the sun went down, towards the time when men loose their oxen, the Cicones got the better of us, and we lost half-a-dozen men from every ship we had; so we got away with those that were left.

"Thence we sailed onward with sorrow in our hearts, but glad to have escaped death though we had lost our comrades, nor did we leave till we had thrice invoked each one of the poor fellows who had perished by the hands of the Cicones. Then Zeus raised the north wind against us till it blew a hurricane, so that land and sky were hidden in thick clouds, and night sprang forth out of the heavens. We let the ships run before the gale, but the force of the wind tore our sails to tatters, so we took them down for fear of shipwreck, and rowed our hardest towards the land. There we lay two days and two nights suffering much alike from toil and distress of mind, but on the morning of the third day we again raised our masts, set sail, and took our places, letting the wind and steersmen direct our ship. I should have got home at that time unharmed had not the north wind and the currents been against me as I was doubling Cape Malea, and set me off my course hard by the island of Cythera.

"I was driven thence by foul winds for a space of nine days upon the sea, but on the tenth day we reached the land of the Lotus-eaters, who live on a food that comes from a kind of flower. Here we landed to take in fresh water, and our crews got their midday meal on the shore near the ships. When they had eaten and drunk, I sent two of my company to see what manner of men the people of the place might be, and they had a third man under them. They started at once and went about among the Lotus-eaters, who did them no hurt, but gave them to eat of the lotus, which was so delicious that those who ate of it left off caring about home, and did not even want to go back and say what had happened to them, but were for staying and munching lotus with the Lotus-eaters without thinking further of their return. Nevertheless, though they wept bitterly I forced them back to the ships and made them fast under the benches. Then I told the rest to go on board at once, lest any of them should taste of the lotus and leave off wanting to get home, so they took their places and smote the gray sea with their oars.

"We sailed hence, always in much distress, till we came to the land of the lawless and inhuman Cyclopes. Now the Cyclopes neither plant nor plow, but trust in providence, and live on such wheat, barley, and grapes as grow wild without any kind of tillage, and their wild grapes yield them wine as the sun and the rain may grow them. They have no laws or assemblies of the people, but live in caves on the tops of high mountains; each is lord and master in his family, and they take no account of their neighbors.

"Now off their harbor there lies a wooded and fertile island not quite close to the land of the Cyclopes, but still not far. It is overrun with wild goats, that breed there in great numbers and are never disturbed by foot of man. For sportsmen—who as a rule will suffer so much hardship in forest or among mountain precipices—do not go there, nor yet again is it ever plowed or fed down, but it lies a wilderness untilled and unsown from year to year, and has no living thing upon it but only goats. For the Cyclopes have no ships, nor yet shipwrights who could make ships for them. They cannot therefore go from city to city, or sail over the sea to one another's country as people who have ships can do. If they had had these they would have colonized the island, for it is a very good one, and would yield everything in due season. There are meadows that in some places come right down to the seashore, well-watered and full of luscious grass; grapes would do there excellently; there is level land for plowing, and it would always yield heavily at harvest time, for the soil is deep. There is a good harbor where no cables are wanted, nor yet anchors, nor need a ship be moored, but all one has to do is to beach one's vessel and stay there till the wind becomes fair for putting out to sea again. At the head of the harbor there is a spring of clear water coming out of a cave, and there are poplars growing all round it.

"Here we entered, but so dark was the night that some god must have brought us in, for there was nothing whatever to be seen. A thick mist hung all round our ships; the moon was hidden behind a mass of clouds so that no one could have seen the island if he had looked for it, nor were there any breakers to tell us we were close in shore before we found ourselves upon the land itself. When, however, we had beached the ships, we took down the sails, went ashore, and camped upon the beach till daybreak.

"When the child of morning, rosy-fingered Dawn, appeared, we admired the island and wandered all over it, while the nymphs, Zeus' daughters, roused the wild goats that we might get some meat for our dinner. On this we fetched our spears and bows and arrows from the ships, and dividing ourselves into three bands began to shoot the goats. Heaven sent us excellent sport; I had twelve ships with me, and each ship got nine goats, while my own ship had ten; thus through the livelong day to the going down of the sun we ate and drank our fill, and we had plenty of wine left, for each one of us had taken many jars full when we sacked the city of the Cicones, and this had not yet run out. While we were feasting we kept turning our eyes towards the land of the Cyclopes, which was hard by, and saw the smoke of their stubble fires. We could almost fancy we heard their voices and the bleating of their sheep and goats, but when the sun went down and it came on dark, we camped down upon the beach, and next morning I called a council.

" 'Stay here, my brave fellows,' said I, 'all the rest of you, while I go with my ship and explore these people myself. I want to see if they are uncivilized savages, or a hospitable and humane race.'

"I went on board, bidding my men to do so also and loose the hawsers; so they took their places and smote the gray sea with their oars. When we got to the land, which was not far, there, on the face of a cliff near the sea, we saw a great cave overhung with laurels. It was a station for a great many sheep and goats, and outside there was a large yard, with a high wall round it made of stones built into the ground and of trees both pine and oak. This was the abode of a huge monster who was then away from home shepherding his flocks. He would have nothing to do with other people, but led the life of an outlaw. He was a horrid creature, not like a human being at all, but resembling rather some crag that stands out boldly against the sky on the top of a high mountain.

"I told my men to draw the ship ashore, and stay where they were, all but the twelve best among them, who were to go along with myself. I also took a goatskin of sweet black wine which had been given me by Maron son of Euanthes, who was priest of Apollo the patron god of Ismarus, and lived within the wooded precincts of the temple. When we were sacking the city we respected him, and spared his life, as also his wife and child; so he made me some presents of great value—seven talents of fine gold, and a bowl of silver, with twelve jars of sweet wine, unblended, and of the most exquisite flavor. Not a man or maid in the house knew about it, but only himself, his wife, and one housekeeper. When he drank it he mixed twenty parts of water to one of wine, and yet the fragrance from the mixing bowl was so exquisite that it was impossible to refrain from drinking. I filled a large skin with this wine, and took a wallet full of provisions with me, for my mind misgave me that I might have to deal with some savage who would be of great strength, and would respect neither right nor law.

"We soon reached his cave, but he was out shepherding, so we went inside and took stock of all that we could see. His cheese-racks were loaded with cheeses, and he had more lambs and kids than his pens could hold. They were kept in separate flocks; first there were the hoggets, then the oldest of the younger lambs, and lastly the very young ones, all kept apart from one another. As for his dairy, all the vessels, bowls, and milk pails into which he milked were swimming with whey. When they saw all this, my men begged me to let them first steal some cheeses, and make off with them to the ship; they would then return, drive down the lambs and kids, put them on board and sail away with them. It would have been indeed better if we had done so, but I would not listen to them, for I wanted to see the owner himself, in the hope that he might give me a present. When, however, we saw him my poor men found him ill to deal with.

"We lit a fire, offered some of the cheeses in sacrifice, ate others of them, and then sat waiting till the Cyclops should come in with his sheep. When he came, he brought in with him a huge load of dry firewood to light the fire for his supper, and this he flung with such a noise on to the floor of his cave that we hid ourselves for fear at the far end of the cavern. Meanwhile he drove all the ewes inside, as well as the she-goats that he was going to milk, leaving the males, both rams and he-goats, outside in the yards. Then he rolled a huge stone to the mouth of the cave—so huge that two and twenty strong four-wheeled wagons would not be enough to draw it from its place against the doorway. When he had so done he sat down and milked his ewes and goats, all in due course, and then let each of them have her own young. He curdled half the milk and set it aside in wicker strainers, but the other half he poured into bowls that he might drink it for his supper. When he had got through with all his work, he lit the fire, and then caught sight of us, whereon he said:

" 'Strangers, who are you? Where do you sail from? Are you traders, or do you sail the sea as rovers, with your hands against every man, and every man's hand against you?'

"We were frightened of our senses by his loud voice and monstrous form, but I managed to say: 'We are Achaeans on our way home from Troy, but by the will of Zeus and stress of weather we have been driven far out of our course. We are the people of Agamemnon son of Atreus, who has won infinite renown throughout the whole world by sacking so great a city and killing so many people. We therefore humbly pray you to show us some hospitality, and otherwise make us such presents as visitors may reasonably expect. May your excellency fear the wrath of heaven, for we are your suppliants, and Zeus takes all respectable travelers under his protection, for he is the avenger of all suppliants and foreigners in distress.'

"To this he gave me but a pitiless answer. 'Stranger,' said he, 'you are a fool, or else you know nothing of this country. Talk to me, indeed, about fearing the gods or shunning their anger? We Cyclopes do not care about Zeus or any of your blessed gods, for we are ever so much stronger than they. I shall not spare either yourself or your companions out of any regard for Zeus, unless I am in the humor for doing so. And now tell me where you made your ship fast when you came on shore. Was it round the point, or is she lying straight off the land?'

"He said this to draw me out, but I was too cunning to be caught in that way, so I answered with a lie. 'Poseidon,' said I, 'sent my ship on the rocks at the far end of your country, and wrecked it. We were driven onto them from the open sea, but I and those who are with me escaped the jaws of death.'

"The cruel wretch vouchsafed me not one word of answer, but with a sudden clutch he gripped up two of my men at once and dashed them down upon the ground as though they had been puppies. Their brains were shed upon the ground, and the earth was wet with their blood. Then he tore them limb from limb and supped upon them. He gobbled them up like a lion in the wilderness, flesh, bones, marrow, and entrails, without leaving anything uneaten. As for us, we wept and lifted up our hands to heaven on seeing such a horrid sight, for we did not know what else to do; but when the Cyclops had filled his huge paunch, and had washed down his meal of human flesh with a drink of neat milk, he stretched himself full length upon the ground among his sheep, and went to sleep. I was at first inclined to seize my sword, draw it, and drive it into his vitals, but I reflected that if I did we should all certainly be lost, for we should never be able to shift the stone which the monster had put in front of the door. So we stayed sobbing and sighing where we were till morning came.

"When the child of morning, rosy-fingered Dawn, appeared, he again lit his fire, milked his goats and ewes, all quite rightly, and then let each have her own young one; as soon as he had got through with all his work, he clutched up two more of my men, and began eating them for his morning's meal. Presently, with the utmost ease, he rolled the stone away from the door and drove out his sheep, but he at once put it back again—as easily as though he were merely clapping the lid on to a quiver full of arrows. As soon as he had done so he shouted and cried, 'Shoo, shoo,' after his sheep to drive them on to the mountain; so I was left to scheme some way of taking my revenge and covering myself with glory.

"In the end I deemed it would be the best plan to do as follows. The Cyclops had a great club which was lying near one of the sheep pens; it was of green olive wood, and he had cut it intending to use it for a staff as soon as it should be dry. It was so huge that we could only compare it to the mast of a twenty-oared merchant vessel of large burden, and able to venture out into open sea. I went up to this club and cut off about six feet of it; I then gave this piece to the men and told them to fine it evenly off at one end, which they proceeded to do, and lastly I brought it to a point myself, charring the end in the fire to make it harder. When I had done this I hid it under the dung, which was lying about all over the cave, and told the men to cast lots which of them should venture along with myself to lift it and bore it into the monster's eye while he was asleep. The lot fell upon the very four whom I should have chosen, and I myself made five. In the evening the wretch came back from shepherding, and drove his flocks into the cave—this time driving them all inside, and not leaving any in the yards; I suppose some fancy must have taken him, or a god must have prompted him to do so. As soon as he had put the stone back to its place against the door, he sat down, milked his ewes and his goats all quite rightly, and then let each have her own young one; when he had got through with all this work, he gripped up two more of my men, and made his supper off them. So I went up to him with an ivy-wood bowl of black wine in my hands:

" 'Look here, Cyclops,' said I, 'you have been eating a great deal of man's flesh, so take this and drink some wine, that you may see what kind of liquor we had on board my ship. I was bringing it to you as a drink offering, in the hope that you would take compassion upon me and further me on my way home, whereas all you do is to go on ranting and raving most intolerably. You ought to be ashamed of yourself. How can you expect people to come and see you anymore if you treat them in this way?'

"He then took the cup and drank. He was so delighted with the taste of the wine that he begged me for another bowl full. 'Be so kind,' he said, 'as to give me some more, and tell me your name at once. I want to make you a present that you will be glad to have. We have wine even in this country, for our soil grows grapes and the sun ripens them, but this drink is like nectar and ambrosia all in one.'

"I then gave him some more; three times did I fill the bowl for him and three times did he drain it without thought or heed. Then, when I saw that the wine had got into his head, I said to him as plausibly as I could: 'Cyclops, you ask my name and I will tell it you; give me, therefore, the present you promised me. My name is Noman; this is what my father and mother and my friends have always called me.'

"But the cruel wretch said, 'Then I will eat all Noman's comrades before Noman himself, and will keep Noman for the last. This is the present that I will make him.'

"As he spoke, he reeled and fell sprawling face upwards on the ground. His great neck hung heavily backwards and a deep sleep took hold upon him. Presently he turned sick, and threw up both vine and the gobbets of human flesh on which he had been gorging, for he was very drunk. Then I thrust the beam of wood far into the embers to heat it, and encouraged my men lest any of them should turn faint-hearted. When the wood, green though it was, was about to blaze, I drew it out of the fire glowing with heat, and my men gathered round me, for heaven had filled their hearts with courage. We drove the sharp end of the beam into the monster's eye, and bearing upon it with all my weight I kept turning it round and round as though I were boring a hole in a ship's plank with an auger, which two men with a wheel and strap can keep on turning as long as they choose. Even thus did we bore the red-hot beam into his eye, till the boiling blood bubbled all over it as we worked it round and round, so that the steam from the burning eyeball scalded his eyelids and eyebrows, and the roots of the eye sputtered in the fire. As a blacksmith plunges an ax or hatchet into cold water to temper it—for it is this that gives strength to the iron—and it makes a great hiss as he does so, even thus did the Cyclops' eye hiss round the beam of olive wood, and his hideous yells made the cave ring again. We ran away in a fright, but he plucked the beam all besmirched with gore from his eye, and hurled it from him in a frenzy of rage and pain, shouting as he did so to the other Cyclopes who lived on the bleak headlands near him. So they gathered from all quarters round his cave when they heard him crying, and asked what was the matter with him.

" 'What ails you, Polyphemus,' said they, 'that you make such a noise, breaking the stillness of the night, and preventing us from being able to sleep? Surely no man is carrying off your sheep? Surely no man is trying to kill you either by fraud or by force?'

"But Polyphemus shouted to them from inside the cave, 'Noman is killing me by fraud! Noman is killing me by force!'

" 'Then,' said they, 'if no man is attacking you, you must be ill; when Zeus makes people ill, there is no help for it, and you had better pray to your father Poseidon.'

"Then they went away, and I laughed inwardly at the success of my clever stratagem, but the Cyclops, groaning and in an agony of pain, felt about with his hands till he found the stone and took it from the door; then he sat in the doorway and stretched his hands in front of it to catch anyone going out with the sheep, for he thought I might be foolish enough to attempt this.

"As for myself I kept on puzzling to think how I could best save my own life and those of my companions. I schemed and schemed, as one who knows that his life depends upon it, for the danger was very great. In the end I deemed that this plan would be the best. The male sheep were well-grown, and carried a heavy black fleece, so I bound them noiselessly in threes together, with some of the withies on which the wicked monster used to sleep. There was to be a man under the middle sheep, and the two on either side were to cover him, so that there were three sheep to each man. As for myself there was a ram finer than any of the others, so I caught hold of him by the back, ensconced myself in the thick wool under his belly, and hung on patiently to his fleece, face upwards, keeping a firm hold on it all the time.

"Thus, then, did we wait in great fear of mind till morning came, but when the child of morning, rosy-fingered Dawn, appeared, the male sheep hurried out to feed, while the ewes remained bleating about the pens waiting to be milked, for their udders were full to bursting; but their master, in spite of all his pain, felt the backs of all the sheep as they stood upright, without being sharp enough to find out that the men were underneath their bellies. As the ram was going out, last of all, heavy with its fleece and with the weight of my crafty self, Polyphemus laid hold of it and said:

" 'My good ram, what is it that makes you the last to leave my cave this morning? You are not wont to let the ewes go before you, but lead the mob with a run whether to flowery mead or bubbling fountain, and are the first to come home again at night; but now you lag last of all. Is it because you know your master has lost his eye, and are sorry because that wicked Noman and his horrid crew have got him down in his drink and blinded him? But I will have his life yet. If you could understand and talk, you would tell me where the wretch is hiding, and I would dash his brains upon the ground till they flew all over the cave. I should thus have some satisfaction for the harm this no-good Noman has done me.'

"As he spoke he drove the ram outside, but when we were a little way out from the cave and yards, I first got from under the ram's belly, and then freed my comrades; as for the sheep, which were very fat, by constantly heading them in the right direction we managed to drive them down to the ship. The crew rejoiced greatly at seeing those of us who had escaped death, but wept for the others whom the Cyclops had killed. However, I made signs to them by nodding and frowning that they were to hush their crying, and told them to get all the sheep on board at once and put out to sea. So they went aboard, took their places, and smote the gray sea with their oars.

Then, when I had got as far out as my voice would reach, I began to jeer at the Cyclops.

" 'Cyclops,' said I, 'you should have taken better measure of your man before eating up his comrades in your cave. You wretch, eat up your visitors in your own house? You might have known that your sin would find you out, and now Zeus and the other gods have punished you.

"He got more and more furious as he heard me, so he tore the top off from a high mountain, and flung it just in front of my ship so that it was within a little of hitting the end of the rudder. The sea quaked as the rock fell into it, and the wash of the wave it raised carried us back towards the mainland, and forced us towards the shore. But I snatched up a long pole and kept the ship off, making signs to my men by nodding my head, that they must row for their lives, whereon they laid out with a will. When we had got twice as far as we were before, I was for jeering at the Cyclops again, but the men begged and prayed of me to hold my tongue.

" 'Do not,' they exclaimed, 'be mad enough to provoke this savage creature further. He has thrown one rock at us already which drove us back again to the mainland, and we made sure it had been the death of us. If he had then heard any further sound of voices he would have pounded our heads and our ship's timbers into a jelly with the rugged rocks he would have heaved at us, for he can throw them a long way.'

"But I would not listen to them, and shouted out to him in my rage, 'Cyclops, if anyone asks you who it was that put your eye out and spoiled your beauty, say it was the valiant warrior Odysseus son of Laertes, who lives in Ithaca.'

"On this he groaned, and cried out, 'Alas, alas, then the old prophecy about me is coming true. There was a prophet here, at one time, a man both brave and of great stature, Telemus son of Eurymus, who was an excellent seer, and did all the prophesying for the Cyclopes till he grew old. He told me that all this would happen to me someday, and said I should lose my sight by the hand of Odysseus. I have been all along expecting someone of imposing presence and superhuman strength, whereas he turns out to be a little insignificant weakling, who has managed to blind my eye by taking advantage of me in my drink. Come here, then, Odysseus, that I may make you presents to show my hospitality, and urge Poseidon to help you forward on your journey—for Poseidon and I are father and son. He, if he so will, shall heal me, which no one else neither god nor man can do.'

"Then I said, 'I wish I could be as sure of killing you outright and sending you down to the house of Hades, as I am that it will take more than Poseidon to cure that eye of yours.'

"On this he lifted up his hands to the firmament of heaven and prayed, saying: 'Hear me, great Poseidon! If I am indeed your own true-begotten son, grant that Odysseus may never reach his home alive; or if he must get back to his friends at last, let him do so late and in sore plight after losing all his men. Let him reach his home in another man's ship and find trouble in his house.'

"Thus did he pray, and Poseidon heard his prayer. Then he picked up a rock much larger than the first, swung it aloft, and hurled it with prodigious force. It fell just short of the ship, but was within a little of hitting the end of the rudder. The sea quaked as the rock fell into it, and the wash of the wave it raised drove us onwards on our way towards the shore of the island.

"When at last we got to the island where we had left the rest of our ships, we found our comrades lamenting us and anxiously awaiting our return. We ran our vessel upon the sands and got out of her on to the seashore. We also landed the Cyclops' sheep, and divided them equitably among us so that none might have reason to complain. As for the ram, my companions agreed that I should have it as an extra share; so I sacrificed it on the seashore, and burned its thighbones to Zeus, who is the lord of all. But he heeded not my sacrifice, and only thought how he might destroy both my ships and my comrades.

"Thus through the livelong day to the going down of the sun we feasted our fill on meat and drink, but when the sun went down and it came on dark, we camped upon the beach. When the child of morning, rosy-fingered Dawn, appeared, I bade my men go on board and loose the hawsers. Then they took their places and smote the gray sea with their oars; so we sailed on with sorrow in our hearts, but glad to have escaped death though we had lost our comrades."

Book X

Odysseus and his fleet came next to the isle of Aeolus. When they departed,
Odysseus was given a bag of the winds, to hold tight until he reached home.
But while he slept, his men wickedly opened the bag, allowing the winds to
escape. The ships were blown back to Aeolus' isle, and thence to the land of
the savage Laestrygonians, who sunk eleven of them and devoured their crews.
Odysseus and the one crew remaining to him sought shelter on Circe's isle.
Here half of his men drank Circe's magic potion and were changed into pigs.
Odysseus compelled Circe to restore them to human shape, and they stayed
feasting with her for a year.

THENCE WE WENT TO THE AEOLIAN ISLAND WHERE LIVES AEOLUS SON of Hippotas, dear to the immortal gods. It is an island that floats (as it were) upon the sea, iron-bound with a wall that girds it. Now Aeolus has six daughters and six lusty sons, so he made the sons marry the daughters, and they all live with their dear father and mother, feasting and enjoying every conceivable kind of luxury. All day long the atmosphere of the house is loaded with the savor of roasting meats till it groans again, yard and all; but by night they sleep on their well-made bedsteads, each with his own wife between the blankets. These were the people among whom we had now come.

"Aeolus entertained me for a whole month asking me questions all the time about Troy, the Argive fleet, and the return of the Achaeans. I told him exactly how everything had happened, and when I said I must go, and asked him to further me on my way, he made no sort of difficulty, but set about doing so at once. Moreover, he flayed me a prime oxhide to hold the ways of the roaring winds, which he shut up in the hide as in a sack—for Zeus had made him captain over the winds, and he could stir or still each one of them according to his own pleasure. He put the sack in the ship, and bound the mouth so tightly with a silver thread that not even a breath of a side-wind could blow from any quarter. The west wind which was fair for us did he alone let blow as it chose; but it all came to nothing, for we were lost through our own folly.

"Nine days and nine nights did we sail, and on the tenth day our native land showed on the horizon. We got so close in that we could see the stubble fires burning, and I, being then dead beat, fell into a light sleep, for I had never let the rudder out of my own hands, that we might get home the faster. On this the men fell to talking among themselves, and said I was bringing back gold and silver in the sack that Aeolus had given me. 'Bless my heart,' would one turn to his neighbor, saying, 'how this man gets honored and makes friends to whatever city or country he may go. See what fine prizes he is taking home from Troy, while we, who have traveled just as far as he has, come back with hands as empty as we set out with—and now Aeolus has given him ever so much more. Quick, let us see what it all is, and how much gold and silver there is in the sack he gave him.'

"Thus they talked and evil counsels prevailed. They loosed the sack, whereupon the winds flew howling forth and raised a storm that carried us weeping out to sea and away from our own country Then I awoke, and knew not whether to throw myself into the sea or to live on and make the best of it; but I bore it, covered myself up, and lay down in the ship, while the men lamented bitterly as the fierce winds bore our fleet back to the Aeolian island.

"When we reached it we went ashore to take in water, and dined hard by the ships. Immediately after dinner I took a herald and one of my men and I went straight to the house of Aeolus, where I found him feasting with his wife and family; so we sat down as suppliants on the threshold. They were astounded when they saw us and said, 'Odysseus, what brings you here? What god has been ill-treating you? We took great pains to further you on your way home to Ithaca, or wherever it was that you wanted to go to.'

"Thus did they speak, but I answered sorrowfully, 'My men have undone me; they and cruel sleep have ruined me. My friends, mend me this mischief, for you can if you will.'

"I spoke as movingly as I could, but they said nothing, till their father answered, 'Vilest of mankind, get you gone at once out of the island; him whom heaven hates will I in no wise help. Be off, for you come here as one abhorred of heaven.' And with these words he sent me sorrowing from his door.

"Thence we sailed sadly on till the men were worn out with long and fruitless rowing, for there was no longer any wind to help them. Six days, night and day, did we toil, and on the seventh day we reached the rocky stronghold of Lamus—Telepylus, the city of the Laestrygonians, where the shepherd who is driving in his sheep and goats to be milked salutes him who is driving out his flock to feed and this last answers the salute. In that country a man who could do without sleep might earn double wages, one as a herdsman of cattle, and another as a shepherd, for they work much the same by night as they do by day.

"When we reached the harbor we found it landlocked under steep cliffs, with a narrow entrance between two headlands. My captains took all their ships inside, and made them fast close to one another, for there was never so much as a breath of wind inside, but it was always dead calm. I kept my own ship outside, and moored it to a rock at the very end of the point; then I climbed a high rock to reconnoiter, but could see no sign either of man or cattle, only some smoke rising from the ground. So I sent two of my company with an attendant to find out what sort of people the inhabitants were.

"The men when they got on shore followed a level road by which the people draw their firewood from the mountains into the town, till presently they met a young woman who had come outside to fetch water, and who was daughter to a Laestrygonian named Antiphates. She was going to the fountain Artacia from which the people bring in their water, and when my men had come close up to her, they asked her who the king of that country might be, and over what kind of people he ruled. So she directed them to her father's house, but when they got there they found his wife to be a giantess as huge as a mountain, and they were horrified at the sight of her.

"She at once called her husband Antiphates from the place of assembly, and forthwith he set about killing my men. He snatched up one of them, and began to make his dinner off him then and there, whereon the other two ran back to the ships as fast as ever they could. But Antiphates raised a hue and cry after them, and thousands of sturdy Laestrygonians sprang up from every quarter—ogres, not men. They threw vast rocks at us from the cliffs as though they had been mere stones, and I heard the horrid sound of the ships crunching up against one another, and the death cries of my men, as the Laestrygonians speared them like fishes and took them home to eat them. While they were thus killing my men within the harbor I drew my sword, cut the cable of my own ship, and told my men to row with all their might if they too would not fare like the rest; so they laid out for their lives, and we were thankful enough when we got into open water out of reach of the rocks they hurled at us. As for the others, there was not one of them left.

Thence we sailed sadly on, glad to have escaped death, though we had lost our comrades, and came to the Aeaean island, where Circe lives, a great and cunning goddess, who is own sister to the magician Aeetes, for they are both children of the sun by Perse, who is daughter to Oceanus. We brought our ship into a safe harbor without a word, for some god guided us thither, and having landed we lay there for two days and two nights, worn out in body and mind. When the morning of the third day came I took my spear and my sword, and went away from the ship to reconnoiter, and see if I could discover signs of human handiwork, or hear the sound of voices. Climbing to the top of a high lookout I espied the smoke of Circe's house rising upwards amid a dense forest of trees, and when I saw this I doubted whether, having seen the smoke, I should not go on at once and find out more. But in the end I deemed it best to go back to the ship, give the men their dinners, and send some of them instead of going myself.

"When I had nearly got back to the ship, some god took pity upon my solitude and sent a fine antlered stag right into the very middle of my path. He was coming down from his pasture in the forest to drink of the river, for the heat of the sun drove him, and as he passed I struck him in the middle of the back; the bronze point of the spear went clean through him, and he lay groaning in the dust until the life went out of him. Then I set my foot upon him, drew my spear from the wound, and laid it down. I also gathered rough grass and rushes and twisted them into a fathom or so of good stout rope with which I bound the four feet of the noble creature together. Having so done I hung him round my neck and walked back to the ship leaning upon my spear, for the stag was much too big for me to be able to carry him on my shoulder, steadying him with one hand. As I threw him down in front of the ship, I called the men and spoke cheeringly man by man to each of them. 'Look here, my friends,' said I, 'we are not going to die so much before our time after all, and at any rate we will not starve so long as we have got something to eat and drink on board.' On this they uncovered their heads upon the seashore and admired the stag, for he was indeed a splendid fellow. Then, when they had feasted their eyes upon him sufficiently, they washed their hands and began to cook him for dinner.

"Thus through the livelong day to the going down of the sun we stayed there eating and drinking our fill, but when the sun went down and it came on dark, we camped upon the seashore. When the child of morning, rosy-fingered Dawn, appeared, I called a council and said, 'My friends, we are in very great difficulties; listen therefore to me. We have no idea where the sun either sets or rises, so that we do not even know east from west. I see no way out of it; nevertheless, we must try and find one. We are certainly on an island, for I went as high as I could this morning, and saw the sea reaching all round it to the horizon; it lies low, but towards the middle I saw smoke rising from out of a thick forest of trees.'

"Their hearts sank as they heard me, for they remembered how they had been treated by the Laestrygonian Antiphates and by the savage ogre Polyphemus. They wept bitterly in their dismay, but there was nothing to be got by crying, so I divided them into two companies and set a captain over each; I gave one company to Eurylochus, while I took command of the other myself. Then we cast lots in a helmet, and the lot fell upon Eurylochus; so he set out with his twenty-two men, and they wept, as also did we who were left behind.

"When they reached Circe's house they found it built of cut stones, on a site that could be seen from far, in the middle of the forest. There were wild mountain wolves and lions prowling all round it—poor bewitched creatures whom she had tamed by her enchantments and drugged into subjection. They did not attack my men, but wagged their great tails, fawned upon them, and rubbed their noses lovingly against them. As hounds crowd round their master when they see him coming from dinner—for they know he will bring them something—even so did these wolves and lions with their great claws fawn upon my men, but the men were terribly frightened at seeing such strange creatures. Presently they reached the gates of the goddess's house, and as they stood there they could hear Circe within, singing most beautifully as she worked at her loom, making a web so fine, so soft, and of such dazzling colors as no one but a goddess could weave. On this Polites, whom I valued and trusted more than any other of my men, said, 'There is someone inside working at a loom and singing most beautifully; the whole place resounds with it, let us call her and see whether she is woman or goddess.'

"They called her and she came down, unfastened the door, and bade them enter. They, thinking no evil, followed her, all except Eurylochus, who suspected mischief and stayed outside. When she had got them into her house, she set them upon benches and seats and mixed them a mess with cheese, honey, meal, and Pramnian wine, but she drugged it with wicked poisons to make them forget their homes, and when they had drunk she turned them into pigs by a stroke of her wand, and shut them up in her pigsties. They were like pigs—head, hair, and all, and they grunted just as pigs do; but their senses were the same as before, and they remembered everything.

"Thus then were they shut up squealing, and Circe threw them some acorns and beech mast such as pigs eat, but Eurylochus hurried back to tell me about the sad fate of our comrades. He was so overcome with dismay that though he tried to speak he could find no words to do so; his eyes filled with tears and he could only sob and sigh, till at last we forced his story out of him, and he told us what had happened to the others.

" 'We went,' said he, 'as you told us, through the forest, and in the middle of it there was a fine house built with cut stones in a place that could be seen from far. There we found a woman, or else she was a goddess, working at her loom and singing sweetly; so the men shouted to her and called her, whereon she at once came down, opened the door, and invited us in. The others did not suspect any mischief so they followed her into the house, but I stayed where I was, for I thought there might be some treachery. From that moment I saw them no more, for not one of them ever came out, though I sat a long time watching for them.'

"Then I took my sword of bronze and slung it over my shoulders; I also took my bow, and told Eurylochus to come back with me and show me the way. But he laid hold of me with both his hands and spoke piteously, saying, 'Sir, do not force me to go with you, but let me stay here, for I know you will not bring one of them back with you, nor even return alive yourself. Let us rather see if we cannot escape at any rate with the few that are left us, for we may still save our lives.'

" 'Stay where you are, then,' answered I, 'eating and drinking at the ship, but I must go, for I am most urgently bound to do so.'

"With this I left the ship and went up inland. When I got through the charmed grove, and was near the great house of the enchantress Circe, I met Hermes with his golden wand, disguised as a young man in the heyday of his youth and beauty with the down just coming upon his face. He came up to me and took my hand within his own, saying: 'My poor unhappy man, whither are you going over this mountain top, alone and without knowing the way? Your men are shut up in Circe's pigsties, like so many wild boars in their lairs. You surely do not fancy that you can set them free? I can tell you that you will never get back and will have to stay there with the rest of them. But never mind, I will protect you and get you out of your difficulty. Take this herb, which is one of great virtue, and keep it about you when you go to Circe's house. It will be a talisman to you against every kind of mischief.

" 'And I will tell you of all the wicked witchcraft that Circe will try to practice upon you. She will mix a mess for you to drink, and she will drug the meal with which she makes it, but she will not be able to charm you, for the virtue of the herb that I shall give you will prevent her spells from working. I will tell you all about it. When Circe strikes you with her wand, draw your sword and spring upon her as though you were going to kill her. She will then be frightened and will desire you to go to bed with her. On this you must not point-blank refuse her, for you want her to set your companions free, and to take good care also of yourself, but you must make her swear solemnly by all the blessed gods that she will plot no further mischief against you, or else when she has got you naked she will unman you and make you fit for nothing.'

"As he spoke he pulled the herb out of the ground and showed me what it was like. The root was black, while the flower was as white as milk; the gods call it Moly, and mortal men cannot uproot it, but the gods can do whatever they like.

"Then Hermes went back to high Olympus, passing over the wooded island; but I fared onward to the house of Circe, and my heart was clouded with care as I walked along. When I got to the gates I stood there and called the goddess, and as soon as she heard me she came down, opened the door, and asked me to come in; so I followed her—much troubled in my mind. She set me on a richly decorated seat inlaid with silver, there was a footstool also under my feet, and she mixed a mess in a golden goblet for me to drink; but she drugged it, for she meant me mischief. When she had given it me, and I had drunk it without its charming me, she struck me with her wand. 'There now,' she cried, 'be off to the pigsty, and make your lair with the rest of them.'

"But I rushed at her with my sword drawn as though I would kill her, whereon she fell with a loud scream, clasped my knees, and spoke piteously, saying: 'Who and whence are you? From what place and people have you come? How can it be that my drugs have no power to charm you? Never yet was any man able to stand so much as a taste of the herb I gave you; you must be spell-proof. Surely you can be none other than the bold hero Odysseus, who Hermes always said would come here someday with his ship while on his way home from Troy. So be it then; sheathe your sword and let us go to bed, that we may make friends and learn to trust each other.'

"And I answered: 'Circe, how can you expect me to be friendly with you when you have just been turning all my men into pigs? And now that you have got me here myself, you mean me mischief when you ask me to go to bed with you, and will unman me and make me fit for nothing. I shall certainly not consent to go to bed with you unless you will first take your solemn oath to plot no further harm against me.'

"So she swore at once as I had told her, and when she had completed her oath, then I went to bed with her.

"Meanwhile her four servants, who are her housemaids, set about their work. They are the children of the groves and fountains, and of the holy waters that run down into the sea. One of them spread a fair purple cloth over a seat, and laid a carpet underneath it. Another brought tables of silver up to the seats, and set them with baskets of gold. A third mixed some sweet wine with water in a silver bowl and put golden cups upon the tables, while the fourth brought in water and set it to boil in a large cauldron over a good fire which she had lighted. When the water in the cauldron was boiling, she poured cold into it till it was just as I liked it, and then she set me in a bath and began washing me from the cauldron about the head and shoulders, to take the tire and stiffness out of my limbs. As soon as she had done washing me and anointing me with oil, she arrayed me in a good cloak and shirt and led me to a richly decorated seat inlaid with silver; there was a footstool also under my feet. A maidservant then brought me water in a beautiful golden ewer and poured it into a silver basin for me to wash my hands, and she drew a clean table beside me. An upper servant brought me bread and offered me many good things of what there was in the house, and then Circe bade me eat, but I would not, and sat without heeding what was before me, still moody and suspicious.

"When Circe saw me sitting there without eating, and in great grief, she came to me and said, 'Odysseus, why do you sit like that as though you were dumb, gnawing at your own heart, and refusing both meat and drink? Is it that you are still suspicious? You ought not to be, for I have already sworn solemnly that I will not hurt you.'

"And I said, 'Circe, no man with any sense of what is right can think of either eating or drinking in your house until you have set his friends free and let him see them. If you want me to eat and drink, you must free my men and bring them to me that I may see them with my own eyes.'

"When I had said this, she went straight through the court with her wand in her hand and opened the pigsty doors. My men came out like so many prime hogs and stood looking at her, but she went about among them and anointed each with a second drug, whereon the bristles that the bad drug had given them fell off, and they became men again, younger than they were before, and much taller and better looking. They knew me at once, seized me each of them by the hand, and wept for joy till the whole house was filled with the sound of their hullabalooing, and Circe herself was so sorry for them that she came up to me and said, 'Odysseus, noble son of Laertes, go back at once to the sea where you have left your ship, and first draw it on to the land. Then hide all your ship's gear and property in some cave, and come back here with your men.'

"I agreed to this, so I went back to the seashore, and found the men at the ship weeping and wailing most piteously. When they saw me, the silly blubbering fellows began frisking round me as calves break out and gambol round their mothers when they see them coming home to be milked after they have been feeding all day, and the homestead resounds with their lowing. They seemed as glad to see me as though they had got back to their own rugged Ithaca, where they had been born and bred. 'Sir,' said the affectionate creatures, 'we are as glad to see you back as though we had got safe home to Ithaca; but tell us all about the fate of our comrades.'

"I spoke comfortingly to them and said, 'We must draw our ship on to the land, and hide the ship's gear with all our property in some cave; then, come with me, all of you, as fast as you can to Circe's house, where you will find your comrades eating and drinking in the midst of great abundance.'

"On this the men would have come with me at once, but Eurylochus tried to hold them back and said: 'Alas, poor wretches that we are, what will become of us? Rush not on your ruin by going to the house of Circe, who will turn us all into pigs or wolves or lions, and we shall have to keep guard over her house. Remember how the Cyclops treated us when our comrades went inside his cave, and Odysseus with them. It was all through his sheer folly that those men lost their lives.'

"When I heard him, I was in two minds whether or no to draw the keen blade that hung by my sturdy thigh and cut his head off in spite of his being a near relation of my own; but the men interceded for him and said, 'Sir, if it may so be, let this fellow stay here and mind the ship, but take the rest of us with you to Circe's house.'

"On this we all went inland, and Eurylochus was not left behind after all, but came on too, for he was frightened by the severe reprimand that I had given him.

"Meanwhile Circe had been seeing that the men who had been left behind were washed and anointed with olive oil; she had also given them woolen cloaks and shirts, and when we came we found them all comfortably at dinner in her house. As soon as the men saw each other face to face and knew one another, they wept for joy and cried aloud till the whole palace rang again. Thereon Circe came up to me and said: 'Odysseus, noble son of Laertes, tell your men to leave off crying. I know how much you have all of you suffered at sea, and how ill you have fared among cruel savages on the mainland, but that is over now. So stay here, and eat and drink till you are once more as strong and hearty as you were when you left Ithaca; for at present you are weakened both in body and mind. You keep all the time thinking of the hardships you have suffered during your travels, so that you have no more cheerfulness left in you.'

"Thus did she speak and we assented. We stayed with Circe for a whole twelvemonth feasting upon an untold quantity both of meat and wine. But when the year had passed in the waning of moons and the long days had come round, my men called me apart and said, 'Sir, it is time you began to think about going home, if so be you are to be spared to see your house and native country at all.'

"Thus did they speak and I assented. Thereon through the livelong day to the going down of the sun we feasted our fill on meat and wine, but when the sun went down and it came on dark the men laid themselves down to sleep in the covered cloisters. I, however, after I had got into bed with Circe, besought her by her knees, and the goddess listened to what I had got to say. 'Circe,' said I, 'please to keep the promise you made me about furthering me on my homeward voyage. I want to get back and so do my men. They are always pestering me with their complaints as soon as ever your back is turned.'

"And the goddess answered, 'Odysseus, noble son of Laertes, you shall none of you stay here any longer if you do not want to, but there is another journey which you have got to take before you can sail homewards. You must go to the house of Hades and of dread Persephone to consult the ghost of the blind Theban prophet Teiresias, whose reason is still unshaken. To him alone has Persephone left his understanding even in death, but the other ghosts flit about aimlessly.'

"I was dismayed when I heard this. I sat up in bed and wept, and would gladly have lived no longer to see the light of the sun. But presently when I was tired of weeping and tossing myself about, I said, 'And who shall guide me upon this voyage—for the house of Hades is a port that no ship can reach.'

" 'You will want no guide,' she answered; 'raise your mast, set your white sails, sit quite still, and the north wind will blow you there of itself. When your ship has traversed the waters of Occanus, you will reach the fertile shore of Persephone's country with its groves of tall poplars and willows that shed their fruit untimely; here beach your ship upon the shore of Oceanus, and go straight on to the dark abode of Hades. You will find it near the place where the rivers Pyriphlegethon and Cocytus (which is a branch of the river Styx) flow into Acheron, and you will see a rock near it, just where the two roaring rivers run into one another.

" 'When you have reached this spot, as I now tell you, dig a trench a cubit or so in length, breadth, and depth, and pour into it as a drink offering to all the dead, first, honey mixed with milk, then wine, and in the third place water—sprinkling white barley meal over the whole. Moreover, you must offer many prayers to the poor feeble ghosts, and promise them that when you get back to Ithaca you will sacrifice a barren heifer to them, the best you have, and will load the pyre with good things. More particularly you must promise that Teiresias shall have a black sheep all to himself, the finest in all your flocks.

" 'When you shall have thus besought the ghosts with your prayers, offer them a ram and a black ewe, bending their heads towards Erebus; but yourself turn away from them as though you would make towards the river. On this, many dead men's ghosts will come to you, and you must tell your men to skin the two sheep that you have just killed, and offer them as a burnt sacrifice with prayers to Hades and to Persephone. Then draw your sword and sit there, so as to prevent any other poor ghost from coming near the spilt blood before Teiresias shall have answered your questions. The seer will presently come to you, and will tell you about your voyage—what stages you are to make, and how you are to sail the sea so as to reach your home.'

"It was daybreak by the time she had done speaking, so she dressed me in my shirt and cloak. As for herself, she threw a beautiful light gossamer fabric over her shoulders, fastening it with a golden girdle round her waist, and she covered her head with a mantle. Then I went about among the men everywhere all over the house, and spoke kindly to each of them man by man: 'You must not lie sleeping here any longer,' said I to them, 'we must be going, for Circe has told me all about it.' And on this they did as I bade them.

"Even so, however, I did not get them away without misadventure. We had with us a certain youth named Elpenor, not very remarkable for sense or courage, who had got drunk and was lying on the house top away from the rest of the men, to sleep off his liquor in the cool. When he heard the noise of the men bustling about, he jumped up on a sudden and forgot all about coming down by the main staircase, so he tumbled right off the roof and broke his neck, and his soul went down to the house of Hades.

"When I had got the men together I said to them, 'You think you are about to start home again, but Circe has explained to me that instead of this, we have got to go to the house of Hades and Persephone to consult the ghost of the Theban prophet Teiresias.'

"The men were brokenhearted as they heard me, and threw themselves on the ground groaning and tearing their hair, but they did not mend matters by crying. When we reached the seashore, weeping and lamenting our fate, Circe brought the ram and the ewe, and we made them fast hard by the ship. She passed through the midst of us without our knowing it, for who can see the comings and goings of a god, if the god does not wish to be seen?

Book XI

Having been told by Circe that he must consult the blind prophet Teiresias in the house of Hades, Odysseus sailed next to the dark underworld, home of the dead. Here he met and conversed with the ghosts of Teiresias, who foretold for him his future; of his mother; of his old comrades in arms, Agamemnon, Achilles, and Ajax; and of Heracles, and saw many dread and fearful things.

THEN, WHEN WE HAD GOT DOWN TO THE SEA SHORE WE DREW OUR ship into the water and got her mast and sails into her. We also put the sheep on board and took our places, weeping and in great distress of mind. Circe, that great and cunning goddess, sent us a fair wind that blew dead aft and stayed steadily with us keeping our sails all the time well-filled; so we did whatever wanted doing to the ship's gear and let her go as the wind and helmsman headed her. All day long her sails were full as she held her course over the sea, but when the sun went down and darkness was over all the earth, we got into the deep waters of the river Oceanus, where lie the land and city of the Cimmerians who live enshrouded in mist and darkness, which the rays of the sun never pierce either at his rising or as he goes down again out of the heavens, but the poor wretches live in one long melancholy night. When we got there we beached the ship, took the sheep out of her, and went along by the waters of Oceanus till we came to the place of which Circe had told us.

"Here Perimedes and Eurylochus held the victims, while I drew my sword and dug the trench a cubit each way. I made a drink offering to all the dead, first with honey and milk, then with wine, and thirdly with water, and I sprinkled white barley meal over the whole, praying earnestly to the poor feckless ghosts, and promising them that when I got back to Ithaca I would sacrifice a barren heifer for them, the best I had, and would load the pyre with good things. I also particularly promised that Teiresias should have a black sheep to himself, the best in all my flocks. When I had prayed sufficiently to the dead, I cut the throats of the two sheep and let the blood run into the trench, whereon the ghosts came trooping up from Erebus—brides, young bachelors, old men worn out with toil, maids who had been crossed in love, and brave men who had been killed in battle, with their armor still smirched with blood; they came from every quarter and flitted round the trench with a strange kind of screaming sound that made me turn pale with fear. When I saw them coming I told the men to be quick and flay the carcasses of the two dead sheep and make burnt offerings of them, and at the same time to repeat prayers to Hades and to Persephone; but I sat where I was with my sword drawn and would not let the poor feckless ghosts come near the blood till Teiresias should have answered my questions.

"The first ghost that came was that of my comrade Elpenor, for he had not yet been laid beneath the earth. We had left his body unwaked and unburied in Circe's house, for we had had too much else to do. I was very sorry for him, and cried when I saw him, 'Elpenor,' said I, 'how did you come down here into this gloom and darkness? You have got here on foot quicker than I have with my ship.'

" 'Sir,' he answered with a groan, 'it was all bad luck, and my own unspeakable drunkenness. I was lying asleep on the top of Circe's house, and never thought of coming down again by the great staircase but fell right off the roof and broke my neck, so my soul came down to the house of Hades. And now I beseech you by all those whom you have left behind you, though they are not here, by your wife, by the father who brought you up when you were a child, and by Telemachus who is the one hope of your house, do what I shall now ask you. I know that when you leave this limbo you will again hold your ship for the Aeaean island. Do not go thence leaving me unwaked and unburied behind you, or I may bring heaven's anger upon you; but burn me with whatever armor I have, build a barrow for me on the seashore, that may tell people in days to come what a poor unlucky fellow I was, and plant over my grave the oar I used to row with when I was yet alive and with my messmates.' And I said, 'My poor fellow, I will do all that you have asked of me.'

"Thus, then, did we sit and hold sad talk with one another, I on the one side of the trench with my sword held over the blood, and the ghost of my comrade saying all this to me from the other side. Then came the ghost of my dead mother Anticlea, daughter to Autolycus. I had left her alive when I set out for Troy and was moved to tears when I saw her, but even so, for all my sorrow I would not let her come near the blood till I had asked my questions of Teiresias.

"Then came also the ghost of Theban Teiresias, with his golden scepter in his hand. He knew me and said, 'Odysseus, noble son of Laertes, why, poor man, have you left the light of day and come down to visit the dead in this sad place? Stand back from the trench and withdraw your sword that I may drink of the blood and answer your questions truly.'

"So I drew back and sheathed my sword, whereon when he had drank of the blood he began with his prophecy.

" 'You want to know,' said he, 'about your return home, but heaven will make this hard for you. I do not think that you will escape the eye of Poseidon, who still nurses his bitter grudge against you for having blinded his son. Still, after much suffering you may get home if you can restrain yourself and your companions when your ship reaches the Thrinacian island,[1] where you will find the sheep and cattle belonging to the sun, who sees and gives ear to everything. If you leave these flocks unharmed and think of nothing but of getting home, you may yet after much hardship reach Ithaca; but if you harm them,

---

[1] Trinacria was the ancient name of the island of Sicily.

then I forewarn you of the destruction both of your ship and of your men. Even though you may yourself escape, you will return in bad plight after losing all your men, in another man's ship, and you will find trouble in your house, which will be overrun by high-handed people, who are devouring your substance under the pretext of paying court and making presents to your wife.

" 'When you get home you will take your revenge on these suitors; and after you have killed them by force or fraud in your own house, you must take a well-made oar and carry it on and on, till you come to a country where the people have never heard of the sea and do not even mix salt with their food, nor do they know anything about ships, and oars that are as the wings of a ship. I will give you this certain token which cannot escape your notice. A wayfarer will meet you and will say it must be a winnowing shovel that you have got upon your shoulder; on this you must fix the oar in the ground and sacrifice a ram, a bull, and a boar to Poseidon.[2] Then go home and offer hecatombs to all the gods in heaven one after the other. As for yourself, death shall come to you from the sea, and your life shall ebb away very gently when you are full of years and peace of mind, and your people shall bless you. All that I have said will come true.'

" 'This,' I answered, 'must be as it may please heaven, but tell me and tell me true, I see my poor mother's ghost close by us; she is sitting by the blood without saying a word, and though I am her own son she does not remember me and speak to me. Tell me, sir, how I can make her know me.'

" 'That,' said he, 'I can soon do. Any ghost that you let taste of the blood will talk with you like a reasonable being, but if you do not let them have any blood they will go away again.'

"On this the ghost of Teiresias went back to the house of Hades, for his prophesyings had now been spoken, but I sat still where I was until my

---

[2]Odysseus was to become a missionary and preach Poseidon to people who knew not his name. I was fortunate enough to meet in Sicily a woman carrying one of these winnowing shovels; it was not much shorter than an oar. and I was able at once to see what the writer of the *Odyssey* intended. (B.)

mother came up and tasted the blood. Then she knew me at once and spoke fondly to me, saying, 'My son, how did you come down to this abode of darkness while you are still alive? It is a hard thing for the living to see these places, for between us and them there are great and terrible waters, and there is Oceanus, which no man can cross on foot, but he must have a good ship to take him. Are you all this time trying to find your way home from Troy, and have you never yet got back to Ithaca, nor seen your wife in your own house?'

" 'Mother,' said I, 'I was forced to come here to consult the ghost of the Theban prophet Teiresias. I have never yet been near the Achaean land nor set foot on my native country, and I have had nothing but one long series of misfortunes from the very first day that I set out with Agamemnon for Ilium, the land of noble steeds, to fight the Trojans. But tell me, and tell me true, in what way did you die? Did you have a long illness, or did heaven vouchsafe you a gentle easy passage to eternity? Tell me also about my father, and the son whom I left behind me. Is my property still in their hands, or has someone else got hold of it, who thinks that I shall not return to claim it? Tell me again what my wife intends doing, and in what mind she is. Does she live with my son and guard my estate securely, or has she made the best match she could and married again?'

"My mother answered: 'Your wife still remains in your house, but she is in great distress of mind and spends her whole time in tears both night and day. No one as yet has got possession of your fine property, and Telemachus still holds your lands undisturbed. He has to entertain largely, as of course he must, considering his position as a magistrate, and how everyone invites him. Your father remains at his old place in the country and never goes near the town. He has no comfortable bed nor bedding; in the winter he sleeps on the floor in front of the fire with the men and goes about all in rags, but in summer, when the warm weather comes on again, he lies out in the vineyard on a bed of vine leaves thrown anyhow upon the ground. He grieves continually about your never having come home, and suffers more and more as he grows older. As for my own end it was in this wise: heaven did not take me swiftly and painlessly in my own house, nor was I attacked by any illness such as those that generally wear people out and kill them, but my longing to know what you were doing and the force of my affection for you—this it was that was the death of me.'[3]

"Then I tried to find some way of embracing my poor mother's ghost. Thrice I sprung towards her and tried to clasp her in my arms, but each time she flitted from my embrace as it were a dream or phantom, and being touched to the quick I said to her, 'Mother, why do you not stay still when I would embrace you? If we could throw our arms around one another we might find sad comfort in the sharing of our sorrows even in the house of Hades. Does Persephone want to lay a still further load of grief upon me by mocking me with a phantom only?

" 'My son,' she answered, 'most ill-fated of all mankind, it is not Persephone that is beguiling you, but all people are like this when they are dead. The sinews no longer hold the flesh and bones together; these perish in the fierceness of consuming fire as soon as life has left the body, and the soul flits away as though it were a dream. Now, however, go back to the light of day as soon as you can, and note all these things that you may tell them to your wife hereafter.'

"Thus did we converse, and anon Persephone sent up the ghosts of the wives and daughters of all the most famous men. They gathered in crowds about the blood, and I considered how I might question them severally. In the end I deemed that it would be best to draw the keen blade that hung by my sturdy thigh, and keep them from all drinking the blood at once. So they came up one after the other, and each one as I questioned her told me her race and lineage.

[3] Tradition says that she had hanged herself. See also Book XV.

"The first I saw was Tyro. She was daughter of Salmoneus and wife of Cretheus the son of Aeolus.[4] She fell in love with the river Enipeus, who is much the most beautiful river in the whole world. Once when she was taking a walk by his side as usual, Poseidon, disguised as her lover, lay with her at the mouth of the river, and a huge blue wave arched itself like a mountain over them to hide both woman and god, whereon he loosed her virgin girdle and laid her in a deep slumber. When the god had accomplished the deed of love, he took her hand in his own and said, 'Tyro, rejoice in all good will; the embraces of the gods are not fruitless, and you will have fine twins about this time twelve months. Take great care of them. I am Poseidon, so now go home, but hold your tongue and do not tell anyone.'

"Then he dived under the sea, and she in due course bore Pelias and Neleus,[5] who both of them served Zeus with all their might. Pelias was a great breeder of sheep and lived in Iolcus, but the other lived in Pylos. The rest of her children were by Cretheus, namely, Aeson, Pheres, and Amythaon, who was a mighty warrior and charioteer.

"Next to her I saw Antiope daughter of Asopus, who could boast of having slept in the arms of even Zeus himself, and who bore him two sons, Amphion and Zethus. These founded Thebes with its seven gates, and built a wall all round it; for strong though they were they could not hold Thebes till they had walled it.

"Then I saw Alcmena, the wife of Amphitryon, who also bore to Zeus indomitable Heracles; and Megara, who was daughter to great King Creon, and married the redoubtable son of Amphitryon.

"I also saw fair Epicaste,[6] mother of King Oedipus, whose awful lot it was to marry her own son without suspecting it. He married her after having

[4] Not to be confounded with Aeolus, king of the winds. (B.)

[5] Father of Nestor.

[6] We know her better as Jocasta, under which name she appears in Sophocles' great tragedy of *Oedipus Tyrannus*.

killed his father, but the gods proclaimed the whole story to the world; whereon he remained king of Thebes, in great grief for the spite the gods had borne him; but Epicaste went to the house of the mighty jailor Hades, having hanged herself for grief, and the avenging spirits haunted him as for an outraged mother—to his ruing bitterly thereafter.

"Then I saw Chloris, whom Neleus married for her beauty, having given priceless presents for her. She was youngest daughter to Amphion, son of Iasus and king of Minyan Orchomenus, and was queen in Pylos. She bore Nestor, Chromius, and Periclymenus, and she also bore that marvelously lovely woman Pero, who was wooed by all the country round; but Neleus would only give her to him who should raid the cattle of Iphicles from the grazing grounds of Phylace, and this was a hard task. The only man who would undertake to raid them was a certain excellent seer,[7] but the will of heaven was against him, for the rangers of the cattle caught him and put him in prison. Nevertheless, when a full year had passed and the same season came round again, Iphicles set him at liberty, after he had expounded all the oracles of heaven. Thus, then, was the will of Zeus accomplished.

"And I saw Leda the wife of Tyndarus, who bore him two famous sons, Castor, breaker of horses, and Pollux, the mighty boxer. Both these heroes are lying under the earth, though they are still alive, for by a special dispensation of Zeus, they die and come to life again, each one of them every other day throughout all time, and they have the rank of gods.

"After her I saw Iphimedeia wife of Aloeus, who boasted the embrace of Poseidon. She bore two sons, Otus and Ephialtes, but both were short-lived. They were the finest children that were ever born in this world, and the best-looking, Orion only excepted; for at nine years old they were nine fathoms high, and measured nine cubits round the chest. They threatened to make war with the gods in Olympus, and tried to set Mount Ossa on the top of Mount Olympus, and Mount Pelion on the top of Ossa, that they might scale

[7] Melampus, see Book XV.

heaven itself, and they would have done it too if they had been grown up. But Apollo son of Leto killed both of them, before they had got so much as a sign of hair upon cheeks or chin.

"Then I saw Phaedra, and Procris, and fair Ariadne, daughter of the magician Minos, whom Theseus was carrying off from Crete to Athens,[8] but he did not enjoy her, for before he could do so Artemis killed her in the island of Dia on account of what Dionysus had said against her.

"I also saw Maera and Clymene and hateful Eriphyle, who sold her own husband for gold. But it would take me all night if I were to name every single one of the wives and daughters of heroes whom I saw, and it is time for me to go to bed, either on board ship with my crew, or here. As for my escort, heaven and yourselves will see to it."

Here he ended, and the guests sat all of them enthralled and speechless throughout the covered cloister. Then Arete said to them:

"What do you think of this man, O Phaeacians? Is he not tall and good-looking, and is he not clever? True, he is my own guest, but you all of you share in the distinction. Do not be in a hurry to send him away, nor niggardly in the presents you make to one who is in such great need, for heaven has blessed all of you with great abundance."

Then spoke the aged hero Echeneus, who was one of the oldest men among them. "My friends," said he, "what our august queen has just said to us is both reasonable and to the purpose, therefore be persuaded by it; but the decision whether in word or deed rests ultimately with King Alcinous."

"The thing shall be done," exclaimed Alcinous, "as surely as I still live and reign over the Phaeacians. Our guest is indeed very anxious to get home; still we must persuade him to remain with us until tomorrow, by which time I shall be able to get together the whole sum that I mean to give him. As regards his escort, it will be a matter for you all, and mine above all others as the chief person among you."

---

[8] Ariadne, it may be remembered, had helped Theseus to escape from the Minotaur.

And Odysseus answered: "King Alcinous, if you were to bid me to stay here for a whole twelve months, and then speed me on my way, loaded with your noble gifts, I should obey you gladly and it would redound greatly to my advantage, for I should return fuller-handed to my own people, and should thus be more respected and beloved by all who see me when I get back to Ithaca."

"Odysseus," replied Alcinous, "not one of us who sees you has any idea that you are a charlatan or a swindler. I know there are many people going about who tell such plausible stories that it is very hard to see through them, but there is a style about your language which assures me of your good disposition. Moreover you have told the story of your own misfortunes, and those of the Argives, as though you were a practiced bard; but tell me, and tell me true, whether you saw any of the mighty heroes who went to Troy at the same time with yourself, and perished there. The evenings are still at their longest, and it is not yet bedtime. Go on, therefore, with your divine story, for I could stay here listening till tomorrow morning, so long as you will continue to tell us of your adventures."

"Alcinous," answered Odysseus, "there is a time for making speeches, and a time for going to bed; nevertheless, since you so desire, I will not refrain from telling you the still sadder tale of those of my comrades who did not fall fighting with the Trojans, but perished on their return, through the treachery of a wicked woman.

"When Persephone had dismissed the female ghosts in all directions, the ghost of Agamemnon son of Atreus came sadly up to me, surrounded by those who had perished with him in the house of Aegisthus. As soon as he had tasted the blood he knew me, and weeping bitterly stretched out his arms towards me to embrace me; but he had no strength or substance anymore, and I too wept and pitied him as I beheld him. 'How did you come by your death,' said I, 'King Agamemnon? Did Poseidon raise his winds and waves against you when you were at sea, or did your enemies make an end of you on the mainland when you were cattle-lifting or sheep-stealing, or while they were fighting in defense of their wives and city?'

" 'Odysseus,' he answered, 'noble son of Laertes, I was not lost at sea in any storm of Poseidon's raising, nor did my foes despatch me upon the mainland, but Aegisthus and my wicked wife were the death of me between them. He asked me to his house, feasted me, and then butchered me most miserably, as though I were a fat beast in a slaughter house, while all around me my comrades were slain like sheep or pigs for the wedding breakfast, or picnic, or gorgeous banquet of some great nobleman. You must have seen numbers of men killed, either in a general engagement or in single combat, but you never saw anything so truly pitiable as the way in which we fell in that cloister, with the mixing bowl and the loaded tables lying all about, and the ground reeking with our blood. I heard Priam's daughter Cassandra [9] scream as Clytemnestra killed her close beside me. I lay dying upon the earth with the sword in my body, and raised my hands to kill the slut of a murderess, but she slipped away from me. She would not even close my lips or my eyes when I was dying, for there is nothing in this world so cruel and so shameless as a woman when she has fallen into such guilt as hers was. Fancy murdering her own husband! I thought I was going to be welcomed home by my children and my servants, but her abominable crime has brought disgrace on herself and all women who shall come after—even on the good ones.'

"And I said, 'In truth Zeus has hated the house of Atreus from first to last in the matter of their women's counsels. See how many of us fell for Helen's sake, and now it seems that Clytemnestra hatched mischief against you too during your absence.'[10]

" 'Be sure, therefore,' continued Agamemnon, 'and not be too friendly even with your own wife. Do not tell her all that you know perfectly well

---

[9] Cassandra had been alloted to Agamemnon as a part of his booty from the sack of Troy.
[10] Menelaus, husband of Helen, whose sin was the cause of the Trojan War, was, it is to be remembered, a son of Atreus and brother of Agamemnon.

yourself. Tell her a part only, and keep your own counsel about the rest. Not that your wife, Odysseus, is likely to murder you, for Penelope is a very admirable woman, and has an excellent nature. We left her a young bride with an infant at her breast when we set out for Troy. This child no doubt is now grown up happily to man's estate, and he and his father will have a joyful meeting and embrace one another as it is right they should do, whereas my wicked wife did not even allow me the happiness of looking upon my son, but killed me ere I could do so. Furthermore I say—and lay my saying to your heart—do not tell people when you are bringing your ship to Ithaca, but steal a march upon them, for after all this there is no trusting women. But now tell me, and tell me true, can you give me any news of my son Orestes? Is he in Orchomenus, or at Pylos, or is he at Sparta with Menelaus? For I presume that he is still living.'

"And I said, 'Agamemnon, why do you ask me? I do not know whether your son is alive or dead, and it is not right to talk when one does not know.'

"As we two sat weeping and talking thus sadly with one another, the ghost of Achilles came up to us with Patroclus, Antilochus, and Ajax, who was the finest and goodliest man of all the Danaans after the son of Peleus. The fleet descendant of Aeacus knew me and spoke piteously, saying, 'Odysseus, noble son of Laertes, what deed of daring will you undertake next, that you venture down to the house of Hades among us silly dead, who are but the ghosts of them that can labor no more?'

"And I said, 'Achilles, son of Peleus, foremost champion of the Achaeans, I came to consult Teiresias, and see if he could advise me about my return home to Ithaca, for I have never yet been able to get near the Achaean land, or to set foot in my own country, but have been in trouble all the time. As for you, Achilles, no one was ever yet so fortunate as you have been, nor ever will be, for you were adored by all us Argives as long as you were alive, and now that you are here you are a great prince among the dead. Do not, therefore, take it so much to heart even if you are dead.'

" 'Say not a word,' he answered, 'in death's favor; I would rather be a paid servant in a poor man's house and be above ground than king of kings among the dead. But give me news about my son; is he gone to the wars and will he be a great soldier, or is this not so? Tell me also if you have heard anything about my father Peleus—does he still rule among the Myrmidons, or do they show him no respect throughout Hellas and Phthia now that he is old and his limbs fail him? Could I but stand by his side, in the light of day, with the same strength that I had when I killed the bravest of our foes upon the plain of Troy—could I but be as I then was and go even for a short time to my father's house, anyone who tried to do him violence or supersede him would soon rue it.'

" 'I have heard nothing,' I answered, 'of Peleus, but I can tell you all about your son Neoptolemus, for I took him in my own ship from Scyros with the Achaeans. In our councils of war before Troy he was always first to speak, and his judgment was unerring. Nestor and I were the only two who could surpass him; and when it came to fighting on the plain of Troy, he would never remain with the body of his men, but would dash on far in front, foremost of them all in valor. Many a man did he kill in battle—I cannot name every single one of those whom he slew while fighting on the side of the Argives, but will only say how he killed that valiant hero Eurypylus son of Telephus, who was the handsomest man I ever saw except Memnon; many others also of the Ceteians fell around him by reason of a woman's bribes. Moreover, when all the bravest of the Argives went inside the horse that Epeus had made, and it was left to me to settle when we should either open the door of our ambuscade, or keep it closed, though all the other leaders and chief men among the Danaans were drying their eyes and quaking in every limb, I never once saw him turn pale or wipe a tear from his cheek. He was all the time urging me to break out from the horse—grasping the handle of his sword and his bronze-shod spear, and breathing fury against the foe. Yet when we had sacked the city of Priam he got his handsome share of the prize money and went on board (such is the fortune of war) without a wound upon him, neither from a thrown spear nor in close combat, for the rage of Ares is a matter of great chance.'

"When I had told him this, the ghost of Achilles strode off across a meadow full of asphodel, exulting over what I had said concerning the prowess of his son.

"The ghosts of other dead men stood near me and told me each his own melancholy tale; but that of Ajax son of Telamon alone held aloof—still angry with me for having won the cause in our dispute about the armor of Achilles. Thetis had offered it as a prize, but the Trojan prisoners and Athene were the judges. Would that I had never gained the day in such a contest, for it cost the life of Ajax, who was foremost of all the Danaans after the son of Peleus, alike in stature and prowess.[11]

"When I saw him I tried to pacify him and said, 'Ajax, will you not forget and forgive even in death, but must the judgment about that hateful armor still rankle with you? It cost us Argives dear enough to lose such a tower of strength as you were to us. We mourned you as much as we mourned Achilles son of Peleus himself, nor can the blame be laid on anything but on the spite which Zeus bore against the Danaans, for it was this that made him counsel your destruction. Come hither, therefore, bring your proud spirit into subjection, and hear what I can tell you.'

"He would not answer, but turned away to Erebus and to the other ghosts. Nevertheless, I should have made him talk to me in spite of his being so angry, or I should have gone on talking to him, only that there were still others among the dead whom I desired to see.

"Then I saw Minos son of Zeus with his golden scepter in his hand, sitting in judgment on the dead, and the ghosts were gathered sitting and standing round him in the spacious house of Hades, to learnt his sentences upon them.

---

[11] After the death of Achilles, his beautiful armor was offered by his mother, the nymph Thetis, to the man who was judged bravest among the surviving Greeks. It was awarded to Odysseus, whereupon Ajax killed himself.

"After him I saw huge Orion in a meadow full of asphodel, driving the ghosts of the wild beasts that he had killed upon the mountains, and he had a great bronze club in his hand, unbreakable for ever and ever.

"And I saw Tityus son of Gaia stretched upon the plain and covering some nine acres of ground. Two vultures on either side of him were digging their beaks into his liver, and he kept on trying to beat them off with his hands, but could not; for he had violated Zeus' mistress Leto as she was going through Panopeus on her way to Pytho.

"I saw also the dreadful fate of Tantalus, who stood in a lake that reached his chin. He was dying to quench his thirst, but could never reach the water, for whenever the poor creature stooped to drink, it dried up and vanished, so that there was nothing but dry ground—parched by the spite of heaven. There were tall trees, moreover, that shed their fruit over his head—pears, pomegranates, apples, sweet figs, and juicy olives, but whenever the poor creature stretched out his hand to take some, the wind tossed the branches back again to the clouds.

"And I saw Sisyphus at his endless task raising his prodigious stone with both his hands. With hands and feet he tried to roll it up to the top of the hill, but always, just before he could roll it over on to the other side, its weight would be too much for him, and the pitiless stone would come thundering down again on to the plain. Then he would begin trying to push it uphill again, and the sweat ran off him and the steam rose after him.

"After him I saw mighty Heracles, but it was his phantom only, for he is feasting ever with the immortal gods, and has lovely Hebe to wife, who is daughter of Zeus and Hera. The ghosts were screaming round him like scared birds flying all whithers. He looked black as night with his bare bow in his hands and his arrow on the string, glaring around as though ever on the point of taking aim. About his breast there was a wondrous golden belt adorned in the most marvelous fashion with bears, wild boars, and lions with gleaming eyes; there was also war, battle, and death. The man who made that belt, do what he might, would never be able to make another like it. Heracles knew me at once when he saw me, and spoke piteously, saying, 'My poor Odysseus, noble son of Laertes, are you too leading the same sorry kind of life that I did when I was above ground? I was son of Zeus, but I went through an infinity of suffering, for I became bondsman to one who was far beneath me—a low fellow who set me all manner of labors. He once sent me here to fetch the hellhound—for he did not think he could find anything harder for me than this, but I got the hound out of Hades and brought him to him, for Hermes and Athene helped me.'

"On this Heracles went down again into the house of Hades, but I stayed where I was in case some other of the mighty dead should come to me. And I should have seen still other of them that are gone before, whom I would fain have seen—Theseus and Pirithoüs—glorious children of the gods, but so many thousands of ghosts came round me and uttered such appalling cries, that I was panic-stricken lest Persephone should send up from the house of Hades the head of that awful monster Gorgon. On this I hastened back to my ship and ordered my men to go on board at once and loose the hawsers; so they embarked and took their places, whereon the ship went down the stream of the river Oceanus. We had to row at first, but presently a fair wind sprang up."

Book XII

From the house of Hades, Odysseus returned to Circe, who warned him of
the dangers ahead and how to meet them. They sailed then, as directed, past
the rocks of the Sirens and Scylla and Charybdis. Landing on the island of
Sicily, Odysseus' men slaughtered the fine cattle there, the property of the
sun-god. In punishment, Zeus destroyed their ship with his thunderbolts.
Odysseus alone escaped drowning and was stranded on Calypso's isle.
With this he brings his tale to an end.

AFTER WE WERE CLEAR OF THE RIVER OCEANUS, AND HAD GOT OUT INTO the open sea, we went on till we reached the Aeaean island where there is dawn and sunrise as in other places. We then drew our ship on to the sands and got out of her on to the shore, where we went to sleep and waited till day should break.

"Then, when the child of morning, rosy-fingered Dawn, appeared, I sent some men to Circe's house to fetch the body of Elpenor. We cut firewood from a wood where the headland jutted out into the sea, and after we had wept over him and lamented him we performed his funeral rites. When his body and armor had been burned to ashes, we raised a cairn, set a stone over it, and at the top of the cairn we fixed the oar that he had been used to row with.

"While we were doing all this, Circe, who knew that we had got back from the house of Hades, dressed herself and came to us as fast as she could; and her maidservants came with her bringing us bread, meat, and wine. Then she stood in the midst of us and said, 'You have done a bold thing in going down alive to the house of Hades, and you will have died twice, to other people's once. Now, then, stay here for the rest of the day, feast your fill, and go on with your voyage at daybreak tomorrow morning. In the meantime I will tell Odysseus about your course, and will explain everything to him so as to prevent your suffering from misadventure either by land or sea.'

"We agreed to do as she had said, and feasted through the livelong day to the going down of the sun, but when the sun had set and it came on dark, the men laid themselves down to sleep by the stern cables of the ship. Then Circe took me by the hand and bade me be seated away from the others, while she reclined by my side and asked me all about our adventures.

" 'So far so good,' said she, when I had ended my story, 'and now pay attention to what I am about to tell you—heaven itself, indeed, will recall it to your recollection. First you will come to the Sirens who enchant all who come near them. If anyone unwarily draws in too close and hears the singing of the Sirens, his wife and children will never welcome him home again, for they sit in a green field and warble him to death with the sweetness of their song. There is a great heap of dead men's bones lying all around, with the flesh still rotting off them. Therefore pass these Sirens by, and stop your men's ears with wax that none of them may hear; but if you like you can listen yourself, for you may get the men to bind you as you stand upright on a cross-piece halfway up the mast, and they must lash the rope's ends to the mast itself, that you may have the pleasure of listening. If you beg and pray the men to unloose you, then they must bind you faster.

" 'When your crew have taken you past these Sirens, I cannot give you coherent directions as to which of two courses you are to take; I will lay the two alternatives before you, and you must consider them for yourself. On the one hand there are some overhanging rocks against which the deep blue waves of Amphitrite beat with terrific fury; the blessed gods call these rocks the Wanderers. Here not even a bird may pass, no, not even the timid doves that bring ambrosia to Father Zeus, but the sheer rock always carries off one of them, and Father Zeus has to send another to make up their number. No ship that ever yet came to these rocks has got away again, but the waves and whirlwinds of fire are freighted with wreckage and with the bodies of dead men. The only vessel that ever sailed and got through was the famous Argo on her way from the house of Aeetes, and she too would have gone against these great rocks, only that Hera piloted her past them for the love she bore to Jason.

" 'Of these two rocks the one reaches heaven and its peak is lost in a dark cloud. This never leaves it, so that the top is never clear not even in summer and early autumn. No man, though he had twenty hands and twenty feet, could get a foothold on it and climb it, for it runs sheer up, as smooth as though it had been polished. In the middle of it there is a large cavern, looking west and turned towards Erebus; you must take your ship this way, but the cave is so high up that not even the stoutest archer could send an arrow into it. Inside it Scylla sits and yelps with a voice that you might take to be that of a young hound, but in truth she is a dreadful monster and no one—not even a god—could face her without being terror-struck. She has twelve misshapen feet, and six necks of the most prodigious length; and at the end of each neck she has a frightful head with three rows of teeth in each, all set very close together, so that they would crunch anyone to death in a moment. She sits deep within her shady cell thrusting out her heads and peering all round the rock, fishing for dolphins or dogfish or any larger monster that she can catch, of the thousands with which Amphitrite teems. No ship ever yet got past her without losing some men, for she shoots out all her heads at once, and carries off a man in each mouth.

" 'You will find the other rock lies lower, but they are so close together that there is not more than a bow-shot between them. A large fig tree in full leaf grows upon it, and under it lies the sucking whirlpool of Charybdis. Three times in the day does she vomit forth her waters, and three times she sucks them down again. See that you be not there when she is sucking, for if you are, Poseidon himself could not save you; you must hug the Scylla side and drive your ship by as fast as you can, for you had better lose six men than your whole crew.'

" 'Is there no way,' said I, 'of escaping Charybdis, and at the same time keeping Scylla off when she is trying to harm my men?'

" 'You daredevil,' replied the goddess, 'you are always wanting to fight somebody or something; you will not let yourself be beaten even by the immortals. For Scylla is not mortal; moreover she is savage, extreme, rude, cruel, and invincible. There is no help for it; your best chance will be to get by her as fast as ever you can, for if you dawdle about her rock while you are putting on your armor, she may catch you with a second cast of her six heads, and snap up another half-dozen of your men. So drive your ship past her at full speed, and roar out lustily to Crataiis who is Scylla's dam, bad luck to her; she will then stop her from making a second raid upon you.

" 'You will now come to the Thrinacian island, and here you will see many herds of cattle and flocks of sheep belonging to the sun-god—seven herds of cattle and seven flocks of sheep, with fifty head in each flock. They do not breed, nor do they become fewer in number, and they are tended by the goddesses Phaethusa and Lampetie, who are children of the sun-god Hyperion by Neaera. Their mother, when she had borne them and had done suckling them, sent them to the Thrinacian island, which was a long way off, to live there and look after their father's flocks and herds. If you leave these flocks unharmed, and think of nothing but getting home, you may yet after much hardship reach Ithaca. But if you harm them, then I forewarn you of the destruction both of your ship and of your comrades; and even though you may yourself escape, you will return late, in bad plight, after losing all your men.'

"Here she ended, and Dawn enthroned in gold began to show in heaven, whereon she returned inland. I then went on board and told my men to loose the ship from her moorings; so they at once got into her, took their places, and began to smite the gray sea with their oars. Presently the great and cunning goddess Circe befriended us with a fair wind that blew dead aft, and stayed steadily with us, keeping oar sails well-filled, so we did whatever wanted doing to the ship's gear, and let her go as wind and helmsman headed her.

"Then, being much troubled in mind, I said to my men, 'My friends, it is not right that one or two of us alone should know the prophecies that Circe has made me, I will therefore tell you about them, so that whether we live or die we may do so with our eyes open. First she said we were to keep clear of the Sirens, who sit and sing most beautifully in a field of flowers; but she said I might hear them myself so long as no one else did. Therefore, take me and bind me to the crosspiece halfway up the mast; bind me as I stand upright, with a bond so fast that I cannot possibly break away, and lash the rope's ends to the mast itself. If I beg and pray you to set me free, then bind me more tightly still.'

"I had hardly finished telling everything to the men before we reached the island of the two Sirens, for the wind had been very favorable. Then all of a sudden it fell dead calm; there was not a breath of wind or a ripple upon the water, so the men furled the sails and stowed them; then taking to their oars they whitened the water with the foam they raised in rowing. Meanwhile I took a large wheel of wax and cut it up small with my sword. Then I kneaded the wax in my strong hands till it became soft, which it soon did between the kneading and the rays of the sun-god son of Hyperion. Then I stopped the ears of all my men, and they bound me hands and feet to the mast as I stood upright on the cross-piece; but they went on rowing themselves. When we had got within earshot of the land, and the ship was going at a good rate, the Sirens saw that we were getting in shore and began with their singing.

" 'Come here,' they sang, 'renowned Odysseus, honor to the Achaean name, and listen to our two voices. No one ever sailed past us without staying to hear the enchanting sweetness of our song—and he who listens will go on his way not only charmed, but wiser, for we know all the ills that the gods laid upon the Argives and Trojans before Troy, and can tell you everything that is going to happen over the whole world.'

"They sang these words most musically, and as I longed to hear them further I made signs by frowning to my men that they should set me free; but they quickened their stroke, and Eurylochus and Perimedes bound me with still stronger bonds till we had got out of hearing of the Sirens' voices. Then my men took the wax from their ears and unbound me.

"Immediately after we had got past the island I saw a great wave from which spray was rising, and I heard a loud roaring sound. The men were so frightened that they loosed hold of their oars, for the whole sea resounded with the rushing of the waters, but the ship stayed where it was, for the men had left off rowing. I went round, therefore, and exhorted them man by man not to lose heart.

" 'My friends,' said I, 'this is not the first time that we have been in danger, and we are in nothing like so bad a case as when the Cyclops shut us up in his cave; nevertheless, my courage and wise counsel saved us then, and we shall live to look back on all this as well. Now, therefore, let us all do as I say, trust in Zeus, and row on with might and main. As for you, coxswain, these are your orders—attend to them, for the ship is in your hands: turn her head away from these steaming rapids and hug the rock, or she will give you the slip and be over yonder before you know where you are, and you will be the death of us.'

"So they did as I told them; but I said nothing about the awful monster Scylla, for I knew the men would not go on rowing if I did, but would huddle together in the hold. In one thing only did I disobey Circe's strict instructions— I put on my armor. Then seizing two strong spears I took my stand on the ship's bows, for it was there that I expected first to see the monster of the rock, who was to do my men so much harm; but I could not make her out anywhere, though I strained my eyes with looking the gloomy rock all over and over.

"Then we entered the Straits[1] in great fear of mind, for on the one hand was Scylla, and on the other dread Charybdis kept sucking up the salt water.

---

[1] These straits are generally understood to be the Straits of Messina.

As she vomited it up, it was like the water in a cauldron when it is boiling over upon a great fire, and the spray reached the top of the rocks on either side. When she began to suck again, we could see the water all inside whirling round and round, and it made a deafening sound as it broke against the rocks. We could see the bottom of the whirlpool all black with sand and mud, and the men were at their wits ends for fear. While we were taken up with this, and were expecting each moment to be our last, Scylla pounced down suddenly upon us and snatched up my six best men. I was looking at once after both ship and men, and in a moment I saw their hands and feet ever so high above me, struggling in the air as Scylla was carrying them off, and I heard them call out my name in one last despairing cry. As a fisherman, seated, spear in hand, upon some jutting rock,[2] throws bait into the water to deceive the poor little fishes, and spears them with the ox's horn with which his spear is shod, throwing them gasping on to the land as he catches them one by one—even so did Scylla land these panting creatures on her rock and munch them up at the mouth of her den, while they screamed and stretched out their hands to me in their mortal agony. This was the most sickening sight that I saw throughout all my voyages.

"When we had passed the [Wandering] rocks, with Scylla and terrible Charybdis, we reached the noble island of the sun-god, where were the goodly cattle and sheep belonging to the sun Hyperion. While still at sea in my ship I could hear the cattle lowing as they came home to the yards, and the sheep bleating. Then I remembered what the blind Theban prophet Teiresias had told me, and how carefully Aeaean Circe had warned me to shun the island of the blessed sun-god. So being much troubled, I said to the men, 'My men, I know you are hard-pressed, but listen while I tell you the prophecy that Teiresias made me, and how carefully Aeaean Circe warned

---

[2] In the islands of Favognana and Marettimo off Sicily I have seen men fish exactly as here described. They chew bread into a paste and throw it into the sea to attract the fish, which they then spear. No line is used. (B.)

me to shun the island of the blessed sun-god, for it was here, she said, that our worst danger would lie. Head the ship, therefore, away from the island.'

"The men were in despair at this, and Eurylochus at once gave me an insolent answer. 'Odysseus', said he, 'you are cruel. You are very strong yourself and never get worn out; you seem to be made of iron, and now, though your men are exhausted with toil and want of sleep, you will not let them land and cook themselves a good supper upon this island, but bid them put out to sea and go faring fruitlessly on through the watches of the flying night. It is by night that the winds blow hardest and do so much damage. How can we escape should one of those sudden squalls spring up from southwest or west, which so often wreck a vessel when our lords the gods are unpropitious? Now, therefore, let us obey the behests of night and prepare our supper here hard by the ship; tomorrow morning we will go on board again and put out to sea.'

"Thus spoke Eurylochus, and the men approved his words. I saw that heaven meant us a mischief and said, 'You force me to yield, for you are many against one, but at any rate each one of you must take his solemn oath that if he meet with a herd of cattle or a large flock of sheep, he will not be so mad as to kill a single head of either, but will be satisfied with the food that Circe has given us.'

"They all swore as I bade them, and when they had completed their oath we made the ship fast in a harbor that was near a stream of fresh water, and the men went ashore and cooked their suppers. As soon as they had had enough to eat and drink, they began talking about their poor comrades whom Scylla had snatched up and eaten; this set them weeping, and they went on crying till they fell off into a sound sleep.

"In the third watch of the night when the stars had shifted their places, Zeus raised a great gale of wind that blew a hurricane so that land and sea were covered with thick clouds, and night sprang forth out of the heavens. When the child of morning, rosy-fingered Dawn, appeared, we brought the ship to land and drew her into a cave wherein the sea-nymphs hold their courts and dances, and I called the men together in council."

" 'My friends,' said I, 'we have meat and drink in the ship, let us mind, therefore, and not touch the cattle, or we shall suffer for it; for these cattle and sheep belong to the mighty sun, who sees and gives ear to everything.' And again they promised that they would obey.

"For a whole month the wind blew steadily from the south, and there was no other wind, but only south and east.[3] As long as corn and wine held out the men did not touch the cattle when they were hungry. When, however, they had eaten all there was in the ship, they were forced to go further afield, fishing with hook and line, catching birds, and taking whatever they could lay their hands on, for they were starving. One day, therefore, I went up inland that I might pray heaven to show me some means of getting away. When I had gone far enough to be clear of all my men, and had found a place that was well sheltered from the wind, I washed my hands and prayed to all the gods in Olympus till by and by they sent me off into a sweet sleep.

"Meanwhile Eurylochus had been giving evil counsel to the men. 'Listen to me,' said he, 'my poor comrades. All deaths are bad enough, but there is none so bad as famine. Why should not we drive in the best of these cows and offer them in sacrifice to the immortal gods? If we ever get back to Ithaca, we can build a fine temple to the sun-god and enrich it with every kind of ornament. If, however, he is determined to sink our ship out of revenge for these horned cattle, and the other gods are of the same mind, I for one would rather drink salt water once for all and have done with it than be starved to death by inches in such a desert island as this is.'

"Thus spoke Eurylochus, and the men approved his words. Now the cattle, so fair and goodly, were feeding not far from the ship; the men, therefore, drove in the best of them, and they all stood round them saying their prayers, and using young oak-shoots instead of barley meal, for there was no barley left. When they had done praying they killed the cows and dressed their carcasses;

[3] The writer evidently regards Odysseus as on a coast that looked east at no great distance south of the Straits of Messina somewhere, say, near Tauromenium, now Taormina. (B.)

they cut out the thighbones, wrapped them round in two layers of fat, and set some pieces of raw meat on the top of them. They had no wine with which to make drink offerings over the sacrifice while it was cooking, so they kept pouring on a little water from time to time while the inward meats were being grilled. Then, when the thighbones were burned and they had tasted the inward meats, they cut the rest up small and put the pieces upon the spits.

"By this time my deep sleep had left me, and I turned back to the ship and to the seashore. As I drew near I began to smell hot roast meat, so I groaned out a prayer to the immortal gods. 'Father Zeus,' I exclaimed, 'and all you other gods who live in everlasting bliss, you have done me a cruel mischief by the sleep into which you have sent me. See what fine work these men of mine have been making in my absence.'

"Meanwhile Lampetie went straight off to the sun and told him we had been killing his cows, whereon he flew into a great rage, and said to the immortals, 'Father Zeus, and all you other gods who live in everlasting bliss, I must have vengeance on the crew of Odysseus' ship. They have had the insolence to kill my cows, which were the one thing I loved to look upon, whether I was going up heaven or down again. If they do not square accounts with me about my cows, I will go down to Hades and shine there among the dead.'

" 'Sun,' said Zeus, 'go on shining upon us gods and upon mankind over the fruitful earth. I will shiver their ship into little pieces with a bolt of white lightning as soon as they get out to sea.'

"I was told all this by Calypso, who said she had heard it from the mouth of Hermes.

"As soon as I got down to my ship and to the seashore, I rebuked each one of the men separately, but we could see no way out of it, for the cows were dead already. And indeed the gods began at once to show signs and wonders among us, for the hides of the cattle crawled about, and the joints upon the spits began to low like cows, and the meat, whether cooked or raw, kept on making a noise just as cows do.

"For six days my men kept driving in the best cows and feasting upon them, but when Zeus the son of Cronus had added a seventh day, the fury of the gale abated; we therefore went on board, raised our masts, spread sail, and put out to sea. As soon as we were well away from the island, and could see nothing but sky and sea, the son of Cronus raised a black cloud over our ship, and the sea grew dark beneath it. We did not get on much further, for in another moment we were caught by a terrific squall from the west that snapped the forestays of the mast so that it fell aft, while all the ship's gear tumbled about at the bottom of the vessel. The mast fell upon the head of the helmsman in the ship's stern, so that the bones of his head were crushed to pieces, and he fell overboard as though he were diving, with no more life left in him.

"Then Zeus let fly with his thunderbolts, and the ship went round and round, and was filled with fire and brimstone as the lightning struck it. The men all fell into the sea; they were carried about in the water round the ship, looking like so many seagulls, but the god presently deprived them of all chance of getting home again.

"I stuck to the ship till the sea knocked her sides from her keel (which drifted about by itself) and struck the mast out of her in the direction of the keel; but there was a backstay of stout ox-thong still hanging about it, and with this I lashed the mast and keel together, and getting astride of them was carried wherever the winds chose to take me.

"The gale from the west had now spent its force, and the wind got into the south again, which frightened me lest I should be taken back to the terrible whirlpool of Charybdis. This indeed was what actually happened, for I was borne along by the waves all night, and by sunrise had reached the rock of Scylla, and the whirlpool. She was then sucking down the salt sea-water, but I was carried aloft toward the fig tree, which I caught hold of and clung on to like a bat. I could not plant my feet anywhere so as to stand securely, for the roots were a long way off and the boughs that overshadowed the whole pool were too high, too vast, and too far apart for me to reach them; so I hung patiently on, waiting till the pool should discharge my mast and raft again— and a very long while it seemed. A juryman is not more glad to get home to supper, after having been long detained in court by troublesome cases, than I was to see my raft beginning to work its way out of the whirlpool again. At last I let go with my hands and feet, and fell heavily into the sea, hard by my raft on to which I then got, and began to row with my hands. As for Scylla, the father of gods and men would not let her get further sight of me—otherwise I should have certainly been lost.

"Hence I was carried along for nine days till on the tenth night the gods stranded me on the Ogygian island, where dwells the great and powerful goddess Calypso. She took me in and was kind to me, but I need say no more about this, for I told you and your noble wife all about it yesterday, and I hate saying the same thing over and over again."

Book XIII

*Odysseus is given more rich gifts by Alcinous and his nobles and sent away
at night in a ship to Ithaca. On arrival he is carried, sleeping, ashore and set
gently down with his treasure on his native soil. The ship on its return is
changed by angry Poseidon into a rock. When Odysseus wakes, Athene
appears to tell him where he is and counsel him to caution. She helps him
conceal his treasure and then transforms him into an ugly old beggar.*

T HUS DID HE SPEAK, AND THEY ALL HELD THEIR PEACE THROUGHOUT THE
covered cloister, enthralled by the charm of his story, till presently
Alcinous began to speak.

"Odysseus," said he, "now that you have reached my house I doubt not
you will get home without further misadventure no matter how much you
have suffered in the past. To you others, however, who come here night after
night to drink my choicest wine and listen to my bard, I would insist as fol-
lows. Our guest has already packed up the clothes, wrought gold, and other
valuables which you have brought for his acceptance; let us now, therefore,
present him further, each one of us, with a large tripod and a cauldron. We
will recoup ourselves by the levy of a general rate; for private individuals can-
not be expected to bear the burden of such a handsome present."

Everyone approved of this, and then they went home to bed each in his
own abode. When the child of morning, rosy-fingered Dawn, appeared, they
hurried down to the ship and brought their cauldrons with them. Alcinous
went on board and saw everything so securely stowed under the ship's benches

that nothing could break adrift and injure the rowers. Then they went to the house of Alcinous to get dinner, and he sacrificed a bull for them in honor of Zeus, who is the lord of all. They set the steaks to grill and made an excellent dinner, after which the inspired bard, Demodocus, who was a favorite with everyone, sang to them; but Odysseus kept on turning his eyes towards the sun, as though to hasten his setting, for he was longing to be on his way. As one who has been all day plowing a fallow field with a couple of oxen keeps thinking about his supper and is glad when night comes that he may go and get it, for it is all his legs can do to carry him, even so did Odysseus rejoice when the sun went down, and he at once said to the Phaeacians, addressing himself more particularly to King Alcinous.

"Sir, and all of you, farewell. Make your drink offerings and send me on my way rejoicing, for you have fulfilled my heart's desire by giving me an escort, and making me presents, which heaven grant that I may turn to good account. May I find my admirable wife living in peace among friends, and may you whom I leave behind me give satisfaction to your wives and children. May heaven vouchsafe you every good grace, and may no evil thing come among your people."

Thus did he speak. His hearers all of them approved his saying and agreed that he should have his escort, inasmuch as he had spoken reasonably. Alcinous therefore said to his servant, "Pontonous, mix some wine and hand it round to everybody, that we may offer a prayer to father Zeus and speed our guest upon his way."

Pontonous mixed the wine and handed it to everyone in turn. The others each from his own seat made a drink offering to the blessed gods that live in heaven, but Odysseus rose and placed the double cup in the hands of Queen Arete.

"Farewell, Queen," said he, "henceforward and forever, till age and death, the common lot of mankind, lay their hands upon you. I now take my leave; be happy in this house with your children, your people, and with King Alcinous."

As he spoke he crossed the threshold, and Alcinous sent a man to conduct him to his ship and to the seashore. Arete also sent some maidservants with him—one with a clean shirt and cloak, another to carry his strong-box, and a third with corn and wine. When they got to the waterside the crew took these things and put them on board, with all the meat and drink; but for Odysseus they spread a rug and a linen sheet on deck that he might sleep soundly in the stern of the ship. Then he too went on board and lay down without a word, but the crew took every man his place and loosed the hawser from the pierced stone to which it had been bound. Thereon, when they began rowing out to sea, Odysseus fell into a deep, sweet, and almost deathlike slumber.

The ship bounded forward on her way as a four-in-hand chariot flies over the course when the horses feel the whip. Her prow curveted as it were the neck of a stallion, and a great wave of dark blue water seethed in her wake. She held steadily on her course, and even a falcon, swiftest of all birds, could not have kept pace with her. Thus, then, she cut her way through the water, carrying one who was as cunning as the gods, but who was now sleeping peacefully, forgetful of all that he had suffered both on the field of battle and by the waves of the weary sea.

When the bright star that heralds the approach of dawn began to show, the ship drew near to land. Now there is in Ithaca a haven of the old merman Phorcys, which lies between two points that break the line of the sea and shut the harbor in. These shelter it from the storms of wind and sea that rage outside, so that, when once within it, a ship may lie without being even moored. At the head of this harbor there is a large olive tree, and at no great distance a fine overarching cavern sacred to the nymphs who are called Naiads. There are mixing bowls within it and wine-jars of stone, and the bees hive there. Moreover, there are great looms of stone on which the nymphs weave their robes of sea purple—very curious to see—and at all times there is water within it. It has two entrances, one facing north by which mortals can go down into the cave, while the other comes from the south and is more mysterious. Mortals cannot possibly get in by it, it is the way taken by the gods.

Into this harbor, then, they took their ship, for they knew the place. She had so much way upon her that she ran half her own length on to the shore. When, however, they had landed, the first thing they did was to lift Odysseus with his rug and linen sheet out of the ship, and lay him down upon the sand still fast asleep. Then they took out the presents which Athene had persuaded the Phaeacians to give him when he was setting out on his voyage homewards. They put these all together by the root of the olive tree, away from the road, for fear some passer-by might come and steal them before Odysseus awoke; and then they made the best of their way home again.

But Poseidon did not forget the threats with which he had already threatened Odysseus, so he took counsel with Zeus. "Father Zeus," said he, "I shall no longer be held in any sort of respect among you gods, if mortals like the Phaeacians, who are my own flesh and blood, show such small regard for me. I said I would let Odysseus get home when he had suffered sufficiently. I did not say that he should never get home at all, for I knew you had already nodded your head about it, and promised that he should do so. But now they have brought him in a ship fast asleep and have landed him in Ithaca, after loading him with more magnificent presents of bronze, gold, and raiment than he would ever have brought back from Troy, if he had had his share of the spoil and got home without misadventure."

And Zeus answered: "What, O Lord of the Earthquake, are you talking about? The gods are by no means wanting in respect for you. It would be monstrous were they to insult one so old and honored as you are. As regards mortals, however, if any of them is indulging in insolence and treating you disrespectfully, it will always rest with yourself to deal with him as you may think proper, so do just as you please."

"I should have done so at once," replied Poseidon, "if I were not anxious to avoid anything that might displease you; now, therefore, I should like to wreck the Phaeacian ship as it is returning from its escort. This will stop them from escorting people in future; and I should also like to bury their city under a huge mountain."

"My good friend," answered Zeus, "I should recommend you at the very moment when the people from the city are watching the ship on her way, to turn it into a rock near the land and looking like a ship. This will astonish everybody, and you can then bury their city under the mountain."

When earth-encircling Poseidon heard this, he went to Scheria where the Phaeacians live and stayed there till the ship, which was making rapid way, had got close in. Then he went up to it, turned it into stone, and drove it down with the flat of his hand so as to root it in the ground. After this he went away.

The Phaeacians then began talking among themselves, and one would turn towards his neighbor, saying, "Bless my heart, who is it that can have rooted the ship in the sea just as she was getting into port? We could see the whole of her only a moment ago."

This was how they talked, but they knew nothing about it; and Alcinous said: "I remember now the old prophecy of my father. He said that Poseidon would be angry with us for taking everyone so safely over the sea, and would one day wreck a Phaeacian ship as it was returning from an escort, and bury our city under a high mountain. This was what my old father used to say, and now it is all coming true. Now therefore let us all do as I say. In the first place we must leave off giving people escorts when they come here, and in the next let us sacrifice twelve picked bulls to Poseidon that he may have mercy upon us, and not bury our city under the high mountain." When the people heard this they were afraid and got ready the bulls.

Thus did the chiefs and rulers of the Phaeacians pray to King Poseidon, standing round his altar; and at the same time Odysseus woke up once more upon his own soil. He had been so long away that he did not know it again. Moreover, Zeus' daughter Athene had made it a foggy day, so that people might not know of his having come, and that she might tell him everything without either his wife or his fellow citizens and friends recognizing him until he had taken his revenge upon the wicked suitors. Everything, therefore, seemed quite different to him—the long straight tracks, the harbors, the precipices, and the goodly trees appeared all changed as he started up and looked upon his native land. So he smote his thighs with the flat of his hands and cried aloud despairingly.

"Alas," he exclaimed, "among what manner of people am I fallen? Are they savage and uncivilized or hospitable and humane? Where shall I put all this treasure, and which way shall I go? I wish I had stayed over there with the Phaeacians; or I could have gone to some other great chief who would have been good to me and given me an escort. As it is I do not know where to put my treasure, and I cannot leave it here for fear somebody else should get hold of it. In good truth the chiefs and rulers of the Phaeacians have not been dealing fairly by me, and have left me in the wrong country; they said they would take me back to Ithaca and they have not done so. May Zeus, the protector of suppliants, chastise them, for he watches over everybody and punishes those who do wrong. Still, I suppose I must count my goods and see if the crew have gone off with any of them."

He counted his goodly coppers and cauldrons, his gold and all his clothes, but there was nothing missing. Still he kept grieving about not being in his own country, and wandered up and down by the shore of the sounding sea bewailing his hard fate. Then Athene came up to him disguised as a young shepherd of delicate and princely mien, with a good cloak folded double about her shoulders; she had sandals on her comely feet and held a javelin in her hand. Odysseus was glad when he saw her, and went straight up to her.

"My friend," said he, "you are the first person whom I have met with in this country. I salute you, therefore, and beg you to be well-disposed towards me. Protect these my goods, and myself too, for I embrace your knees and pray to you as though you were a god. Tell me, then, and tell me truly, what land and country is this? Who are its inhabitants? Am I on an island, or is this the seaboard of some continent?"

Athene answered: "Stranger, you must be very simple, or must have come from somewhere a long way off, not to know what country this is. It is a very celebrated place, and everybody knows it both east and west. It is rugged and not a good driving country, but it is by no means a bad island for what there is of it. It grows any quantity of corn and also wine, for it is watered both by rain and dew; it breeds cattle also and goats. All kinds of timber grow here, and there are watering places where the water never runs dry. So, sir, the name of Ithaca is known even as far as Troy, which I understand to be a long way off from this Achaean country."

Odysseus was glad at finding himself, as Athene told him, in his own country, and he began to answer, but he did not speak the truth, and made up a lying story in the instinctive wiliness of his heart.

"I heard of Ithaca," said he, "when I was in Crete beyond the seas, and now it seems I have reached it with all these treasures. I have left as much more behind me for my children, but am flying because I killed Orsilochus son of Idomeneus, the fleetest runner in Crete. I killed him because he wanted to rob me of the spoils I had got from Troy with so much trouble and danger both on the field of battle and by the waves of the weary sea. He said I had not served his father loyally at Troy as vassal, but had set myself up as an independent ruler, so I lay in wait for him with one of my followers by the roadside, and speared him as he was coming into town from the country. It was a very dark night and nobody saw us. It was not known, therefore, that I had killed him, but as soon as I had done so I went to a ship and besought the owners, who were Phoenicians, to take me on board and set me in Pylos or in Elis where the Epeans rule, giving them as much spoil as satisfied them. They meant no guile, but the wind drove them off their course, and we sailed on till we came hither by night. It was all we could do to get inside the harbor, and none of us said a word about supper though we wanted it badly, but we all went on shore and lay down just as we were. I was very tired and fell asleep directly, so they took my goods out of the ship and placed them beside me where I was lying upon the sand. Then they sailed away to Sidonia, and I was left here in great distress of mind."

Such was his story, but Athene smiled and caressed him with her hand. Then she took the form of a woman, fair, stately, and wise. "He must be indeed a shifty lying fellow," said she, "who could surpass you in all manner of craft even though you had a god for your antagonist. Daredevil that you are, full of guile, unwearying in deceit, can you not drop your tricks and your instinctive falsehood, even now that you are in your own country again? We will say no more, however, about this, for we can both of us deceive upon occasion. You are the most accomplished counselor and orator among all mankind, while I for diplomacy and subtlety have no equal among the gods. Did you not know Zeus' daughter Athene—me, who have been ever with you, who kept watch over you in all your troubles, and who made the Phaeacians take so great a liking to you? And now, again, I am come here to talk things over with you, and help you to hide the treasure I made the Phaeacians give you. I want to tell you about the troubles that await you in your own house; you have got to face them, but tell no one, neither man nor woman, that you have come home again. Bear everything and put up with every man's insolence without a word."

And Odysseus answered: "A man, goddess, may know a great deal, but you are so constantly changing your appearance that when he meets you it is a hard matter for him to know whether it is you or not. This much, however, I know exceedingly well; you were very kind to me as long as we Achaeans were fighting before Troy, but from the day on which we went on board ship after having sacked the city of Priam, and heaven dispersed us—from that day, Athene, I saw no more of you, and cannot ever remember your coming to my ship to help me in a difficulty. I had to wander on sick and sorry till the gods delivered me from evil and I reached the city of the Phaeacians, where you encouraged me and took me into the town. And now, I beseech you in your father's name, tell me the truth, for I do not believe I am really back in Ithaca. I am in some other country and you are mocking me and deceiving me in all you have been saying. Tell me then truly, have I really got back to my own country?"

"You are always taking something of that sort into your head," replied Athene, "and that is why I cannot desert you in your afflictions; you are so plausible, shrewd, and shifty. Anyone but yourself on returning from so long a voyage would at once have gone home to see his wife and children, but you do not seem to care about asking after them or hearing any news about them till you have made sure of your wife, who remains at home vainly grieving for you, and having no peace night or day for the tears she sheds on your behalf. As for my not coming near you, I was never uneasy about you, for I was certain you would get back safely, though you would lose all your men. I did not wish to quarrel with my uncle Poseidon, who never forgave you for having blinded his son.[1] I will now, however, point out to you the lie of the land, and you will then perhaps believe me. This is the haven of the old merman Phorcys, and here is the olive tree that grows at the head of it; near it is the cave sacred to the Naiads; here too is the overarching cavern in which you have offered many an acceptable hecatomb to the nymphs, and this is the wooded mountain Neritum."

As she spoke, the goddess dispersed the mist and the land appeared. Then Odysseus rejoiced at finding himself again in his own land, and kissed the bounteous soil. He lifted up his hands and prayed to the nymphs, saying, "Naiad nymphs, daughters of Zeus, I made sure that I was never again to see you, now therefore I greet you with all loving salutations, and I will bring you offerings as in the old days, if Zeus' redoubtable daughter will grant me life, and bring my son to manhood."

"Take heart, and do not trouble yourself about that," rejoined Athene, "let us rather set about stowing your things at once in the cave, where they will be quite safe. Let us see how we can best manage it all."

[1] That is, the Cyclops Polyphemus.

Therewith she went down into the cave to look for the safest hiding places, while Odysseus brought up all the treasure of gold, bronze, and good clothing which the Phaeacians had given him. They stowed everything carefully away, and Athene set a stone against the door of the cave. Then the two sat down by the root of the great olive, and consulted how to compass the destruction of the wicked suitors.

"Odysseus," said Athene, "noble son of Laertes, think how you can lay hands on these disreputable people who have been lording it in your house these three years, courting your wife and making wedding presents to her, while she does nothing but lament your absence, giving hope and sending encouraging messages to every one of them, but meaning the very opposite of all she says."

And Odysseus answered: "In good truth, goddess, it seems I should have come to much the same bad end in my own house as Agamemnon did, if you had not given me such timely information. Advise me how I shall best avenge myself. Stand by my side and put your courage into my heart as on the day when we loosed Troy's fair diadem from her brow. Help me now as you did then, and I will fight three hundred men, if you, goddess, will be with me."

"Trust me for that," said she, "I will not lose sight of you when once we set about it, and I imagine that some of those who are devouring your substance will then bespatter the pavement with their blood and brains. I will begin by disguising you so that no human being shall know you. I will cover your body with wrinkles; you shall lose all your yellow hair. I will clothe you in a garment that shall fill all who see it with loathing; I will blear your fine eyes for you, and make you an unseemly object in the sight of the suitors, of your wife, and of the son whom you left behind you. Then go at once to the swineherd who is in charge of your pigs; he has been always well-affected towards you, and is devoted to Penelope and your son. You will find him feeding his pigs near the rock that is called Raven by the fountain Arethusa, where they are fattening on beech mast and spring water after their manner. Stay with him and find out how things are going, while I proceed to Sparta and see your son, who is with Menelaus at Sparta, where he has gone to try and find out whether you are still alive."

"But why," said Odysseus, "did you not tell him, for you knew all about it? Did you want him too to go sailing about amid all kinds of hardship while others are eating up his estate?"

Athene answered: "Never mind about him, I sent him that he might be well spoken of for having gone. He is in no sort of difficulty, but is staying quite comfortably with Menelaus, and is surrounded with abundance of every kind. The suitors have put out to sea and are lying in wait for him, for they mean to kill him before he can get home. I do not much think they will succeed, but rather that some of those who are now eating up your estate will first find a grave themselves."

As she spoke Athene touched him with her wand and covered him with wrinkles, took away all his yellow hair, and withered the flesh over his whole body. She bleared his eyes, which were naturally very fine ones; she changed his clothes and threw an old rag of a wrap about him, and a tunic, tattered, filthy, and begrimed with smoke. She also gave him an undressed deerskin as an outer garment, and furnished him with a staff and a wallet all in holes, with a twisted thong for him to sling it over his shoulder.

When the pair had thus laid their plans they parted, and the goddess went straight to Sparta to fetch Telemachus.

Book XIV

Odysseus finds the hut of his swineherd Eumaeus. He is made welcome and learns the news of home. He does not reveal himself to Eumaeus, but tells him a long lying story with a feigned report in it of Odysseus' probable return. They make sacrifices and eat together. Odysseus spends the night comfortably in Eumaeus' hut.

ODYSSEUS NOW LEFT THE HAVEN, AND TOOK THE ROUGH TRACK UP through the wooded country and over the crest of the mountain till he reached the place where Athene had said that he would find the swineherd, who was the most thrifty servant he had. He found him sitting in front of his hut, which was by the yards that he had built on a site which could be seen from far. He had made them spacious and fair to see, with a free run for the pigs all round them; he had built them during his master's absence, of stones which he had gathered out of the ground, without saying anything to Penelope or Laertes, and he had fenced them on top with thorn bushes. Outside the yard he had run a strong fence of oaken posts, split, and set pretty close together, while inside he had built twelve sties near one another for the sows to lie in. There were fifty pigs wallowing in each sty, all of them breeding sows; but the boars slept outside and were much fewer in number, for the suitors kept on eating them, and the swineherd had to send them the best he had continually. There were three hundred and sixty boar pigs, and the herdsman's four hounds, which were as fierce as wolves, slept always with them. The swineherd was at that moment cutting

595

out a pair of sandals from a good stout oxhide. Three of his men were out herding the pigs in one place or another, and he had sent the fourth to town with a boar that he had been forced to send the suitors that they might sacrifice it and have their fill of meat.

When the hounds saw Odysseus they set up a furious barking and flew at him, but Odysseus was cunning enough to sit down and loose his hold of the stick that he had in his hand. Still, he would have been torn by them in his own homestead had not the swineherd dropped his oxhide, rushed full speed through the gate of the yard, and driven the dogs off by shouting and throwing stones at them. Then he said to Odysseus; "Old man, the dogs were likely to have made short work of you, and then you would have got me into trouble. The gods have given me quite enough worries without that, for I have lost the best of masters, and am in continual grief on his account. I have to attend swine for other people to eat, while he, if he yet lives to see the light of day, is starving in some distant land. But come inside, and when you have had your fill of bread and wine, tell me where you come from, and all about your misfortunes."

On this the swineherd led the way into the hut and bade him sit down. He strewed a good thick bed of rushes upon the floor, and on the top of this he threw the shaggy chamois skin—a great thick one—on which he used to sleep by night. Odysseus was pleased at being made thus welcome, and said, "May Zeus, sir, and the rest of the gods grant you your heart's desire in return for the kind way in which you have received me."

To this you answered, O swineherd Eumaeus: "Stranger, though a still poorer man should come here, it would not be right for me to insult him, for all strangers and beggars are from Zeus. You must take what you can get and be thankful, for servants live in fear when they have young lords for their masters. And this is my misfortune now, for heaven has hindered the return of him who would have been always good to me and given me something of my own—a house, a piece of land, a good-looking wife, and all else that a

liberal master allows a servant who has worked hard for him, and whose labor
the gods have prospered as they have mine in the situation which I hold. If my
master had grown old here he would have done great things by me, but he is
gone, and I wish that Helen's whole race were utterly destroyed, for she has
been the death of many a good man. It was this matter that took my master
to Ilium, the land of noble steeds, to fight the Trojans in the cause of King
Agamemnon."

As he spoke he bound his girdle round him and went to the sties where
the young sucking pigs were penned. He picked out two which he brought
back with him and sacrificed. He singed them, cut them up, and spitted them;
when the meat was cooked he brought it all in and set it before Odysseus, hot
and still on the spit, whereon Odysseus sprinkled it over with white barley
meal. The swineherd then mixed wine in a bowl of ivy wood, and taking a
seat opposite Odysseus told him to begin.

"Fall to, stranger," said he, "on a dish of servant's pork. The fat pigs have
to go to the suitors, who eat them up without shame or scruple; but the
blessed gods love not such shameful doings, and respect those who do what
is lawful and right. Even the fierce freebooters who go raiding on other peo-
ple's land, and Zeus gives them their spoil—even they, when they have filled
their ships and got home again, live conscience-stricken, and look fearfully
for judgment. But some god seems to have told these people that Odysseus is
dead and gone. They will not, therefore, go back to their own homes and
make their offers of marriage in the usual way, but waste his estate by force,
without fear or stint. Not a day or night comes out of heaven, but they sacri-
fice not one victim or two only, and they take the run of his wine, for he was
exceedingly rich. No other great man either in Ithaca or on the mainland is
as rich as he was; he had as much as twenty men put together. I will tell you
what he had. There are twelve herds of cattle upon the mainland, and as
many flocks of sheep, there are also twelve droves of pigs, while his own men
and hired strangers feed him twelve widely spreading herds of goats. Here in

Ithaca he runs eleven large flocks of goats on the far end of the island, and they are in the charge of excellent goatherds. Each one of these sends the suitors the best goat in the flock every day. As for myself, I am in charge of the pigs that you see here, and I have to keep picking out the best I have and sending it to them."

This was his story, but Odysseus went on eating and drinking ravenously without a word, brooding his revenge. When he had eaten enough and was satisfied, the swineherd took the bowl from which he usually drank, filled it with wine, and gave it to Odysseus, who was pleased, and said as he took it in his hands, "My friend, who was this master of yours that bought you and paid for you, so rich and so powerful as you tell me? You say he perished in the cause of King Agamemnon; tell me who he was, in case I may have met with such a person. Zeus and the other gods know, but I may be able to give you news of him, for I have traveled much."

Eumaeus answered: "Old man, no traveler who comes here with news will get Odysseus' wife and son to believe his story. Nevertheless, tramps in want of a lodging keep coming with their mouths full of lies, and not a word of truth. Everyone who finds his way to Ithaca goes to my mistress and tells her falsehoods, whereon she takes them in, makes much of them, and asks them all manner of questions, crying all the time as women will when they have lost their husbands. And you too, old man, for a shirt and cloak would doubtless make up a very pretty story. But the wolves and birds of prey have long since torn Odysseus to pieces, or the fishes of the sea have eaten him, and his bones are lying buried deep in sand upon some foreign shore. He is dead and gone, and a bad business it is for all his friends—for me especially. Go where I may I shall never find so good a master, not even if I were to go home to my father and mother where I was bred and born. I do not so much care, however, about my parents now, though I should dearly like to see them again in my own country. It is the loss of Odysseus that grieves me most; I cannot speak of him without reverence though he is here no longer, for he was very fond of me, and took such care of me that wherever he may be I shall always honor his memory."

"My friend," replied Odysseus, "you are very positive, and very hard of belief about your master's coming home again; nevertheless, I will not merely say, but will swear, that he is coming. Do not give me anything for my news till he has actually come, you may then give me a shirt and cloak of good wear if you will. I am in great want, but I will not take anything at all till then, for I hate a man, even as I hate hell fire, who lets his poverty tempt him into lying. I swear by King Zeus, by the rites of hospitality, and by that hearth of Odysseus to which I have now come, that all will surely happen as I have said it will. Odysseus will return in this selfsame year; with the end of this moon and the beginning of the next he will be here to do vengeance on all those who are ill-treating his wife and son."

To this you answered, O swineherd Eumaeus: "Old man, you will neither get paid for bringing good news, nor will Odysseus ever come home. Drink your wine in peace, and let us talk about something else. Do not keep on reminding me of all this; it always pains me when anyone speaks about my honored master. As for your oath, we will let it alone, but I only wish he may come, as do Penelope, his old father Laertes, and his son Telemachus. I am terribly unhappy too about this same boy of his. He was running up fast into manhood, and bade fare to be no worse man, face and figure, than his father, but someone, either god or man, has been unsettling his mind, so he has gone off to Pylos to try and get news of his father, and the suitors are lying in wait for him as he is coming home, in the hope of leaving the house of Arceisius without a name in Ithaca. But let us say no more about him, and leave him to be taken, or else to escape, if the son of Cronus holds his hand over him to protect him. And now, old man, tell me your own story; tell me also, for I want to know, who you are and where you come from. Tell me of your town and parents, what manner of ship you came in, how your crew brought you to Ithaca, and from what country they professed to come—for you cannot have come by land."

And Odysseus answered: "I will tell you all about it. If there were meat and wine enough, and we could stay here in the hut with nothing to do but to eat and drink while the others go to their work, I could easily talk on for a whole twelve months without ever finishing the story of the sorrows with which it has pleased heaven to visit me.

"I am by birth a Cretan; my father was a well-to-do man, who had many sons born in marriage, whereas I was the son of a slave whom he had purchased for a concubine. Nevertheless, my father Castor son of Hylax (whose lineage I claim, and who was held in the highest honor among the Cretans for his wealth, prosperity, and the valor of his sons) put me on the same level with my brothers who had been born in wedlock. When, however, death took him to the house of Hades, his sons divided his estate and cast lots for their shares, but to me they gave a holding and little else. Nevertheless, my valor enabled me to marry into a rich family, for I was not given to bragging, or shirking on the field of battle. It is all over now; still, if you look at the straw you can see what the ear was, for I have had trouble enough and to spare. Ares and Athene made me doughty in war. When I had picked my men to surprise the enemy with an ambuscade, I never gave death so much as a thought, but was the first to leap forward and spear all whom I could overtake. Such was I in battle, but I did not care about farm work, nor the frugal home life of those who would bring up children. My delight was in ships, fighting, javelins, and arrows—things that most men shudder to think of. But one man likes one thing and another another, and this was what I was most naturally inclined to. Before the Achaeans went to Troy, nine times was I in command of men and ships on foreign service, and I amassed much wealth. I had my pick of the spoil in the first instance, and much more was allotted to me later on.

"My house grew apace and I became a great man among the Cretans, but when Zeus counseled that terrible expedition in which so many perished, the people required me and Idomeneus to lead their ships to Troy, and there was no way out of it, for they insisted on our doing so. There we fought for nine whole years, but in the tenth we sacked the city of Priam and sailed home again as heaven dispersed us. Then it was that Zeus devised evil against me. I spent but one month happily with my children, wife, and property, and then I conceived the idea of making a descent on Egypt, so I fitted out a fine fleet and manned it. I had nine ships, and the people flocked to fill them. For six days I and my men made feast, and I found them many victims both for sacrifice to the gods and for themselves, but on the seventh day we went on board and set sail from Crete with a fair north wind behind us as though we were going down a river. Nothing went ill with any of our ships, and we had no sickness on board, but sat where we were and let the ships go as the wind and steersmen took them. On the fifth day we reached the river Aegyptus; there I stationed my ships in the river, bidding my men stay by them and keep guard over them while I sent out scouts to reconnoiter from every point of vantage.

"But the men disobeyed my orders, took to their own devices, and ravaged the land of the Egyptians, killing the men, and taking their wives and children captive. The alarm was soon carried to the city, and when they heard the war cry, the people came out at daybreak till the plain was filled with horsemen and foot soldiers and with the gleam of armor. Then Zeus spread panic among my men, and they would no longer face the enemy, for they found themselves surrounded. The Egyptians killed many of us, and took the rest alive to do forced labor for them. Zeus, however, put it in my mind to do thus—and I wish I had died then and there in Egypt instead, for there was much sorrow in store for me. I took off my helmet and shield and dropped my spear from my hand; then I went straight up to the king's chariot, clasped his knees and kissed them, whereon he spared my life, bade me get into his chariot, and took me weeping to his own home. Many made at me with their ashen spears and tried to kill me in their fury, but the king protected me, for he feared the wrath of Zeus, the protector of strangers, who punishes those who do evil.

"I stayed there for seven years and got together much money among the Egyptians, for they all gave me something. But when it was now going on for eight years there came a certain Phoenician, a cunning rascal, who had already committed all sorts of villainy, and this man talked me over into going with him to Phoenicia, where his house and his possessions lay. I stayed there for a whole twelve months, but at the end of that time when months and days had gone by till the same season had come round again, he set me on board a ship bound for Libya, on a pretense that I was to take a cargo along with him to that place, but really that he might sell me as a slave and take the money I fetched. I suspected his intention, but went on board with him, for I could not help it.

"The ship ran before a fresh north wind till we had reached the sea that lies between Crete and Libya. There, however, Zeus counseled their destruction, for as soon as we were well out from Crete and could see nothing but sea and sky, he raised a black cloud over our ship and the sea grew dark beneath it. Then Zeus let fly with his thunderbolts and the ship went round and round and was filled with fire and brimstone as the lightning struck it. The men fell all into the sea; they were carried about in the water round the ship looking like so many seagulls, but the god presently deprived them of all chance of getting home again. I was all dismayed; Zeus, however, sent the ship's mast within my reach, which saved my life, for I clung to it, and drifted before the fury of the gale. Nine days did I drift but in the darkness of the tenth night a great wave bore me on to the Thesprotian coast. There Pheidon, king of the Thesprotians, entertained me hospitably without charging me anything at all—for his son found me when I was nearly dead with cold and fatigue, whereon he raised me by the hand, took me to his father's house and gave me clothes to wear.

"There it was that I heard news of Odysseus, for the king told me he had entertained him, and shown him much hospitality while he was on his homeward journey. He showed me also the treasure of gold, bronze, and wrought iron that Odysseus had got together. There was enough to keep his family for ten generations, so much had he left in the house of King Pheidon. But the king said Odysseus had gone to Dodona that he might learn Zeus' mind from the god's high oak tree, and know whether after so long an absence he should return to Ithaca openly, or in secret. Moreover, the king swore in my presence, making drink offerings in his own house as he did so, that the ship was by the waterside, and the crew found, that should take him to his own country. He sent me off, however, before Odysseus returned, for there happened to be a Thesprotian ship sailing for the wheat-growing island of Dulichium, and he told those in charge of her to be sure and take me safely to King Acastus.

"These men hatched a plot against me that would have reduced me to the very extreme of misery, for when the ship had got some way out from land they resolved on selling me as a slave. They stripped me of the shirt and cloak that I was wearing, and gave me instead the tattered old clouts in which you now see me. Then, towards nightfall, they reached the tilled lands of Ithaca, and there they bound me with a strong rope fast in the ship, while they went on shore to get supper by the seaside. But the gods soon undid my bonds for me, and having drawn my rags over my head I slid down the rudder into the sea, where I struck out and swam till I was well clear of them, and came ashore near a thick wood in which I lay concealed. They were very angry at my having escaped and went searching about for me, till at last they thought it was no further use and went back to their ship. The gods, having hidden me thus easily, then took me to a good man's door—for it seems that I am not to die yet a while."

To this you answered, O swineherd Eumaeus: "Poor unhappy stranger, I have found the story of your misfortunes extremely interesting, but that part about Odysseus is not right; and you will never get me to believe it. Why should a man like you go about telling lies in this way? I know all about the return of my master. The gods, one and all of them, detest him, or they would have taken him before Troy, or let him die with friends around him when the days of his fighting were done; for then the Achaeans would have built a mound over his ashes and his son would have been heir to his renown, but now the storm winds have spirited him away we know not whither.

"As for me, I live out of the way here with the pigs, and never go to the town unless when Penelope sends for me on the arrival of some news about Odysseus. Then they all sit round and ask questions, both those who grieve over the king's absence, and those who rejoice at it because they can eat up his property without paying for it. For my own part, I have never cared about asking anyone else since the time when I was taken in by an Aetolian, who had killed a man and come a long way till at last he reached my station, and I was very kind to him. He said he had seen Odysseus with Idomeneus among the Cretans, refitting his ships which had been damaged in the gale. He said Odysseus would return in the following summer or autumn with his men, and that he would bring back much wealth. And now you, you unfortunate old man, since fate has brought you to my door, do not try to flatter me in this way with vain hopes. It is not for any such reason that I shall treat you kindly, but only out of respect for Zeus the god of hospitality, as fearing him and pitying you."

Odysseus answered: "I see that you are of an unbelieving mind; I have given you my oath, and yet you will not credit me. Let us then make a bargain, and call all the gods in heaven to witness it. If your master comes home, give me a cloak and shirt of good wear, and send me to Dulichium where I want to go; but if he does not come as I say he will, set your men on to me, and tell them to throw me from yonder precipice, as a warning to tramps not to go about the country telling lies."

"And a pretty figure I should cut then," replied Eumaeus, "both now and hereafter, if I were to kill you after receiving you into my hut and showing you hospitality. I should have to say my prayers in good earnest if I did. But it is just supper time and I hope my men will come in directly, that we may cook something savory for supper."

Thus did they converse, and presently the swineherds came up with the pigs, which were then shut up for the night in their sties, and a tremendous squealing they made as they were being driven into them. But Eumaeus called to his men and said, "Bring in the best pig you have, that I may sacrifice him for this stranger, and we will take toll of him ourselves. We have had trouble enough this long time feeding pigs, while others reap the fruit of our labor."

On this he began chopping firewood, while the others brought in a fine fat five-year-old boar pig, and set it at the altar. Eumaeus did not forget the gods, for he was a man of good principles, so the first thing he did was to cut bristles from the pig's face and throw them into the fire, praying to all the gods as he did so that Odysseus might return home again. Then he clubbed the pig with a billet of oak which he had kept back when he was chopping the firewood, and stunned it, while the others slaughtered and singed it. Then they cut it up, and Eumaeus began by putting raw pieces from each joint on to some of the fat; these he sprinkled with barley meal, and laid upon the embers; they cut the rest of the meat up small, put the pieces upon the spits, and roasted them till they were done; when they had taken them off the spits they threw them on to the dresser in a heap. The swineherd, who was a most equitable man, then stood up to give everyone his share. He made seven portions; one of these he set apart for Hermes the son of Maia and the nymphs, praying to them as he did so; the others he dealt out to the men, man by man. He gave Odysseus some slices cut lengthways down the loin as a mark of especial honor, and Odysseus was much pleased. 'I hope, Eumaeus," said he, "that Zeus will be as well-disposed towards you as I am, for the respect you are showing to an outcast like myself."

To this you answered, O swineherd Eumaeus, "Eat, my good fellow, and enjoy your supper, such as it is. God grants this and withholds that, just as he thinks right, for he can do whatever he chooses."

As he spoke he cut off the first piece and offered it as a burnt sacrifice to the immortal gods; then he made them a drink offering, put the cup in the hands of Odysseus, and sat down to his own portion. Mesaulius brought them their bread. The swineherd had bought this man on his own account from among the Taphians during his master's absence, and had paid for him with his own money without saying anything either to his mistress or Laertes. They then laid their hands upon the good things that were before them, and when they had had enough to eat and drink, Mesaulius took away what was left of the bread, and they all went to bed after having made a hearty supper.

Now the night came on stormy and very dark, for there was no moon. It poured without ceasing, and the wind blew strong from the west, which is a wet quarter, so Odysseus thought he would see whether Eumaeus, in the excellent care he took of him, would take off his own cloak and give it him, or make one of his men give him one. "Listen to me," said he, "Eumaeus and the rest of you; when I have said a prayer I will tell you something. It is the wine that makes me talk in this way. Wine will make even a wise man fall to singing; it will make him chuckle and dance and say many a word that he had better leave unspoken; still, as I have begun, I will go on. Would that I were still young and strong as when we got up an ambuscade before Troy. Menelaus and Odysseus were the leaders, but I was in command also, for the other two would have it so. When we had come up to the wall of the city we crouched down beneath our armor and lay there under cover of the reeds and thick brushwood that grew about the swamp. It came on to freeze with a north wind blowing; the snow fell small and fine like hoar frost, and our shields were coated thick with rime. The others had all got cloaks and shirts, and slept comfortably enough with their shields about their shoulders, but I had carelessly left my cloak behind me, not thinking that I should be too cold, and had gone off in nothing but my shirt and shield. When the night was two thirds through and the stars had shifted their places, I nudged Odysseus, who was close to me, with my elbow, and he at once gave me his ear.

" 'Odysseus,' said I, 'this cold will be the death of me, for I have no cloak. Some god fooled me into setting off with nothing on but my shirt, and I do not know what to do.'

"Odysseus, who was as crafty as he was valiant, hit upon the following plan:"

" 'Keep still,' said he in a low voice, 'or the others will hear you.' Then he raised his head on his elbow.

" 'My friends,' said he, 'I have had a dream from heaven in my sleep. We are a long way from the ships: I wish someone would go down and tell Agamemnon to send us up more men at once.'

"On this Thoas son of Andraemon threw off his cloak and set out running to the ships, whereon I took the cloak and lay in it comfortably enough till morning. Would that I were still young and strong as I was in those days, for then some one of you swineherds would give me a cloak both out of good will and for the respect due to a brave soldier; but now people look down upon me because my clothes are shabby."

And Eumaeus answered: "Old man, you have told us an excellent story, and have said nothing so far but what is quite satisfactory. For the present, therefore, you shall want neither clothing nor anything else that a stranger in distress may reasonably expect, but tomorrow morning you will have to shake your own old rags about your body again, for we have not many spare cloaks or shirts up here, but every man has only one. When Odysseus' son comes home again he will give you both cloak and shirt, and send you wherever you may want to go."

With this he got up and made a bed for Odysseus by throwing some goat-skins and sheepskins on the ground in front of the fire. Here Odysseus lay down, and Eumaeus covered him over with a great heavy cloak that he kept for a change in case of extraordinarily bad weather.

Thus did Odysseus sleep, and the young men slept beside him. But the swineherd did not like sleeping away from his pigs, so he got ready to go outside, and Odysseus was glad to see that he looked after his property during his master's absence. First he slung his sword over his brawny shoulders and put on a thick cloak to keep out the wind. He also took the skin of a large and well-fed goat, and a javelin in case of attack from men or dogs. Thus equipped he went to his rest where the pigs were camping under an overhanging rock that gave them shelter from the north wind.

Book XV

Athene meanwhile appears to Telemachus at Menelaus' house, bidding him return home. Helen and Menelaus give him parting gifts. Accompanied by Pisistratus, he drives back to his boat in Pylos and thence sets sail for Ithaca. Odysseus stays on with the swineherd Eumaeus, who tells him the story of his life. Telemachus lands and comes straight to the swineherd's hut.

B UT ATHENE WENT TO THE FAIR CITY OF SPARTA TO TELL ODYSSEUS' SON that he was to return at once. She found him and Pisistratus sleeping in the forecourt of Menelaus' house. Pisistratus was fast asleep, but Telemachus could get no rest all night for thinking of his unhappy father, so Athene went close up to him and said:

"Telemachus, you should not remain so far away from home any longer, or leave your property with such dangerous people in your house; they will eat up everything you have among them, and you will have been on a fool's errand. Ask Menelaus to send you home at once if you wish to find your excellent mother still there when you get back. Her father and brothers are already urging her to marry Eurymachus, who has given her more than any of the others, and has been greatly increasing his wedding presents. I hope nothing valuable may have been taken from the house in spite of you, but you know what women are—they always want to do the best they can for the man who marries them, and never give another thought to the children of their first husband, or to their father either when he is dead and done with. Go home, therefore, and put everything in charge of the most respectable womanservant that you have, until it shall please heaven to send you a wife of your own.

"Let me tell you also of another matter which you had better attend to. The chief men among the suitors are lying in wait for you in the Strait between Ithaca and Same, and they mean to kill you before you can reach home. I do not much think they will succeed; it is more likely that some of those who are now eating up your property will find a grave themselves. Sail night and day, and keep your ship well away from the islands. The god who watches over you and protects you will send you a fair wind. As soon as you get to Ithaca, send your ship and men on to the town, but yourself go straight to the swineherd who has charge of your pigs; he is well-disposed towards you. Stay with him, therefore, for the night, and then send him to Penelope to tell her that you have got back safe from Pylos."

Then she went back to Olympus; but Telemachus stirred Pisistratus with his heel to rouse him, and said, "Wake up, Pisistratus, and yoke the horses to the chariot, for we must set off home."

But Pisistratus said: "No matter what hurry we are in, we cannot drive in the dark. It will be morning soon; wait till Menelaus has brought his presents and put them in the chariot for us; and let him say good-by to us in the usual way. So long as he lives a guest should never forget a host who has shown him kindness."

As he spoke day began to break, and Menelaus, who had already risen, leaving Helen in bed, came towards them. When Telemachus saw him he put on his shirt as fast as he could, threw a great cloak over his shoulders, and went out to meet him. "Menelaus," said he, "let me go back now to my own country, for I want to get home."

And Menelaus answered: "Telemachus, if you insist on going I will not detain you. I do not like to see a host either too fond of his guest or too rude to him. Moderation is best in all things, and not letting a man go when he wants to do so is as bad as telling him to go if he would like to stay. One should treat a guest well as long as he is in the house and speed him when he wants to leave it. Wait, then, till I can get your beautiful presents into your chariot, and till you have yourself seen them. I will tell the women to prepare a sufficient dinner for you of what there may be in the house; it will be at once more proper and cheaper for you to get your dinner before setting out on such a long journey. If, moreover, you have a fancy for making a tour in Hellas or in the Peloponnese, I will yoke my horses, and will conduct you myself through all our principal cities. No one will send us away empty-handed; everyone will give us something—a bronze tripod, a couple of mules, or a gold cup."

"Menelaus," replied Telemachus, "I want to go home at once, for when I came away I left my property without protection, and fear that while looking for my father I shall come to ruin myself, or find that something valuable has been stolen during my absence."

When Menelaus heard this he immediately told his wife and servants to prepare a sufficient dinner from what there might be in the house. At this moment Eteoneus joined him, for he lived close by and had just got up; so Menelaus told him to light the fire and cook some meat, which he at once did. Then Menelaus went down into his fragrant storeroom, not alone, but Helen went too, with Megapenthes. When he reached the place where the treasures of his house were kept, he selected a double cup, and told his son Megapenthes to bring also a silver mixing bowl. Meanwhile Helen went to the chest where she kept the lovely dresses which she had made with her own hands, and took out one that was largest and most beautifully enriched with embroidery; it glittered like a star, and lay at the very bottom of the chest. Then they all came back through the house again till they got to Telemachus, and Menelaus said, "Telemachus, may Zeus, the mighty husband of Hera, bring you safely home according to your desire. I will now present you with the finest and most precious piece of plate in all my house. It is a mixing bowl of pure silver, except the rim, which is inlaid with gold, and it is the work of Hephaestus. Phaedimus, king of the Sidonians, made me a present of it in the course of a visit that I paid him while I was on my return home. I should like to give it to you."

With these words he placed the double cup in the hands of Telemachus, while Megapenthes brought the beautiful mixing bowl and set it before him. Hard by stood lovely Helen with the robe ready in her hand.

"I too, my son," said she, "have something for you as a keepsake from the hand of Helen; it is for your bride to wear upon her wedding day. Till then, get your dear mother to keep it for you. Thus may you go back rejoicing to your own country and to your home."

So saying she gave the robe over to him and he received it gladly. Then Pisistratus put the presents into the chariot, and admired them all as he did so. Presently Menelaus took Telemachus and Pisistratus into the house, and they both of them sat down to table. A maidservant brought them water in a beautiful golden ewer, and poured it into a silver basin for them to wash their hands, and she drew a clean table beside them; an upper servant brought them bread and offered them many good things of what there was in the house. Eteoneus carved the meat and gave them each their portions, while Megapenthes poured out the wine. Then they laid their hands upon the good things that were before them. But as soon as they had had enough to eat and drink Telemachus and Pisistratus yoked the horses, and took their places in the chariot. They drove out through the inner gateway and under the echoing gatehouse of the outer court, and Menelaus came after them with a golden goblet of wine in his right hand that they might make a drink offering before they set out. He stood in front of the horses and pledged them, saying, "Farewell to both of you; see that you tell Nestor how I have treated you, for he was as kind to me as any father could be while we Achaeans were fighting before Troy."

"We will be sure, sir," answered Telemachus, "to tell him everything as soon as we see him. I wish I were as certain of finding Odysseus returned when I get back to Ithaca, that I might tell him of the very great kindness you have shown me and of the many beautiful presents I am taking with me."

As he was thus speaking a bird flew by on his right hand—an eagle with a great white goose in its talons which it had carried off from the farmyard— and all the men and women were running after it and shouting. It came quite close up to them and flew away on their right hands in front of the horses. When they saw it they were glad, and their hearts took comfort within them, whereon Pisistratus said, "Tell me, Menelaus, has heaven sent this omen for us or for you?"

Menelaus was thinking what would be the most proper answer for him to make, but Helen was too quick for him and said, "I will read this matter as heaven has put it in my heart, and as I doubt not that it will come to pass. The eagle came from the mountain where it was bred and has its nest, and in like manner Odysseus, after having traveled far and suffered much, will return to take his revenge—if indeed he is not back already and hatching mischief for the suitors."

"May Zeus so grant it," replied Telemachus. "If it should prove to be so, I will make vows to you as though you were a god, even when I am at home."

As he spoke he lashed his horses and they started off at full speed through the town towards the open country. They swayed the yoke upon their necks and traveled the whole day long till the sun set and darkness was over all the land. Then they reached Pherae, where Diocles lived who was son of Ortilochus the son of Alpheus. There they passed the night and were treated hospitably. When the child of morning, rosy-fingered Dawn, appeared, they again yoked their horses and took their places in the chariot. They drove out through the inner gateway and under the echoing gatehouse of the outer court. Then Pisistratus lashed his horses on and they flew forward nothing loath; ere long they came to Pylos, and then Telemachus said:

"Pisistratus, I hope you will promise to do what I am going to ask you. You know our fathers were old friends before us; moreover, we are both of an age, and this journey has brought us together still more closely. Do not, there- fore, take me past my ship, but leave me there, for if I go to your father's house he will try to keep me in the warmth of his good will towards me, and I must go home at once."

Pisistratus thought how he should do as he was asked, and in the end he deemed it best to turn his horses towards the ship, and put Menelaus' beautiful presents of gold and raiment in the stem of the vessel. Then he said, "Go on board at once and tell your men to do so also before I can reach home to tell my father. I know how obstinate he is, and am sure he will not let you go; he will come down here to fetch you, and he will not go back without you. But he will be very angry."

With this he drove his goodly steeds back to the city of the Pylians and soon reached his home. But Telemachus called the men together and gave his orders. "Now, my men," said he, "get everything in order on board the ship, and let us set out at once."

Thus did he speak, and they went on board even as he had said. But as Telemachus was thus busied, praying also and sacrificing to Athene in the ship's stern, there came to him a man from a distant country, a seer, who was flying from Argos because he had killed a man. He was descended from Melampus, who used to live in Pylos, the land of sheep. He was rich and owned a great house, but he was driven into exile by the great and powerful King Neleus. Neleus seized his goods and held them for a whole year, during which he was a close prisoner in the house of King Phylacus, and in much distress of mind both on account of the daughter of Neleus and because he was haunted by a great sorrow that dread Erinys had laid upon him. In the end, however, he escaped with his life, drove the cattle from Phylace to Pylos, avenged the wrong that had been done him, and gave the daughter of Neleus to his brother. Then he left the country and went to Argos, where it was ordained that he should reign over much people. There he married, established himself, and had two famous sons, Antiphates and Mantius. Antiphates became father of Oicleus, and Oicleus of Amphiaraus, who was dearly beloved both by Zeus and by Apollo, but he did not live to old age, for he was killed in Thebes by reason of a woman's gifts. His sons were Alcmaeon and Amphilochus. Mantius, the other son of Melampus, was father to Polypheides and Cleitus. Aurora, throned in gold, carrried off Cleitus for his beauty's sake, that he might dwell among the immortals, but Apollo made Polypheides the greatest seer in the whole world now that Amphiaraus was dead. He quarreled with his father and went to live in Hyperesia, where he remained and prophesied for all men.

His son Theoclymenus it was who now came up to Telemachus as he was making drink offerings and praying in his ship. "Friend," said he, "now that I find you sacrificing in this place, I beseech you by your sacrifices themselves, and by the god to whom you make them, I pray you also by your own head and by those of your followers, tell me the truth and nothing but the truth. Who and whence are you? Tell me also of your town and parents."

Telemachus said, "I will answer you quite truly. I am from Ithaca, and my father is Odysseus, as surely as that he ever lived. But he has come to some miserable end. Therefore I have taken this ship and got my crew together to see if I can hear any news of him, for he has been away a long time."

"I too," answered Theoclymenus, "am an exile, for I have killed a man of my own race. He has many brothers and kinsmen in Argos, and they have great power among the Argives. I am flying to escape death at their hands, and am thus doomed to be a wanderer on the face of the earth. I am your suppliant; take me, therefore, on board your ship that they may not kill me, for I know they are in pursuit."

"I will not refuse you," replied Telemachus, "if you wish to join us. Come, therefore, and in Ithaca we will treat you hospitably according to what we have."

On this he received Theoclymenus' spear and laid it down on the deck of the ship. He went on board and sat in the stern, bidding Theoclymenus sit beside him; then the men let go the hawsers. Telemachus told them to catch hold of the ropes, and they made all haste to do so. They set the mast in its socket in the cross-plank, raised it and made it fast with the forestays, and they hoisted their white sails with sheets of twisted oxhide. Athene sent them a fair wind that blew fresh and strong to take the ship on her course as fast as possible. Thus then they passed by Crouni and Chalcis.

Presently the sun set and darkness was over all the land. The vessel made a quick passage to Pheae and thence on to Elis, where the Epeans rule. Telemachus then headed her for the flying islands, wondering within himself whether he should escape death or should be taken prisoner.

Meanwhile Odysseus and the swineherd were eating their meal in the hut, and the men ate with them. As soon as they had had enough to eat and drink, Odysseus began trying to prove the swineherd and see whether he would continue to treat him kindly, and ask him to stay on at the station or pack him off to the city; so he said:

"Eumaeus, and all of you, tomorrow I want to go away and begin begging about the town, so as to be no more trouble to you or to your men. Give me your advice therefore, and let me have a good guide to go with me and show me the way. I will go the round of the city begging as I needs must, to see if anyone will give me a drink and a piece of bread. I should like also to go to the house of Odysseus and bring news of her husband to Queen Penelope. I could then go about among the suitors and see if out of all their abundance they will give me a dinner. I should soon make them an excellent servant in all sorts of ways. Listen and believe when I tell you that by the blessing of Hermes, who gives grace and good name to the works of all men, there is no one living who would make a more handy servant than I should—to put fresh wood on the fire, chop fuel, carve, cook, pour out wine, and do all those services that poor men have to do for their betters."

The swineherd was very much disturbed when he heard this. "Heaven help me," he exclaimed, "whatever can have put such a notion as that into your head? If you go near the suitors you will be undone to a certainty, for their pride and insolence reach the very heavens. They would never think of taking a man like you for a servant. Their servants are all young men, well-dressed, wearing good cloaks and shirts, with well-looking faces and their hair always tidy. The tables are kept quite clean and are loaded with bread, meat, and wine. Stay where you are, then; you are not in anybody's way. I do not mind your being here, no more do any of the others, and when Telemachus comes home he will give you a shirt and cloak and will send you wherever you want to go."

Odysseus answered: "I hope you may be as dear to the gods as you are to me, for having saved me from going about and getting into trouble; there is nothing worse than being always on the tramp. Still, when men have once got low down in the world they will go through a great deal on behalf of their miserable bellies. Since, however, you press me to stay here and await the return of Telemachus, tell me about Odysseus' mother, and his father whom he left on the threshold of old age when he set out for Troy. Are they still living or are they already dead and in the house of Hades?"

"I will tell you all about them," replied Eumaeus. "Laertes is still living and prays heaven to let him depart peacefully in his own house, for he is terribly distressed about the absence of his son, and also about the death of his wife, which grieved him greatly and aged him more than anything else did. She came to an unhappy end through sorrow for her son. May no friend or neighbor who has dealt kindly by me come to such an end as she did. As long as she was still living, though she was always grieving, I used to like seeing her and asking her how she did, for she brought me up along with her daughter, Ctimene, the youngest of her children. We were boy and girl together, and she made little difference between us. When, however, we both grew up, they sent Ctimene to Same and received a splendid dowry for her. As for me, my mistress gave me a good shirt and cloak with a pair of sandals for my feet, and sent me off into the country, but she was just as fond of me as ever. This is all over now. Still it has pleased heaven to prosper my work in the situation which I now hold. I have enough to eat and drink, and can find something for any respectable stranger who comes here; but there is no getting a kind word or deed out of my mistress, for the house has fallen into the hands of wicked people. Servants want sometimes to see their mistress and have a talk with her; they like to have something to eat and drink at the house, and something too to take back with them into the country. This is what will keep servants in a good humor."

Odysseus answered: "Then you must have been a very little fellow, Eumaeus, when you were taken so far away from your home and parents. Tell me, and tell me true, was the city in which your father and mother lived sacked and pillaged, or did some enemies carry you off when you were alone tending sheep or cattle, ship you off here, and sell you for whatever your master gave them?"

"Stranger," replied Eumaeus, "as regards your question: sit still, make yourself comfortable, drink your wine, and listen to me. The nights are now at their longest; there is plenty of time both for sleeping and sitting up talking together; you ought not to go to bed till bedtime, too much sleep is as bad as too little. If any one of the others wishes to go to bed, let him leave us and do so; he can then take my master's pigs out when he has done breakfast in the morning. We two will sit here eating and drinking in the hut, and telling one another stories about our misfortunes; for when a man has suffered much and been buffeted about in the world, he takes pleasure in recalling the memory of sorrows that have long gone by. As regards your question, then, my tale is as follows:

"You may have heard of an island called Syra that lies over above Ortygia,[1] where the land begins to turn round and look in another direction. It is not very thickly peopled, but the soil is good, with much pasture fit for cattle and

[1] Assuming, as we may safely do, that the Syra and Ortygia of the *Odyssey* refer to the islands on which Syracuse was originally built, it is the fact that not far to the south of these places the land turns sharply round, so that mariners following the coast would find the sun upon the other side of their ship to that on which they had had it hitherto. (B.)

sheep, and it abounds with wine and wheat. Dearth never comes there, nor are the people plagued by any sickness, but when they grow old Apollo comes with Artemis and kills them with his painless shafts. It contains two communities, and the whole country is divided between these two. My father Ctesius son of Ormenus, a man comparable to the gods, reigned over both.

"Now to this place there came some cunning traders from Phoenicia (for the Phoenicians are great mariners) in a ship which they had freighted with gewgaws of all kinds. There happened to be a Phoenician woman in my father's house, very tall and comely, and an excellent servant. These scoundrels got hold of her one day when she was washing near their ship, seduced her, and cajoled her in ways that no woman can resist, no matter how good she may be by nature. The man who had seduced her asked her who she was and where she came from, and on this she told him her father's name. 'I come from Sidon,' said she, 'and am daughter to Arybas, a man rolling in wealth. One day as I was coming into the town from the country some Taphian pirates seized me and took me here over the sea, where they sold me to the man who owns this house, and he gave them their price for me.'

"The man who had seduced her then said, 'Would you like to come along with us to see the house of your parents and your parents themselves? They are both alive and are said to be well off.'

" 'I will do so gladly,' answered she, 'if you men will first swear me a solemn oath that you will do me no harm by the way.'

"They all swore as she told them, and when they had completed their oath the woman said, 'Hush; and if any of your men meets me in the street or at the well, do not let him speak to me, for fear someone should go and tell my master, in which case he would suspect something. He would put me in prison, and would have all of you murdered; keep your own counsel therefore. Buy your merchandise as fast as you can, and send me word when you have done loading. I will bring as much gold as I can lay my hands on, and there is something else also that I can do towards paying my fare. I am nurse to the son of the good man of the house, a funny little fellow just able to run about. I will carry him off in your ship, and you will get a great deal of money for him if you take him and sell him in foreign parts.'

"On this she went back to the house. The Phoenicians stayed a whole year till they had loaded their ship with much precious merchandise, and then, when they had got freight enough, they sent to tell the woman. Their messenger, a very cunning fellow, came to my father's house bringing a necklace of gold with amber beads strung among it; and while my mother and the servants had it in their hands admiring it and bargaining about it, he made a sign quietly to the woman and then went back to the ship, whereon she took me by the hand and led me out of the house. In the fore part of the house she saw the tables set with the cups of guests who had been feasting with my father, as being in attendance on him; these were now all gone to a meeting of the public assembly, so she snatched up three cups and carried them off in the bosom of her dress, while I followed her, for I knew no better. The sun was now set, and darkness was over all the land, so we hurried on as fast as we could till we reached the harbor, where the Phoenician ship was lying. When they had got on board they sailed their ways over the sea, taking us with them, and Zeus sent them a fair wind. Six days did we sail both night and day, but on the seventh day Artemis struck the woman and she fell heavily down into the ship's hold as though she were a seagull alighting on the water; so they threw her overboard to the seals and fishes, and I was left all sorrowful and alone. Presently the winds and waves took the ship to Ithaca, where Laertes gave sundry of his chattels for me, and thus it was that ever I came to set eyes upon this country."

Odysseus answered, "Eumaeus, I have heard the story of your misfortunes with the most lively interest and pity, but Zeus has given you good as well as evil, for in spite of everything you have a good master, who sees that you always have enough to eat and drink; and you lead a good life, whereas I am still going about begging my way from city to city."

Thus did they converse, and they had only a very little time left for sleep, for it was soon daybreak. In the meantime Telemachus and his crew were nearing land, so they loosed the sails, took down the mast, and rowed the ship into the harbor. They cast out their mooring stones and made fast the hawsers; they then got out upon the seashore, mixed their wine, and got dinner ready. As soon as they had had enough to eat and drink Telemachus said, "Take the ship on to the town, but leave me here, for I want to look after the herdsmen on one of my farms. In the evening, when I have seen all I want, I will come down to the city, and tomorrow morning in return for your trouble I will give you all a good dinner with meat and wine."

Then Theoclymenus said, "And what, my dear young friend, is to become of me? To whose house, among all your chief men, am I to repair? or shall I go straight to your own house and to your mother?"

"At any other time," replied Telemachus, "I should have bidden you go to my own house, for you would find no want of hospitality; at the present moment, however, you would not be comfortable there, for I shall be away, and my mother will not see you. She does not often show herself even to the suitors, but sits at her loom weaving in an upper chamber, out of their way. But I can tell you a man whose house you can go to—I mean Eurymachus the son of Polybus, who is held in the highest estimation by everyone in Ithaca. He is much the best man and the most persistent wooer of all those who are paying court to my mother and trying to take Odysseus' place. Zeus, however, in heaven alone knows whether or no they will come to a bad end before the marriage takes place."

As he was speaking a bird flew by upon his right hand—a hawk, Apollo's messenger. It held a dove in its talons, and the feathers, as it tore them off, fell to the ground midway between Telemachus and the ship. On this Theoclymenus called him apart and caught him by the hand. "Telemachus," said he, "that bird did not fly on your right hand without having been sent there by some god. As soon as I saw it I knew it was an omen. It means that you will remain powerful and that there will be no house in Ithaca more royal than your own."

"I wish it may prove so," answered Telemachus. "If it does, I will show you so much good will and give you so many presents that all who meet you will congratulate you."

Then he said to his friend, Piraeus, "Piraeus son of Clytius, you have throughout shown yourself the most willing to serve me of all those who have accompanied me to Pylos. I wish you would take this stranger to your own house and entertain him hospitably till I can come for him."

And Piraeus answered, "Telemachus, you may stay away as long as you please, but I will look after him for you, and he shall find no lack of hospitality."

As he spoke he went on board, and bade the others do so also and loose the hawsers, so they took their places in the ship. But Telemachus bound on his sandals, and took a long and doughty spear with a head of sharpened bronze from the deck of the ship. Then they loosed the hawsers, thrust the ship off from land, and made on towards the city as they had been told to do, while Telemachus strode on as fast as he could, till he reached the homestead where his countless herds of swine were feeding, and where dwelt the excellent swineherd, who was so devoted a servant to his master.

Book XVI

*Telemachus sends Eumaeus into the town to tell Penelope that her son is safely
back. Athene then restores Odysseus back to his own likeness. He reveals himself
to Telemachus, and instructs his son in his plan for the destruction of the suitors.
The suitors confer uneasily together and Eumaeus returns to his hut.*

MEANWHILE ODYSSEUS AND THE SWINEHERD HAD LIT A FIRE IN
the hut and were getting breakfast ready at daybreak, for they
had sent the men out with the pigs. When Telemachus came
up, the dogs did not bark but fawned upon him, so Odysseus, hearing the
sound of feet and noticing that the dogs did not bark, said to Eumaeus:

"Eumaeus, I hear footsteps; I suppose one of your men or someone of
your acquaintance is coming here, for the dogs are fawning upon him and
not barking."

The words were hardly out of his mouth before his son stood at the door.
Eumaeus sprang to his feet, and the bowls in which he was mixing wine fell
from his hands, as he made towards his master. He kissed his head and both
his beautiful eyes, and wept for joy. A father could not be more delighted at
the return of an only son, the child of his old age, after ten years' absence in
a foreign country and after having gone through much hardship. He embraced
him, kissed him all over as though he had come back from the dead, and
spoke fondly to him, saying:

"So you are come, Telemachus, light of my eyes that you are. When I
heard you had gone to Pylos I made sure I was never going to see you any-

more. Come in, my dear child, and sit down, that I may have a good look at you now you are home again. It is not very often you come into the country to see us herdsmen; you stick pretty close to the town generally. I suppose you think it better to keep an eye on what the suitors are doing."

"So be it, old friend," answered Telemachus, "but I am come now because I want to see you, and to learn whether my mother is still at her old home or whether someone else has married her, so that the bed of Odysseus is without bedding and covered with cobwebs."

"She is still at the house," replied Eumaeus, "grieving and breaking her heart, and doing nothing but weep, both night and day continually."

As he spoke he took Telemachus' spear, whereon he crossed the stone threshold and came inside. Odysseus rose from his seat to give him place as he entered, but Telemachus checked him. "Sit down, stranger," said he, "I can easily find another seat, and there is one here who will lay it for me."

Odysseus went back to his own place, and Eumaeus strewed some green brushwood on the floor and threw a sheepskin on top of it for Telemachus to sit upon. Then the swineherd brought them platters of cold meat, the remains from what they had eaten the day before, and he filled the bread baskets with bread as fast as he could. He mixed wine also in bowls of ivy wood, and took his seat facing Odysseus. Then they laid their hands on the good things that were before them, and as soon as they had had enough to eat and drink, Telemachus said to Eumaeus, "Old friend, where does this stranger come from? How did his crew bring him to Ithaca, and who were they?—for assuredly he did not come here by land."

To this you answered, O swineherd Eumaeus: "My son, I will tell you the real truth. He says he is a Cretan, and that he has been a great traveler. At this moment he is running away from a Thesprotian slip, and has taken refuge at my station, so I will put him into your hands. Do whatever you like with him, only remember that he is your suppliant."

"I am very much distressed," said Telemachus, "by what you have just told me. How can I take this stranger into my house? I am as yet young, and am not strong enough to hold my own if any man attacks me. My mother cannot make up her mind whether to stay where she is and look after the house out of respect for public opinion and the memory of her husband, or whether the time is now come for her to take the best man of those who are wooing her, and the one who will make her the most advantageous offer. Still, as the stranger has come to your station I will find him a cloak and shirt of good wear, with a sword and sandals, and will send him wherever he wants to go. Or if you like, you can keep him here at the station, and I will send him clothes and food that he may be no burden on you and on your men. But I will not have him go near the suitors, for they are very insolent, and are sure to ill-treat him in a way that would greatly grieve me. No matter how valiant a man may be he can do nothing against numbers, for they will be too strong for him."

Then Odysseus said: "Sir, it is right that I should say something myself. I am much shocked by what you have said about the insolent way in which the suitors are behaving in despite of such a man as you are. Tell me, do you submit to such treatment tamely, or has some god set your people against you? May you not complain of your brothers—for it is to these that a man may look for support, however great his quarrel may be? I wish I were as young as you are and in my present mind. If I were son to Odysseus, or, indeed, Odysseus himself, I would rather someone came and cut my head off, but I would go to the house and be the bane of every one of these men. If they were too many for me—I being single-handed—I would rather die fighting in my own house than see such disgraceful sights day after day, strangers grossly maltreated, and men dragging the womenservants about the house in an unseemly way, wine drawn recklessly, and bread wasted all to no purpose for an end that shall never be accomplished."

And Telemachus answered: "I will tell you truly everything. There is no enmity between me and my people, nor can I complain of brothers, to whom a man may look for support however great his quarrel may be. Zeus has made us a race of only sons. Laertes was the only son of Arceisius, and Odysseus only son of Laertes. I am myself the only son of Odysseus, who left me behind him when he went away, so that I have never been of any use to him. Hence it comes that my house is in the hands of numberless marauders; for the chiefs from all the neighboring islands, Dulichium, Same, Zacynthus, as also all the principal men of Ithaca itself, are eating up my house under the pretext of paying court to my mother, who will neither say point-blank that she will not marry, nor yet bring matters to an end; so they are making havoc of my estate, and before long will do so with myself into the bargain. The issue, however, rests with heaven. But do you, old friend Eumaeus, go at once and tell Penelope that I am safe and have returned from Pylos. Tell it to herself alone, and then come back here without letting anyone else know, for there are many who are plotting mischief against me."

"I understand and heed you," replied Eumaeus; "you need instruct me no further, only as I am going that way say whether I had not better let poor Laertes know that you are returned. He used to superintend the work on his farm in spite of his bitter sorrow about Odysseus, and he would eat and drink at will along with his servants; but they tell me that from the day on which you set out for Pylos he has neither eaten nor drunk as he ought to do, nor does he look after his farm, but sits weeping and wasting the flesh from off his bones."

"More's the pity," answered Telemachus, "I am sorry for him, but we must leave him to himself just now. If people could have everything their own way, the first thing I should choose would be the return of my father. But go, and give your message; then make haste back again, and do not turn out of your way to tell Laertes. Tell my mother to send one of her women secretly with the news at once, and let him hear it from her."

Thus did he urge the swineherd. Eumaeus, therefore, took his sandals, bound them to his feet, and started for the town. Athene watched him well off the station, and then came up to it in the form of a woman—fair, stately, and wise. She stood against the side of the entry, and revealed herself to Odysseus, but Telemachus could not see her, and knew not that she was there, for the gods do not let themselves be seen by everybody. Odysseus saw her, and so did the dogs, for they did not bark, but went scared and whining off to the other side of the yards. She nodded her head and motioned to Odysseus with her eyebrows, whereon he left the hut and stood before her outside the main wall of the yards. Then she said to him:

"Odysseus, noble son of Laertes, it is now time for you to tell your son; do not keep him in the dark any longer, but lay your plans for the destruction of the suitors, and then make for the town. I will not be long in joining you, for I too am eager for the fray."

As she spoke she touched him with her golden wand. First she threw a fair clean shirt and cloak about his shoulders; then she made him younger and of more imposing presence; she gave him back his color, filled out his cheeks, and let his beard become dark again. Then she went away and Odysseus came back inside the hut. His son was astounded when he saw him, and turned his eyes away for fear he might be looking upon a god.

"Stranger," said he, "how suddenly you have changed from what you were a moment or two ago. You are dressed differently and your color is not the same. Are you some one or other of the gods that live in heaven? If so, be propitious to me till I can make you due sacrifice and offerings of wrought gold. Have mercy upon me."

And Odysseus said, "I am no god; why should you take me for one? I am your father, on whose account you grieve and suffer so much at the hands of lawless men."

As he spoke he kissed his son, and a tear fell from his cheek on to the ground, for he had restrained all tears till now. But Telemachus could not yet believe that it was his father, and said:

"You are not my father, but some god is flattering me with vain hopes that I may grieve the more hereafter. No mortal man could of himself contrive to do as you have been doing, and make yourself old and young at a moment's notice, unless a god were with him. A second ago you were old and all in rags, and now you are like some god come down from heaven."

Odysseus answered: "Telemachus, you ought not to be so immeasurably astonished at my being really here. There is no other Odysseus who will come hereafter. Such as I am, it is I, who after long wandering and much hardship have got home in the twentieth year to my own country. What you wonder at is the work of the redoubtable goddess Athene, who does with me whatever she will, for she can do what she pleases. At one moment she makes me like a beggar, and the next I am a young man with good clothes on my back. It is an easy matter for the gods who live in heaven to make any man look either rich or poor."

As he spoke he sat down, and Telemachus threw his arms about his father and wept. They were both so much moved that they cried aloud like eagles or vultures with crooked talons that have been robbed of their half-fledged young by peasants. Thus piteously did they weep, and the sun would have gone down upon their mourning if Telemachus had not suddenly said, "In what ship, my dear father, did your crew bring you to Ithaca? Of what nation did they declare themselves to be—for you cannot have come by land?"

"I will tell you the truth, my son," replied Odysseus. "It was the Phaeacians who brought me here. They are great sailors, and are in the habit of giving escorts to anyone who reaches their coasts. They took me over the sea while I was fast asleep, and landed me in Ithaca, after giving me many presents in bronze, gold, and raiment. These things by heaven's mercy are lying concealed in a cave, and I am now come here on the suggestion of Athene that we may consult about killing our enemies. First, therefore, give me a list of the suitors, with their number, that I may learn who, and how many, they are. I can then turn the matter over in my mind, and see whether we two can fight the whole body of them ourselves, or whether we must find others to help us."

To this Telemachus answered: "Father, I have always heard of your renown both in the field and in council, but the task you talk of is a very great one: I am awed at the mere thought of it; two men cannot stand against many and brave ones. There are not ten suitors only, nor twice ten, but ten many times over; you shall learn their number at once. There are fifty-two chosen youths from Dulichium, and they have six servants; from Same there are twenty-four, twenty young Achaeans from Zacynthus, and twelve from Ithaca itself, all of them well-born. They have with them a servant Medon, a bard, and two men who can carve at table. If we face such numbers as this, you may have bitter cause to rue your coming, and your revenge. See whether you cannot think of someone who would be willing to come and help us."

"Listen to me," replied Odysseus, "and think whether Athene and her father Zeus may seem sufficient, or whether I am to try and find someone else as well."

"Those whom you have named," answered Telemachus, "are a couple of good allies, for though they dwell high up among the clouds they have power over both gods and men."

"These two," continued Odysseus, "will not keep long out of the fray, when the suitors and we join fight in my house. Now, therefore, return home early tomorrow morning, and go about among the suitors as before. Later on the swineherd will bring me to the city disguised as a miserable old beggar. If you see them ill-treating me, steel your heart against my sufferings; even though they drag me feet foremost out of the house, or throw things at me, look on and do nothing beyond gently trying to make them behave more reasonably. They will not listen to you, for the day of their reckoning is at hand. Furthermore I say, and lay my saying to your heart, when Athene shall put it in my mind, I will nod my head to you, and on seeing me do this you must collect all the armor that is in the house and hide it in the strong storeroom. Make some excuse when the suitors ask you why you are removing it; say that you have taken it to be out of the way of the smoke, inasmuch as it is no longer what it was when Odysseus went away, but has become soiled and begrimed with soot. Add to this more particularly that you are afraid Zeus may set them on to quarrel over their wine, and that they may do each other some harm which may disgrace both banquet and wooing, for the sight of arms sometimes tempts people to use them. But leave a sword and a spear apiece for yourself and me, and a couple of oxhide shields so that we can snatch them up at any moment; Zeus and Athene will then soon quiet these people. There is also another matter; if you are indeed my son and my blood runs in your veins, let no one know that Odysseus is within the house—neither Laertes, nor yet the swineherd, nor any of the servants, nor even Penelope herself. Let you and me test out the women alone, and let us also make trial of some other of the menservants, to see who is on our side and whose hand is against us."

"Father," replied Telemachus, "you will come to know me by and by, and when you do you will find that I can keep your counsel. I do not think, however, the plan you propose will turn out well for either of us. Think it over. It will take us a long time to go the round of the farms and find out about the men, and all the time the suitors will be wasting your estate with impunity and without compunction. Prove the women by all means, to see who are disloyal and who guiltless, but I am not in favor of going round and trying the men. We can attend to that later on, if you really have some sign from Zeus that he will support you."

Thus did they converse, and meanwhile the ship which had brought Telemachus and his crew from Pylos had reached the town of Ithaca. When they had come inside the harbor they drew the ship on to the land. Their servants came and took their armor from them, and they left all the presents at the house of Clytius. Then they sent a servant to tell Penelope that Telemachus had gone into the country, but had sent the ship to the town to prevent her from being alarmed and made unhappy. This servant and Eumaeus happened to meet when they were both on the same errand of going to tell Penelope. When they reached the house, the servant stood up and said to the queen in the presence of the waiting-women, "Your son, madam, is now returned from Pylos"; but Eumaeus went close up to Penelope, and said privately all that her son had bidden him tell her. When he had given his message he left the house with its outbuildings and went back to his pigs again.

The suitors were surprised and angry at what had happened, so they went outside the great wall that ran round the outer court, and held a council near the main entrance. Eurymachus son of Polybus was the first to speak.

"My friends," said he, "this voyage of Telemachus' is a very serious matter; we had made sure that it would come to nothing. Now, however, let us draw a ship into the water, and get a crew together to send after the others and tell them to come back as fast as they can."

He had hardly done speaking when Amphinomus turned in his place and saw the ship inside the harbor, with the crew lowering her sails, and putting by their oars; so he laughed, and said to the others, "We need not send them any message, for they are here. Some god must have told them, or else they saw the ship go by, and could not overtake her."

On this they rose and went to the waterside. The crew then drew the ship on shore; their servants took their armor from them, and they went up in a body to the place of assembly, but they would not let anyone, old or young, sit along with them, and Antinous son of Eupeithes spoke first.

"Good heavens," said he, "see how the gods have saved this man from destruction! We kept a succession of scouts upon the headlands all day long, and when the sun was down we never went on shore to sleep, but waited in the ship all night till morning in the hope of capturing and killing him; but some god has conveyed him home in spite of us. Let us consider how we can make an end of him. He must not escape us; our affair is never likely to come off while he is alive, for he is very shrewd, and public feeling is by no means all on our side. We must make haste before he can call the Achaeans in assembly. He will lose no time in doing so, for he will be furious with us, and will tell all the world how we plotted to kill him, but failed to take him. The people will not like this when they come to know of it; we must see that they do us no hurt, nor drive us from our own country into exile. Let us try and lay hold of him either on his farm away from the town, or on the road hither. Then we can divide up his property among us, and let his mother and the man who marries her have the house. If this does not please you, and you wish Telemachus to live on and hold his father's property, then we must not gather here and eat up his goods in this way, but must make our offers to Penelope each from his own house, and she can marry the man who will give the most for her, and whose lot it is to win her."

They all held their peace until Amphinomus rose to speak. He was the son of Nisus, who was son to King Aretias, and he was foremost among all the suitors from the wheat-growing and well-grassed island of Dulichium. His conversation, moreover, was more agreeable to Penelope than that of any of the other suitors, for he was a man of good natural disposition. "My friends," said he, speaking to them plainly and in all honesty, "I am not in favor of killing Telemachus. It is a heinous thing to kill one who is of noble blood. Let us first take counsel of the gods, and if the oracles of Zeus advise it, I will both help to kill him myself, and will urge everyone else to do so; but if they dissuade us, I would have you hold your hands."

Thus did he speak, and his words pleased them well, so they rose forthwith and went to the house of Odysseus, where they took their accustomed seats.

Then Penelope resolved that she would show herself to the suitors. She knew of the plot against Telemachus, for the servant Medon had overheard their counsels and had told her; she went down therefore to the court attended by her maidens, and when she reached the suitors she stood by one of the bearing-posts supporting the roof of the cloister holding a veil before her face, and rebuked Antinous, saying:

"Antinous, insolent and wicked schemer, they say you are the best speaker and counselor of any man your own age in Ithaca, but you are nothing of the kind. Madman, why should you try to compass the death of Telemachus, and take no need of suppliants, whose witness is Zeus himself? It is not right for you to plot thus against one another. Do you not remember how your father fled to this house in fear of the people, who were enraged against him for having gone with some Taphian pirates and plundered the Thesprotians, who were at peace with us? They wanted to tear him in pieces and eat up everything he had, but Odysseus stayed their hands although they were infuriated, and now you devour his property without paying for it, and break my heart by wooing his wife and trying to kill his son. Leave off doing so, and stop the others also."

To this Eurymachus son of Polybus answered: "Take heart, Queen Penelope daughter of Icarius, and do not trouble yourself about these matters. The man is not yet born, nor never will be, who shall lay hands upon your son Telemachus, while I yet live to look upon the face of the earth. I say—and it shall surely be—that my spear shall be reddened with his blood; for many a time has Odysseus taken me on his knees, held wine up to my lips to drink, and put pieces of meat into my hands. Therefore Telemachus is much the dearest friend I have, and has nothing to fear from the hands of us suitors. Of course, if death comes to him from the gods, he cannot escape it." He said this to quiet her, but in reality he was plotting against Telemachus.

Then Penelope went upstairs again and mourned her husband till Athene shed sleep over her eyes. In the evening Eumaeus got back to Odysseus and his son, who had just sacrificed a young pig of a year old and were helping one another to get supper ready. Athene therefore came up to Odysseus, turned him into an old man with a stroke of her wand, and clad him in his old clothes again, for fear that the swineherd might recognize him and not keep the secret, but go and tell Penelope.

Telemachus was the first to speak. "So you have got back, Eumaeus," said he. "What is the news of the town? Have the suitors returned, or are they still waiting over yonder, to take me on my way home?"

"I did not think of asking about that," replied Eumaeus, "when I was in the town. I thought I would give my message and come back as soon as I could.

I met a man sent by those who had gone with you to Pylos, and he was the first to tell the news to your mother, but I can say what I saw with my own eyes. I had just got on to the crest of the hill of Hermes above the town when I saw a ship coming into harbor with a number of men in her. They had many shields and spears, and I thought it was the suitors, but I cannot be sure."

On hearing this Telemachus smiled to his father, but so that Eumaeus could not see him.

Then, when they had finished their work and the meal was ready, they ate it, and every man had his full share so that all were satisfied. As soon as they had had enough to eat and drink, they laid down to test and enjoyed the boon of sleep.

Book XVII

Telemachus is welcomed home by his mother Penelope and tells her what he heard from Menelaus about Odysseus. Odysseus, again in the guise of an aged beggar, sets out with Eumaeus for the town. On the threshold of his house, he is recognized by his old dog, Argos, who wags his tail and dies. Odysseus is given food by Telemachus, but a suitor, Antinous, is abusive and strikes him.

WHEN THE CHILD OF MORNING, ROSY-FINGERED DAWN, APPEARED, Telemachus bound on his sandals and took a strong spear that suited his hands, for he wanted to go into the city. "Old friend," said he to the swineherd, "I will now go to the town and show myself to my mother, for she will never leave off grieving till she has seen me. As for this unfortunate stranger, take him to the town and let him beg there of anyone who will give him a drink and a piece of bread. I have trouble enough of my own, and cannot be burdened with other people. If this makes him angry, so much the worse for him, but I like to say what I mean."

Then Odysseus said: "Sir, I do not want to stay here. A beggar can always do better in town than country, for anyone who likes can give him something. I am too old to care about remaining here at the beck and call of a master. Therefore let this man do as you have just told him, and take me to the town as soon as I have had a warm by the fire, and the day has got a little heat in it. My clothes are wretchedly thin, and this frosty morning I shall be perished with cold, for you say the city is some way off."

On this Telemachus strode off through the yards, brooding his revenge upon the suitors. When he reached home he stood his spear against a bearing-post of the cloister, crossed the stone floor of the cloister itself, and went inside.

Nurse Euryclea saw him long before anyone else did. She was putting the fleeces on to the seats, and she burst out crying as she ran up to him; all the other maids came up too, and covered his head and shoulders with their kisses. Penelope came out of her room looking like Artemis or Aphrodite, and wept as she flung her arms about her son. She kissed his forehead and both his beautiful eyes. "Light of my eyes," she cried, as she spoke fondly to him, "so you are come home again! I made sure I was never going to see you anymore. To think of your having gone off to Pylos without saying anything about it or obtaining my consent. But come, tell me what you saw."

"Do not scold me, mother," answered Telemachus, "nor vex me, seeing what a narrow escape I have had, but wash your face, change your dress, go upstairs with your maids, and promise full and sufficient hecatombs to all the gods if Zeus will only grant us our revenge upon the suitors. I must now go to the place of assembly to invite a stranger who has come back with me from Pylos. I sent him on with my crew, and told Piraeus to take him home and look after him till I could come for him myself."

She heeded her son's words, washed her face, changed her dress, and vowed full and sufficient hecatombs to all the gods if they would only vouchsafe her revenge upon the suitors.

Telemachus went through and out of the cloisters spear in hand—not alone, for his two fleet dogs went with him. Athene endowed him with a presence of such divine comeliness that all marveled at him as he went by, and the suitors gathered round him with fair words in their mouths and malice in their hearts. But he avoided them, and went to sit with Mentor, Antiphus, and Halitherses, old friends of his father's house, and they made him tell them all that had happened to him. Then Piraeus came up with Theoclymenus, whom he had escorted through the town to the place of assembly, whereon Telemachus at once joined them. Piraeus was first to speak: "Telemachus," said he, "I wish you would send some of your women to my house to take away the presents Menelaus gave you."

"We do not know, Piraeus," answered Telemachus, "what may happen. If the suitors kill me in my own house and divide my property among them, I would rather you had the presents than that any of those people should get hold of them. If on the other hand I manage to kill them, I shall be much obliged if you will kindly bring me my presents."

With these words he took Theoclymenus to his own house. When they got there they laid their cloaks on the benches and seats, went into the baths, and washed themselves. When the maids had washed and anointed them, and had given them cloaks and shirts, they took their seats at table. A maidservant then brought them water in a beautiful golden ewer, and poured it into a silver basin for them to wash their hands; and she drew a clean table beside them. An upper servant brought them bread and offered them many good things of what there was in the house. Opposite them sat Penelope, reclining on a couch by one of the bearing-posts of the cloister, and spinning. Then they laid their hands on the good things that were before them, and as soon as they had had enough to eat and drink Penelope said:

"Telemachus, I shall go upstairs and lie down on that sad couch, which I have not ceased to water with my tears, from the day Odysseus set out for Troy with the sons of Atreus. You failed, however, to make it clear to me, before the suitors came back to the house, whether or no you had been able to hear anything about the return of your father."

"I will tell you the truth," replied her son. "We went to Pylos and saw Nestor, who took me to his house and treated me as hospitably as though I were a son of his own who had just returned after a long absence; so also did his sons; but he said he had not heard a word from any human being about Odysseus, whether he was alive or dead. He sent me, therefore, with a chariot and horses to Menelaus. There I saw Helen, for whose sake so many, both Argives and Trojans, were in heaven's wisdom doomed to suffer. Menelaus asked me what it was that had brought me to Sparta, and I told him the whole truth, whereon he said 'So, then, these cowards would usurp a brave man's bed? A hind might as well lay her newborn young in the lair of a lion, and then go off to feed in the forest or in some grassy dell. The lion, when he comes back to his lair, will make short work with the pair of them, and so will Odysseus with these suitors. By father Zeus, Athene, and Apollo, if Odysseus is still the man that he was when he wrestled with Philomeleides in Lesbos, and threw him so heavily that all the Greeks cheered him—if he is still such, and were to come near these suitors, they would have a short shrift and a sorry wedding. As regards your question, however, I will not prevaricate or deceive you, but what the old man of the sea told me, so much will I tell you in full. He said he could see Odysseus on an island sorrowing bitterly in the house of the nymph Calypso, who was keeping him prisoner, and he could not reach his home, for he had no ships or sailors to take him over the sea.' This was what Menelaus told me, and when I had heard his story I came away. The gods then gave me a fair wind and soon brought me safe home again."

With these words he moved the heart of Penelope. Then Theoclymenus said to her:

"Madam, wife of Odysseus, Telemachus does not understand these things. Listen therefore to me, for I can divine them surely, and will hide nothing from you. May Zeus the king of heaven be my witness, and the rites of hospitality, with that hearth of Odysseus to which I now come, that Odysseus himself is even now in Ithaca, and, either going about the country or staying in one place, is inquiring into all these evil deeds and preparing a day of reckoning for the suitors. I saw an omen when I was on the ship which meant this, and I told Telemachus about it."

"May it be even so," answered Penelope; "if your words come true, you shall have such gifts and such good will from me that all who see you shall congratulate you."

Thus did they converse. Meanwhile, the suitors were throwing discs, or aiming with spears at a mark on the leveled ground in front of the house and behaving with all their old insolence. But when it was now time for dinner, and the flock of sheep and goats had come into the town from all the country round,[1] with their shepherds as usual, then Medon, who was their favorite servant, and who waited upon them at table, said, "Now then, my young masters, you have had enough sport, so come inside that we may get dinner ready. Dinner is not a bad thing, at dinner time."

They left their sports as he told them, and when they were within the house, they laid their cloaks on the benches and seats inside, and then sacrificed some sheep, goats, pigs, and a heifer, all of them fat and well-grown.[2] Thus they made ready for their meal. In the meantime Odysseus and the swineherd were about starting for the town, and the swineherd said: "Stranger, I suppose you still want to go to town today, as my master said you were to do. For my own part, I should have liked you to stay here as a station hand, but I must do as my master tells me, or he will scold me later on, and a scolding from one's master is a very serious thing. Let us then be off, for it is now broad day; it will be night again directly and then you will find it colder."

"I know, and understand you," replied Odysseus; "you need say no more. Let us be going, but if you have a stick ready cut, let me have it to walk with, for you say the road is a very rough one."

As he spoke he threw his shabby old tattered wallet over his shoulders, by the cord from which it hung, and Eumaeus gave him a stick to his liking. The two then started, leaving the station in charge of the dogs and herdsmen who

---

[1] That is, to be milked, as in South Italian and Sicilian towns at the present day. (B.)

[2] The butchering and making ready the carcasses took place partly in the outer yard and partly in the open part of the inner court. (B.)

remained behind. The swineherd led the way and his master followed after, looking like some broken-down old tramp as he leaned upon his staff, and his clothes were all in rags. When they had got over the rough steep ground and were nearing the city, they reached the fountain from which the citizens drew their water. This had been made by Ithacus, Neritus, and Polyctor. There was a grove of water-loving poplars planted in a circle all round it, and the clear cold water came down to it from a rock high up, while above the fountain there was an altar to the nymphs, at which all wayfarers used to sacrifice. Here Melanthius son of Dolius overtook them as he was driving down some goats, the best in his flock, for the suitors' dinner, and there were two shepherds with him. When he saw Eumaeus and Odysseus, he reviled them with outrageous and unseemly language, which made Odysseus very angry.

"There you go," cried he, "and a precious pair you are. See how heaven brings birds of the same feather to one another. Where, pray, master swineherd, are you taking this poor miserable object? It would make anyone sick to see such a creature at table. A fellow like this never won a prize for anything in his life, but will go about rubbing his shoulders against every man's doorpost, and begging, not for swords and cauldrons[3] like a man, but only for a few scraps not worth begging for. If you would give him to me for a hand on my station, he might do to clean out the folds, or bring a bit of sweet feed to the kids, and he could fatten his thighs as much as he pleased on whey; but he has taken to bad ways and will not go about any kind of work; he will do nothing but beg victuals all the town over, to feed his insatiable belly. I say, therefore—and it shall surely be—if he goes near Odysseus' house he will get his head broken by the stools they will fling at him, till they turn him out."

---

[3] From this and other passages in the *Odyssey* it appears that we are in an age anterior to the use of coined money—an age when cauldrons, tripods, swords, cattle, chattels of all kinds, measures of corn, wine, or oil, etc., not to say pieces of gold, silver, bronze, or even iron, wrought more or less, but unstamped, were the nearest approach to a currency that had as yet been reached. (B.)

On this, as he passed, he gave Odysseus a kick on the hip out of pure wantonness, but Odysseus stood firm, and did not budge from the path. For a moment he doubted whether or no to fly at Melanthius and kill him with his staff, or fling him to the ground and beat his brains out. He resolved, however, to endure it and keep himself in check, but the swineherd looked straight at Melanthius and rebuked him, lifting up his hands and praying to heaven as he did so.

"Fountain nymphs," he cried, "children of Zeus, if ever Odysseus burned you thighbones covered with fat whether of lambs or kids, grant my prayer that heaven may send him home. He would soon put an end to the swaggering threats with which such men as you go about insulting people—gadding all over the town while your flocks are going to ruin through bad shepherding."

Then Melanthius the goatherd answered: "You ill-conditioned cur, what are you talking about? Some day or other I will put you on board ship and take you to a foreign country, where I can sell you and pocket the money you will fetch. I wish I were as sure that Apollo would strike Telemachus dead this very day, or that the suitors would kill him, as I am that Odysseus will never come home again."

With this he left them to come on at their leisure, while he went quickly forward and soon reached the house of his master. When he got there he went in and took his seat among the suitors opposite Eurymachus, who liked him better than any of the others. The servants brought him a portion of meat, and an upper womanservant set bread before him that he might eat. Presently Odysseus and the swineherd came up to the house and stood by it, amid a sound of music, for Phemius was just beginning to sing to the suitors. Then Odysseus took hold of the swineherd's hand, and said:

"Eumaeus, this house of Odysseus is a very fine place. No matter how far you go you will find few like it. One building keeps following on after another. The outer court has a wall with battlements all round it; the doors are double folding, and of good workmanship; it would be a hard matter to take it by force of arms. I perceive, too, that there are many people banqueting within it, for there is a smell of roast meat, and I hear a sound of music, which the gods have made to go along with feasting."

Then Eumaeus said: "You have perceived aright, as indeed you generally do; but let us think what will be our best course. Will you go inside first and join the suitors, leaving me here behind you, or will you wait here and let me go in first? But do not wait long, or someone may see you loitering about outside, and throw something at you. Consider this matter, I pray you."

And Odysseus answered: "I understand and heed. Go in first and leave me here where I am. I am quite used to being beaten and having things thrown at me. I have been so much buffeted about in war and by sea that I am case-hardened, and this too may go with the rest. But a man cannot hide away the cravings of a hungry belly; this is an enemy which gives much trouble to all men. It is because of this that ships are fitted out to sail the seas, and to make war upon other people."

As they were thus talking, a dog that had been lying asleep raised his head and pricked up his ears. This was Argos, whom Odysseus had bred before setting out for Troy, but he had never had any work out of him. In the old days he used to be taken out by the young men when they went hunting wild goats, or deer, or hares, but now that his master was gone he was lying neglected on the heaps of mule and cow dung that lay in front of the stable doors till the men should come and draw it away to manure the great close; and he was full of fleas. As soon as he saw Odysseus standing there, he dropped his ears and wagged his tail, but he could not get close up to his master. When Odysseus saw the dog on the other side of the yard, he dashed a tear from his eyes without Eumaeus seeing it, and said:

"Eumaeus, what a noble hound that is over yonder on the manure heap; his build is splendid. Is he as fine a fellow as he looks, or is he only one of those dogs that come begging about a table and are kept merely for show?"

"This hound," answered Eumaeus, "belonged to him who has died in a far country. If he were what he was when Odysseus left for Troy, he would soon show you what he could do. There was not a wild beast in the forest that could get away from him when he was once on its tracks. But now he has fallen on evil times, for his master is dead and gone, and the women take no care of him. Servants never do their work when their master's hand is no longer over them, for Zeus takes half the goodness out of a man when he makes a slave of him."

As he spoke he went inside the buildings to the cloister where the suitors were, but Argos died as soon as he had recognized his master.

Telemachus saw Eumaeus long before anyone else did, and beckoned him to come and sit beside him. So he looked about and saw a seat: lying near where the carver sat serving out their portions to the suitors; he picked it up, brought it to Telemachus' table, and sat down opposite him. Then the servant brought him his portion, and gave him bread from the bread-basket.

Immediately afterwards Odysseus came inside, looking like a poor miserable old beggar, leaning on his staff and with his clothes all in rags. He sat down upon the threshold of ash wood just inside the doors leading from the outer to the inner court, and against a bearing-post of cypress wood which the carpenter had skillfully planed, and had made to join truly with rule and line. Telemachus took a whole loaf from the bread-basket, with as much meat as he could hold in his two hands, and said to Eumaeus, "Take this to the stranger, and tell him to go the round of the suitors, and beg from them. A beggar must not be shamefaced."

So Eumaeus went up to him and said, "Stranger, Telemachus sends you this, and says you are to go the round of the suitors begging, for beggars must not be shamefaced."

Odysseus answered, "May King Zeus grant all happiness to Telemachus, and fulfill the desire of his heart."

Then with both hands he took what Telemachus had sent him, and laid it on the dirty old wallet at his feet. He went on eating it while the bard was singing, and had just finished his dinner as he left off. The suitors applauded the bard, whereon Athene went up to Odysseus and prompted him to beg pieces of bread from each one of the suitors, that he might see what kind of people they were, and tell the good from the bad. But come what might she was not going to save a single one of them. Odysseus, therefore, went on his round, going from left to right, and stretched out his hands to beg as though he were a real beggar. Some of them pitied him, and were curious about him, asking one another who he was and where he came from; whereon the goatherd Melanthius said, "Suitors of my noble mistress, I can tell you something about him, for I have seen him before. The swineherd brought him here, but I know nothing about the man himself, nor where he comes from."

On this Antinous began to abuse the swineherd. "You precious idiot," he cried, "what have you brought this man to town for? Have we not tramps and beggars enough already to pester us as we sit at meat? Do you think it a small thing that such people gather here to waste your master's property—and must you needs bring this man as well?"

And Eumaeus answered: "Antinous, your birth is good but your words evil. It was no doing of mine that he came here. Who is likely to invite a stranger from a foreign country, unless it be one of those who can do public service as a seer, a healer of hurts, a carpenter, or a bard who can charm us with his singing? Such men are welcome all the world over, but no one is likely to ask a beggar who will only worry him. You are always harder on Odysseus' servants than any of the other suitors are, and above all on me, but I do not care so long as Telemachus and Penelope are alive and here."

But Telemachus said, "Hush, do not answer him. Antinous has the bitterest tongue of all the suitors, and he makes the others worse."

Then turning to Antinous he said: "Antinous, you take as much care of my interests as though I were your son. Why should you want to see this stranger turned out of the house? Heaven forbid. Take something and give it him yourself; I do not grudge it; I bid you take it. Never mind my mother, or any of the other servants in the house. But I know you will not do what I say, for you are more fond of eating things yourself than of giving them to other people."

"What do you mean, Telemachus," replied Antinous, "by this swaggering talk? If all the suitors were to give him as much as I will, he would not come here again for another three months."

As he spoke he drew the stool on which he rested his dainty feet from under the table and made as though he would throw it at Odysseus, but the other suitors all gave him something, and filled his wallet with bread and meat. He was about, therefore, to go back to the threshold and eat what the suitors had given him, but he first went up to Antinous and said:

"Sir, give me something. You are not, surely, the poorest man here. You seem to be a chief, foremost among them all; therefore you should be the better giver, and I will tell far and wide of your bounty. I too was a rich man once, and had a fine house of my own. In those days I gave to many a tramp such as I now am, no matter who he might be or what he wanted. I had any number of servants, and all the other things which people have who live well and are accounted wealthy, but it pleased Zeus to take all away from me. He sent me with a band of roving robbers to Egypt; it was a long voyage and I was undone by it. I stationed my ships in the river Aegyptus, and bade my men stay by them and keep guard over them, while I sent out scouts to reconnoiter from every point of vantage.

"But the men disobeyed my orders, took to their own devices, and ravaged the land of the Egyptians, killing the men, and taking their wives and children captives. The alarm was soon carried to the city, and when they heard the war cry, the people came out at daybreak till the plain was filled with soldiers horse and foot, and with the gleam of armor. Then Zeus spread panic among my men, and they would no longer face the enemy, for they found themselves surrounded. The Egyptians killed many of us, and took the rest alive to do forced labor for them. As for myself, they gave me to a friend who met them, to take to Cyprus, Dmetor by name, son of Iasus, who was a great man in Cyprus. Thence I am come hither in a state of great misery."

Then Antinous said: "What god can have sent such a pestilence to plague us during our dinner? Get out, into the open part of the court, or I will give you Egypt and Cyprus over again for your insolence and importunity. You have begged of all the others, and they have given you lavishly, for they have abundance round them, and it is easy to be free with other people's property when there is plenty of it."

On this Odysseus began to move off, and said: "Your looks, my fine sir, are better than your breeding. If you were in your own house, you would not spare a poor man so much as a pinch of salt, for though you are in another man's, and surrounded with abundance, you cannot find it in you to give him even a piece of bread."

This made Antinous very angry, and he scowled at him, saying, "You shall pay for this before you get clear of the court." With these words he threw a footstool at him, and hit him on the right shoulder blade near the top of his back. Odysseus stood firm as a rock and the blow did not even stagger him, but he shook his head in silence as be brooded on his revenge. Then he went back to the threshold and sat down there, laying his well-filled wallet at his feet.

"Listen to me," he cried, "you suitors of Queen Penelope, that I may speak even as I am minded. A man knows neither ache nor pain if he gets hit while fighting for his money, or for his sheep or his cattle. Even so Antinous has hit me while in the service of my miserable belly, which is always getting people into trouble. Still, if the poor have gods and avenging deities at all, I pray them that Antinous may come to a bad end before his marriage."

"Sit where you are, and eat your victuals in silence, or be off elsewhere," shouted Antinous. "If you say more, I will have you dragged hand and foot through the courts, and the servants shall flay you alive."

The other suitors were much displeased at this, and one of the young men said, "Antinous, you did ill in striking that poor wretch of a tramp. It will be worse for you if he should turn out to be some god. And we know the gods go about disguised in all sorts of ways as people from foreign countries, and travel about the world to see who do amiss and who righteously."

Thus said the suitors, but Antinous paid them no heed. Meanwhile Telemachus was furious about the blow that had been given to his father, and though no tear fell from him, he shook his head in silence and brooded on his revenge.

Now when Penelope heard that the beggar had been struck in the banqueting cloister, she said before her maids, "Would that Apollo would so strike you, Antinous," and her waiting-woman Eurynome answered, "If our prayers were answered not one of the suitors would ever again see the sun rise." Then Penelope said, "Nurse, I hate every single one of them, for they mean nothing but mischief, but I hate Antinous like the darkness of death itself. A poor unfortunate tramp has come begging about the house for sheer want. Everyone else has given him something to put in his wallet, but Antinous has hit him on the right shoulder blade with a footstool."

Thus did she talk with her maids as she sat in her own room, and in the meantime Odysseus was getting his dinner. Then she called for the swineherd and said, "Eumaeus, go and tell the stranger to come here. I want to see him and ask him some questions. He seems to have traveled much, and he may have seen or heard something of my unhappy husband."

To this you answered, O swineherd Eumaeus: "If these Achaeans, madam, would only keep quiet, you would be charmed with the history of his adventures. I had him three days and three nights with me in my hut, which was the first place he reached after running away from his ship, and he has not yet completed the story of his misfortunes. If he had been the most heaven-taught minstrel in the whole world, on whose lips all hearers hang entranced, I could not have been more charmed as I sat in my hut and listened to him. He says there is an old friendship between his house and that of Odysseus, and that he comes from Crete where the descendants of Minos live, after having been driven hither and thither by every kind of misfortune. He also declares that he has heard of Odysseus as being alive and near at hand among the Thesprotians, and that he is bringing great wealth home with him."

"Call him here, then," said Penelope, "that I too may hear his story. As for the suitors, let them take their pleasure indoors or out as they will, for they have nothing to fret about. Their corn and wine remain unwasted in their houses with none but servants to consume them, while they keep hanging about our house day after day, sacrificing our oxen, sheep, and fat goats for their banquets, and never giving so much as a thought to the quantity of wine they drink. No estate can stand such recklessness, for we have now no Odysseus to protect us. If he were to come again, he and his son would soon have their revenge."

As she spoke Telemachus sneezed so loudly that the whole house resounded with it. Penelope laughed when she heard this, and said to Eumaeus, "Go and call the stranger. Did you not hear how my son sneezed just as I was speaking? This can only mean that all the suitors are going to be killed, and that not one of them shall escape. Furthermore I say, and lay my saying to your heart: if I am satisfied that the stranger is speaking the truth I shall give him a shirt and cloak of good wear."

When Eumaeus heard this he went straight to Odysseus and said: "Father stranger, my mistress Penelope, mother of Telemachus, has sent for you. She is in great grief, but she wishes to hear anything you can tell her about her husband, and if she is satisfied that you are speaking the truth, she will give you a shirt and cloak, which are the very things that you are most in want of. As for bread, you can get enough of that to fill your belly by begging about the town, and letting those give that will."

"I will tell Penelope," answered Odysseus, "nothing but what is strictly true. I know all about her husband, and have been partner with him in afflic-tion, but I am afraid of passing through this crowd of cruel suitors, for their pride and insolence reach heaven. Just now, moreover, as I was going about the house without doing any harm, a man gave me a blow that hurt me very much, but neither Telemachus nor anyone else defended me. Tell Penelope, therefore, to be patient and wait till sundown. Let her give me a seat close up to the fire, for my clothes are worn very thin. You know they are, for you have seen them ever since I first asked you to help me. She can then ask me about the return of her husband."

The swineherd went back when he heard this, and Penelope said as she saw him cross the threshold, "Why do you not bring him here, Eumaeus? Is he afraid that someone will ill-treat him, or is he shy of coming inside the house at all? Beggars should not be shamefaced."

To this you answered, O swineherd Eumaeus, "The stranger is quite reasonable. He is avoiding the suitors, and is only doing what anyone else would do. He asks you to wait till sundown, and it will be much better, madam, that you should have him all to yourself, when you can hear him and talk to him as you will."

"The man is no fool," answered Penelope, "it would very likely be as he says, for there are no such abominable people in the whole world as these men are."

When she had done speaking Eumaeus went back to the suitors, for he had explained everything. Then he went up to Telemachus and said in his ear so that none could overhear him, "My dear sir, I will now go back to the pigs, to see after your property and my own business. You will look to what is going on here, but above all be careful to keep out of danger, for there are many who bear you ill will. May Zeus bring them to a bad end before they do us a mischief."

"Very well," replied Telemachus, "go home when you have had your dinner, and in the morning come here with the victims we are to sacrifice for the day. Leave the rest to heaven and me."

On this Eumaeus took his seat again, and when he had finished his dinner he left the courts and the cloister with the men at table, and went back to his pigs. As for the suitors, they presently began to amuse themselves with singing and dancing, for it was now getting on towards evening.

Book XVIII

Odysseus is insulted by Irus, a beggar, who challenges him to fight. While the suitors look on, Odysseus thrashes Irus soundly. Penelope upbraids her son for allowing the stranger to be ill-treated. The suitor Eurymachus gibes at Odysseus, and hurls a footstool at him. Telemachus censures the suitors for their behavior, and they go home to bed.

NOW THERE CAME A CERTAIN COMMON TRAMP WHO USED TO GO begging all over the city of Ithaca, and was notorious as an incorrigible glutton and drunkard. This man had no strength or stay in him, but he was a great hulking fellow to look at. His real name, the one his mother gave him, was Arnaeus, but the young men of the place called him Irus, because he used to run errands for anyone who would send him.[1] As soon as he came he began to insult Odysseus, and to try and drive him out of his own house.

"Be off, old man," he cried, "from the doorway, or you shall be dragged out neck and heels. Do you not see that they are all giving me the wink, and wanting me to turn you out by force, only I do not like to do so? Get up then, and go of yourself, or we shall come to blows."

Odysseus frowned on him and said: "My friend, I do you no manner of harm; people give you a great deal, but I am not jealous. There is room enough in this doorway for the pair of us, and you need not grudge me things that are not yours to give. You seem to be just such another tramp

[1] Iris was the messenger of the gods.

as myself, but perhaps the gods will give us better luck by and by. Do not, however, talk too much about fighting, or you will incense me, and old though I am, I shall cover your mouth and chest with blood. I shall have more peace tomorrow if I do, for you will not come to the house of Odysseus anymore."

Irus was very angry and answered: "You filthy glutton, you run on trippingly like an old fish-fag. I have a good mind to lay both hands about you, and knock your teeth out of your head like so many boar's tusks. Get ready, therefore, and let these people here stand by and look on. You will never be able to fight one who is so much younger than yourself."

Thus roundly did they rate one another on the smooth pavement in front of the doorway,[2] and when Antinous saw what was going on he laughed heartily and said to the others, "This is the finest sport that you ever saw; heaven never yet sent anything like it into this house. The stranger and Irus have quarreled and are going to fight. Let us set them on to do so at once."

The suitors all came up laughing, and gathered round the two ragged tramps. "Listen to me," said Antinous, "there are some goats' paunches down at the fire, which we have filled with blood and fat, and set aside for supper. He who is victorious and proves himself to be the better man shall have his pick of the lot. He shall be free of our table and we will not allow any other beggar about the house at all."

The others all agreed, but Odysseus, to throw them off the scent, said, "Sirs, an old man like myself, worn out with suffering, cannot hold his own against a young one. But my irrepressible belly urges me on, though I know it can only end in my getting a drubbing. You must swear, however, that none of you will give me a foul blow to favor Irus and secure him the victory."

They swore as he told them, and when they had completed their oath Telemachus put in a word and said, "Stranger, if you have a mind to settle with this fellow, you need not be afraid of anyone here. Whoever strikes you will have

[2] The doorway leading from the inner to the outer court. (B.)

to fight more than one. I am host, and the other chiefs, Antinous and Eurymachus, both of them men of understanding, are of the same mind as I am."

Everyone assented, and Odysseus girded his old rags about his loins, thus baring his stalwart thighs, his broad chest and shoulders, and his mighty arms. Athene came up to him and made his limbs even stronger still. The suitors were beyond measure astonished, and one would turn towards his neighbor saying, "The stranger has brought such a thigh out of his old rags that there will soon be nothing left of Irus."

Irus began to be very uneasy as he heard them, but the servants girded him by force, and brought him into the open part of the court in such a fright that his limbs were all of a tremble. Antinous scolded him and said, "You swaggering bully, you ought never to have been born at all if you are afraid of such an old broken-down creature as this tramp is. I say, therefore—and it shall surely be—if he beats you and proves himself the better man, I shall pack you off on board ship to the mainland and send you to king Echetus, who kills everyone that comes near him. He will cut off your nose and ears, and draw out your entrails for the dogs to eat."

This frightened Irus still more, but they brought him into the middle of the court, and the two men raised their hands to fight. Then Odysseus considered whether he should let drive so hard at him as to make an end of him then and there, or whether he should give him a lighter blow that should only knock him down. In the end he deemed it best to give the lighter blow for fear the Achaeans should begin to suspect who he was. Then they began to fight, and Irus hit Odysseus on the right shoulder, but Odysseus gave Irus a blow on the neck under the ear that broke in the bones of his skull, and the blood came gushing out of his mouth. He fell groaning in the dust, gnashing his teeth and kicking on the ground. The suitors threw up their hands and nearly died of laughter, as Odysseus caught hold of him by the foot and dragged him into the outer court as far as the gatehouse. There he propped him up against the wall and put his staff in his hands. "Sit here," said he, "and keep the dogs and pigs off. You are a pitiful creature, and if you try to make yourself king of the beggars anymore you shall fare still worse."

Then he threw his dirty old wallet, all tattered and torn, over his shoulder with the cord by which it hung, and went back to sit down upon the threshold. But the suitors went within the cloisters, laughing and saluting him, "May Zeus, and all the other gods," said they, "grant you whatever you want for having put an end to the importunity of this insatiable tramp. We will take him over to the mainland presently, to king Echetus, who kills everyone that comes near him."

Odysseus hailed this as of good omen, and Antinous set a great goat's paunch before him filled with blood and fat. Amphinomus took two loaves out of the bread-basket and brought them to him, pledging him as he did so in a golden goblet of wine. "Good luck to you," he said, "father stranger. You are very badly off at present, but I hope you will have better times by and by."

To this Odysseus answered: "Amphinomus, you seem to be a man of good understanding, as indeed you may well be, seeing whose son you are. I have heard your father well spoken of; he is Nisus of Dulichium, a man both brave and wealthy. They tell me you are his son, and you appear to be a considerable person. Listen, therefore, and take heed to what I am saying. Man is the vainest of all creatures that have their being upon earth. As long as heaven vouchsafes him health and strength, he thinks that he shall come to no harm hereafter, and even when the blessed gods bring sorrow upon him, he bears it as he needs must, and makes the best of it; for God almighty gives men their daily minds day by day. I know all about it, for I was a rich man once, and did much wrong in the stubbornness of my pride, and in the confidence that my father and my brothers would support me. Therefore let a man fear God in all things always, and take the good that heaven may see fit to send him without vainglory. Consider the infamy of what these suitors are doing. See how they are wasting the estate, and doing dishonor to the wife, of one who is certain to return someday, and that, too, not long hence. Nay, he will be here soon. May heaven send you home quietly first that you may not meet with him in the day of his coming, for once he is here the suitors and he will not part bloodlessly."

With these words he made a drink offering, and when he had drunk he put the gold cup again into the hands of Amphinomus, who walked away serious and bowing his head, for he foreboded evil. But even so he did not escape destruction, for Athene had doomed him to fall by the hand of Telemachus. So he took his seat again at the place from which he had come.

Then Athene put it into the mind of Penelope to show herself to the suitors, that she might make them still more enamored of her, and win still further honor from her son and husband. So she feigned a mocking laugh and said, "Eurynome, I have changed my mind, and have a fancy to show myself to the suitors although I detest them. I should like also to give my son a hint that he had better not have anything more to do with them. They speak fairly enough but they mean mischief."

"My dear child," answered Eurynome, "all that you have said is true. Go and tell your son about it, but first wash yourself and anoint your face. Do not go about with your cheeks all covered with tears. It is not right that you should grieve so incessantly; for Telemachus, whom you always prayed that you might live to see with a beard, is already grown up."

"I know, Eurynome," replied Penelope, "that you mean well, but do not try and persuade me to wash and to anoint myself, for heaven robbed me of all my beauty on the day my husband sailed. Nevertheless, tell Autonoe and Hippodamia that I want them. They must be with me when I am in the cloister. I am not going among the men alone; it would not be proper for me to do so."

On this the old woman went out of the room to bid the maids go to their mistress. In the meantime Athene bethought her of another matter, and sent Penelope off into a sweet slumber; so she lay down on her couch and her limbs became heavy with sleep. Then the goddess shed grace and beauty over her that all the Achaeans might admire her. She washed her face with the ambrosial loveliness that Aphrodite wears when she goes dancing with the Graces;

she made her taller and of a more commanding figure, while as for her complexion it was whiter than sawn ivory. When Athene had done all this she went away, whereon the maids came in from the women's room and woke Penelope with the sound of their talking.

"What an exquisitely delicious sleep I have been having," said she, as she passed her hands over her face, "in spite of all my misery. I wish Artemis would let me die so sweetly now at this very moment, that I might no longer waste in despair for the loss of my dear husband, who possessed every kind of good quality and was the most distinguished man among the Achaeans."

With these words she came down from her upper room, not alone but attended by two of her maidens, and when she reached the suitors she stood by one of the bearing-posts supporting the roof of the cloister, holding a veil before her face, and with a staid maidservant on either side of her. As they beheld her the suitors were so overpowered and became so desperately enamored of her that each one prayed he might win her for his own bedfellow.

"Telemachus," said she, addressing her son, "I fear you are no longer so discreet and well-conducted as you used to be. When you were younger you had a greater sense of propriety; now, however, that you are grown up, though a stranger to look at you would take you for the son of a well-to-do father as far as size and good looks go, your conduct is by no means what it should be. What is all this disturbance that has been going on, and how came you to allow a stranger to be so disgracefully ill-treated? What would have happened if he had suffered serious injury while a suppliant in our house? Surely this would have been very discreditable to you."

"I am not surprised, my dear mother, at your displeasure," replied Telemachus, "I understand all about it and know when things are not as they should be, which I could not do when I was younger. I cannot, however, behave with perfect propriety at all times. First one and then another of these wicked people here keeps driving me out of my mind, and I have no one to stand by me. After all, however, this fight between Irus and the stranger did not turn out as the suitors meant it to do, for the stranger got the best of it. I wish Father Zeus, Athene, and Apollo would break the neck of every one of these wooers of yours, some inside the house and some out; and I wish they might all be as limp as Irus is over yonder in the gate of the outer court. See how he nods his head like a drunken man. He has had such a thrashing that he cannot stand on his feet nor get back to his home, wherever that may be, for he has no strength left in him."

Thus did they converse. Eurymachus then came up and said, "Queen Penelope, daughter of Icarius, if all the Achaeans in Iasian Argos could see you at this moment, you would have still more suitors in your house by tomorrow morning, for you are the most admirable woman in the whole world both as regards personal beauty and strength of understanding."

To this Penelope replied: "Eurymachus, heaven robbed me of all my beauty whether of face or figure when the Argives set sail for Troy and my dear husband with them. If he were to return and look after my affairs, I should both be more respected and show a better presence to the world. As it is, I am oppressed with care, and with the afflictions which heaven has seen fit to heap upon me. My husband foresaw it all, and when he was leaving home he took my right wrist in his hand—'Wife,' he said, 'we shall not all of us come safe home from Troy, for the Trojans fight well both with bow and spear. They are excellent also at fighting from chariots, and nothing decides the issue of a fight sooner than this. I know not, therefore, whether heaven will send me back to you, or whether I may not fall over there at Troy. In the meantime do you look after things here. Take care of my father and mother as at present, and even more so during my absence, but when you see our son growing a beard, then marry whom you will, and leave this your present home.' This is what he said and now it is all coming true. A night will come when I shall have to yield myself to a marriage which I detest, for Zeus has taken from me all hope of happiness. This further grief, moreover, cuts me to the very heart. You suitors are not wooing me after the custom of my country.

When men are courting a woman who they think will be a good wife to them and who is of noble birth, and when they are each trying to win her for himself, they usually bring oxen and sheep to feast the friends of the lady, and they make her magnificent presents, instead of eating up other people's property without paying for it."

This was what she said, and Odysseus was glad when he heard her trying to get presents out of the suitors, and flattering them with fair words which he knew she did not mean.

Then Antinous said, "Queen Penelope, daughter of Icarius, take as many presents as you please from anyone who will give them to you. It is not well to refuse a present. But we will not go about our business or stir from where we are, till you have married the best man among us, whoever he may be."

The others applauded what Antinous had said, and each one sent his servant to bring his present. Antinous' man returned with a large and lovely dress most exquisitely embroidered. It had twelve beautifully made brooch pins of pure gold with which to fasten it. Eurymachus immediately brought her a magnificent chain of gold and amber beads that gleamed like sunlight. Eurydamas' two men returned with some earrings fashioned into three brilliant pendants which glistened most beautifully; while King Pisander son of Polyctor gave her a necklace of the rarest workmanship, and everyone else brought her a beautiful present of some kind.

Then the queen went back to her room upstairs, and her maids brought the presents after her. Meanwhile, the suitors took to singing and dancing, and stayed till evening came. They danced and sang till it grew dark; they then brought in three braziers [3] to give light, and piled them up with chopped firewood very old and dry, and they lit torches from them, which the maids held up turn and turn about. Then Odysseus said:

[3] These, I imagine, must have been in the open part of the inner courtyard, where the maids also stood, and threw the light of their torches into the covered cloister that ran all round it. The smoke would otherwise have keen intolerable. (B.)

"Maids, servants of Odysseus, who has so long been absent, go to the queen inside the house. Sit with her and amuse her, or spin, and pick wool. I will hold the light for all these people. They may stay till morning, but shall not beat me, for I can stand a great deal."

The maids looked at one another and laughed, while pretty Melantho began to gibe at him contemptuously. She was daughter to Dolius, but had been brought up by Penelope, who used to give her toys to play with, and looked after her when she was a child. But in spite of all this she showed no consideration for the sorrows of her mistress, and used to misconduct herself with Eurymachus, with whom she was in love.

"Poor wretch," said she, "are you gone clean out of your mind? Go and sleep in some smithy, or place of public gossips, instead of chattering here. Are you not ashamed of opening your mouth before your betters—so many of them too? Has the wine been getting into your head, or do you always babble in this way? You seem to have lost your wits because you beat the tramp Irus; take care that a better man than he does not come and cudgel you about the head till he pack you bleeding out of the house."

"Vixen," replied Odysseus, scowling at her, "I will go and tell Telemachus what you have been saying, and he will have you torn limb from limb."

With these words he scared the women, and they went off into the body of the house. They trembled all over, for they thought he would do as he said. But Odysseus took his stand near the burning braziers, holding up torches and looking at the people—brooding the while on things that should surely come to pass.

But Athene would not let the suitors for one moment cease their insolence, for she wanted Odysseus to become even more bitter against them; she therefore set Eurymachus son of Polybus on to gibe at him, which made the others laugh. "Listen to me," said he, "you suitors of Queen Penelope, that I may speak even as I am minded. It is not for nothing that this man has come to the house of Odysseus. I believe the light has not been coming from the torches, but from his own head—for his hair is all gone, every bit of it."

Then turning to Odysseus he said, "Stranger, will you work as a servant, if I send you to the wolds and see that you are well paid? Can you build a stone fence, or plant trees? I will have you fed all the year round and provide you with shoes and clothing. Will you go, then? Not you; for you have got into bad ways, and do not want to work! You had rather fill your belly by going round the country begging."

"Eurymachus," answered Odysseus, "if you and I were to work one against the other in early summer when the days are at their longest—give me a good scythe, and take another yourself, and let us see which will fast the longer or mow the stronger, from dawn till dark when the mowing grass is about. Or if you will plow against me, let us each take a yoke of tawny oxen, well-mated and of great strength and endurance: turn me into a four-acre field, and see whether you or I can drive the straighter furrow. If, again, war were to break out this day, give me a shield, a couple of spears, and a helmet fitting well upon my temples—you would find me foremost in the fray, and would cease your gibes about my belly. You are insolent and cruel, and think yourself a great man because you live in a little world, and that a bad one. If Odysseus comes to his own again, the doors of his house are wide, but you will find them narrow when you try to fly through them."

Eurymachus was furious at all this. He scowled at him and cried: "You wretch, I will soon pay you out for daring to say such things to me, and in public too! Has the wine been getting into your head or do you always babble in this way? You seem to have lost your wits because you beat the tramp Irus." With this he caught hold of a footstool, but Odysseus sought protection at the knees of Amphinomus of Dulichium, for he was afraid. The stool hit the cup-bearer on his right hand and knocked him down: the man fell with a cry flat on his back, and his wine-jug fell ringing to the ground. The suitors in the covered cloister were now in an uproar, and one would turn towards his neighbor, saying, "I wish the stranger had gone somewhere else. Bad luck to him, for all the trouble he gives us. We cannot permit such disturbance about a beggar; if such ill counsels are to prevail we shall have no more pleasure at our banquet."

On this Telemachus came forward and said, "Sirs, are you mad? Can you not carry your meat and your liquor decently? Some evil spirit has possessed you. I do not wish to drive any of you away, but you have had your suppers, and the sooner you all go home to bed the better."

The suitors bit their lips and marveled at the boldness of his speech; but Amphinomus the son of Nisus, who was son to Aretias, said, "Do not let us take offense; it is reasonable, so let us make no answer. Neither let us do violence to the stranger nor to any of Odysseus' servants. Let the cupbearer go round with the drink offerings, that we may make them and go home to our rest. As for the stranger, let us leave Telemachus to deal with him, for it is to his house that he has come."

Thus did he speak, and his saying pleased them well. So Mulius of Dulichium, servant to Amphinomus, mixed them a bowl of wine and water and handed it round to each of them man by man, whereon they made their drink offerings to the blessed gods. Then, when they had made their drink offerings and had drunk each one as he was minded, they took their several ways each of them to his own abode.

Book XIX

*Inventing a plausible excuse, Telemachus and Odysseus remove all armor
from the court to the storeroom. Penelope talks with Odysseus, not knowing
him, and he tries to encourage her by foretelling the early return of the
wanderer. The old nurse Euryclea washes Odysseus' feet and recognizes him
by a scar on his leg. She is overjoyed, but he commands her to keep silent as to
her discovery. Penelope tells him of the archery test she is to set for the suitors.*

ODYSSEUS WAS LEFT IN THE CLOISTER, PONDERING ON THE MEANS whereby with Athene's help he might be able to kill the suitors. Presently he said to Telemachus: "Telemachus, we must get the armor together and take it down inside. Make some excuse when the suitors ask you why you have removed it. Say that you have taken it to be out of the way of the smoke, inasmuch as it is no longer what it was when Odysseus went away, but has become soiled and begrimed with soot. Add to this more particularly that you are afraid Zeus may set them on to quarrel over their wine, and that they may do each other some harm which may disgrace both banquet and wooing, for the sight of arms sometimes tempts people to use them."

Telemachus approved of what his father had said, so he called nurse Euryclea and said, "Nurse, shut the women up in their room, while I take the armor that my father left behind him down into the storeroom. No one looks after it now my father is gone, and it has got all smirched with soot during my own boyhood. I want to take it down where the smoke cannot reach it."

"I wish, child," answered Euryclea, "that you would take the management of the house into your own hands altogether, and look after all the property yourself. But who is to go with you and light you to the storeroom? The maids would have done so, but you would not let them."

"The stranger," said Telemachus, "shall show me a light. When people eat my bread they must earn it, no matter where they come from."

Euryclea did as she was told, and bolted the women inside their room. Then Odysseus and his son made all haste to take the helmets, shields, and spears inside; and Athene went before them with a gold lamp in her hand that shed a soft and brilliant radiance. Whereon Telemachus said, "Father, my eyes behold a great marvel: the walls, with the rafters, crossbeams, and the supports on which they rest are all aglow as with a flaming fire. Surely there is some god here who has come down from heaven."

"Hush," answered Odysseus, "hold your peace and ask no questions, for this is the manner of the gods. Get you to your bed, and leave me here to talk with your mother and the maids. Your mother in her grief will ask me all sorts of questions."

On this Telemachus went by torchlight to the other side of the inner court, to the room in which he always slept. There he lay in his bed till morning, while Odysseus was left in the cloister pondering on the means whereby with Athene's help he might be able to kill the suitors.

Then Penelope came down from her room looking like Aphrodite or Artemis, and they set her a seat inlaid with scrolls of silver and ivory near the fire in her accustomed place. It had been made by Icmalius and had a footstool all in one piece with the seat itself; and it was covered with a thick fleece; on this she now sat, and the maids came from the women's room to join her. They set about removing the tables at which the wicked suitors had been dining, and took away the bread that was left, with the cups from which they had drunk. They emptied the embers out of the braziers and heaped much wood upon them to give both light and heat. But Melantho began to rail at Odysseus a second time and said, "Stranger, do you mean to plague us by hanging about the house all night and spying upon the women? Be off, you wretch, outside, and eat your supper there, or you shall be driven out with a firebrand."

Odysseus scowled at her and answered: "My good woman, why should you be so angry with me? Is it because I am not clean, and my clothes are all in rags, and because I am obliged to go begging about after the manner of tramps and beggars generally? I too was a rich man once, and had a fine house of my own; in those days I gave to many a tramp such as I now am, no matter who he might be nor what he wanted. I had any number of servants, and all the other things which people have who live well and are accounted wealthy, but it pleased Zeus to take all away from me. Therefore, woman, beware lest you too come to lose that pride and place in which you now wanton above your fellows. Have a care lest you get out of favor with your mistress, and lest Odysseus should come home, for there is still a chance that he may do so. Moreover, though he be dead as you think he is, yet by Apollo's will he has left a son behind him, Telemachus, who will note anything done amiss by the maids in the house, for he is now no longer in his boyhood."

Penelope heard what he was saying and scolded the maid. "Impudent baggage," said she, "I see how abominably you are behaving, and you shall smart for it. You knew perfectly well, for I told you myself, that I was going to see the stranger and ask him about my husband, for whose sake I am in such continual sorrow."

Then she said to her head waiting-woman Eurynome, "Bring a seat with a fleece upon it, for the stranger to sit upon while he tells his story, and listens to what I have to say. I wish to ask him some questions."

Eurynome brought the seat at once and set a fleece upon it, and as soon as Odysseus had sat down Penelope began by saying, "Stranger, I shall first ask you who and whence are you? Tell me of your town and parents."

"Madam," answered Odysseus, "who on the face of the whole earth can dare to chide with you? Your fame reaches the firmament of heaven itself. You are like some blameless king, who upholds righteousness, as the monarch over a great and valiant nation. The earth yields its wheat and barley, the trees are loaded with fruit, the ewes bring forth lambs, and the sea abounds with fish by reason of his virtues, and his people do good deeds under him. Nevertheless, as I sit here in your house, ask me some other question and do not seek to know my race and family, or you will recall memories that will yet more increase my sorrow. I am full of heaviness, but I ought not to sit weeping and wailing in another person's house, nor is it well to be thus grieving continually. I shall have one of the servants or even yourself complaining of me, and saying that my eyes swim with tears because I am heavy with wine."

Then Penelope answered: "Stranger, heaven robbed me of all beauty, whether of face or figure, when the Argives set sail for Troy and my dear husband with them. If he were to return and look after my affairs I should be both more respected and should show a better presence to the world. As it is, I am oppressed with care, and with the afflictions which heaven has seen fit to heap upon me. The chiefs from all our islands—Dulichium, Same, and Zacynthus, as also from Ithaca itself—are wooing me against my will and are wasting my estate. I can therefore show no attention to strangers, or suppliants, or to people who say that they are skilled artisans, but am all the time brokenhearted about Odysseus. They want me to marry again at once, and I have to invent stratagems in order to deceive them.

"In the first place heaven put it in my mind to set up a great tambour-frame in my room, and to begin working upon an enormous piece of fine needlework. Then I said to them, 'Sweethearts, Odysseus is indeed dead, still, do not press me to marry again immediately. Wait—for I would not have my skill in needlework perish unrecorded—till I have finished making a pall for the hero Laertes, to be ready against the time when death shall take him. He is very rich, and the women of the place will talk if he is laid out without a pall.'

This was what I said, and they assented; whereon I used to keep working at my great web all day long, but at night I would unpick the stitches again by torch light. I fooled them in this way for three years without their finding it out, but as time wore on and I was now in my fourth year, in the waning of moons, and many days had been accomplished, those good-for-nothing hussies my maids betrayed me to the suitors, who broke in upon me and caught me; they were very angry with me, so I was forced to finish my work whether I would or no.

"And now I do not see how I can find any further shift for getting out of this marriage. My parents are putting great pressure upon me, and my son chafes at the ravages the suitors are making upon his estate, for he is now old enough to understand all about it and is perfectly able to look after his own affairs, for heaven has blessed him with an excellent disposition. Still, notwithstanding all this, tell me who you are and where you come from—for you must have had father and mother of some sort; you cannot be the son of an oak or of a rock."

Then Odysseus answered: "Madam, wife of Odysseus, since you persist in asking me about my family, I will answer, no matter what it costs me. People must expect to be pained when they have been exiles as long as I have, and suffered as much among as many peoples. Nevertheless, as regards your question I will tell you all you ask. There is a fair and fruitful island in midocean called Crete. It is thickly peopled and there are ninety cities in it. The people speak many different languages which overlap one another, for there are Achaeans, brave Eteocretans, Dorians of three-fold race, and noble Pelasgi. There is a great town there, Cnossus, where Minos reigned who every nine years had a conference with Zeus himself. Minos was father to Deucalion, whose son I am, for Deucalion had two sons, Idomeneus and myself. Idomeneus sailed for Troy, and I, who am the younger, am called Aethon; my brother, however, was at once the older and the more valiant of the two.

"Hence it was in Crete that I saw Odysseus and showed him hospitality, for the winds took him there as he was on his way to Troy, carrying him out of his course from cape Malea and leaving him in Amnisus off the cave of Ilithuia, where the harbors are difficult to enter and he could hardly find shelter from the winds that were then raging. As soon as he got there he went into the town and asked for Idomeneus, claiming to be his old and valued friend, but Idomeneus had already set sail for Troy some ten or twelve days earlier, so I took him to my own house and showed him every kind of hospitality, for I had abundance of everything. Moreover, I fed the men who were with him with barley meal from the public store, and got subscriptions of wine and oxen for them to sacrifice to their heart's content. They stayed with me twelve days, for there was a gale blowing from the north so strong that one could hardly keep one's feet on land. I suppose some unfriendly god had raised it for them, but on the thirteenth day the wind dropped, and they got away."

Many a plausible tale did Odysseus further tell her, and Penelope wept as she listened, for her heart was melted. As the snow wastes upon the mountain tops when the winds from southeast and west have breathed upon it and thawed it till the rivers run bank full with water, even so did her cheeks overflow with tears for the husband who was all the time sitting by her side. Odysseus felt for her and was sorry for her, but he kept his eyes as hard as horn or iron without letting them so much as quiver, so cunningly did he restrain his tears. Then, when she had relieved herself by weeping, she turned to him again and said: "Now, stranger, I shall put you to the test and see whether or no you really did entertain my husband and his men, as you say you did. Tell me, then, how he was dressed, what kind of a man he was to look at, and so also with his companions."

"Madam," answered Odysseus, "it is such a long time ago that I can hardly say. Twenty years are come and gone since he left my home, and went elsewhither; but I will tell you as well as I can recollect. Odysseus wore a mantle of purple wool, double lined, and it was fastened by a gold brooch with two catches for the pin. On the face of this there was a device that showed a dog holding a spotted fawn between his forepaws, and watching it as it lay panting upon the ground. Everyone marveled at the way in which these things had been done in gold, the dog looking at the fawn, and strangling it, while the fawn was struggling convulsively to escape. As for the shirt that he wore next his skin, it was so soft that it fitted him like the skin of an onion, and glistened in the sunlight to the admiration of all the women who beheld it.

"Furthermore I say, and lay my saying to your heart, that I do not know whether Odysseus wore these clothes when he left home, or whether one of his companions had given them to him while he was on his voyage; or possibly someone at whose house he was staying made him a present of them, for he was a man of many friends and had few equals among the Achaeans. I myself gave him a sword of bronze and a beautiful purple mantle, double lined, with a shirt that went down to his feet, and I sent him on board his ship with every mark of honor. He had a servant with him, a little older than himself, and I can tell you what he was like; his shoulders were hunched, he was dark, and he had thick curly hair. His name was Eurybates, and Odysseus treated him with greater familiarity than he did any of the others, as being the most like-minded with himself."

Penelope was moved still more deeply as she heard the indisputable proofs that Odysseus laid before her; and when she had again found relief in tears she said to him: "Stranger, I was already disposed to pity you, but henceforth you shall be honored and made welcome in my house. It was I who gave Odysseus the clothes you speak of. I took them out of the storeroom and folded them up myself, and I gave him also the gold brooch to wear as an ornament. Alas! I shall never welcome him home again. It was by an ill fate that he ever set out for that detested city whose very name I cannot bring myself even to mention."

Then Odysseus answered: "Madam, wife of Odysseus, do not disfigure yourself further by grieving thus bitterly for your loss, though I can hardly blame you for doing so. A woman who has loved her husband and borne him children would naturally be grieved at losing him, even though he were a worse man than Odysseus, who they say was like a god. Still, cease your tears and listen to what I can tell you. I will hide nothing from you, and can say with perfect truth that I have lately heard of Odysseus as being alive and on his way home. He is among the Thesprotians, and is bringing back much valuable treasure that he has begged from one and another of them. But his ship and all his crew were lost as they were leaving the Thrinacian island, for Zeus and the sun-god were angry with him because his men had slaughtered the sun-god's cattle, and they were all drowned to a man. But Odysseus stuck to the keel of the ship and was drifted on to the land of the Phaeacians, who are near of kin to the immortals, and who treated him as though he had been a god, giving him many presents, and wishing to escort him home safe and sound. In fact Odysseus would have been here long ago had he not thought better to go from land to land gathering wealth; for there is no man living who is so wily as he is; there is no one can compare with him. Pheidon, king of the Thesprotians, told me all this, and he swore to me—making drink offerings in his house as he did so—that the ship was by the waterside and the crew found who would take Odysseus to his own country. He sent me off first, for there happened to be a Thesprotian ship sailing for the wheat-growing island of Dulichium, but he showed me all the treasure Odysseus had got together, and he had enough lying in the house of King Pheidon to keep his family for ten generations. The king said Odysseus had gone to Dodona that he might learn Zeus' mind from the high oak tree, and know whether after so long an absence he should return to Ithaca openly or in secret. So you may know he is safe and will be here shortly; he is close at hand and cannot remain away from home much longer. Furthermore, I will confirm my words with an oath, and call Zeus who is the first and mightiest of all gods to witness, as also that hearth of Odysseus to which I have now come, that all I have spoken shall surely come to pass. Odysseus will return in this selfsame year; with the end of this moon and the beginning of the next he will be here."

"May it be even so," answered Penelope. "If your words come true, you shall have such gifts and such good will from me that all who see you shall congratulate you; but I know very well how it will all be. Odysseus will not return, neither will you get your escort hence, for so surely as that Odysseus ever was, there are now no longer any such masters in the house as he was, to receive honorable strangers or to further them on their way home. And now, you maids, wash his feet for him, and make him a bed on a couch with rugs and blankets, that he may be warm and quiet till morning. Then, at daybreak wash him and anoint him again, that he may sit in the cloister and take his meals with Telemachus. It shall be the worse for any one of these hateful people who is uncivil to him; like it or not, he shall have no more to do in this house. For how, sir, shall you be able to learn whether or no I am superior to others of my sex both in goodness of heart and understanding, if I let you dine in my cloisters squalid and ill-clad? Men live but for a little season; if they are hard, and deal hardly, people wish them ill so long as they are alive, and speak contemptuously of them when they are dead, but he that is righteous and deals righteously, the people tell of his praise among all lands, and many shall call him blessed."

Odysseus answered: "Madam, I have foresworn rugs and blankets from the day that I left the snowy ranges of Crete to go on shipboard. I will lie as I have lain on many a sleepless night hitherto. Night after night have I passed in any rough sleeping place, and waited for morning. Nor, again, do I like having my feet washed. I shall not let any of the young hussies about your house touch my feet; but, if you have any old and respectable woman who has gone through as much trouble as I have, I will allow her to wash them."

To this Penelope said: "My dear sir, of all the guests who ever yet came to my house there never was one who spoke in all things with such admirable propriety as you do. There happens to be in the house a most respectable old woman—the same who received my poor dear husband in her arms the night he was born, and nursed him in infancy. She is very feeble now, but she shall wash your feet. Come here," said she, "Euryclea, and wash your master's age-mate; I suppose Odysseus' hands and feet are very much the same now as his are, for trouble ages all of us dreadfully fast."

On these words the old woman covered her face with her hands. She began to weep and made lamentation, saying, "My dear child, I cannot think whatever I am to do for you. I am certain no one was ever more god-fearing than yourself, and yet Zeus hates you. No one in the whole world ever burned him more thighbones, nor gave him finer hecatombs when you prayed you might come to a green old age yourself and see your son grow up to take your place after you: yet see how he has prevented you alone from ever getting back to your own home! I have no doubt the women in some foreign palace which Odysseus has got to are gibing at him as all these sluts here have been gibing at you. I do not wonder at your not choosing to let them wash you after the manner in which they have insulted you. I will wash your feet myself gladly enough, as Penelope has said that I am to do so; I will wash them both for Penelope's sake and for your own, for you have raised the most lively feelings of compassion in my mind. And let me say this moreover, which pray attend to: we have had all kinds of strangers in distress come here before now, but I make bold to say that no one ever yet came who was so like Odysseus in figure, voice, and feet as you are."

"Those who have seen us both," answered Odysseus, "have always said we were wonderfully like each other, and now you have noticed it too."

Then the old woman took the cauldron in which she was going to wash his feet, and poured plenty of cold water into it, adding hot till the bath was warm enough. Odysseus sat by the fire, but ere long he turned away from the light, for it occurred to him that when the old woman had hold of his leg she would recognize a certain scar which it bore, whereon the whole truth would come out. And indeed as soon as she began washing her master, she at once knew the scar as one that had been given him by a wild boar when he was hunting on Mount Parnassus with his excellent grandfather Autolycus—who was the most accomplished thief and perjurer in the whole world—and with the sons of Autolycus. Hermes himself had endowed him with this gift, for he used to burn the thighbones of goats and kids to him, so he took pleasure in his companionship. It happened once that Autolycus had gone to Ithaca and had found the child of his daughter just born. As soon as he had done supper Euryclea set the infant upon his knees and said, "Autolycus, you must find a name for your grandson; you greatly wished that you might have one."

"Son-in-law and daughter," replied Autolycus, "call the child thus. I am highly displeased with a large number of people in one place and another, both men and women; so name the child 'Odysseus,' or the child of anger. When he grows up and comes to visit his mother's family on Mount Parnassus, where my possessions lie, I will make him a present and will send him on his way rejoicing."

Odysseus, therefore, went to Parnassus to get the presents from Autolycus, who with his sons shook hands with him and gave him welcome. His grandmother Amphithea threw her arms about him, and kissed his head, and both his beautiful eyes, while Autolycus desired his sons to get dinner ready, and they did as he told them. They brought in a five-year-old bull, flayed it, made it ready, and divided it into joints; these they then cut carefully up into smaller pieces and spitted them; they roasted them sufficiently and served the portions round. Thus through the livelong day to the going down of the sun they feasted, and every man had his full share so that all were satisfied; but when the sun set and it came on dark, they went to bed and enjoyed the boon of sleep.

When the child of morning, rosy-fingered Dawn, appeared, the sons of Autolycus went out with their hounds hunting, and Odysseus went too. They climbed the wooded slopes of Parnassus and soon reached its breezy upland valleys; but as the sun was beginning to beat upon the fields, fresh-risen from the slow still currents of Oceanus, they came to a mountain dell. The dogs were in front searching for the tracks of the beast they were chasing, and after them came the sons of Autolycus, among whom was Odysseus, close behind the dogs, and he had a long spear in his hand. Here was the lair of a huge boar among some thick brushwood, so dense that the wind and rain could not get through it, nor could the sun's rays pierce it, and the ground underneath lay thick with fallen leaves. The boar heard the noise of the men's feet, and the hounds baying on every side as the huntsmen came up to him, so he rushed from his lair, raised the bristles on his neck, and stood at bay with fire flashing from his eyes. Odysseus was the first to raise his spear and try to drive it into the brute, but the boar was too quick for him, and charged him sideways, ripping him above the knee with a gash that tore deep though it did not reach the bone. As for the boar, Odysseus hit him on the right shoulder, and the point of the spear went right through him, so that he fell groaning in the dust until the life went out of him. The sons of Autolycus busied themselves with the carcass of the boar, and bound Odysseus' wound; then, after saying a spell to stop the bleeding, they went home as fast as they could. But when Autolycus and his sons had thoroughly healed Odysseus, they made him some splendid presents, and sent him back to Ithaca with much mutual good will. When he got back, his father and mother were rejoiced to see him, and asked him all about it, and how he had hurt himself to get the scar, so he told them how the boar had ripped him when he was out hunting with Autolycus and his sons on Mount Parnassus.

As soon as Euryclea had got the scarred limb in her hands and had well hold of it, she recognized it and dropped the foot at once. The leg fell into the bath, which rang out and was overturned, so that all the water was spilt on the ground. Euryclea's eyes between her joy and her grief filled with tears, and she could not speak, but she caught Odysseus by the beard and said, "My dear child; I am sure you must be Odysseus himself, only I did not know you till I had actually touched and handled you."

As she spoke she looked towards Penelope, as though wanting to tell her that her dear husband was in the house, but Penelope was unable to look in that direction and observe what was going on, for Athene had diverted her attention. So Odysseus caught Euryclea by the throat with his right hand and with his left drew her close to him, and said, "Nurse, do you wish to be the ruin of me, you who nursed me at your own breast, now that after twenty years of wandering I am at last come to my own home again? Since it has been borne in upon you by heaven to recognize me, hold your tongue, and do not say a word about it to anyone else in the house, for if you do I tell you— and it shall surely be—that if heaven grants me to take the lives of these suitors, I will not spare you, though you are my own nurse, when I am killing the other women."

"My child," answered Euryclea, "what are you talking about? You know very well that nothing can either bend or break me. I will hold my tongue like a stone or a piece of iron. Furthermore let me say, and lay my saying to your heart, when heaven has delivered the suitors into your hand, I will give you a list of the women in the house who have been ill-behaved and of those who are guiltless."

And Odysseus answered, "Nurse, you ought not to speak in that way; I am well able to form my own opinion about one and all of them. Hold your tongue and leave everything to heaven."

As he said this Euryclea left the cloister to fetch some more water, for the first had been all spilt. And when she had washed him and anointed him with oil, Odysseus drew his seat nearer to the fire to warm himself, and hid the scar under his rags. Then Penelope began talking to him and said:

"Stranger, I should like to speak with you briefly about another matter. It is indeed nearly bedtime—for those, at least, who can sleep in spite of sorrow. As for myself, heaven has given me a life of such unmeasurable woe, that even by day when I am attending to my duties and looking after the servants, I am still weeping and lamenting during the whole time; then, when night comes, and we all of us go to bed, I lie awake thinking, and my heart becomes a prey to the most incessant and cruel tortures. As the dun nightingale, daughter of

Pandareus, sings in the early spring from her seat in shadiest covert hid, and with many a plaintive trill pours out the tale how by mishap she killed her own child Itylus, son of king Zethus, even so does my mind toss and turn in its uncertainty whether I ought to stay with my son here, and safeguard my substance, my bondsmen, and the greatness of my house, out of regard to public opinion and the memory of my late husband, or whether it is not now time for me to go with the best of these suitors who are wooing me and making me such magnificent presents. As long as my son was still young, and unable to understand, he would not hear of my leaving my husband's house, but now that he is full grown he begs and prays me to do so, being incensed at the way in which the suitors are eating up his property.

"Listen, then, to a dream that I have had and interpret it for me if you can. I have twenty geese about the house that eat mash out of a trough, and of which I am exceedingly fond. I dreamed that a great eagle came swooping down from a mountain, and dug his curved beak into the neck of each of them till he had killed them all. Presently he soared off into the sky, and left them lying dead about the yard; whereon I wept in my dream till all my maids gathered round me, so piteously was I grieving because the eagle had killed my geese. Then he came back again, and perching on a projecting rafter spoke to me with human voice, and told me to leave off crying. 'Be of good courage,' he said, 'daughter of Icarius; this is no dream, but a vision of good omen that shall surely come to pass. The geese are the suitors, and I am no longer an eagle, but your own husband, who am come back to you, and who will bring these suitors to a disgraceful end.' On this I woke, and when I looked out I saw my geese at the trough eating their mash as usual."

"This dream, madam," replied Odysseus, "can admit but of one interpretation, for has not Odysseus himself told you how it shall be fulfilled? The death of the suitors is portended, and not one single one of them will escape."

And Penelope answered: "Stranger, dreams are very curious and unaccountable things, and they do not by any means invariably come true. There are two gates through which these unsubstantial fancies proceed; the one is of horn, and the other ivory. Those that come through the gate of ivory are fatuous, but those from the gate of horn mean something to those that see them. I do not think, however, that my own dream came through the gate of horn, though I and my son should be most thankful if it proves to have done so. Furthermore I say—and lay my saying to your heart—the coming dawn will usher in the ill-omened day that is to sever me from the house of Odysseus, for I am about to hold a tournament of axes. My husband used to set up twelve axes in the court, one in front of the other, like the stays upon which a ship is built; he would then go back from them and shoot an arrow through the whole twelve. I shall make the suitors try to do the same thing, and whichever of them can string the bow most easily, and send his arrow through all the twelve axes, him will I follow, and quit this house of my lawful husband, so goodly and so abounding in wealth. But even so, I doubt not that I shall remember it in my dreams."

Then Odysseus answered, "Madam, wife of Odysseus, you need not defer your tournament, for Odysseus will return ere ever they can string the bow, handle it how they will, and send their arrows through the iron."

To this Penelope said: "As long, sir, as you will sit here and talk to me, I can have no desire to go to bed. Still, people cannot do permanently without sleep, and heaven has appointed us dwellers on earth a time for all things. I will therefore go upstairs and recline upon that couch which I have never ceased to flood with my tears from the day Odysseus set out for the city with a hateful name."

She then went upstairs to her own room, not alone, but attended by her maidens, and when there, she lamented her dear husband till Athene shed sweet sleep over her eyelids.

Book XX

Both Odysseus and Penelope pass a restless night. In the morning Odysseus is heartened by omens from Zeus. At the feast Telemachus seats the ragged Odysseus in an honorable place, but he is again abused by the suitors. The stranger Theoclymenus, seeing signs of impending disaster, takes his leave.

ODYSSEUS SLEPT IN THE CLOISTER UPON AN UNDRESSED BULLOCK'S HIDE, on the top of which he threw several skins of the sheep the suitors had eaten, and Eurynome threw a cloak over him after he had laid himself down. There, then, Odysseus lay wakefully brooding upon the way in which he should kill the suitors; and by and by, the women who had been in the habit of misconducting themselves with them left the house giggling and laughing with one another. This made Odysseus very angry, and he doubted whether to get up and kill every single one of them then and there, or to let them sleep one more and last time with the suitors. His heart growled within him, and as a bitch with puppies growls and shows her teeth when she sees a stranger, so did his heart growl with anger at the evil deeds that were being done. But he beat his breast and said, "Heart, be still! You had worse than this to bear on the day when the terrible Cyclops ate your brave companions; yet you bore it in silence till your cunning got you safe out of the cave, though you made sure of being killed."

Thus he chided with his heart, and checked it into endurance, but he tossed about as one who turns a paunch full of blood and fat in front of a hot fire, doing it first on one side and then on the other, that he may get it cooked as soon as possible. Even so did he turn himself about from side to side, thinking all the time how, single-handed as he was, he should contrive to kill so large a body of men as the wicked suitors. But by and by Athene came down from heaven in the likeness of a woman, and hovered over his head saying, "My poor unhappy man, why do you lie awake in this way? This is your house; your wife is safe inside it, and so is your son who is just such a young man as any father may be proud of."

"Goddess," answered Odysseus, "all that you have said is true, but I am in some doubt as to how I shall be able to kill these wicked suitors single-handed, seeing what a number of them there always are. And there is this further difficulty, which is still more considerable. Supposing that with Zeus' and your assistance I succeed in killing them, I must ask you to consider where I am to escape from their avengers when it is all over."

"For shame," replied Athene, "why, anyone else would trust a worse ally than myself, even though that ally were only a mortal and less wise than I am. Am I not a goddess, and have I not protected you throughout in all your troubles? I tell you plainly that even though there were fifty bands of them surrounding us and eager to kill us, you should take all their sheep and cattle, and drive them away with you. But go to sleep; it is a very bad thing to lie awake all night, and you shall be out of your troubles before long."

As she spoke she shed sleep over his eyes, and then went back to Olympus.

While Odysseus was thus yielding himself to a very deep slumber that eased the burden of his sorrows, his admirable wife awoke, and sitting up in her bed began to cry. When she had relieved herself by weeping she prayed to Artemis, saying, "Great Goddess Artemis, daughter of Zeus, drive an arrow into my heart and slay me; or let some whirlwind snatch me up and hear me through paths of darkness till it drop me into the mouths of overflowing Oceanus, as it did the daughters of Pandareus. The daughters of Pandareus lost their father and mother, for the gods killed them, so they were left orphans. But Aphrodite took care of them, and fed them on cheese, honey, and sweet wine. Hera taught them to excell all women in beauty of form and understanding; Artemis gave them an imposing presence, and Athene endowed them with every kind of accomplishment. But one day when Aphrodite had gone up to Olympus to see Zeus about getting them married (for well does he know both what shall happen and what not happen to every-one) the storm winds came and spirited them away to become handmaids to the dread Furies. Even so I wish that the gods who live in heaven would hide me from mortal sight, or that fair Artemis might strike me, for I would fain go even beneath the sad earth if I might do so still looking towards Odysseus only, and without having to yield myself to a worse man than he was. Besides, no matter how much people may grieve by day, they can put up with it so long as they can sleep at night, for when the eyes are closed in slumber people for-get good and ill alike; whereas my misery haunts me even in my dreams. This very night me thought there was one lying by my side who was like Odysseus as he was when he went away with his host, and I rejoiced, for I believed that it was no dream, but the very truth itself."

On this the day broke, but Odysseus heard the sound of her weeping, and it puzzled him, for it seemed as though she already knew him and was by his side. Then he gathered up the cloak and the fleeces on which he had lain, and set them on a seat in the cloister, but he took the bullock's hide out into the open. He lifted up his hands to heaven, and prayed, saying, "Father Zeus, since you have seen fit to bring me over land and sea to my own home after all the afflictions you have laid upon me, give me a sign out of the mouth of some one or other of those who are now waking within the house, and let me have another sign of some kind from outside."

Thus did he pray. Zeus heard his prayer and forthwith thundered high up among the clouds from the splendor of Olympus, and Odysseus was glad when he heard it. At the same time within the house, a miller-woman from hard by in the mill room lifted up her voice and gave him another sign. There were twelve miller-women whose business it was to grind wheat and barley which are the staff of life. The others had ground their task and had gone to take their rest, but this one had not yet finished, for she was not so strong as they were, and when she heard the thunder she stopped grinding and gave the sign to her master. "Father Zeus," said she, "you who rule over heaven and earth, you have thundered from a clear sky without so much as a cloud in it, and this means something for somebody. Grant the prayer, then, of me your poor servant who calls upon you, and let this be the very last day that the suitors dine in the house of Odysseus. They have worn me out with the labor of grinding meal for them, and I hope they may never have another dinner anywhere at all."

Odysseus was glad when he heard the omens conveyed to him by the woman's speech, and by the thunder, for he knew they meant that he should avenge himself on the suitors.

Then the other maids in the house rose and lit the fire on the hearth. Telemachus also rose and put on his clothes. He girded his sword about his shoulder, bound his sandals on his comely feet, and took a doughty spear with a point of sharpened bronze; then he went to the threshold of the cloister and said to Euryclea, "Nurse, did you make the stranger comfortable both as regards bed and board, or did you let him shift for himself?—for my mother, good woman though she is, has a way of paying great attention to second-rate people, and of neglecting others who are in reality much better men."

"Do not find fault, child," said Euryclea, "when there is no one to find fault with. The stranger sat and drank his wine as long as he liked. Your mother did ask him if he would take any more bread and he said he would not. When he wanted to go to bed she told the servants to make one for him, but he said he was such a wretched outcast that he would not sleep on a bed and under blankets. He insisted on having an undressed bullock's hide and some sheepskins put for him in the cloister, and we threw a cloak over him."

Then Telemachus went out of the court to the place where the Achaeans were meeting in assembly. He had his spear in his hand, and he was not alone, for his two dogs went with him. But Euryclea called the maids and said, "Come, wake up; set about sweeping the cloisters and sprinkling them with water to lay the dust. Put the covers on the seats; wipe down the tables, some of you, with a wet sponge; clean out the mixing-jugs and the cups, and go for water from the fountain at once. The suitors will be here directly; they will be here early, for it is a feast day."

Thus did she speak, and they did even as she had said. Twenty of them went to the fountain for water, and the others set themselves busily to work about the house. The men who were in attendance on the suitors also came up and began chopping firewood. By and by the women returned from the fountain, and the swineherd came after them with the three best pigs he could pick out. These he let feed about the premises, and then he said good-humoredly to Odysseus, "Stranger, are the suitors treating you any better now, or are they as insolent as ever?"

"May heaven," answered Odysseus, "requite to them the wickedness with which they deal high-handedly in another man's house without any sense of shame."

Thus did they converse. Meanwhile, Melanthius the goatherd came up, for he too was bringing in his best goats for the suitors' dinner, and he had two shepherds with him. They tied the goats up under the gatehouse, and then Melanthius began gibing at Odysseus. "Are you still here, stranger," said he, "to pester people by begging about the house? Why can you not go elsewhere? You and I shall not come to an understanding before we have given each other a taste of our fists. You beg without any sense of decency. Are there not feasts elsewhere among the Achaeans, as well as here?"

Odysseus made no answer, but bowed his head and brooded. Then a third man, Philoetius, joined them, who was bringing in a barren heifer and some goats. These were brought over by the boatmen who are there to take people over when anyone comes to them. So Philoetius made his heifer and his goats secure under the gatehouse, and then went up to the swineherd. "Who, swineherd," said he, "is this stranger that is lately come here? Is he one of your men? What is his family? Where does he come from? Poor fellow, he looks as if he had been some great man, but the gods give sorrow to whom they will—even to kings if it so pleases them."

As he spoke he went up to Odysseus and saluted him with his right hand. "Good day to you, father stranger," said he, "you seem to be very poorly off now, but I hope you will have better times by and by. Father Zeus, of all gods you are the most malicious. We are your own children, yet you show us no mercy in all our misery and afflictions. A sweat came over me when I saw this man, and my eyes filled with tears, for he reminds me of Odysseus, who I fear is going about in just such rags as this man's are, if indeed he is still among the living. If he is already dead and in the house of Hades, then, alas! for my good master, who made me his stockman when I was quite young among the Cephallenians, and now his cattle are countless. No one could have done better with them than I have, for they have bred like ears of corn; nevertheless, I have to keep bringing them in for others to eat, who take no heed of his son though he is in the house, and fear not the wrath of heaven, but are already eager to divide Odysseus' property among them because he has been away so long. I have often thought—only it would not be right while his son is living—of going off with the cattle to some foreign country. Bad as this would be, it is still harder to stay here and be ill-treated about other people's herds. My position is intolerable, and I should long since have run away and put myself under the protection of some other chief, only that I believe my poor master will yet return, and send all these suitors flying out of the house."

"Stockman," answered Odysseus, "you seem to be a very well-disposed person, and I can see that you are a man of sense. Therefore I will tell you, and will confirm my words with an oath: by Zeus, the chief of all gods, and by that hearth of Odysseus to which I am now come, Odysseus shall return before you leave this place, and if you are so minded you shall see him killing the suitors who are now masters here."

"If Zeus were to bring this to pass," replied the stockman, "you should see how I would do my very utmost to help him."

And in like manner Eumaeus prayed that Odysseus might return home.

Thus did they converse. Meanwhile the suitors were hatching a plot to murder Telemachus: but a bird flew near them on their left hand—an eagle with a dove in its talons. On this Amphinomus said, "My friends, this plot of ours to murder Telemachus will not succeed; let us go to dinner instead."

The others assented, so they went inside and laid their cloaks on the benches and seats. They sacrificed the sheep, goats, pigs, and the heifer, and when the inward meats were cooked they served them round. They mixed the wine in the mixing bowls, and the swineherd gave every man his cup, while Philoetius handed round the bread in the bread-baskets, and Melanthius poured them out their wine. Then they laid their hands upon the good things that were before them.

Telemachus purposely made Odysseus sit in the part of the cloister that was paved with stone;[1] he gave him a shabby-looking seat at a little table to himself, and had his portion of the inward meats brought to him, with his wine in a gold cup. "Sit there," said he, "and drink your wine among the great people. I will put a stop to the gibes and blows of the suitors, for this is no public house, but belongs to Odysseus, and has passed from him to me. Therefore, suitors, keep your hands and your tongues to yourselves, or there will be mischief."

The suitors bit their lips, and marveled at the boldness of his speech; then Antinous said, "We do not like such language but we will put up with it, for Telemachus is threatening us in good earnest. If Zeus had let us we should have put a stop to his brave talk ere now."

Thus spoke Antinous, but Telemachus heeded him not. Meanwhile the heralds were bringing the holy hecatomb through the city, and the Achaeans gathered under the shady grove of Apollo.

---

[1] This, I take it, was immediately in front of the main entrance from the inner courtyard into the body of the house. (B.)

Then they roasted the outer meat, drew it off the spits, gave every man his portion, and feasted to their hearts' content; those who waited at table gave Odysseus exactly the same portion as the others had, for Telemachus had told them to do so.

But Athene would not let the suitors for one moment drop their insolence, for she wanted Odysseus to become still more bitter against them. Now there happened to be among them a ribald fellow, whose name was Ctesippus, and who came from Same. This man, confident in his great wealth, was paying court to the wife of Odysseus, and said to the suitors, "Hear what I have to say. The stranger has already had as large a portion as anyone else. This is well, for it is not right or reasonable to ill-treat any guest of Telemachus who comes here. I will, however, make him a present on my own account, that he may have something to give to the bath-woman, or to some other of Odysseus' servants."

As he spoke he picked up a heifer's foot from the meat-basket in which it lay, and threw it at Odysseus, but Odysseus turned his head a little aside, and avoided it, smiling grimly Sardinian fashion as he did so, and it hit the wall, not him. On this Telemachus spoke fiercely to Ctesippus. "It is a good thing for you," said he, "that the stranger turned his head so that you missed him. If you had hit him I should have run you through with my spear, and your father would have had to see about getting you buried rather than married in this house. So let me have no more unseemly behavior from any of you, for I am grown up now to the knowledge of good and evil and understand what is going on, instead of being the child that I have been heretofore. I have long seen you killing my sheep and making free with my corn and wine. I have put up with this, for one man is no match for many, but do me no further violence. Still, if you wish to kill me, kill me; I would far rather die than see such disgraceful scenes day after day—guests insulted, and men dragging the womenservants about the house in an unseemly way."

They all held their peace till at last Agelaus son of Damastor said: "No one should take offense at what has just been said, nor gainsay it, for it is quite reasonable. Leave off, therefore, ill-treating the stranger, or anyone else of the servants who are about the house. I would say, however, a friendly word to Telemachus and his mother, which I trust may commend itself to both. 'As long,' I would say, 'as you had ground for hoping that Odysseus would one day come home, no one could complain of your waiting and suffering the suitors to be in your house. It would have been better that he should have returned, but it is now sufficiently clear that he will never do so. Therefore talk all this quietly over with your mother, and tell her to marry the best man, and the one who makes her the most advantageous offer. Thus you will yourself be able to manage your own inheritance, and to eat and drink in peace, while your mother will look after some other man's house, not yours.'"

To this Telemachus answered: "By Zeus, Agelaus, and by the sorrows of my unhappy father, who has either perished far from Ithaca, or is wandering in some distant land, I throw no obstacles in the way of my mother's marriage. On the contrary, I urge her to choose whomsoever she will, and I will give her numberless gifts into the bargain, but I dare not insist point-blank that she shall leave the house against her own wishes. Heaven forbid that I should do this."

Athene now made the suitors fall to laughing immoderately, and set their wits wandering; but they were laughing with a forced laughter. Their meat became smeared with blood, their eyes filled with tears, and their hearts were heavy with forebodings. Theoclymenus saw this and said, "Unhappy men, what is it that ails you? There is a shroud of darkness drawn over you from head to foot, your cheeks are wet with tears. The air is alive with wailing voices; the walls and roof-beams drip blood; the gate of the cloisters and the court beyond them are full of ghosts trooping down into the night of hell. The sun is blotted out of heaven, and a blighting gloom is over all the land."

Thus did he speak, and they all of them laughed heartily. Eurymachus then said, "This stranger who has lately come here has lost his senses. Servants, turn him out into the streets, since he finds it so dark here."

But Theoclymenus said, "Eurymachus, you need not send anyone with me. I have eyes, ears, and a pair of feet of my own, to say nothing of an understanding mind. I will take these out of the house with me, for I see mischief overhanging you, from which not one of you men who are insulting people and plotting ill deeds in the house of Odysseus will be able to escape."

He left the house as he spoke, and went back to Piraeus who gave him welcome, but the suitors kept looking at one another and provoking Telemachus by laughing at the strangers. One insolent fellow said to him, "Telemachus, you are not happy in your guests. First you have this importunate tramp, who comes begging bread and wine and has no skill for work or for hard fighting, but is perfectly useless, and now here is another fellow who is setting himself up as a prophet. Let me persuade you, for it will be much better, to put them on board ship and send them off to the Sicels to sell for what they will bring."

Telemachus gave him no heed, but sat silently watching his father, expecting every moment that he would begin his attack upon the suitors.

Meanwhile the daughter of Icarius, wise Penelope, had had a rich seat placed for her facing the court and cloisters, so that she could hear what everyone was saying. The dinner indeed had been prepared amid much merriment; it had been both good and abundant, for they had sacrificed many victims. But the supper was yet to come, and nothing can be conceived more gruesome than the meal which a goddess and a brave man were soon to lay before them—for they had brought their doom upon themselves.

Book XXI

*The banquet being over, Penelope brings forth Odysseus' bow, which first
Telemachus and then the suitors try to string without success. Odysseus,
going outside, reveals himself to Eumaeus and Philoetus, the stockman.
They bar the outer doors and send the women to their quarters, in
preparation for the fray. Odysseus now strings the bow with ease and shoots it
with perfection. The suitors watch him, fearful and dismayed.*

ATHENE NOW PUT IT IN PENELOPE'S MIND TO MAKE THE SUITORS TRY
their skill with the bow and with the iron axes, in contest among
themselves, as a means of bringing about their destruction. She
went upstairs and got the storeroom key, which was made of bronze and had
a handle of ivory. She then went with her maidens into the storeroom at the
end of the house, where her husband's treasures of gold, bronze, and wrought
iron were kept, and where was also his bow, and the quiver full of deadly
arrows that had been given him by a friend whom he had met in Sparta—
Iphitus the son of Eurytus. The two fell in with one another in Messene at the
house of Ortilochus, where Odysseus was staying in order to recover a debt
that was owing from the whole people; for the Messenians had carried off
three hundred sheep from Ithaca, and had sailed away with them and with
their shepherds. In quest of these Odysseus took a long journey while still
quite young, for his father and the other chieftains sent him on a mission to
recover them. Iphitus had gone there also to try and get back twelve brood
mares that he had lost, and the mule foals that were running with them. These
mares were the death of him in the end, for when he went to the house of

Zeus' son, mighty Heracles, who performed such prodigies of valor, Heracles to his shame killed him, though he was his guest. For he feared not heaven's vengeance, nor yet respected his own table which he had set before Iphitus, but killed him in spite of everything, and kept the mares himself.

It was when claiming these that Iphitus met Odysseus, and gave him the bow which mighty Eurytus had been used to carry, and which on his death had been left by him to his son. Odysseus gave him in return a sword and a spear, and this was the beginning of a fast friendship, although they never visited at one another's houses, for Zeus' son Heracles killed Iphitus ere they could do so. This bow, then, given him by Iphitus, had not been taken with him by Odysseus when he sailed for Troy; he had used it so long as he had been at home, but had left it behind as having been a keepsake from a valued friend.

Penelope presently reached the oak threshold of the storeroom. The carpenter had planed this duly, and had drawn a line on it so as to get it quite straight; he had then set the door posts into it and hung the doors. She loosed the strap from the handle of the door, put in the key, and drove it straight home to shoot back the bolts that held the doors; these flew open with a noise like a bull bellowing in a meadow, and Penelope stepped upon the raised platform, where the chests stood in which the fair linen and clothes were laid by along with fragrant herbs. Reaching thence, she took down the bow with its bow case from the peg on which it hung. She sat down with it on her knees, weeping bitterly as she took the bow out of its case. When her tears had relieved her, she went to the cloister where the suitors were, carrying the bow and the quiver, with the many deadly arrows that were inside it. Along with her came her maidens, bearing a chest that contained much iron and bronze which her husband had won as prizes. When she reached the suitors, she stood by one of the bearing-posts supporting the roof of the cloister, holding a veil before her face, and with a maid on either side of her. Then she said:

"Listen to me you suitors, who persist in abusing the hospitality of this house because its owner has been long absent, and without other pretext than that you want to marry me. This, then, being the prize that you are contending for, I will bring out the mighty bow of Odysseus, and whosoever of you shall string it most easily and send his arrow through each one of twelve axes, him will I follow and quit this house of my lawful husband, so goodly, and so abounding in wealth. But even so I doubt not that I shall remember it in my dreams."

As she spoke, she told Eumaeus to set the bow and the pieces of iron before the suitors, and Eumaeus wept as he took them to do as she had bidden him. Hard by, the stockman wept also when he saw his master's bow, but Antinous scolded them. "You country louts," said he, "silly simpletons; why should you add to the sorrows of your mistress by crying in this way? She has enough to grieve her in the loss of her husband. Sit still, therefore, and eat your dinners in silence, or go outside if you want to cry, and leave the bow behind you. We suitors shall have to contend for it with might and main, for we shall find it no light matter to string such a bow as this is. There is not a man of us all who is such another as Odysseus; for I have seen him and remember him, though I was then only a child."

This was what he said, but all the time he was expecting to be able to string the bow and shoot through the iron, whereas in fact he was to be the first that should taste of the arrows from the hands of Odysseus, whom he was dishonoring in his own house—egging the others on to do so also.

Then Telemachus spoke. "Great heavens!" he exclaimed. "Zeus must have robbed me of my senses. Here is my dear and excellent mother saying she will quit this house and marry again, yet I am laughing and enjoying myself as though there were nothing happening. But, suitors, as the contest has been agreed upon, let it go forward. It is for a woman whose peer is not to be found in Pylos, Argos, or Mycene, nor yet in Ithaca nor on the mainland. You know this as well as I do; what need have I to speak in praise of my mother? Come on, then, make no excuses for delay, but let us see whether you can string the bow or no. I too will make trial of it, for if I can string it and shoot through the iron, I shall not suffer my mother to quit this house with a stranger, not if I can win the prizes which my father won before me."

As he spoke he sprang from his seat, threw his crimson cloak from him, and took his sword from his shoulder. First he set the axes in a row, in a long groove which he had dug for them, and had made straight by line.[1] Then he stamped the earth tight round them, and everyone was surprised when they saw him set them up so orderly, though he had never seen anything of the kind before. This done, he went on to the pavement to make trial of the bow. Thrice did he tug at it, trying with all his might to draw the string, and thrice he had lo leave off, though he had hoped to string the bow and shoot through the iron. He was trying for the fourth time, and would have strung it had not Odysseus made a sign to check him in spite of all his eagerness. So he said:

"Alas! I shall either be always feeble and of no prowess, or I am too young, and have not yet reached my full strength so as to be able to hold my own if anyone attacks me. You others, therefore, who are stronger than I, make trial of the bow and get this contest settled."

On this he put the bow down, letting it lean against the door that led into the house with the arrow standing against the top of the bow. Then he sat down on the seat from which he had risen, and Antinous said:

"Come on, each of you in his turn, going towards the right from the place at which the cupbearer begins when he is handing round the wine."

The rest agreed, and Leiodes son of Oenops was the first to rise. He was sacrificial priest to the suitors, and sat in the corner near the mixing bowl. He was the only man who hated their evil deeds and was indignant with the others. He was now the first to take the bow and arrow, so he went on to the pavement to make his trial. But he could not string the bow, for his hands were weak and unused to hard work; they therefore soon grew tired, and he said to the suitors: "My friends, I cannot string it; let another have it. This bow shall take the life and soul out of many a chief among us, for it is better to die than

---

[1] It is evident that the open part of the court had no flooring, but the natural soil. (B.)

to live after having missed the prize that we have so long striven for, and which has brought us so long together. Some one of us is even now hoping and praying that he may marry Penelope, but when he has seen this bow and tried it, let him woo and make bridal offerings to some other woman, and let Penelope marry whoever makes her the best offer and whose lot it is to win her."

On this he put the bow down, letting it lean against the door,[2] with the arrow standing against the tip of the bow. Then he took his seat again on the seat from which he had risen; and Antinous rebuked him, saying:

"Leiodes, what are you talking about? Your words are monstrous and intolerable; it makes me angry to listen to you. Shall, then, this bow take the life of many a chief among us, merely because you cannot bend it yourself? True, you were not born to be an archer, but there are others who will soon string it."

Then he said to Melanthius the goatherd, "Look sharp, light a fire in the court, and set a seat hard by with a sheepskin on it; bring us also a large ball of lard, from what they have in the house. Let us warm the bow and grease it. We will then make trial of it again, and bring the contest to an end."

Melanthius lit the fire, and set a seat covered with sheepskins beside it. He also brought a great ball of lard from what they had in the house, and the suitors warmed the bow and again made trial of it, but they were none of them nearly strong enough to string it. Nevertheless there still remained Antinous and Eurymachus, who were the ringleaders among the suitors and much the foremost among them all.

Then the swineherd and the stockman left the cloisters together, and Odysseus followed them. When they had got outside the gates and the outer yard, Odysseus said to them quietly:

"Stockman, and you swineherd, I have something in my mind which I am in doubt whether to say or no; but I think I will say it. What manner of men would you be to stand by Odysseus, if some god should bring him back here

---

[2] The door that led into the body of the house.

all of a sudden? Say which you are disposed to do—to side with the suitors, or with Odysseus?"

"Father Zeus," answered the stockman, "would indeed that you might so ordain it. If some god were but to bring Odysseus back, you should see with what might and main I would fight for him."

In like words Eumaeus prayed to all the gods that Odysseus might return. When, therefore, he saw for certain what mind they were of, Odysseus said: "It is I, Odysseus, who am here. I have suffered much, but at last, in the twentieth year, I am come back to my own country. I find that you two alone of all my servants are glad that I should do so, for I have not heard any of the others praying for my return. To you two, therefore, will I unfold the truth as it shall be. If heaven shall deliver the suitors into my hands, I will find wives for both of you, will give you house and holding close to my own, and you shall be to me as though you were brothers and friends of Telemachus. I will now give you convincing proofs that you may know me and be assured. See, here is the scar from the boar's tooth that ripped me when I was out hunting on Mount Parnassus with the sons of Autolycus."

As he spoke he drew his rags aside from the great scar, and when they had examined it thoroughly, they both of them wept about Odysseus, threw their arms round him, and kissed his head and shoulders, while Odysseus kissed their hands and faces in return. The sun would have gone down upon their mourning if Odysseus had not checked them and said:

"Crease your weeping, lest someone should come outside and see us, and tell those who are within. When you go in, do so separately, not both together; I will go first, and do you follow afterwards. Let this moreover be the token between us; the suitors will all of them try to prevent me from getting hold of the bow and quiver. Do you, therefore, Eumaeus, place it in my hands when you are carrying it about, and tell the women to close the doors of their apartment. If they hear any groaning or uproar as of men fighting about the house, they must not come out; they must keep quiet, and stay where they are at their work. And I charge you, Philoetius, to make fast the doors of the outer court, and to bind them securely at once."

When he had thus spoken, he went back to the house and took the seat that he had left. Presently, his two servants followed him inside.

At this moment the bow was in the hands of Eurymachus, who was warming it by the fire, but even so he could not string it, and he was greatly grieved. He heaved a deep sigh and said, "I grieve for myself and for us all. I grieve that I shall have to forego the marriage, but I do not care nearly so much about this, for there are plenty of other women in Ithaca and elsewhere. What I feel most is the fact of our being so inferior to Odysseus in strength that we cannot string his bow. This will disgrace us in the eyes of those who are yet unborn."

"It shall not be so, Eurymachus," said Antinous, "and you know it yourself. Today is the feast of Apollo throughout all the land; who can string a bow on such a day as this? Put it on one side! As for the axes, they can stay where they are, for no one is likely to come to the house and take them away. Let the cupbearer go round with his cups, that we may make our drink offerings and drop this matter of the bow. We will tell Melanthius to bring us in some goats tomorrow—the best he has; we can then offer thighbones to Apollo the mighty archer, and again make trial of the bow, so as to bring the contest to an end."

The rest approved his words, and thereon menservants poured water over the hands of the guests, while pages filled the mixing bowls with wine and water and handed it round after giving every man his drink offering. Then, when they had made their offerings and had drunk each as much as he desired, Odysseus craftily said.

"Suitors of the illustrious queen, listen that I may speak even as I am minded. I appeal more especially to Eurymachus, and to Antinous who has just spoken with so much reason. Cease shooting for the present and leave the matter to the gods, but in the morning let heaven give victory to whom it will. For the moment, however, give me the bow that I may prove the power of my hands among you all, and see whether I still have as much strength as I used to have, or whether travel and neglect have made an end of it."

This made them all very angry, for they feared he might string the bow. Antinous therefore rebuked him fiercely, saying: "Wretched creature, you have not so much as a grain of sense in your whole body. You ought to think yourself lucky in being allowed to dine unharmed among your betters, without having any smaller portion served you than we others have had, and in being allowed to hear our conversation. No other beggar or stranger has been allowed to hear what we say among ourselves. The wine must have been doing you a mischief, as it does with all those who drink immoderately. It was wine that inflamed the Centaur Eurytion when he was staying with Peirithous among the Lapithae. When the wine had got into his head, he went mad and did ill deeds about the house of Peirithous; this angered the heroes who were there assembled, so they rushed at him and cut off his ears and nostrils; then they dragged him through the doorway out of the house. So he went away crazed, and bore the burden of his crime, bereft of understanding. Henceforth, therefore, there was war between mankind and the centaurs, but he brought it upon himself through his own drunkenness. In like manner I can tell you that it will go hardly with you if you string the bow. You will find no mercy from anyone here, for we shall at once ship you off to King Echetus, who kills everyone that comes near him; you will never get away alive. So drink and keep quiet without getting into a quarrel with men younger than yourself."

Penelope then spoke to him. "Antinous," said she, "it is not right that you should ill-treat any guest of Telemachus who comes to this house. If the stranger should prove strong enough to string the mighty bow of Odysseus, can you suppose that he would take me home with him and make me his wife? Even the man himself can have no such idea in his mind. None of you need let that disturb his feasting; it would be out of all reason."

"Queen Penelope," answered Eurymachus, "we do not suppose that this man will take you away with him; it is impossible. But we are afraid lest some of the baser sort, men or women among the Achaeans, should go gossiping about and say, 'These suitors are a feeble folk; they are paying court to the wife of a brave man whose bow not one of them was able to string. Yet a beggarly tramp who came to the house strung it at once and sent an arrow through the iron.' This is what will be said, and it will be a scandal against us."

"Eurymachus," Penelope answered, "people who persist in eating up the estate of a great chieftain and dishonoring his house must not expect others to speak well of them. Why then should you mind if men talk as you think they will? This stranger is strong and well-built; he says moreover that he is of noble birth. Give him the bow, and let us see whether he can string it or no. I say—and it shall surely be—that if Apollo vouchsafes him the glory of stringing it, I will give him a cloak and shirt of good wear, with a javelin to keep off dogs and robbers, and a sharp sword. I will also give him sandals, and will see him sent safely wherever he wants to go."

Then Telemachus said: "Mother, I am the only man either in Ithaca or in the islands that are over against Elis who has the right to let anyone have the bow or to refuse it. No one shall force me one way or the other, not even though I choose to make the stranger a present of the bow outright, and let him take it away with him. Go, then, within the house and busy yourself with your daily duties, your loom, your distaff, and the ordering of your servants. This bow is a man's matter, and mine above all others, for it is I who am master here."

She went wondering back into the house, and laid her son's saying in her heart. Then going upstairs with her handmaids into her room, she mourned her dear husband till Athene sent sweet sleep over her eyelids.

The swineherd now took up the bow and was for taking it to Odysseus, but the suitors clamored at him from all parts of the cloisters, and one of them said, "You idiot, where are you taking the bow to? Are you out of your wits? If Apollo and the other gods will grant our prayer, your own boarhounds shall get you into some quiet little place, and worry you to death."

Eumaeus was frightened at the outcry they all raised, so he put the bow down then and there. But Telemachus shouted out at him from the other side of the cloisters and threatened him, saying, "Father Eumaeus, bring the bow on in spite of them, or young as I am I will pelt you with stones back to the country, for I am the better man of the two. I wish I was as much stronger than all the other suitors in the house as I am than you. I would soon send some of them off sick and sorry, for they mean mischief."

Thus did he speak, and they all of them laughed heartily, which put them in a better humor with Telemachus. So Eumaeus brought the bow on and placed it in the hands of Odysseus. When he had done this, he called Euryclea apart and said to her, "Euryclea, Telemachus says you are to close the doors of the women's apartments. If they hear any groaning or uproar as of men fighting about the house, they are not to come out, but are to keep quiet and stay where they are at their work."

Euryclea did as she was told and closed the doors of the women's apartments.

Meanwhile Philoetius slipped quietly out and made fast the gates of the outer court. There was a ship's cable of byblus fiber lying in the gatehouse, so he made the gates fast with it. Then he came in again, resuming the seat that he had left, and keeping an eye on Odysseus, who had now got the bow in his hands, and was turning it every way about, and proving it all over to see whether the worms had been eating into its two horns during his absence. Then would one turn towards his neighbor, saying, "This is some tricky old bow-fancier. Either he has got one like it at home, or he wants to make one; in such workmanlike style does the old vagabond handle it."

Another said, "I hope he may be no more successful in other things than he is likely to be in stringing this bow."

But Odysseus, when he had taken it up and examined it all over, strung it as easily as a skilled bard strings a new peg of his lyre and makes the twisted gut fast at both ends. Then he took it in his right hand to prove the string, and it sang sweetly under his touch like the twittering of a swallow. The suitors were dismayed, and turned color as they heard it; at that moment, moreover, Zeus thundered loudly as a sign, and the heart of Odysseus rejoiced as he heard the omen that the son of scheming Cronus had sent him.

He took an arrow that was lying upon the table—for those which the Achaeans were so shortly to taste were all inside the quiver. He laid it on the center-piece of the bow, and drew the notch of the arrow and the string toward him, still seated on his seat. When he had taken aim he let fly, and his arrow pierced every one of the handle-holes of the axes from the first onwards till it had gone right through them,[3] and into the outer courtyard. Then he said to Telemachus:

"Your guest has not disgraced you, Telemachus. I did not miss what I aimed at, and I was not long in stringing my bow. I am still strong, and not as the suitors twit me with being. Now, however, it is time for the Achaeans to prepare supper while there is still daylight, and then otherwise to disport themselves with song and dance, which are the crowning ornaments of a banquet."

As he spoke he made a sign with his eyebrows, and Telemachus girded on his sword, grasped his spear, and stood armed beside his father's seat.

---

[3] I suppose the iron part of the ax to have been wedged into the handle, or bound securely to it—the handle being half buried in the ground. The ax would be placed edgeways towards the archer, and he would have to shoot his arrow through the hole into which the handle was fitted when the ax was in use. Twelve axes were placed in a row all at the same height, all exactly in front of one another, all edgeways to Odysseus whose arrow passed through all the holes from the first onward. (B.)

Book XXII

*Odysseus tears off his rags and begins the slaughter of the suitors.
Telemachus brings armor from the storeroom, and Athene appears to help
her favorite. The suitors try to defend themselves, but all finally are slain.
Odysseus learns from Euryclea which of the housemaids have been guilty of
misbehavior and these are hung. The banqueting cloister is then thoroughly
cleansed and purified.*

THEN ODYSSEUS TORE OFF HIS RAGS, AND SPRANG ON TO THE BROAD
pavement with his bow and his quiver full of arrows. He shed the
arrows on to the ground at his feet and said, "The mighty contest is
at an end. I will now see whether Apollo will vouchsafe it to me to hit another
mark which no man has yet hit."

On this he aimed a deadly arrow at Antinous, who was about to take up
a two-handled gold cup to drink his wine and already had it in his hands. He
had no thought of death—who among all the revelers would think that one
man, however brave, would stand alone among so many and kill him? The
arrow struck Antinous in the throat, and the point went clean through his
neck, so that he fell over and the cup dropped from his hand, while a thick
stream of blood gushed from his nostrils. He kicked the table from him and
upset the things on it, so that the bread and roasted meats were all soiled as
they fell over on to the ground. The suitors were in an uproar when they saw
that a man had been hit. They sprang in dismay one and all of them from their
seats and looked everywhere towards the walls, but there was neither shield

nor spear, and they rebuked Odysseus very angrily. "Stranger," said they, "you shall pay for shooting people in this way. You shall see no other contest; you are a doomed man. He whom you have slain was the foremost youth in Ithaca, and the vultures shall devour you for having killed him."

Thus they spoke, for they thought that he had killed Antinous by mistake, and did not perceive that death was hanging over the head of every one of them. But Odysseus glared at them and said:

"Dogs, did you think that I should not come back from Troy? You have wasted my substance, have forced my womenservants to lie with you, and have wooed my wife while I was still living. You have feared neither God nor man, and now you shall die."

They turned pale with fear as he spoke, and every man looked round about to see whether he might fly for safety, but Eurymachus alone spoke.

"If you are Odysseus," said he, "then what you have said is just. We have done much wrong on your lands and in your house. But Antinous who was the head and front of the offending lies low already. It was all his doing. It was not that he wanted to marry Penelope; he did not so much care about that. What he wanted was something quite different, and Zeus has not vouchsafed it to him; he wanted to kill your son and to be chief man in Ithaca. Now, therefore, that he has met the death which was his due, spare the lives of your people. We will make everything good among ourselves, and pay you in full for all that we have eaten and drunk. Each one of us shall pay you a fine worth twenty oxen, and we will keep on giving you gold and bronze till your heart is softened. Until we have done this no one can complain of your being enraged against us."

Odysseus again glared at him and said: "Though you should give me all you have in the world both now and all that you ever shall have, I will not stay my hand till I have paid all of you in full. You must fight, or fly for your lives; and fly, not a man of you shall."

Their hearts sank as they heard him, but Eurymachus again spoke, saying:

"My friends, this man will give us no quarter. He will stand where he is and shoot us down till he has killed every man among us. Let us then show fight; draw your swords, and hold up the tables to shield you from his arrows. Let us have at him with a rush, to drive him from the pavement and doorway. We can then get through into the town, and raise such an alarm as shall soon stay his shooting."

As he spoke he drew his keen blade of bronze, sharpened on both sides, and with a loud cry sprang towards Odysseus, but Odysseus instantly shot an arrow into his breast that caught him by the nipple and fixed itself in his liver. He dropped his sword and fell doubled up over his table. The cup and all the meats went over on to the ground as he smote the earth with his forehead in the agonies of death, and he kicked the stool with his feet until his eyes were closed in darkness.

Then Amphinomus drew his sword and made straight at Odysseus to try and get him away from the door, but Telemachus was too quick for him, and struck him from behind. The spear caught him between the shoulders and went right through his chest, so that he fell heavily to the ground and struck the earth with his forehead. Then Telemachus sprang away from him, leaving his spear still in the body, for he feared that if he stayed to draw it out, some one of the Achaeans might come up and hack at him with his sword, or knock him down, so he set off at a run, and immediately was at his father's side. Then he said:

"Father, let me bring you a shield, two spears, and a brass helmet for your temples. I will arm myself as well, and will bring other armor for the swineherd and the stockman, for we had better be armed."

"Run and fetch them," answered Odysseus, "while my arrows hold out, or when I am alone they may get me away from the door."

Telemachus did as his father said, and ran off to the storeroom where the armor was kept. He chose four shields, eight spears, and four brass helmets with horsehair plumes. He brought them with all speed to his father, and armed himself first, while the stockman and the swineherd also put on their armor, and took their places near Odysseus. Meanwhile Odysseus, as long as his arrows lasted, had been shooting the suitors one by one, and they fell thick on one another. When his arrows gave out, he set the bow to stand against the end wall of the house by the door post, and hung a shield four hides thick about his shoulders; on his comely head he set his helmet, well-wrought with a crest of horsehair that nodded menacingly above it, and he grasped two redoubtable bronze-shod spears.

Now there was a window in the wall, while at one end of the pavement[1] there was an exit leading to a narrow passage, and this exit was closed by a well-made door. Odysseus told Philoetius to stand by this door and guard it, for only one person could attack it at a time. But Agelaus shouted out, "Cannot someone go up to the window and tell the people outside what is going on? Help would come at once, and we should soon make an end of this man and his shooting."

"This may not be, Agelaus," answered Melanthius, "the mouth of the narrow passage is dangerously near the entrance to the outer court. One brave man could prevent any number from getting in. But I know what I will do, I will bring you arms from the storeroom, for I am sure it is there that Odysseus and his son have put them."

On this the goatherd Melanthius went by back passages to the storeroom of Odysseus' house. There he chose twelve shields, with as many helmets and spears, and brought them back as fast as he could to give them to the suitors. Odysseus' heart began to fail him when he saw the suitors putting on their armor and brandishing their spears. He saw the greatness of the danger, and said to Telemachus, "Some one of the women inside is helping the suitors against us, or it may be Melanthius."

Telemachus answered: "The fault, father, is mine, and mine only. I left the storeroom door open, and they have kept a sharper lookout than I have.

[1] The pavement on which Odysseus was standing.

Go, Eumaeus, put the door to, and see whether it is one of the women who is doing this, or whether, as I suspect, it is Melanthius the son of Dolius."

Thus did they converse. Meanwhile Melanthius was again going to the storeroom to fetch more armor, but the swineherd saw him and said to Odysseus who was beside him, "Odysseus, noble son of Laertes, it is that scoundrel Melanthius, just as we suspected, who is going to the storeroom. Say, shall I kill him, if I can get the better of him, or shall I bring him here that you may take your own revenge for all the many wrongs that he has done in your house?"

Odysseus answered: "Telemachus and I will hold these suitors in check, no matter what they do. Go back, both of you, and bind Melanthius' hands and feet behind him. Throw him into the storeroom and make the door fast behind you; then fasten a noose about his body, and string him close up to the rafters from a high bearing-post, that he may linger on in an agony."

Thus did he speak, and they did even as he had said. They went to the storeroom, which they entered before Melanthius saw them, for he was busy searching for arms in the innermost part of the room, so the two took their stand on either side of the door and waited. By and by Melanthius came out with a helmet in one hand, and an old dry-rotted shield in the other, which had been borne by Laertes when he was young, but which had been long since thrown aside, and the straps had become unsewn. On this the two seized him, dragged him back by the hair, and threw him struggling to the ground. They bent his hands and feet well behind his back, and bound them tight with a painful bond as Odysseus had told them; then they fastened a noose about his body and strung him up from a high pillar till he was close up to the rafters. And over him did you then vaunt, O swineherd Eumaeus, saying, "Melanthius, you will pass the night on a soft bed as you deserve. You will know very well when morning comes from the streams of Oceanus, and it is time for you to be driving in your goats for the suitors to feast on."

There, then, they left him in very cruel bondage, and having put on their armor they closed the door behind them and went back to take their places by the side of Odysseus; whereon the four men stood in the cloister, fierce and full of fury. Nevertheless, those who were in the body of the court were still both brave and many. Then Zeus' daughter Athene came up to them, having assumed the voice and form of Mentor. Odysseus was glad when he saw her and said, "Mentor, lend me your help, and forget not your old comrade, or the many good turns he has done you. Besides, you are my age-mate."

But all the time he felt sure it was Athene, and the suitors from the other side raised an uproar when they saw her. Agelaus was the first to reproach her. "Mentor," he cried, "do not let Odysseus beguile you into siding with him and fighting the suitors. This is what we will do: when we have killed these people, father and son, we will kill you too. You shall pay for it with your head, and when we have killed you, we will take all you have, indoors or out, and bring it into hotch-pot with Odysseus' property. We will not let your sons live in your house, nor your daughters, nor shall your widow continue to live in the city of Ithaca."

This made Athene still more furious, so she scolded Odysseus very angrily. "Odysseus," she said, "your strength and prowess are no longer what they were when you fought for nine long years among the Trojans about the noble lady Helen. You killed many a man in those days, and it was through your stratagem that Priam's city was taken. How comes it that you are so lamentably less valiant now that you are on your own ground, face to face with the suitors in your own house? Come on, my good fellow, stand by my side and see how Mentor son of Alcimus shall fight your foes and requite your kindnesses conferred upon him."

But she would not give him full victory as yet, for she wished still further to prove his own prowess and that of his brave son, so she flew up to one of the rafters in the roof of the cloister and sat upon it in the form of a swallow.

Meanwhile Agelaus son of Damastor, Eurynomus, Amphimedon, Demoptolemus, Pisander, and Polybus son of Polyctor bore the brunt of the fight upon the suitors' side. Of all those who were still fighting for their lives they were by far the most valiant, for the others had already fallen under the arrows of Odysseus. Agelaus shouted to them and said: "My friends, he will soon have to leave off, for Mentor has gone away after having done nothing for him but brag. They are standing at the doors unsupported. Do not aim at him all at once, but six of you throw your spears first, and see if you cannot cover yourselves with glory by killing him. When he has fallen we need not be uneasy about the others."

They threw their spears as he bade them, but Athene made them all of no effect. One hit the door post; another went against the door; the pointed shaft of another struck the wall. As soon as they had avoided all the spears of the suitors Odysseus said to his own men, "My friends, I should say we too had better let drive into the middle of them, or they will crown all the harm they have done us by killing us outright."

They therefore aimed straight in front of them and threw their spears. Odysseus killed Demoptolemus, Telemachus Euryades, Eumaeus Elatus, while the stockman killed Pisander. These all bit the dust, and as the others drew back into a corner Odysseus and his men rushed forward and regained their spears by drawing them from the bodies of the dead.

The suitors now aimed a second time, but again Athene made their weapons for the most part without effect. One hit a bearing-post of the cloister; another went against the door; while the pointed shaft of another struck the wall. Still, Amphimedon just took a piece of the top skin from off Telemachus' wrist, and Ctesippus managed to graze Eumaeus' shoulder above his shield; but the spear went on and fell to the ground. Then Odysseus and his men let drive into the crowd of suitors. Odysseus hit Eurydamas, Telemachus Amphimedon, and Eumaeus Polybus. After this the stockman hit Ctesippus in the breast, and taunted him, saying, "Foul-mouthed son of Polytherses, do not be so foolish as to talk wickedly another time, but let heaven direct your speech, for the gods are far stronger than men. I make you a present of this advice to repay you for the foot which you gave Odysseus when he was begging about in his own house."

Thus spoke the stockman, and Odysseus struck the son of Damastor with a spear in close fight, while Telemachus hit Leiocritus son of Evenor in the belly, and the dart went clean through him, so that he fell forward full on his face upon the ground. Then Athene from her seat on the rafter held up her deadly aegis, and the hearts of the suitors quailed. They fled to the other end of the court like a herd of cattle maddened by the gadfly in early summer when the days are at their longest. As eagle-beaked, crook-taloned vultures from the mountains swoop down on the smaller birds that cower in flocks upon the ground, and kill them, for they cannot either fight or fly, and lookers-on enjoy the sport—even so did Odysseus and his men fall upon the suitors and smite them on every side. They made a horrible groaning as their brains were being battered in, and the ground seethed with their blood.

Leiodes then caught the knees of Odysseus and said, "Odysseus, I beseech you have mercy upon me and spare me. I never wronged any of the women in your house either in word or deed, and I tried to stop the others. I saw them, but they would not listen, and now they are paying for their folly. I was their sacrificing priest. If you kill me, I shall die without having done anything to deserve it, and shall have got no thanks for all the good that I did."

Odysseus looked sternly at him and answered, "If you were their sacrificing priest, you must have prayed many a time that it might be long before I got home again, and that you might marry my wife and have children by her. Therefore you shall die."

With these words he picked up the sword that Agelaus had dropped when he was being killed, and which was lying upon the ground. Then he struck Leiodes on the back of his neck, so that his head fell rolling in the dust while he was yet speaking.

The minstrel Phemius son of Terpes—he who had been forced by the suitors to sing to them—now tried to save his life. He was standing near towards the window and held his lyre in his hand. He did not know whether to fly out of the cloister and sit down by the altar of Zeus that was in the outer court, and on which both Laertes and Odysseus had offered up the thighbones of many an ox, or whether to go straight up to Odysseus and embrace his knees, but in the end he deemed it best to embrace Odysseus' knees. So he laid his lyre on the ground between the mixing bowl and the silver-studded seat; then going up to Odysseus he caught hold of his knees and said: "Odysseus, I beseech you have mercy on me and spare me. You will be sorry for it afterwards if you kill a bard who can sing both for gods and men as I can. I make all my lays myself, and heaven visits me with every kind of inspiration. I would sing to you as though you were a god; do not therefore be in such a hurry to cut my head off. Your own son Telemachus will tell you that I did not want to frequent your house and sing to the suitors after their meals, but they were too many and too strong for me, so they made me."

Telemachus heard him, and at once went up to his father. "Hold!" he cried. "The man is guiltless, do him no hurt; and we will spare Medon too, who was always good to me when I was a boy, unless Philoetius or Eumaeus has already killed him, or he has fallen in your way when you were raging about the court."

Medon caught these words of Telemachus, for he was crouching under a seat beneath which he had hidden by covering himself up with a freshly flayed heifer's hide, so he threw off the hide, went up to Telemachus, and laid hold of his knees.

"Here I am, my dear sir," said he. "Stay your hand therefore, and tell your father, or he will kill me in his rage against the suitors for having wasted his substance and been so foolishly disrespectful to yourself."

Odysseus smiled at him and answered, "Fear not! Telemachus has saved your life, that you may know in future, and tell other people, how greatly better good deeds prosper than evil ones. Go, therefore, outside the cloisters into the outer court, and be out of the way of the slaughter—you and the bard—while I finish my work here inside."

The pair went into the outer court as fast as they could, and sat down by Zeus' great altar, looking fearfully round, and still expecting that they would be killed. Then Odysseus searched the whole court carefully over, to see if anyone had managed to hide himself and was still living, but he found them all lying in the dust and weltering in their blood. They were like fishes which fishermen have netted out of the sea, and thrown upon the beach to lie gasping for water till the heat of the sun makes an end of them. Even so were the suitors lying all huddled up one against the other.

Then Odysseus said to Telemachus, "Call nurse Euryclea. I have something to say to her."

Telemachus went and knocked at the door of the women's room. "Make haste," said he, "you old woman who have been set over all the other women in the house. Come outside; my father wishes to speak to you."

When Euryclea heard this she unfastened the door of the women's room and came out, following Telemachus. She found Odysseus among the corpses bespattered with blood and filth like a lion that has just been devouring an ox, and his breast and both his cheeks are all bloody, so that he is a fearful sight; even so was Odysseus besmirched from head to foot with gore. When she saw all the corpses and such a quantity of blood, she was beginning to cry out for joy, for she saw that a great deed had been done; but Odysseus checked her. "Old woman," said he, "rejoice in silence. Restrain yourself, and do not make any noise about it; it is an unholy thing to vaunt over dead men. Heaven's doom and their own evil deeds have brought these men to destruction, for they respected no man in the whole world, neither rich nor poor, who came near them, and they have come to a bad end as a punishment for their wickedness and folly. Now, however, tell me which of the women in the house have misconducted themselves, and who are innocent."

"I will tell you the truth, my son," answered Euryclea. "There are fifty women in the house whom we teach to do things, such as carding wool, and all kinds of household work. Of these, twelve in all[2] have misbehaved, and have been wanting in respect to me, and also to Penelope. They showed no

[2] There were a hundred and eight suitors.

disrespect to Telemachus, for he has only lately grown up, and his mother never permitted him to give orders to the female servants. But let me go upstairs and tell your wife all that has happened, for some god has been sending her to sleep."

"Do not wake her yet," answered Odysseus, "but tell the women who have misconducted themselves to come to me."

Euryclea left the cloister to tell the women, and make them come to Odysseus; in the meantime he called Telemachus, the stockman, and the swineherd. "Begin," said he, "to remove the dead, and make the women help you. Then, get sponges and clean water to swill down the tables and seats. When you have thoroughly cleansed the whole cloisters, take the women into the space between the domed room and the wall of the outer court, and run them through with your swords till they are quite dead, and have forgotten all about love and the way in which they used to lie in secret with the suitors."

On this the women came down in a body, weeping and wailing bitterly. First they carried the dead bodies out, and propped them up against one another in the gatehouse. Odysseus ordered them about and made them do their work quickly, so they had to carry the bodies out. When they had done this, they cleaned all the tables and seats with sponges and water, while Telemachus and the two others shoveled up the blood and dirt from the ground, and the women carried it all away and put it out of doors. Then when they had made the whole place quite clean and orderly, they took the women out and hemmed them in the narrow space between the wall of the domed room and that of the yard, so that they could not get away. And Telemachus said to the other two, "I shall not let these women die a clean death, for they were insolent to me and my mother, and used to sleep with the suitors."

So saying he made a ship's cable fast to one of the bearing-posts that supported the roof of the domed room, and secured it all around the building, at a good height, lest any of the women's feet should touch the ground. And as thrushes or doves beat against a net that has been set for them in a thicket just as they were getting to their nest, and a terrible fate awaits them, even so did the women have to put their heads in nooses one after the other and die most miserably. Their feet moved convulsively for a while, but not for very long.

As for Melanthius, they took him through the cloister into the inner court. There they cut off his nose and his ears; they drew out his vitals and gave them to the dogs raw, and then in their fury they cut off his hands and his feet.

When they had done this they washed their hands and feet and went back into the house, for all was now over. And Odysseus said to the dear old nurse Euryclea, "Bring me sulfur, which cleanses all pollution, and fetch fire also that I may burn it, and purify the cloisters. Go, moreover, and tell Penelope to come here with her attendants, and also all the maidservants that are in the house."

"All that you have said is true," answered Euryclea, "but let me bring you some clean clothes—a shirt and cloak. Do not keep these rags on your back any longer. It is not right."

"First light me a fire," replied Odysseus.

She brought the fire and sulfur, as he had bidden her, and Odysseus thoroughly purified the cloisters and both the inner and outer courts. Then she went inside to call the women and tell them what had happened; whereon they came from their apartment with torches in their hands, and pressed round Odysseus to embrace him, kissing his head and shoulders and taking hold of his hands. It made him feel as if he should like to weep, for he remembered every one of them.

Book XXIII

Euryclea now tells her mistress that the beggar who has rid the house of the plague of suitors is Odysseus. Unbelieving, Penelope questions him, and is at last convinced that it is indeed he. They embrace and converse happily through much of the night. The following day, Odysseus, accompanied by Telemachus and their faithful retainers, goes to tell his father Laertes of his return.

E URYCLEA NOW WENT UPSTAIRS LAUGHING, TO TELL HER MISTRESS THAT her dear husband had come home. Her aged knees became young again and her feet were nimble for joy as she went up to her mistress and bent over her head to speak to her. "Wake up, Penelope, my dear child," she exclaimed, "and see with your own eyes something that you have been wanting this long time past. Odysseus has at last indeed come home again, and has killed the suitors who were giving so much trouble in his house, eating up his estate, and ill-treating his son."

"My good nurse," answered Penelope, "you must be mad. The gods sometimes send some very sensible people out of their minds, and make foolish people become sensible. This is what they must have been doing to you; for you always used to be a reasonable person. Why should you thus mock me when I have trouble enough already—talking such nonsense, and waking me up out of a sweet sleep that had taken possession of my eyes and closed them? I have never slept so soundly from the day my poor husband went to that city with the ill-omened name. Go back again into the women's room! If it had been anyone else who had woke me up to bring me such absurd news, I should have sent her away with a severe scolding. As it is, your age shall protect you."

"My dear child," answered Euryclea, "I am not mocking you. It is quite true as I tell you that Odysseus is come home again. He was the stranger whom they all kept on treating so badly in the cloister. Telemachus knew all the time that he was come back, but kept his father's secret that he might have his revenge on all these wicked people."

Then Penelope sprang up from her couch, threw her arms round Euryclea, and wept for joy. "But my dear nurse," said she, "explain this to me: if he has really come home as you say, how did he manage to overcome the wicked suitors single-handed, seeing what a number of them there always were?"

"I was not there," answered Euryclea, "and do not know; I only heard them groaning while they were being killed. We sat crouching and huddled up in a corner of the women's room with the doors closed, till your son came to fetch me because his father sent him. Then I found Odysseus standing over the corpses that were lying on the ground all round him, one on top of the other. You would have enjoyed it if you could have seen him standing there all bespattered with blood and filth, and looking just like a lion. But the corpses are now all piled up in the gatehouse that is in the outer court, and Odysseus has lit a great fire to purify the house with sulfur. He has sent me to call you, so come with me that you may both be happy together after all; for now at last the desire of your heart has been fulfilled. Your husband is come home to find both wife and son alive and well, and to take his revenge in his own house on the suitors who behaved so badly to him."

"My dear nurse," said Penelope, "do not exult too confidently over all this. You know how delighted everyone would be to see Odysseus come home—more particularly myself, and the son who has been born to both of us; but what you tell cannot be really true. It is some god who is angry with the suitors for their great wickedness, and has made an end of them; for they respected no man in the whole world, neither rich nor poor, who came near them, and they have come to a bad end in consequence of their iniquity. Odysseus is dead far away from the Achaean land; he will never return home again."

Then nurse Euryclea said: "My child, what are you talking about? But you were always hard of belief, and have made up your mind that your husband is never coming, although he is in the house and by his own fireside at this very moment. Besides, I can give you another proof. When I was washing him I perceived the scar which the wild boar gave him, and I wanted to tell you about it, but in his wisdom he would not let me, and clapped his hands over my mouth. So come with me and I will make this bargain with you—if I am deceiving you, you may have me killed by the most cruel death you can think of."

"My dear nurse," said Penelope, "however wise you may be, you can hardly fathom the counsels of the gods. Nevertheless, we will go in search of my son, that I may see the corpses of the suitors, and the man who has killed them."

On this she came down from her upper room, and while doing so she considered whether she should keep at a distance from her husband and question him, or whether she should at once go up to him and embrace him. When, however, she had crossed the stone floor of the cloister, she sat down opposite Odysseus by the fire, against the wall at right angles to that by which she had entered, while Odysseus sat near one of the bearing-posts, looking upon the ground, and waiting to see what his brave wife would say to him when she saw him. For a long time she sat silent and as one lost in amazement. At one moment she looked him full in the face, but then again directly, she was misled by his shabby clothes and failed to recognize him, till Telemachus began to reproach her and said:

"Mother—but you are so hard that I cannot call you by such a name— why do you keep away from my father in this way? Why do you not sit by his side and begin talking to him and asking him questions? No other woman could bear to keep away from her husband when he had come back to her after twenty years of absence, and after having gone through so much. But your heart always was as hard as a stone."

Penelope answered: "My son, I am so lost in astonishment that I can find no words in which either to ask questions or to answer them. I cannot even look him straight in the face. Still, if he really is Odysseus come back to his own home again, we shall get to understand one another better by and by, for there are tokens with which we two are alone acquainted, and which are hidden from all others."

Odysseus smiled at this, and said to Telemachus: "Let your mother put me to any proof she likes; she will make up her mind about it presently. She rejects me for the moment and believes me to be somebody else, because I am covered with dirt and have such bad clothes on. Let us, however, consider what we had better do next. When one man has killed another, even though he was not one who would leave many friends to take up his quarrel, the man who has killed him must still say good-by to his friends and fly the country; whereas we have been killing the stay of a whole town, and all the picked youth of Ithaca. I would have you consider this matter."

"Look to it yourself, father," answered Telemachus, "for they say you are the wisest counselor in the world, and that there is no other mortal man who can compare with you. We will follow you with right good will, nor shall you find us fail you in so far as our strength holds out."

"I will say what I think will be best," answered Odysseus. "First wash and put your shirts on; tell the maids also to go to their own room and dress. Phemius shall then strike up a dance tune on his lyre, so that if people outside hear, or any of the neighbors, or someone going along the street happens to notice it, they may think there is a wedding in the house, and no rumors about the death of the suitors will get about in the town, before we can escape to the woods upon my own land. Once there, we will settle which of the courses heaven vouchsafes us shall seem wisest."

Thus did he speak, and they did even as he had said. First they washed and put their shirts on, while the women got ready. Then Phemius took his lyre and set them all longing for sweet song and stately dance. The house reechoed with the sound of men and women dancing, and the people outside said, "I suppose the queen has been getting married at last. She ought to be ashamed of herself for not continuing to protect her husband's property until he comes home."

This was what they said, but they did not know what it was that had been happening. The upper servant Eurynome washed and anointed Odysseus in his own house and gave him a shirt and cloak, while Athene made him look taller and stronger than before. She also made the hair grow thick on the top of his head, and flow down in curls like hyacinth blossoms; she glorified him about the head and shoulders just as a skillful workman who has studied art of all kinds under Hephaestus or Athene—and his work is full of beauty— enriches a piece of silver plate by gilding it. He came from the bath looking like one of the immortals, and sat down opposite his wife on the seat he had left. "My dear," said he, "heaven has endowed you with a heart more unyielding than woman ever yet had. No other woman could bear to keep away from her husband when he had come back to her after twenty years of absence, and after having gone through so much. But come, nurse, get a bed ready for me. I will sleep alone, for this woman has a heart as hard as iron."

"My dear," answered Penelope, "I have no wish to set myself up, nor to depreciate you, but I am not struck by your appearance, for I very well remember what kind of a man you were when you set sail from Ithaca. Nevertheless, Euryclea, take his bed outside the bedchamber that he himself built. Bring the bed outside this room, and put bedding upon it with fleeces, good coverlets, and blankets."

She said this to try him, but Odysseus was very angry and said: "Wife, I am much displeased at what you have just been saying. Who has been taking my bed from the place in which I left it? He must have found it a hard task, no matter how skilled a workman he was, unless some god came and helped him to shift it. There is no man living, however strong and in his prime, who could move it from its place, for it is a marvelous curiosity which I made with my very own hands. There was a young olive growing within the precincts of the house, in full vigor, and about as thick as a bearing-post. I built my room round this with strong walls of stone and a roof to cover them, and I made the doors strong and well-fitting. Then I cut off the top boughs of the olive tree and left the stump standing. This I dressed roughly from the root upwards and then worked with carpenter's tools well and skillfully, straightening my work by drawing a line on the wood, and making it into a bed-prop. I then bored a hole down the middle, and made it the center-post of my bed, at which I worked till I had finished it, inlaying it with gold and silver; after this I stretched a hide of crimson leather from one side of it to the other. So you see I know all about it, and I desire to learn whether it is still there, or whether anyone has been removing it by cutting down the olive tree at its roots."

When she heard the sure proofs Odysseus now gave her, she fairly broke down. She flew weeping to his side, flung her arms about his neck, and kissed him. "Do not be angry with me, Odysseus," she cried, "you, who are the wisest of mankind. We have suffered, both of us. Heaven has denied us the happiness of spending our youth and growing old together; do not then be aggrieved or take it amiss that I did not embrace you thus as soon as I saw you. I have been shuddering all the time through fear that someone might come here and deceive me with a lying story; for there are many very wicked people going about. Zeus' daughter Helen would never have yielded herself to a man from a foreign country, if she had known that the sons of Achaeans would come after her and bring her back. Heaven put it in her heart to do wrong, and she gave no thought to that sin, which has been the source of all our sorrows. Now, however, that you have convinced me by showing that you know all about our bed (which no human being has ever seen but you and I and a single maidservant, the daughter of Actor, who was given me by my father on my marriage and who keeps the doors of our room), hard of belief though I have been, I can mistrust no longer."

Then Odysseus in his turn melted, and wept as he clasped his dear and faithful wife to his bosom. As the sight of land is welcome to men who are swimming towards the shore, when Poseidon has wrecked their ship with the fury of his winds and waves—a few alone reach the land, and these, covered with brine, are thankful when they find themselves on firm ground and out of danger—even so was her husband welcome to her as she looked upon him, and she could not tear her two fair arms from about his neck. Indeed they would have gone on indulging their sorrow till rosy-fingered morn appeared had not Athene determined otherwise, and held night back in the far west, while she would not suffer Dawn to leave Oceanus, nor to yoke the two steeds Lampus and Phaethon that bear her onward to break the day upon mankind.

At last, however, Odysseus said: "Wife, we have not yet reached the end of our troubles. I have an unknown amount of toil still to undergo. It is long and difficult, but I must go through with it, for thus the shade of Teiresias prophesied concerning me, on the day when I went down into Hades to ask about my return and that of my companions. But now let us go to bed, that we may lie down and enjoy the blessed boon of sleep."

"You shall go to bed as soon as you please," replied Penelope, "now that the gods have sent you home to your own good house and to your country. But as heaven has put it in your mind to speak of it, tell me about the task that lies before you. I shall have to hear about it later, so it is better that I should be told at once."

"My dear," answered Odysseus, "why should you press me to tell you? Still, I will not conceal it from you, though you will not like it. I do not like it myself, for Teiresias bade me travel far and wide, carrying an oar, till I came to a country where the people have never heard of the sea, and do not even mix salt with their food, They know nothing about ships, nor oars that are as the wings of a ship. He gave me this certain token which I will not hide from you. He said that a wayfarer should meet me and ask me whether it was a winnowing shovel that I had on my shoulder. On this, I was to fix my oar in the ground and sacrifice a ram, a bull, and a boar to Poseidon; after which I was to go home and offer hecatombs to all the gods in heaven, one after the other. As for myself, he said that death should come to me from the sea, and that my life should ebb away very gently when I was full of years and peace of mind, and my people should bless me. All this, he said, should surely come to pass."

And Penelope said, "If the gods are going to vouchsafe you a happier time in your old age, you may hope then to have some respite from misfortune."

Thus did they converse. Meanwhile Eurynome and the nurse took torches and made the bed ready with soft coverlets. As soon as they had laid them, the nurse went back into the house to go to her rest, leaving the bedchamber woman Eurynome to show Odysseus and Penelope to bed by torchlight. When she had conducted them to their room she went back, and they then came joyfully to the rites of their own old bed. Telemachus, Philoetius, and the swineherd now left off dancing, and made the women leave off also. They then laid themselves down to sleep in the cloisters.

When Odysseus and Penelope had had their fill of love, they fell talking with one another. She told him how much she had had to bear in seeing the house filled with a crowd of wicked suitors who had killed so many sheep and oxen on her account, and had drunk so many casks of wine. Odysseus in his turn told her what he had suffered, and how much trouble he had himself given to other people. He told her everything, and she was so delighted to listen that she never went to sleep till he had ended his whole story.

He began with his victory over the Cicones, and how he thence reached the fertile land of the Lotus-eaters. He told her all about the Cyclops and how he had punished him for having so ruthlessly eaten his brave comrades; how he then went on to Aeolus, who received him hospitably and furthered him on his way, but even so he was not to reach home, for to his great grief a hurricane carried him out to sea again; how he went on to the Laestrygonian city Telepylos, where the people destroyed all his ships with their crews, save himself and his own ship only. Then he told of cunning Circe and her craft, and how he sailed to the chill house of Hades, to consult the ghost of the Theban prophet Teiresias, and how he saw his old comrades in arms, and his mother who bore him and brought him up when he was a child; how he then heard the wondrous singing of the Sirens, and went on to the wandering rocks and terrible Charybdis and to Scylla, whom no man had ever yet passed in safety; how his men then ate the cattle of the sun-god, and how Zeus therefore struck the ship with his thunderbolts, so that all his men perished together, himself alone being left alive; how at last he reached the Ogygian island and the nymph Calypso, who kept him there in a cave, and fed him, and wanted him to marry her, in which case she intended making him immortal so that he should never grow old, but she could not persuade him to let her do so; and how after much suffering he had found his way to the Phaeacians, who had treated him as though he had been a god, and sent him back in a ship to his own country after having given him gold, bronze, and raiment in great abundance. This was the last thing about which he told her, for here a deep sleep took hold upon him and eased the burden of his sorrows.

Then Athene bethought her of another matter. When she deemed that Odysseus had had enough both of his wife and of repose, she bade gold-enthroned Dawn rise out of Oceanus that she might shed light upon mankind. On this, Odysseus rose from his comfortable bed and said to Penelope: "Wife, we have both of us had our full share of troubles, you, here, in lamenting my absence, and I in being prevented from getting home though I was longing all the time to do so. Now, however, that we have at last come together, take care of the property that is in the house. As for the sheep and goats which the wicked suitors have eaten, I will take many myself by force from other people, and will compel the Achaeans to make good the rest till they shall have filled all my yards. I am now going to the wooded lands out in the country to see my father who has so long been grieved on my account, and to yourself I will give these instructions, though you have little need of them. At sunrise it will at once get abroad that I have been killing the suitors;

go upstairs, therefore, and stay there with your women. See nobody and ask no questions."

As he spoke he girded on his armor. Then he roused Telemachus, Philoetius, and Eumaeus, and told them all to put on their armor also. This they did, and armed themselves. When they had done so, they opened the gates and sallied forth, Odysseus leading the way. It was now daylight, but Athene nevertheless concealed them in darkness and led them quickly out of the town.

Book XXIV

The ghosts of the suitors gather miserably in the house of Hades and tell of
their deaths to the spirits of Agamemnon and Achilles. Meanwhile,
Odysseus finds his father working humbly in his orchard and reveals himself
to him. Certain men of Ithaca, bent on avenging the suitors, march to attack
Odysseus. The battle begins, but Athene stops it, bidding them make
a covenant of peace.

THEN HERMES OF CYLLENE SUMMONED THE GHOSTS OF THE SUITORS, and in his hand he held the fair golden wand with which he seals men's eyes in sleep or wakes them just as he pleases; with this he roused the ghosts and led them, while they followed whining and gibbering behind him. As bats fly squealing in the hollow of some great cave, when one of them has fallen out of the cluster in which they hang, even so did the ghosts whine and squeal as Hermes the healer of sorrow led them down into the dark abode of death. When they had passed the waters of Oceanus and the rock Leucas, they came to the gates of the sun and the land of dreams, whereon they reached the meadow of asphodel where dwell the souls and shadows of them that can labor no more.

Here they found the ghost of Achilles son of Peleus, with those of Patroclus, Antilochus, and Ajax, who was the finest and handsomest man of all the Danaans after the son of Peleus himself.

They were gathered round the ghost of the son of Peleus, and the ghost of Agamemnon joined them, sorrowing bitterly. Round him were gathered also the ghosts of those who had perished with him in the house of Aegisthus. The ghost of Achilles spoke first.

"Son of Atreus," it said, "we used to say that Zeus had loved you better from first to last than any other hero, for you were captain over many and brave men, when we were all fighting together before Troy; yet the hand of death, which no mortal can escape, was laid upon you all too early. Better for you had you fallen at Troy in the heyday of your renown, for the Achaeans would have built a mound over your ashes, and your son would have been heir to your good name, whereas it has now been your lot to come to a most miserable end."

"Happy son of Peleus," answered the ghost of Agamemnon, "for having died at Troy far from Argos, while the bravest of the Trojans and the Achaeans fell round you fighting for your body. There you lay in the whirling clouds of dust, all huge and hugely, heedless now of your chivalry. We fought the whole of the livelong day, nor should we ever have left off if Zeus had not sent a hurricane to stay us. Then, when we had borne you to the ships out of the fray, we laid you on your bed and cleansed your fair skin with warm water and with ointments. The Danaans tore their hair and wept bitterly round about you. Your mother, when she heard, came with her immortal nymphs from out of the sea, and the sound of a great wailing went forth over the waters so that the Achaeans quaked for fear. They would have fled panic-stricken to their ships had not wise old Nestor whose counsel was ever truest checked them, saying, 'Hold, Argives, fly not, sons of the Achaeans! This is his mother coming from the sea with her immortal nymphs to view the body of her son.'

"Thus he spoke, and the Achaeans feared no more. The daughters of the old man of the sea stood round you weeping bitterly, and clothed you in immortal raiment. The nine muses also came and lifted up their sweet voices in lament—calling and answering one another. There was not an Argive but wept for pity of the dirge they chanted. Days and nights seven and ten we mourned you, mortals and immortals, but on the eighteenth day we gave you to the flames, and many a fat sheep with many an ox did we slay in sacrifice around you. You were burnt in raiment of the gods, with rich resins and with honey, while heroes, horse and foot, clashed their armor round the pile as you were burning, with the tramp as of a great multitude. But when the flames of heaven had done their work, we gathered your white bones at daybreak and laid them in ointments and in pure wine. Your mother brought us a golden vase to hold them—gift of Dionysus, and work of Hephaestus himself. In this we mingled your bleached bones with those of Patroclus who had gone before you, and separate we enclosed also those of Antilochus who had been closer to you than any other of your comrades now that Patroclus was no more.

"Over these the host of the Argives built a noble tomb, on a point jutting out over the open Hellespont, that it might be seen from far out upon the sea by those now living and by them that shall be born hereafter. Your mother begged prizes from the gods, and offered them to be contended for by the noblest of the Achaeans. You must have been present at the funeral of many a hero, when the young men gird themselves and make ready to contend for prizes on the death of some great chieftain, but you never saw such prizes as silver-footed Thetis offered in your honor; for the gods loved you well. Thus even in death your fame, Achilles, has not been lost, and your name lives evermore among all mankind. But as for me, what solace had I when the days of my fighting were done? For Zeus willed my destruction on my return, by the hands of Aegisthus and those of my wicked wife."

Thus did they converse, and presently Hermes came up to them with the ghosts of the suitors who had been killed by Odysseus. The ghosts of Agamemnon and Achilles were astonished at seeing them, and went up to them at once. The ghost of Agamemnon recognized Amphimedon son of Melaneus, who lived in Ithaca and had been his host, so it began to talk to him.

"Amphimedon," it said, "what has happened to all you fine young men—all of an age too—that you are come down here under the ground? One could pick no finer body of men from any city. Did Poseidon raise his winds and waves against you when you were at sea, or did your enemies make an end of you on the mainland when you were cattle-lifting or sheep-stealing, or while fighting in defense of their wives and city? Answer my question, for I have been your guest. Do you not remember how I came to your house with Menelaus, to persuade Odysseus to join us with his ships against Troy? It was a whole month ere we could resume our voyage, for we had hard work to persuade Odysseus to come with us."

And the ghost of Amphimedon answered: "Agamemnon son of Atreus, king of men, I remember everything that you have said, and will tell you fully and accurately about the way in which our end was brought about. Odysseus had been long gone, and we were courting his wife, who did not say pointblank that she would not marry, nor yet bring matters to an end, for she meant to compass our destruction. This, then, was the trick she played us. She set up a great tambour frame in her room and began to work on an enormous piece of fine needlework. 'Sweethearts,' said she, 'Odysseus is indeed dead, still, do not press me to marry again immediately. Wait—for I would not have my skill in needlework perish unrecorded—till I have completed a pall for the hero Laertes, against the time when death shall take him. He is very rich, and the women of the place will talk if he is laid out without a pall.' This is what she said, and we assented; whereupon we could see her working upon her great web all day long, but at night she would unpick the stitches again by torchlight. She fooled us in this way for three years without our finding it out. But as time wore on and she was now in her fourth year, in the waning of moons and many days had been accomplished, one of her maids who knew what she was doing told us, and we caught her in the act of undoing her work, so she had to finish it whether she would or no. And when she showed us the robe she had made, after she had had it washed, its splendor was as that of the sun or moon.

"Then some malicious god conveyed Odysseus to the upland farm where his swineherd lives. Thither presently came also his son, returning from a voyage to Pylos, and the two came to the town when they had hatched their plot for our destruction. Telemachus came first, and then after him, accompanied by the swineherd, came Odysseus, clad in rags and leaning on a staff as though he were some miserable old beggar. He came so unexpectedly that none of us knew him, not even the older ones among us, and we reviled him and threw things at him. He endured both being struck and insulted without a word, though he was in his own house; but when the will of aegis-bearing Zeus inspired him, he and Telemachus took the armor and hid it in an inner chamber, bolting the doors behind them. Then he cunningly made his wife offer his bow and a quantity of iron to be contended for by us ill-fated suitors. And this was the beginning of our end, for not one of us could string the bow—nor nearly do so. When it was about to reach the hands of Odysseus, we all of us shouted out that it should not be given him, no matter what he might say, but Telemachus insisted on his having it. When he had got it in his hands he strung it with ease and sent his arrow through the iron. Then he stood on the floor of the cloister and poured his arrows on the ground, glaring fiercely about him. First he killed Antinous, and then, aiming straight before him, he let fly his deadly darts and they fell thick on one another. It was plain that some one of the gods was helping them, for they fell upon us with might and main throughout the cloisters, and there was a hideous sound of groaning as our brains were being battered in, and the ground seethed with our blood. This, Agamemnon, is how we came by our end, and our bodies are lying still uncared for in the house of Odysseus. For our friends at home do not yet know what has happened, so that they cannot lay us out and wash the black blood from our wounds, making moan over us according to the offices due to the departed."

"Happy Odysseus son of Laertes," replied the ghost of Agamemnon, "you are indeed blessed in the possession of a wife endowed with such rare excellence of understanding, and so faithful to her wedded lord as Penelope the daughter of Icarius. The fame, therefore, of her virtue shall never die, and the immortals shall compose a song that shall be welcome to all mankind in honor of the constancy of Penelope. How far otherwise was the wickedness of the daughter of Tyndareus, who killed her lawful husband; her song shall be hateful among men, for she has brought disgrace on all womankind, even on the good ones."

Thus did they converse in the house of Hades, deep down within the bowels of the earth. Meanwhile Odysseus and the others passed out of the town and soon reached the fair and well-tilled farm of Laertes, which he had reclaimed with infinite labor. Here was his house, with a lean-to running all round it, where the slaves who worked for him slept and sat and ate, while inside the house there was an old Sicel woman, who looked after him in this his country farm. When Odysseus got there, he said to his son and to the other two:

"Go to the house, and kill the best pig that you can find for dinner. Meanwhile I want to see whether my father will know me, or fail to recognize me after so long an absence."

He then took off his armor and gave it to Eumaeus and Philoetius, who went straight on to the house, while he turned off into the vineyard to make trial of his father. As he went down into the great orchard, he did not see Dolius, or any of his sons or other bondsmen, for they were all gathering thorns to make a fence for the vineyard, at the place where the old man had told them. He therefore found his father alone, hoeing a vine. He had on a dirty old shirt, patched and very shabby; his legs were bound round with thongs of oxhide to save him from the brambles, and he also wore sleeves of leather. He had a goatskin cap on his head, and was looking very woebegone. When Odysseus saw him so worn, so old and full of sorrow, he stood still under a tall pear tree and began to weep. He doubted whether to embrace him, kiss him, and tell him all about his having come home, or whether he should first question him and see what he would say. In the end he deemed it best to be crafty with him, so in this mind he went up to his father, who was bending down and digging about a plant.

"I see, sir," said Odysseus, "that you are an excellent gardener. What pains you take with it, to be sure. There is not a single plant, not a fig tree, vine, olive, pear, or flower bed, but bears the trace of your attention. I trust, however, that you will not be offended if I say that you take better care of your garden than of yourself. You are old, unsavory, and very meanly clad. It cannot be because you are idle that your master takes such poor care of you. Indeed your face and figure have nothing of the slave about them, and proclaim you of noble birth. I should have said that you were one of those who should wash well, eat well, and lie soft at night, as old men have a right to do. But tell me, and tell me true, whose bondman are you, and in whose garden are you working? Tell me also about another matter. Is this place that I have come to really Ithaca? I met a man just now who said so, but he was a dull fellow, and had not the patience to hear my story out when I was asking him about an old friend of mine, whether he was still living, or was already dead and in the house of Hades. Believe me when I tell you that this man came to my house once when I was in my own country and never yet did any stranger come to me whom I liked better. He said that his family came from Ithaca and that his father was Laertes, son of Arceisius. I received him hospitably, making him welcome to all the abundance of my house, and when he went away I gave him all customary presents. I gave him seven talents of fine gold, and a cup of solid silver with flowers chased upon it. I gave him twelve light cloaks, and as many pieces of tapestry. I also gave him twelve cloaks of single fold, twelve rugs, twelve fair mantles, and an equal number of shirts. To all this I added four good-looking women skilled in all useful arts, and I let him take his choice."

His father shed tears and answered: "Sir, you have indeed come to the country that you have named, but it is fallen into the hands of wicked people. All this wealth of presents has been given to no purpose. If you could have found your friend here alive in Ithaca, he would have entertained you hospitably and would have requited your presents amply when you left him—as would have been only right considering what you had already given him. But tell me, and tell me true, how many years is it since you entertained this guest—my unhappy son, as ever was? Alas! He has perished far from his own country; the fishes of the sea have eaten him, or he has fallen a prey to the birds and wild beasts of some continent. Neither his mother nor I his father, who were his parents, could throw our arms about him and wrap him in his shroud, nor could his excellent and richly dowered wife Penelope bewail her husband as was natural upon his deathbed, and close his eyes according to the offices due to the departed. But now, tell me truly, for I want to know: Who and whence are you? Tell me of your town and parents. Where is the ship lying that has brought you and your men to Ithaca? Or were you a passenger on some other man's ship, and those who brought you here have gone on their way and left you?"

"I will tell you everything," answered Odysseus, "quite truly. I come from Alybas where I have a fine house. I am son of King Apheidas, who is the son of Polypemon. My own name is Eperitus. Heaven drove me off my course as I was leaving Sicania, and I have been carried here against my will. As for my ship, it is lying over yonder, off the open country outside the town. And this is the fifth year since Odysseus left my country. Poor fellow, yet the omens were good for him when he left me. The birds all flew on our right hands, and both he and I rejoiced to see them as we parted, for we had every hope that we should have another friendly meeting and exchange presents."

A dark cloud of sorrow fell upon Laertes as he listened. He filled both hands with the dust from off the ground and poured it over his gray head, groaning heavily as he did so. The heart of Odysseus was touched, and his nostrils quivered as he looked upon his father; then he sprang towards him, flung his arms about him, and kissed him, saying, "I am he, father, about whom you are asking! I have returned after having been away for twenty years. But cease your sighing and lamentation—we have no time to lose, for I should tell you that I have been killing the suitors in my house, to punish them for there insolence and crimes."

"If you really are my son Odysseus," replied Laertes, "and have come back again, you must give me such manifest proof of your identity as shall convince me."

"First observe this scar," answered Odysseus, "which I got from a boar's tusk when I was hunting on Mount Parnassus. You and my mother had sent me to Autolycus, my mother's father, to receive the presents which when he was over here he had promised to give me. Furthermore, I will point out to you the trees in the vineyard which you gave me, and I asked you all about them as I followed you round the garden. We went over them all, and you told me their names and what they all were. You gave me thirteen pear trees, ten apple trees, and forty fig trees; you also said you would give me fifty rows of vines. There was corn planted between each row, and they yield grapes of every kind when the heat of heaven has been laid heavy upon them."

Laertes' strength failed him when he heard the convincing proofs which his son had given him. He threw his arms about him, and Odysseus had to support him, or he would have gone off into a swoon. But as soon as he came to, and was beginning to recover his senses, he said, "O father Zeus, then you gods are still in Olympus, after all, if the suitors have really been punished for their insolence and folly. Nevertheless, I am much afraid that I shall have all the townspeople of Ithaca up here directly, and they will be sending messengers everywhere throughout the cities of the Cephallenians."

Odysseus answered, "Take heart and do not trouble yourself about that, but let us go into the house hard by your garden. I have already told Telemachus, Philoetius, and Eumaeus to go on there and get dinner ready as soon as possible."

Thus conversing the two made their way towards the house. When they got there they found Telemachus with the stockman and the swineherd cutting up meat and mixing wine with water. Then the old Sicel woman took Laertes inside and washed him and anointed him with oil. She put on him a good cloak, and Athene came up to him and gave him a more imposing presence, making him taller and stouter than before. When he came back his son was surprised to see him looking so like an immortal, and said to him, "My dear father, some one of the gods has been making you much taller and better-looking."

Laertes answered, "Would, by Father Zeus, Athene, and Apollo, that I were the man I was when I ruled among the Cephallenians, and took Nericum, that strong fortress on the foreland. If I were still what I then was and had been in our house yesterday with my armor on, I should have been able to stand by you and help you against the suitors. I should have killed a great many of them, and you would have rejoiced to see it."

Thus did they converse. But the others, when they had finished their work and the feast was ready, left off working, and took each his proper place on the benches and seats; then they began eating. By and by old Dolius and his sons left their work and came up, for their mother, the Sicel woman who looked after Laertes now that he was growing old, had been to fetch them. When they saw Odysseus and were certain it was he, they stood there lost in astonishment; but Odysseus scolded them good-naturedly and said, "Sit down to your dinner, old man, and never mind about your surprise. We have been wanting to begin for some time and have been waiting for you."

Then Dolius put out both his hands and went up to Odysseus. "Sir," said he, seizing his master's hand and kissing it at the wrist, "we have long been wishing you home, and now heaven has restored you to us after we had given up hoping. All hail, therefore, and may the gods prosper you. But tell me, does Penelope already know of your return, or shall we send someone to tell her?"

"Old man," answered Odysseus, "she knows already, so you need not trouble about that." On this he took his seat, and the sons of Dolius gathered round Odysseus to give him greeting and embrace him one after the other. Then they took their seats in due order near Dolius their father.

While they were thus busy getting their dinner ready, Rumor went round the town, and noised abroad the terrible fate that had befallen the suitors. As soon, therefore, as the people heard of it they gathered from every quarter, groaning and hooting before the house of Odysseus. They took the dead away, buried every man his own, and put the bodies of those who came from elsewhere on board the fishing vessels, for the fishermen to take each of them to his own place. They then met angrily in the place of assembly, and when they were got together Eupeithes rose to speak. He was overwhelmed with grief for the death of his son Antinous, who had been the first man killed by Odysseus, so he said, weeping bitterly: "My friend, this man has done the Achaeans great wrong. He took many of our best men away with him in his fleet, and he has lost both ships and men, Now, moreover, on his return he has been killing all the foremost men among the Cephallenians. Let us be up and doing before he can get away to Pylos or to Elis where the Epeans rule, or we shall be ashamed of ourselves forever afterwards. It will be an everlasting disgrace to us if we do not avenge the murder of our sons and brothers. For my own part, I should have no more pleasure in life, but had rather die at once. Let us be up, then, and after them, before they can cross over to the mainland."

He wept as he spoke and everyone pitied him. But Medon and the bard Phemius had now woke up, and came to them from the house of Odysseus. Everyone was astonished at seeing them, but they stood firm in the middle of the assembly, and Medon said, "Hear me, men of Ithaca. Odysseus did not do these things against the will of heaven. I myself saw an immortal god take the form of Mentor and stand beside him. This god appeared, now in front of him encouraging him, and now going furiously about the court and attacking the suitors, whereon they fell thick on one another."

On this pale fear laid hold of them, and old Halitherses son of Mastor rose to speak, for he was the only man among them who knew both past and future. So he spoke to them plainly and in all honesty, saying:

"Men of Ithaca, it is all your own fault that things have turned out as they have. You would not listen to me, nor yet to Mentor, when we bade you check the folly of your sons who were doing much wrong in the wantonness of their hearts—wasting the substance and dishonoring the wife of a chieftain who they thought would not return. Now, however, let it be as I say, and do as I tell you. Do not go out against Odysseus, or you may find that you have been drawing down evil on your own heads."

This was what he said, and more than half raised a loud shout, and at once left the assembly. But the rest stayed where they were, for the speech of Halitherses displeased them, and they sided with Eupeithes. They therefore hurried off for their armor, and when they had armed themselves, they met together in front of the city, and Eupeithes led them on in their folly. He thought he was going to avenge the murder of his son, whereas in truth he was never to return, but was himself to perish in his attempt.

Then Athene said to Zeus, "Father, son of Cronus, king of kings, answer me this question: What do you propose to do? Will you set them fighting still further, or will you make peace between them?"

And Zeus answered: "My child, why should you ask me? Was it not by your own arrangement that Odysseus came home and took his revenge upon the suitors? Do whatever you like, but I will tell you what I think will be the most reasonable arrangement. Now that Odysseus is revenged, let them swear to a solemn covenant, in virtue of which he shall continue to rule, while we cause the others to forgive and forget the massacre of their sons and brothers. Let them then all become friends as heretofore, and let peace and plenty reign."

This was what Athene was already eager to bring about, so down she darted from off the topmost summits of Olympus.

Now when Laertes and the others had done dinner, Odysseus began by saying, "Some of you go out and see if they are not getting close up to us." So one of Dolius' sons went as he was bid. Standing on the threshold he could see them all quite near, and said to Odysseus, "Here they are, let us put on our armor at once."

They put on their armor as fast as they could—that is to say Odysseus, his three men, and the six sons of Dolius. Laertes also and Dolius did the same—warriors by necessity in spite of their gray hair. When they had all put on their armor, they opened the gate and sallied forth, Odysseus leading the way.

Then Zeus' daughter Athene came up to them, having assumed the form and voice of Mentor. Odysseus was glad when he saw her, and said to his son Telemachus, "Telemachus, now that you are about to fight in an engagement which will show every man's mettle, be sure not to disgrace your ancestors, who were eminent for their strength and courage all the world over."

"You say truly, my dear father," answered Telemachus, "and you shall, see, if you will, that I am in no mind to disgrace your family."

Laertes was delighted when he heard this. "Good heavens," he exclaimed, "what a day I am enjoying! I do indeed rejoice at it. My son and grandson are vying with one another in the matter of valor."

On this Athene came close up to him and said, "Son of Arceisius—best friend I have in the world—pray to the blue-eyed damsel, and to Zeus her father; then poise your spear and hurl it."

As she spoke she infused fresh vigor into him, and when he had prayed to her he poised his spear and hurled it. He hit Eupeithes' helmet, and the spear went right through it, for the helmet stayed it not, and his armor rang rattling round him as he fell heavily to the ground. Meantime Odysseus and his son fell upon the front line of the foe and smote them with their swords and spears. Indeed, they would have killed every one of them, and prevented them from ever getting home again, only Athene raised her voice aloud, and made everyone pause. "Men of Ithaca," she cried, "cease this dreadful war, and settle the matter at once without further bloodshed."

On this pale fear seized everyone; they were so frightened that their arms dropped from their hands and fell upon the ground at the sound of the goddess' voice, and they fled back to the city for their lives. But Odysseus gave a great cry, and gathering himself together swooped down like a soaring eagle. Then the son of Cronus sent a thunderbolt of fire that fell just in front of Athene, so she said to Odysseus, "Odysseus, noble son of Laertes, stop this warful strife, or Zeus will be angry with you."

Thus spoke Athene, and Odysseus obeyed her gladly. Then Athene assumed the form and voice of Mentor, and presently made a covenant of peace between the two contending parties.

About the Author

Homer may have been merely the vague personification of a school of epic poets. If an actual person, he probably lived during the first half of the eighth century B.C. The ancient belief that he was a native of Ionia—the central part of the western seaboard of modern Turkey—seems reasonable since the poems are in Ionian dialect. He may have dictated his poems to a literate associate, written them down himself, noted down lines or passages to cue his memory, or never used writing at all. Aristotle believed that Homer wrote *The Odyssey* in his old age; linguistic evidence does suggest that *The Iliad* came first, and that *The Odyssey* followed after a significant lapse of time. According to the philosopher Heraclitus, Homer died from a fit of anger at not being able to solve a boys' riddle about lice—an anecdote that seems to mock the curiosity of scholars. Among modern speculations concerning Homer are the various assertions that he was a doctor, a general, and a woman.

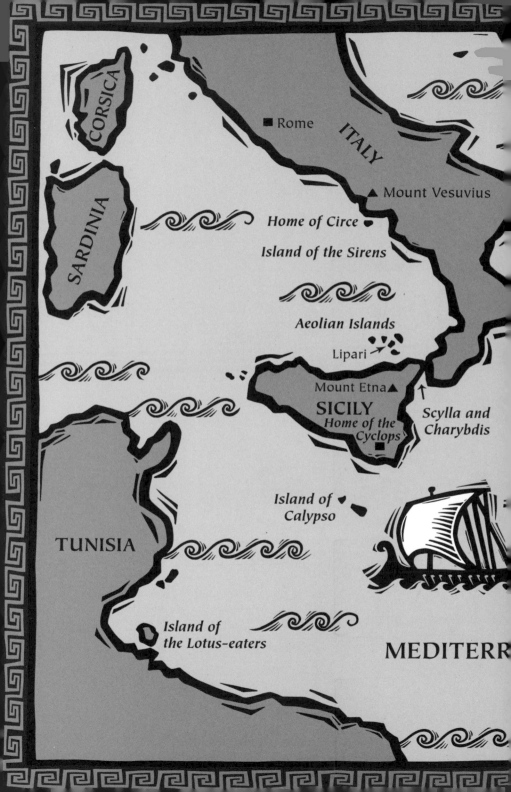